Contents

Renault 21 GTX

Renault 21 Savanna GTS

Renault 21 Owners Workshop Manual

I M Coomber

Models covered

Renault 21 TL, TS, RS, GTS, Savanna TL, Savanna TS
& Savanna GTS; 1721 cc

Renault 21 RX, TXE, GTX, Monaco, TI, Turbo &
Savanna GTX; 1995 cc

Does not cover Diesel engine variants

ABCDE
FGHIJ
KLMNO
PQRST

Haynes Publishing Group
Sparkford Nr Yeovil
Somerset BA22 7JJ England

Haynes Publications, Inc
861 Lawrence Drive
Newbury Park
California 91320 USA

Acknowledgements

Thanks are due to the Champion Sparking Plug Company Limited who supplied the illustrations showing the spark plug conditions, and to Duckhams Oils who provided lubrication data. Certain other illustrations are the copyright of Renault UK Limited, and are used with their permission. Thanks are also due to Sykes-Pickavant, who supplied some of the workshop tools, and to all those people at Sparkford who helped in the production of this manual.

A book in the **Haynes Owners Workshop Manual Series**

Printed by J. H. Haynes & Co. Ltd, Sparkford, Nr Yeovil, Somerset BA22 7JJ, England

ISBN 1 85010 397 6

British Library Cataloguing in Publication Data
Coomber, Ian. *1943-*
    Renault 21 owners workshop manual.
    1. Cars. Maintenance and repair – Amateurs' manuals
    I. Title   II. Series
    629.28'722
    ISBN 1-85010-397-6

About this manual

Its aim

The aim of this manual is to help you get the best value from your vehicle. It can do so in several ways. It can help you decide what work must be done (even should you choose to get it done by a garage), provide information on routine maintenance and servicing, and give a logical course of action and diagnosis when random faults occur. However, it is hoped that you will use the manual by tackling the work yourself. On simpler jobs it may even be quicker than booking the car into a garage and going there twice, to leave and collect it. Perhaps most important, a lot of money can be saved by avoiding the costs a garage must charge to cover its labour and overheads.

The manual has drawings and descriptions to show the function of the various components so that their layout can be understood. Then the tasks are described and photographed in a step-by-step sequence so that even a novice can do the work.

Its arrangement

The manual is divided into 12 Chapters, each covering a logical sub-division of the vehicle. The Chapters are each divided into Sections, numbered with single figures, eg 5; and the Sections into paragraphs (or sub-sections), with decimal numbers following on from the Section they are in, eg 5.1, 5.2, 5.3 etc.

It is freely illustrated, especially in those parts where there is a detailed sequence of operations to be carried out. There are two forms of illustration: figures and photographs. The figures are numbered in sequence with decimal numbers, according to their position in the Chapter – eg Fig. 6.4 is the fourth drawing/illustration in Chapter 6. Photographs carry the same number (either individually or in related groups) as the Section or sub-section to which they relate.

There is an alphabetical index at the back of the manual as well as a contents list at the front. Each Chapter is also preceded by its own individual contents list.

References to the 'left' or 'right' of the vehicle are in the sense of a person in the driver's seat facing forwards.

Unless otherwise stated, nuts and bolts are removed by turning anti-clockwise, and tightened by turning clockwise.

Vehicle manufacturers continually make changes to specifications and recommendations, and these, when notified, are incorporated into our manuals at the earliest opportunity.

Whilst every care is taken to ensure that the information in this manual is correct, no liability can be accepted by the authors or publishers for loss, damage or injury caused by any errors in, or omissions from, the information given.

Project vehicles

The project vehicles used in the preparation of this manual, and appearing in many of the photographic sequences, were a Renault 21 GTX, Renault 21 Savanna TS and Renault 21 2.0 litre Turbo.

Introduction to the Renault 21

The Renault 21 series was first introduced in June 1986 and filled the mid-range gap between the Renault 11 and Renault 25 models. Initially available only in Saloon form, in April 1987, an Estate version known as the Savanna was added to the range.

A 1.7 or 2.0 litre OHC, water-cooled engine is used together with a five-speed manual transmission or a three-speed automatic transmission. On 1.7 litre models the engine and transmission are transversely-mounted whilst on 2.0 litre models the engine and transmission are mounted longitudinally.

Independent front suspension and rack and pinion steering (power assisted on some models) is used, but the layout and specifications differ according to engine type and model.

All 1.7 litre models are fitted with a carburettor, whilst 2.0 litre models have fuel injection, with a turbocharger on the top of the range 2.0 litre Turbo model. An electronic engine management system is employed, and the fuel and ignition systems are jointly controlled by a computer module in accordance with engine demands.

All models are well built and fully equipped. They provide a combination of comfort, reliability and economy.

General dimensions, weights and capacities

Dimensions
Overall length:
- Saloon (except RS, RX and Turbo) .... 4462 mm (175.6 in)
- Saloon RS and RX .... 4465 mm (175.7 in)
- Turbo .... 4498 mm (177.0 in)
- Savanna .... 4644 mm (182.8 in)

Overall width:
- Saloon and Savanna (except TL, TS and Turbo) .... 1715 mm (67.5 in)
- Saloon and Savanna TL and TS .... 1706 mm (67.1 in)
- Turbo .... 1714 mm (67.4 in)

Overall height:
- Saloon (except Turbo) .... 1414 mm (55.6 in)
- Turbo .... 1385 mm (54.5 in)
- Savanna (except GTX and TXE) .... 1427 mm (56.1 in)
- Savanna GTX and TXE .... 1430 mm (56.2 in)

Ground clearance (at kerb weight):
- All models .... 120 mm (4.7 in)

Wheelbase:
- Saloon (except RX, TXE and Turbo) .... 2695 mm (104.6 in)
- Saloon RX and TXE .... 2600 mm (102.3 in)
- Turbo .... 2597 mm (102.2 in)
- Savanna (except GTX and TXE) .... 2809 mm (110.6 in)
- Savanna GTX and TXE .... 2750 mm (108.2 in)

Front track:
- Saloon (except RX, TXE and Turbo) and Savanna (except GTX and TXE) .... 1429 mm (56.2 in)
- Saloon RX and TXE .... 1454 mm (57.2 in)
- Savanna GTX and TXE .... 1454 mm (57.2 in)
- Turbo .... 1450 mm (57.0 in)

Rear track:
- Saloon (except RX, TXE and Turbo) .... 1402 mm (55.2 in)
- Saloon RX and TXE and all Savanna models .... 1406 mm (55.3 in)
- Turbo .... 1402 mm (55.2 in)

Weights
Kerb weight:
- Saloon models:
  - TL .... 985 kg (2172 lb)
  - TS, GTS, RS and TSE .... 1040 kg (2293 lb)
  - RX and TXE .... 1130 kg (2491 lb)
  - Turbo .... 1190 kg (2624 lb)
- 5-seat Savanna models*:
  - TL .... 1015 kg (2238 lb)
  - TS .... 1030 kg (2271 lb)
  - GTS .... 1040 kg (2293 lb)
  - GTX .... 1135 kg (2502 lb)
  - TXE .... 1155 kg (2546 lb)

For 7-seat Savanna models add 20 kg (44 lb)

Maximum roof rack load:
- Saloon .... 60 kg (132 lb)
- Savanna .... 70 kg (154 lb)

Maximum towing weight .... Consult a Renault dealer

Capacities
Engine oil:
- 1.7 litre engine (excluding filter) .... 4.7 litres (8.0 pints)
- 2.0 litre engine (excluding filter) .... 5.7 litres (10.0 pints)
- Oil filter .... 0.5 litre (0.88 pint)

Cooling system:
- 1.7 litre models .... 5.2 litres (9.2 pints)
- 2.0 litre non-Turbo models .... 6.8 litres (12.0 pints)
- 2.0 litre Turbo model .... 6.2 litres (11.0 pints)

Fuel tank:
- All models .... 66 litres (14.5 gals)

Manual transmission oil:
- JB3 type .... 3.4 litres (6.0 pints)
- NG9 type .... 2.2 litres (4.0 pints)
- UN1 type .... 3.0 litres (5.2 pints)

Automatic transmission fluid:
- Fluid renewal .... 2.5 litres (4.4 pints)
- Dry fill .... 6.0 litres (10.6 pints)

Jacking, towing and wheel changing

1 To avoid repetition, the procedure for raising the vehicle, in order to carry out work under it, is not included before each relevant operation described in this Manual.

2 It is to be preferred, and it is certainly recommended, that the vehicle is positioned over an inspection pit or raised on a lift. Where these facilities are not available, use ramps or jack up the vehicle strictly in accordance with the following guide. Once the vehicle is raised, supplement the jack with axle stands.

Wheel changing

3 To change a roadwheel, remove the jack and wheelbrace from their compartment under the luggage area floor.

4 Where a wheel trim is fitted, prise it free using a screwdriver inserted in the lever opening on its outer rim. Some models are fitted with an anti-theft type wheel and in this instance the trim can only be removed using the special key supplied for this purpose.

5 Place the car in gear (preferably 1st or reverse), or on automatic transmission model engage 'P'.

6 Make sure that the handbrake is fully applied and if possible chock the roadwheel opposite to the one being removed.

7 Release but do not remove the roadwheel bolts.

8 Locate the jack under the sill jacking point nearest to the wheel being changed. If the ground is soft, a base plate should be located under the jack.

9 Using the wheelbrace, turn the jack screw and raise the wheel off the floor.

10 Remove the bolts and wheel, and bolt on the spare wheel.

11 If a smaller emergency only type wheel is fitted, or if a steel type roadwheel is fitted as a replacement for an alloy type, the vehicle speed should not exceed 50 mph (80 kph) during their use. The normal roadwheel should be repaired and put back into service as soon as possible.

12 When the spare wheel is fitted, moderately tighten the bolts, lower the vehicle, then fully tighten the bolts. Refit the trim where applicable.

Jacking

13 When raising the car for repair or maintenance work, preferably use a trolley jack, or a hydraulic bottle or heavy screw type jack.

14 Place the jack under the sill jacking points using a shaped wooden block with a groove into which the weld flange of the sill will locate.

15 The front end may be raised if a substantial wooden baulk of timber is placed transversally under the subframe as shown. Place the jack under the centre of the timber.

16 **Never** attempt to jack the car under the front crossmember or front or rear suspension arms, or the rear axle unit.

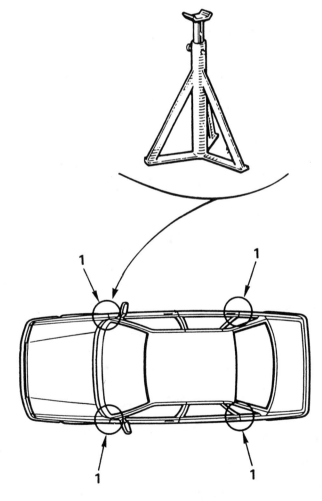

Jacking and support points for axle stands (1)

Front and jacking point – note use of shaped wooden block
(arrowed), between jack and sill

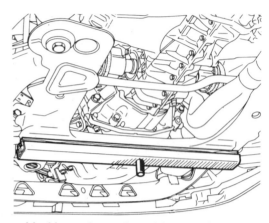

Front end jacking point under subframe using support beam
located as shown – longitudinal engine models

Towing

17 The towing hooks may be used for towing or being towed on
normal road surfaces.

18 When being towed, remember to unlock the steering column by
turning the ignition key to the 'M' position.

19 Vehicles equipped with automatic transmission should preferably
be towed with the front wheels off the ground. However, towing with
the front wheels on the ground is permissible if an extra 2.0 litres (3.5
pints) of the specified transmission fluid is poured into the transmission, the speed is restricted to 30 km/h (18 mph) and the distance
towed kept below 50 km (30 miles).

20 Keep the selector lever in 'M' during towing and remove the
surplus fluid after the vehicle has been made serviceable again; a
syphon is the best way to do this.

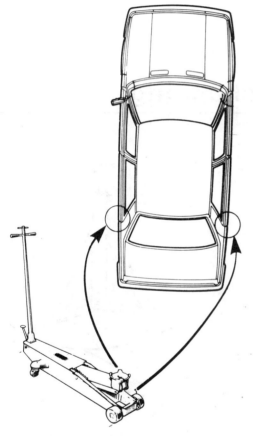

Rear end jacking points (arrowed)

Front towing eye

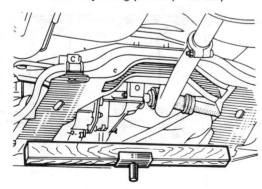

**Front end jacking point under subframe using support beam
located as shown – transverse engine models**

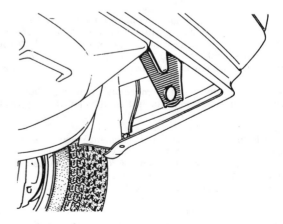

Rear towing eye

Buying spare parts and vehicle identification numbers

Buying spare parts

Spare parts are available from many sources, for example: Renault garages, other garages and accessory shops, and motor factors. Our advice regarding spare part is as follows.

Officially appointed Renault garages – These will be the best source for parts which are peculiar to your car, and are otherwise not generally available (eg complete cylinder heads, internal gearbox components, badges, interior trim etc). It is also the only place at which you should buy parts if your car is still under warranty – non-Renault components may invalidate the warranty. To be sure of obtaining the correct parts, it will always be necessary to give the storeman your car's vehicle identification number, and if possible to take the old part along for positive identification. Remember that many parts are available under a factory exchange scheme – any parts returned should always be clean! It obviously makes good sense to go straight to the specialists on your car for this type of part, as they are best equipped to supply you.

Other garages and accessory shops – These are often very good places to buy materials and components needed for the maintenance of your car (eg oil filters, spark plugs, bulbs, drivebelts, oils and greases, touch-up paint, filler paste, etc). They also sell general accessories, usually have convenient opening hours, charge lower prices and can often be found not far from home.

Motor factors – Good factors will stock all the more important components which wear out relatively quickly (eg clutch components, pistons, valves, exhaust systems, brake cylinders/pipes/hoses/seals/shoes and pads etc). Motor factors will often provide new or reconditioned components on a part exchange basis – this can save a considerable amount of money.

Vehicle identification numbers

Modifications are a continuing and unpublicised process in vehicle manufacture, quite apart from their major model changes. Spare parts manuals and lists are compiled on a numerical basis, the individual vehicle numbers being essential for correct identification of the component concerned.

When ordering spare parts it will usually be necessary to quote the numbers on the oval plate under all circumstances and often those on the manufacturer's plate. If engine or gearbox parts are being ordered the engine plate or gearbox plate numbers will be needed. The paint code may be required if the colour of the car is not easily described. All these numbers with the exception of those on the gearbox plate are located in readily visible places in the engine compartment. The gearbox plate is affixed to the transmission housing.

The model type code numbers used in some Chapters of this manual appear on the manufacturer's plate – eg L485 identifies a 2.0 litre Turbo model.

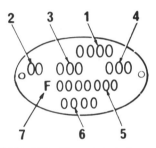

Oval identification plate information

1 Factory symbol
2 Transmission type
3 Equipment number
4 Optional equipment fitted (in production)
5 Fabrication number
6 Original paint reference (not all models)
7 Place of manufacture (Factory)

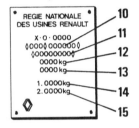

Manufacturer's information plate identification

10 Vehicle type
11 Chassis number
12 Gross vehicle weight
13 Gross total weight (loaded vehicle and loaded trailer)
14 Maximum permissible front axle loading
15 Maximum permissible rear axle loading

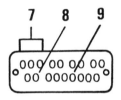

Engine plate

7 Engine type
8 Engine suffix
9 Engine number

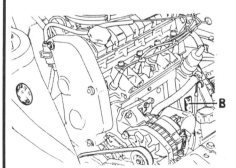

Engine plate location (B) – transverse (1.7 litre) engine

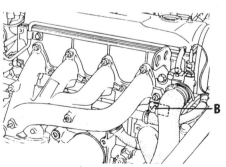

Engine plate location (B) – longitudinal (2.0 litre) engine

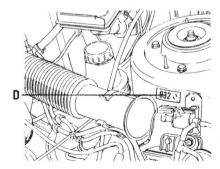

Alternative paint code plate location (D)

General repair procedures

Whenever servicing, repair or overhaul work is carried out on the car or its components, it is necessary to observe the following procedures and instructions. This will assist in carrying out the operation efficiently and to a professional standard of workmanship.

Joint mating faces and gaskets

Where a gasket is used between the mating faces of two components, ensure that it is renewed on reassembly, and fit it dry unless otherwise stated in the repair procedure. Make sure that the mating faces are clean and dry with all traces of old gasket removed. When cleaning a joint face, use a tool which is not likely to score or damage the face, and remove any burrs or nicks with an oilstone or fine file.

Make sure that tapped holes are cleaned with a pipe cleaner, and keep them free of jointing compound if this is being used unless specifically instructed otherwise.

Ensure that all orifices, channels or pipes are clear and blow through them, preferably using compressed air.

Oil seals

Whenever an oil seal is removed from its working location, either individually or as part of an assembly, it should be renewed.

The very fine sealing lip of the seal is easily damaged and will not seal if the surface it contacts is not completely clean and free from scratches, nicks or grooves. If the original sealing surface of the component cannot be restored, the component should be renewed.

Protect the lips of the seal from any surface which may damage them in the course of fitting. Use tape or a conical sleeve where possible. Lubricate the seal lips with oil before fitting and, on dual lipped seals, fill the space between the lips with grease.

Unless otherwise stated, oil seals must be fitted with their sealing lips toward the lubricant to be sealed.

Use a tubular drift or block of wood of the appropriate size to install the seal and, if the seal housing is shouldered, drive the seal down to the shoulder. If the seal housing is unshouldered, the seal should be fitted with its face flush with the housing top face.

Screw threads and fastenings

Always ensure that a blind tapped hole is completely free from oil, grease, water or other fluid before installing the bolt or stud. Failure to do this could cause the housing to crack due to the hydraulic action of the bolt or stud as it is screwed in.

When tightening a castellated nut to accept a split pin, tighten the nut to the specified torque, where applicable, and then tighten further to the next split pin hole. Never slacken the nut to align a split pin hole unless stated in the repair procedure.

When checking or retightening a nut or bolt to a specified torque setting, slacken the nut or bolt by a quarter of a turn, and then retighten to the specified setting.

Locknuts, locktabs and washers

Any fastening which will rotate against a component or housing in the course of tightening should always have a washer between it and the relevant component or housing.

Spring or split washers should always be renewed when they are used to lock a critical component such as a big-end bearing retaining nut or bolt.

Locktabs which are folded over to retain a nut or bolt should always be renewed.

Self-locking nuts can be reused in non-critical areas, providing resistance can be felt when the locking portion passes over the bolt or stud thread.

Split pins must always be replaced with new ones of the correct size for the hole.

Special tools

Some repair procedures in this manual entail the use of special tools such as a press, two or three-legged pullers, spring compressors etc. Wherever possible, suitable readily available alternatives to the manufacturer's special tools are described, and are shown in use. In some instances, where no alternative is possible, it has been necessary to resort to the use of a manufacturer's tool and this has been done for reasons of safety as well as the efficient completion of the repair operation. Unless you are highly skilled and have a thorough understanding of the procedure described, never attempt to bypass the use of any special tool when the procedure described specifies its use. Not only is there a very great risk of personal injury, but expensive damage could be caused to the components involved.

Tools and working facilities

Introduction

A selection of good tools is a fundamental requirement for anyone contemplating the maintenance and repair of a motor vehicle. For the owner who does not possess any, their purchase will prove a considerable expense, offsetting some of the savings made by doing-it-yourself. However, provided that the tools purchased are of good quality, they will last for many years and prove an extremely worthwhile investment.

To help the average owner to decide which tools are needed to carry out the various tasks detailed in this manual, we have compiled three lists of tools under the following headings: *Maintenance and minor repair, Repair and overhaul,* and *Special.* The newcomer to practical mechanics should start off with the *Maintenance and minor repair* tool kit and confine himself to the simpler jobs around the vehicle. Then, as his confidence and experience grow, he can undertake more difficult tasks, buying extra tools as, and when, they are needed. In this way, a *Maintenance and minor repair* tool kit can be built-up into a *Repair and overhaul* tool kit over a considerable period of time without any major cash outlays. The experienced do-it-yourselfer will have a tool kit good enough for most repair and overhaul procedures and will add tools from the *Special* category when he feels the expense is justified by the amount of use to which these tools will be put.

It is obviously not possible to cover the subject of tools fully here. For those who wish to learn more about tools and their use there is a book entitled *How to Choose and Use Car Tools* available from the publishers of this manual.

Maintenance and minor repair tool kit

The tools given in this list should be considered as a minimum requirement if routine maintenance, servicing and minor repair operations are to be undertaken. We recommend the purchase of combination spanners (ring one end, open-ended the other); although more expensive than open-ended ones, they do give the advantages of both types of spanner.

Combination spanners - 10, 11, 12, 13, 14 & 17 mm
Adjustable spanner - 9 inch
Engine sump/gearbox/rear axle drain plug key
Spark plug spanner (with rubber insert)
Spark plug gap adjustment tool
Set of feeler gauges
Brake adjuster spanner
Brake bleed nipple spanner
Screwdriver - 4 in long x $^1/4$ in dia (flat blade)
Screwdriver - 4 in long x $^1/4$ in dia (cross blade)
Combination pliers - 6 inch
Hacksaw (junior)
Tyre pump
Tyre pressure gauge
Grease gun
Oil can

Fine emery cloth (1 sheet)
Wire brush (small)
Funnel (medium size)

Repair and overhaul tool kit

These tools are virtually essential for anyone undertaking any major repairs to a motor vehicle, and are additional to those given in the *Maintenance and minor repair* list. Included in this list is a comprehensive set of sockets. Although these are expensive they will be found invaluable as they are so versatile - particularly if various drives are included in the set. We recommend the ½ in square-drive type, as this can be used with most proprietary torque wrenches. If you cannot afford a socket set, even bought piecemeal, then inexpensive tubular box spanners are a useful alternative.

It should be noted that many of the fixing bolts and screws on the Renault 21 are of the Torx type and it is therefore essential that a suitable set of Torx keys and sockets is obtained before starting any service or repair procedures.

The tools in this list will occasionally need to be supplemented by tools from the *Special* list.

Torx tool set
Sockets (or box spanners) to cover range in previous list
Reversible ratchet drive (for use with sockets)
Extension piece, 10 inch (for use with sockets)
Universal joint (for use with sockets)
Torque wrench (for use with sockets)
'Mole' wrench - 8 inch
Ball pein hammer
Soft-faced hammer, plastic or rubber
Screwdriver - 6 in long x $^5/16$ in dia (flat blade)
Screwdriver - 2 in long x $^5/16$ in square (flat blade)
Screwdriver - 1$^1/2$ in long x $^1/4$ in dia (cross blade)
Screwdriver - 3 in long x $^1/8$ in dia (electrician's)
Pliers - electrician's side cutters
Pliers - needle nosed
Pliers - circlip (internal and external)
Cold chisel - $^1/2$ inch
Scriber
Scraper
Centre punch
Pin punch
Hacksaw
Valve grinding tool
Steel rule/straight-edge
Allen keys (inc. splined/Torx type if necessary)
Selection of files
Wire brush (large)
Axle-stands
Jack (strong trolley or hydraulic type)

Special tools

The tools in this list are those which are not used regularly, are expensive to buy, or which need to be used in accordance with their manufacturers' instructions. Unless relatively difficult mechanical jobs are undertaken frequently, it will not be economic to buy many of these tools. Where this is the case, you could consider clubbing together with friends (or joining a motorists' club) to make a joint purchase, or borrowing the tools against a deposit from a local garage or tool hire specialist.

The following list contains only those tools and instruments freely available to the public, and not those special tools produced by the vehicle manufacturer specifically for its dealer network. You will find occasional references to these manufacturers' special tools in the text of this manual. Generally, an alternative method of doing the job without the vehicle manufacturers' special tool is given. However, sometimes, there is no alternative to using them. Where this is the case and the relevant tool cannot be bought or borrowed, you will have to entrust the work to a franchised garage.

Valve spring compressor (where applicable)
Piston ring compressor
Balljoint separator
Universal hub/bearing puller
Impact screwdriver
Micrometer and/or vernier gauge
Dial gauge
Stroboscopic timing light
Dwell angle meter/tachometer
Universal electrical multi-meter
Cylinder compression gauge
Lifting tackle
Trolley jack
Light with extension lead

Buying tools

For practically all tools, a tool factor is the best source since he will have a very comprehensive range compared with the average garage or accessory shop. Having said that, accessory shops often offer excellent quality tools at discount prices, so it pays to shop around.

Remember, you don't have to buy the most expensive items on the shelf, but it is always advisable to steer clear of the very cheap tools. There are plenty of good tools around at reasonable prices, so ask the proprietor or manager of the shop for advice before making a purchase.

Care and maintenance of tools

Having purchased a reasonable tool kit, it is necessary to keep the tools in a clean serviceable condition. After use, always wipe off any dirt, grease and metal particles using a clean, dry cloth, before putting the tools away. Never leave them lying around after they have been used. A simple tool rack on the garage or workshop wall, for items such as screwdrivers and pliers is a good idea. Store all normal wrenches and sockets in a metal box. Any measuring instruments, gauges, meters, etc, must be carefully stored where they cannot be damaged or become rusty.

Take a little care when tools are used. Hammer heads inevitably become marked and screwdrivers lose the keen edge on their blades from time to time. A little timely attention with emery cloth or a file will soon restore items like this to a good serviceable finish.

Working facilities

Not to be forgotten when discussing tools, is the workshop itself. If anything more than routine maintenance is to be carried out, some form of suitable working area becomes essential.

It is appreciated that many an owner mechanic is forced by circumstances to remove an engine or similar item, without the benefit of a garage or workshop. Having done this, any repairs should always be done under the cover of a roof.

Wherever possible, any dismantling should be done on a clean, flat workbench or table at a suitable working height.

Any workbench needs a vice: one with a jaw opening of 4 in (100 mm) is suitable for most jobs. As mentioned previously, some clean dry storage space is also required for tools, as well as for lubricants, cleaning fluids, touch-up paints and so on, which become necessary.

Another item which may be required, and which has a much more general usage, is an electric drill with a chuck capacity of at least 5/16 in (8 mm). This, together with a good range of twist drills, is virtually

essential for fitting accessories such as mirrors and reversing lights.

Last, but not least, always keep a supply of old newspapers and clean, lint-free rags available, and try to keep any working area as clean as possible.

Spanner jaw gap comparison table

Jaw gap (in)	Spanner size
0.250	1/4 in AF
0.276	7 mm
0.313	5/16 in AF
0.315	8 mm
0.344	11/32 in AF; 1/8 in Whitworth
0.354	9 mm
0.375	3/8 in AF
0.394	10 mm
0.433	11 mm
0.438	7/16 in AF
0.445	3/16 in Whitworth; 1/4 in BSF
0.472	12 mm
0.500	1/2 in AF
0.512	13 mm
0.525	1/4 in Whitworth; 5/16 in BSF
0.551	14 mm
0.563	9/16 in AF
0.591	15 mm
0.600	5/16 in Whitworth; 3/8 in BSF
0.625	5/8 in AF
0.630	16 mm
0.669	17 mm
0.686	11/16 in AF
0.709	18 mm
0.710	3/8 in Whitworth; 7/16 in BSF
0.748	19 mm
0.750	3/4 in AF
0.813	13/16 in AF
0.820	7/16 in Whitworth; 1/2 in BSF
0.866	22 mm
0.875	7/8 in AF
0.920	1/2 in Whitworth; 9/16 in BSF
0.938	15/16 in AF
0.945	24 mm
1.000	1 in AF
1.010	9/16 in Whitworth; 5/8 in BSF
1.024	26 mm
1.063	1 1/16 in AF; 27 mm
1.100	5/8 in Whitworth; 11/16 in BSF
1.125	1 1/8 in AF
1.181	30 mm
1.200	11/16 in Whitworth; 3/4 in BSF
1.250	1 1/4 in AF
1.260	32 mm
1.300	3/4 in Whitworth; 7/8 in BSF
1.313	1 5/16 in AF
1.390	13/16 in Whitworth; 15/16 in BSF
1.417	36 mm
1.438	1 7/16 in AF
1.480	7/8 in Whitworth; 1 in BSF
1.500	1 1/2 in AF
1.575	40 mm; 15/16 in Whitworth
1.614	41 mm
1.625	1 5/8 in AF
1.670	1 in Whitworth; 1 1/8 in BSF
1.688	1 11/16 in AF
1.811	46 mm
1.813	1 13/16 in AF
1.860	1 1/8 in Whitworth; 1 1/4 in BSF
1.875	1 7/8 in AF
1.969	50 mm
2.000	2 in AF
2.050	1 1/4 in Whitworth; 1 3/8 in BSF
2.165	55 mm
2.362	60 mm

Conversion factors

Length (distance)
Inches (in)	X 25.4	= Millimetres (mm)	X 0.0394	= Inches (in)
Feet (ft)	X 0.305	= Metres (m)	X 3.281	= Feet (ft)
Miles	X 1.609	= Kilometres (km)	X 0.621	= Miles

Volume (capacity)
Cubic inches (cu in; in³)	X 16.387	= Cubic centimetres (cc; cm³)	X 0.061	= Cubic inches (cu in; in³)
Imperial pints (Imp pt)	X 0.568	= Litres (l)	X 1.76	= Imperial pints (Imp pt)
Imperial quarts (Imp qt)	X 1.137	= Litres (l)	X 0.88	= Imperial quarts (Imp qt)
Imperial quarts (Imp qt)	X 1.201	= US quarts (US qt)	X 0.833	= Imperial quarts (Imp qt)
US quarts (US qt)	X 0.946	= Litres (l)	X 1.057	= US quarts (US qt)
Imperial gallons (Imp gal)	X 4.546	= Litres (l)	X 0.22	= Imperial gallons (Imp gal)
Imperial gallons (Imp gal)	X 1.201	= US gallons (US gal)	X 0.833	= Imperial gallons (Imp gal)
US gallons (US gal)	X 3.785	= Litres (l)	X 0.264	= US gallons (US gal)

Mass (weight)
Ounces (oz)	X 28.35	= Grams (g)	X 0.035	= Ounces (oz)
Pounds (lb)	X 0.454	= Kilograms (kg)	X 2.205	= Pounds (lb)

Force
Ounces-force (ozf; oz)	X 0.278	= Newtons (N)	X 3.6	= Ounces-force (ozf; oz)
Pounds-force (lbf; lb)	X 4.448	= Newtons (N)	X 0.225	= Pounds-force (lbf; lb)
Newtons (N)	X 0.1	= Kilograms-force (kgf; kg)	X 9.81	= Newtons (N)

Pressure
Pounds-force per square inch (psi; lbf/in²; lb/in²)	X 0.070	= Kilograms-force per square centimetre (kgf/cm²; kg/cm²)	X 14.223	= Pounds-force per square inch (psi; lbf/in²; lb/in²)
Pounds-force per square inch (psi; lbf/in²; lb/in²)	X 0.068	= Atmospheres (atm)	X 14.696	= Pounds-force per square inch (psi; lbf/in²; lb/in²)
Pounds-force per square inch (psi; lbf/in²; lb/in²)	X 0.069	= Bars	X 14.5	= Pounds-force per square inch (psi; lbf/in²; lb/in²)
Pounds-force per square inch (psi; lbf/in²; lb/in²)	X 6.895	= Kilopascals (kPa)	X 0.145	= Pounds-force per square inch (psi; lbf/in²; lb/in²)
Kilopascals (kPa)	X 0.01	= Kilograms-force per square centimetre (kgf/cm²; kg/cm²)	X 98.1	= Kilopascals (kPa)
Millibar (mbar)	X 100	= Pascals (Pa)	X 0.01	= Millibar (mbar)
Millibar (mbar)	X 0.0145	= Pounds-force per square inch (psi; lbf/in²; lb/in²)	X 68.947	= Millibar (mbar)
Millibar (mbar)	X 0.75	= Millimetres of mercury (mmHg)	X 1.333	= Millibar (mbar)
Millibar (mbar)	X 0.401	= Inches of water (inH₂O)	X 2.491	= Millibar (mbar)
Millimetres of mercury (mmHg)	X 0.535	= Inches of water (inH₂O)	X 1.868	= Millimetres of mercury (mmHg)
Inches of water (inH₂O)	X 0.036	= Pounds-force per square inch (psi; lbf/in²; lb/in²)	X 27.68	= Inches of water (inH₂O)

Torque (moment of force)
Pounds-force inches (lbf in; lb in)	X 1.152	= Kilograms-force centimetre (kgf cm; kg cm)	X 0.868	= Pounds-force inches (lbf in; lb in)
Pounds-force inches (lbf in; lb in)	X 0.113	= Newton metres (Nm)	X 8.85	= Pounds-force inches (lbf in; lb in)
Pounds-force inches (lbf in; lb in)	X 0.083	= Pounds-force feet (lbf ft; lb ft)	X 12	= Pounds-force inches (lbf in; lb in)
Pounds-force feet (lbf ft; lb ft)	X 0.138	= Kilograms-force metres (kgf m; kg m)	X 7.233	= Pounds-force feet (lbf ft; lb ft)
Pounds-force feet (lbf ft; lb ft)	X 1.356	= Newton metres (Nm)	X 0.738	= Pounds-force feet (lbf ft; lb ft)
Newton metres (Nm)	X 0.102	= Kilograms-force metres (kgf m; kg m)	X 9.804	= Newton metres (Nm)

Power
Horsepower (hp)	X 745.7	= Watts (W)	X 0.0013	= Horsepower (hp)

Velocity (speed)
Miles per hour (miles/hr; mph)	X 1.609	= Kilometres per hour (km/hr; kph)	X 0.621	= Miles per hour (miles/hr; mph)

Fuel consumption*
Miles per gallon, Imperial (mpg)	X 0.354	= Kilometres per litre (km/l)	X 2.825	= Miles per gallon, Imperial (mpg)
Miles per gallon, US (mpg)	X 0.425	= Kilometres per litre (km/l)	X 2.352	= Miles per gallon, US (mpg)

Temperature

Degrees Fahrenheit = (°C x 1.8) + 32

Degrees Celsius (Degrees Centigrade; °C) = (°F - 32) x 0.56

*It is common practice to convert from miles per gallon (mpg) to litres/100 kilometres (l/100km), where mpg (Imperial) x l/100 km = 282 and mpg (US) x l/100 km = 235

Safety first!

Professional motor mechanics are trained in safe working procedures. However enthusiastic you may be about getting on with the job in hand, do take the time to ensure that your safety is not put at risk. A moment's lack of attention can result in an accident, as can failure to observe certain elementary precautions.

There will always be new ways of having accidents, and the following points do not pretend to be a comprehensive list of all dangers; they are intended rather to make you aware of the risks and to encourage a safety-conscious approach to all work you carry out on your vehicle.

Essential DOs and DON'Ts

DON'T rely on a single jack when working underneath the vehicle. Always use reliable additional means of support, such as axle stands, securely placed under a part of the vehicle that you know will not give way.

DON'T attempt to loosen or tighten high-torque nuts (e.g. wheel hub nuts) while the vehicle is on a jack; it may be pulled off.

DON'T start the engine without first ascertaining that the transmission is in neutral (or 'Park' where applicable) and the parking brake applied.

DON'T suddenly remove the filler cap from a hot cooling system – cover it with a cloth and release the pressure gradually first, or you may get scalded by escaping coolant.

DON'T attempt to drain oil until you are sure it has cooled sufficiently to avoid scalding you.

DON'T grasp any part of the engine, exhaust or catalytic converter without first ascertaining that it is sufficiently cool to avoid burning you.

DON'T allow brake fluid or antifreeze to contact vehicle paintwork.

DON'T syphon toxic liquids such as fuel, brake fluid or antifreeze by mouth, or allow them to remain on your skin.

DON'T inhale dust – it may be injurious to health (see *Asbestos* below).

DON'T allow any spilt oil or grease to remain on the floor – wipe it up straight away, before someone slips on it.

DON'T use ill-fitting spanners or other tools which may slip and cause injury.

DON'T attempt to lift a heavy component which may be beyond your capability – get assistance.

DON'T rush to finish a job, or take unverified short cuts.

DON'T allow children or animals in or around an unattended vehicle.

DO wear eye protection when using power tools such as drill, sander, bench grinder etc, and when working under the vehicle.

DO use a barrier cream on your hands prior to undertaking dirty jobs – it will protect your skin from infection as well as making the dirt easier to remove afterwards; but make sure your hands aren't left slippery. Note that long-term contact with used engine oil can be a health hazard.

DO keep loose clothing (cuffs, tie etc) and long hair well out of the way of moving mechanical parts.

DO remove rings, wristwatch etc, before working on the vehicle – especially the electrical system.

DO ensure that any lifting tackle used has a safe working load rating adequate for the job.

DO keep your work area tidy – it is only too easy to fall over articles left lying around.

DO get someone to check periodically that all is well, when working alone on the vehicle.

DO carry out work in a logical sequence and check that everything is correctly assembled and tightened afterwards.

DO remember that your vehicle's safety affects that of yourself and others. If in doubt on any point, get specialist advice.

IF, in spite of following these precautions, you are unfortunate enough to injure yourself, seek medical attention as soon as possible.

Asbestos

Certain friction, insulating, sealing, and other products – such as brake linings, brake bands, clutch linings, torque converters, gaskets, etc – contain asbestos. *Extreme care must be taken to avoid inhalation of dust from such products since it is hazardous to health.* If in doubt, assume that they *do* contain asbestos.

Fire

Remember at all times that petrol (gasoline) is highly flammable. Never smoke, or have any kind of naked flame around, when working on the vehicle. But the risk does not end there – a spark caused by an electrical short-circuit, by two metal surfaces contacting each other, by careless use of tools, or even by static electricity built up in your body under certain conditions, can ignite petrol vapour, which in a confined space is highly explosive.

Always disconnect the battery earth (ground) terminal before working on any part of the fuel or electrical system, and never risk spilling fuel on to a hot engine or exhaust.

It is recommended that a fire extinguisher of a type suitable for fuel and electrical fires is kept handy in the garage or workplace at all times. Never try to extinguish a fuel or electrical fire with water.

Note: *Any reference to a 'torch' appearing in this manual should always be taken to mean a hand-held battery-operated electric lamp or flashlight. It does NOT mean a welding/gas torch or blowlamp.*

Fumes

Certain fumes are highly toxic and can quickly cause unconsciousness and even death if inhaled to any extent. Petrol (gasoline) vapour comes into this category, as do the vapours from certain solvents such as trichloroethylene. Any draining or pouring of such volatile fluids should be done in a well ventilated area.

When using cleaning fluids and solvents, read the instructions carefully. Never use materials from unmarked containers – they may give off poisonous vapours.

Never run the engine of a motor vehicle in an enclosed space such as a garage. Exhaust fumes contain carbon monoxide which is extremely poisonous; if you need to run the engine, always do so in the open air or at least have the rear of the vehicle outside the workplace.

If you are fortunate enough to have the use of an inspection pit, never drain or pour petrol, and never run the engine, while the vehicle is standing over it; the fumes, being heavier than air, will concentrate in the pit with possibly lethal results.

The battery

Never cause a spark, or allow a naked light, near the vehicle's battery. It will normally be giving off a certain amount of hydrogen gas, which is highly explosive.

Always disconnect the battery earth (ground) terminal before working on the fuel or electrical systems.

If possible, loosen the filler plugs or cover when charging the battery from an external source. Do not charge at an excessive rate or the battery may burst.

Take care when topping up and when carrying the battery. The acid electrolyte, even when diluted, is very corrosive and should not be allowed to contact the eyes or skin.

If you ever need to prepare electrolyte yourself, always add the acid slowly to the water, and never the other way round. Protect against splashes by wearing rubber gloves and goggles.

When jump starting a car using a booster battery, for negative earth (ground) vehicles, connect the jump leads in the following sequence: First connect one jump lead between the positive ($+$) terminals of the two batteries. Then connect the other jump lead first to the negative ($-$) terminal of the booster battery, and then to a good earthing (ground) point on the vehicle to be started, at least 18 in (45 cm) from the battery if possible. Ensure that hands and jump leads are clear of any moving parts, and that the two vehicles do not touch. Disconnect the leads in the reverse order.

Mains electricity

When using an electric power tool, inspection light etc, which works from the mains, always ensure that the appliance is correctly connected to its plug and that, where necessary, it is properly earthed (grounded). Do not use such appliances in damp conditions and, again, beware of creating a spark or applying excessive heat in the vicinity of fuel or fuel vapour.

Ignition HT voltage

A severe electric shock can result from touching certain parts of the ignition system, such as the HT leads, when the engine is running or being cranked, particularly if components are damp or the insulation is defective. Where an electronic ignition system is fitted, the HT voltage is much higher and could prove fatal.

Routine maintenance

Maintenance is essential for ensuring safety, and desirable for the purpose of getting the best in terms of performance and economy from your car. Over the years the need for periodic lubrication – oiling, greasing and so on – has been drastically reduced, if not totally eliminated. This has unfortunately tended to lead some owners to think that because no such action is required, components either no longer exist, or will last forever. This is a serious delusion. It follows therefore that the largest initial element of maintenance is visual examination and a general sense of awareness. This may lead to repairs or renewals, but should help to avoid roadside breakdowns.

Although fluid levels and brakepad wear are monitored by sensors, there is still no real substitute for visual inspection. This is a precautionary operation to be able to anticipate the illumination of a warning lamp which may well otherwise occur at a time when topping-up, rectification of a leak, or brake overhaul may at least be inconvenient if not expensive or dangerous.

The following service schedules are a list of the maintenance requirements and the intervals at which they should be carried out, as recommended by the manufacturers. Where applicable these procedures are covered in greater detail throughout this manual, near the beginning of each Chapter.

Every 400 km (250 miles) or weekly, whichever comes first

Check engine oil level (Chapter 1)
Check coolant level (Chapter 2)
Check tyre pressures (Chapter 8)
Check operation of all lights and horn (Chapter 12)
Check washer bottle level (Chapter 12)

After first 1600 km (1000 miles) – new cars or after major engine overhaul

Renew engine oil and filter (Chapter 1)
Adjust valve clearances (after overhaul only) (Chapter 1)
Check torque of cylinder head bolts (after overhaul only) (Chapter 1)
Renew manual transmission oil (Chapter 6)

Every 10 000 km (6 000 miles) or 6 months, whichever comes first

Renew the engine oil. On Turbo models, also renew the oil filter (Chapter 1)
Check the cooling system hoses for condition and security (Chapter 2)
Check and clean the crankcase ventilation system hoses and jets (Chapter 1)
Check the condition and tension of the drivebelts (Chapter 2)
On Turbo models, have the Turbo boost pressure circuits checked for leaks. This task must be entrusted to a Renault dealer
Clean and regap the spark plugs (Chapter 4)
Check the manual transmission oil level (Chapter 6)
Check the automatic transmission fluid level (Chapter 7)
Check the fluid level in the brake/clutch master cylinder and top up if necessary (Chapter 9)
Check the fluid level in the power steering fluid reservoir and top up if necessary (Chapter 10)
Inspect the front brake pads for excessive wear and renew if necessary
Check the brake system circuits for damage, corrosion and signs of leakage (Chapter 9)
Check the battery terminals for security and signs of corrosion
Where applicable, check the battery electrolyte level and top up if required (Chapter 12)
Check the headlamps for satisfactory operation and adjustment (Chapter 12)
Check the windscreen wipers and washers for satisfactory operation and the wiper blades for condition (Chapter 12)
Check all the instruments for satisfactory operation

Every 20 000 km (12 000 miles) or annually, whichever comes first

Renew the engine oil and filter – all models (Chapter 1)
Renew the air filter element (Chapter 3)
Renew the spark plugs (Chapter 4)
Check the rear brake linings (or pads if applicable) for wear (Chapter 9)
Check the driveshaft bellows for condition (Chapter 8)
Check the underbody for corrosion (Chapter 11)

Every 50 000 km (30 000 miles) or 2¹/₂ years whichever comes first

Renew the fuel filter (Chapter 3)
Drain and renew the manual transmission oil (Chapter 6)
Drain and renew the automatic transmission fluid. Renew the gauze filter (Chapter 7)
Drain and renew the brake fluid (Chapter 9)
Check and if necessary adjust the handbrake (Chapter 9)
Check the condition of the steering and suspension components
Check the wheel alignment (Chapter 10)
Drain and renew the engine coolant (Chapter 2)

Every 65 000 km (40 000 miles)

Renew the timing belt (Chapter 1)

Engine and underbonnet component locations – 1.7 litre model

1 Engine oil dipstick	8 Fuel filter	13 Shock absorber turret
2 Radiator and cooling fan	9 Brake master cylinder	14 Ignition control module
3 Oil filter	reservoir	15 Battery
4 Radiator expansion tank cap	10 Air cleaner	16 Washer reservoir
5 Alternator	11 Coolant/heater feed and	17 Gearbox
6 Vehicle identification plates	return hoses	18 Gearbox breather
7 Oil filler cap	12 Ignition distributor	19 Clutch cable

Engine and underbonnet component locations – 2.0 litre non-Turbo model

1 Engine oil dipstick
2 Battery
3 Vehicle identification plates
4 Shock absorber turret
5 Brake master cylinder reservoir
6 Steering gear unit
7 Engine oil filler cap

8 Ignition coil module
9 Heater coolant hose and bleed valve
10 Cooling system expansion bottle
11 Power steering fluid reservoir

12 Engine management computer
13 Air cleaner
14 Throttle casing
15 Throttle control linkage
16 Cooling system top hose/bleed valve/thermostat
17 Washer reservoir

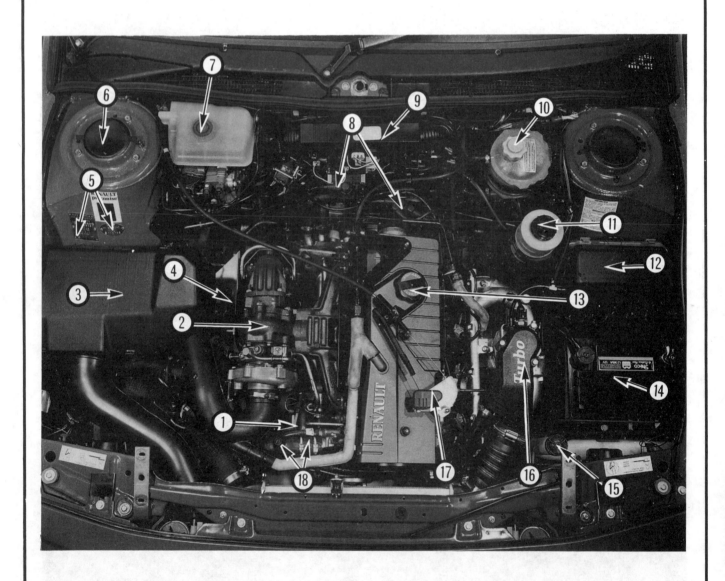

Engine and underbonnet component locations – 2.0 litre Turbo model (turbocharger heat shield removed for clarity)

1 Engine oil dipstick	8 Ignition coil module and distributor	13 Engine oil filler cap
2 Turbocharger	9 ABS relays	14 Battery
3 Air cleaner	10 Cooling system expansion bottle	15 Washer reservoir
4 Engine oil filter mounting		16 Throttle casing
5 Vehicle identification plates	11 Power steering fluid reservoir	17 Throttle control linkage
6 Shock absorber turret		18 Coolant top hose/bleed valve/thermostat
7 Brake/clutch master cylinder reservoir	12 Engine management computer	

Front underside view – 1.7 litre model (undershield removed)

1 Exhaust
2 Subframe
3 Steering gear
4 Driveshaft
5 Sump drain plug
6 Transmission undershield
7 Brake caliper
8 Suspension lower arm
9 Anti-roll bar
10 Steering arm
11 Gearchange rod

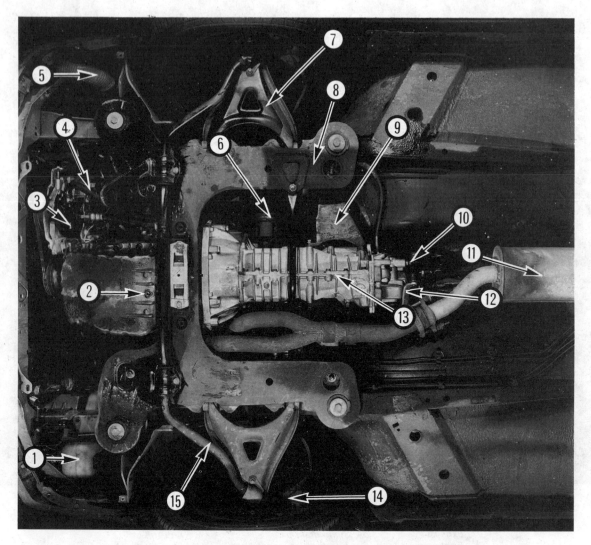

Front underside view – 2.0 litre model (undershield removed)

1 Washer reservoir
2 Sump and drain plug
3 Power steering pump unit
4 Alternator
5 Air cleaner intake hose
6 Driveshaft

7 Suspension lower arm
8 Subframe
9 Transmission mounting
10 Reverse selector cable
11 Exhaust

12 Gearchange selector
13 Transmission (undershield removed)
14 Brake caliper
15 Anti-roll bar

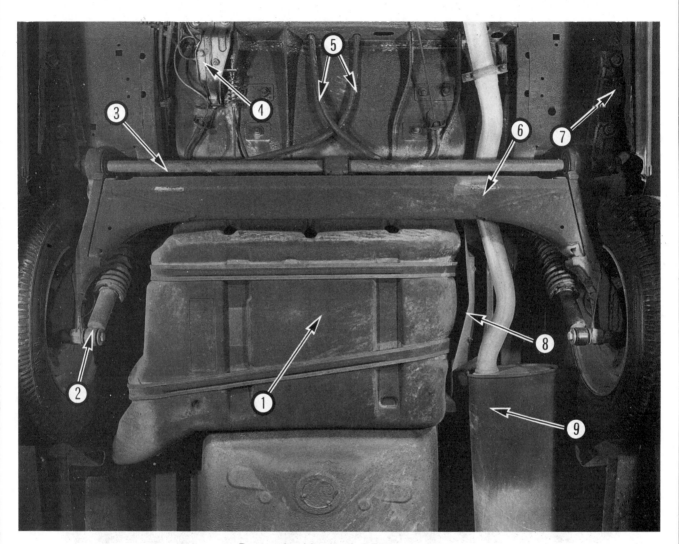

Rear underside view – 1.7 litre model

1	Fuel tank	4	Brake compensator unit	7	Rear axle mounting
2	Shock absorber	5	Handbrake cables	8	Heat shield
3	Torsion bar	6	Rear axle beam	9	Exhaust

Rear underside view – 2.0 litre model

1	Fuel tank	5	Fuel pulse damper	9	Torsion bar
2	Shock absorber	6	Fuel filter	10	Exhaust
3	Rear axle beam	7	Brake compensator unit	11	Rear axle mounting
4	Fuel pump	8	Handbrake cables	12	Heat shield

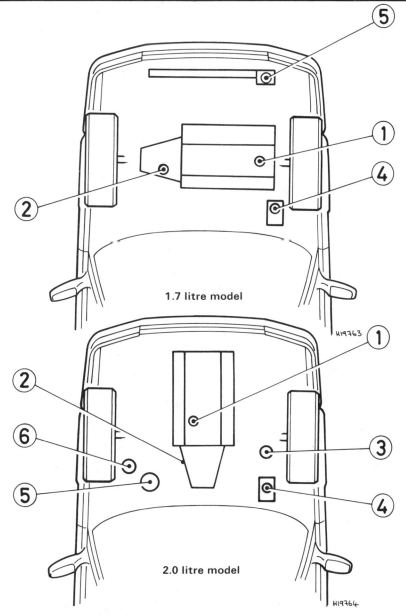

1.7 litre model

2.0 litre model

Recommended lubricants and fluids

Component or system	Lubricant type/specification	Duckhams recommendation
1 Engine	Multigrade engine oil, viscosity SAE 10W/40, 15W/50, or 20W/50	Duckhams QXR Hypergrade, or 10W/40 Motor Oil
2 Manual transmission JB3 and NG9	Hypoid gear oil, viscosity SAE 80W to API GL5	Duckhams Hypoid 80S
UN1	Hypoid gear oil, viscosity SAE 75W/90	Duckhams Hypoid 75W/90S
3 Automatic transmission	Dexron type ATF	Duckhams D-Matic
4 Brake/clutch fluid reservoir	Hydraulic fluid to SAE J1703F, DOT3 or DOT4	Duckhams Universal Brake and Clutch Fluid
5 Cooling system	Ethylene glycol based antifreeze with corrosion inhibitor to BS 3151, 3152, or 6580	Duckhams Universal Antifreeze and Summer Coolant
6 Power steering fluid reservoir	Dexron type ATF	Duckhams D-Matic

Fault diagnosis

Introduction

The vehicle owner who does his or her own maintenance according to the recommended schedules should not have to use this section of the manual very often. Modern component reliability is such that, provided those items subject to wear or deterioration are inspected or renewed at the specified intervals, sudden failure is comparatively rare. Faults do not usually just happen as a result of sudden failure, but develop over a period of time. Major mechanical failures in particular are usually preceded by characteristic symptoms over hundreds or even thousands of miles. Those components which do occasionally fail without warning are often small and easily carried in the vehicle.

With any fault finding, the first step is to decide where to begin investigations. Sometimes this is obvious, but on other occasions a little detective work will be necessary. The owner who makes half a dozen haphazard adjustments or replacements may be successful in curing a fault (or its symptoms), but he will be none the wiser if the fault recurs and he may well have spent more time and money than was necessary. A calm and logical approach will be found to be more satisfactory in the long run. Always take into account any warning signs or abnormalities that may have been noticed in the period preceding the fault – power loss, high or low gauge readings, unusual noises or smells, etc – and remember that failure of components such as fuses or spark plugs may only be pointers to some underlying fault.

The pages which follow here are intended to help in cases of failure to start or breakdown on the road. There is also a Fault Diagnosis Section at the end of each Chapter which should be consulted if the preliminary checks prove unfruitful. Whatever the fault, certain basic principles apply. These are as follows:

Verify the fault. This is simply a matter of being sure that you know what the symptoms are before starting work. This is particularly important if you are investigating a fault for someone else who may not have described it very accurately.

Don't overlook the obvious. For example, if the vehicle won't start, is there petrol in the tank? (Don't take anyone else's word on this particular point, and don't trust the fuel gauge either!) If an electrical fault is indicated, look for loose or broken wires before digging out the test gear.

Cure the disease, not the symptom. Substituting a flat battery with a fully charged one will get you off the hard shoulder, but if the underlying cause is not attended to, the new battery will go the same way. Similarly, changing oil-fouled spark plugs for a new set will get you moving again, but remember that the reason for the fouling (if it wasn't simply an incorrect grade of plug) will have to be established and corrected.

Don't take anything for granted. Particularly, don't forget that a 'new' component may itself be defective (especially if it's been rattling round in the boot for months), and don't leave components out of a fault diagnosis sequence just because they are new or recently fitted. When you do finally diagnose a difficult fault, you'll probably realise that all the evidence was there from the start.

Electrical faults

Electrical faults can be more puzzling than straightforward mechanical failures, but they are no less susceptible to logical analysis if the basic principles of operation are understood. Vehicle electrical wiring exists in extremely unfavourable conditions – heat, vibration and chemical attack – and the first things to look for are loose or corroded connections and broken or chafed wires, especially where the wires pass through holes in the bodywork or are subject to vibration.

All metal-bodied vehicles in current production have one pole of the battery 'earthed', ie connected to the vehicle bodywork, and in nearly all modern vehicles it is the negative (–) terminal. The various electrical components – motors, bulb holders etc – are also connected to earth, either by means of a lead or directly by their mountings. Electric current flows through the component and then back to the battery via the bodywork. If the component mounting is loose or corroded, or if a good path back to the battery is not available, the circuit will be incomplete and malfunction will result. The engine and/or gearbox are also earthed by means of flexible metal straps to the body or subframe; if these straps are loose or missing, starter motor, generator and ignition trouble may result.

Assuming the earth return to be satisfactory, electrical faults will be due either to component malfunction or to defects in the current supply. Individual components are dealt with in Chapter XX. If supply wires are broken or cracked internally this results in an open-circuit, and the easiest way to check for this is to bypass the suspect wire temporarily with a length of wire having a crocodile clip or suitable connector at each end. Alternatively, a 12V test lamp can be used to verify the presence of supply voltage at various points along the wire and the break can be thus isolated.

If a bare portion of a live wire touches the bodywork or other earthed metal part, the electricity will take the low-resistance path thus formed back to the battery: this is known as a short-circuit. Hopefully a short-circuit will blow a fuse, but otherwise it may cause burning of the insulation (and possibly further short-circuits) or even a fire. This is why it is inadvisable to bypass persistently blowing fuses with silver foil or wire.

Spares and tool kit

Most vehicles are supplied only with sufficient tools for wheel changing; the *Maintenance and minor repair* tool kit detailed in *Tools*

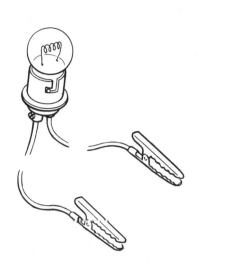

A simple test lamp is useful for tracing electrical faults

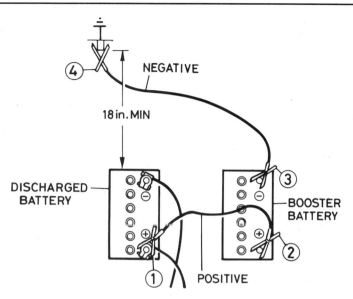

Jump start lead connections for negative earth vehicles –
connect leads in order shown

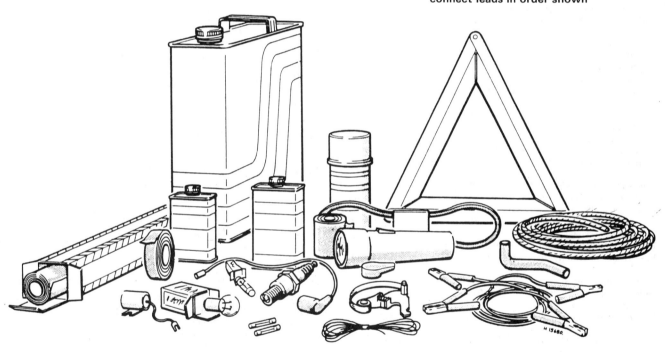

Carrying a few spares can save you a long walk

and working facilities, with the addition of a hammer, is probably sufficient for those repairs that most motorists would consider attempting at the roadside. In addition a few items which can be fitted without too much trouble in the event of a breakdown should be carried. Experience and available space will modify the list below, but the following may save having to call on professional assistance:

Spark plugs, clean and correctly gapped
HT lead and plug cap – long enough to reach the plug furthest from the distributor
Distributor rotor
Drivebelt(s) – emergency type may suffice
Spare fuses
Set of principal light bulbs
Tin of radiator sealer and hose bandage
Exhaust bandage
Roll of insulating tape

Length of soft iron wire
Length of electrical flex
Torch or inspection lamp (can double as test lamp)
Battery jump leads
Tow-rope
Ignition waterproofing aerosol
Litre of engine oil
Sealed can of hydraulic fluid
Emergency windscreen
'Jubilee' clips
Tube of filler paste

If spare fuel is carried, a can designed for the purpose should be used to minimise risks of leakage and collision damage. A first aid kit and a warning triangle, whilst not at present compulsory in the UK, are obviously sensible items to carry in addition to the above.

When touring abroad it may be advisable to carry additional spares which, even if you cannot fit them yourself, could save having to wait while parts are obtained. The items below may be worth considering:

Clutch and throttle cables
Cylinder head gasket
Alternator brushes
Tyre valve core

One of the motoring organisations will be able to advise on availability of fuel etc in foreign countries.

Engine will not start

Engine fails to turn when starter operated
Flat battery (recharge, use jump leads, or push start)
Battery terminals loose or corroded
Battery defective
Engine earth strap loose or broken
Starter motor (or solenoid) wiring loose or broken
Automatic transmission selector in wrong position, or inhibitor switch faulty
Ignition/starter switch faulty
Major mechanical failure (seizure)
Starter or solenoid internal fault (see Chapter 12)

Starter motor turns engine slowly
Partially discharged battery (recharge, use jump leads, or push start)
Battery terminals loose or corroded
Battery earth to body defective
Engine earth strap loose
Starter motor (or solenoid) wiring loose
Starter motor internal fault (see Chapter 12)

Starter motor spins without turning engine
Flat battery
Starter motor pinion sticking on sleeve
Flywheel gear teeth damaged or worn
Starter motor mounting bolts loose

Engine turns normally but fails to start
Damp or dirty HT leads and distributor cap (crank engine and check for spark)
No fuel in tank (check for delivery at carburettor or fuel injectors on carburettor models)
Excessive choke (hot engine) or insufficient choke (cold engine)
Fouled or incorrectly gapped spark plugs (remove, clean and regap)
Other ignition system fault (see Chapter 4)
Other fuel system fault (see Chapter 3)
Poor compression
Major mechanical failure (eg camshaft drive)

Engine fires but will not run
Insufficient choke (cold engine on carburettor models)
Air leaks at carburettor or inlet manifold
Fuel starvation (see Chapter 3)
Ignition fault (see Chapter 4)

Engine cuts out and will not restart

Engine cuts out suddenly – ignition fault
Loose or disconnected LT wires
Wet HT leads or distributor cap (after traversing water splash)
Coil or condenser failure (check for spark)
Other ignition fault (see Chapter 4)

Engine misfires before cutting out – fuel fault
Fuel tank empty
Fuel pump defective or filter blocked (check for delivery)
Fuel tank filler vent blocked (suction will be evident on releasing cap)
Carburettor needle valve sticking
Carburettor jets or fuel injectors blocked (fuel contaminated)

Other fuel system fault (see Chapter 3)

Engine cuts out – other causes
Serious overheating
Major mechanical failure (eg camshaft drive)

Engine overheats

Ignition (no-charge) warning light illuminated
Slack or broken drivebelt – retension or renew (Chapter 2)

Ignition warning light not illuminated
Coolant loss due to internal or external leakage (see Chapter 2)
Thermostat defective
Low oil level
Brakes binding
Radiator clogged externally or internally
Electric cooling fan not operating correctly
Engine waterways clogged
Ignition timing incorrect or automatic advance malfunctioning
Mixture too weak

Note: *Do not add cold water to an overheated engine or damage may result*

Low engine oil pressure

Gauge reads low or warning light illuminated with engine running
Oil level low or incorrect grade
Defective gauge or sender unit
Wire to sender unit earthed
Engine overheating
Oil filter clogged or bypass valve defective
Oil pressure relief valve defective
Oil pick-up strainer clogged
Oil pump worn or mountings loose
Worn main or big-end bearings

Note: *Low oil pressure in a high-mileage engine at tickover is not necessarily a cause for concern. Sudden pressure loss at speed is far more significant. In any event, check the gauge or warning light sender before condemning the engine.*

Engine noises

Pre-ignition (pinking) on acceleration
Incorrect grade of fuel
Ignition timing incorrect
Worn or maladjusted carburettor or fuel injection components
Excessive carbon build-up in engine

Whistling or wheezing noises
Leaking vacuum hose
Leaking carburettor or inlet manifold gasket
Blowing head gasket

Tapping or rattling
Incorrect valve clearances
Worn valve gear
Worn timing belt
Broken piston ring (ticking noise)

Knocking or thumping
Unintentional mechanical contact (eg fan blades)
Worn drivebelt
Peripheral component fault (generator, water pump etc)
Worn big-end bearings (regular heavy knocking, perhaps less under load)
Worn main bearings (rumbling and knocking, perhaps worsening under load)
Piston slap (most noticeable when cold)

Chapter 1 Engine

Contents

Specifications

Part A – 1721 cc (1.7 litre) engines
General
Type	Four cylinder, in-line, belt-driven overhead camshaft. Engine transversely mounted
Engine type designation	F2N
Engine code numbers and maximum power output:	
F2N 712	76 bhp at 5000 rpm
F2N 710	90 bhp at 5500 rpm
Compression ratio:	
F2N 712	9.2 : 1
F2N 710	10 : 1
Firing order	1-3-4-2 (No 1 cylinder at flywheel end)
Bore	81.0 mm
Stroke	83.5 mm
Capacity	1721 cc

Crankshaft
Number of main bearings	5
Main journal diameter	54.794 mm
Main journal minimum regrind diameter	54.545 mm
Crankpin journal diameter	48 mm
Crankpin journal minimum regrind diameter	47.75 mm
Crankshaft endfloat	0.07 to 0.23 mm
Thrust washer thicknesses available	2.30, 2.35, 2.40, 2.45 and 2.50 mm

Connecting rods
Connecting rod endfloat	0.22 to 0.40 mm

Pistons
Piston fitted direction	V or arrow on crown towards flywheel
Gudgeon pin fit in piston	Hand push-fit
Gudgeon pin fit in connecting rod	Interference
Gudgeon pin length	64.7 to 65.0 mm
Gudgeon pin outside diameter	21 mm
Piston clearance in cylinder bore	0.023 to 0.047 mm

Piston rings
Number	Three (two compression, one oil control)
Compression ring thickness:	
Top ring	1.75 mm
Second ring	2.0 mm
Oil control ring thickness	3.0 mm
Piston ring end gaps	Supplied pre-set

Camshaft
Number of bearings	5
Endfloat	0.048 to 0.133 mm

Auxiliary shaft
Bush diameter:	
Inner	39.5 mm
Outer	40.5 mm
Endfloat	0.07 to 0.15 mm

Valves
Seat included angle:	
Inlet	120°
Exhaust	90°
Head diameter:	
Inlet	38.1 mm
Exhaust	32.5 mm
Stem diameter	8.0 mm
Valve seat width in cylinder head	1.5 to 1,9 mm
Valve head-to-cylinder head face recess depth (inlet and exhaust)	0.8 to 1.1 mm
Valve guides:	
Bore diameter in cylinder head	12.99 mm
Fitted height above joint face	42.8 to 43.2 mm
Valve springs:	
Free height	44.9 mm
Valve clearances (cold):	
Inlet	0.20 mm (0.0079 in)
Exhaust	0.40 mm (0.0158 in)

Tappets
Diameter	34.99 to 35.04 mm

Cylinder head

Maximum permitted warp .... 0.05 mm
Cylinder head height .... 169.3 to 169.7 mm

Lubrication system

Oil pump:
    Gear-to-body clearance .... 0.02 mm (maximum)
    Gear endfloat .... 0.085 mm (maximum)
System pressure (at 80°C):
    Idling .... 2.0 bar (29.0 lbf/in²)
    Running (at 3000 rpm) .... 3.5 bar (50.8 lbf/in²)
Oil type/specification .... Multigrade engine oil, viscosity SAE 10W/40, 15W/50, or 20W/50
                  (Duckhams QXR, Hypergrade, or 10W/40 Motor Oil)
Oil capacity (with filter renewal) .... 5.2 litres (9.15 pints)

Torque wrench settings

	Nm	lbf ft
Cylinder head bolts:		
1st tightening	30	22
2nd tightening	70	52
1st retightening – wait 3 minutes, slacken all bolts then tighten to	20	15
2nd retightening	Turn through 123°	Turn through 123°
Main bearing cap bolts	65	48
Big-end bearing cap bolts	50	37
Flywheel retaining bolts	55	41
Camshaft bearing cap bolts:		
8 mm diameter	20	15
6 mm diameter	10	7
Camshaft sprocket bolt	50	37
Idler puller bolt	20	15
Tensioner pulley nut	40	30
Auxiliary shaft sprocket bolt	50	37
Crankshaft pulley bolt	95	70
Oil pump-to-crankcase retaining bolts	25	18
Sump retaining bolts	15	11
Engine mounting nuts and bolts	40	30
Piston cooler oil jet bolts	30	22

Part B – 1995 cc (2.0 litre) engines

General

Type .... Four-cylinder, in-line, belt-driven overhead camshaft, light alloy
                  construction with wet cylinder liners. Engine and transmission
                  longitudinally mounted at the front of vehicle
Engine type designation J7R
Engine code numbers and maximum power output:
    J7R 750 .... 120 bhp at 5500 rpm
    J7R 750 (TXE model) .... 124 bhp at 5500 rpm
    J7R 752 (Turbo model) .... 175 bhp at 5200 rpm
Compression ratio:
    J7R 750 models .... 10 : 1
    J7R 752 model .... 8 : 1
Firing order .... 1-3-4-2 (No 1 cylinder at the flywheel end)
Bore .... 88.0 mm
Stroke .... 82.0 mm
Capacity .... 1995 cc
Compression pressure:
    Minimum .... 10.3 bar (149.4 lbf/in²)
    Maximum difference between cylinders .... 1.4 bar (20.3 lbf/in²)

Cylinder block

Material .... Light alloy
Overall depth .... 149.25 to 149.75 mm

Cylinder liners

Height .... 143.5 mm
Bore .... 88.0 mm
Base locating diameter .... 93.6 mm
Protrusion without O-ring .... 0.008 to 0.150 mm

Crankshaft

Number of main bearings 5
Main bearing journal diameter .... 62.892 mm
Main bearing journal minimum
regrind diameter (0.050 mm undersize) .... 62.642 mm
Crankpin diameter .... 52.296 mm
Crankpin minimum regrind diameter (0.025 mm undersize) .... 52.271 mm
Crankshaft endfloat .... 0.07 to 0.25 mm

Connecting rods and gudgeon pins
Small-end play .... 0.31 to 0.57 mm
Gudgeon pins (press fit in small-end):
    Length .... 75.0 mm
    Diameter .... 23.0 mm

Piston rings
Piston ring thickness:
    Top compression .... 1.75 mm
    Second compression .... 2.0 mm
    Oil control .... 4.0 mm

Camshaft
Number of bearings 5
Endfloat:
    J6R .... 0.07 to 0.13 mm

Cylinder head
Material .... Light alloy
Overall height .... 111.6 mm
Maximum permitted surface distortion .... 0.05 mm

Timing belt
Deflection at midway point between auxiliary
shaft sprocket and camshaft sprocket .... 5.5 to 7.0 mm

Valves
Stem diameter .... 8.0 mm
Head diameter:
    Inlet .... 44.0 mm
    Exhaust .... 38.5 mm
Valve seat included angle:
    Inlet .... 120°
    Exhaust .... 90°
Valve seat width:
    Inlet .... 1.8 mm
    Exhaust .... 1.6 mm
Valve guides:
    Bore .... 8.0 mm
    Outside diameter (nominal) .... 13.0 m
    Repair oversizes:
        With one groove .... 13.10 mm
        With two grooves .... 13.25 mm
Valve springs:
    Free height:
        Later models .... 46.0 mm
Valve clearances (cold):
    Inlet .... 0.10 mm (0.0039 in)
    Exhaust .... 0.25 mm (0.0099 in)

Lubrication system
Oil pump:
    Type .... Gear, driven from auxiliary shaft
    Clearances:
        Gear teeth to body .... 0.05 to 0.12 mm
        Gear endfloat .... 0.02 to 0.10 mm
Oil pressure (at 80°C 176°F):
    At idle .... 0.8 bar (11.6 lbf/in²)
    At 3000 rpm .... 3.0 bar (43.5 lbf/in²)
Oil type/specification .... Multigrade engine oil, viscosity SAE 10W/40, 15W/50, or 20W/50
                                  (Duckhams QXR, Hypergrade or 10W/40 Motor Oil)
Oil capacity (with filter renewal) .... 6.2 litres (10.9 pints)

Torque wrench setting	Nm	lbf/ft
Cylinder head bolts:		
Stage 1	49	36
Stage 2	79	58
Stage 3	95	70
Run engine for 20 minutes, allow to cool fully then retighten bolts as described in Section 88		
Main bearing cap bolts	95	70
Big-end cap nuts	49	36
*Flywheel bolts	60	44
*Driveplate-to-crankshaft bolts	68	50
Driveplate-to-torque converter bolts	30	22
Crankshaft pulley bolt	79	58
Auxiliary shaft sprocket bolt	49	36

Camshaft sprocket bolt	49	36
Oil pump fixing bolts	44	32
Oil pump cover bolts	12	9
Timing belt tensioner bolt and nut	25	18
Sump pan bolts	10	7
Flywheel or torque converter housing-to-engine bolts	54	40
Rocker shaft filter bolt	20	15
Engine mounting nuts and bolts	40	30

* Smear bolt threads with locking fluid

PART A: 1721 CC (1.7 LITRE) ENGINE

1   General description

The engine is of four-cylinder, in-line overhead camshaft type, mounted transversely at the front of the car.

The crankshaft is supported in five shell type main bearings. Thrust washers are fitted to No 2 main bearing to control crankshaft endfloat.

The connecting rods are attached to the crankshaft by horizontally split shell type big-end bearings, and to the pistons by interference fit gudgeon pins. The aluminium alloy pistons are of the slipper type and are fitted with three piston rings; two compression rings and a scraper type oil control ring.

The overhead camshaft is mounted directly in the cylinder head, and is driven by the crankshaft via a toothed rubber timing belt. The camshaft operated the valves via inverted bucket type tappets which

Fig. 1.1 Cutaway view of the 1.7 litre engine (Sec 1)

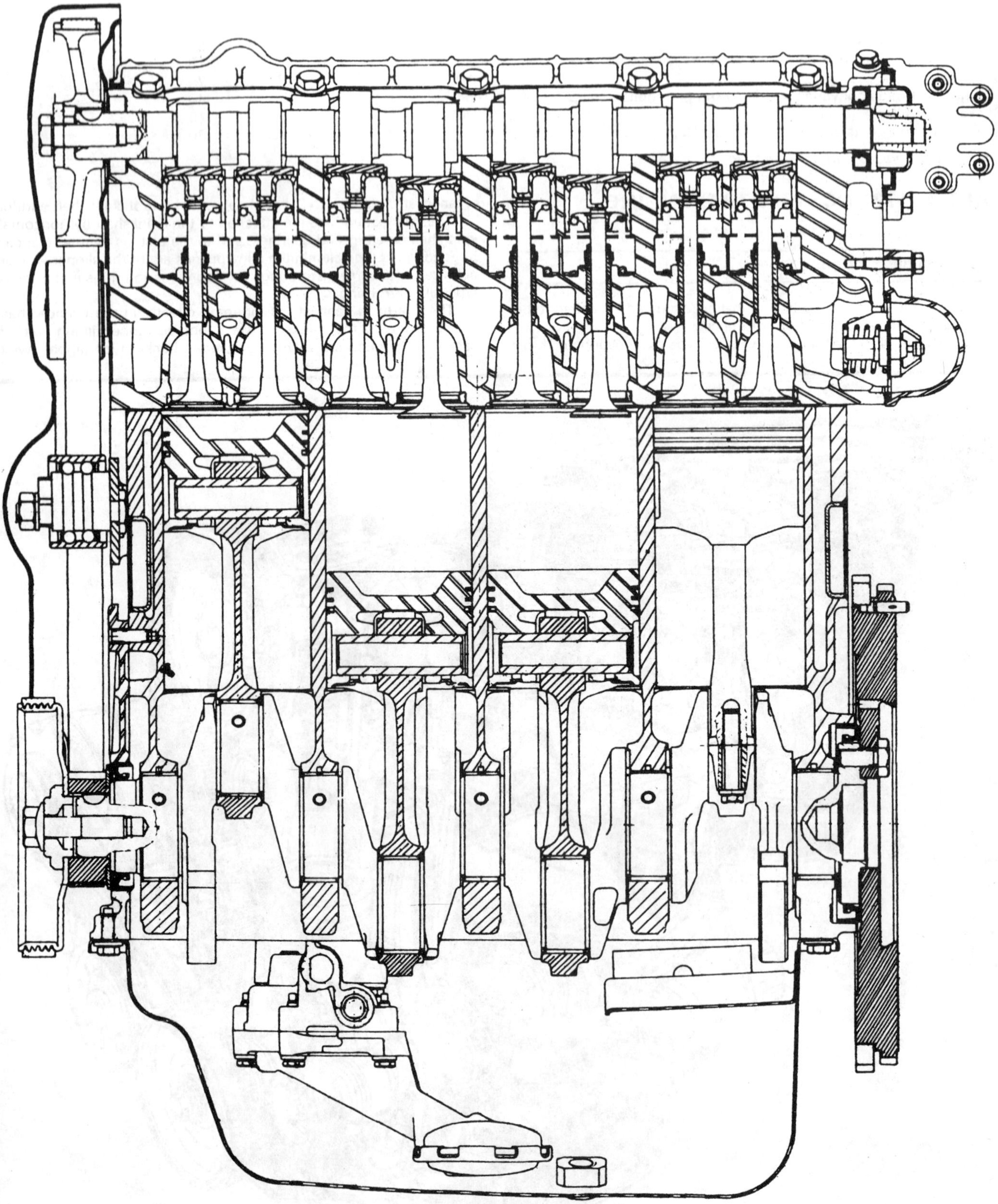

Fig. 1.2 Sectional view of the 1.7 litre engine (Sec 1)

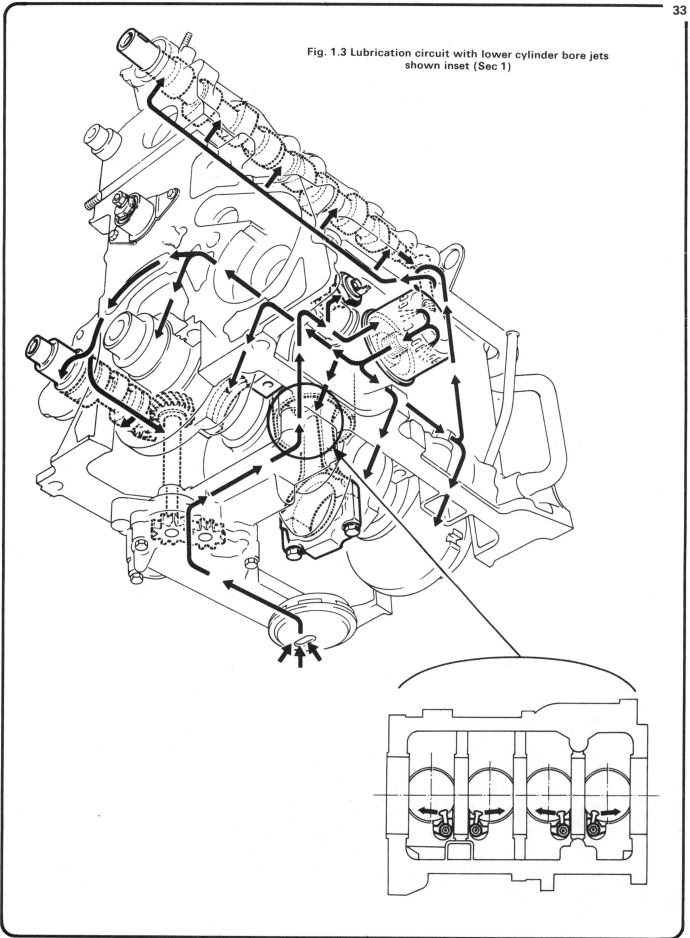

Fig. 1.3 Lubrication circuit with lower cylinder bore jets shown inset (Sec 1)

operate in bores machined directly in the cylinder head. Valve clearance adjustment is by selected shims located externally between the tappet bucket and the cam lobe. The inlet and exhaust valves are mounted vertically in the cylinder head and are each closed by a single valve spring.

An auxiliary shaft located alongside the crankshaft is also driven by the toothed timing belt, and actuates the oil pump via a skew gear.

A semi-closed crankcase ventilation system is employed, and crankcase fumes are drawn from an oil separator on the cylinder block and passed via a hose to the inlet manifold.

Engine lubrication is by pressure feed from a gear type oil pump located beneath the crankshaft. Engine oil is fed through an externally-mounted oil filter to the main oil gallery feeding the crankshaft auxiliary shaft and camshaft. Oil jets are fitted to the lower end of each cylinder bore to lubricate and cool the pistons.

The distributor rotor and the fuel pump are driven by the camshaft; the rotor directly and the fuel pump via an eccentric and plunger.

2 Maintenance

Carry out the following procedures at the intervals specified in the 'Routine maintenance' Section at the start of this manual.

General checks
1   At weekly intervals, check the engine oil level, preferably when the engine is cold.
2   Withdraw the dipstick, wipe it clean and re-insert it. Withdraw it for the second time and read off the oil level which should be between the low and high marks.
3   Top up if necessary through the cap on the camshaft cover.
4   Visually inspect the engine joint faces, gaskets, seals and related hoses for any sign of oil or water leaks. Pay particular attention to the areas around the camshaft cover, crankshaft oil seal carrier and sump joint faces. Rectify any leaks by referring to the appropriate Sections of this Chapter.

Engine oil and filter renewal
5   Run the engine for a few minutes to warm the oil, enabling it to drain more easily. Switch off, and remove the cap from the camshaft cover.
6   Position a suitable container underneath the engine sump drain plug. Unscrew and remove the plug using an 8 mm square head key as shown (photo).
7   When the oil has drained, unscrew and discard the oil filter. A filter removal tool (strap wrench) will be require for this. If one is not available, drive a large screwdriver through the filter canister and use it as a lever to unscrew the filter (photo).
8   Smear the rubber sealing ring of the new filter with clean engine oil and tighten it fully by hand only.
9   Refit and tighten the sump drain plug. Refill the engine with the specified type and quantity of oil (photo), and refit the cap to the rocker cover.
10 Start the engine, and run it for a few seconds to allow time for the new filter to fill with oil. Check for signs of any oil leaks from the filter joint.

11 Switch off, wait a few minutes and check the oil level on the dipstick. Top up as necessary to the full mark.

Fig. 1.4 Engine oil level dipstick location (1) and oil filler cap (3) (Sec 2)

3 Major operations possible with the engine in the car

The following operations can be carried out without having to remove the engine from the car:

(a) *Removal and refitting of the timing belt*
(b) *Removal and refitting of the camshaft*
(c) *Removal and refitting of the cylinder head*
(d) *Removal and refitting of the sump*
(e) *Removal and refitting of the oil pump*
(f) *Removal and refitting of the connecting rod and piston assemblies*
(g) *Removal and refitting of the engine mountings*

Warning: *Vehicles equipped with air conditioning:*

Whenever overhaul of a major nature is being undertaken to the engine, and components of the air conditioning system obstruct the work, and such items of the system cannot be unbolted and moved aside sufficiently far within the limits of their flexible connecting pipes, before any components are disconnected or removed the system should be discharged by your dealer or a competent refrigeration engineer.

As the system must be completely evacuated before recharging, the necessary vacuum equipment to do this is only likely to be available at a specialist establishment.

The refrigerant fluid is Freon 12 and although harmless under normal conditions, contact with the eyes or skin must be avoided. If Freon comes into contact with a naked flame, then a poisonous gas will be created which is injurious to health.

2.6 Sump plug removal using 8 mm square head key

2.7 Oil filter removal using a strap wrench

2.9 Topping-up the engine oil level

4 Major operations requiring engine removal

The following operations can only be carried out after removal of the engine from the car:

    (a) Removal and refitting of the flywheel
    (b) Removal and refitting of the crankshaft and main bearings
    (c) Removal and refitting of the crankshaft rear oil seal
    (d) Removal and refitting of the auxiliary shaft

Warning: *Vehicles equipped with air conditioning*
Refer to the warning note at the end of the previous Section.

5 Methods of engine removal

The engine and gearbox assembly can be lifted from the car as a complete unit, as described in the following Section, or the gearbox may first be removed, as described in Chapter 6.

Although it may be feasible to remove the engine leaving the transmission in position, it is not considered practical. The reason for this is that most of the transmission fittings and attachments will need to be disconnected in order to allow the engine and transmission to be separated (and subsequently reconnected). It is therefore considered more practical to remove the two units as an assembly and then to separate them.

6 Engine and transmission – removal

Warning: *Vehicles equipped with air conditioning*
Refer to the warning note at the end of Section 3.
1 Disconnect the battery negative terminal, then remove the bonnet, as described in Chapter 11.
2 Remove the radiator, as described in Chapter 2.
3 Remove the air cleaner, as described in Chapter 3.
4 Drain the engine oil into a suitable container for disposal. An 8 mm square head key is required to remove the sump drain plug. When the oil has drained, refit and tighten the drain plug and remove the container.
5 Unbolt and detach the undershield from the transmission, then unscrew the gearbox drain plug and drain the oil into a suitable container. When the oil has drained, refit and tighten the drain plug.
6 Improved access to some components may be gained by unbolting and removing the front undershield from the underside of the vehicle.
7 Slacken the hose clips and disconnect the two heater hoses at their connections on the engine.
8 Release the clip securing the choke cable to its support bracket on the carburettor and disconnect the cable end loop from the stud on the linkage.
9 Open the throttle and slip the accelerator cable out of the slot on the linkage bellcrank. Release the outer cable from its support bracket and move the cable to one side.
10 Disconnect the fuel feed and return pipes at the fuel pump and plug their ends (photo).
11 Disconnect the ignition HT cable from the centre of the distributor cap.
12 Detach the ignition vacuum pipe at the carburettor.
13 Detach the brake servo vacuum hose from the rear of the inlet manifold.
14 Note the locations of the wiring at the rear of the alternator and disconnect the wires.
15 Note the wiring locations at the starter motor solenoid and disconnect the wires (photo).
16 Disconnect the lead at the water temperature gauge sender unit on the cylinder head, and the lead at the oil pressure switch on the front facing side of the cylinder block (photo).
17 Undo the two shouldered bolts and remove the angular position/speed sensor from its location at the top of the bellhousing (photo). Unclip the sensor lead from the transmission breather hose, then fold the lead back out of the way.
18 Disconnect the engine and transmission earth straps (photos).
19 Disconnect the reversing light switch lead from the transmission.
20 All the wiring to the engine and transmission should now have been disconnected and, after releasing the clips and ties, it should be

6.10 Detach the hoses from the fuel pump (arrowed)

6.15 Disconnect the starter motor solenoid wires (arrowed)

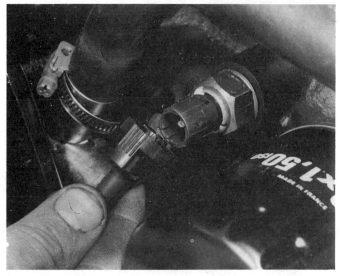
6.16 Detach the lead from the oil pressure switch

possible to move the complete wiring harness to one side.

21 Withdraw the spring wire and retaining clip securing the speedometer cable to the transmission at the rear, and remove the cable. Note the fitted direction of the clip (photos).

22 Disconnect the clutch cable from the release fork and the bracket on the bellhousing.

23 Apply the handbrake, and raise and support the front end of the vehicle on axle stands. Unbolt and remove the front roadwheels.

24 Undo the two retaining nuts and detach the exhaust downpipe from the manifold (photo).

25 Disconnect the gearchange rod from the fork control shaft. To do this, cut free the nylon retainer strap from the gaiter (taking care not to damage the gaiter), fold back the gaiter, then undo the link nut (photo).

26 Drive out the roll pin securing the right-hand driveshaft inner joint to the differential stub shaft, using a pin punch. Note that there are in fact two roll pins, one inside the other.

27 Undo the three bolts securing the left-hand driveshaft inner joint bellows and retaining plate to the side of the transmission.

28 Disconnect the steering arm outer balljoints as described in Chapter 10.

29 On each side of the vehicle, undo the two retaining nuts securing the shock absorber to the hub carrier, and remove the upper bolt. This will allow the hub carrier to pivot sufficiently to enable the driveshaft to be withdrawn from the transmission, leaving it attached to the hub carrier at its outboard end. Take care not to strain the brake hydraulic hoses. Allow for oil leakage from the transmission as the driveshafts are disengaged.

30 Temporarily reconnect the shock absorbers and the steering arm balljoints to the hub carriers to enable the vehicle to rest on its roadwheels during engine and transmission removal. Refit the front roadwheels.

31 Lower the car to the ground and make a final check that all cables, pipes and components likely to impede removal have been detached and moved aside.

32 Attach a crane or hoist to the engine using chain or rope slings, or secure the chains or ropes to the engine lifting brackets.

33 Undo the retaining nuts and detach the engine stabilizer from the front of the subframe.

34 Unbolt and detach the rear engine mounting.

35 Unbolt and detach the right-hand engine mounting (underneath the alternator).

36 Unbolt and detach the left-hand engine/transmission mounting.

37 Check that all engine and transmission fittings and associated attachments are disconnected and out of the way.

38 Slowly lift the engine and transmission assembly, moving it around as necessary to clear all obstructions. When high enough, lift it over the front body panel and lower the unit to the ground (photo).

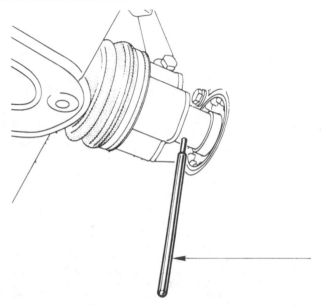

Fig. 1.5 Drive the roll pins from the right-hand driveshaft using a pin punch (arrowed) (Sec 6)

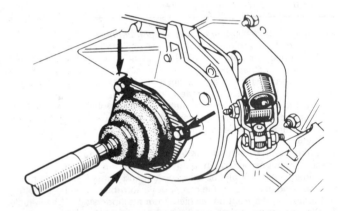

Fig. 1.6 Undo the three retaining bolts (arrowed) to detach the left-hand driveshaft (Sec 6)

6.17 Engine angular position sensor and retaining bolts

6.18A Earth strap connection to transmission

6.18B Earth strap connection to transmission mounting

6.21A Extract the retaining clip (arrowed) ...

6.21B   and withdraw the speedometer cable

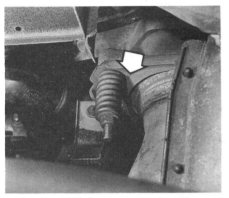

6.24 Exhaust downpipe connection to manifold (arrowed)

6.25 Fold back gaiter and disconnect the gearchange rod

6.38 Engine and transmission removal

7 Engine – separation from transmission

1   Unbolt and remove the 'U'-shaped support bar from the underside of the sump. It is secured by five bolts, one on each side of the crankcase, one on each side of the transmission housing, and one underneath the transmission housing (photos).

2   Unbolt and remove the starter motor heat shield. Unbolt and remove the starter motor.

3   Undo the retaining bolts and remove the cover plate from the base of the transmission bellhousing.

4   Unscrew and remove the remaining engine-to-transmission bellhousing bolts, noting the bolt lengths and locations, also the location of wiring retainer clips and the rear engine mounting bracket.

5   Support the engine and withdraw the transmission from it, supporting its weight so that the input shaft is not strained. The transmission may initially be stuck on the location dowels, in which case tap it free using a piece of wood.

7.1A Undo the support bar mounting bolts at the side (arrowed) ...

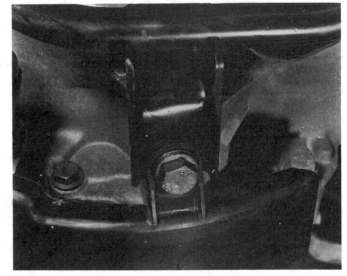

7.1B ... and underneath (undershield shown still fitted)

8 Engine dismantling – general

1 If possible, mount the engine on a stand for the dismantling procedure, but, failing this, support it in an upright position with blocks of wood placed under each side of the sump or crankcase.
2 Drain any remaining oil into a suitable container before cleaning the engine for major dismantling.
3 Cleanliness is most important, and if the engine is dirty it should be cleaned with paraffin or a suitable solvent while keeping it in an upright position.
4 Avoid working with the engine directly on a concrete floor, as grit presents a real source of trouble.
5 As parts are removed, clean them in a paraffin bath. However, do not immerse parts with internal oilways in paraffin as it is difficult to remove, usually requiring a high pressure hose. Clean oilways with nylon pipe cleaners.
6 It is advisable to have suitable containers to hold small items, as this will help when reassembling the engine and also prevent possible losses.
7 Always obtain complete sets of gaskets when the engine is being dismantled, but retain the old gaskets with a view to using them as a pattern to make a replacement if a new one is not available. Note that in many instances a gasket is not used, but instead the joints are sealed with an RTV sealant. It is recommended that a tube of CAF 4/60 THIXO paste, obtainable from Renault dealers, be obtained as it is specially formulated for this purpose.
8 When possible, refit nuts, bolts and washers in their location after being removed, as this helps to protect the threads and will also be helpful when reassembling the engine.
9 Retain unserviceable components in order to compare them with the new parts supplied.
10 The operations described in this Chapter are a step by step sequence, assuming that the engine is to be completely dismantled for major overhaul or repair. Where an operation can be carried out with the engine in the car, the dismantling necessary to gain access to the component concerned is described separately.
11 Socket-headed multi-point 'Torx' bolts and screws are used extensively in the construction of the engine, and a set of suitable wrenches will be essential.

9 Ancillary components – removal

With the engine separated from the gearbox or transmission the externally-mounted ancillary components, as given in the following list, can be removed. In most cases removal is straightforward, but further information will be found in the relevant Chapters.

Inlet and exhaust manifolds and carburettor (Chapter 3)
Fuel pump (Chapter 3)
Alternator (Chapter 12)
Spark plugs (Chapter 4)
Distributor (Chapter 4)
Water pump (Chapter 2)
Clutch (Chapter 5)
Oil filter (Section 2 of this Chapter)
Engine front mounting bracket (Section 23 of this Chapter)

10 Timing belt – removal

1 If the engine is in the car, first carry out the following operations:

   (a) *Disconnect the battery negative lead*
   (b) *Remove the air cleaner*
   (c) *Remove the alternator drivebelt*
   (d) *Pull free the fuel filter from its mounting clip on the side face of the timing belt cover, and position it out of the way, leaving the fuel lines attached*

2 Undo the four bolts and lift off the timing belt cover (photo).
3 Note the location of the timing mark on the outer edge of the camshaft sprocket. Using a socket or spanner on the crankshaft pulley bolt, turn the crankshaft until the camshaft sprocket timing mark is uppermost and in line with a corresponding mark or notch on the metal plate behind the sprocket.
4 Again using a socket or spanner, undo the crankshaft pulley retaining bolt and withdraw the pulley. If the engine is in the car, the crankshaft can be prevented from turning by engaging top gear and firmly applying the handbrake. If the engine is out of the car, lock the

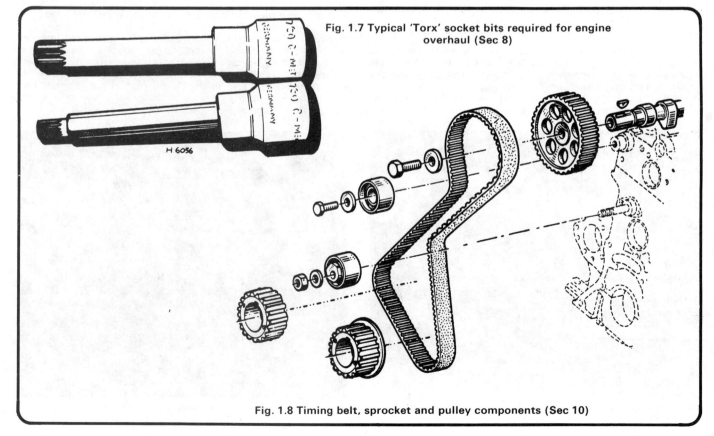

Fig. 1.7 Typical 'Torx' socket bits required for engine overhaul (Sec 8)

H.6056

Fig. 1.8 Timing belt, sprocket and pulley components (Sec 10)

10.2 Timing belt cover removal

flywheel ring gear using a wide-bladed screwdriver or strip of angle iron between the ring gear teeth and the long stud on the side of the cylinder block.

5   Remove the plug on the lower front facing side of the engine, at the flywheel end, and obtain a metal rod which is a snug fit in the plug hole. Turn the crankshaft slightly as necessary to the TDC position then push the rod through the hole to locate in the slot in the crankshaft web. Make sure that the crankshaft is exactly at TDC for No 1 piston by aligning the timing notch on the flywheel with the bellhousing mark, or the mark on the camshaft sprocket with the corresponding mark on the metal plate. If the crankshaft is not positioned accurately, it is possible to engage the rod with a balance hole in the crankshaft web which is not the TDC slot (Fig. 1.9).

6   Double check that the camshaft sprocket timing mark is aligned with the corresponding mark on the metal plate. If the plate does not have a mark, make one now using paint or by accurately scribing a line aligned with the mark on the sprocket. Also check that there are arrows indicating the running direction of the belt, located between the auxiliary shaft sprocket and the idler pulley. Some belts also have their own timing marks and if so these marks should also be aligned with the marks on the sprocket and plate.

7   Slacken the tensioner pulley retaining nut and rotate the tensioner body until the belt is slack.

8   Slip the timing belt off the sprockets and pulleys and remove it from the engine.

11 Cylinder head – removal (engine in car)

1   Disconnect the battery earth (negative) lead.

2   Drain the engine coolant as described in Chapter 2.

3   Remove the air cleaner unit as described in Chapter 3.

4   Detach the HT leads from the spark plugs, then detach and remove the distributor cap.

5   Remove the timing belt as described in the previous Section.

6   Disconnect the lead at the water temperature gauge sender on the cylinder head.

7   Disconnect the fuel feed and return pipes at the fuel pump and plug their ends.

8   Open the throttle linkage by hand and slip the accelerator cable end out of the slot on the linkage bellcrank connector. Release the accelerator cable from its support bracket and move the cable clear.

9   Release the choke cable looped end from the stud on the linkage and detach the support clip from the carburettor bracket.

10   Disconnect the brake servo vacuum hose from the inlet manifold.

11   Disconnect the heater hoses, crankcase ventilation hoses and the two nuts securing the support plate to the rear facing side of the cylinder head (photo).

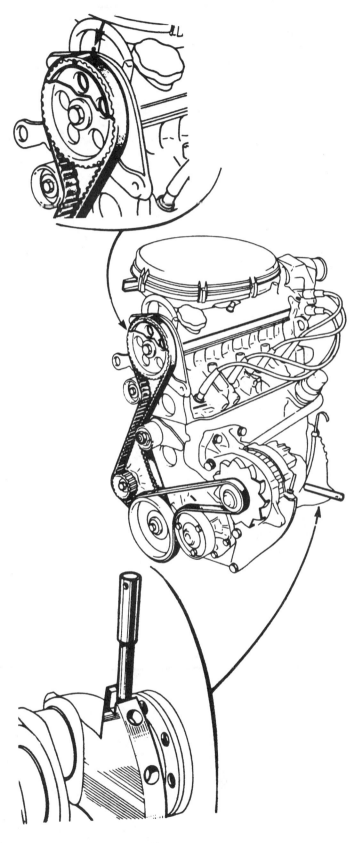

Fig. 1.9 Timing marks on belt and sprocket must align with those on backing plate when crankshaft is at TDC (No1 cylinder on compression). Note metal rod used to locate crankshaft (Sec 10)

11.11 Hose support plate on the side of the cylinder head (securing nuts arrowed)

12 Disconnect the radiator top hose from the thermostat housing.
13 Undo the two bolts and withdraw the tension springs securing the exhaust front section to the manifold.
14 Undo the three domed nuts, lift off the washers and withdraw the the camshaft cover from the cylinder head. Recover the gasket.
15 Undo the top retaining bolt securing the timing case backing plate to the end face of the cylinder head.
16 Using a suitable hexagon-headed socket bit, slacken the cylinder head retaining bolts, half a turn at a time in the reverse order to that shown in Fig. 1.34. When the tension has been relieved, remove all the bolts.
17 Lift the cylinder head, complete with manifolds and carburettor upwards and off the engine. If it is stuck, tap it upwards using a hammer and block of wood (Fig. 1.11). Do not try to turn it as it is located by two dowels and make no attempt whatsoever to prise it free using a screwdriver inserted between the block and head faces.

12 Cylinder head – removal (engine on bench)

The procedure for removing the cylinder head with the engine on the bench is similar to that for removal when the engine is in the car, with the exception of disconnecting the controls and services. Remove the timing belt, as described in Section 10, then refer to Section 11 and follow the procedure given in paragraphs 11, then 14 to 17.

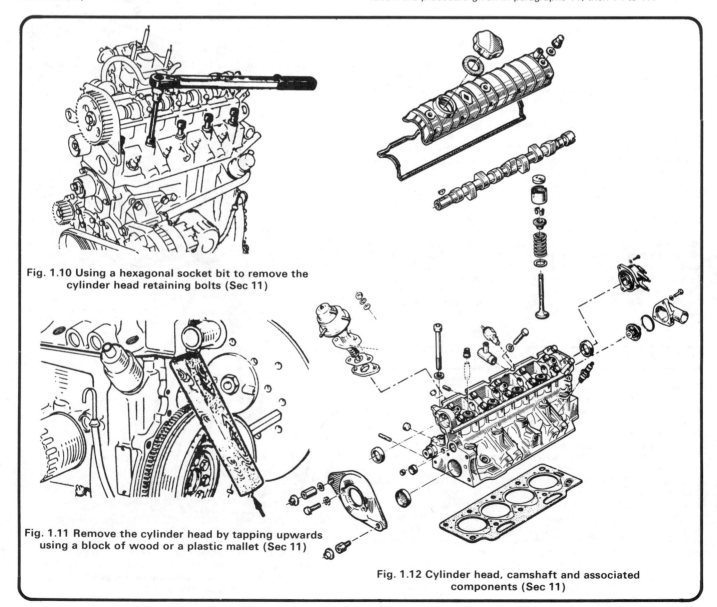

Fig. 1.10 Using a hexagonal socket bit to remove the cylinder head retaining bolts (Sec 11)

Fig. 1.11 Remove the cylinder head by tapping upwards using a block of wood or a plastic mallet (Sec 11)

Fig. 1.12 Cylinder head, camshaft and associated components (Sec 11)

13 Camshaft and tappets – removal

1 If the engine is in the car, first carry out the following operations:

   (a) *Remove the timing belt*
   (b) *Remove the distributor cap (Chapter 4)*
   (c) *Remove the camshaft cover*
   (d) *Remove the fuel pump (Chapter 3)*

2 Undo the bolt securing the camshaft sprocket to the camshaft and withdraw the sprocket. The camshaft may be prevented from turning during this operation by holding it between the cam lobes using grips or, preferably, by wrapping an old timing belt around the sprocket, clamping the belt tight and holding securely (Fig. 1.13). With the sprocket removed, check whether the locating Woodruff key is likely to drop out of its camshaft groove and if it is, remove it and store it safely.

3 Undo the two bolts securing the metal sprocket backing plate to the cylinder head and remove the plate.

4 Number the camshaft bearing caps 1 to 5 with No 1 nearest the flywheel, and also mark them with an arrow pointing towards the flywheel, to indicate their fitted direction.

5 Progressively slacken all the camshaft bearing cap retaining bolts and, when all are slack, remove them from the caps.

6 Lift off the five bearing caps and then remove the camshaft complete with oil seals from the cylinder head.

7 Withdraw the tappet buckets, complete with shims, from their bores in the head. Lay the buckets out on a sheet of cardboard numbered 1 to 8 with No 1 at the flywheel end. It is a good idea to write the shim thickness size on the card alongside each bucket in case the shims are accidentally knocked off their buckets and mixed up. The size is stamped on the shim bottom face.

14 Cylinder head – dismantling

1 If the cylinder head has been removed with the engine in the car, remove the following associated components from it, referring to the appropriate Chapter for further details where necessary.

   (a) *Carburettor, inlet and exhaust manifolds (Chapter 3)*
   (b) *Fuel pump (Chapter 3)*
   (c) *Water temperature gauge sender unit*
   (d) *Hose support bracket on the side face of the cylinder head*
   (e) *Camshaft and tappets (see previous Section)*
   (f) *Thermostat (Chapter 2)*

2 Using a valve spring compressor, compress each valve spring in turn until the split collets can be removed. Release the compressor and lift off the cap, spring and spring seat.

3 If, when the valve spring compressor is screwed down, the valve spring cap refuses to free and expose the split collets, gently tap the top of the tool, directly over the cap with a light hammer. This will free the cap.

4 Withdraw the oil seal off the top of the valve guide, and then remove the valve through the combustion chamber.

5 It is essential that the valves are kept in their correct sequence unless they are so badly worn that they are to be renewed. If they are going to be kept and used again, place them in a sheet of card having eight holes numbered 1 to 8 – corresponding to the relative fitted positions of the valves. Note that No 1 valve is nearest to the flywheel end of the engine.

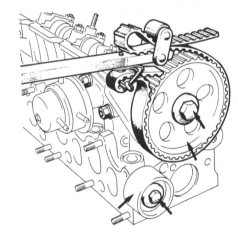

Fig. 1.13 Hold the camshaft sprocket with an old timing belt, then remove the sprocket retaining bolt followed, if necessary, by the idler pulley (Sec 13)

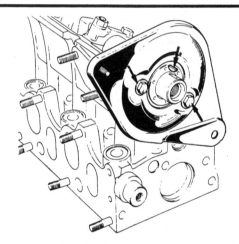

Fig. 1.14 Undo the two bolts and remove the sprocket metal backing plate. Also remove the Woodruff key if loose (Sec 13)

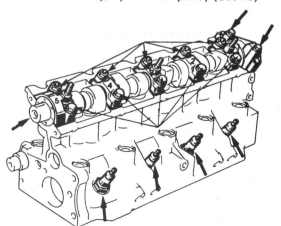

Fig. 1.15 Mark the camshaft bearing caps, then remove the retaining bolts (Sec 13)

Fig. 1.16 Keep the tappet buckets and shims in strict order of removal (Sec 13)

15 Sump – removal

1   If the engine is in the car, first carry out the following operations:

   (a) *Unscrew the drain plug and drain the engine oil into a suitable container for disposal*
   (b) *Detach and remove the undertray just forward of the engine for improved access (if necessary)*
   (c) *Undo the retaining bolts and remove the 'U'-shaped support bracket from the underside of the sump (see Section 7, paragraph 1)*

2   Undo and remove the bolts securing the sump to the crankcase. Tap the sump with a hide or plastic mallet to break the seal between sump flange and crankcase, and remove the sump. Note that a gasket is not used, only a sealing compound.

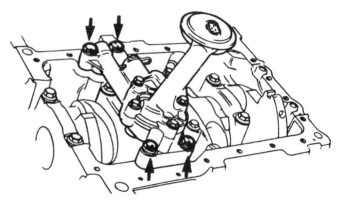

Fig. 1.17 Oil pump retaining bolt locations (Sec 16)

16 Oil pump – removal

1   If the oil pump is to be removed with the engine in the car, first remove the sump (see previous Section).
2   Undo the four retaining bolts at the ends of the pump body and withdraw the pump from the crankcase and drivegear. Note that no gasket is fitted between the mating faces of the pump and crankcase.

17 Auxiliary shaft – removal

1   The engine must be removed from the car for this operation to allow clearance for the withdrawal of the auxiliary shaft.
2   Remove the timing belt as described in Section 10.
3   Undo the retaining bolt and remove the washer securing the sprocket to the auxiliary shaft. Hold the sprocket with an old timing belt, tightly clamped and securely held while undoing the bolt.
4   Withdraw the sprocket using two screwdrivers as levers to ease it off. If it is very tight use a two-legged puller. Recover the Woodruff key if it is not securely located in its groove.
5   Undo the retaining bolts and remove the timing case backing plate.
6   Undo the four bolts and withdraw the auxiliary shaft housing.
7   At the top undo the two bolts and withdraw the oil pump drivegear cover plate. Screw a suitable bolt into the oil pump drivegear or use a tapered wooden shaft and withdraw the drivegear from its location.
8   Undo the two bolts and washers and lift out the auxiliary shaft retaining plate and the auxiluary shaft.

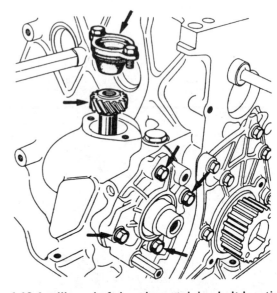

Fig. 1.18 Auxiliary shaft housing retaining bolt locations, oil pump driveshaft and cover plate (Sec 17)

18 Crankshaft front plate – removal

1   If the engine is in the car, first carry out the following operations:

   (a) *Remove the timing belt (Section 10) and the timing case backing plate*
   (b) *Remove the sump (Section 15)*

2   Withdraw the crankshaft sprocket using two screwdrivers carefully as levers, or by using a suitable puller. Remove the Woodruff key.
3   Undo the bolts securing the front plate to the cylinder block and withdraw the plate, noting that it is located by dowels in the two lower bolt hole locations (Fig. 1.19).

19 Pistons, connecting rods and big-end bearings – removal

1   If the engine is in the car, first carry out the following operations:

   (a) *Remove the sump (Section 15)*
   (b) *Remove the oil pump (Section 16)*
   (c) *Remove the cylinder head (not necessary if only the big-end bearings are to be removed) (Section 11 or 12)*

2   Rotate the crankshaft so that No 1 big-end cap (nearest the flywheel) is at the lowest point of its travel. Using a centre punch, number the cap and rod on the auxiliary shaft side to indicate the cylinder to which they are fitted.

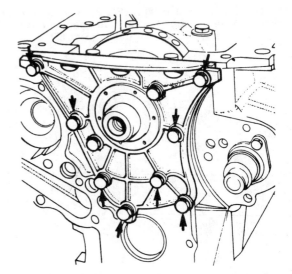

Fig. 1.19 Crankshaft front plate retaining bolt locations (Sec 18)

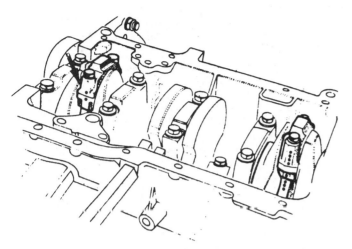

Fig. 1.20 Number the connecting rods and caps before removal (Sec 19)

3   Undo and remove the big-end bearing cap bolts and withdraw the cap, complete with shell bearing from the connecting rod. If only the bearing shells are being attended to, push the connecting rod up and off the crankpin then remove the upper bearing shell. Keep the bearing shells and cap together in their correct sequence if they are to be refitted.
4   Push the connecting rod up and withdraw the piston and connecting rod assembly from the top of the cylinder block.
5   Now repeat these operations on the remaining three piston and connecting rod assemblies.

20 Flywheel – removal

1   Lock the crankshaft using a strip of angle iron between the ring gear teeth and the engine dowel bolt, or a block of wood between one of the crankshaft counterweights and the crankcase.
2   The flywheel retaining bolt holes are not symmetrical so there is no need to mark the fitting position of the flywheel. Undo the retaining bolts and withdraw the flywheel.

21 Crankshaft and main bearings – removal

1   Before removing the crankshaft and bearings, first check the endfloat of the crankshaft to assess for excessive wear. This procedure is described in Section 28.
2   Identification numbers should be cast onto the base of each main bearing cap, but if not, number the cap and crankcase using a centre punch.
3   Undo and remove the main bearing cap retaining bolts, noting that a hexagonal socket bit will be needed for No 1 main bearing cap bolts. Withdraw the caps and the bearing shell lower halves.
4   Carefully lift the crankshaft from the crankcase.
5   Remove the thrust washers from each side of No 2 main bearing, then remove the bearing shell upper halves from the crankcase. Place each shell with its respective bearing cap.
6   Oil jets are located within the crankcase at the lower end of each cylinder bore. These can be unbolted and removed for cleaning in petrol if necessary, but note the fitted position of each jet (see inset in Fig. 1.3).

22 Crankshaft rear oil seal – renewal

1   With the engine removed from the car and separated from the gearbox (if applicable), remove the flywheel.
2   Clean the area around the crankshaft rear oil seal, then use a screwdriver to prise it from the block and bearing cap.
3   Wipe clean the oil seal recess. Dip the new oil seal in clean engine

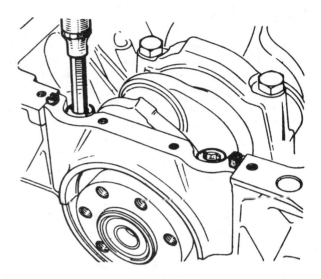

Fig. 1.21 Removing the No 1 main bearing cap bolts (Sec 21)

22.3 Crankshaft rear seal installation. Note protective polythene shim – remove once the seal is fitted

oil and carefully install it over the crankshaft rear journal. Take great care not to damage the delicate lip of the seal and make sure that the seal open face is towards the engine. A polythene shim can be temporarily used to protect the seal when fitting (photo).
4   Using a tube of suitable diameter, a block of wood or the old seal, install the new seal squarely into its location until the outer face is flush with the block and bearing cap. If the original seal has worn a groove in the journal, drive the seal in a further 3 mm (0.12 in).
5   Refit the flywheel and the engine, as described in the applicable Sections of this Chapter.

23 Engine/transmission mountings – renewal

1   The engine and transmission flexible mountings may be renewed with the units in the car.
2   Support the engine or transmission securely on a jack using a block of wood as an insulator.
3   Renew only one mounting at a time by unscrewing the through-bolt nuts and unbolting the mounting bracket from the crankcase, transmission casing or body member (photos).
4   A stabilizer/bracket is fitted, and is located at the front between

23.3A Engine mounting bracket removal

23.3B Transmission mounting

23.4A Engine stabilizer bracket removal from subframe

23.4B Engine stabilizer and retaining bolts

engine and subframe. Removal is simply a matter of undoing the retaining bolts (photos).

5   Refitting is the reverse sequence to removal.

24 Crankcase ventilation system – description

The layout of the crankcase ventilation system is shown in the accompanying illustration (Fig. 1.22).

When the engine is idling, or under partial load conditions, the high depression in the inlet manifold draws the crankcase fumes (diluted by air from the air cleaner) through the calibrated restrictor and into the combustion chambers.

The system ensures that there is always a partial vacuum in the crankcase, and so prevents a build-up of pressure which could cause oil contamination, fume emission and oil leakage past seals. An oil separator unit is fitted between the crankcase (to which it is attached) and the main hose to the three-way union.

The only maintenance required on this system is to ensure that the hoses and connections are in good condition, secure and clean.

25 Examination and renovation

1   With the engine completely stripped, clean all the components and examine them for wear. Each part should be checked and, where necessary, renewed or renovated, as described in the following Sections.

Cylinder block and crankcase

2   The cylinder bores must be examined for taper, ovality, scoring and scratches. Start by examining the top of the bores; if these are worn, a slight ridge will be found which marks the top of the piston ring travel. If the wear is excessive, the engine will have had a high oil consumption rate accompanied by blue smoke from the exhaust.

3   If available, use an inside dial gauge to measure the bore diameter just below the ridge and compare it with the diameter at the bottom of the bore, which is not subject to wear. If the difference is more than 0.152 mm, the cylinders will normally require boring with new oversize pistons fitted.

4   Provided the cylinder bore wear does not exceed 0.203 mm, special

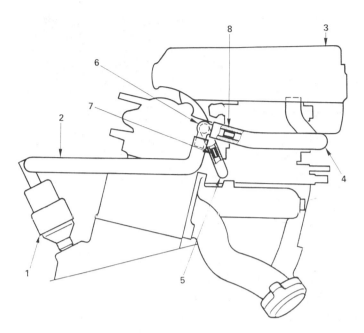

Fig. 1.22 Engine crankcase ventilation system (Sec 24)

1 *Oil separator*
2 *Hose from oil separator to 3-way union*
3 *Air filter unit*
4 *Filter to 3-way union hose*
5 *Hose from 3-way union to carburettor*
6 *3-way union*
7 *1.7 mm diameter jet*
8 *7.0 mm diameter jet*

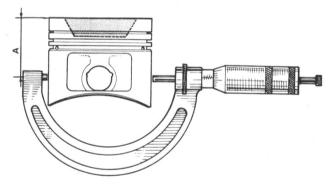

Fig. 1.23 Piston diameter measuring point – A = 53.8 mm (Sec 25)

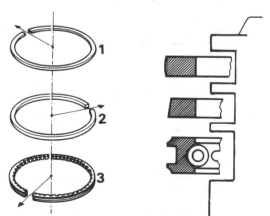

Fig. 1.24 Piston ring fitting diagram (Sec 25)

1 *Top compression ring*
2 *Second compression ring*
3 *Oil control ring*

oil control rings and pistons can be fitted to restore compression and stop the engine burning oil.

5 If new pistons are being fitted to old bores, it is essential to roughen the bore walls slightly with fine glasspaper to enable the new piston rings to bed in properly. Only a crosshatch diagonal honing pattern must be used (not vertical).

6 Thoroughly examine the crankcase and cylinder bores for cracks and damage and use a piece of wire to probe all oilways and waterways to ensure they are unobstructed.

Pistons and connecting rods

7 Examine the pistons for ovality, scoring and scratches, and for wear of the piston ring grooves.

8 If the pistons or connecting rods are to be renewed it is necessary to have this work carried out by a Renault dealer or suitable engineering works who will have the necessary tooling to remove the gudgeon pins.

9 If a single piston only is being renewed, ensure that the replacement has identical type markings on its crown to the piston it replaces (photo). The piston diameter is measured at the point indicated in Fig. 1.23.

10 If new rings are to be fitted to the original pistons, expand the old rings over the top of the pistons (photo). The use of two or three old feeler blades will be helpful in preventing the rings dropping into empty grooves.

11 Before fitting the new rings, ensure that the ring grooves in the piston are free of carbon by cleaning them using an old ring. Break the ring in half to do this.

12 Install the new rings by fitting them over the top of the piston, starting with the oil control scraper ring. Note that the second compression ring is tapered and must be fitted with the word TOP uppermost (photo).

13 With all the rings in position, space the ring gaps at 120° to each other (Fig. 1.24).

Crankshaft

14 Examine the crankpin and main journal surfaces for signs of scoring or scratches, and check the ovality and taper of the crankpins and main journals. If the bearing surface dimensions do not fall within the tolerance ranges given in the Specifications at the beginning of this Chapter, the crankpins and/or main journals will have to be reground.

15 Big-end and crankpin wear is accompanied by distinct metallic knocking, particularly noticeable when the engine is pulling from low revs, and some loss of oil pressure.

16 Main bearing and main journal wear is accompanied by severe engine vibration rumble – getting progressively worse as engine revs increase – and again by loss of oil pressure.

17 If the crankshaft requires regrinding take it to an engine reconditioning specialist, who will machine it for you and supply the correct undersize bearing shells.

25.9 Marks on piston crown

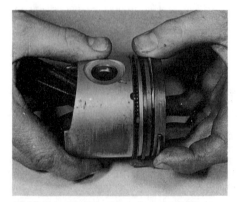

25.10 Remove the piston rings from the top of the pistons

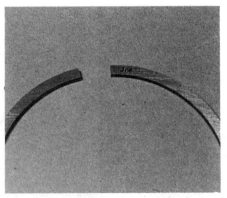

25.12 The word TOP (arrowed) indicates the second compression ring upper face

25.25 Auxiliary shaft components

25.27 Auxiliary shaft housing and oil seal

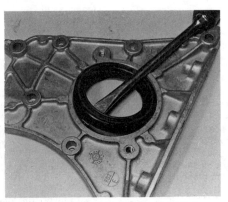

25.28 Prising out oil seal from crankshaft front plate

25.29 Oil seal installed in crankshaft front plate. Note orientation

Big-end and main bearing shells

18 Inspect the big-end and main bearing shells for signs of general wear, scoring pitting and scratches. The bearings should be matt grey in colour. With lead-indium bearings, should a trace of copper colour be noticed, the bearings are badly worn as the lead bearing material has worn away to expose the indium underlay. Renew the bearings if they are in this condition or if there are any signs of scoring or pitting. **You are strongly advised to renew the bearings – regardless of their condition at time of major overhaul. Refitting used bearings is a false economy.**

19 The undersizes available are designed to correspond with crankshaft regrind sizes. The bearings are in fact, slightly more than the stated undersize as running clearances have been allowed for during their manufacture.

20 Main and big-end bearing shells can be identified as to size by the marking on the back of the shell. Standard size shell bearings are marked STD or .00, undersize shells are marked with the undersize such as 0.020 u/s. This marking method applies only to replacement bearing shells and not to those used during production.

Camshaft and tappets

21 Examine the camshaft bearing surfaces and cam lobes for wear ridges, pitting or scoring. Renew the camshaft if any of these conditions are apparent.

22 The oil seals at each end of the camshaft should be renewed as a matter of course. To change the oil seal at the flywheel end of the camshaft, the distributor rotor and endplate must first be removed. Unfortunately the rotor is bonded to the end of the camshaft with a special adhesive and can only be removed by breaking it. Having done this the seal and endplate can be slid off. With two new oil seals, new rotor and a quantity of the special adhesive, available from Renault dealers, the new seals can be fitted. Lubricate their seal lips, then carefully slip them over the camshaft journals, ensuring that their open sides face the camshaft. Refit the endplate, then bond the new rotor to the camshaft. After fitting the new oil seals, store the camshaft in such

a way that the weight of the camshaft is not resting on the oil seals.

23 Examine the camshaft bearings and bearing caps in the cylinder head. The camshaft runs directly in the aluminium housings and separate bearing shells are not used. Check the housings and caps for signs of wear ridges or deep scoring. Any excessive wear in these areas will mean a new cylinder head.

24 Finally, inspect the tappet buckets and the shims for scoring, pitting, especially on the shims, and wear ridges. Renew any components as necessary. Note that some scuffing and discolouration of the tappets is to be expected and is acceptable providing that the tappets are not scored.

Auxiliary shaft and bearings

25 Examine the auxiliary shaft and oil pump driveshaft for pitting, scoring or wear ridges on the bearing journals and for chipping or wear of the gear teeth. Renew as necessary (photo).

26 Check the auxiliary shaft bearings in the cylinder block for wear and, if worn, have these renewed by your Renault dealer or a suitably equipped engineering works.

27 Clean off all traces of old gasket from the auxiliary shaft housing and tap out the oil seal using a tube of suitable diameter. Install the new oil seal using a block of wood and tap it in until it is flush with the outer face of the housing. The open side of the seal must be towards the engine (photo).

Crankshaft front plate

28 Check the front plate for signs of distortion or damage to the threads. If serviceable, clean off all traces of sealant and prise or tap out the oil seal using a tube of suitable diameter (photo).

29 Fit a new seal so that it is flush with the outer face of the front plate using a block of wood. Ensure that the open side of the seal is fitted towards the engine (photo).

Timing belt, sprockets and tensioner

30 Examine the timing belt carefully for any signs of cracking, fraying

or general wear, particularly at the roots of the teeth. Renew the belt if there is any sign of deterioration of this nature, or if there is any oil or grease contamination.

31 Also inspect the timing sprockets for cracks or chipping of the teeth. Handle the sprockets with care as they may easily fracture if they are dropped or sharply knocked. Renew the sprockets if they are in any way damaged.

32 Check that the idler and tensioner pulleys rotate freely with no trace of roughness or harshness and without excessive free play. Renew if necessary.

Oil pump

33 Undo the retaining bolts and lift off the pump cover.

34 Withdraw the idler gear and the drivegear and shaft.

35 Extract the retaining clip and remove the oil pressure relief valve spring retainer, spring, spring seat and plunger.

36 Clean the components and carefully examine the gears, pump body and relief valve plunger for any signs of scoring or wear. Renew the pump if these conditions are apparent.

37 If the components appear serviceable, measure the clearance between the pump body and the gears and also the gear endfloat using feeler gauges. If the clearances exceed the specified tolerance, the pump must be renewed (Figs. 1.26 and 1.27).

38 If the pump is satisfactory, reassemble the components in the order of removal, fill the pump with oil and refit the cover.

Flywheel

39 Examine the flywheel for scoring of the clutch face and for chipping of the ring gear teeth. If the clutch face is scored, the flywheel may be machined until flat, but renewal is preferable. If the ring gear is worn or damaged it may be renewed separately, but this job is best left to a Renault dealer or engineering works. The temperature to which the new ring gear must be heated for installation is critical, and if not done accurately the hardness of the teeth will be destroyed.

26 Cylinder head and pistons – decarbonizing, valve grinding and renovation

1 The operation will normally only be required at comparatively high mileages. However, if persistent pinking occurs and performance has deteriorated, even though the engine adjustments are correct, decarbonizing and valve grinding may be required.

2 With the cylinder head removed, use a scraper to remove the carbon from the combustion chambers and ports. Remove all traces of gasket from the cylinder head surface, then wash it thoroughly with paraffin.

3 Use a straight-edge and feeler blade to check that the cylinder head surface is not distorted. If it is, it must be resurfaced by a suitably equipped engineering works.

4 If the engine is still in the car, clean the piston crowns and cylinder bore upper edges, but make sure that no carbon drops between the pistons and bores. To do this, locate two of the pistons at the top of their bores and seal off the remaining bores with paper and masking tape. Press a little grease between the two pistons and their bores to collect any carbon dust; this can be wiped away when the piston is lowered. To prevent carbon build-up, polish the piston crown with metal polish, but remove all traces of polish afterwards.

5 Examine the heads of the valves for pitting and burning, expecially the exhaust valve heads. Renew any valve which is badly burnt. Examine the valve seats at the same time. If the pitting is very slight, it can be removed by grinding the valve heads and seats together with coarse, then fine grinding paste.

6 Where excessive pitting has occurred, the valve seats must be recut or renewed by a suitably equipped engineering works.

7 Valve grinding is carried out as follows: place the cylinder head upside down on a bench with a block of wood at each end to give clearance for the valve stems.

8 Smear a trace of coarse carborundum paste on the seat face and press a suction grinding tool onto the valve head. With a semi-rotary action, grind the valve head to its seat, lifting the valve occasionally to redistribute the grinding paste. When a dull matt even surface is produced on both the valve seat and the valve, wipe off the paste and repeat the process with fine carborundum paste. A light spring placed under the valve head will greatly ease this operation. When a smooth

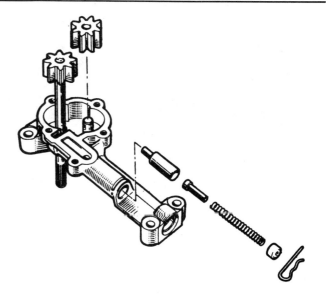

Fig. 1.25 Exploded view of the oil pump components (Sec 25)

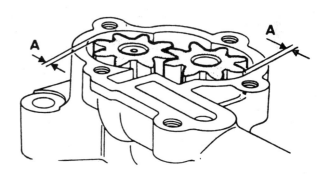

Fig. 1.26 Check clearance between the gears and oil pump body (A) (Sec 25)

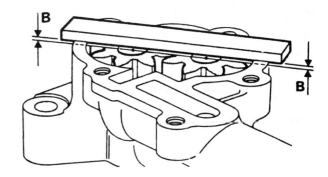

Fig. 1.27 Check the oil pump gear endfloat (B) (Sec 25)

unbroken ring of light grey matt finish is produced on both the valve and seat, the grinding operation is complete.

9 Scrape away all carbon from the valve head and stem, and clean away all traces of grinding compound. Clean the valves and seats with a paraffin-soaked rag, then wipe with a clean rag.

10 When each valve head has been ground to the required finish, insert it into its location in the cylinder head and check the amount the valve head is recessed beneath the cylinder head face, using a feeler gauge and steel rule across the head face and valve. It is important to retain the valve head recessing within the specified limits, as the valve seats have a step (C in Fig. 1.28) which must be kept intact. If the valve

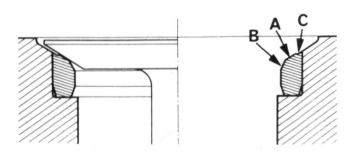

Fig. 1.28 Valve seat profile (Sec 26)

A   Valve seating surface   C   Seat step – upper
B   Seat step – lower

28.1A Oil jet and retaining bolt

and/or seat are worn beyond the specified limit, they will need renewal, in which case consult a Renault dealer.

11 If the valve guides are worn, indicated by a side-to-side motion of the valve, new guides must be fitted. To do this, use a suitable mandrel to press the worn guides downwards and out through the combustion chamber. Press the new guides into the cylinder head in the same direction until they are at the specified fitted height.

12 Check that all valve springs are intact. If any one is broken, all should be renewed. Check the free height of the springs against new ones. If some springs are not within specifications, replace them all. Springs suffer from fatigue and it is a good idea to renew them even if they look serviceable.

27 Engine reassembly – general

1 To ensure maximum life with minimum trouble from a rebuilt engine, not only must everything be correctly assembled, but it must also be spotlessly clean. All oilways must be clear, and locking washers and spring washers must be fitted where indicated. Oil all bearings and other working surfaces thoroughly with engine oil during assembly.

2 Before assembly begins, renew any bolts or studs with damaged threads and have all new components at hand ready for assembly.

3 Gather together a torque wrench, oil can, clean rags and a set of engine gaskets, together with a new oil filter. A tube of RTV sealing compound will also be required for the joint faces that are fitted without gaskets. It is recommended that CAF 4/60 THIXO paste, obtainable from Renault dealers, is used, as it is specially formulated for this purpose.

28 Crankshaft and main bearings – refitting

1 If they were removed, refit the oil jets to their positions in the crankcase, at the bottom end of each cylinder bore (photo). Ensure that the fitted position of each is as noted during removal, otherwise it is possible for contact to occur between the jets and pistons as the pistons reach the bottom of their strokes. Tighten the retaining bolts to the specified torque wrench setting.

2 Before fitting the crankshaft or main bearings, it is necessary to determine the correct thickness of side seals to be fitted to No 1 main bearing cap. To do this, place the bearing cap in position without any seals and secure it with the two retaining bolts. Locate a twist drill, dowel rod, or any other suitable implement which will just fit, in the side seal groove. Now measure the implement, and this dimension is the side seal groove size. If the dimension is less than or equal to 5 mm, a 5.1 mm thick side seal is needed. If the dimension is more than 5 mm, a 5.3 mm thick side seal is required. Having determined the side seal size and obtained the necessary seals, proceed as follows.

3 Clean the backs of the bearing shells and the bearing recesses in both the cylinder block and main bearing caps.

4 Press the bearing shells without oil holes into the caps, ensuring that the tag on the shell engages in the notch in the cap (photo).

5 Press the bearing shells with the oil holes into the recesses in the

28.1B Oil jet in position

28.4 Main bearing shells without oil holes fit to caps

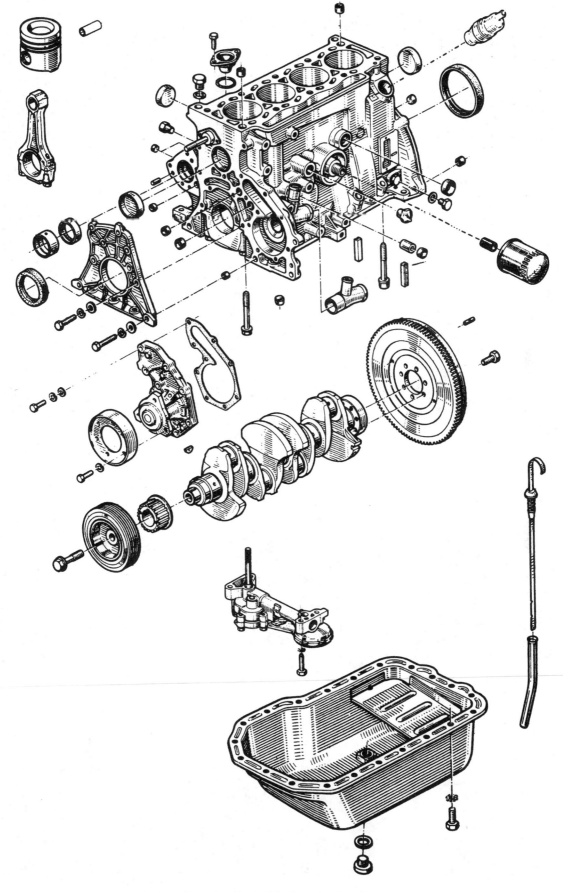

Fig. 1.29 Exploded view of cylinder block and related components (Sec 28)

cylinder block (photo).

6   If the original bearing shells are being refitted, these must be placed in their original locations.

7   Using a little grease, stick the thrust washers to each side of No 2 main bearing, so that the oilway grooves on each thrust washer face outwards (photo).

8   Lubricate the lips of a new crankshaft rear oil seal and carefully slip it over the crankshaft journal. Do this carefully as the seal lips are very delicate. Ensure that the open side of the seal faces the engine.

9   Liberally lubricate each bearing shell in the cylinder block and lower the crankshaft into position (photo).

10 Fit all the bearing caps, with the exception of No 1, in their numbered or previously noted locations, so that the bearing shell locating notches in the cap and block are both on the same side (photo). Fit the retaining bolts and tighten them hand tight at this stage.

11 Check the crankshaft endfloat using a dial gauge or feeler gauges inserted between the thrust washers and the side of the bearing journal (photos). If new thrust washers have been fitted, the endfloat should be in accordance with the dimension given in the Specifications. If the

original washers have been refitted and the endfloat is excessive, new thrust washers must be obtained. These are available in a number of oversizes.

12 Fit the side seals to No 1 main bearing cap with their seal groove facing outwards. Position the seals so that approximately 0.2 mm (0.008 in) of seal protrudes at the bottom facing side (the side towards the crankcase) (photo).

13 Apply some CAF 4/60 THIXO paste to the bottom corners of the cap and then place the retaining bolts through the cap bolt holes.

14 Place the cap in position and just start the bolts two or three turns into their threads. These will now serve as guide studs.

15 Press the cap firmly into place taking care not to displace the side seals. When the cap is nearly home, check that the side seals are still protruding at the bottom, push the cap down fully and tighten the bolts hand tight to hold it.

16 Position the oil seal so that its face is flush with the bearing cap and block, then tighten all the retaining bolts to the specified torque (photo). Check that the crankshaft is free to turn.

17 When all components have been fitted and tightened, trim off the protruding ends of the side seals, flush with the block face (photo).

28.5 Main bearing shells with oil grooves and holes fit to block

28.7 Locate the thrust washers each side of No 2 main bearing – note oilway grooves face outwards

28.9 Lowering the crankshaft into position

28.10 Fit the main bearing caps (except No1)

28.11A Check the crankshaft endfloat using a dial gauge ...

28.11B ... or feeler gauges

28.12 Fit the side seals to No 1 main bearing cap

28.16 Tighten the main bearing cap bolts to the specified torque

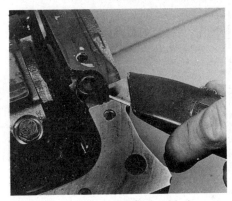

28.17 Trim the side seals flush with the block face

29 Pistons, connecting rods and big-end bearings – refitting

1 Clean the backs of the bearing shells and the recesses in the connecting rods and big-end caps. If new shells are being fitted, ensure that all traces of the protective grease are cleaned off using paraffin (photo).

2 Press the big-end bearing shells into the connecting rods and caps in their correct positions and oil them liberally.

3 Lubricate the pistons and rings with engine oil, then fit a ring compressor to No 1 piston. Insert the piston and connecting rod into No 1 cylinder (at the flywheel end). With No 1 crankpin at its lowest point, drive the piston carefully into the cylinder with the wooden handle of a hammer and at the same time guide the connecting rod onto the crankpin (photo). Make sure that the V mark on the piston crown, or arrow, is facing the flywheel end of the engine.

4 Fit the big-end bearing cap in its previously noted position, then tighten the bolts to the specified torque (photoo).

5 Check that the crankshaft turns freely.

6 Repeat the procedure given in paragraphs 3 to 5 for No 4 piston and connecting rod, then turn the crankshaft through half a turn and repeat the procedure on No 2 and No 3 pistons.

7 If the engine is in the car, refit the oil pump, sump and cylinder head.

30 Flywheel – refitting

1 Clean the flywheel and crankshaft faces, then fit the flywheel. The flywheel retaining bolts are not symmetrical, so the flywheel can only be fitted in one position.

2 Apply a few drops of thread locking compound to the retaining bolt threads, fit the bolts and tighten them in a diagonal sequence to the specified torque (photo).

31 Crankshaft front plate – refitting

1 Apply a bead of CAF 4/60 THIXO paste to the mating face of the front plate and liberally lubricate the oil seal lips (photo).

2 Refit the front plate and the retaining bolts. Do not fit the two bolts around the oil seal opening at the 2 o'clock and 8 o'clock positions at this stage, as they also secure the timing case backing plate.

3 Tighten the retaining bolts in a progressive sequence.

32 Auxiliary shaft – refitting

1 Liberally lubricate the auxiliary shaft and slide it into its bearings (photo).

2 Place the retaining plate in position with its curved edge away from the crankshaft and refit the two retaining bolts (photo). Tighten the bolts fully.

3 Place a new gasket in position over the dowels of the cylinder block (photo). If a gasket was not used previously, apply a bead of CAF 4/60 THIXO paste to the housing mating face.

4 Liberally lubricate the oil seal lips and then locate the housing in place (photo). Refit and tighten the housing retaining bolts progressively in a diagonal sequence.

5 Lubricate the oil pump drivegear and lower the gear into its location.

6 Position a new O-ring seal on the drivegear cover plate, fit the plate and secure with the two retaining bolts.

7 Fit the drivebelt tensioner pulley unit to the front face of the block.

8 Refit the timing case backing plate. The two bolts around the crankshaft front plate oil seal opening at the 2 o'clock and 8 o'clock positions should also have a small quantity of the sealant paste applied to their threads, as they protrude into the crankcase (photo).

9 Locate the special spacer bolt at the 7 o'clock position under the auxiliary shaft.

29.1 Piston, connecting rod, bearing shells, cap and bolts ready for refitting

29.3 Using a piston ring compressor and a wooden drift to refit the piston and connecting rod assembly

29.4A Locate the connecting rod big-end bearing cap ...

29.4B ... and fit and tighten the retaining bolts

30.2 Tighten the flywheel retaining bolts to the specified torque

31.1 Apply sealant to the front plate. Do not block the oilway in zone C

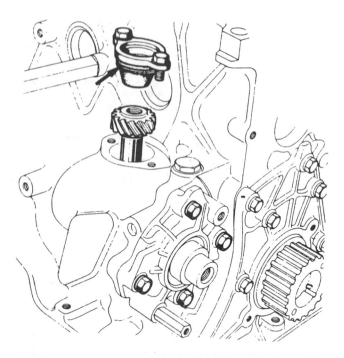

Fig. 1.30 Fit a new O-ring seal (arrowed) to the cover plate (Sec 32)

10 With the Woodruff key in place, refit the auxiliary shaft sprocket, washer and retaining bolt. Hold the sprocket using the method employed for removal, and tighten the bolt to the specified torque.
11 If the engine is in the car, refit the timing belt and, if removed, the engine undertray.

33 Oil pump – refitting

1 Place the oil pump in position with its shaft engaged with the drivegear.
2 Refit the retaining bolts and tighten them securely (photo).
3 If the engine is in the car, refit the sump.

34 Sump – refitting

1 Ensure that the mating faces of the sump and crankcase are clean and dry.
2 Apply a bead of CAF 4/60 THIXO paste to the sump face and place the sump in position (photo). Refit the retaining bolts and tighten them progressively in a diagonal sequence.
3 Refit the 'U'-shaped support bracket to the underside of the sump.
4 Refit the undertray, and fill the engine with oil.

35 Cylinder head – reassembly

1 Using a suitable tube, fit new oil seals to each of the valve guides (photos).
2 Lubricate the stems of the valves and insert them into their original locations. If new valves are being fitted, insert them into the locations to which they have been ground (photo).
3 Working on the first valve, fit the spring seat to the cylinder head followed by the valve spring and cap (photos).
4 Compress the valve spring and locate the split collets in the recess in the valve stem (photo). Release the compressor, then repeat the procedure on the remaining valves.
5 With all the valves installed, lay the cylinder head on one side and tap each valve stem with a plastic mallet to settle the components.
6 If the cylinder head has been removed with the engine in the car, refit the camshaft and tappets, the fuel pump, carburettor and manifolds, water temperature gauge sender unit, hose support bracket, and thermostat.

32.1 Insert the auxiliary shaft ...

32.2 ... and fit the retaining plate

32.3 Fit the auxiliary shaft housing gasket over the dowels ...

32.4 ... then locate the housing

32.8 Fit the timing case backing plate. Note the special spacer bolt location (A). Apply sealant to bolts (B)

33.2 Refit the oil pump and tighten the retaining bolts

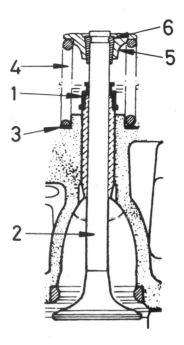

Fig. 1.31 Valve components (Sec 35)

1	Oil seal	4	Spring
2	Valve	5	Cap
3	Spring seat	6	Split collets

36 Camshaft and tappets – refitting

1   Lubricate the tappet buckets and insert them into their respective locations as noted during removal. Make sure that each bucket has its correct tappet shim in place on its upper face (photos).

2   Lubricate the camshaft bearings, then lay the camshaft in position. Position the oil seals so that they are flush with the cylinder head faces and refit the bearing caps. Ensure that the caps are fitted facing the same way as noted during removal and in their original locations (photos).

3   Apply a thread locking compound to the bearing cap retaining bolts, refit the bolts and progressively tighten them to the specified torque (photo).

4   Refit the camshaft sprocket backing plate to the cylinder head and secure with the retaining bolts (photo).

5   With the Woodruff key in its groove, fit the camshaft sprocket and retaining bolts. Prevent the camshaft turning using the same method as for removal and tighten the sprocket retaining bolt to the specified torque (photo).

6   If the engine is in the car, refit the fuel pump, timing belt and distributor cap, then check the valve clearances before refitting the camshaft cover.

37 Cylinder head – refitting

1   Ensure that the mating faces of the cylinder block and head are spotlessly clean, that the retaining bolt threads are also clean and dry and that they screw easily in and out of their locations.

2   Turn the crankshaft as necessary to bring No 1 piston to the TDC position. Retain the crankshaft in this position using a metal rod in the TDC locating hole in the cylinder block (photo).

3   Place a new gasket on the block face and located over the studs. Do not use any jointing compound on the gasket (photo).

34.2 Refit the sump

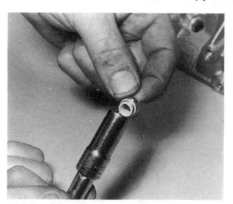

35.1A Using a socket ...

35.1B ... to fit the valve oil seals (arrowed)

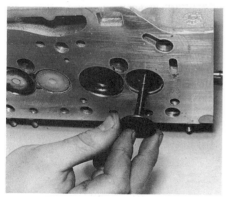

35.2 Inserting a valve ...

35.3A ... valve spring seat ...

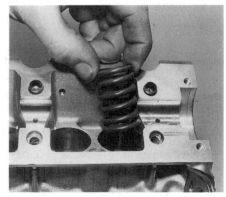

35.3B ... and valve spring

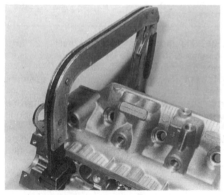

35.4 Using a valve spring compressor

36.1A Underside of a tappet bucket

36.1B Underside of tappet shim showing the thickness identification number

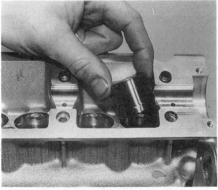

36.1C Refitting a tappet bucket

36.2A Refit the camshaft to the cylinder head

36.2B Fit the camshaft oil seals and bearing caps

36.3 Camshaft bearing cap and retaining bolts

36.4 Fit the camshaft sprocket backing plate

36.5 Camshaft sprocket bolt tightening method

4   Turn the camshaft sprocket until the mark on its outer face is aligned with the mark on the sprocket backing plate.
5   Lower the cylinder head into position on the block and engage the dowels (photo).
6   Lightly lubricate the cylinder head retaining bolt threads and under the bolt heads with clean engine oil and screw in the bolts finger tight.
7   Tighten the retaining bolts in the sequence shown in Fig. 1.32 to the 1st tightening setting given in the Specifications. Now repeat the sequence, but this time to the 2nd tightening setting.
8   Wait 3 minutes then loosen all the bolts completely. Tighten them again this time to the 1st retightening setting, still in the correct sequence.
9   The final, or 2nd, retightening is done using an angular measurement. To do this, draw two lines at 123° to each other on a sheet of card and punch a hole for the socket bit at the point where the lines intersect. Starting with bolt No 1, engage the socket through the

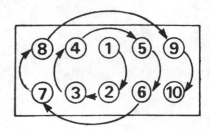

Fig. 1.32 Cylinder head bolt tightening sequence (Sec 37)

card and into the bolt head. Position the first line on the card under, and directly in line with, the socket extension bar. Hold the card, and in one movement tighten the bolt until the extension bar is aligned with the second line on the card. Repeat this procedure for the remaining bolts in the correct sequence (photo).

10 Fit and tighten the bolt securing the top end of the timing case backing plate to the end face of the cylinder head.

11 Refit the timing belt and check the valve clearances. If the engine is in the car, refit the control cables and services using the reverse of the removal procedure described in Section 11, but bearing in mind the following points:

(a) Tighten the exhaust front section-to-manifold retaining bolts so that the tension springs are compressed and coil bound (see Chapter 3)
(b) Adjust the choke and accelerator cables, as described in Chapter 3
(c) Adjust the drivebelt tension, as described in Chapter 2
(d) Refill the cooling system, as described in Chapter 2

38 Timing belt – refitting

1 Check that the crankshaft is at the TDC position for No 1 cylinder and that the crankshaft is locked in this position using the metal rod through the hole in the crankcase (photo 37.2).

2 Check that the timing mark on the camshaft sprocket is in line with the corresponding mark on the metal backing plate (photo).

3 Align the timing marks on the belt with those on the sprockets, noting that the running direction arrows on the belt should be positioned between the auxiliary shaft sprocket and the idler pulley (photos).

4 Hold the belt in this position and slip it over the crankshaft, auxiliary shaft and camshaft sprockets in that order, then around the idler tensioner pulleys.

5 Check that all the timing marks are still aligned, then temporarily tension the belt by turning the tensioner pulley anti-clockwise and tightening the retaining nut (photo).

6 Remove the TDC locating rod.

37.2 Insert bolts through TDC locating hole in cylinder block

37.3 Locate the cylinder head gasket over the studs

37.5 Refitting the cylinder head

37.9 Cylinder head bolt tightening method using an angle gauge

38.2 Align timing marks on camshaft sprocket and backing plate

38.3A Fit the timing belt, aligning the timing marks ...

38.3B ... and ensure correct running direction (indicated by arrows which must point in direction of normal rotation)

38.5 Timing belt tensioner

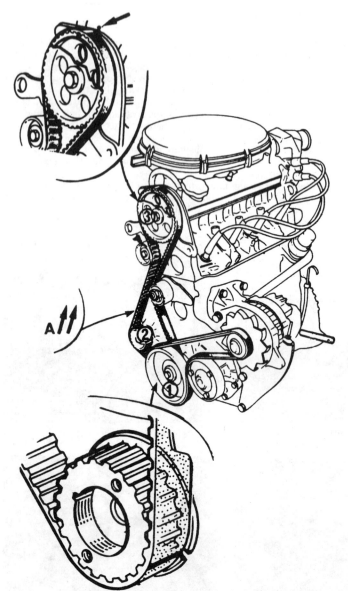

Fig. 1.33 Arrangement of the timing belt, sprockets, timing marks and belt direction arrows – A (Sec 38)

39 Valve clearances – adjustment

1   If the engine is in the car, remove the air cleaner and disconnect the choke cable, as described in Chapter 3. Undo the three domed retaining nuts and lift off the camshaft cover and gasket.

2   Using a socket or spanner on the crankshaft pulley bolt, turn the engine until the peak of the cam lobe for valve No 1 (nearest the flywheel) is uppermost. Using feeler gauges measure and record the clearance between the heel of the cam lobe and the shim on the top of the tappet bucket. Repeat this procedure for the remaining valves in turn.

3   Once all the clearances have been recorded, compare the figures with the specified valve clearances given in the Specifications, noting that valve Nos 2, 4, 5 and 7 are inlet and valve Nos 1, 3, 6 and 8 are exhaust.

4   If the clearance of any of the valves differs from the specified value, then the shim for that valve must be replaced with a thinner or thicker shim accordingly. The size of shim required can be calculated as follows: If the measured clearance is less than specified, subtract the measured clearance from the specified clearance. A shim thinner by this amount from the one now in place than is needed. If the measured clearance is greater than specified, subtract the specified clearance from the measured clearance. A shim thicker by this amount than the one now in place, is needed. The shim size is stamped on the bottom face of the shim.

5   The shims can be removed from their locations on top of the tappet buckets without removing the camshaft if the Renault tool shown in the accompanying illustrations can be borrowed, or a suitable alternative fabricated. To remove the shim the tappet bucket has to be

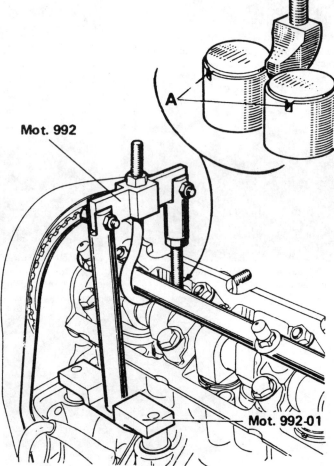

Fig. 1.34 Renault tool for compressing tappet buckets to change tappet shims (Sec 39)

Fit slots (A) at right-angles to the camshaft

7   Refit the crankshaft pulley and retaining bolt. Prevent the crankshaft turning by whichever method was used during removal and tighten the pulley bolt to the specified torque.

8   Using a socket or spanner on the pulley bolt, turn the crankshaft at least two complete turns in the normal direction of rotation; then return it to the TDC position with No 1 cylinder on compression.

9   Check that the timing marks are still aligned. If not, slacken the tensioner, move the belt one tooth as necessary on the camshaft sprocket and check again.

10   With the timing correct, tension the belt by turning the tensioner as necessary so that under moderate pressure applied at a point midway between the auxiliary sprocket and idler pulley, the belt deflects by 7.5 mm (0.3 in). When the tension is correct, tighten the tensioner pulley retaining nut.

11   Refit the timing belt cover and secure with the four retaining bolts.

12   If the engine is in the car, refit the alternator drivebelt, air cleaner, and fuel filter, then reconnect the battery.

pressed down against valve spring pressure just far enough to allow the shim to be slid out. Theoretically this could be done by levering against the camshaft between the cam lobes with a suitable pad to push the bucket down, but this is not recommended by the manufacturers. Alternatively an arrangement similar to the Renault tool can be made by bolting a bar to the camshaft bearing studs and levering down against this with a stout screwdriver. The contact pad should be a triangular-shaped metal block with a lip filed along each side to contact the edge of the bucket. Levering down against this will open the valve and allow the shim to be withdrawn. Make sure that the cam lobe peaks are uppermost when doing this and rotate the buckets so that the notches are at right angles to the camshaft centreline.

6 If the Renault tool cannot be borrowed or a suitable alternative made up then it will be necessary to remove the camshaft, as described in Section 13 to gain access to the shims.

7 When refitting the shims ensure that the size markings face the tappet buckets (ie downwards).

8 On completion refit the camshaft cover using a new gasket. If the engine is in the car refit the air cleaner and choke cable with reference to Chapter 3.

40 Ancillary components – refitting

Refer to Section 9, and refit all the components listed with reference to the Chapters indicated.

41 Engine – attachment to transmission

Refer to Section 7 and attach the engine using the reverse of the removal procedure. Apply a trace of molybdenum disulphide grease to the end of the transmission input shaft before fitting.

42 Engine and transmission – refitting

Refitting the engine is a reverse of the removal procedure contained in Section 6, but bear in mind the following additional points:

(a) Tighten the exhaust front section-to-manifold retaining bolts so that the tension springs are compressed and coil bound (see Chapter 3)

(b) Reconnect the driveshafts and front steering/suspension components as described in Chapters 8 and 10 respectively

(c) Refill the cooling system with reference to Chapter 2

(d) Adjust the choke and accelerator cables with reference to Chapter 3

(e) Refill the transmission with oil as described in Chapter 6, and the engine, as described in Section 2 of this Chapter.

43 Engine – adjustments after major overhaul

1 With the engine and transmission refitted to the car, make a final check to ensure that everything has been reconnected and that no rags or tools have been left in the engine compartment.

2 Make sure that the oil and water levels are topped up and then start the engine; this may take a little longer than usual as the fuel pump and carburettor float chamber may be empty.

3 As soon as the engine starts, watch for the oil pressure light to go out and check for any oil, fuel or water leaks. Don't be alarmed if there are some odd smells and smoke from parts getting hot and burning off oil deposits.

4 If new pistons, rings or crankshaft bearings have been fitted, the engine must be run-in for the first 500 miles (800 km). Do not exceed 45 mph (72 kph), operate the engine at full throttle or allow it to labour in any gear.

PART B: 1995 CC (2.0 LITRE) ENGINE

44 General description

The 2.0 litre engine is a four-cylinder in-line unit mounted at the front of the vehicle. It incorporates a crossflow design head, having the inlet valves and manifold on the left-hand side of the engine and the exhaust on the right. The inclined valves are operated by a single rocker shaft assembly which is mounted directly above the camshaft. The rocker arms have a stud and locknut type of adjuster for the valve clearances, providing easy adjustment. No special tools are required to set the clearances. The camshaft is driven via its sprocket from the timing belt, which in turn is driven by the crankshaft sprocket.

This belt also drives an auxiliary shaft, which in turn drives the oil pump by means of a short driveshaft geared to it.

The distributor is driven from the rear end of the camshaft by means of an offset dog.

A spring-loaded jockey wheel assembly provides the timing belt tension adjustment. A single, twin or triple pulley is mounted on the front of the crankshaft and this drives the alternator/water pump drivebelt, the power steering pump drivebelt and the air conditioning compressor drivebelt, as applicable. The crankshaft runs in the main bearings which are shell type aluminium/tin material. The crankshaft endfloat is taken up by side thrust washers. The connecting rods also have aluminium/tin shell bearing type big-ends.

Aluminium pistons are employed, the gudgeon pins being a press fit in the connecting rod small-ends and a sliding fit in the pistons. The No 1 piston is located at the flywheel end of the engine (at the rear).

Fig. 1.35 Cutaway view of the 2.0 litre (L483) engine (Sec 44)

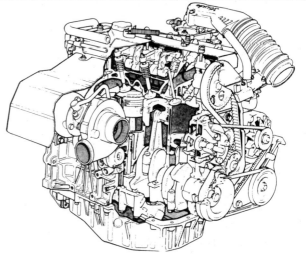

Fig. 1.36 Cutaway view of the 2.0 litre Turbo (L485) engine (Sec 44)

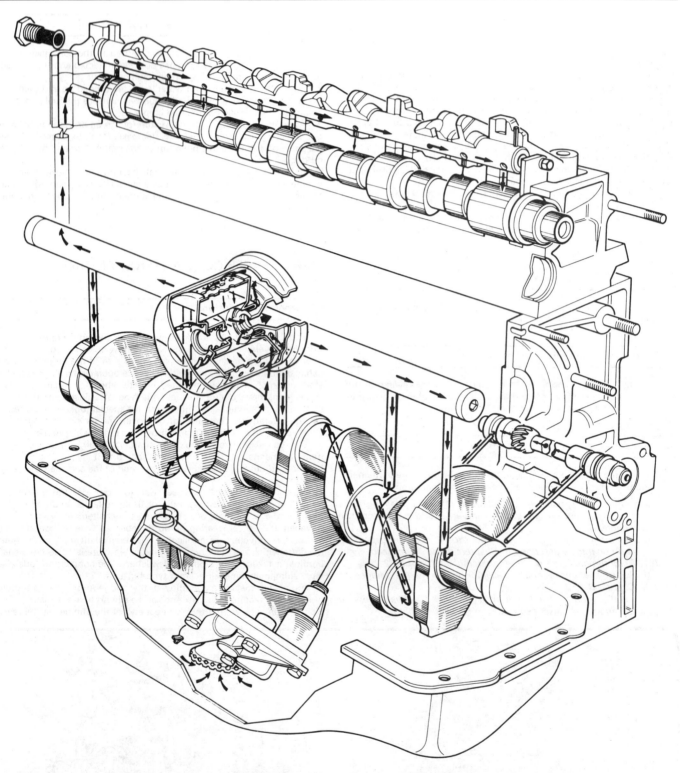

Fig. 1.37 Engine lubrication circuit (Sec 44)

Removable wet cylinder liners are employed, each being sealed in the crankcase by a flange and O-ring. The liner protrusion above the top surface of the crankcase is crucial; when the cylinder head and gasket are tightened down they compress the liners to provide the upper and lower seal of the engine coolant circuit within the engine. The cylinder head and crankcase are manufactured in light alloy.

This engine is available in both normally aspirated and turbocharged forms.

45 Maintenance

1   The engine servicing procedures for 2.0 litre models are much the same as those outlined for the 1.7 litre engine variants. Reference should therefore be made to Section 2 in Part A of this Chapter for details. As with the 1.7 litre engine, the maintenance intervals are given in the *'Routine maintenance'* Section at the start of this manual.
2   The accompanying photos illustrate the main items for servicing on the 2.0 litre engine.

45.2A Topping up the engine oil – 2.0 litre engine

45.2B Engine oil drain plug – 2.0 litre engine

45.2C Engine oil filter renewal using a strap wrench – 2.0 litre engine

46 Major operations possible with the engine in the car

The following operations are possible without the need to remove the engine from the car.

(a) Removal and refitting of the timing belt
(b) Removal and refitting of the camshaft
(c) Removal and refitting of the cylinder head
(d) Removal and refitting of the sump
(e) Removal and refitting of the auxiliary shaft
(f) Removal and refitting of the oil pump
(g) Removal and refitting of the connecting rod and piston assemblies
(h) Removal and refitting of the engine/transmission mountings
(i) Removal and refitting of the cylinder liners
(j) Removal and refitting of the injection, induction and exhaust manifolds

Warning: *Vehicles equipped with air conditioning*
Refer to the warning note in Part A, Section 2 of this Chapter.

47 Major operations requiring engine removal

The following operations can only be carried out after removal of the engine from the car:

(a) Removal and refitting of the flywheel
(b) Removal and refitting of the crankshaft and main bearings

Warning: *Vehicles equipped with air conditioning*
Refer to the warning note in Part A, Section 2 of this Chapter.

48 Methods of engine removal

The engine may be removed on its own or withdrawn complete with transmission for separation later.

If the transmission is not in need of overhaul, it will be easier to remove the engine and leave the transmission in the car.

Suitable lifting equipment will be required, also a trolley jack to support the units during removal. An assistant will also be required to assist with the actual removal of the units.

Where applicable, additional items for disconnection and/or removal on Turbo models are included in the removal instructions.

49 Engine – removal (leaving manual transmission in the car)

Warning: *Vehicles equipped with air conditioning*
Refer to the warning note in Part A, Section 2 of this Chapter.

1 Open the bonnet, mark the position of the hinges on its underside using a pencil or masking tape and with the help of an assistant, unbolt and remove the bonnet.

2 Disconnect the battery.
3 Drain the engine oil.
4 Drain the cooling system, and then remove the radiator as described in Chapter 2. On Turbo models it will also be necessary to detach and remove the following items. Refer to the accompanying illustrations for details:

(a) Front grille panel
(b) Upper front panel
(c) Upper crossmember and intercooler
(d) Headlight units (refer to Chapter 12)
(e) Front grille mounting

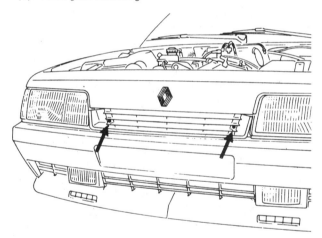

Fig. 1.38 Front grille retaining screw locations – arrowed (Sec 49)

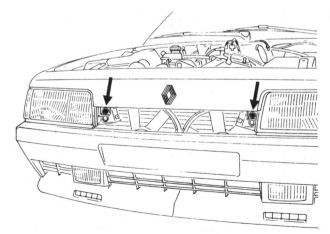

Fig. 1.39 Upper front panel front retaining bolt locations – arrowed (Sec 49)

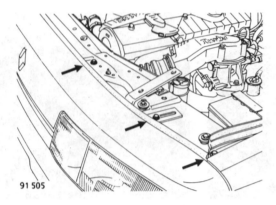

**Fig. 1.40 Upper front panel top retaining bolt locations –
arrowed (Sec 49)**

5   Disconnect the throttle cable as described in Chapter 3.
6   Disconnect and remove the air cleaner unit as described in Chapter 3.
7   Disconnect the clutch cable from the operating lever as described in Chapter 5.
8   Unbolt and remove the engine angular position/speed sensor from the top of the clutch bellhousing (photo). Disconnect the HT lead from the coil.
9   Undo the retaining nut and remove the protective cover from the computer unit on the inner left-hand wing panel. Undo the computer unit retaining screw at the bottom and release the retaining clip at the top. Detach the appropriate wiring connections, and then move the computer unit and rest it on top of the engine. The computer unit can then be removed together with the engine.
10 Disconnect the fuel feed and return hoses at the bulkhead, and plug them to prevent leakage (photo).
11 Disconnect the appropriate heater coolant hoses and the coolant hose to the expansion bottle (photo).
12 Disconnect the vacuum hose to the brake servo unit at the manifold.
13 Disconnect the various wiring connectors to the engine sensors, switches, starter motor and alternator (photos). Note and label the wiring runs and connections to avoid confusion during reassembly.
14 Remove the starter motor – see Chapter 12 for details.
15 Raise and support the front of the vehicle on axle stands.
16 Detach and remove the engine undershield.
17 Disconnect the power steering hoses at the pump. Clamp the hoses and plug the ports to prevent fluid leakage.
18 Unbolt and disconnect the exhaust downpipe at the exhaust manifold. On Turbo models also remove the turbocharger heat shield and the intercooler hoses (see Chapter 3). Unbolt the downpipe at the lower end and remove it.
19 Disconnect the engine earth lead.
20 Attach a suitable hoist and lifting gear to the engine lifting lugs, using the inner hole of the front lug, and just take the weight of the engine. The computer unit should be securely tied to the engine to avoid any possibility of damage during the subsequent lifting operation.
21 Position a jack to support the weight of the transmission.
22 Unbolt and remove the engine mountings at the points indicated in Fig. 1.43.
23 Unscrew the bolts which hold the reinforcement brackets and cover plate to the lower face of the clutch bellhousing.
24 Unscrew and remove the engine-to-transmission connecting bolts. Note the locations of the various brackets, wiring harness clips and other attachments held by some of the bolts.
25 Make a final check to ensure that any components, hoses etc affecting engine removal have been removed or disconnected as applicable.
26 Carefully raise the engine to clear the mounting brackets, then withdraw it forwards, swivelling the engine slightly about the crankshaft axis to enable the clutch release fork to be released from its bearing. As the two units are separated, support the weight of the transmission with the jack to prevent any unnecessary force being applied to the input shaft.
27 Lift the engine carefully from the engine compartment.

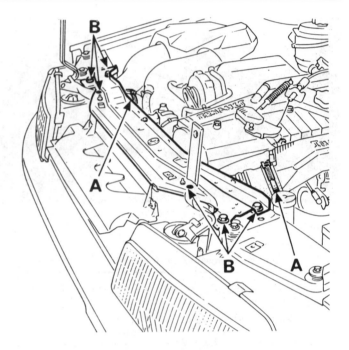

**Fig. 1.41 Upper crossmember bolts (B) and intercooler clips
(A) (Sec 49)**

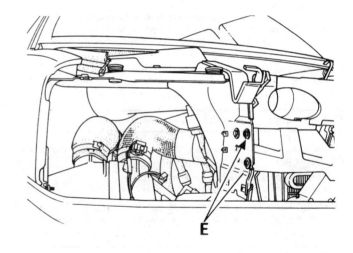

Fig. 1.42 Front grille mounting bolts (E) (Sec 49)

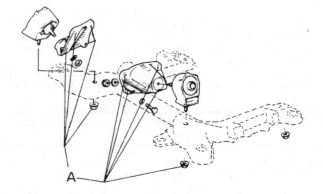

Fig. 1.43 Unbolt engine mountings at points 'A' (Sec 49)

49.8 Engine angular position/speed sensor location on clutch bellhousing

49.10 Detach the fuel hoses at the bulkhead

49.11 Detach the heater coolant hoses

49.13A Wiring connector to oil level indicator

49.13B Wiring connector to coolant temperature sensor (arrowed)

50 Engine and manual transmission – removal and separation

1 Proceed as described in paragraphs 1 to 18 inclusive of the previous Section, then continue as follows.
2 Remove the transmission undershield, then drain the transmission oil.
3 Apply the handbrake, then raise and support the vehicle at the front on axle stands so that there is sufficient clearance to work underneath the transmission. Unbolt and remove the front roadwheels.
4 Disconnect the gearchange link rods and reverse interlock operating cable, as described in Chapter 6.
5 Disconnect the reversing light switch leads.
6 Disconnect the speedometer cable by pulling the nylon retainer pin downwards using suitable pliers, and disengaging the cable from the transmission.
7 Using a suitable pin punch, drive out the roll pins which secure the driveshafts to the transmission (see Chapter 8).
8 On each side of the vehicle, loosen, but do not remove at this stage, the two nuts securing the front shock absorber-to-hub carrier bolts. Drive each bolt rearwards so that the splined section under its head is clear of the hub carrier, then remove the nut from the upper bolt only.
9 Withdraw the upper bolt to enable the hub carrier to be pivoted outwards sufficiently to allow the driveshaft on the side concerned to be withdrawn. Take care not to strain the brake hydraulic hoses. If necessary, detach the steering arm outer balljoint as described in Chapter 10.
10 Position a trolley jack under the transmission to support its weight.
11 Undo the retaining bolts, and remove the transmission mountings on each side.
12 Unbolt and remove the transverse bar from the subframe.
13 Attach a suitable hoist and lifting gear to the engine lifting lugs. Use the inner hole of the front lug. Arrange the lifting gear to give a lift angle of 15° from the horizontal – see Fig. 1.44.

14 Take the weight of the engine and transmission, then unbolt and remove the engine mountings.
15 Withdraw the engine/transmission forward and upwards from the engine compartment (photo).
16 Clean away external dirt using paraffin and a stiff brush or a water soluble solvent.

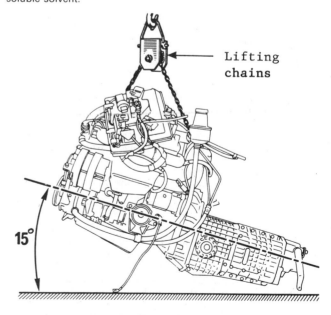

Lifting chains

15°

Fig. 1.44 Engine and transmission lift angle (Sec 50)

50.15 Engine and transmission removal

17 To separate the engine from the transmission, proceed as follows.
18 Unscrew the bolts which hold the reinforcement brackets and cover plate to the lower face of the clutch bellhousing.
19 Unscrew and remove the engine-to-transmission connecting bolts. Note the location of the various brackets, wiring harness clips and other attachments held by some of the bolts.
20 Support the engine with wooden blocks under the sump pan so that the transmission has a clear gap underneath, and then withdraw the transmission from the engine. **Do not** allow the weight of the transmission to hang upon the input shaft while the latter is still engaged with the clutch driven plate. As the two units are separated, swivel the gearbox slightly about the input shaft axis to enable the clutch release fork to be released from its bearing.

51 Engine – removal (leaving automatic transmission in the car)

1 Carry out the operations described in paras 1 to 6 and 8 to 19 of Section 49.
2 Working through the starter motor aperture, lock the teeth of the ring gear using a suitable tool and unscrew the driveplate-to-torque converter fixing bolts.
3 In order to bring each bolt into view, the crankshaft will have to be turned by means of a socket on its pulley bolt while the ring gear locking
tool is temporarily removed.
4 Unscrew and remove the bolts which hold the torque converter lower cover plate. The cover plate will drop off its dowels only after the engine and transmission are separated.
5 Unscrew and remove the engine-to-transmission bolts.
6 Attach a hoist to the engine lifting lugs and just take the weight of the engine.
7 Place a jack under the transmission.
8 Unscrew the engine mounting through-bolt nuts.
9 Raise the engine to clear the mounting brackets, then withdraw it forward to disconnect it from the transmission and lift it up and out of the engine compartment.
10 Bolt a retaining bar to one of the torque converter housing flange bolts in order to retain the converter in full engagement with the transmission and to prevent damage to the oil seal.

52 Engine and automatic transmission – removal and separation

1 Carry out the operations described in paras 1 to 6 and 8 to 18 of Section 49.

2 Disconnect the earth straps.
3 Remove the transmission dipstick tube.
4 Disconnect the fluid hoses from the transmission fluid cooler and plug them.
5 Disconnect reversing lamp switch lead.
6 Disconnect the speedometer cable.
7 Disconnect the driveshafts from the transmission as described in paragraphs 7 to 9 of Section 50.
8 Disconnect the speed selector control cable and kick-down cable after reference to Chapter 7, also the vacuum pipe and computer wiring plugs.
9 With a hoist attached to the lifting lugs and taking the weight of the engine and transmission, remove the transmission mountings and unscrew the nuts from the engine mounting through-bolts. Prepare to guide the computer out with the transmission.
10 Withdraw the engine/transmission forward and upwards out of the engine compartment.
11 Clean away external dirt using paraffin and a stiff brush or a water soluble solvent.
12 Separate the transmission from the engine as described in paragraphs 5 to 7 of Section 51. Pull the transmission from the engine and then fit a torque converter retaining bar as described in paragraph 10 of Section 51.

53 Engine dismantling – general

Refer to Part A, Section 8 of this Chapter.

54 Ancillary components – removal

Before complete engine dismantling begins, remove the following ancillary items:

Exhaust manifold and where applicable, turbocharger unit (Chapter 3)
Power steering unit (Chapter 10)
Alternator (Chapter 12)
Distributor cap and plug leads (Chapter 4)
Engine mounting and reinforcement brackets
Timing belt cover
Coolant pump (Chapter 2)
Clutch (Chapter 5)
Injection and induction manifold (Chapter 3)
Coolant hoses and thermostat housing (Chapter 2)
Starter motor (Chapter 12)

55 Timing belt – removal

1 If the engine has been removed from the car, proceed from paragraph 7.
2 Apply the handbrake, raise the car so that the front roadwheels are clear of the ground and support with axle stands. Detach and remove the engine undertray.
3 Remove the power steering pump drivebelt.
4 Loosen the alternator retaining bolts and remove its drivebelt.
5 Remove the camshaft cover.
6 Detach the battery earth terminal.
7 Remove the spark plugs and keep them in order for refitting.
8 Remove the timing belt cover (photo).
9 Turn the crankshaft (using a suitable spanner on the crankshaft pulley bolt) until No 1 piston (flywheel end) is at TDC. The correct setting will be established when the square cut-out in the camshaft sprocket is at its lowest point and the dimple is in line with the camshaft cover stud. The dimple and keyway on the crankshaft sprocket will be at their highest point (see Fig. 1.63). An alternative way to set TDC is to remove the brass plug from the crankcase and insert a rod to engage in the slot which is located in the crankshaft counterbalance weight. Obviously, to find this slot, the engine No 1 piston must be approaching TDC. This can be checked by removing No 1 spark plug and feeling the compression being generated. Yet a further means of checking TDC is to observe the timing mark on the flywheel is in line with the 'O' mark on the graduated scale at the clutch housing aperture (photos).

55.8 Remove the timing belt cover. Note the wiring harness duct (arrowed)

55.9A Camshaft sprocket dimple aligned with rocker cover stud (No 1 piston at TDC)

55.9B Crankshaft sprocket (No 1 piston at TDC)

55.9C Timing rod plug location

55.9D Timing rod inserted into plug hole

55.9E Timing rod slot in crankshaft counterbalance weight (sump removed)

55.9F Flywheel timing mark at TDC position

55.11 Timing belt tensioner retaining bolt and nut (arrowed)

10 Lock the flywheel or driveplate (auto. trans.) starter ring gear teeth with a suitable tool, unscrew the crankshaft pulley bolt and take off the pulley. Never use the TDC sensor teeth on the flywheel as a means of preventing it rotating. If the timing belt is to be used again, mark its running direction (if not already marked).
11 Loosen the tensioner retaining bolt and nut and remove the belt (photo).
12 Take care if removing the tensioner, as it is operated by a spring and piston in the crankcase side, and the tensioner is under considerable pressure. As the tensioner is unbolted, take care that the spring and piston do not fly out of their aperture at high speed.

56 Cylinder head – removal (engine in car)

1 Disconnect the battery earth lead.
2 On Turbo models, unbolt and remove the heat shield from the top of the turbocharger unit/exhaust manifold assembly (photo).
3 Disconnect the throttle cable from the pivot quadrant on top of the camshaft cover. Detach the cable adjuster at the retaining bracket on top of the cover and prise free the throttle connecting rod from the balljoint at the throttle housing.
4 Drain the cooling system as described in Chapter 2.
5 Unclip and detach the air intake duct from the throttle case cover. For improved access underneath the manifolds, remove the air filter (Chapter 3) and on Turbo models, the battery (Chapter 12).
6 Disconnect the appropriate cooling system hoses, vacuum hoses, and wiring connections to the cylinder head and its associated components. Take note of and label their respective connections as they are detached to avoid confusion on refitting. Note that the thermostat is positioned within the cylinder head end of the coolant top hose.
7 Disconnect and plug the fuel hoses to prevent leakage and the ingress of dirt.
8 Unbolt and disconnect the exhaust downpipe at its connection to the manifold or turbocharger unit, as applicable (Chapter 3). If the turbocharger and exhaust are to be removed as a unit together with the cylinder head, detach the turbocharger support bracket, working from underneath. If required, the manifolds can be removed with reference to Chapter 3.
9 Detach the distributor cap and HT leads from the cylinder head, and remove the rotor arm (Chapter 4). Position the cap and leads out of the way.
10 Unbolt and remove the camshaft cover. Disconnect the coolant hose, vacuum hose and HT lead support brackets as applicable (photos).
11 Remove the timing belt as described in Section 55.
12 The cylinder head retaining bolts can now be progressively

loosened, and with the exception of the front right-hand bolt, removed. Loosen off the bolts in the sequence shown in Fig. 1.45.
13 The cylinder head is now ready for removal from the block, and it is essential that it is detached in the correct manner. **Do not** lift the head directly upwards from the block. The head must be swivelled from the rear in a horizontal manner, pivoting on the remaining head dowel and bolt at the front. You will probably have to tap the head round on its rear corner, using a soft-headed mallet or wood block to break the seal between the head, gasket and block. Once the head is pivoted round and the seal broken, it can be lifted clear. This action is necessary because if the head were to be lifted directly from the block, the seal between the head gasket and block would be unbroken and the liners would thus be disturbed. Each liner has a seal around its lower flange; where the liners are not being removed, it is essential that this seal is not broken or disturbed. If the liners are accidentally disturbed they must be removed and new lower seals fitted.
14 The rocker shaft assembly and final bolt can be removed from the cylinder head once it is withdrawn from the engine.
15 To prevent the possibility of movement by the respective cylinder liners whilst the head is removed, it is advisable to place a clamp-plate over the top edges of the liners. A suitable plate (or bar) can be fastened temporarily in position using the existing head bolt holes, using shorter bolts of the desired thread and diameter with large, flat washers under the heads. Alternatively, use a block of wood with two bolts and spacers, clamping it in position in diagonal fashion (photo).
16 Refer to Section 69 for details of dismantling and decarbonising the cylinder head.

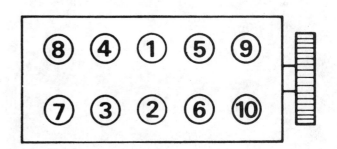

Fig. 1.45 Cylinder head bolt loosening and tightening sequence (Sec 56)

56.2 Remove the heat shield from the turbocharger and exhaust manifold

56.10A Detach the hoses and support brackets ...

56.10B ... and the HT leads support bracket from the rocker cover

56.15 Fabricated liner clamps

57 Cylinder head – removal (engine on bench)

1 Carry out the operations described in paragraph 9 onwards of the previous Section.
2 If required, the manifolds and associated components can be removed from the cylinder head prior to its removal, as described in Chapter 3.

58 Camshaft – removal

1 Disconnect the battery earth lead.
2 Drain the engine coolant (see Chapter 2).
3 Disconnect the throttle cable from the pivot quadrant on top of the camshaft cover. Detach the cable adjuster at the retaining bracket on top of the cover and prise free the throttle connecting rod from the balljoint at the throttle housing.
4 Remove the camshaft cover.
5 Remove the radiator together with the electric cooling fan unit (see Chapter 2).
6 Remove the drivebelts to the alternator, the power steering pump

and air conditioning pump, as applicable.
7 Unbolt and remove the timing cover.
8 Disconnect the respective HT leads and remove the sparking plugs. Next, rotate the crankshaft to locate the No 1 piston (flywheel end) at TDC or firing stroke. This can be checked by ensuring the timing mark on the flywheel is in line with the 'O' graduation marked on the aperture in the clutch housing (see Section 55, paragraph 9). Rotate the crankshaft by means of a spanner applied to the crankshaft pulley retaining bolt.
9 Remove the timing belt as described in Section 55.
10 To remove the camshaft sprocket, pass a suitable rod or screwdriver through a hole in the sprocket and jam against the top surface of the cylinder head to prevent the camshaft from turning.
Unscrew the retaining bolt and remove the sprocket. Take great care as the sprocket is manufactured in sintered metal and is therefore relatively fragile. Also, take care not to damage or distort the cylinder head. Remove the Woodruff key.
11 Remove the camshaft cover and unscrew the cylinder head retaining bolts in a progressive manner in the sequence shown in Fig. 1.45. With the bolts extracted, remove the rocker assembly and relocate some of the bolts with spacers to the same depth as the rocker pedestals fitted under the bolt heads, to ensure that the cylinder head is

not disturbed during subsequent operations. If for any reason the head is disturbed, then the head gasket and respective liner seals will have to be renewed.

12 Unclip the distributor cap and place it to one side.

13 Remove the rotor arm.

14 Unbolt and remove the distributor body.

15 Remove the camshaft retaining thrustplate (two bolts).

16 Unbolt and remove the timing belt rear cover plate.

17 The camshaft front oil seal can now be extracted from its housing. Carefully prise out from the front or preferably drift out from the rear. Take great care not to damage the seal location bore in the head.

18 The camshaft can now be withdrawn carefully through the seal aperture in the front of the cylinder head. Take care during its removal not to snag any of the lobe corners on the bearings as they are passed through the cylinder head.

59 Cylinder head – dismantling

1 With the cylinder head removed to the bench, dismantle in the following way.

2 If not already done, remove the manifolds, as described in Chapter 3.

3 Unscrew and remove the spark plugs.

4 Remove the distributor body from the rear of the cylinder head (Chapter 4).

5 Remove the camshaft sprocket and key.

6 Extract the camshaft front oil seal, and remove the rocker assembly.

7 Lift the camshaft from the cylinder head.

8 Using a valve spring compressor, compress the first valve spring and remove the split collets.

9 Gently release the compressor and remove it.

10 Take off the spring retainer, the spring and the spring seat.

11 Remove all the other valves in a similar way, keeping them in their original fitted sequence together with their associated components. Remove and discard the valve stem oil seals.

12 Bearing in mind that the cylinder head is of light alloy construction and is easily damaged, use a blunt scraper or rotary wire brush to clean all traces of carbon deposits from combustion spaces and the ports. The valve stems and valve guides should also be freed from any carbon deposits. Wash the combustion spaces and ports down with paraffin and scrape the cylinder head surface free of any foreign matter with the side of a steel rule, or a similar article.

60 Sump – removal

1 If the engine has been removed from the car, proceed from paragraph 5.

2 Drain the engine oil as described in Section 45.

3 Apply the handbrake, and raise and support the car at the front end on axle stands.

4 Detach and remove the engine undertray. This is secured by screws and clips. Loosen the engine mountings and raise the engine slightly using a hoist and lifting gear attached to the inner hole of the front engine lifting lug.

5 Unscrew the securing screws and remove the sump pan. If it is stuck tight, tap it gently with a wooden or plastic-faced hammer.

6 Remove the original gasket and clean the mating surfaces.

7 It should be noted that on Turbo models, bolt A shown in Fig. 1.49, cannot be withdrawn and removed when undoing the retaining bolts of the aluminium type sump.

61 Oil pump – removal

1 If the engine is in the car, remove the sump as described in Section 60.

2 Unbolt and remove the cover plate from the left-hand side of the crankcase.

3 Withdraw the drive pinion and then the oil pump driveshaft, noting that the circlip is at its lower end.

4 Unbolt and remove the oil pump. The pump flange is located on dowels, so pull it straight off.

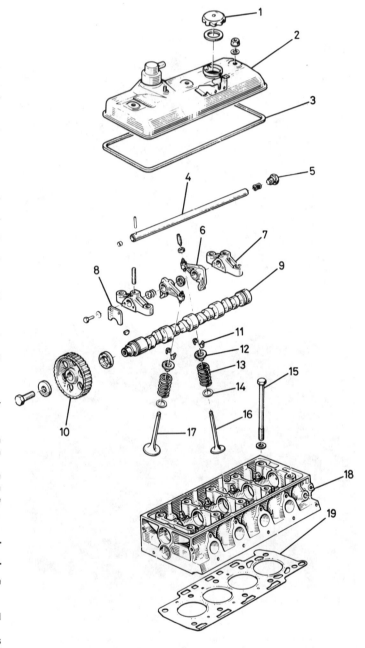

Fig. 1.46 Cylinder head and associated components (Sec 59)

1 Oil filler cap	11 Split collets
2 Camshaft cover	12 Spring retaining cap
3 Gasket	13 Valve spring
4 Rocker shaft	14 Spring seat
5 End plug and oil filter	15 Cylinder head bolt
6 Rocker arm	16 Exhaust valve
7 Rocker shaft pedestal	17 Inlet valve
8 Camshaft retaining plate	18 Cylinder head
9 Camshaft	19 Gasket
10 Sprocket	

62 Auxiliary shaft – removal

1 If the engine is in the car, disconnect the battery earth lead.

2 Remove the timing belt as described in Section 55.

3 Unscrew the auxiliary shaft sprocket bolt, passing a screwdriver

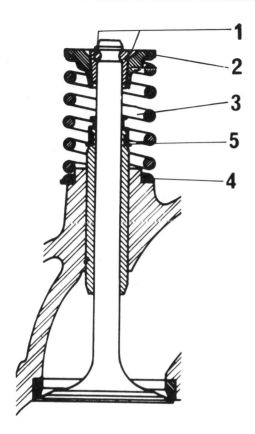

Fig. 1.47 Sectional view of valve components (Sec 59)

1	Split collets	4	Spring seat
2	Spring retaining cap	5	Oil seal
3	Valve spring		

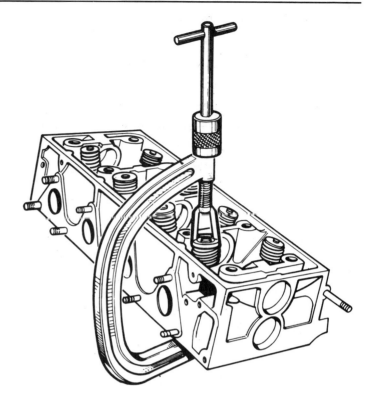

Fig. 1.48 Using a valve spring compressor (Sec 59)

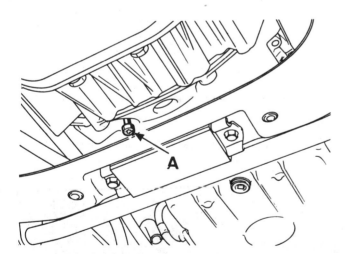

Fig. 1.49 On Turbo models, bolt 'A' cannot be withdrawn from the sump (Sec 60)

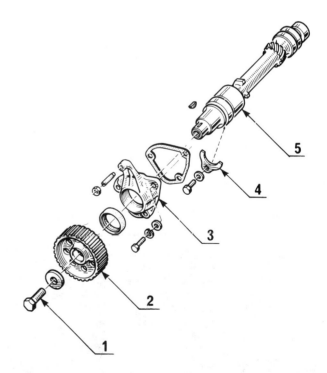

Fig. 1.50 Auxiliary shaft components (Sec 62)

1	Bolt	4	Forked lockplate
2	Sprocket	5	Shaft
3	Front housing cover		

shaft or rod through one of the holes in the sprocket to lock against the front of the block and retain the sprocket in position whilst it is being unscrewed.

4 Withdraw the sprocket and remove the Woodruff key from the shaft.

5 Unbolt and remove the auxiliary shaft housing cover and the forked lockplate.

6 The oil seal can now be extracted. Prise it free with a screwdriver, but take care not to damage the housing.

7   Before the auxiliary shaft can be withdrawn, the oil pump drive pinion must first be extracted. To do this, unscrew the two cover plate retaining bolts and remove the cover. The oil pump drive pinion is now accessible and can be extracted.
8   The auxiliary shaft can now be removed from the front of the crankcase.

63 Flywheel (or driveplate) – removal

1   Jam the flywheel teeth and unscrew the flywheel bolts (or driveplate – automatic transmission). The flywheel bolt holes are offset so it can only be fitted one way.
2   It should be noted that the flywheel retaining bolts must be renewed when refitting.

64 Crankshaft and main bearings – removal

1   Remove the cylinder head as described in Section 57, and the flywheel as described in Section 63.
2   Turn the engine on its side and remove the sump as described in Section 60, and the oil pump as described in Section 61.
3   The main and big-end bearing caps are numbered from 1 to 4, from the flywheel end of the block. The main bearing cap numbers are read from the oil filter side of the crankcase (photo).
4   The big-end bearing caps and their connecting rods are not very clearly marked, so it is best to centre punch them at adjacent points and on the oil filter side so that there is no doubt as to their position and orientation in the block.
5   The connecting rod big-ends will not pass out through the cylinder liners, so each liner/piston/connecting rod must be removed as an assembly out of the top of the cylinder block. Before doing this however, centre punch each liner rim and adjacent surface on the top of the cylinder block so that they will be refitted in their original position and orientation if of course they are not being renewed completely.
6   Unbolt the big-end bearing caps, keeping the bearing shells taped to their original cap or connecting rod if they are to be used again, although this is not to be recommended (see Section 68 for bearing renewal).
7   Withdraw the cylinder liner/piston/connecting rod assemblies.
8   Unbolt and remove the main bearing caps, again keeping their bearing shells with their respective caps if they are to be refitted, again not to be recommended.
9   Note that the front and rear main bearing caps are located on dowels so if they are tight, tap them straight off, **not** in a sideways direction.
10 Withdraw the crankshaft, noting the two semi-circular thrust washers located in the crankcase. Remove the bearing shells and identify them by marking with numbered tape if they are to be used again.
11 Using two screwdrivers inserted at opposite points, lever off the crankshaft sprocket. Extract the Woodruff key and remove the belt guide.

12 Remove the crankshaft front and rear oil seals and discard them.

65 Piston/connecting rod/cylinder liner assembly – removal

1   These assemblies can be removed with the engine in the car once the cylinder head, sump and oil pump have been removed, as described in previous Sections.
2   Rotate the crankshaft, using a spanner on the crankshaft pulley, so that No 1 big-end (nearest the flywheel) is at the lowest point of its travel.
3   The remainder of the procedure is as described in Section 64, paragraphs 4 to 7.

66 Engine/transmission mountings – renewal

1   The procedure for the 2.0 litre engine variants is similar to that for the 1.7 litre variants described in Part A, Section 23 of this Chapter.
2   The engine undertray will have to be removed for access to the mountings, and to allow the engine/transmission to be supported with a jack.
3   Refer to the accompanying photos. Note that there is no stabilizer bracket fitted to 2.0 litre models.

67 Crankcase ventilation system – description

The system is designed to extract oil fumes and blow-by gas from within the crankcase and burn them in the combustion chambers. This ensures that there is always a partial vacuum in the crankcase, and so prevents a build-up of pressure which could cause oil contamination, fume emission, and oil leakage post seals.
Periodically clean out the connecting hoses and jets and make sure that the hoses are a tight fit on their connectors.
The system layouts for non-Turbo and Turbo models are shown in Figs. 1.52 and 1.53.

68 Examination and renovation

1   With the engine stripped down and all parts thoroughly clean, it is now time to examine everything for wear. The following items should be checked and where necessary renewed or renovated as described in the following Sections.

Cylinder block and crankcase
2   Clean away all old gasket material and then examine the casting for cracks particularly about bolt holes. If they are found, specialist welding or cold repair will be required.
3   Clean out the oilways and galleries with compressed air or wire.
4   If the cylinder bores are worn, this will be evident by the emission of exhaust smoke and general deterioration in engine performance together with increased oil consumption. A good way to test the

64.3 Crankshaft main bearing cap identification number

66.3A Left-hand engine mounting

66.3B Transmission mounting

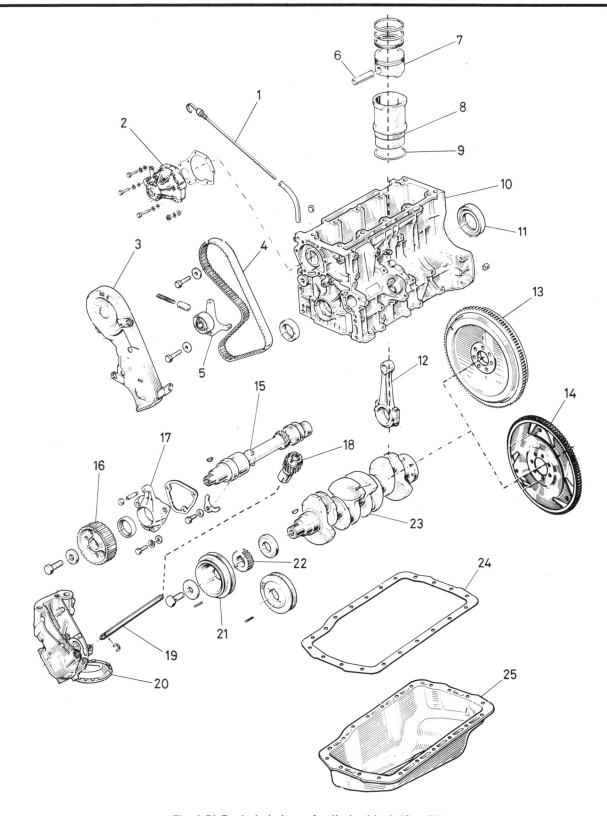

Fig. 1.51 Exploded view of cylinder block (Sec 64)

1 Dipstick
2 Coolant pump
3 Timing belt cover
4 Timing belt
5 Timing belt tensioner
6 Gudgeon pin
7 Piston

8 Cylinder liner
9 O-ring seal
10 Crankcase
11 Oil seal
12 Connecting rod
13 Flywheel (manual transmission)

14 Driveplate (automatic transmission
15 Auxiliary shaft
16 Sprocket
17 Housing
18 Oil pump drive pinion
19 Oil pump driveshaft

20 Oil pump
21 Crankshaft pulley
22 Crankshaft timing belt sprocket
23 Crankshaft
24 Gasket
25 Sump pan

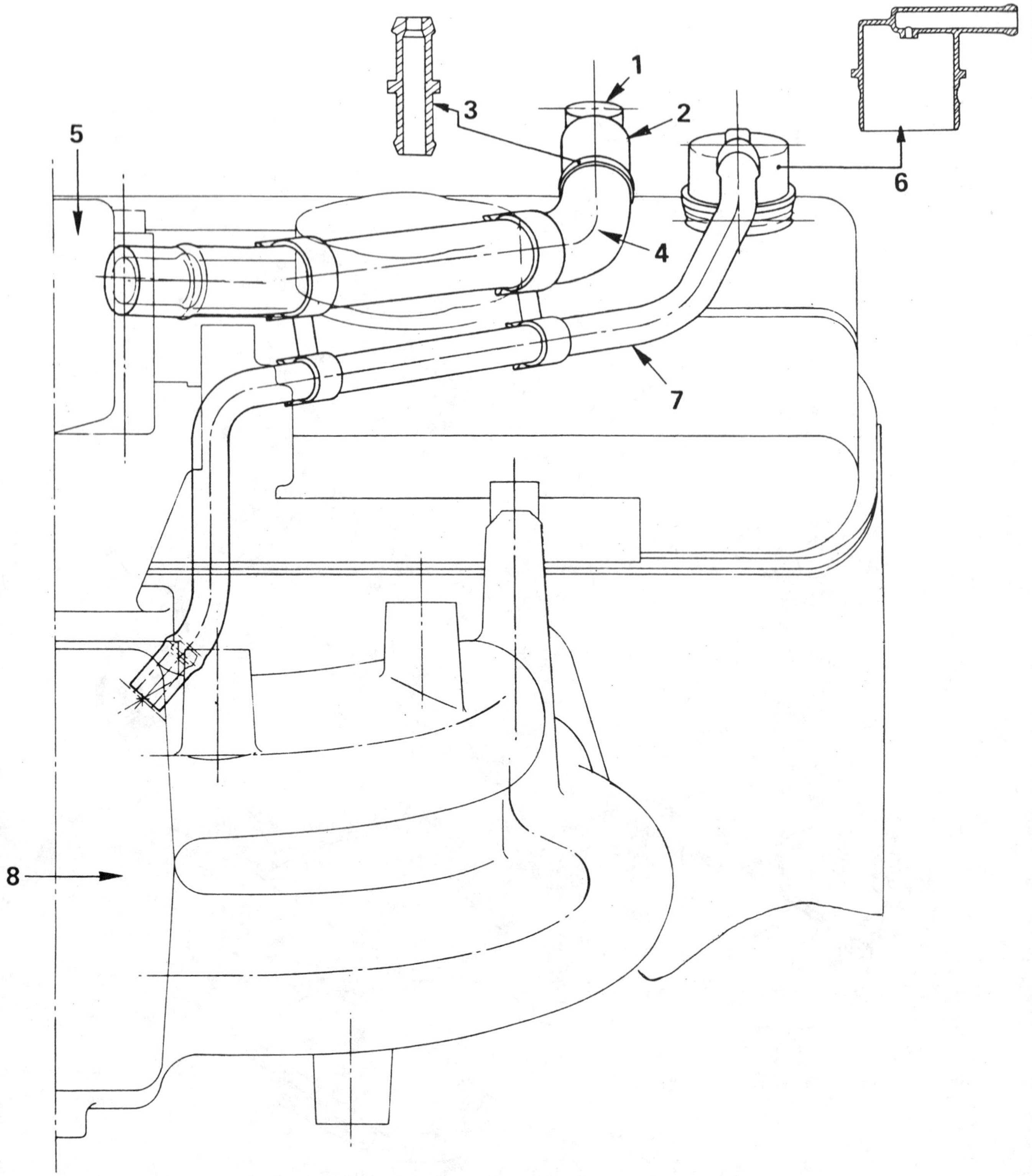

Fig. 1.52 Crankcase ventilation system hoses – non-Turbo
(Sec 67)

1   2-way union
2   Calibrated
    connector-to-2-way union
    hose
3   Calibrated connector (red)
4   Calibrated connector-to-air
    intake casing hose
5   Air intake casing
6   2-way union with internal
    restrictor
7   2-way union-to-mixer
    casing hose
8   Mixer casing

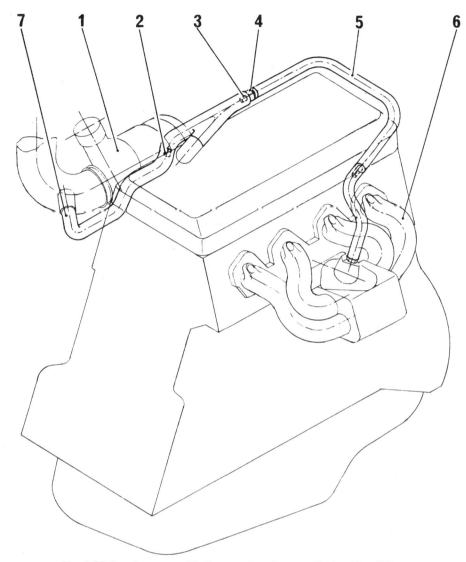

Fig. 1.53 Crankcase ventilation system hoses – Turbo (Sec 67)

1	Turbocharger	3	Restrictor	5	Downstream circuit	7	Upstream circuit
2	Restrictor	4	Valve	6	Inlet manifold		

condition of the engine when it is still in the car is to have it at normal operating temperature with the spark plugs removed. Screw a compression tester (available from most modern accessory stores) into the first plug hole. Hold the accelerator pedal fully depressed and crank the engine on the starter motor for several revolutions. Record the reading. Zero the tester and check the remaining cylinders in the same way. All four compression figures should be approximately equal and within the tolerance given in the Specifications. If they are all low, suspect piston ring or cylinder bore wear. If only one reading is down, suspect a valve not seating.

5 The cylinder bores must be checked for taper, ovality, scoring and scratching. Start by examining the top of the cylinder bores. If they are at all worn, a ridge will be felt on the thrust side. This ridge marks the limit of piston ring travel.

6 An internal micrometer or dial gauge can be used to check bore wear and taper against Specifications, but this is a pointless operation if the engine is obviously worn as indicated by excessive oil consumption.

7 The engine is fitted with renewable 'wet' cylinder liners and these are supplied complete with piston, rings and gudgeon pin.

Pistons and connecting rods

8 The gudgeon pin is an interference fit in the connecting rod small end and removal or refitting and changing a piston is a job best left to

your dealer or engine reconditioner. This is owing to the need for a press and jig and careful heating of the connecting rod.

9 Removal and refitting piston rings is described in the following paragraphs.

10 Remove the piston rings from the top of the piston. To avoid breaking a ring either during removal or refitting, slide two or three old feeler blades at equidistant points behind the top ring and slide it up them. Remove the other rings in a similar way.

11 Clean carbon from the ring grooves, a segment of old piston ring is useful for this purpose.

12 Clean out the oil return holes in the piston ring grooves and fit the new piston rings.

13 If proprietary rings are being fitted to old pistons, the top ring will be supplied stepped so that it does not impinge on the wear ridge.

14 Insert each piston ring in turn squarely into its bore. New rings supplied as part of Renault piston/liner sets are pre-gapped and must not be altered.

15 Now check each compression ring in its groove and measure the clearances with a feeler gauge. If it is tight the ring may be rubbed flat on a sheet of wet and dry paper laid flat on a piece of plate glass.

16 Fit the rings to the piston using the feeler blade method as described for removal. Work from the top of the piston, fitting the oil control ring first.

17 Lubricate the piston rings and locate their end gaps at 120° apart.

Crankshaft

18 Examine the crankpin and main journal surfaces for signs of scoring or scratches, and check for ovality and taper of the crankpins and main journals. If the bearing surface dimensions do not fall within the tolerance ranges given in the Specifications at the beginning of this Chapter, the crankpins and/or main journals will have to be reground.

19 Big-end and crankpin wear is accompanied by distinct metallic knocking, particularly noticeable when the engine is pulling from low revs, and some loss of oil pressure.

20 Main bearing and main journal wear is accompanied by severe engine vibration rumble – getting progressively worse as engine revs increase – again by loss of oil pressure.

21 If the crankshaft requires regrinding, take it to an engine reconditioning specialist, who will machine it for you and supply the correct undersize bearing shells.

Big-end and main bearing shells

22 Inspect the big-end and main bearing shells for signs of general wear, scoring, pitting and scratches. The bearings should be matt grey in colour. With lead-indium bearings, should a trace of copper colour be noticed, the bearings are badly worn as the lead bearing material has worn away to expose the indium underlay. Renew the bearings if they are in this condition or if there are any signs of scoring or pitting. **You are strongly advised to renew the bearings – regardless of their condition at time of major overhaul. Refitting used bearings is a false economy.**

23 The undersizes available are designed to corrspond with crankshaft regrind sizes. The bearings are in fact, slightly more than the stated undersize as running clearances have been allowed for during their manufacture.

24 Main and big-end bearing shells can be identified as to size by the marking on the back of the shell. Standard size shell bearings are marked STD or .00, undersize shells are marked with the undersize such as 0.020 u/s. This marking method applies only to replacement bearing shells and not to those used during production.

Flywheel/driveplate and starter ring gear

25 If the starter ring gear teeth on the flywheel (manual transmission) or torque converter driveplate (automatic transmission) are excessively worn, it will be necessary to obtain complete new assemblies. It is not possible to obtain separate ring gears.

26 On manual transmission models, examine the clutch mating surface of the flywheel and renew the flywheel if scoring or cracks are evident.

27 On automatic transmission models, the driveplate face should be checked for run-out, using a dial gauge. The maximum permissible run-out is 0.3 mm (0.012 in). Renew the plate if this figure is exceeded.

28 The flywheel/driveplate retaining bolts must be renewed on reassembly.

Camshaft

29 Check the bearings in the cylinder head. If worn, a new head will be required.

30 Inspect the camshaft journals and lobes. Scoring or general wear will indicate the need for new parts.

31 The camshaft sprocket teeth should be unchipped and free from wear.

32 The camshaft thrust plate should be free from scoring otherwise camshaft endfloat will be excessive.

Auxiliary shaft

33 Check the journals and gear teeth for wear, chipping or scoring.

34 The sprocket teeth should be free from wear and damage.

35 The forked thrust plate should be unworn, otherwise excessive shaft endfloat will occur.

36 Wear in the shaft bearings can only be rectified by the purchase of a new crankcase.

Timing belt and tensioner

37 The belt should be without any sign of fraying, cuts or splits and no deformation of the teeth.

38 Even if the timing belt appears to be in good condition, it is recommended that it is renewed at the intervals specified in the Routine Maintenance Section at the beginning of the Manual.

39 Check the belt tensioner pulley. It should spin freely without noise. If it does not, renew it.

Rocker gear

40 Slight wear in the heels of the rocker arms can be removed using an oilstone, but ensure that the contour is maintained.

41 Scoring or wear in the components can only be rectified by dismantling and renewing the defective components.

42 Unscrew the end plug from the shaft and extract the plug and filter. This filter must be renewed at the specified intervals, or whenever it is removed.

43 Number the rocker arms and pedestals/bearings. Note that bearing No 5 has two threaded holes to retain the thrust plate which controls the camshaft endfloat, and a hole for the roll pin which locates the shaft and pedestal. Renew the roll pin if it is not the solid type.

44 Keep the respective parts in order as they are removed from the shaft and note their respective locations. Note also that the machined flat section on top of pedestals 1 to 4 all face towards the camshaft sprocket.

45 Lubricate each component as it is assembled with engine oil. Lay the pedestals, spacers, springs and rockers out in order.

46 Support the rocker shaft in a soft-jawed vice and insert the new filter into the end of it, fit the retaining bolt and tighten it to the specified torque.

47 Assemble the respective pedestals, rocker arms, springs and spacers onto the shaft. When the shaft assembly is complete, compress

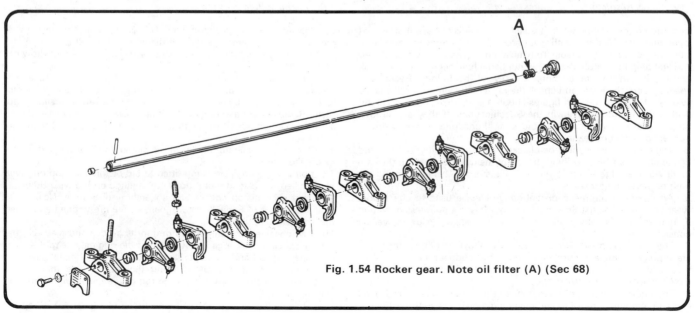

Fig. 1.54 Rocker gear. Note oil filter (A) (Sec 68)

the last pedestal to align the retaining pin hole in the shaft and pedestal. Drive a new pin into position to secure it. Early models fitted with a hollow type roll pin should have the later solid type pin fitted on reassembly.

Oil pump

48 It is essential that all parts of the pump are in good condition for the pump to work effectively.

49 To dismantle the pump, remove the cover retaining bolts and detach the cover.

50 Extract the gears and clean the respective components (photos).

51 Inspect for any signs of damage or excessive wear. Use a feeler gauge and check the clearance between the rotor (gear) tips and the inner housing.

52 Also, check the rotor endfloat using a straight-edge rule laid across the body of the pump and feeler gauge inserted between the rule and gears.

53 Compare the clearances with the allowable tolerance given in the Specifications at the start of this Chapter and, if necessary, renew any defective parts, or possibly the pump unit.

54 Do not overlook the relief valve assembly. To extract it, remove the split pin and withdraw the cup, spring, guide and piston. Again, look for signs of excessive wear or damage and renew as applicable.

55 Check the pump driveshaft for signs of wear or distortion and renew if necessary.

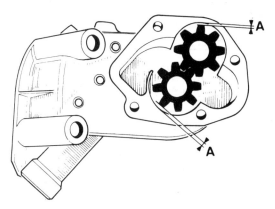

Fig. 1.55 Oil pump rotor-to-body clearance (A) (Sec 68)

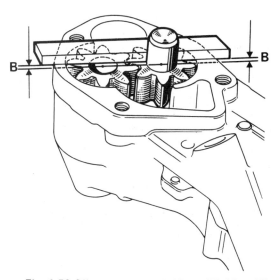

Fig. 1.56 Oil pump rotor endfloat (B) (Sec 68)

68.50A Oil pump gear

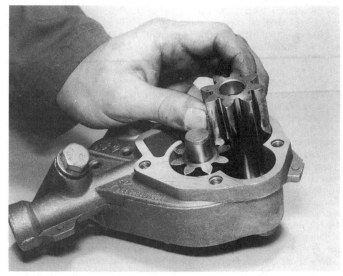

68.50B Removing the oil pump drive gear

Fig. 1.57 Oil pump pressure relief valve (Sec 68)

69 Cylinder head and pistons – decarbonizing, valve grinding and renovation

1   Proceed as described in Part A, Section 26 of this Chapter, but ignore the instructions given in paragraph 10.
2   The valve seat profile should be as shown in Fig. 1.58.

70 Piston rings – renewal (engine in car)

1   The piston rings can be renewed with the engine in the car, but a ring compressor and some suitable liner clamps will be required unless the liner seals are to be renewed also. In the latter instance, remove the pistons and liners as an assembly as described in Section 65.
2   Although the pistons cannot be withdrawn through the top of the block independently of the cylinder liners, new piston rings can be fitted, but the normal process of cylinder bore glaze removal cannot be carried out to enable the new rings to bed in properly. Despite this, the procedure is useful if a broken ring has to be renewed.
3   Remove the cylinder head (Section 56).
4   Remove the sump and oil pump (Sections 60 and 61).
5   Disconnect the big-end bearing caps (Section 64).
6   Before pushing the piston and rod assemblies up their respective bores, ensure that the cylinder liners are clamped down to prevent the liner seals from being disturbed. Refer to Section 56 for details.
7   Push each connecting rod upwards until the piston rings are out of the bore. If a wear ridge is evident, then this must be removed by careful scraping or using a ridge reamer.
8   Remove the piston rings by sliding two or three feeler blades behind the top ring and removing it upwards using a twisting motion. Refit using the same method.
9   If the top compression ring is being renewed, a stepped replacement should be obtained to prevent it making contact with the wear ridge.
10 A piston ring compressor should be fitted to the rings (well lubricated with engine oil) and the wooden handle of a hammer placed on the piston crown while the head of the hammer is given a sharp blow with the hand. This will drive the piston/rod assembly down the cylinder bore out of the compressor which will be left standing on the liner rim.
11 Reconnect the big-ends, remove the liner clamps and refit the cylinder head (see Sections 73 and 80). Refit the oil pump and sump with reference to Sections 76 and 77.

71 Engine – reassembly (general)

1   To ensure maximum life with minimum trouble from a rebuilt engine, not only must everything be correctly assembled, but everything must be spotlessly clean, all the oilways must be clear, locking washers and spring washers must always be fitted where indicated and all bearing and other working surfaces must be thoroughly lubricated during assembly.
2   Before assembly begins renew any bolts or studs the threads of which are in any way damaged, and whenever possible use the new spring washers.
3   Apart from your normal tools, a supply of clean rag, an oil can filled with engine oil (an empty plastic detergent bottle, thoroughly cleaned and washed out, will do just as well), a new supply of assorted spring washers, a set of new gaskets and a torque wrench should be collected together.

72 Crankshaft and main bearings – refitting

1   Invert the block and locate the main bearing upper shells into position, engaging the lock tabs into the cut-outs in the bearing recesses. Note that the bearing shells for bearings Nos 1, 3 and 5 are identical and have two oil holes in them whilst the Nos 2 and 4 bearing shells have three holes and an oil groove in them. However, all new shells incorporate grooves (photo).
2   Lubricate the shells with clean engine oil (photo), fit the thrust washers to No 2 main bearing so that the oil grooves are visible

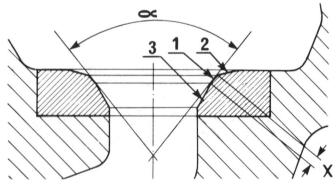

Fig. 1.58 Valve seat profile (Sec 69)

1   Valve seating surface
2   Upper seat step
3   Lower seat step
X = 1.8 mm for inlet valve, 1.6 mm for exhaust valve
α = 120° for inlet valve, 90° for exhaust valve

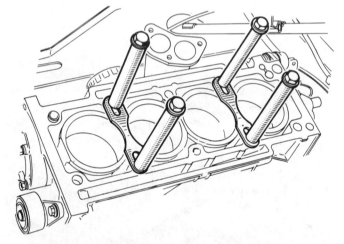

Fig. 1.59 Cylinder liner clamp arrangement (Sec 70)

(photo) and lower the crankshaft into position.
3   Locate the shells in the main bearing caps in a similar manner to that of the block, and lubricate.
4   Fit the bearing caps into position, and torque tighten the retaining bolts (photo).
5   Now check the crankshaft endfloat using a dial gauge or feeler gauge (photo). Select a thrust washer of suitable thickness to provide the correct endfloat (see Specifications).
6   Remove the main bearing caps and crankshaft, and insert the selected thrust washers, with their grooved side towards the crankshaft.
7   Refit the main bearing caps again and tighten their bolts to the specified torque (photo).
8   The grooves at the sides of the front and rear main bearing caps must be sealed with RTV type sealant (instant gasket). Make sure that the sealant is forced in under sustained pressure to prevent any air pockets. Cease injecting when the sealant begins to seep from the joints (photo).
9   Lubricate the new front and rear crankshaft oil seals and carefully locate them into their apertures tapping them fully into position using a tubular drift of a suitable diameter. Ensure that the seals face the correct way round with the cavity/spring side towards the engine. Should the seal lip accidentally become damaged during fitting, remove and discard it and fit another new seal (photos).
10 If a new clutch spigot bearing is being fitted, now is the time to do it. Drive it home using a suitable diameter tubular drift. **Note**: *When fitting this bearing to the crankshaft, smear the outer bearing surface with a suitable thread locking compound.* To the crankshaft front end fit the belt guide, the Woodruff key and sprocket (rollpins visible) (photos).

72.1 Locate the main shells into position in the block

72.2A Lubricating main bearing shell

72.2B Crankshaft thrust washer

72.2C Lowering the crankshaft into position

72.4 Fitting a main bearing cap. Note the locating dowel (arrowed)

72.5 Checking crankshaft endfloat using a feeler gauge

72.7 Tightening a main bearing cap bolt

72.8 Sealing main bearing cap groove

72.9A Locate a new crankshaft front oil seal

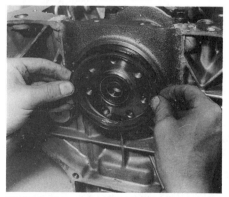

72.9B Locate a new crankshaft rear oil seal

72.10A Clutch spigot bearing in crankshaft rear flange

72.10B Timing belt guide

72.10C Crankshaft sprocket Woodruff key

72.10D Fitting crankshaft sprocket

73 Piston/connecting rod/cylinder liner assembly

1   Before fitting the piston and connecting rod assemblies into the liners, the liners must be checked in the crankcase for depth of fitting. This is carried out as follows.
2   Although the cylinder liners fit directly onto the crankcase inner flange, O-ring seals are fitted between the chamfered flange and the lower cylinder section, as shown in Fig. 1.60. New O-rings must always be used once the cylinders have been disturbed from the crankcase.
3   First, insert a liner into the crankcase *without its O-ring* and measure how far it protrudes from the top face of the crankcase. Lay a straight-edge rule across its top face and measure the gap to the top face of the cylinder block with feeler gauges. It should be as given in the Specifications.
4   Now check the height on the other cylinders in the same way and note each reading. Check that the variation in protrusion on adjoining liners does not exceed 0.0016 in (0.04 mm).
5   New liners can be interchanged for position to achieve this if necessary, and when in position should be marked accordingly 1 to 4 from the flywheel end.
6   Remove each liner in turn and position an O-ring seal onto its lower section so that it butts into the corner, taking care not to twist or distort it (see Fig. 1.60).
7   Wipe the liners and pistons clean and smear with clean engine oil, prior to their respective fitting.
8   Refit the pistons to the liners, using a piston ring compressor tightened around well oiled rings to install the piston into the lower end of the cylinder liners. Fit the liners/pistons into the cylinder block. Fit the big-end caps with shells (photos).
9   Observe the following important points:
(a) *the arrows on top of the pistons must point towards the flywheel (photo)*
(b) *the connecting rod and cap bolts must be tightened to the specified torque with the numbered markings in alignment (photo)*
(c) *When assembled, reclamp the liners and rotate the crankshaft to ensure it rotates smoothly*

74 Flywheel (or driveplate) – refitting

1   Locate the flywheel or driveplate on the crankshaft mounting flange. The bolt holes are offset so it will only go on one way (photo).
2   Use new fixing bolts, and having cleaned their threads, apply thread locking fluid to them. Refit the clutch (Chapter 5) (photos).

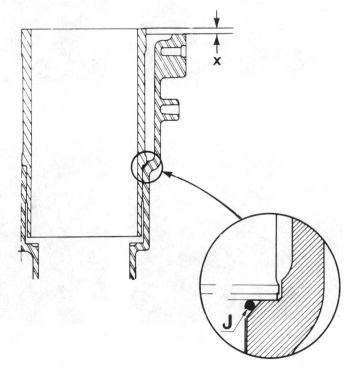

Fig. 1.60 Cylinder liner protrusion (Sec 73)

J   O-ring seal   X   Protrusion above block face

75 Auxiliary shaft – refitting

1   Lubricate the shaft and insert it through the front of the crankcase (photo).
2   Slide the lockplate fork into the protruding shaft location groove and secure the plate with the bolt and washer. Check that the shaft is free to rotate on completion (photos).
3   Fit the new oil seal into the auxiliary shaft front cover and lubricate its lips. Locate the new gasket onto the cover face.
4   Refit the auxiliary shaft cover (photos).
5   Fit the Woodruff key into its groove in the shaft and carefully locate the auxiliary shaft drive sprocket into position with its large offset inner face towards the crankcase. Use a suitable diameter drift to tap the sprocket into position over the key (photo).

73.8A Fitting a piston/connecting rod into cylinder liner

73.8B Fitting a cylinder liner/piston/connecting rod assembly into the block

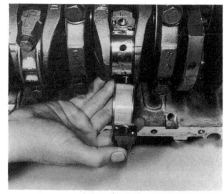

73.8C Fitting a big-end cap

73.9A Piston directional arrow

73.9B Tightening a big-end cap bolt

74.1 Fitting the flywheel

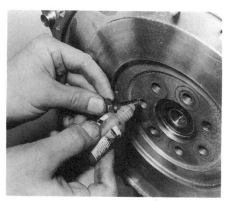

74.2A Applying thread locking fluid to a flywheel bolt

74.2B Tightening a flywheel bolt

75.1 Insert the auxiliary shaft ...

75.2A ... fit the locking plate ...

75.2B ... and its retaining bolt and washer

75.4A Auxiliary shaft cover and gasket

75.4B Fitting auxiliary shaft cover and retaining bolts

75.5 Fitting the auxiliary shaft sprocket ...

75.6 ... and its retaining bolt and washer

75.7A Oil pump driveshaft and circlip

75.7B Oil pump drive pinion

75.9 Crankcase cover plate being fitted

6   Prevent the sprocket from rotating by inserting a screwdriver blade or similar through a sprocket hole, and tighten the retaining nut (complete with flat washer) to the specified torque (photo).
7   The oil pump drive pinion and shaft can now be inserted through the side cover hole in the crankcase. Make sure that the limiting circlip is in position on the oil pump end of the shaft (photos).
8   Once in position lubricate with engine oil to prevent pinion 'pick-up' on restarting the engine.
9   Ensure that the auxiliary shaft and oil pump drive rotate freely then refit the cover plate. This should be sealed by applying a thick bead of RTV sealant (instant gasket) to its underside flange edge (photo).

76 Oil pump – refitting

1   Lubricate the respective parts of the oil pump and reassemble.
2   Insert the rotors and refit the cover. No gasket is fitted on this face.
3   Tighten the retaining bolts to secure the cover.
4   Insert the oil pressure relief valve assembly, fitting the piston into the spring and the cup over the spring at the opposing end. Compress into the cylinder and insert a new split pin to retain the valve assembly in place.
5   Fit the assembled pump into position. Tighten the retaining bolts (photos).
6   If not already done, refit the oil pump drive pinion and driveshaft, ensuring that the circlip is in position on the lower end of the shaft. Refit the cover plate.

77 Sump – refitting

1   Check that the mating surfaces of the sump and crankcase are perfectly clean, with no sections of old gasket remaining.
2   Locate the new sump gasket, which should be fitted dry (photo).
3   Fit the sump carefully into position and locate the retaining bolts.

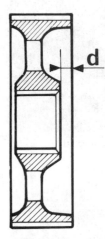

Fig. 1.61 Auxiliary shaft sprocket orientation. Large offset (d) must face towards crankcase (Sec 75)

Note that three types of retaining bolts are used on the aluminium sumps fitted to non-Turbo models, and these should be located as shown in Fig. 1.62.
On Turbo models, two types of retaining bolts are used, and these should be located as shown in Fig. 1.63. Tighten the three bolts securing the sump to the clutch housing first, then tighten the remaining bolts. On Turbo models, remember to tighten the captive bolt ('A' in Fig. 1.49).
4   Fit and tighten the sump drain plug.

76.5A Locate the oil pump

76.5D ... and tighten its retaining bolts

77.2 Sump gasket located

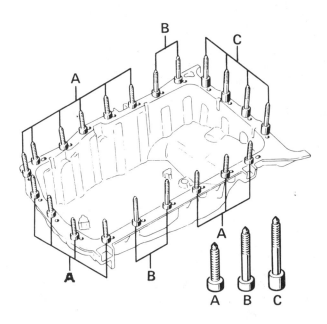
Fig. 1.62 Sump retaining bolt identification and location –
non-Turbo models (Sec 77)

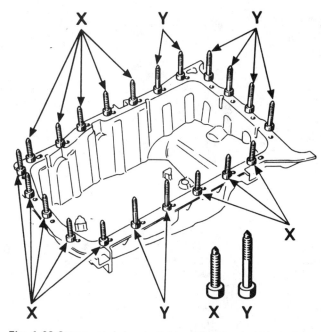
Fig. 1.63 Sump retaining bolt identification and location –
Turbo models (Sec 77)

78 Cylinder head – reassembly

1   Commence reassembly by oiling the stem of the first valve and pushing it into its guide which should have been fitted with a new oil seal (photo).
2   Fit the spring seat, the valve spring so that the close coils are towards the cylinder head and then the spring retaining cap (photos).
3   Compress the valve spring and using a little grease locate the split in the valve stem cut-out (photo).
4   Gently release the compressor, checking to see that the collets are not displaced.
5   Fit the remaining valves in the same way.
6   Tap the end of each valve stem with a plastic or copper-faced hammer to settle the components.
7   Refit the camshaft to the cylinder head as described in Section 79.

79 Camshaft – refitting

1   Check that the respective camshaft location bearings in the cylinder head are perfectly clean and lubricate with some engine oil. Similarly lubricate the camshaft journals and lobes.
2   Insert the camshaft carefully into the cylinder head, guiding the

cam sections through the bearing apertures so as not to score the bearing surfaces (photo).
3   With the camshaft in position, the front oil seal can be carefully drifted into position. Lubricate the seal lips with oil and drive into its location using a suitable tube drift (photo).
4   Refit the rocker assembly and tighten the cylinder head bolts to the specified torque in the sequence shown in Fig. 1.45. Bolt on the timing belt rear cover plate (photo).
5   Refit the camshaft sprocket with Woodruff key and tighten the retaining bolt to the specified torque. Note that the offset (d) in Fig. 1.64 faces towards the cylinder head. The square cut-out in the sprocket will be at its lowest point when No 4 cam lobes are pointing downwards. Bolt on the camshaft thrust plate (photos).
6   Refit the timing belt as described in Section 81.
7   Refit the distributor body, rotor arm and cap.
8   Refit and connect the spark plugs.
9   Refit the timing cover.
10   Refit and tension the drivebelt.
11   Fit the radiator and cooling fan unit.
12   Reconnect the throttle cable and linkage.
13   Refill the cooling system.
14   Check and adjust the valve clearances as described in Section 82, then refit the camshaft cover.
15   Reconnect the battery.

78.1 Fitting a valve into its guide

78.2A Valve stem oil seal and spring seat

78.2B Fitting a valve spring

78.2C Valve spring retaining cap

78.3 Compressing a valve spring

79.2 Inserting the camshaft into the cylinder head

79.3 Camshaft front oil seal

79.4 Timing belt rear cover plate

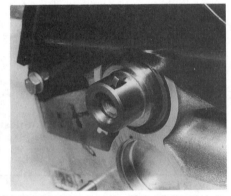

79.5A Camshaft sprocket Woodruff key

79.5B Tightening the camshaft sprocket bolt

79.5C Tightening the camshaft thrust plate bolt

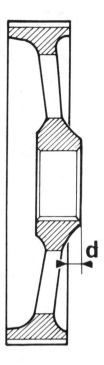

Fig. 1.64 Camshaft sprocket orientation. Offset (d) must face towards cylinder head (Sec 79)

80 Cylinder head – refitting

1   Before refitting the cylinder head, check that all the mating surfaces are perfectly clean. Loosen the rocker arm adjuster screws fully back. Also ensure that the cylinder head bolt holes in the crankcase are clean and free of oil. Syringe or soak up any oil left in the bolt holes, and in the oil feed hole on the rear left-hand corner of the block. This is most important in order that the correct bolt tightening torque can be applied.
2   Prior to removing the liner clamps, rotate the crankshaft to locate the pistons halfway down the bores. Check that the location dowel is in position at the front right-hand corner.
3   Remove the liner clamps.
4   Fit the cylinder head gasket onto the cylinder block upper face and ensure that it is exactly located (photo). If possible, screw a couple of guide studs into position. They must be long enough to pass through the cylinder head so that they can be removed when it is in position.
5   Lower the cylinder head into position, engaging with the location dowel, and then locate the rocker assembly (photos).
6   Lubricate the cylinder head bolt threads and washers sparingly with engine oil, then screw them into position. Tighten them progressively in the sequence given in Fig. 1.45. Tighten all the bolts to the initial torque then to the stage two and stage three torque wrench settings given in the Specifications at the start of this Chapter (photo). Further tightening of the cylinder head bolts will be necessary once the engine has been restarted and run for an initial period of twenty minutes – see Section 88.
7   Refit the timing belt as described in Section 81 and check the valve clearances as described in Section 82.
8   Reconnect the coolant hose, vacuum hose and HT lead brackets as applicable, and refit the camshaft cover.
9   Refit the rotor arm, distributor cap and HT leads.
10 If the engine is in the car, refer to Section 56, and refit or reconnect as applicable the items removed or disconnected in paragraphs 1 to 8.

81 Timing belt – refitting

1   Locate the timing belt tensioner by inserting the spring into its

80.4 Locating the cylinder head gasket

80.5A Lowering the cylinder head onto the block

80.5B Locating the rocker assembly

80.6 Tighten the cylinder head bolts

81.1A Timing belt tensioner spring and plunger

81.1B Fitting tensioner pulley

81.1C Tensioner pulley fully retracted

81.5 Tightening the belt tensioner nut

81.9 Fitting the timing belt cover

housing in the side of the crankcase, and locate the plunger over it. Compress the spring and locate the tensioner pulley arm, retaining it with the bolt and nut. The spring tension is quite strong and an assistant will probably be required here. Fully retract the tensioner (photos).

2   If the engine is being reassembled after a comprehensive rebuild, or the sprockets have been moved from the position to which they were set during removal of the timing belt, reset them so the No 1 piston is at TDC, as described in paragraph 9 of Section 55.

3   Slip the belt over the sprocket teeth, making sure that it is taut from the crankshaft sprocket around the intermediate shaft sprocket and camshaft sprocket – see Fig. 1.66.

4   Refit the crankshaft pulley.

5   Release the tensioner bolt and nut so that the tensioner pulley is spring-loaded against the timing belt, retighten the tensioner bolt and nut (photo).

6   Now turn the crankshaft two complete turns in a clockwise direction, never turn it anti-clockwise.

7   Release the tensioner bolt and nut about a quarter of a turn each, then retighten them to the specified torque (bolt first).

8   Check that the drivebelt deflection at the mid-way point between the camshaft and auxiliary shaft pulleys is as specified, then refit the timing belt cover (photo).

9   Refit the spark plugs and reconnect the battery earth terminal.

10 Refit the camshaft cover.

11 Refit the alternator and power steering pump drivebelts.

82 Valve clearances – adjustment

1   Remove the camshaft cover, with reference to Section 56, paragraphs 3 and 10 if the engine is in the car.

2   The precise adjustment of the valve/rocker clearances is of utmost importance for two main reasons. The first, to enable the valves to be opened and fully closed at the precise moment required by the cycle of

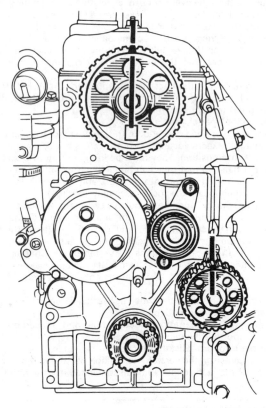

Fig. 1.65 Timing sprockets set with No 1 piston at TDC (Sec 81)

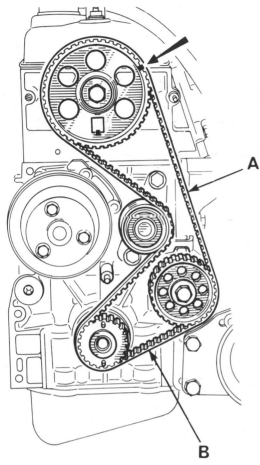

Fig. 1.66 The timing belt must be taut at points A and B (Sec 81)

82.6 Adjusting a valve clearance

the engine. The second, to ensure quiet operation and minimum wear of the valve gear components.

3   Settings made when the engine is on the bench will require rotation of the engine and this may be done by turning the exposed crankshaft pulley bolt. If the engine is in the car and a manual gearbox fitted, remove the spark plugs, select top gear, then jack up the front so that one front wheel is clear of the ground and can be turned. With automatic transmission, this method is not possible and 'inching' the engine using the starter motor will have to be resorted to. Alternatively the crankshaft pulley bolt can be turned as described previously.

4   Turn the engine using one of the methods described until the exhaust valve of no 1 cylinder is fully open. The clearance for No 3 cylinder inlet valve and No 4 cylinder exhaust valve can now be checked and adjusted using a feeler blade.

5   Remember No 1 cylinder is at the flywheel end of the engine and of course the inlet and exhaust valves on the side adjacent to their respective manifolds.

6   If the clearance requires adjustment, loosen the locknut and with the feeler in position turn the adjuster screw until the feeler blade is nipped and will not move. Now unscrew the adjuster until the feeler blade is a stiff sliding fit. Tighten the locknut and recheck the clearance. Refer to the Specifications for the correct clearances (photo).

7   Repeat the adjustment procedure using the following sequence:

Exhaust valve fully open on cylinder:	Inlet valve to adjust on cylinder:	Exhaust valve to adjust on cylinder:
1	3	4
3	4	2
4	2	1
2	1	3

8   On completion refit the camshaft cover.

83 Ancillary components – refitting

1   Depending on the extent of the engine overhaul, refit the applicable items listed in Section 54, referring to the appropriate Sections in the Chapters concerned for details.

2   Where applicable, use new gaskets and seals and if specified, apply the recommended sealant.

3   Tighten the various components to the specified torque wrench settings (where given).

4   Adjust the drivebelt(s) as described in Chapter 2.

5   Arrange the wiring and hoses so that they will not interfere with the engine refitting procedures.

6   The starter motor can be bolted in position before refitting the engine, and held by its support bracket (see Chapter 12).

7   Oil the sealing ring of a new engine oil filter and screw it into position using hand pressure only.

84 Engine – refitting (manual transmission in car)

1   The operations are reversals of those described in Section 49, but observe the following points.

2   Make sure that the clutch driven plate has been centralised, and smear the clutch shaft splines with a little molybdenum disulphide grease.

3   Refill the engine with oil and coolant.

4   Ensure that all wires and hoses have been reconnected in their correct positions.

5   Reconnect the exhaust downpipe to the manifold, fitting a new Thermoplastic seal, and tighten the clamp bolts/nuts to the point where the coil springs are fully compressed (coil bound). Refer to Chapter 3 for details.

85 Engine and manual transmission – reconnection and refitting

1   The operations are reversals of those described in Section 50, but observe the following points. Refer to the relevant Sections and Chapters where necessary for refitting details.

2   Make sure that the clutch driven plate has been centralised, and

smear the input shaft splines with molybdenum disulphide grease.

3 As the engine/transmission units are lowered into the engine bay, the transmission must be raised and supported with a jack, as the engine is lowered onto its mouldings. Initially, only loosely fit the engine mounting nuts to allow for minor adjustments when connecting the transmission mountings. Fit the transmission mountings to the subframe first, then move the transmission as required to align the retaining bolts and holes. When all of the mounting bolts are located, tighten them to the specified torque wrench setting.

4 Lubricate the gearchange linkage. and reconnect as described in Chapter 6.

5 Reconnect the driveshafts as described in Chapter 8 and, if applicable, the steering arm outer balljoints as described in Chapter 10.

6 Reconnect the exhaust system as described in Chapter 3, ensuring that the coil springs at the joint are coil bound.

7 Top up the cooling system, the engine oil and transmission oil with reference to Chapters 2, 1 and 6 respectively.

8 Check that all connections are secure. Leave fitting the bonnet and undershields until the engine has been started, so that checks can be made for any leaks.

86 Engine – refitting (automatic transmission in car)

1 Apply a smear of molybdenum disulphide grease to the locating boss on the torque converter.

2 Remove the temporary holding bar from the torque converter.

3 lower the engine into the car, making sure that the torque converter does not move forward as the engine is connected and bolted to the transmission. The upper bellhousing bolts must be in position before the engine is connected to the transmission as they cannot be fitted afterwards.

4 The bellhousing lower cover must be located on the dowels before the engine and transmission are brought together, and the alignment mark on the driveplate must be between the two marks on the torque converter.

5 The remaining reconnection and refitting operations are reversals of removal and separation (Section 51) but observe the following points.

6 Reconnect the vacuum pipe and the control linkage before connecting the transmission mountings. The control cable must have the notches towards the balljoint.

7 Refill the engine with oil and coolant and top up the transmission fluid if necessary.

87 Engine/automatic transmission – reconnection and refitting

1 The reconnection operations are as described in the preceding Section.

2 Once the engine/automatic transmission has been installed, refill with oil and coolant and adjust controls and cables as described in Chapter 7.

3 Top up the transmission fluid if necessary.

88 Engine – adjustments after major overhaul

1 Before starting the engine, check that all hoses, controls and electrical leads have been connected.

2 Make sure that tools and rags have been removed from the engine compartment.

3 If the majority of internal components have been renewed, treat the engine as a new one and restrict speed for the first 500 miles (800 km).

4 Once the engine has been restarted, run it for a period of 20 minutes, then switch off and remove the rocker cover. The cylinder head bolts must now be progressively loosened off in the sequence shown in Fig. 1.45 by one half turn, then retightened to the final torque wrench setting given in the Specifications.

5 On completion, refit the rocker cover.

PART C: ALL ENGINES

89 Fault diagnosis

Symptom	Reason(s)
Engine will not crank or cranks very slowly	Discharged battery Poor battery connections Starter motor fault
Engine cranks but will not start	No fuel Ignition circuit fault Fuel system fault Leak in crankcase vent system hoses Leak in intake manifold
Engine stalls or rough idle	Leak in crankcase vent system hoses Leak in intake manifold Very weak mixture Incorrect valve clearances
Hesitation or poor acceleration	Incorrectly adjusted mixture (1.7 litre) Clogged air cleaner Incorrect valve clearances

Chapter 2 Cooling, heating and air conditioning systems

Contents

Specifications

System type .... Pressurized, pump assisted thermosyphon system with electric cooling fan(s)

Filler cap
Blow-off pressure:
    1.7 and 2.0 litre non-Turbo .... 1.2 bar (17.4 lbf/in²)
    2.0 litre Turbo .... 1.6 bar (23.2 lbf/in²)

Thermostat
Starts to open .... 89°C
Fully open .... 101°C

Coolant
Type/specification .... Ethylene glycol based antifreeze with corrosion inhibitor to BS 3151, 3152, or 6580 (Duckhams Universal Antifreeze and Summer Coolant)

Capacity:
    1.7 litre .... 5.2 litres (9.2 pints)
    2.0 litre non-Turbo .... 6.8 litres (11.9 pints)
    2.0 litre Turbo .... 6.2 litres (10.9 pints)

1 General description

The system is of pressurised semi-sealed type with the inclusion of an expansion bottle or chamber to accept coolant displaced from the system when hot and to return it when the system cools.

Coolant is circulated by thermosyphon action and is assisted by means of the impeller in the belt-driven coolant pump.

A thermostat is fitted. When the engine is cold, the thermostat valve remains closed so that the coolant flow which occurs at normal operating temperatures through the radiator matrix is interrupted.

As the coolant warms up, the thermostat valve starts to open and allows the coolant flow through the radiator to resume.

The engine temperature will always be maintained at a constant level (according to the thermostat rating) whatever the ambient air temperature.

The coolant circulates around the engine block and cylinder head and absorbs heat as it flows, then travels out into the radiator to pass across the matrix. As the coolant flows across the radiator matrix, air flow created by the forward motion of the car cools it, and it returns via the bottom tank of the radiator to the cylinder block. This is a continuous process, assisted by the coolant pump impeller.

All models are fitted with an electric cooling fan which is actuated by the thermostat switch according to coolant temperature. Certain models are equipped with two cooling fans.

The car interior heater operates by means of coolant from the engine cooling system. Coolant flow through the heater is constant, as there is no coolant on/off valve fitted to the system. This improves engine cooling.

On carburettor models, the system incorporates coolant connections to permit coolant from the cooling system to circulate to the carburettor base. Coolant also circulates to the automatic choke operating mechanism.

On models with automatic transmission, a fluid cooler is built into the cooling system circuit.

An additional coolant pump is fitted in the cooling system circuit on Turbo models. This pump is electrically-operated and is located adjacent to the right-hand shock absorber turret within the engine compartment. This pump supplies coolant to the turbocharger unit when activated by a timed relay in the computer casing.

The cooling system circuits are shown in Figs. 2.1, 2.2 and 2.3.

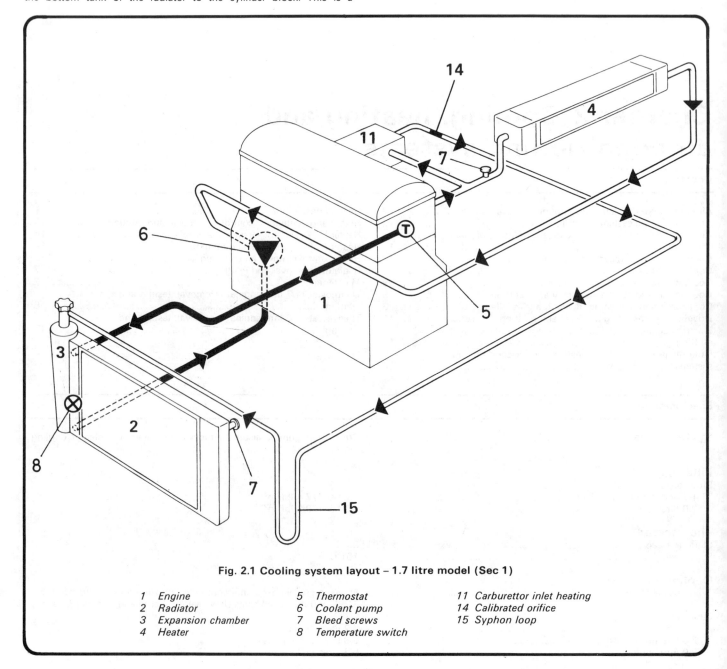

Fig. 2.1 Cooling system layout – 1.7 litre model (Sec 1)

1	Engine	5	Thermostat
2	Radiator	6	Coolant pump
3	Expansion chamber	7	Bleed screws
4	Heater	8	Temperature switch
		11	Carburettor inlet heating
		14	Calibrated orifice
		15	Syphon loop

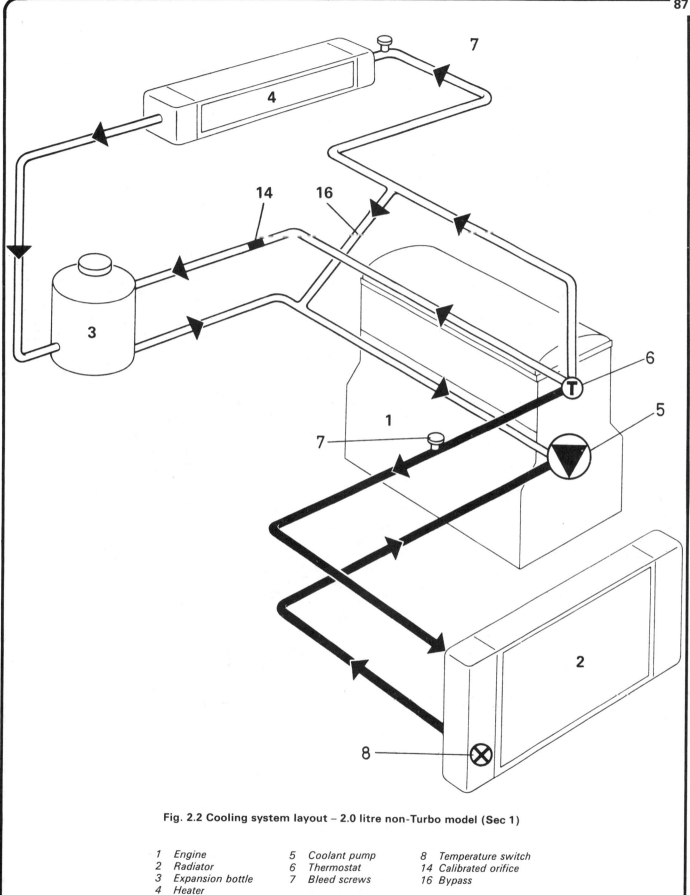

Fig. 2.2 Cooling system layout – 2.0 litre non-Turbo model (Sec 1)

1 Engine	5 Coolant pump	8 Temperature switch
2 Radiator	6 Thermostat	14 Calibrated orifice
3 Expansion bottle	7 Bleed screws	16 Bypass
4 Heater		

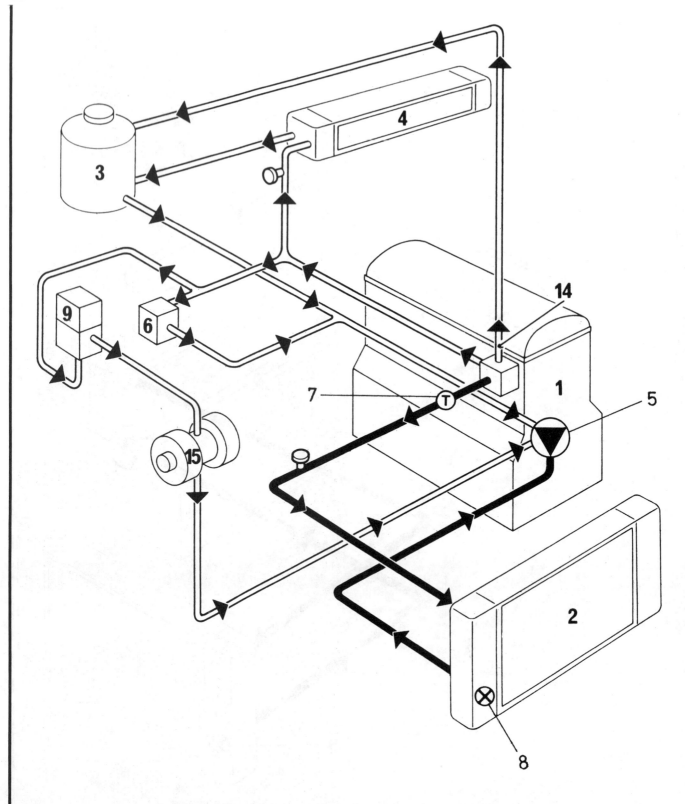

Fig. 2.3 Cooling system layout – Turbo models (Sec 1)

1 Engine	5 Coolant pump	9 Electric coolant pump
2 Radiator	6 Intercooler (oil-to-water)	14 Calibrated orifice
3 Expansion bottle	7 Thermostat	15 Turbocharger
4 Heater	8 Temperature switch	

2 Maintenance

1 Apart from renewing the coolant at the prescribed intervals, maintenance is mainly confined to checking the coolant level in the expansion bottle.

2 Check the level when cold. It should be maintained between the MINI and MAXI marks on the expansion bottle or radiator expansion chamber, as applicable (photos).

3 If topping-up is required, use only coolant made up in similar proportions to the original mixture.

4 Only very infrequent topping-up should be required, anything more will indicate a leak in the system which should be rectified immediately.

5 The hoses and their clamps should also be inspected regularly for security and good condition.

6 The radiator should be brushed periodically, or a compressed air jet or cold water hose directed onto it to remove insects and leaves from its cooling tubes and fins. This will ensure the maximum cooling effect from the radiator.

7 Blanking off the radiator or grille in very cold weather is not recommended. Provided the correct thermostat is used with a suitable antifreeze mixture in the system, the correct engine operating temperature will be maintained whatever the climatic conditions.

8 Check the condition and adjustment of the drivebelt(s) at the specified intervals, as described in Section 11.

9 If air conditioning is fitted, refer to Section 18 for maintenance procedures. If disconnecting any part of the air conditioning system any time, it is important that the precautionary notes given in Section 17 are adhered to.

3 Cooling system – draining, flushing and refilling

1 If the coolant is to be saved for further use, place a suitable container under the radiator bottom hose connection. If the coolant is to be renewed, it may be allowed to run to waste.

2 Remove the expansion bottle or chamber cap, as applicable.

3 Disconnect the radiator bottom hose and drain the coolant.

4 If the coolant has been renewed regularly, then the system may be refilled immediately. If the cooling system has been neglected, remove the cylinder block drain plug (photo) and place a cold water hose in the radiator top hose. Flush the system through until the water comes out clear from the drain plug hole and the radiator hose. If contamination is severe, the radiator may have to be removed and cleaned out; see Section 7.

5 Reconnect the radiator hose and tighten its clip. Tighten the cylinder block drain plug if removed.

6 Open the system bleed screws. On 1.7 litre models, these are located in the radiator and heater hose. On 2.0 litre models, the bleed screws are located in the radiator top hose and the heater hose (photos). It should be noted that the bleed screw must not be opened with the engine running.

7 On 1.7 litre models, disconnect the syphon loop hose at the radiator and lay it out flat.

8 Fill the system slowly through the expansion bottle or tank opening. Use only coolant made up as an antifreeze mixture as described in the next Section.

9 As soon as coolant is ejected from the bleed screws, close them (photo). Proceed as described in the following paragraphs for 1.7 or 2.0 litre models, as applicable.

1.7 litre models

10 Start and run the engine at a speed of 1500 rpm.

11 Depress the accelerator 3 or 4 times to increase the engine speed to between 3000 and 4000 rpm, then top up the expansion chamber until it overflows.

12 Repeat this procedure for approximately 4 minutes, then switch off the engine and refit the expansion chamber cap and reconnect the syphon hose.

13 Run the engine for a further 10 minutes at 1500 rpm, until the cooling fan(s) have cut in at least 3 times (this is necessary for automatic degassing of the system).

14 Check that the coolant level is near the MAXI mark. It is permissible for the coolant level to be just above this mark.

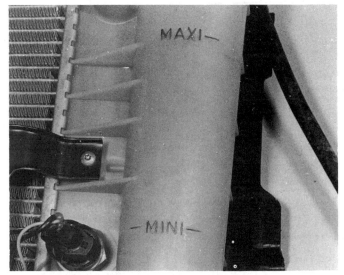

2.2A Coolant level markings – 1.7 litre model (radiator expansion chamber)

2.2B Topping up the cooling system – 2.0 litre model (expansion bottle)

3.4 Cylinder block drain plug (arrowed) – 1.7 litre engine

Fig. 2.4 Bleed screw locations – 1.7 litre model (Sec 3)

A *Radiator*   B *Heater hose*

3.6A Bleed screw in top hose (arrowed) – 2.0 litre engine

3.6B Bleed screw in heater hose (arrowed) – 2.0 litre engine

3.9 Coolant bleeding from top hose – 2.0 litre engine

2.0 litre models

15 Start and run the engine at a speed of 1500 rpm.

16 Run the engine at a constant 1500 rpm, and fill the expansion bottle until it overflows.

17 Continue this procedure for approximately 4 minutes, then switch off the engine and refit the expansion bottle cap.

18 Run the engine for a further 10 minutes at 1500 rpm until the cooling fan(s) cut in (this is necessary for automatic degassing of the system).

19 Check that the coolant level is near the MAXI mark.

4 Coolant mixtures

1 It is essential that an approved type of antifreeze is employed, in order that the necessary antifreeze and anticorrosion proportions are maintained.

2 The radiator matrix of some models is made of aluminium and it is essential to use an antifreeze product suitable for this material.

3 Whilst the life of the coolant originally used in the vehicle is stated to be 3 years or 40 000 miles (60 000 km), owners are advised to consider renewing the coolant yearly to ensure that all the essential properties of the solution are fully maintained.

4 Make up the solution, ideally using distilled water or rain water, in the proportions necessary to give protection in the prevailing climate. Percentages of antifreeze necessary are usually found on the container. Do not use too low a percentage of antifreeze, or the anticorrosion properties will not be sufficiently effective.

5 If it is suspected that the coolant strength is unsatisfactory, a check may be made using a hydrometer. Employ the instrument as instructed by the manufacturer, and using the correction tables normally supplied. If the protection is found to be insufficient, drain off some of the coolant and replace it with pure antifreeze. Recheck the coolant with the hydrometer.

6 Even in territories where the climate does not require the use of antifreeze, never use plain water in the cooling system; always add a suitable corrosion inhibitor.

5 Thermostat (1.7 litre engine) – removal, testing and refitting

1 The thermostat is located in a housing bolted to the left-hand side of the cylinder head beneath the distributor (photo).
2 To remove the thermostat, first unscrew the expansion chamber filler cap. If the engine is hot, place a cloth over the cap and unscrew it slowly allowing all the pressure to escape before removing the cap completely.
3 Place a suitable container beneath the radiator bottom hose outlet. Disconnect the bottom hose and drain approximately 1 litre (1.76 pints) of the coolant. Reconnect the bottom hose and tighten the clip.
4 Slacken the clip securing the radiator top hose to the thermostat housing and remove the hose.
5 Undo the three bolts, lift off the housing and take out the thermostat (photo). Remove the thermostat rubber sealing ring.
6 To test whether the unit is serviceable, suspend it on a string in a saucepan of cold water together with a thermometer. Heat the water and note the temperature at which the thermostat begins to open. Continue heating the water until the thermostat is fully open and then remove it from the water.
7 The temperature at which the thermostat should start to open is stamped on the unit. If the thermostat does not start to open at the specified temperature, does not fully open in boiling water, or does not fully close when removed from the water, then it must be discarded and a new one fitted.
8 Refitting is the reverse sequence to removal, but renew the thermostat rubber sealing ring if it shows any signs of deterioration. After fitting, fill the cooling system, with reference to Section 3.

6 Thermostat (2.0 litre engine) – removal, testing and refitting

1 The thermostat is located within the cylinder head end of the coolant top hose.
2 Proceed as described in paragraphs 2 to 4 of the previous Section. When the top hose is detached from the cylinder head, extract the thermostat from the hose (photos).
3 To test the thermostat, proceed as described in paragraphs 6 and 7 of the previous Section.
4 Refit in the reverse order of removal, then top up the cooling system as described in Section 3.

7 Radiator – removal and refitting

1 Drain the engine coolant as described in Section 3.
2 Unclip and detach the top, bottom and, on 1.7 litre models, the syphon hose from the radiator (photos).
3 Undo the four retaining bolts and remove the crossmember from above the radiator (photos).
4 Disconnect the wiring harnesses and connectors from the coolant temperature switches and the cooling fan(s), then lift out the radiator together with the cooling fan unit (photos).
5 If required, the cooling fan unit can be detached from the radiator as described in the following Section.
6 If the radiator is clogged, reverse flush it with a cold water hose. In severe cases of contamination, use a radiator cleaner but strictly in accordance with the manufacturer's instructions. The product must be suitable for aluminium radiators.
7 If the radiator is leaking, it may be repairable using one of the numerous proprietary liquid sealants available. These sealants are usually diluted with water and run through the cooling system for a set period of time in accordance with the manufacturer's instructions. The radiator will need to be in position for this repair method. Failing this method, consult a radiator repair specialist for advice on any possible repairs, as it is not a task recommended for the home mechanic.

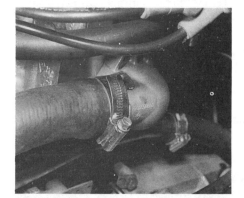

5.1 Thermostat housing location – 1.7 litre engine

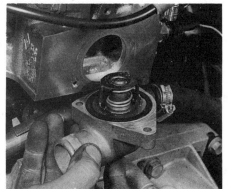

5.5 Thermostat and housing removal – 1.7 litre engine

6.2 Thermostat removal from the top hose – 2.0 litre engine

7.2A Detach the radiator top and syphon hoses ...

7.2B ... and the bottom hose – 1.7 litre model

7.3A Remove the top crossmember bolts (arrowed) ...

7.3B ... and remove the crossmember – 1.7 litre model shown

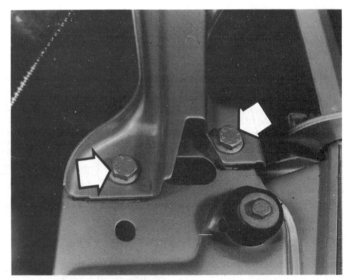

7.3C Top crossmember bolts (arrowed) – 2.0 litre model

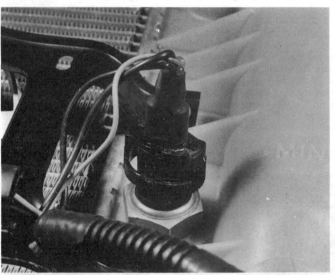

7.4A Coolant temperature switch – 1.7 litre model

7.4B Coolant temperature switch – 2.0 litre non-Turbo model

7.4C Coolant temperature switch and associated wiring connections – Turbo model

7.4D Radiator and fan removal – 1.7 litre model

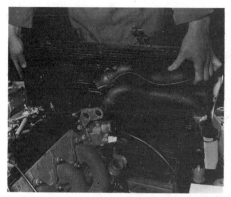

7.4E Radiator and fan removal – 2.0 litre model (fan is mounted on front face of radiator)

7.9A Engage location pegs when refitting radiator – 1.7 litre model

7.9B Radiator location peg and bush – 2.0 litre model

8 Do not leave the radiator empty for more than 48 hours or the aluminium will start to corrode.

9 Refitting is a reversal of removal, but ensure that the bottom locating pegs are engaged in their bushes (photos).

10 Refill and bleed the cooling system, as described in Section 3.

8 Cooling fan and switch – removal and refitting

Note: *On Turbo models, and those equipped with air conditioning, twin cooling fans are used as a means of dissipating the additional heat generated.*

1 The fan assembly is clipped and riveted to the radiator and its removal will require withdrawal of the radiator and drilling out the pop rivets (photos).

2 The temperature switch which regulates the operation of the electric cooling fan(s) is fitted into the radiator (see previous Section). Ideally, tests to the switch should be carried out after it has been removed from its location. If this is done, the cooling system will have to be drained and refilled, but the following alternative method may be used.

3 Connect a test light to the fan switch. When the engine is cold (ie switch contacts open), it should not light up.

4 Start the engine and blank off the radiator to ensure quick warming up.

5 When the temperature reaches the cut-in point, the lamp should light.

6 Switch off the engine and allow the temperature of the radiator to drop. When the cut-out temperature is reached the lamp should go out.

7 If the switch does not operate, renew it.

8 If the switch does operate correctly, then the fault must lie in the fan assembly or the connecting wiring or relay.

9 Refitting is a reversal of removal. Use a new seal when screwing in the temperature switch and avoid overtightening it.

9 Coolant temperature sensor – testing

1 Where an engine coolant temperature sensor unit is suspected of being faulty, the only simple way to test it is by substitution.

2 The temperature sensor unit is located in the side of the cylinder head near the thermostat housing (1.7 litre models), or in the front left-hand side of the cylinder head (2.0 litre models).

3 Removal necessitates partial draining of the cooling system, whilst the gauge removal necessitates removal of the instrument panel (see Chapter 12).

4 It is not possible to repair the gauge or temperature sensor unit and they must therefore be renewed if faulty.

5 A simple test of the gauge may be made by touching the temperature sensor unit wire to earth (ignition on) whilst an assistant observes the gauge. The gauge should read 'hot'; if not, either there is a break in the wiring or the gauge itself is at fault.

10 Coolant pump – removal and refitting

Note: *Coolant pump failure is indicated by water leaking from the gland at the front of the pump, or by rough and noisy operation. This is usually accompanied by excessive play of the pump spindle which can be checked by moving the pulley from side to side. Repair or overhaul of a faulty pump is not possible, as internal parts are not available separately. In the event of failure a replacement pump must be obtained.*

1.7 litre engine

1 Disconnect the battery negative terminal and then refer to Section 3 and drain the cooling system.

2 Refer to Section 11 and remove the drivebelt.

3 Undo the three bolts and remove the pump pulley (photo).

4 Undo the bolts securing the pump to the cylinder block and

8.1A Radiator and cooling fan assembly – 1.7 litre model

8.1B Radiator and cooling fan assembly – 2.0 litre non-Turbo model

8.1C Radiator and twin cooling fan assembly – Turbo model

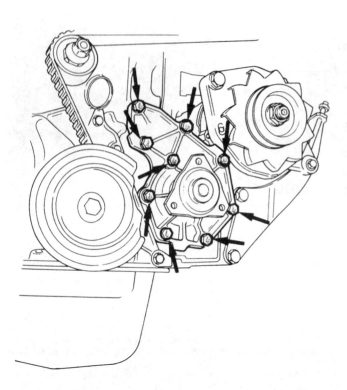

Fig. 2.5 Coolant pump retaining bolts (arrowed) – 1.7 litre model (Sec 9)

10.3 Coolant pump and pulley – 1.7 litre model

withdraw the pump from its location. If it is stuck, strike it sharply with a plastic or hide mallet.

5 Refitting is the reverse sequence to removal, but note the following:

 (a) Remove all traces of old gasket from the cylinder head and pump faces, and ensure that both mating surfaces are clean and dry

 (b) The gasket must be fitted dry, without jointing compound (photo)

 (c) Adjust the drivebelt tension, as described in Section 11, and refill the cooling system, as described in Section 3

2.0 litre engine

6 Disconnect the battery negative lead.
7 Drain the cooling system as described in Section 3.
8 Remove the radiator as described in Section 7.
9 Disconnect the hoses from the coolant pump.
10 Slacken the drivebelt and unbolt and remove the coolant pump pulley.
11 Unscrew the coolant pump fixing bolts, tap the pump gently to break its gasket seal and remove the pump, at the same time compressing the timing belt tensioner plunger spring.
12 The pump is of disposable type and if worn or leaking it must be renewed, no repair being possible (photo).
13 Clean away all old gasket material from the cylinder block and locate a new gasket in position. Bolt the pump into position, holding the timing belt tensioner spring compressed.
14 Refit the pulley, and the drivebelt. Tension the belt (Section 11).
15 Fill and bleed the cooling system. Reconnect the battery.

11 Drivebelts – tensioning, removal and refitting

1 Drivebelts are used to drive the coolant pump, alternator, and where applicable, the power steering pump and/or air conditioning compressor.
2 On 1.7 litre models, a single drivebelt is used to drive all ancillaries. On 2.0 litre models, a single, double, or triple drivebelt arrangement is

10.5 Refitting the coolant pump with new gasket – 1.7 litre model

10.12 Rear view of coolant pump – 2.0 litre model

11.1 Dual drivebelt arrangement for coolant pump, alternator and power steering pump – 2.0 litre model

11.3 Checking drivebelt deflection

11.4A Alternator drivebelt tension adjuster – 2.0 litre model

11.4B Power steering pump drivebelt tension adjuster (viewed from underneath) – 2.0 litre model

used depending on equipment.

3   At the intervals specified in the 'Routine maintenance' Section at the start of this manual, check the tension of the belt(s) by measuring the deflection at the relevant point(s) indicated in the accompanying figures (photo). Adjustment of the belt(s) will be necessary if the deflection is not as specified.

4   To adjust the tension of a drivebelt, loosen the adjuster and mounting bolts of an appropriate driven component (such as the alternator). Move the component to adjust the drivebelt tension as required, and tighten the adjuster and mounting bolts (photos).

5   Take care not to overtighten a drivebelt, as its life and that of the relevant component bearings will be reduced.

6   Check the belts regularly for cuts or fraying, and if evident, renew them.

7   To remove a drivebelt, release the driven component adjuster and mounting bolts and move the component fully in towards the engine. With the drivebelt slack, slip it off the pulleys. If there is any difficulty doing this, turn the crankshaft pulley and at the same time press the belt against the pulley rim when it will ride up and over the rim.

8   It will be obvious that before an inner belt can be removed the outer one will have to be taken off.

9   Fit the new belt, again turning the crankshaft pulley if the belt is difficult to prise over the pulley rim.

10 Tension the belt as described earlier in this Section.

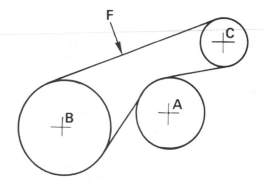

Fig. 2.6 Drivebelt deflection checking point – 1.7 litre models without power steering or air conditioning (Sec 11)

A   Coolant pump drive pulley   C   Alternator pulley
B   Crankshaft pulley   F = 3.0 mm (engine cold)

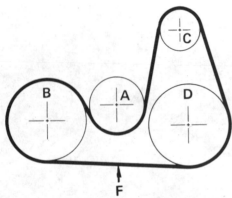

Fig. 2.7 Drivebelt deflection checking point – 1.7 litre models with power steering or air conditioning (Sec 11)

A   Coolant pump drive pulley
B   Crankshaft pulley
C   Alternator pulley

D   Power steering pump or air conditioning compressor pulley
F = 2.5 to 3.0 mm (engine cold)

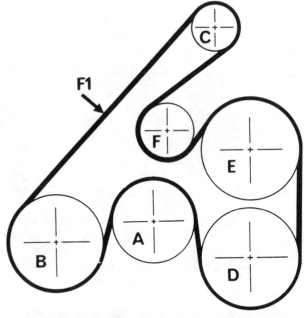

Fig. 2.8 Drivebelt deflection checking point – 1.7 litre models with power steering and air conditioning (Sec 11)

A   Coolant pump pulley
B   Crankshaft pulley
C   Alternator pulley
D   Power steering pump pulley

E   Air conditioning compressor pulley
F   Tensioner pulley
F_1 = 4.0 to 5.0 mm (run engine for 5 minutes before checking)

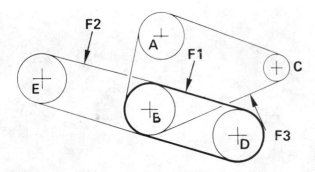

Fig. 2.9 Drivebelt deflection checking points – 2.0 litre models (Sec 11)

A   Coolant pump pulley
B   Crankshaft pulley
C   Alternator pulley
D   Power steering pump pulley
E   Air conditioning compressor pulley

F_1 = 3.0 to 3.5 mm (engine cold)
F_2 = 4.0 mm (engine cold)
F_3 = 4.5 to 5.0 mm (engine cold)

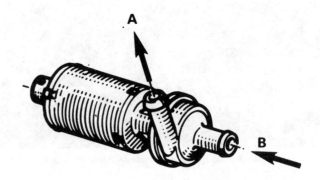

Fig. 2.10 Electric coolant pump fitted to Turbo models showing delivery pipe (A) and inlet pipe (B) (Sec 12)

12 Electric coolant pump (Turbo models) – removal and refitting

1   Disconnect the battery earth lead.
2   Drain the cooling system as described in Section 3.
3   Disconnect the coolant inlet and delivery hoses from the pump unit, which is located next to the front right-hand suspension turret in the engine bay.
4   Detach the pump unit, disconnect the wiring to it, then remove it from the car.
5   Refitting is a reversal of the removal procedure, but ensure that the delivery pipe is vertical as shown in Fig. 2.10.
6   Refill the cooling system as described in Section 3.

13 Heater unit – removal and refitting

1   Disconnect the battery earth lead.
2   Drain the engine coolant as described in Section 3.
3   Remove the facia unit as described in Chapter 11.
4   Unclip and detach the coolant heater hoses at the engine compartment bulkhead. If the manufacturer's retaining clips are still fitted, they will need to be cut free and renewed when refitting.

5   Disconnect the control unit (Section 15).
6   Detach the ducts from each side of the heater unit (photo).
7   Undo the three heater retaining bolts and lower the heater unit, taking care not to spill any remaining coolant as the inlet and outlet pipes are passed through the bulkhead aperture (photo).
8   Refit in the reverse order of removal. Refill the cooling system as described in Section 3.

14 Heater matrix – removal and refitting

1   Remove the heater unit as described in Section 13.
2   Disconnect the control valve return spring from the end of the matrix (photo).
3   Undo the two retaining screws and withdraw the matrix from the heater unit (photo).
4   Refit in the reverse order of removal. Refit the heater unit as described in Section 13.

15 Heater and ventilation controls – removal and refitting

1 Disconnect the battery earth lead.
2 Remove the lower facia panels for access to the underside of the heater/ventilation control unit.
3 Undo the three heater/ventilation control unit retaining screws.
4 Release the unit retaining clips (one each side), then lower the unit for withdrawal.
5 Disconnect the control cables and the wiring connector to fully remove the control unit (photo).
6 Refit in the reverse order of removal. Check for satisfactory operation on completion.

16 Heater blower motor – removal and refitting

1 The blower motor can be removed from the heater unit leaving the heater in position. Proceed as follows.
2 Disconnect the battery earth lead.
3 Detach and remove the glovebox for access to the underside of the heater unit.
4 Prise free the insulator cover from the base of the heater unit casing.
5 Unscrew the three retaining bolts and lower the heater blower motor from the heater casing. Disconnect the wiring (photos).
6 Refit in the reverse order of removal.

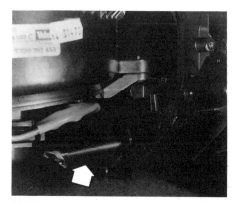

13.6 Detaching a duct (arrowed) from the heater

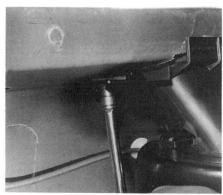

13.7 Undo the heater retaining bolts

14.2 Heater control valve lever and return spring

14.3 Withdrawing the heater matrix

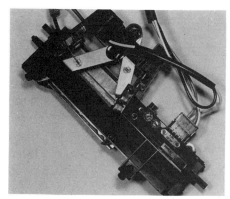

15.5 Heater/ventilation control unit and connections

16.5A Undo the blower motor retaining screws ...

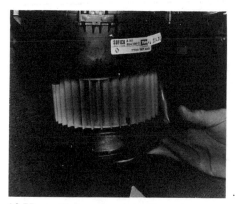

16.5B ... withdraw the motor/fan unit ...

16.5C ... and detach the wiring connector

17 Air conditioning system – description and precautions

1   When an air conditioning system is fitted, it is necessary to observe special precautions whenever dealing with any part of the system, its associated components and any items which necessitate disconnection of the system.

2   The refrigeration circuit contains a liquid refrigerant (Freon) and it is therefore dangerous to disconnect any part of the system without specialised knowledge and equipment. If for any reason the system must be disconnected (engine removal for example), entrust this task to your Renault dealer or a refrigeration engineer.

3   The layout of the air conditioning system is shown in Fig. 2.11. The air conditioner unit is located under the passenger side facia panel.

4   The refrigerant must not be allowed to come in contact with a naked flame or a poisonous gas will be created. Do not allow the fluid to come in contact with the skin or eyes.

5   Whenever the refrigerant lines are disconnected, all pipe lines and openings must be plugged or capped to prevent the entry of moisture.

6   After the system pipe lines have been reconnected, always have the system evacuated and recharged by your dealer or a competent refrigeration engineer.

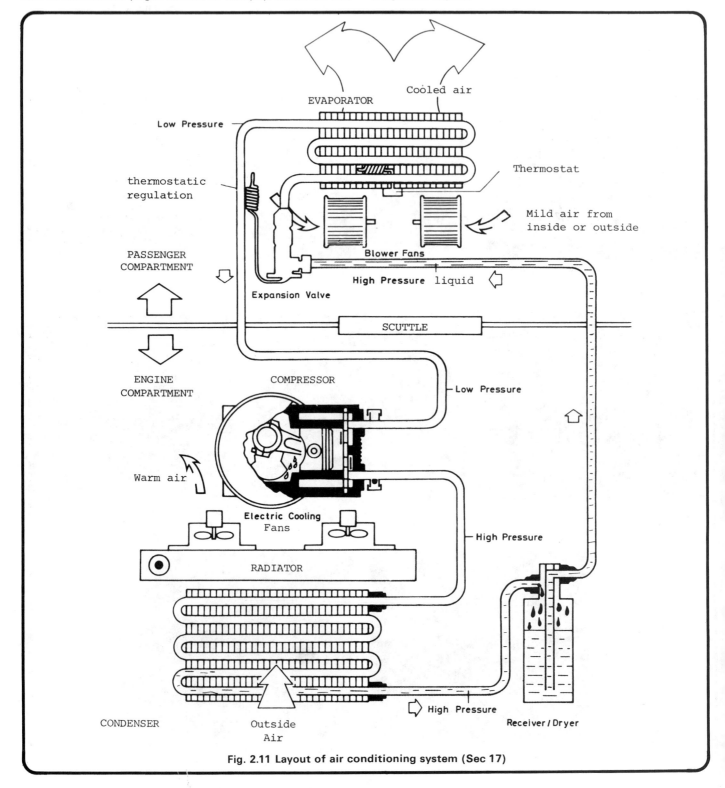

Fig. 2.11 Layout of air conditioning system (Sec 17)

18 Air conditioning system – maintenance

1 Regularly inspect the condition of hoses and the security of connections.
2 A sight glass is located on top of the receiver/dryer chamber. If bubbles are evident immediately after switching on the system, a fluid leak is indicated.
3 Keep the fins of the condenser free from flies and dirt and keep the compressor drivebelt in good condition and correctly tensioned (Section 11).
4 Water dripping or collecting on the floor under the car is quite normal, and is the result of condensation.
5 Run the system for a few minutes each week when it is not generally in use.

19 Air conditioning system – removal and refitting of main components

Note: *The system should be professionally discharged before carrying out any of the following work. Cap or plug the pipe lines as soon as they are disconnected. Refer to the precautions given in Section 17 before proceeding.*

Compressor
1 Disconnect the battery earth lead.
2 Disconnect the refrigerant lines from the compressor.
3 Unbolt and remove the compressor, slipping its pulley out of the drivebelt.
4 Refitting is a reversal of the removal procedure. Tension the belt as described in Section 11.

Condenser
5 Disconnect the battery earth lead.

6 Drain the engine cooling system as described in Section 3.
7 With reference to Fig. 2.13, disconnect the coolant hoses at the radiator, and the freon hoses at the condenser. Note that the condenser connections are easily damaged, so take care. Plug the condenser pipes and ports to prevent the ingress of dirt.
8 Unbolt and remove the crossmember from the top of the radiator.
9 Disconnect the wiring from the cooling fan unit, then carefully lift out the radiator and condenser unit.
10 Refitting is a reversal of the removal procedure. Top up and bleed the cooling system as described in Section 11. Have the refrigerant system recharged by a competent specialist.

Evaporator
11 This unit is combined with the heater/air conditioning unit, therefore refer to Section 13 and remove the heater unit. It will also be necessary to disconnect the following items:

   (a) *Detach the freon hoses from the expansion valve and the vacuum pipe from the vacuum reservoir small diameter connector. Plug the freon hoses and expansion valve ports*
   (b) *Remove the expansion chamber and vacuum reservoir*
   (c) *Unscrew the two expansion valve-to-scuttle retaining nuts (Fig. 2.14)*

12 Refitting is a reversal of the removal procedure. Have the air conditioning circuit recharged by a competent specialist.

Air conditioning unit electrical components
13 The following electrical components of the system are attached to the heater/air conditioning unit and can be removed if required:

   (a) *Relays and diodes (Fig. 2.15)*
   (b) *Recycling flap solenoid valve (Fig. 2.16)*
   (c) *Thermostat – regulates temperature of air leaving the evaporator (Fig. 2.17)*

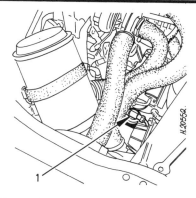

Fig. 2.12 Air conditioning system receiver/dryer chamber sight glass location (1) (Sec 18)

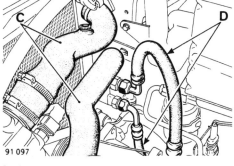

Fig. 2.13 Disconnect engine coolant hoses (C) at the radiator and air conditioning freon hoses (D) at the condenser (Sec 19)

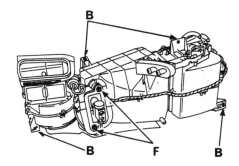

Fig. 2.14 Heater/air conditioning unit showing mounting screw location points (B) and expansion valve-to-scuttle retaining nut locations (F) (Sec 19)

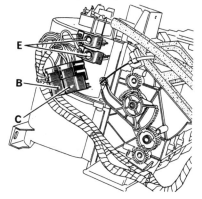

Fig. 2.15 Air conditioning system relays (B and C) and diodes (E) (Sec 19)

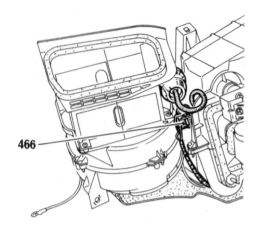

Fig. 2.16 Air conditioning system recycling flap solenoid valve (466) (Sec 19)

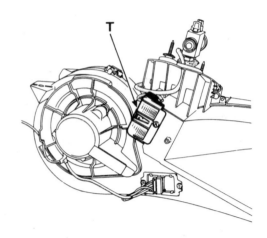

Fig. 2.17 Air conditioning system thermostat (T) (Sec 19)

20 Fault diagnosis – cooling, heating and air conditioning systems

Symptom	Reason(s)
Cooling	
Overheating	Insufficient coolant in system
	Pump ineffective due to slack drivebelt
	Radiator blocked either internally or externally
	Kinked or collapsed hose causing coolant flow restriction
	Thermostat not working properly
	Engine out of tune
	Ignition timing retarded or auto advance malfunction
	Cylinder head gasket blown
	Engine not yet run-in
	Exhaust system partially blocked
	Engine oil level too low
	Brakes binding
	Electric cooling fan or switch faulty
Engine running too cool	Faulty, incorrect or missing thermostat
	Electric cooling fan switch faulty
Loss of coolant	Loose hose clips
	Hoses perished or leaking
	Radiator leaking
	Expansion tank pressure cap defective
	Blown cylinder head gasket
	Cracked cylinder block or head
Heater	
Heater gives insufficient output	Engine overcooled (see above)
	Heater matrix blocked
	Heater controls maladjusted or broken
Air conditioner	
Bubbles observed in sight glass of receiver drier	Leak in system
	Low refrigerant level
No cooling	No refrigerant
Expansion valve frosted over on evaporator	Faulty or clogged expansion valve
	Thermal bulb leaking
Insufficient cooling	Faulty expansion valve
	Air in refrigerant circuit
	Clogged condenser
	Receiver drier clogged
	Faulty compressor
	Compressor overfilled with oil

Chapter 3 Fuel and exhaust systems

Contents

Specifications

Part A: Fuel system – general
Fuel

Grade	98 octane (4-star) – for information on the suitability of unleaded fuel, refer to a Renault dealer
Fuel tank contents	66 litres (14.5 gals)

Part B: Carburettor fuel system
General

Carburettor type	Solex 2834 Z10 twin choke
Code No application:	
F2N 712 engine	867
F2N 710 engine	889/889D*

*Non adjustable

Carburettor data

Type 867:	Primary	Secondary
Venturi	20	26
Main jet	97.5	122
Air correction jet	200	145
Idle jet	47	45
Econostat	–	120
Enrichener	50	–
Accelerator pump injector	40	35

Needle valve	1.8	
Float level	33.0 to 34.0 mm	
Positive throttle opening	0.8 to 1.0 mm	
Mechanical initial opening	2.1 to 2.3 mm	
Degas valve	1.0 to 3.0 mm	
Idle speed	675 to 725 rpm	
CO mixture	0.5 to 1.5%	
Type 889/889D:	**Primary**	**Secondary**
Venturi	20	27
Main jet	100	145
Air correction jet	210	190
Idle jet	45 (889) or 47 (889D)	50
Econostat	–	120
Enrichener	50	–
Accelerator pump injector	40	35
Needle valve	1.8	1.8
Float level	33.0 to 34.0 mm	33.0 to 34.0 mm
Positive throttle opening	0.9 to 1.1 mm	0.9 to 1.1 mm
Mechanical initial opening	2.1 to 2.3 mm	2.1 to 2.3 mm
Degas valve	1.0 to 3.0 mm	1.0 to 3.0 mm
Idle speed	675 to 725 rpm	675 to 725 rpm
CO mixture	1.0 to 2.0%	1.0 to 2.0%

Part C: Renix fuel injection system

Type	Computer-controlled in conjunction with ignition system

Calibration and settings

Idle speed:	
Non-Turbo models	725 to 825 rpm
Turbo	775 to 825 rpm
CO at idle	1.0 to 2.0%
Fuel injector resistance	2.0 to 3.0 ohms

Part D: Turbocharger

Type	Garrett T3

Calibration

Boost pressure:	
At 2500 to 4000 rpm	850 to 950 mbar
At max engine speed	750 to 850 mbar
Boost limiting pressostat operating pressure	1300 to 1480 mbar
Air bypass valve opening vacuum	180 to 220 mbar

Torque wrench settings

	Nm	lbf ft
Turbocharger mounting strut fixings	30	22
Turbocharger-to-exhaust manifold nuts	45	33
Turbocharger coolant pipe connections	35	26
Turbocharger oil pipe retainer clamp	20	15
Turbocharger oil pipe flange screws	20	15

PART A: FUEL AND EXHAUST SYSTEMS – GENERAL

1 General

The type of fuel system fitted is dependent on model. 1.7 litre models use a carburettor based system, whilst 2.0 litre models use a Renix fuel injection system, in the case of Turbo models in conjunction with a Garrett turbocharger. Both carburettor and fuel injection systems are electronically controlled by an engine management computer. The Renix system also has control over ignition advance characteristics.

The details of the carburettor, fuel injection and turbocharger systems will be found in Parts B, C and D respectively. Part A deals with general components which are applicable to all models, such as the fuel tank.

Warning: *Many of the procedures in this Chapter entail the removal of fuel pipes and connections which may result in some fuel spillage. Before carrying out any operation on the fuel system refer to the precautions given in Safety First! at the beginning of this manual and follow them implicitly. Petrol is a highly dangerous and volatile liquid and the precautions necessary when handling it cannot be over-stressed.*

*Remember that fuel lines in the fuel injection system may contain fuel under pressure, even if the engine has not been running for some time. **Do not** smoke or allow any naked flame nearby when there is any risk of fuel spillage. Take care to avoid spilling fuel onto a hot engine, and keep a fire extinguisher handy.*

2 Maintenance

1 At the service intervals shown in *'Routine maintenance'* the following checks and adjustments should be carried out on fuel and exhaust system components.

2 With the car over a pit, raised on a vehicle lift or securely supported on axle stands, carefully inspect the underbody fuel pipes, hoses and unions for chafing, leaks and corrosion. Renew any pipes which are severely pitted with corrosion or in any way damaged. Renew any hoses which show signs of cracking or other deterioration.

3 Check the fuel tank for leaks, for any signs of corrosion or damage, and the security of the mountings.

4 Check the exhaust system condition, as described in Section 9.

5 From within the engine compartment, check the security of all fuel hose attachments and inspect them for chafing, kinks, leaks or deterioration.

6 Renew the air cleaner element as described in Section 3.

7 Check the operation of the accelerator and choke control linkages (as applicable) and lubricate the linkages, cables and accelerator pedal pivot with a few drops of a good quality multi-purpose oil (photos).

8 Renew the fuel filter, as described in Section 24 for fuel injection models, or as follows for carburettor models. On carburettor models the filter is a separate renewable unit held in a spring bracket next to the fuel pump (photo). Clamp and detach the hoses, then remove the filter from the bracket. When refitting, ensure that the direction of flow arrows on the filter body are correctly orientated.

3 Air cleaner – element renewal

1.7 litre models

1 To remove the air cleaner element, release the seven retaining clips around the cover rim, undo the three nuts and the single screw, and then lift the cover clear. Withdraw the element from the casing (photo).

2 Wipe clean the inside of the casing.

3 Insert the new element into the casing, refit the cover, and fasten it with the screw, nuts and clips.

2.0 litre non-Turbo models

4 Unscrew the wing nut, remove the nut and its flat washer, then lift clear the air cleaner cover. Withdraw the element from the casing (photos).

5 Wipe clean the inside of the casing.

6 Insert the new element and refit the cover, fastening it with the nut and washer.

2.0 litre Turbo models

7 Release the retaining clips and remove the outer cover from the air cleaner casing.

8 Detach the air intake hoses from the air cleaner casing, release the four clips securing the end cover, then separate the end cover from the casing and withdraw the element (photos).

9 Wipe clean the inside of the casing.

10 Insert the new element and refit the covers in the reverse order of removal.

Air cleaner assembly (all models)

11 If it is necessary to remove the complete air cleaner assembly at any time, the procedure is the same for all models, although the assemblies differ in appearance according to model.

12 Note their connections, and then detach the air intake and vacuum hoses and any wiring connectors from the air cleaner casing.

13 On some models it may be necessary to remove the cover(s) and/or element, as described earlier in this Section, to gain access to the casing fixings.

14 Undo the retaining nuts and/or bolts, and remove the casing (photos).

15 Refit in the reverse order to removal. Ensure that all hose and wiring connections are securely made.

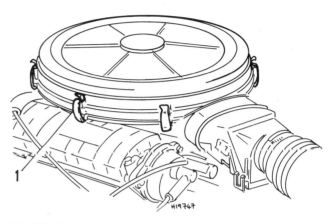

Fig. 3.1 Air cleaner cover securing clips (1) – 1.7 litre model (Sec 3)

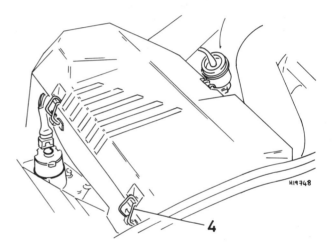

Fig. 3.2 Air cleaner outer cover and retaining clips – 2.0 litre Turbo model (Sec 3)

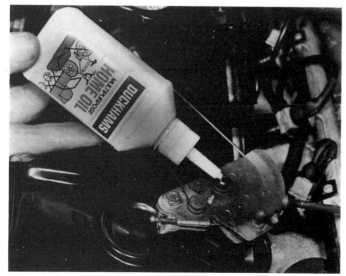

2.7 Lubricate the accelerator control linkage

2.8 Renew the in-line fuel filter – 1.7 litre model

3.1 Air cleaner element removal – 1.7 litre model

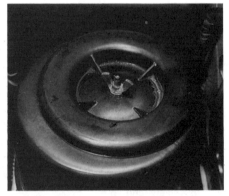

3.4A Air cleaner unit cover and retaining nut – 2.0 litre non-Turbo model

3.4B Withdrawing the air cleaner element – 2.0 litre non-Turbo model

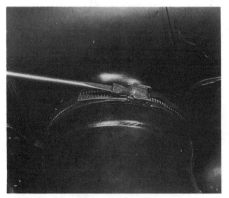

3.8A Detach the air intake hoses ...

3.8B ... and separate the air cleaner casing from the end cover – 2.0 litre Turbo model

3.14A Air cleaner casing removal – 1.7 litre model

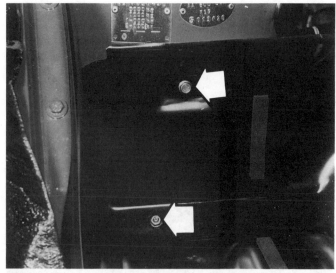

3.14B Air cleaner casing retaining bolt and nut (arrowed) – 2.0 litre Turbo model

3   Detach the outer cable adjuster from the support bracket by removing the retaining clip and unscrewing the adjuster. Take note of the set position of the adjuster in the bracket as a guide to general adjustment when refitting the cable.
4   According to model, the cable will be secured by a locating clip to the suspension strut turret or to the brake master cylinder. Detach the cable according to its method of retension, then withdraw it through the bulkhead from the engine compartment side.
5   If required, the throttle link rod can be removed by simply prising it free from the balljoints.
6   The accelerator pivot quadrant can be removed by releasing the C-clip using suitable circlip pliers, then lifting the pivot quadrant from the pivot pin.
7   Refitting of the accelerator cable and its associated components is a reversal of the removal procedure. Lubricate the pivot points.
8   When securing the outer cable to the support bracket, adjust its position so that there is a small amount of slack in the cable when the throttle is closed (photos).

5   Accelerator pedal – removal and refitting

1   Working inside the car, release the accelerator cable end fitting, which is a push fit in the pedal rod.
2   Undo the bolt securing the pedal assembly to the bulkhead and withdraw it from inside the car.
3   Refitting is the reverse sequence to removal.

6   Fuel tank – removal and refitting

Note: *Refer to the warning note in Section 1 before proceeding*
1   A drain plug is not provided on the fuel tank and it is therefore preferable to carry out the removal operation when the tank is nearly empty. Before proceeding, disconnect the battery negative terminal,

4   Accelerator cable – removal and refitting

1   Working from inside the car, release the cable end fitting by prising or pulling it free from the accelerator pedal rod (photo).
2   Detach the throttle return spring, open the throttle by hand, and withdraw the cable end from the linkage (photos).

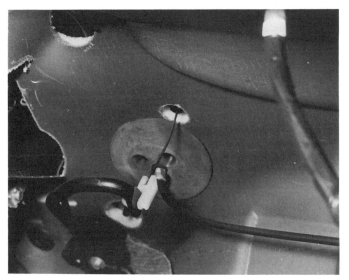

4.1 Accelerator cable-to-pedal fitting

4.2A Accelerator cable and throttle linkage – 1.7 litre model
1   Throttle return spring   3   Outer cable adjuster support bracket
2   Cable end fitting   4   Pivot C-clip

4.2B Accelerator cable and throttle linkage – 2.0 litre non-Turbo model
1   Throttle return spring   3   Outer cable adjuster support bracket
2   Cable end fitting   4   Pivot C-clip

4.8A Accelerator cable adjuster and clip (arorwed) – 1.7 litre model

4.8B Accelerator cable adjuster – 2.0 litre non-Turbo model

and then syphon or hand pump the remaining fuel from the tank.

2   Jack up the rear of the car and securely support it on axle stands.

3   On models fitted with split rear seats, tilt the rear seats forward and fold back the luggage area carpet. On models fitted with a standard type bench seat, remove the seat as described in Chapter 11, then unfasten and fold back the luggage area carpet.

4   Prise free the circular plastic cover from the fuel level sender unit access hole in the floor.

5   Disconnect the battery earth lead, then detach the wires from the fuel level sender unit (photo).

6   Disconnect the fuel feed, return and vent hoses from the top of the sender unit. Mark them for identification if necessary.

7   Remove the right-hand rear wheel.

8   Unclip and detach the two hoses from the double connector on the fuel tank – see Fig. 3.5.

9   Unbolt and remove the protector plate (photo).

10   Take the weight of the tank on a suitable jack, with a block of wood interposed to prevent damage.

11   Undo the tank retaining strap bolts and detach the fuel filler pipe connector hose (photos). An assistant may be required at this point to help in steadying the tank as it is lowered.

12   Carefully lower the fuel tank and withdraw it from under the vehicle.

13   If the tank is contaminated with sediment or water, remove the fuel level sender unit as described in Section 7 and swill out the tank with clean fuel. If the tank is damaged, or leaks, it should be repaired by a specialist or renewed. **Do not** under any circumstances solder or weld the tank.

14   Refit the tank in the reverse sequence to removal. Check for any signs of leaks when topping-up the fuel level.

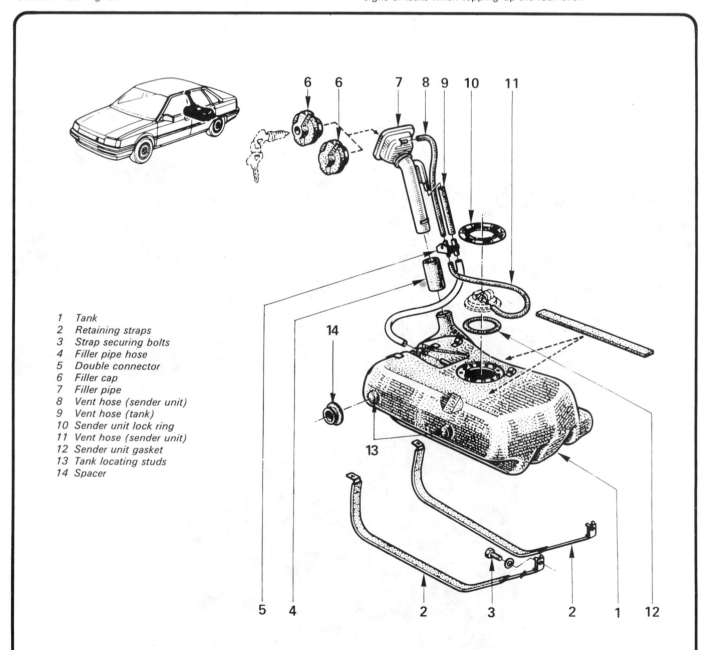

1   Tank
2   Retaining straps
3   Strap securing bolts
4   Filler pipe hose
5   Double connector
6   Filler cap
7   Filler pipe
8   Vent hose (sender unit)
9   Vent hose (tank)
10   Sender unit lock ring
11   Vent hose (sender unit)
12   Sender unit gasket
13   Tank locating studs
14   Spacer

Fig. 3.3 Fuel tank and associated components (Sec 6)

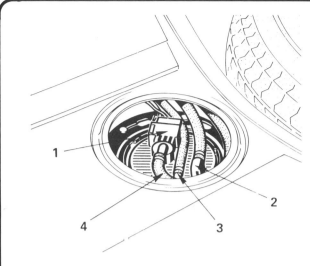

Fig. 3.4 Fuel level sender unit connections (Sec 6)

1 Wiring connector   3 Return hose
2 Feed hose   4 Vent hose

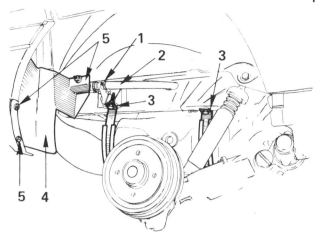

Fig. 3.5 Fuel tank associated fittings (Sec 6)

1 Double connector   4 Protector plate
2 Vent pipes   5 Protector plate securing
3 Tank securing strap bolts   bolts

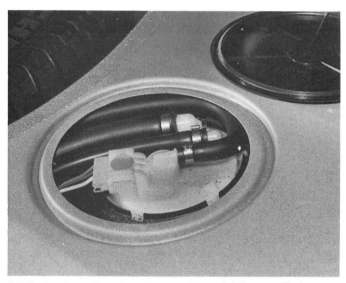

6.5 Fuel tank sender unit and connections – 2.0 litre non-Turbo model shown

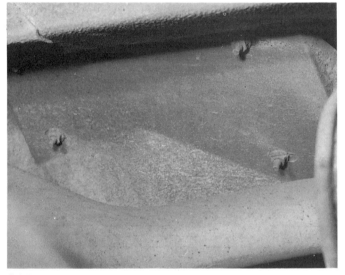

6.9 Fuel tank protector plate and securing nuts – 1.7 litre Savanna model shown

6.11A Rear fuel tank retaining strap and bolt

6.11B Front fuel tank retaining strap and bolt

7 Fuel level sender unit – removal and refitting

1   Refer to the previous Section, observe the warning note and then proceed as described in paragraphs 1 to 6 inclusive.

2   Twist the sender unit body to disengage the retaining pegs. The judicious use of a suitable screwdriver or similar implement will be required to turn the unit. Withdraw the sender unit with care as it is easily damaged. On some models it may be necessary to lower the fuel tank slightly in order to allow the sender unit to be withdrawn. Tie a length of string to the lock ring to prevent it from getting lost between the body and tank.

3   If the sender unit is to be removed for an extensive period, seal off the tank and fuel hoses to prevent petrol fumes escaping.

4   Two types of sender unit are fitted depending on whether conventional or electronic instrumentation is fitted. If an ohmmeter is available, the sender unit can be tested by measuring the resistance produced against the corresponding float heights as follows (see Fig. 3.6):

Float height (H) (electronic instrument panel)	Resistance at terminals 1 and 4
Highest point (31.5 mm)	310 to 350 ohms
Intermediate point (96 mm)	210 to 250 ohms
Lowest point (216 mm)	0 to 40 ohms

Float height (H) (conventional instrument panel)	Resistance at terminals 2 and 4
Highest point (31.5 mm)	6 to 8 ohms
Intermediate point (122.5 mm)	80 to 120 ohms
Lowest point (216 mm)	270 to 330 ohms

6   The minimum fuel level detector on the conventional type sender unit can be checked by holding the unit vertically with an ohmmeter connected to terminals 3 and 4. The resistance reading should be 0 to 30 ohms. If the unit is inverted, the ohmmeter should read infinity.

7   The movable gauze filter can be checked on the electronic type sender unit as follows. Connect the ohmmeter to terminals 1 and 4, hold the float in its highest position and progressively press down the filter. A resistance reading of 20 to 30 ohms should be produced.

8   Renew the sender unit with a replacement of the correct type if necessary.

9   Refitting is a reversal of the removal procedure. Renew the seal and ensure that the sender unit engages in its notch. Ensure that all connections are securely made.

8 Fuel filler pipe – removal and refitting

Note: *Refer to the warning note in Section 1 of this Chapter before proceeding*

1   The upper section of the fuel filler pipe (filler neck) is secured to the body by pop rivets. These rivets are 4.8 mm in diameter and will need to be drilled out for removal.

2   Raise and support the vehicle at the rear. Remove the rear right-hand roadwheel for access.

3   Unbolt and remove the protector plate from under the wing.

4   Release the hose clips and detach the connector hose from the filler pipe. The filler pipe can then be withdrawn.

5   Refitting is a reversal of the removal procedure. The four aluminium pop rivets required to secure the pipe at the top end should be 4.8 mm in diameter, 12 mm long, with 12 mm diameter heads.

9 Exhaust system

1   The exhaust system differs in design according to the engine used.

2   The complete system or just part of it can be removed for repair or renewal. The respective pipe section joints will either be of the flanged type, such as the manifold-to-downpipe joint, or a collared sleeve and clamp joint such as the downpipe-to-secondary expansion box pipe joint.

3   The flanged type joints can normally easily be separated by simply removing the clamping nuts of the joint and withdrawing the pipe from the manifold or mating pipe as the case may be. It may, however, be necessary to apply some rust penetrating fluid to the nuts and joints to ease removal (photo).

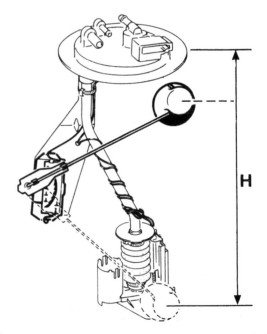

Fig. 3.6 Fuel level sender unit showing float height dimension (H) (Sec 7)

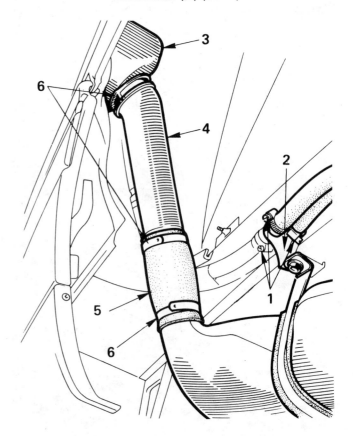

Fig. 3.7 Fuel filler pipe components (Sec 8)

1 Vent pipes	4 Filler pipe
2 Double connector	5 Connector hose
3 Filler neck	6 Clips

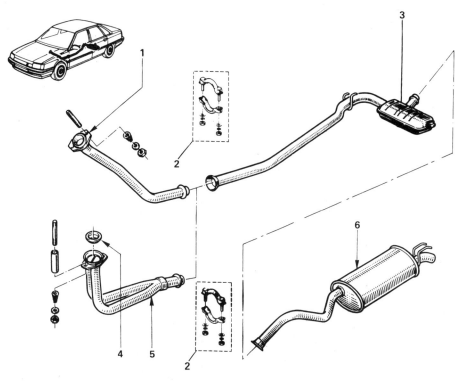

Fig. 3.8 Exhaust system components – 1.7 litre models (Sec 9)

1 Downpipe
2 Flange clamp
3 Intermediate section
4 Thermo-fusing seal
5 Downpipe (alternative)
6 Rear silencer

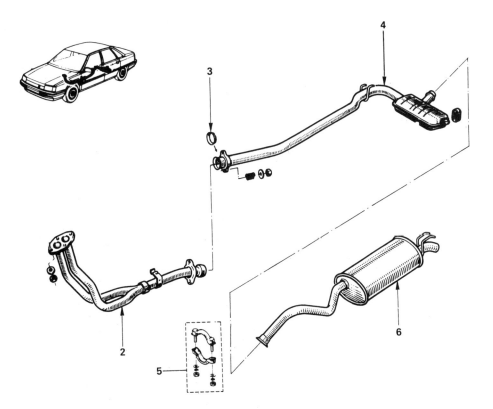

Fig. 3.9 Exhaust system components – 2.0 litre non-Turbo models (Sec 9)

2 Downpipe
3 Thermo-fusing seal
4 Intermediate section
5 Flange clamp
6 Rear silencer

4 The collared sleeve joint is not so easily separated and a certain amount of heat from a gas torch may be required to separate the two pipes after the clamp has been removed. In this instance special care must be taken to guard against fire whenever working underneath the vehicle, particularly at the petrol tank end or near fuel lines!

5 If a pipe section is being renewed it is usually far quicker to cut it through close to the joint concerned to ease removal.

6 The system is suspended in position by means of brackets and rubber mounting straps or rings and these can be levered from their mounting brackets when necessary (photo).

7 The foregoing operations should be followed if only certain sections of the system are to be renewed. If the complete system must be renewed, then it will be much easier if the old pipes are sawn through with a hacksaw in short lengths for removal.

8 When fitting the new system de-burr the connecting sockets and smear the pipe ends with an exhaust system sealant. New mounting clips and rubber suspension rings should be fitted, also new pipe clamps.

9 Do not fully tighten the retaining clamps and joint clamp/flange nuts until the complete system is in position and fully suspended.

10 The downpipe joint has a spring-loaded flange joint at the manifold on 1.7 litre models, or at the lower end of the downpipe on 2.0 litre models (photo). When assembling this joint, a new thermo-fusing seal must be used and the joint retaining nuts must be tightened to the point where the springs are coilbound as shown in Fig. 3.10 (photos).

11 On Turbo models, access to the exhaust downpipe-to-turbocharger elbow flange joint will necessitate the removal of the heat shield mounted above the turbocharger unit. An additional heat shield is also attached to the downpipe-to-turbocharger joint (photo).

12 Check that the pipes do not foul any electrical leads or other components before final tightening of the fastenings.

13 Run the engine on completion and check for any signs of leakage.

10 Manifolds (1.7 litre engine) – removal and refitting

1 The inlet and exhaust manifolds on this engine share a common gasket and they must therefore be removed and refitted as a combined unit.

2 Remove the carburettor as described in Part B, Section 17 of this Chapter.

3 Disconnect the exhaust downpipe from the manifold as described in Section 9.

4 Unbolt and remove the hot air duct from the exhaust manifold (photo).

5 Unbolt and remove the throttle linkage support plate from the top of the inlet manifold (photo).

6 Unbolt and remove the baseplate from the inlet manifold (photo).

7 Undo the retaining nuts and withdraw the inlet and exhaust manifolds from the cylinder head.

8 To separate the inlet and exhaust manifolds, undo the retaining screws on the top face of the inlet manifold.

9 Refitting is a reversal of the removal procedure, but ensure that the joint faces are perfectly clean and always use a new gasket (photo).

10 Refit the carburettor as described in Part B, Section 17 of this Chapter.

11 Reconnect the exhaust downpipe to the manifold as described in Section 9.

11 Manifolds (2.0 litre engine) – removal and refitting

Air induction and fuel injection manifolds

1 Refer to Part C, Sections 30 and 31 of this Chapter.

Exhaust manifold (non-Turbo models)

2 Unbolt and disconnect the downpipe from the manifold.

3 Undo the retaining nuts and withdraw the manifold (photo).

4 Ensure that the joint faces are perfectly clean and renew the gasket.

5 Refitting is a reversal of the removal procedure. Refit the downpipe to the manifold with reference to Section 9.

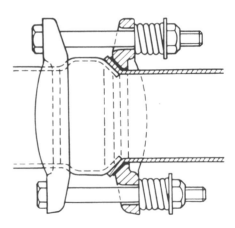

Fig. 3.10 Spring-loaded flange joint – tighten nuts so that springs are coilbound as shown (Sec 9)

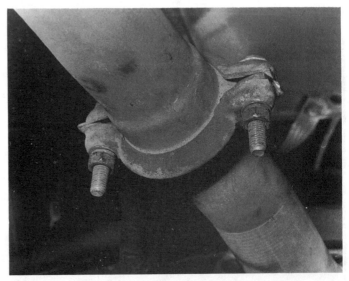

9.3 Exhaust system flanged joint connection – 1.7 litre model shown

9.6A Exhaust system forward mounting bracket

9.6B Exhaust system rear mounting bracket

9.10A Spring-loaded flange joint at the lower end of the downpipe – 2.0 litre non-Turbo model

9.10B Manifold joint thermo-fusing seal – 1.7 litre model

9.11 Downpipe-to-turbocharger elbow flange joint and heat shield

10.4 Remove the hot air duct from the exhaust manifold – 1.7 litre engine

10.5 Throttle linkage support plate retaining bolts (arrowed) – 1.7 litre engine

10.6 Remove the baseplate from the inlet manifold. Note inlet-to-exhaust manifold retaining screws (arrowed) – 1.7 litre engine

10.9 Refitting the inlet and exhaust manifolds with a new gasket – 1.7 litre engine

11.3 Exhaust manifold and retaining nuts – 2.0 litre non-Turbo model

Exhaust manifold (Turbo models)

6   Remove the turbocharger unit as described in Part D, Section 37 of this Chapter.

7   The exhaust manifold can now be removed and refitted as described in paragraphs 3 to 5 of this Section.

8   Refit the turbocharger unit and associated fittings as described in Part D, Section 37 of this Chapter.

PART B: CARBURETTOR AND ASSOCIATED FUEL SYSTEM COMPONENTS

12 Automatic air temperature system – removal, checking and refitting

1   This system is fitted in the air cleaner intake duct on carburettor engine models. Its function is to regulate the air temperature entering the carburettor, thereby assisting in the air/fuel mixture control.

2   A mixer flap directs hot or cold air as required into the air cleaner, the flap valve position being regulated by a wax element thermostat. The hot air is drawn from the area around the exhaust manifold through a hot air duct.

3   This system requires no maintenance, but if suspected of malfunction it can be tested and if necessary renewed as follows.

4   Remove the air cleaner and take out the element as described in Section 3.

5   Immerse the air cleaner body in water at 26°C (79°F) or less, ensuring that the wax capsule in the intake spout is completely submerged. After 5 minutes observe the position of the flap valve which should be blanking off the cold air intake.

6   Now repeat the test in water at 36°C (97°F) and after 5 minutes check that the flap is blanking off the hot air intake. If the flap valve does not operate as described at the specified temperatures, the wax

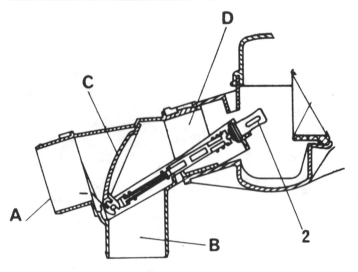

Fig. 3.11 Air cleaner automatic air temperature control
system (Sec 12)

A   Cold air intake
B   Hot air intake
C   Flap valve
D   Air cleaner body intake
    spout
2   Wax capsule

capsule control assembly is faulty and must be renewed.
7   After completing the tests, dry off the air cleaner body and refit the
hot air duct.
8   Refit the element and the air cleaner as described in Section 3.

13 Solex 28/34 Z10 carburettor – description

1   The Solex 28/34 Z10 carburettor is a twin choke downdraught
carburettor mounted direct on the top of the inlet manifold (photos).
2   The carburettor base is heated or cooled according to prevailing
conditions, and the design of the carburettor is such that optimum fuel
flow is obtained over extreme temperature variations. The throttle
butterfly valve in the second stage venturi opens later than that in the
first, giving improved fuel consumption. The carburettor is fitted with
an idle solenoid which cuts off the fuel supply when the ignition is
turned off. To aid cold starting a manual choke, operated by cable, is
fitted.
3   Later models from (1987), are fitted with an electrically heated
primary idle circuit in place of the coolant heated system used on
previous models. To prevent stalling, a cold start diaphragm is also
fitted to later models. An idle cut-off solenoid is also fitted which cuts
off the fuel supply when the ignition is switched off.
4   Models fitted with power steering and/or air conditioning have an
anti-stall valve fitted to increase the idle speed when additional
loading is placed on the engine (eg when the steering is moved to full
lock at idle speed).
5   Another improvement made to later models is the fitting of an
anti-percolation chamber between the carburettor and the fuel pump.
This device improves engine starting when the engine is hot.

14 Carburettor – maintenance

1   Before blaming the carburettor for any shortcomings in engine
performance, remember that there is no reason why the carburettor
should lose tune, and in fact what usually happens is that, as the
engine gets older and less efficient, more or less fruitless attempts are
made to restore performance by interfering with the carburettor. In
those parts of the world where exhaust emission is regulated by law it
is inadvisable and may be illegal to alter carburettor settings without
monitoring exhaust emission levels using special equipment.
2   The ultimate cause of most carburettor problems is wear in moving
parts or dirt in the jets. The Solex carburettors have no continuously
moving parts, except for the float and the throttle spindle, which makes
it a very reliable device so long as dirt does not get in.

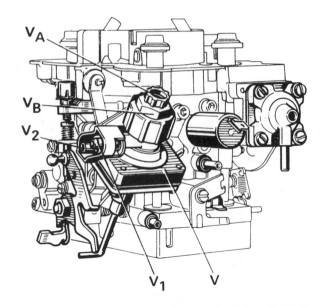

Fig. 3.12 Additional items fitted to later Solex 28/34 Z10
carburettor (Sec 13)

a   Vacuum connection
1   Cold start diaphragm unit
2   Idle cut-off solenoid
3   Circuit heating resistor
4   Anti-stall valve (where
    applicable)

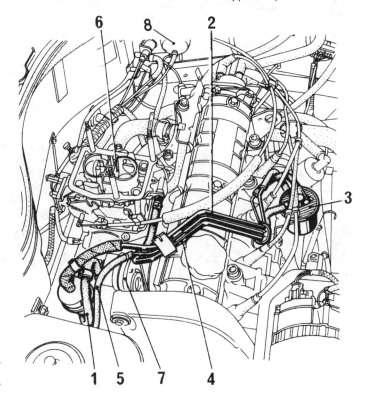

Fig. 3.13 Carburettor fuel line connections and layout on
later models (Sec 13)

1   Feed hose (from tank to
    pump)
2   Fuel
    pump-to-anti-percolation
    chamber hose
3   Anti-percolation chamber
4   Anti-percolation
    chamber-to-carburettor hose
5   Return hose (to fuel tank)
6   Carburettor
7   Fuel pump
8   Cold start diaphragm
    vacuum chamber

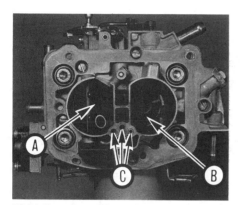

13.1A Top view of Solex 28/34 Z10 carburettor
A 1st choke barrel   C Air correction, main
B 2nd choke barrel   and idle jets

13.1B Side view of Solex 28/34 Z10 carburettor
A Idle speed adjustment screw C Full load
B Choke control linkage   enrichment unit

13.1C Side view of Solex 28/34 Z10 carburettor
A Accelerator pump   C Coolant pipe
B Cold start diaphragm

13.1D Underside view of Solex 28/34 Z10 carburettor showing heat insulating flange

14.3 Inspecting the carburettor integral fuel filter

15.6 Carburettor idle speed adjustment through air cleaner housing aperture

3   Periodically unscrew the plug and extract the integral fuel filter. Wash it in clean petrol and refit it to the carburettor (photos).
4   Check the fuel feed and return hoses, the vacuum and the coolant hoses and connections at the carburettor for condition and security.
5   Occasionally apply a drop of oil to the various linkages and the throttle spindle to ensure that they do not wear prematurely.

15 Carburettor – idle speed and mixture adjustments

1   Generally speaking, unless the carburettor is obviously out of tune or is malfunctioning it is not advisable to tamper with it.
2   Correct adjustment can only be achieved provided that the engine is in generally good condition. The valve clearances must be correct and the ignition system must also be in good condition.
3   An independent tachometer is necessary to make accurate adjustment and it should be connected to the engine in accordance with the maker's instructions. The air filter must be fitted. Run the engine at 2000 rpm until warm, as indicated by the engagement of the cooling fan. On automatic transmission models, engage P. Allow the engine to run; when the cooling fan cuts out, adjustments can be made. During prolonged adjustments take care as the cooling fan will cut-in again periodically.
4   Check and ensure that the manual choke is in the fully retracted position (off).
5   During the adjustment checks, all electrical consumers should be switched off, including the thermally switched radiator fan.
6   Check the idling speed is as given in the Specifications. Adjust using a thin screwdriver inserted through the hole in the air cleaner housing (photo) which allows access to the idle screw.
7   Mixture adjustment can only be made accurately using an exhaust gas analyser. If this is available, connect it to the vehicle exhaust in accordance with the manufacturer's instructions, and proceed as follows if the CO percentage is not as specified.
8   If fitted, remove the tamperproof plug for access to the mixture adjustment screw. Slowly turn the mixture screw in the required

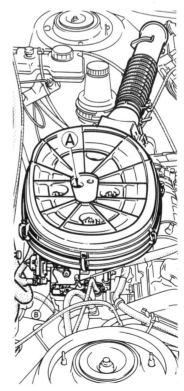

Fig. 3.14 Carburettor idle speed (A) and mixture (B) adjustment points (Sec 15)

direction to weaken or richen the mixture. The engine idle speed will change as this adjustment is made and this should therefore be readjusted as described previously in paragraph 6. Alternate the adjustments in this manner until the specified idle speed and CO percentage readings are obtained. During a prolonged adjustment, it will be necessary to occasionally blip the throttle to clear excess fuel in the inlet manifold so that correct readings can be obtained. Fit a new tamperproof plug on completion.

9   If an exhaust gas analyser is not available, but mixture adjustment is necessary, an approximate adjustment can be made as follows.

10 Turn the mixture screw to the position which provides the highest engine speed. Now reduce the engine speed to approximately 50 rpm above the specified idle speed.

11 Repeat the procedures outlined in paragraph 10, then screw in the mixture control screw to reduce the engine speed by 30 to 50 rpm. Further minor adjustment to the idle speed may be necessary to bring the engine speed to within the idle speed range specified.

16 Anti-stall system – checking and adjustment

1   This system is fitted to models from 1987 on fitted with power steering and/or air conditioning, the function of the system being to prevent the engine from stalling when under additional loading from these systems (eg steering moved to full lock at idle speed). The system operation and adjustment is as described below according to type.

Models with power steering

2   A pressostat mounted in the steering hydraulic circuit activates a solenoid valve, and this supplies manifold pressure to a butterfly opening device which increases the engine speed and prevents stalling. To check the system operation, use the following test method.

3   Detach the wiring connector from the pressostat unit, then connect a length of wire between the female terminals of the wiring connector. The engine speed should increase to between 1000 and 1100 rpm. If necessary, adjust to this speed by turning the adjuster screw (VA) shown in Fig. 3.15, then remove the bridging wire and reconnect the wiring connector to the pressostat.

Models with air conditioning

4   The system is similar to that used on models with power steering, but the solenoid valve is mounted on the compressor. When the compressor is started, the solenoid valve supplies manifold pressure to

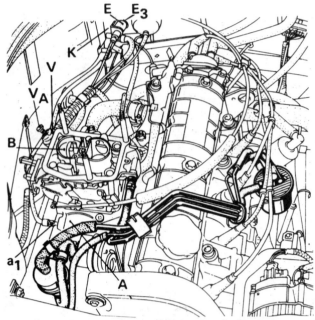

Fig. 3.15 Single-stage butterfly opening device components (Sec 16)

V	Single-stage opening device	E	Solenoid valve
VA	Opening device adjustment screw	E₃	Solenoid valve air filter
K	Solenoid valve mounting plate	B	Carburettor
		A	Inlet manifold
		a1	Manifold vacuum

the butterfly opening device on the carburettor to increase engine speed and prevent stalling.

5   The same check and adjustment method described for the system on models with power steering applies to the system on models with air conditioning, but note that the engine speed should be set to between 1400 and 1600 rpm. An additional check method can be used for the system on models with air conditioning, as follows.

6   Disconnect the wiring connections from the solenoid valve, then

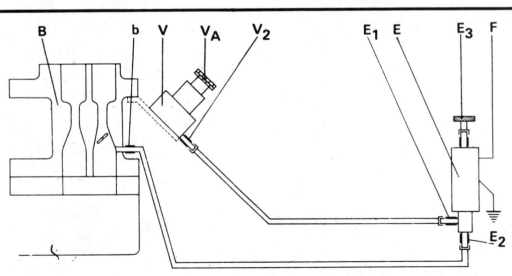

Fig. 3.16 Single-stage butterfly opening device system layout (schematic) (Sec 16)

V	Single stage opening device	V₂	Hose (marked blue)	E₃	Air filter	B	Carburettor
VA	Opening device adjustment screw	E	Solenoid valve	F	Power steering and/or air conditioning data	b	Hose (marked red)
		E₁	Hose (marked blue)				
		E₂	Hose (marked red)				

connect the valve directly to the battery earth and positive terminals, and check the increase in engine speed. If the speed is not as specified in paragraph 5, turn the adjusting screw as necessary.

7 Disconnect the leads from the battery, and reconnect the original wiring connections on completion.

Models with power steering and air conditioning

8 On these models, a two-stage butterfly opening device is used, each stage being separately controlled by its own solenoid in the system concerned. The two-stage device and its associated components are shown in Fig. 3.17.

9 When checking and adjusting either system, both systems must be checked as previously described in this Section, starting with the power steering system, then the air conditioning system.

10 The anti-stall speeds for the two systems should be as follows:

Power steering system – 1000 to 1100 rpm
Air conditioning system – 1400 to 1600 rpm

11 When checking the power steering system speed, disconnect the vacuum hose from the air conditioning system (V1 in Fig. 3.17). When checking the air conditioning system speed, disconnect the vacuum hose from the power steering system (V2 in Fig. 3.17).

17 Carburettor – removal and refitting

1 Remove the air cleaner unit as described in Part A, Section 3 of this Chapter.
2 Disconnect the throttle link rod (photo).
3 Disconnect the choke cable from the carburettor as described in Section 19.
4 Disconnect the fuel supply hose to the carburettor. Plug or clamp the hose to prevent leakage.
5 Disconnect the vacuum and coolant hoses from the carburettor. Clamp the coolant hoses to prevent leakage (photo).
6 Disconnect the crankcase breather hose.

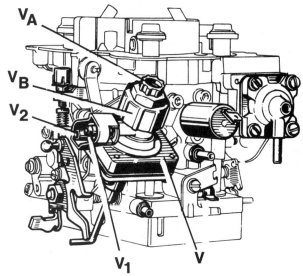

Fig. 3.17 Two-stage butterfly opening device components (Sec 16)

V Two-stage opening device	V_1 Take-off (for air
V_A Air conditioning system	conditioning)
adjustment screw	V_2 Take-off (for power
V_B Power steering system	steering)
adjustment screw	

7 Where applicable, disconnect the idle solenoid lead.
8 Remove the gasket from the air cleaner mating face on the top of the carburettor.
9 Undo and remove the four bolts securing the carburettor to the inlet manifold.

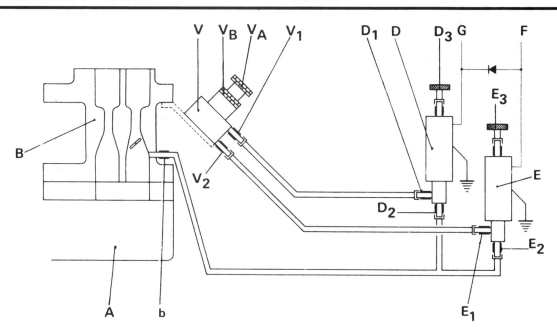

Fig. 3.18 Two-stage butterfly opening device system layout (schematic) (Sec 16)

V Two-stage opening device	E Power steering solenoid	D_1 Hose (marked grey)
V_A Air conditioning system	valve	D_2 Hose (marked white)
adjustment screw	E_1 Hose (marked blue)	D_3 Air filter
V_B Power steering system	E_2 Hose (marked red)	B Carburettor
adjustment screw	E_3 Air filter	A Inlet manifold
V_1 Take-off for air	F Power steering data	b Hose (marked red)
conditioning (marked grey)	G Air conditioning data	
V_2 Take-off for power steering	D Air conditioning solenoid	
(marked blue)	valve	

17.2 Disconnect the throttle link rod (arrowed)

17.5 Disconnect the hoses from the carburettor

17.11A Locate the new gasket piece over the dowels on the manifold face ...

17.11B ... then refit the carburettor

10 Lift the carburettor from the inlet manifold.
11 Refitting is a reversal of removal. A new gasket piece must be fitted between the manifold and the carburettor. Ensure that both mating surfaces are clean (photos).

18 Solex 28/34 Z10 carburettor – dismantling and reassembly

Note: *Little information was available at the time of writing regarding overhaul of the Solex 28/34 Z10 carburettor. The following will serve as a guide should dismantling and reassembly prove absolutely necessary.*
1 Invert the carburettor and remove the insulating flange from the base by removing its retaining screw (see photo 13.1D).
2 Thoroughly clean the exterior of the carburettor in clean petrol and then dry it, preferably using an air line.
3 Remove the cover bolt from the fuel inlet flange, remove the filter and wash the filter in clean fuel (see photo 14.3).
4 Remove the five retaining screws and carefully lift off the cover.
5 Carefully knock the pin from the float hinge brackets, remove the

float and the cover gasket (photo).
6 Check the float assembly for leaks (photo).
7 Remove the needle valve (photo) and check that the needle is free to move.
8 On refitting the float, check the float height with the cover inverted and the float resting lightly against the needle valve. Float height is the distance from the float cover with gasket in place, to the highest point of the float (photo).
9 Adjust the height by bending the tongue (B in photo 18.8).
10 Remove the idle cut-off solenoid (where applicable) and check its operation by connecting it to a 12 volt supply, switching on and seeing whether the needle is drawn in. If not the solenoid is defective and should be renewed.
11 Remove the three screws from the pneumatic full load enrichment unit and recover the spring, diaphragm and idle speed adjusting rod. Check the diaphragm for splits and renew if evident.
12 Remove the cover from the cold start diaphragm assembly (where applicable) and recover the spring, then unhook the diaphragm operating rod. Check the diaphragm for splits and renew if evident.
13 Remove the nut from the end of the throttle butterfly spindle, and remove the lever assembly and the float chamber ventilation valve.

Check that the face of the rubber valve is sound and in good condition, renewing as necessary.

14 Remove the cover from the accelerator pump, recover the spring and diaphragm and inspect the diaphragm as described previously.

15 Carefully lever out the accelerator pump injector and fuel feed pipe, then unscrew the air jets, which will give access to the main fuel jets which can be removed using a long thin screwdriver. Identify them for position.

16 Remove the mixture adjustment screw from the base flange of the carburettor. This will be hidden under a tamperproof plug which should be removed using a sharp instrument (photo).

17 If necessary, the auxiliary venturis may be pulled up out of the carburettor body by carefully using pliers.

18 Reassembly is a reversal of removal, bearing in mind the following points:

   (a) The auxiliary venturis must be located with their bores opposite the bores in the carburettor body. The first stage venturi has an interrupted bridge

   (b) The mixture screw should be screwed in lightly to its full extent, then backed off 1^1/2 to 2 turns. Do not refit the tamperproof cap until after the mixture has been set (Section 15).

   (c) Use a new O-ring seal under the head of the accelerator pump injector, and the idle solenoid.

19 Choke cable – removal and refitting

1 Remove the air cleaner unit for improved access to the cable at the carburettor end. Refer to Section 3 for details.

2 Release the choke outer cable from its support bracket on the carburettor by carefully prising the retaining clip tangs out of the bracket slots (photo).

3 Disconnect the cable end from the carburettor by prising the spring loop off the stud on the linkage (photo).

4 Undo the two retaining screws at the choke knob end, pull the cable through from inside the vehicle and disconnect the 'choke-on' warning light lead. An assistant may be required to help feed the cable through the bulkhead (photo).

5 Refitting is the reverse sequence to removal. Adjust the position of the outer cable in its carburettor support bracket clip as necessary so that the choke linkage opens fully when the knob is pushed in, and closes fully when the knob is pulled out.

20 Fuel pump – removal, testing and refitting

Note: *Refer to the warning note in Section 1 before proceeding*

1 Disconnect the battery negative terminal.

2 Note the location of the fuel inlet, outlet and return pipes and disconnect them from the pump.

3 Undo the two nuts and washers securing the pump to the engine and withdraw it from its location (photo).

4 Remove the insulating block and gaskets from the underside of the pump.

5 If the pump is suspected of malfunctioning, it can be tested as follows. If found to be faulty, the pump is not repairable and must therefore be renewed.

6 Refit the fuel inlet pipe to the pump and hold a wad of rag near the outlet. Operate the pump lever by hand and if the pump is in a satisfactory condition a strong jet of fuel be ejected from the pump outlet as the lever is released. If this is not the case, check that fuel will flow from the inlet pipe when it is held below tank level; if so the pump is faulty.

7 Before refitting the pump, thoroughly clean the pump and cylinder head mating faces.

8 Locate the gaskets and the insulator block over the pump studs on the cylinder head, then refit the pump and secure with the two nuts and washers.

9 Reconnect the fuel pipes to their original positions, as noted during removal. If crimp type retaining clips were used to secure the fuel pipes, these should be replaced by screw type clips.

18.5 Knock out the float hinge pin

18.6 Float assembly

18.7 Remove the needle valve (arrowed)

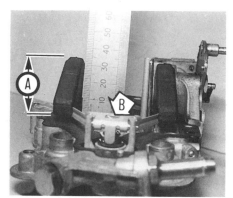

18.8 Measuring the float height (A). Bend tongue (B) to adjust if required

18.16 Mixture adjustment screw

19.2 Release the choke outer cable from its support bracket (retaining clip arrowed)

19.3 Prise the ring loop off the stud on the linkage

19.4 Choke cable removal

20.3 Fuel pump removal (fuel filter removed for clarity)

21 Fault diagnosis – carburettor fuel system

Unsatisfactory engine performance and excessive fuel consumption are not necessarily the fault of the fuel system. In fact they more commonly occur as a result of ignition and timing faults. Before acting on the following it is necessary to check the ignition system first. Even though a fault may lie in the fuel system it will be difficult to trace unless the ignition is correct. The faults below, therefore, assume that this has been attended to first (where appropriate).

Symptom	Reason(s)
Smell of petrol when engine is stopped	Leaking fuel lines or unions Leaking fuel tank
Smell of petrol when engine is idling	Leaking fuel line unions between pump and carburettor Overflow of fuel from float chamber due to wrong level setting, ineffective needle valve or punctured float
Excessive fuel consumption for reasons not covered by leaks or float chamber faults	Worn jets Over-rich setting Sticking mechanism Dirty air cleaner element Sticking air cleaner thermostatic mechanism
Difficult starting, uneven running, lack of power, cutting out	One or more jets blocked or restricted Float chamber fuel level too low or needle valve sticking Fuel pump not delivering sufficient fuel Faulty solenoid fuel shut-off valve Induction leak
Difficult starting when cold	Choke malfunction Weak mixture
Difficult starting when hot	Choke malfunction Accelerator pedal pumped before starting Vapour lock (especially in hot weather or at high altitude) Rich mixture
Engine does not respond properly to throttle	Faulty accelerator pump Blocked jet(s) Slack in accelerator cable
Engine idle speed drops when hot	Overheated fuel pump
Engine runs on	Faulty fuel cut-off valve

PART C: RENIX FUEL INJECTION SYSTEM

22 Description

This fuel system is of the pressure/speed type. The quantity of fuel injected is determined by both the vacuum in the inlet manifold and the engine speed.

The inlet vacuum pressure controls the basic injection time which is then corrected to suit other engine conditions and requirements. These include coolant temperature, air temperature, battery voltage and atmospheric pressure.

The Renix system also calculates the ignition advance requirements to suit any particular set of engine conditions.

A computer controls both the fuel injection and ignition systems.

A warning light on the instrument panel will illuminate should a fault develop in the Renix system.

23 Maintenance

1 Renew the air cleaner element at the specified intervals given in the

'Routine maintenance' Section at the start of this manual. Refer to Part A, Section 3 of this Chapter for details.

2 Remove and renew the fuel filter at the specified intervals. Refer to Section 24 for details.

3 Periodically inspect the fuel injection system lines and hoses (fuel, air and vacuum) to ensure that they are in good condition and securely attached.

24 Fuel filter – removal and refitting

1 The fuel filter is located adjacent to the electric fuel pump on the underside of the vehicle, inboard of the right-hand rear suspension mounting. For access, raise the vehicle at the rear and support on safety stands (photo).

2 Disconnect the battery earth lead.

3 Clamp the inlet and outlet hose each side of the filter to prevent fuel leakage, then disconnect the hoses from the filter by releasing their retaining clips.

4 Undo the retaining clamp nut, release the clamp and remove the filter.

5 Fit the new filter making sure that the direction of flow arrow marked on its body is pointing towards the engine, and the plastic sleeve is fitted between the filter and the clamp.

Fig. 3.19 General view of engine compartment showing positions of main injection and ignition system components
(Sec 22)

1 Coolant temperature sensor	4 Computer casing	7 Throttle switch	10 Diagnostic socket
2 Engine angular	5 Air cleaner unit	8 Air temperature sensor	11 Ignition module
position/speed sensor	6 Throttle casing	9 Idle speed air regulator valve	12 Distributor (ignition)
3 Computer		

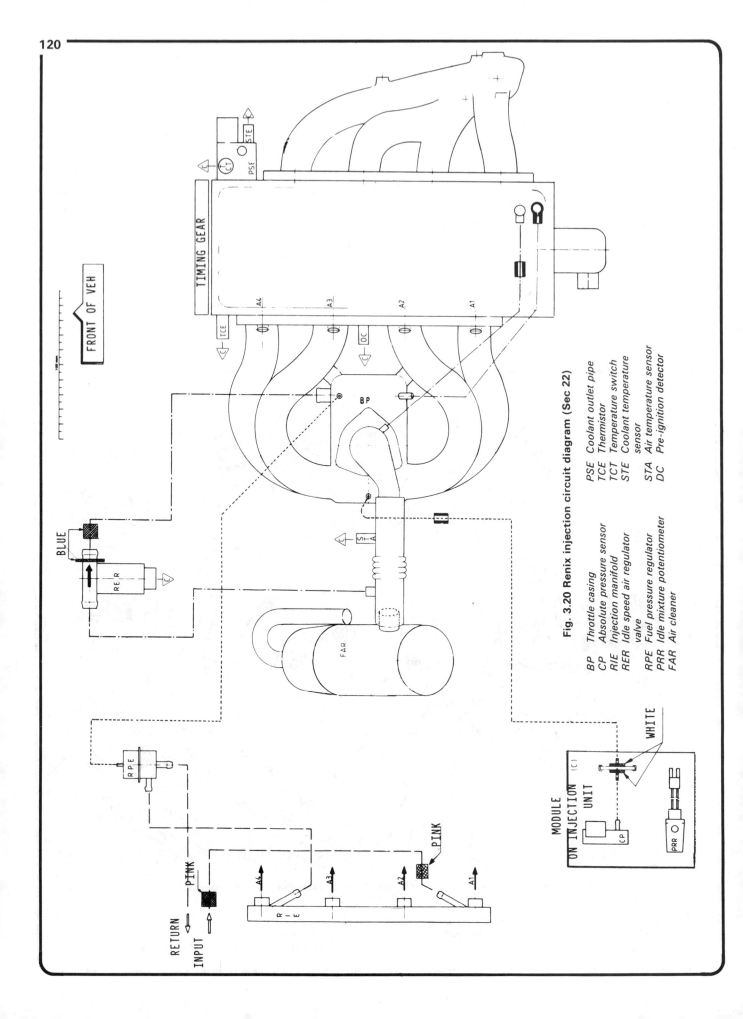

Fig. 3.20 Renix injection circuit diagram (Sec 22)

BP Throttle casing
CP Absolute pressure sensor
RIE Injection manifold
RER Idle speed air regulator valve
RPE Fuel pressure regulator
PRR Idle mixture potentiometer
FAR Air cleaner

PSE Coolant outlet pipe
TCE Thermistor
TCT Temperature switch
STE Coolant temperature sensor
STA Air temperature sensor
DC Pre-ignition detector

24.1 Underside view of the fuel filter (1), fuel pump (2) and pulse damper (3)

25 Fuel pump – removal and refitting

1 The fuel pump unit is mounted on the same plate as the fuel filter (see paragraph 1 of the previous Section).
2 The removal procedure is similar to that described previously for the fuel filter, but in addition, fold back the rubber covers and disconnect the wiring connectors.
3 Refitting is a reversal of the removal procedure. Ensure that the wiring connections are secure. Renew the hoses if they are perished or in poor condition.
4 If required, the fuel pulse damper, located between the pump and the filter, can be removed and refitted in the same manner as that described for the filter in Section 24.

26 Fuel injection system – adjustments

1 As mentioned previously, the Renix type fuel injection system is managed by the computer unit and therefore no manual adjustments are normally required. However the following checks and adjustments are possible if required. If checking the idle mixture adjustment, an exhaust gas analyser will be required.

Idle speed

2 The idle speed cannot be altered as it is controlled by an air regulating solenoid valve monitored by a power module and throttle switch to form an electronic idling system.
3 Main components of this system comprise a computer, an air regulating valve located at the front left-hand side of the engine near the alternator, and a three-position throttle switch.
4 The computer incorporates an integrated idling adjustment circuit.
5 The air regulating (idle speed adjusting) valve consists of two coils which are fed by signals which position the valve between the closed and fully open position according to requirements.
6 The computer controls the idle speed – faster at cold start and then reducing it as the engine warms up.

Idle mixture

7 The engine must be at its normal running temperature for this check and an exhaust gas analyser (CO meter) should be connected in accordance with the manufacturer's instructions.
8 Remove the cover from the computer unit, then detach the idle mixture adjustment potentiometer (see Fig. 3.22).

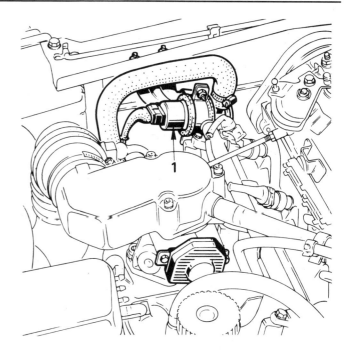

Fig. 3.21 Idle speed air regulator valve location (1) (Sec 26)

9 Remove the tamperproof cap by prising it free, then using a suitable screwdriver, turn the adjustment screw as required to set the idle mixture at the specified CO level.
10 Refit the potentiometer tamperproof cap on completion, then refit the potentiometer and the computer cover.

27 Component testing

Note: *An ohmmeter will be needed for full component testing*

Fuel injectors

1 Disconnect the wiring plugs from the injectors.
2 Remove the injection manifold (see Section 30), leaving the fuel hoses connected, and place each injector in turn over a small container. Ensure that the manifold is held securely.
3 Switch on the ignition; there should be no ejection of fuel. Now apply battery voltage to each injector in turn; fuel should be ejected.
4 Refit the injection manifold, and reconnect the wiring plugs.

Coolant temperature sensor

5 Remove the sensor from the engine and leave it to stabilise for ten minutes (refer to Section 33 for removal details).
6 Now measure its resistance with an ohmmeter. At a temperature of between 19 and 21°C (66 and 70°F) resistance should be between 2.2 and 2.8 Kohms. At a temperature of between 79 and 81°C (174 and 178°F) resistance should be between 0.28 and 0.37 Kohms.

Air temperature sensor

7 Place an accurate thermometer in the air cleaner air intake as a means of measuring the sensor temperature level.
8 Using an ohmmeter, check the resistance using the following table (photo).

Temperature	Resistance (Kohms)
0°C (32°F)	254 to 266
20°C (68°F)	283 to 297
40°C (104°F)	315 to 329

Absolute pressure sensor

9 First check the vacuum pipe and its connections, also make sure that the calibrated jet is correctly located.
10 Check for continuity between terminal (A) on the sensor connector

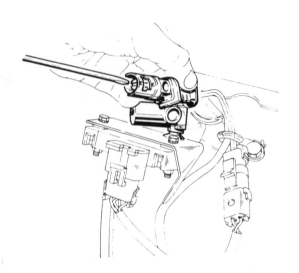

Fig. 3.22 Fuel mixture potentiometer adjustment screw
(Sec 26)

Fig. 3.23 Air temperature sensor removed (Sec 27)

and terminal (17) on the computer connector (Fig. 3.24).
11 Check the computer earth between terminals 1, 2 and 10 and a
good earth.

28 Three position throttle switch – removal, refitting and adjustment

1   The switch can be removed if the wiring plug is pulled off and the
two fixing screws removed (photo).
2   When refitting, align the flat on the switch to coincide with the flat
on the throttle butterfly spindle and then move it in the direction of the
arrow until the light throttle 'click' is heard.
3   Tighten the fixing screws.
4   A check of the throttle switch operation can be made using an
ohmmeter and a set of feeler gauges as follows.
5   When the throttle is set at the normal idle speed position the
clearance 'X' in Fig. 3.25 should be 1 mm (0.039 in). With the throttle
in this position, use the ohmmeter to measure the resistance across the
switch terminals. The resistance across terminals A and B should be O,
and the resistance across terminals B and C should be infinite.
6   Move the throttle to the part open position. The clearance 'X'
should be 1.2 mm (0.047 in) and the resistance across terminals A and
B, and terminals B and C should be infinite.
7   Fully open the throttle. With the upper throttle plate open by 70°,
the throttle plate-to-body clearance should be 22 mm (0.858 in). Use
a gauge rod or twist drill to check this clearance. The resistance across
terminals A and B should be infinite, and the resistance across
terminals B and C should be O.
8   If in any of the preceding tests the resistance measured is not as
specified, then the switch is faulty and should be renewed.

29 Throttle casing – removal and refitting

1   Detach the throttle link rod by carefully prising it free at the balljoint
(photo). Disconnect the throttle switch wire connector.

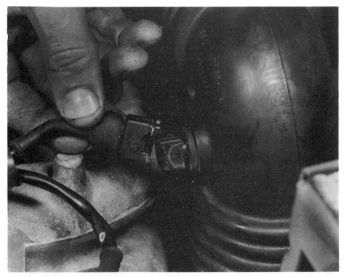

27.8 Air temperature sensor and wiring connector

28.1 Three position throttle switch

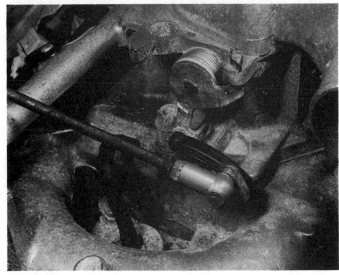

29.1 Disconnect the throttle link rod at the balljoint

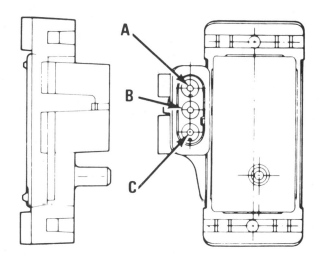

Fig. 3.24 Absolute pressure sensor and terminals (Sec 27)

A   Earth
B   Output voltage
C   + 5V

2 Unclip and remove the air intake duct and the crankcase ventilation hose from the throttle casing.
3 Undo the three retaining screws and remove the air intake casing and the throttle casing.
4 Clean the mating surfaces and refit in the reverse order of removal. New sealing gaskets must always be fitted during reassembly and the crankcase ventilation hose should be inspected before refitting to ensure that its orifice is clear.

30 Fuel injection manifold – removal and refitting

1 Disconnect the wiring plugs from the fuel injectors (photo).
2 Disconnect the fuel hoses from the injection manifold.
3 Unscrew the manifold fixing bolts and remove the manifold.
4 The injectors are held to the manifold by a clamp for each pair of injectors. Remove the clamps.
5 When refitting, fit new 'O'-ring seals (4), and also new caps (5 – Fig. 3.28) if necessary.

30.1 Fuel injectors, injection manifold and injector wiring plugs

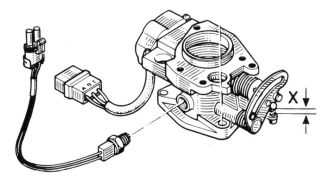

Fig. 3.25 Checking the throttle switch operation (Sec 28)

For X see text

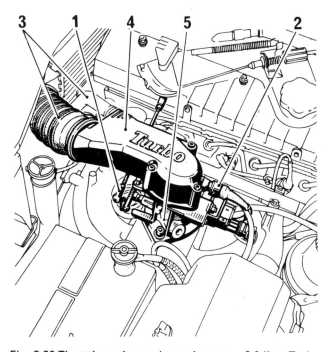

Fig. 3.26 Throttle casing and attachments – 2.0 litre Turbo model (Sec 29)

1 Throttle link rod
2 Air temperature sensor connector
3 Air intake ducts
4 Throttle casing cover
5 Throttle casing

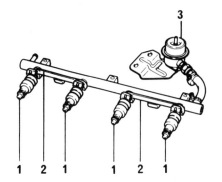

Fig. 3.27 Fuel injection manifold (Sec 30)

1 Injectors
2 Securing clamps
3 Fuel pressure regulator

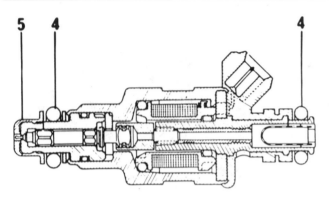

Fig. 3.28 Sectional view of fuel injector (Sec 30)

4   O-rings   5   Cap

31 Air induction manifold – removal and refitting

1   Disconnect the battery earth lead.
2   Detach the throttle link rod at the balljoint.
3   Remove the fuel injection manifold as described in Section 30.
4   Remove the throttle casing as described in Section 29.
5   Unbolt and remove the air regulating valve from the front end face of the manifold.
6   Detach the clutch cable and grommet from their location bracket on the manifold.
7   Disconnect the remaining hoses and wires from the manifold. Note the connection point of each to avoid the possibility of confusion when reassembling.
8   Unbolt and remove the manifold.
10 Refit the manifold in the reverse order of removal. Ensure that the mating surfaces are perfectly clean and be sure to use a new gasket. Ensure that all hoses and wires are connected in their previously noted locations.

32 Fuel pressure regulator – removal and refitting

1   This is located on the inlet manifold side of the engine, just below the front of the throttle housing (photo).
2   If available, fit suitable clamps to the fuel hoses to prevent fuel leakage when the hoses are disconnected from the regulator. Failing this, the hoses will need to be plugged as they are detached, so have suitable plugs ready.
3   Unclip and detach the fuel and vacuum hoses from the regulator unit, then undo the retaining screws and remove the regulator unit.
4   Refit in the reverse order of removal.

33 Sensors – removal and refittings

Coolant temperature sensor

1   This should only be removed when the engine is cold.
2   Disconnect the electrical leads.
3   Remove the expansion tank cap to release any pressure in the cooling system.
4   Unscrew the sensor and quickly plug the hole to minimise coolant loss (photo).
5   Smear the threads with a little gasket cement before screwing in the new sensor.

Air temperature sensor

6   Disconnect the wiring plug from the sensor.
7   Remove the air intake duct from the throttle casing.
8   Remove the sensor.
9   Refitting is a reversal of removal.

Absolute pressure sensor

10 Remove the cover from the computer.

32.1 Fuel pressure regulator (arrowed)

33.4 Coolant temperature sensor location (arrowed)

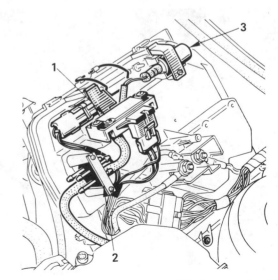

Fig. 3.29 Absolute pressure sensor (1), 4-way union (2), and idle mixture adjustment potentiometer (3) (Sec 33)

11 Disconnect the wiring harness connector, then withdraw the absolute pressure sensor from the support. Detach the pipe at the four-way union and then lever off the pipe at the sensor. Do not pull on the pipe to detach it.
12 Refitting is a reversal of removal.

Engine angular position/speed sensor

13 This sensor is located on the transmission bellhousing, and measures the flywheel angular position and speed (see Chapter 1, photo 49.8).
14 To remove the sensor, disconnect the wiring plug, and remove the two sensor retaining bolts.
15 Refitting is a reversal of removal. No adjustment is necessary.

Pre-ignition detector

16 Disconnect the wiring from the air temperature sensor.
17 Detach the air cleaner-to-air intake casing duct and remove the air cleaner.
18 Disconnect the wiring, then unscrew the pre-ignition detector.
19 Refit in the reverse order of removal.

---

34 Idle mixture potentiometer – removal and refitting

1 This device is located with the absolute pressure sensor under the computer cover (see Fig. 3.29).
2 Remove the cover from the computer, undo the idle mixture potentiometer retaining screw, detach the wiring connector and remove the potentiometer.
3 Refit in the reverse order of removal. Ensure that the potentiometer is positioned correctly with the tamperproof cap on the opposite side to that of the retaining lug.
4 After refitting, adjust the idle mixture as described in Section 26.

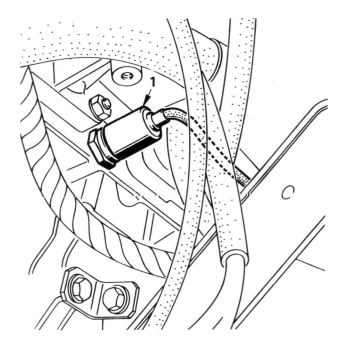

Fig. 3.30 Pre-ignition detector (1) (Sec 33)

---

35 Fault diagnosis – Renix fuel injection system

Symptom	Reason(s)
Engine will not start or starts then stops	Defective injection system relay Faulty fuel pump Leak in intake system Defective fuel injectors Defective absolute pressure sensor Defective engine angular position/speed sensor Defective ignition power module Defective coolant temperature sensor Defective computer Wiring fault
Uneven idling	Throttle not closing Low fuel pressure Defective fuel injector Leak in air intake system Defective or incorrectly adjusted idle mixture potentiometer
Poor acceleration	Defective or incorrectly adjusted idle mixture potentiometer Leak in air intake system Defective computer Wiring fault
Misfiring	Poor central earth connection
Excessive fuel usage	Defective injectors High fuel pressure Defective coolant temperature sensor Defective computer Wiring fault Defective air temperature sensor

PART D: TURBOCHARGER

36 Description

1   A Garrett T3 turbocharger is used on the engine fitted to 2.0 litre Turbo models. The turbocharger uses the exhaust gas pressure to drive a turbine which pressurises the intake system. This increases engine efficiency and power.

2   The turbocharger is mounted directly above the exhaust manifold. A cooling circuit operating under pressure from the main cooling system passes coolant through the turbocharger unit to assist in cooling the central turbine bearing. When the engine is switched off, a separate electric coolant pump switches on for a few minutes to prevent the turbine bearing from overheating.

3   To assist the main engine cooling system, an additional electric cooling fan is fitted in front of the radiator. The two units are thermostatically-controlled and run in unison.

4   The air intake system incorporates two air-to-air intercoolers, one located at the bottom of the air cleaner, the other adjacent to the radiator.

5   Regulation of boost pressure is achieved by an exhaust system wastegate operated by a pressure sensor in the intake manifold.

6   A bypass circuit prevents the turbocharger supplying boost during deceleration (photo).

7   A safety feature is the provision of a pressure sensor to cut the fuel supply off if boost pressure becomes excessive.

8   Engine oil is cooled by passing it through a cooler incorporated in the oil filter base (photo).

9   The fuel system used on Turbo versions is the Renix Type described in Part C of this Chapter.

10   The locations of the system main components are shown in Fig. 3.31 and the accompanying photo. The system hoses and sensors are shown in Figs. 3.32 and 3.33.

11   Testing and adjustment of the turbocharger system can only be carried out by a Renault dealer, as special gauges and adaptors are required.

37 Turbocharger – removal and refitting

1   Remove the air cleaner unit with reference to Part A, Section 3 of this Chapter.

2   Unbolt and remove the heat shield (photo).

3   Detach the remove the turbocharger air intake and outlet hoses.

4   Drain the cooling system (Chapter 2), or clamp the coolant hoses securely so that they cannot leak when disconnected. Unclip and detach the coolant hoses from the turbocharger unit (photo).

5   Disconnect the oil feed and return pipes, and the turbocharger mounting strut (photo).

6   Undo the retaining nuts and detach the right-angled elbow from the exhaust downpipe and the turbocharger.

7   To unscrew the turbocharger retaining nuts a special spanner (Facom No 40 or similar) will be required – see Fig. 3.35. Undo the nuts and remove the turbocharger.

8   Prior to refitting the turbocharger, ensure that the joint faces of the turbocharger and manifold are thoroughly clean.

9   The following items must be renewed when refitting the turbocharger unit:

  (a) The turbocharger-to-manifold self-locking nuts
  (b) The turbocharger-to-manifold joint face O-ring seal
  (c) The oil feed and return pipe seals

10   Refit the turbocharger in the reverse order of removal, tightening the retaining bolts to the specified torque.

11   Before reconnecting the oil feed pipe, prime the turbocharger unit with engine oil through the inlet aperture. Disconnect three-way connector from the ignition power module and then operate the starter motor until oil starts to run out of the hole. Reconnect the oil feed pipe union with a new sealing gasket.

12   Reconnect the three-way connector and then run the engine at idling speed for a few minutes to re-establish the oil flow.

13   Never run the engine with the air intake system disconnected.

36.6 Deceleration air bypass valve

36.8 Engine oil filter and oil cooler connections

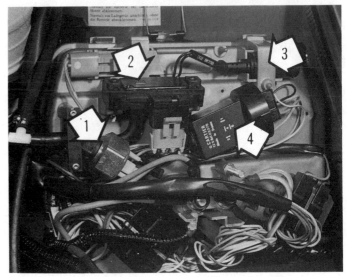

36.10 Boost pressure limiting pressostat (1), absolute pressure sensor (2), mixture adjustment potentiometer (3) and electric cooling pump timer relay (4) (computer cover removed)

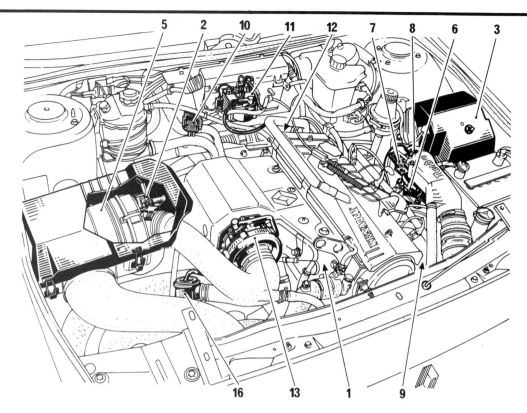

Fig. 3.31 Turbocharger and associated components (Sec 36)

1 Coolant temperature sensor
2 Boost pressure regulating solenoid valve
3 Computer unit
5 Air cleaner
6 Throttle casing
7 Throttle switch
8 Air temperature sensor
9 Idle speed air regulator valve
10 Diagnostic socket
11 Ignition module
12 Distributor
13 Turbocharger
16 Air bypass valve

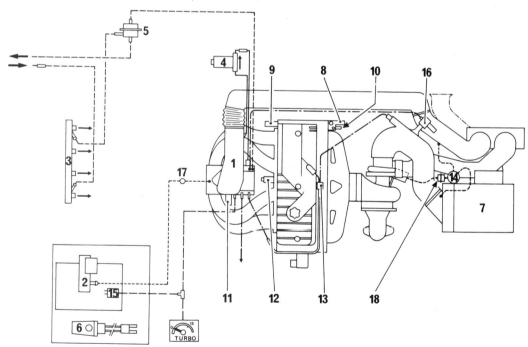

Fig. 3.32 Turbocharger system hoses and sensors (schematic) (Sec 36)

1 Throttle casing
2 Absolute pressure sensor
3 Fuel injection manifold
4 Idle speed air regulator valve
5 Fuel pressure regulator
6 Idle mixture adjustment potentiometer
7 Air cleaner
8 Coolant outlet pipe
9 Thermistor
10 Coolant temperature sensor
11 Air temperature sensor
12 Pre-ignition sensor
13 Valve
14 Boost pressure solenoid valve
15 Boost pressure limiting pressostat
16 Air bypass valve
17 Restrictor (1.5 mm diameter)
18 Air cleaner resonator

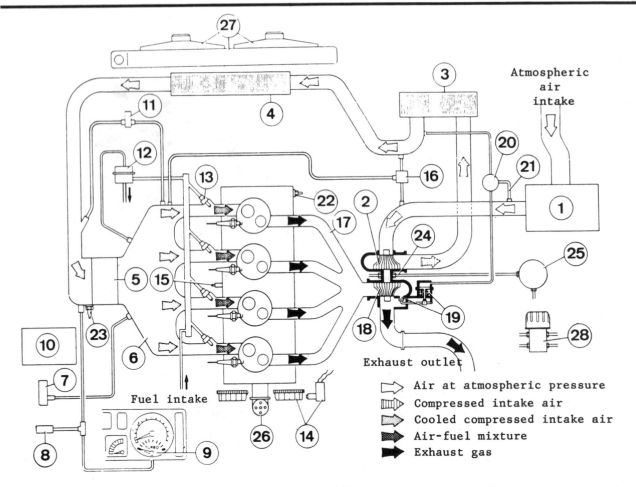

Fig. 3.33 Fuel injection and turbocharger system layout (Sec 36)

1 Air cleaner	9 Boost pressure gauge	16 Air bypass valve	22 Coolant temperature sensor
2 Turbocharger compressor	10 Computer	17 Exhaust manifold	23 Air temperature sensor
3 Air-to-air intercooler	11 Idle speed air regulator valve	18 Turbocharger turbine	24 Turbocharger bearing
4 Air-to-air intercooler	12 Fuel pressure regulator	19 Turbocharger wastegate	cooling system
5 Throttle casing	13 Injectors	20 Boost pressure regulating	25 Electric coolant pump
6 Inlet manifold	14 Engine angular	solenoid valve	26 Distributor
7 Air pressure sensor	position/speed sensor	21 Variable 'leak' from solenoid	27 Radiator
8 Boost pressure limiting	15 Pre-ignition sensor	valve 20	28 Oil cooler
pressostat			

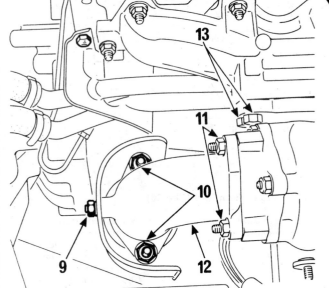

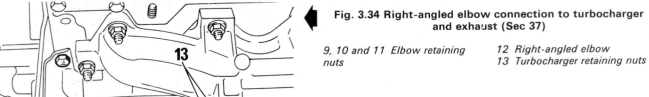

Fig. 3.34 Right-angled elbow connection to turbocharger and exhaust (Sec 37)

9, 10 and 11 Elbow retaining nuts

12 Right-angled elbow
13 Turbocharger retaining nuts

Fig. 3.35 Special spanner (Focom No 40) for turbocharger retaining nuts (Sec 37)

37.2 Remove the heat shield (arrowed)

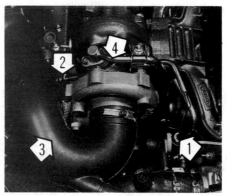

37.4 Turbocharger unit hose connections – coolant hoses (1 and 2), air intake hose (3), and oil feed pipe (4)

37.5 Underside view of turbocharger unit showing oil return pipe (1), mounting strut (2) and wastegate actuator (3)

38 Turbocharger wastegate actuator – adjusting, removal and refitting

1 The wastegate actuator, when correctly adjusted, is vital to the correct operation of the turbocharger.

2 Due to the need for special gauges, it is not possible for the home mechanic to adjust it, but for information purposes, if the wastegate actuator adjusting rod locknut is released and the end fitting screwed further onto the rod, the turbocharger pressure is increased. If it is unscrewed, the pressure is reduced.

3 To remove the wastegate actuator, first disconnect the oil supply and return pipes from the turbocharger as described in the preceding Section.

4 Disconnect the hose from the wastegate actuator.

5 Extract the circlip (2 – Fig. 3.36) and disconnect the adjusting rod (3) from the valve operating arm (6).

6 Unscrew and remove the mounting bolts (4) and withdraw the wastegate actuator by rotating it and passing it downwards beside the turbocharger.

7 Refitting is a reversal of the removal procedure.

39 Boost pressure solenoid valve – removal and refitting

1 Remove the air cleaner outer cover.

2 Detach the wiring connector and the air hoses from the valve unit. Mark and take note of the hose positions as they are disconnected to ensure correct refitting (photo).

3 Detach the solenoid valve and remove it together with its mounting.

4 Refit in the reverse order of removal, ensuring that the hoses are correctly reconnected as noted during removal.

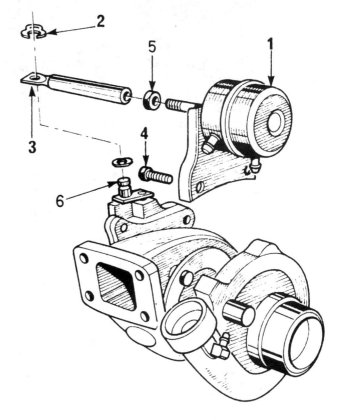

Fig. 3.36 Turbocharger wastegate actuator (Sec 38)

1 Wastegate actuator	4 Fixing bolt
2 Circlip	5 Locknut
3 Threaded rod	6 Wastegate operating arm

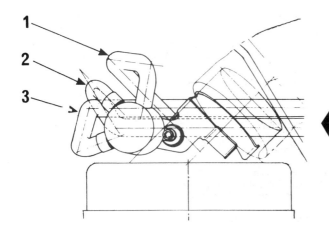

Fig. 3.37 Boost pressure solenoid valve hose connections (Sec 39)

| 1 Air outlet | 3 Wastegate actuator outlet |
| 2 Air-to-air intercooler outlet | |

40 Air-to-air intercoolers – removal and refitting

1   Two air-to-air intercoolers are fitted, one located under the air cleaner, the other adjacent to the radiator.

2   To remove the intercooler from under the air cleaner, first remove the air cleaner unit and mounting, then detach the air ducts, unclip the retaining strap and withdraw the intercooler from the housing (photo).

3   Refit in the reverse order of temoval.

4   To remove the intercooler from adjacent to the radiator, first remove the front grill and the upper crossmember for access.

5   Undo the retaining clips, detach the unit and lift it clear.

6   Refit in the reverse order of removal.

39.2 Detach the wiring connector from the boost pressure solenoid valve

40.3 Intercooler mounted under air cleaner

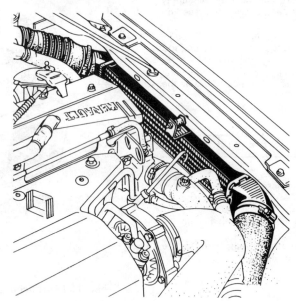

Fig. 3.38 Air-to-air intercooler location adjacent to radiator
(Sec 40)

41 Fault diagnosis – turbocharger

Symptom	Reason(s)
Noisy operation	Worn bearings Intake or exhaust leaks Poor lubrication
Poor acceleration	Air filter clogged Wastegate actuator faulty Leaks in manifold or ducts
Blue smoke in exhaust	Internal oil seals leaking

Chapter 4 Ignition system

Contents

Specifications

System type .... Breakerless, computer controlled

Distributor
Make .... Renix
Direction of rotation .... Anti-clockwise
Firing order .... 1-3-4-2 (No 1 cylinder nearest flywheel)

Ignition timing (with vacuum disconnected)
1.7 litre engine .... 5 to 9° BTDC at idle speed
2.0 litre engine .... Computer controlled

Spark plugs
Type:
    1.7 litre .... Champion N279YC
    2.0 litre non-Turbo .... Champion S6YC
    2.0 litre Turbo .... Eyquem 803 LJSP
Electrode gap:
    Non-Turbo models .... 0.8 mm (0.031 in)
    Turbo models .... 0.6 mm (0.023 in)

Torque wrench settings	Nm	lbf ft
Spark plugs:		
1.7 litre engine	20	15
2.0 litre engine	25	18

1 General description

The electronic ignition system operates on an advanced principle whereby the main functions of the distributor are replaced by a computer module.

The system consists of three main components, namely the computer module which incorporates an ignition coil and a vacuum advance unit, the distributor, which directs the HT voltage received from the coil to the appropriate spark plug, and an angular position/speed sensor which determines the position and speed of the crankshaft by sensing special teeth on the flywheel periphery.

The computer module receives information on crankshaft position relative to TDC and BDC and also engine speed from the angular position/speed sensor, and receives information on engine load from the vacuum advance unit. From these constantly changing variables,

the computer calculates the precise instant at which HT voltage should be supplied and triggers the coil accordingly. The voltage then passes from the coil to the appropriate spark plug, via the distributor in the conventional way. The functions of the centrifugal and vacuum advance mechanisms, as well as the contact breaker points normally associated with a distributor, are all catered for by the computer module, so that the sole purpose of the distributor is to direct the HT voltage from the coil to the appropriate spark plug.

Depending on model, the computer also receives information on the engine coolant temperature and the engine oil temperature, and this information is then collated together with the other factors to control the ignition advance as required.

On Turbo models, a pre-ignition sensor is fitted in the cylinder head. In the event of pre-ignition ('pinking'), the ignition timing is retarded by the computer to compensate.

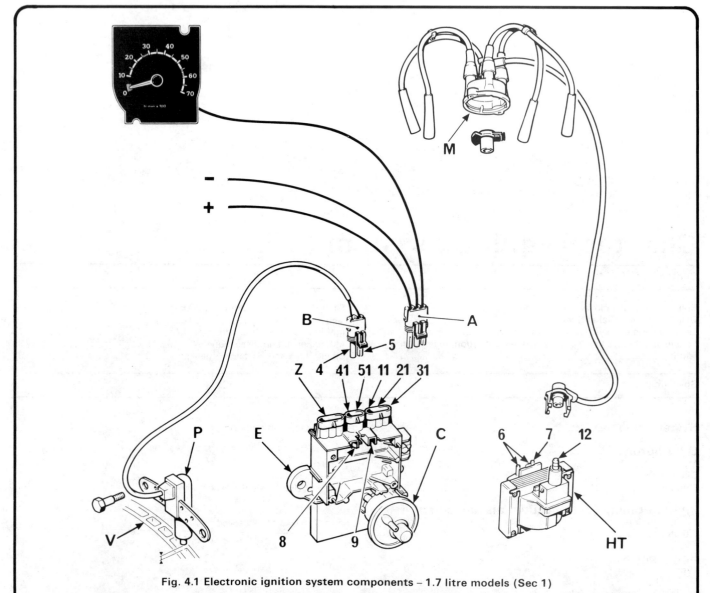

Fig. 4.1 Electronic ignition system components – 1.7 litre models (Sec 1)

4	Sensor winding	9	Coil – switch	51	Sensor information	V	Flywheel

4   Sensor winding
5   Sensor winding
6   Coil + terminal and suppressor capacitor terminal
7   Coil – terminal
8   Coil + switch

9   Coil – switch
11 Computer + input
12 Secondary pin
21 Computer earth
31 Rev counter output
41 Sensor information

51 Sensor information
M   Distributor cap
HT HT coil
C   Vacuum capsule
E   Computer
P   Angular position/speed

V   Flywheel
A   Feed connector
B   Sensor connector
Z   Coolant and engine oil temperature sensor information (not all models)

Terminals 8 and 11 are directly interconnected within the unit

2 Electronic ignition system – precautions

Note: *Due to the sophisticated nature of the electronic ignition system the following precautions must be observed to prevent damage to the components and reduce the risk of personal injury.*

1 Ensure that the ignition is switched off before disconnecting any of the ignition wiring.
2 Ensure that the ignition is switched off before connecting or disconnecting any ignition test equipment such as a timing light.
3 Do not connect a suppression condenser or test lamp to the ignition coil negative terminal.
4 Do not connect any test appliance or stroboscopic timing light requiring a 12 volt supply to the ignition coil positive terminal.
5 Do not allow an HT lead to short out or spark against the computer module body.

3 Maintenance and inspection

1 The only components of the electronic ignition system which require periodic maintenance are the distributor cap, HT leads and spark plugs. These should be treated in the same way as on a conventional system and reference should be made to Section 8.
2 At the intervals specified in *'Routine maintenance'* at the start of this manual, clean or renew the spark plugs and check the high tension (HT) leads.
3 Remove the distributor cap and inspect it for cracks, and the condition of the centre carbon brush.
4 Check the rotor contact end and the cap contacts for erosion. They may be cleaned carefully to remove deposits but, if badly eroded, renew the components.
5 On this system dwell angle and ignition timing are a function of the computer module and there is no provision for adjustment. It is possible to check the ignition timing on 1.7 litre models using a stroboscopic timing light, but this should only be necessary as part of a

fault finding procedure, as any deviation from the specified setting would indicate a possible fault in the computer module.

4 Distributor – removal and refitting

1 On all models, the distributor simply comprises a rotor arm driven from the end of the camshaft, and a distributor cap attached to the end face of the cylinder head.
2 To remove the distributor cap, undo the retaining screws and withdraw it together with the HT leads (photos).
3 The rotor arm and shield can now be pulled free and removed (photos).
4 On 2.0 litre models, undo the three retaining screws to remove the rotor housing if required (photo). If necessary renew the O-ring seal.
5 Wipe clean the cap and leads. If the camshaft oil seal requires renewal, refer to Chapter 1.
6 Carefully inspect the HT leads and cap for signs of deterioration. Check the cap for hairline cracks, and the electrodes for excessive wear. Renew if necessary.
7 Refit in the reverse order of removal. When fitting the rotor arm, ensure that its single inner tooth engages with the slot in the end of the camshaft (photo).

5 Computer unit – removal and refitting

1 The computer unit is located in the engine compartment on the left-hand side just forward of the suspension turret. Whenever the computer unit is removed, handle it with care as it is fragile and easily damaged.
2 Disconnect the battery earth lead.
3 On 1.7 litre models proceed as follows. Disconnect the vacuum hose and the wiring connectors, noting their respective locations. Undo the retaining nuts and remove the unit (photo). If required the

4.2A Distributor cap – 1.7 litre model

4.2B Distributor cap – 2.0 litre model

4.3A Rotor arm and shield – 1.7 litre model

4.3B Rotor arm and shield – 2.0 litre model

4.3C Removing the shield – 2.0 litre model

4.4 Rotor housing retaining screws (arrowed) – 2.0 litre model

4.7 Rotor engagement slot in camshaft (arrowed) – 1.7 litre model

5.3 Ignition computer unit location (coil arrowed) – 1.7 litre model

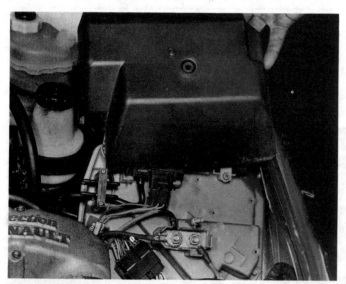

5.4A Removing the computer unit outer casing – 2.0 litre model

5.4B Computer unit location within plastic case – 2.0 litre model

coil can be removed as decribed in Section 7. Do not attempt to remove the vacuum unit.

4   On 2.0 litre models proceed as follows. Undo the retaining screw and remove the outer casing from the computer unit. Release the retaining clip at the top and undo the retaining screw at the bottom, then withdraw the plastic case containing the computer unit (photos).

5   On all models, if removing the unit completely from the car, trace the routeings of the wiring harnesses and disconnect their connectors. Note the positions of the harnesses and connectors to avoid confusion when refitting.

6   Refitting is a reversal of the removal procedure.

6   Engine angular position/speed sensor – description, removal and refitting

1   An angular position/speed sensor is used to monitor the TDC and BDC positions of the crankshaft from the tooth gaps on the periphery of the flywheel (or driveplate).

2   The sensor is secured to the bellhousing by special shouldered bolts and its position is preset in production to provide the required clearance. No adjustment of this clearance is necessary or possible.

3   To remove the sensor, proceed as follows.

4   Disconnect the battery negative terminal.

5   Disconnect the smaller of the two wiring multi-plugs from the front of the computer module.

6   Undo and remove the two bolts securing the sensor to the top of the clutch bellhousing and lift off the sensor. Note that the two retaining bolts are of the shouldered type and must not be replaced with ordinary bolts. When handling the sensor, take care not to damage it.

7   Refitting is the reverse sequence to removal.

7   Ignition coil – removal and refitting

1   The location of the ignition coil is dependent on model. On 1.7 litre models it is attached to the computer unit mounted forward of the left-hand suspension turret (see Section 5). Whilst on 2.0 litre models it is attached to the engine compartment bulkhead. In each case the removal procedure is the same (photos).

2   Disconnect the HT and LT wires from the coil unit, then undo the retaining nuts or bolts (as applicable) and remove the coil units from

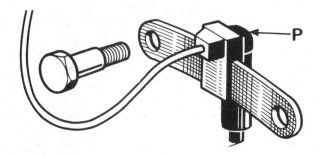

Fig. 4.2 Angular position/speed sensor (P) and special bolt
(Sec 6)

7.1A Ignition coil – 2.0 litre non-Turbo model

7.1B Ignition coil (arrowed) – 2.0 litre Turbo model

8 Spark plugs and HT leads – general

1   The correct functioning of the spark plugs is vital for the proper running and efficiency of the engine. The spark plugs should be renewed at the intervals given in 'Routine maintenance'. If misfiring or bad starting is experienced within the service period, they must be removed, cleaned and regapped.

2   To remove the plugs, first mark the HT leads to ensure correct refitment, and then pull them off the plugs. Using a spark plug spanner, or suitable deep socket and extension bar, unscrew the plugs and remove them from the engine. It will be noted that on 2.0 litre models the plugs are of the tapered seat type and therefore no washers are fitted (photo).

3   The condition of the spark plugs will also tell much about the overall condition of the engine.

4   If the insulator nose of the spark plug is clean and white, with no deposits, this is indicative of a weak mixture, or too hot a plug. (A hot plug transfers heat away from the electrode slowly – a cold plug transfers it away quickly).

5   If the tip and insulator nose are covered with hard black-looking deposits, then this is indicative that the mixture is too rich. Should the plug be black and oily, then it is likely that the engine is fairly worn, as well as the mixture being too rich.

6   If the insulator nose is covered with light tan to greyish brown deposits, then the mixture is correct and it is likely that the engine is in good condition.

7   If there are any traces of long brown tapering stains on the outside of the white portion of the plug, then the plug will have to be renewed, as this shows that there is a faulty joint between the plug body and the insulator, and compression is being lost.

8   Plugs should be cleaned by a sand blasting machine, which will free them from carbon more thoroughly than cleaning by hand. The machine will also test the condition of the plugs under compression. Any plug that fails to spark at the recommended pressure should be renewed.

9   The spark plug gap is of considerable importance as, if it is too large or too small, the size of spark and its efficiency will be seriously impaired. The spark plug gap should be set to the figure given in the Specifications at the beginning of this Chapter.

10   To set it, measure the gap with a feeler gauge, and then bend open, or close, the *outer* plug electrode until the correct gap is achieved. The centre electrode should **never** be bent as this may crack the insulation and cause plug failure, if nothing worse.

11   To refit the plugs, screw them in by hand initially and then fully tighten to the specified torque. If a torque wrench is not available, tighten the plugs until initial resistance is felt as the sealing washer or plug taper (as applicable) contacts its seat and then tighten by a further eighth of a turn. Refit the HT leads in the correct order, ensuring that they are a tight fit over the plug ends. Periodically wipe the leads clean to reduce the risk of HT leakage by arcing (photo).

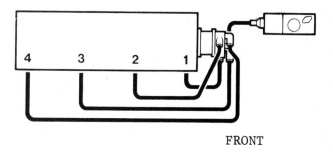

FRONT

Fig. 4.3 Ignition HT lead connections – 1.7 litre engine
(Sec 8)

its location.

3   Refit in the reverse order of removal. Ensure that the wiring connections are securely made.

8.2 Spark plug removal – 2.0 litre engine

8.11 Spark plug installation – 1.7 litre engine

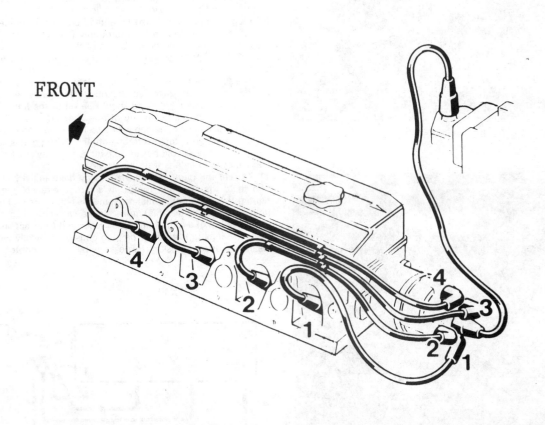

FRONT

Fig. 4.4 Ignition HT lead connections – 2.0 litre engine (Sec 8)

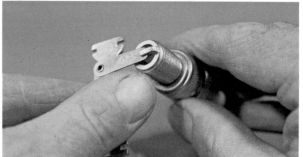

Measuring plug gap. A feeler gauge of the correct size (see ignition system specifications) should have a slight 'drag' when slid between the electrodes. Adjust gap if necessary

Adjusting plug gap. The plug gap is adjusted by bending the earth electrode inwards, or outwards, as necessary until the correct clearance is obtained. Note the use of the correct tool

Normal. Grey-brown deposits, lightly coated core nose. Gap increasing by around 0.001 in (0.025 mm) per 1000 miles (1600 km). Plugs ideally suited to engine, and engine in good condition

Carbon fouling. Dry, black, sooty deposits. Will cause weak spark and eventually misfire. Fault: over-rich fuel mixture. Check: carburettor mixture settings, float level and jet sizes; choke operation and cleanliness of air filter. Plugs can be re-used after cleaning

Oil fouling. Wet, oily deposits. Will cause weak spark and eventually misfire. Fault: worn bores/piston rings or valve guides; sometimes occurs (temporarily) during running-in period. Plugs can be re-used after thorough cleaning

Overheating. Electrodes have glazed appearance, core nose very white – few deposits. Fault: plug overheating. Check: plug value, ignition timing, fuel octane rating (too low) and fuel mixture (too weak). Discard plugs and cure fault immediately

Electrode damage. Electrodes burned away; core nose has burned, glazed appearance. Fault: pre-ignition. Check: as for 'Overheating' but may be more severe. Discard plugs and remedy fault before piston or valve damage occurs

Split core nose (may appear initially as a crack). Damage is self-evident, but cracks will only show after cleaning. Fault: pre-ignition or wrong gap-setting technique. Check: ignition timing, cooling system, fuel octane rating (too low) and fuel mixture (too weak). Discard plugs, rectify fault immediately

9 Fault diagnosis – electronic ignition system

1 Problems associated with the electronic ignition system can usually be grouped into one of two areas, those caused by the more conventional HT side of the system, such as spark plugs, HT leads, rotor arm and distributor cap, and those caused by the LT circuitry including the computer module and its related components.

Prior to making any diagnostic checks on the system, observe the precautionary notes given in Section 2 of this Chapter.

Engine fails to start

2 If the engine fails to start and the car was running normally when it was last used, first check that there is fuel in the petrol tank. If the engine turns over normally on the starter motor and the battery is evidently well charged, then the fault may be in either the high or low tension circuits. First check the HT circuit. If the battery is known to be fully charged, the ignition light comes on, and the starter motor fails to turn the engine, check the tightness of the leads on the battery terminals and also the security of the earth lead to its connection on the body. It is quite common for the leads to have worked loose, even if they look and feel secure. If one of the battery terminal posts gets very hot when trying to work the starter motor this is a sure indication of a faulty connection to that terminal.

3 Check the wiring connections at the plug sockets A and B shown in Fig. 4.1. The terminal connections must be clean and secure. Detach and reconnect them several times to overcome a poor contact.

4 One of the commonest reasons for bad starting is wet or damp spark plug leads and distributor. Remove the distributor cap. If condensation is visible internally, dry the cap with a rag and also wipe over the leads. Refit the cap.

5 If the engine still fails to start, check that the current is reaching the plugs, by dsconnecting each plug lead in turn at the spark plug end, and holding the end of the cable about 5 mm (0.2 in) away from the cylinder block. Spin the engine on the starter motor.

6 Sparking between the end of the cable and the block should be fairly strong with a good, regular blue spark. (Hold the lead with rubber insulated pliers to avoid electric shocks.) If current is reaching the plugs, then remove them and clean and regap them. The engine should now start.

7 If there is no spark at the plug leads, take off the HT lead from the centre of the distributor cap and hold it to the block as before. Spin the engine on the starter once more. A rapid succession of blue sparks between the end of the lead and the block indicates that the coil is in order and that the distributor cap is cracked, the rotor arm faulty, or the carbon brush in the top of the distributor cap is not making good contact with the rotor arm.

8 If there are no sparks from the end of the lead from the coil check the connections at the coil end of the lead. If no fault is apparent in the HT circuit, it is likely that the fault lies in the computer unit which can only be checked by a suitably equipped dealer.

Engine misfires

9 If the engine misfires regularly, run it at a fast idling speed. Pull off each of the plug caps in turn and listen to the note of the engine. Hold the plug cap in a dry cloth or with a rubber glove as additional protection against a shock from the HT supply.

10 No difference in engine running will be noticed when the lead from the defective circuit is removed. Removing the lead from one of the good cylinders will accentuate the misfire.

11 Remove the plug lead from the end of the defective plug and hold it about 5 mm (0.2 in) away from the block. Restart the engine. If the sparking is fairly strong and regular the fault must lie in the spark plug.

12 The plug may be loose, the insulation may be cracked, or the electrodes may have burnt away, giving too wide a gap for the spark to jump. Worse still, one of the electrodes may have broken off.

13 If there is no spark at the end of the plug lead, or if it is weak and intermittent, check the ignition lead from the distributor to the plug. If the insulation is cracked or perished, renew the lead. Check the connections at the distributor cap.

14 If there is still no spark, examine the distributor cap carefully for tracking. This can be recognised by a very thin black line running between two or more electrodes, or between an electrode and some other part of the distributor. These lines are paths which now conduct electricity across the cap, thus letting it run to earth. The only answer is a new distributor cap.

Chapter 5 Clutch

Contents

Specifications

Type .... Single dry plate with diaphragm spring. Sealed release bearing in constant contact with the diaphragm spring fingers.

Actuation

Turbo model .... Hydraulic
Non-Turbo models .... Cable

Driven plate (disc) diameter

1.7 litre models .... 200 mm 7.8 in)
2.0 litre non-Turbo models .... 215 mm (8.4 in)
2.0 litre Turbo models .... 228 mm (8.9 in)

Torque wrench setting

	Nm	lbf/ft
Clutch cover-to-flywheel bolts	24	18

1 Description

The clutch is of single dry plate type with a diaphragm spring pressure plate.

The driven plate incorporates torsion springs to give resilience to the hub.

The release bearing is of sealed ball type, self-centring and in constant contact with the diaphragm spring fingers.

Clutch actuation may be hydraulic or by cable according to model; refer to Specifications. On hydraulic clutches, the master cylinder is fed by fluid from the brake fluid reservoir.

On 1.7 litre models the clutch is of a push-type actuation whilst on the 2.0 litre models it has a pull-type actuation.

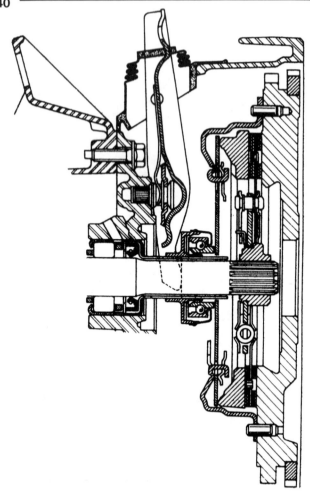

Fig. 5.1 Sectional view of clutch unit on 1.7 litre models
(Sec 1)

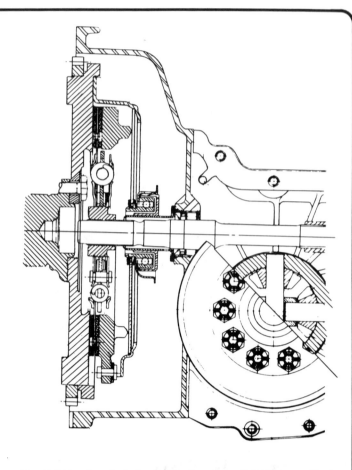

Fig. 5.2 Sectional view of clutch unit on 2.0 litre non-Turbo
models (Sec 1)

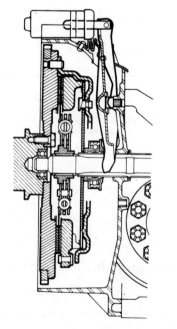

Fig. 5.3 Sectional view of clutch unit on 2.0 litre Turbo
models (Sec 1)

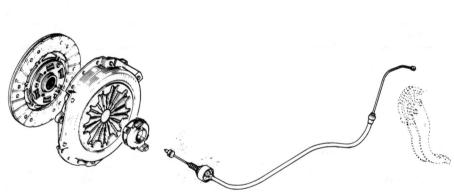

Fig. 5.4 Push-type actuation clutch mechanism – 1.7 litre
models (Sec 1)

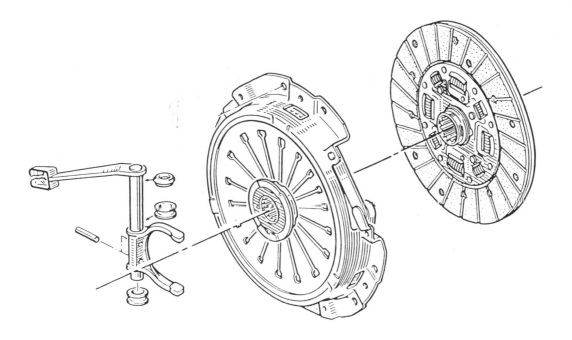

Fig. 5.5 Pull-type actuation clutch mechanism – 2.0 litre models (Sec 1)

2 Clutch cable – removal and refitting

1 Disconnect the battery earth lead.

2 Detach the cable end from the release fork and disengage the outer cable from the bracket on the bellhousing (photos).

3 With reference to Fig. 5.6, undo the retaining screws from the positions indicated and remove the lower facia trim panels on the driver's side.

4 Pull on the cable by pressing down on the pedal, hold the cable, then release the pedal and extract the cable end fitting from the pedal quadrant to free the cable (photo). Withdraw the cable through the scuttle from the engine side.

5 Refit in the reverse order of removal. Ensure that the outer cable end stop is in correct alignment with the scuttle. The outer cable is clipped into the scuttle by depressing the pedal. Adjustment is automatic.

6 Before refitting the lower facia trim panels, check that the clutch operates in a satisfactory manner. The toothed cam of the automatic adjuster must pivot on its shaft and there must be at least 20 mm (0.78 in) free play at the clutch operating fork when the cable is pulled.

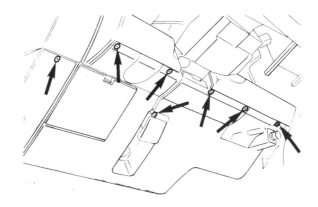

Fig. 5.6 Remove screws from positions indicated to remove lower facia trim panels (Sec 2)

2.2A Detach the clutch cable from the release fork – 1.7 litre model

2.2B Detach the clutch cable from the release fork – 2.0 litre model

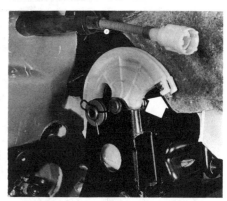

2.4 Clutch cable end fitting (arrowed) and pedal quadrant

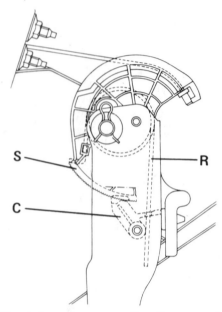

Fig. 5.7 Clutch free play automatic adjuster mechanism at clutch pedal (Sec 2)

R   *Spring*   C   *Toothed cam*
S   *Toothed quadrant section*

3   Hydraulic clutch slave cylinder – removal and refitting

1   The clutch slave cylinder cannot be overhauled; if defective it must be renewed.
2   Before proceeding, fit a suitable clamp onto the hydraulic hose at the master cylinder end as shown in Fig. 5.8. This will prevent excessive fluid spillage when the pipe is detached from the cylinder.
3   Unbolt and remove the turbocharger heat shield.
4   Unbolt and remove the heat shield from the clutch slave cylinder (see Fig. 5.9).
5   Unscrew and detach the hydraulic fluid feed pipe from the slave cylinder, then undo the mounting bolts and withdraw the slave cylinder unit.
6   Refitting is a reversal of the removal procedure. When the slave cylinder is bolted in position and the hydraulic hose reconnected, release the clamp from the hydraulic hose and top up the hydraulic fluid level in the fluid reservoir, then bleed the clutch hydraulic system as described in Section 4.
7   On completion ensure that the clutch pedal returns to its full height position and that the operating lever travel is as shown in Fig. 5.11.

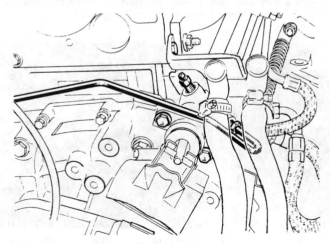

Fig. 5.10 Hydraulic fluid feed pipe to the clutch slave cylinder (Sec 3)

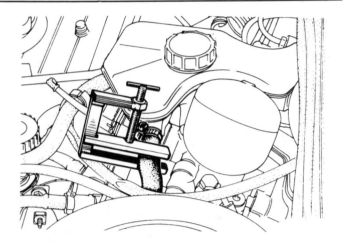

Fig. 5.8 Clamp the hydraulic hose at the master cylinder (Sec 3)

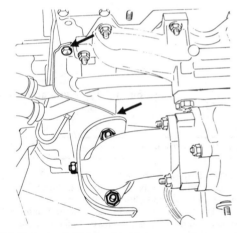

Fig. 5.9 Unbolt the heat shield (arrowed) from the clutch slave cylinder (Sec 3)

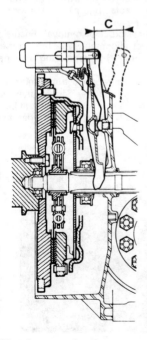

Fig. 5.11 Clutch operating lever travel (Sec 3)

C = 11.0 mm (0.429 in)

4 Clutch hydraulic system – bleeding

Note: *Bleeding of the hydraulic system is necessary whenever air has entered the system, after disconnecting any component or as a result of leakage (which should first be rectified).*

1 Gather together a clean jar, a length of rubber or plastic tubing which fits tightly over the bleed nipple on the slave cylinder and a supply of fresh hydraulic fluid. An assistant will also be required to operate the clutch pedal and to keep the fluid level in the master cylinder topped up.

2 Check that the master cylinder reservoir is full – if not, fill it – and also cover the bottom inch of the jar with hydraulic fluid. Note that the ignition must be switched on when checking the fluid level in the reservoir. When the fluid level reaches the 'MAXI' mark, the reservoir is full.

3 Remove the dust cap (if present) from the bleed nipple on the slave cylinder and place one end of the tube securely over it (photo). Place the other end of the tube in the jar, ensuring that the tube orifice is below the level of the fluid.

4 Using a ring or open-ended spanner, unscrew the bleed nipple approximately one turn and then slowly depress the clutch pedal.

5 Tighten the bleed nipple while the pedal is held in the fully depressed position.

6 Release the clutch pedal slowly, allowing it to return fully. After waiting four seconds to allow the master cylinder to recuperate, repeat the above procedure.

7 Keep the master cylinder reservoir topped up throughout this bleeding operation, otherwise further air will be introduced into the system.

8 When clean hydraulic fluid free from air bubbles can be seen coming from the end of the tube, tighten the bleed nipple, remove the rubber tube and refit the dust cap.

9 Finally top up the master cylinder reservoir and refit the cap. Discard the old hydraulic fluid as it is contaminated and must not be re-used in the system.

10 Reference should be made to Chapter 9, Section 15 for details of bleeding using one-way valve or pressure bleeding equipment which is also suitable for the clutch hydraulic system.

5 Clutch unit – removal and refitting

Removal – all models

1 Access to the clutch may be gained in one of two ways. Either the engine, or engine/transmission unit, can be removed, as described in Chapter 1, and the transmission separated from the engine, or the engine may be left in the car and the transmission unit removed independently, as described in Chapter 6.

2 Having separated the transmission from the engine, undo and remove the clutch cover retaining bolts, working in a diagonal sequence and slackening the bolts only a few turns at a time.

3 Ease the clutch cover off its locating dowels and be prepared to catch the clutch disc which will drop out as the cover is removed. Note which way round the disc is fitted.

4 It is important that no oil or grease is allowed to come into contact with the friction material of the clutch disc or the pressure plate and flywheel faces during inspection and refitting. The inspection procedures are outlined in Section 6.

5 It is advisable to refit the clutch assembly with clean hands and to wipe down the pressure plate and flywheel faces with a clean dry rag before assembly begins.

Refitting – 1.7 litre and 2.0 litre non-Turbo models

6 Fit the clutch disc into its cover orientated so that the central hub is as shown in Fig. 5.1 or 5.2 according to model (photo). As the clutch disc is a snug fit within its cover, it is virtually self-centralising.

7 Fit the combined disc and hub assembly to the flywheel, align the cover plate over the dowels on the flywheel, then locate the cover plate retaining bolts.

8 Align the disc so that it is central within the cover, with reference to paragraphs 13 to 16 of this Section if necessary, then tighten the retaining bolts to the specified torque wrench setting (photos). Tighten the bolts progressively in a diagonal sequence.

4.3 Clutch slave cylinder bleed nipple fitted with dust cap (arrowed)

5.6 Clutch disc orientation – 2.0 litre non-Turbo model

5.8A Tightening the clutch cover bolts – 1.7 litre model

5.8B Tightening the clutch cover bolts – 2.0 litre non-Turbo model

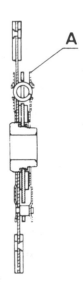

Fig. 5.12 Clutch disc orientation on 2.0 litre Turbo models – larger offset side (A) must face towards gearbox (Sec 5)

9   The transmission can now be mated to the engine by referring to the relevant Sections and Chapters.

Refitting – 2.0 litre Turbo models
10   The clutch disc must be fitted so that its hub is orientated as shown in Figs. 5.3 and 5.12.
11   Locate the disc, then place the clutch cover over the dowels, refit the retaining bolts and tighten them finger tight so that the clutch disc is gripped, but can still be moved.
12   The clutch disc must now be centralised so that, when the engine and transmission are mated, the splines of the gearbox input shaft will pass through the splines in the centre of the clutch disc hub.
13   Centralisation can be carried out quite easily by inserting a round bar or long screwdriver through the hole in the centre of the clutch disc so that the end of the bar rests in the hole in the end of the crankshaft containing the input shaft support bearing.
14   Using the support bearing as a fulcrum, moving the bar sideways or up and down will move the clutch disc in whichever direction is necessary to achieve centralisation.
15   Centralisation is easily judged by removing the bar and viewing the clutch disc hub in relation to the support bearing. When the support bearing appears exactly in the centre of the clutch disc hub, all is correct.
16   An alternative and more accurate method of centralisation is to use a commercially available clutch aligning tool obtainable from most accessory shops.
17   Once the clutch is centralised, progressively tighten the cover bolts in a diagonal sequence to the torque setting given in the Specifications.

6   Clutch unit – inspection

1   With the clutch assembly removed, clean off all traces of asbestos dust using a dry cloth. This is best done outside or in a well ventilated area; *asbestos dust is harmful, and must not be inhaled.*
2   Examine the linings of the clutch disc for wear and loose rivets, and the disc rim for distortion, cracks, broken torsion springs and worn splines. The surface of the friction linings may be highly glazed, but, as long as the friction material pattern can be clearly seen, this is satisfactory. If there is any sign of oil contamination, indicated by a continuous, or patchy, shiny black discolouration, the disc must be renewed and the source of the contamination traced and rectified. This will be either a leaking crankshaft oil seal or gearbox input shaft oil seal – or both. Renewal procedures are given in Chapter 1 and Chapter 6 respectively. The disc must also be renewed if the lining thickness has worn down to, or just above, the level of the rivet heads.
3   Check the machined faces of the flywheel and pressure plate. If

6.3 Examine the machined contact face of the pressure plate – 2.0 litre non-Turbo model

either is grooved, or heavily scored, renewal is necessary (photo). The pressure plate must also be renewed if any cracks are apparent, or if the diaphragm spring is damaged or its pressure suspect.
4   With the gearbox removed it is advisable to check the condition of the release bearing, as described in the following Sections.

7   Clutch release bearing (1.7 litre models) – removal, inspection and refitting

1   To gain access to the release bearing it is necessary to separate the engine and transmission either by removing the engine or transmission individually, or by removing both units as an assembly and separating them after removal. Depending on the method chosen, the appropriate procedures will be found in Chapter 1 or Chapter 6.
2   With the transmission removed from the engine, tilt the release fork and slide the bearing assembly off the gearbox input shaft guide tube (photo).
3   To remove the bearing from its holder, release the four tags of the spring retainer, lift off the retainer and remove the bearing.

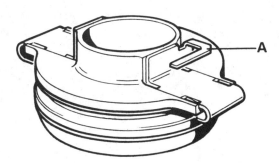

Fig. 5.13 Clutch release bearing. Lug (A) must engage with release fork – 1.7 litre models (Sec 7)

4   Check the bearing for smoothness of operation and renew it if there is any roughness or harshness as the bearing is spun.

5   To remove the release fork, disengage the rubber cover and then pull the fork upwards to release it from its ball pivot stud.

6   Refitting the release fork and release bearing is the reverse sequence to removal, but note the following points:

(a)   *Lubricate the release fork pivot ball stud and the release bearing-to-diaphragm spring contact areas sparingly with molybdenum disulphide grease*

(b)   *Ensure that the release fork spring retainer locates behind the flat shoulder of the ball pivot stud*

8   Clutch release bearing (2.0 litre models) – removal, inspection and refitting

Non-Turbo models

1   The release bearing is attached to the clutch cover/pressure plate diaphragm springs and, if renewal is necessary, the two must be obtained as a unit part (photo).

2   Check the bearing for smoothness of operation. If any harshness is felt when the bearing is spun, it must be renewed.

3   If required, the release fork can be removed by driving out the retaining roll pins. It is recommended that Renault special tools B Vi 606 and Cor 41 are used for this operation.

4   When refitting the release fork, lubricate the fork shaft with a liberal amount of grease and fit it with its seal rubber. Locate the fork with the plastic spacers and ensure that it is correctly orientated before fitting the new roll pins. Double roll pins are fitted, and they must be orientated as shown in Fig. 5.15 when refitting.

Turbo models

5   Proceed as described in Section 7.

9   Clutch pedal – removal and refitting

1   The clutch and brake pedals share a common mounting and pivot shaft. Remove the clutch pedal as follows.

2   Detach the battery earth lead. For improved access, remove the driver's seat or at least move it fully rearwards.

3   Undo the fastenings and remove the trim panels from the lower facia on the driver's side. Unclip the fuse holder and remove the ventilation duct.

4   Disconnect the clutch cable from the pedal with reference to Section 2.

5   On Turbo models, detach the spring capsule as described in Section 10.

6   Withdraw the pedal shaft retaining clip on the clutch pedal end of the shaft, then carefully withdraw the shaft from the brake pedal side just enough to allow the clutch pedal to be removed (photo). If the shaft is withdrawn too far, the brake pedal will become detached as well, so take care.

7   Refit in the reverse order of removal. Lubricate the pedal, and cable

7.2 Clutch release bearing – 1.7 litre model

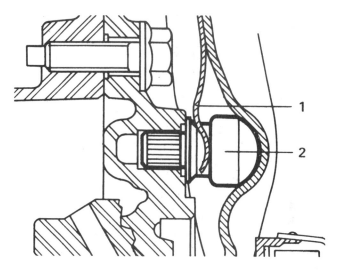

Fig. 5.14 Clutch release fork spring retainer (1) and ball stud (2) – 1.7 litre models (Sec 7)

Fig. 5.15 Release fork retaining roll pin orientation – 2.0 litre non-Turbo models (Sec 8)

8.1 Clutch release bearing location in clutch cover – 2.0 litre non-Turbo model

9.6 Pedal shaft retaining clip (arrowed)

or spring capsule pivots (as applicable). Check the clutch pedal for satisfactory operation before refitting the ventilation duct, fuse holder, and lower facia trim panels.

10 Clutch spring capsule (Turbo models) – description, removal and refitting

1   This device is mounted between the clutch pedal mounting and the pedal, and serves the purpose of a clutch pedal return spring. As the pedal is depressed beyond the dotted line shown in Fig. 5.16, the pedal pressure required to operate the clutch is reduced by approximately 18%. This results in a 'lighter' clutch pedal.
2   When removing the spring capsule, a special spring compressor tool (Renault No Emb 1082) or similar will be required to secure the unit in the compressed position during removal.
3   Detach the battery earth lead. For improved access in the car, remove the driver's seat or at least move it fully rearwards.
4   Undo the fastenings and remove the trim panels from the lower

facia on the driver's side. Unclip the fuse holder and remove the ventilation duct.
5   With the clutch pedal now accessible, locate the special spring compressor tool as shown in Fig. 5.18.
6   Extract the circlip retaining the capsule lower pivot pin and the roll pin securing the upper pivot pin to the pedal and pushrod.
7   Press the pedal downwards and withdraw the lower pivot pin. Remove the capsule unit complete with the spring compressor tool.
8   To remove the spring compressor tool from the capsule unit, locate the unit in a vice, release the tool, then slowly unscrew the vice and remove the capsule unit from it.
9   Refitting is a reversal of removal. Lubricate the pivot pins with grease. If fitting a new capsule, locate the unit in a vice and fit the spring compressor tool.
10 When fitting the capsule, ensure that its larger diameter is at the pushrod end. Locate the pushrod (and plastic bushes) into the capsule and pedal, fit the upper pivot pin and roll pin, then slightly depress the pedal to enable the lower pivot pin to be fitted. Ensure that the circlip is correctly fitted on the lower pivot pin.

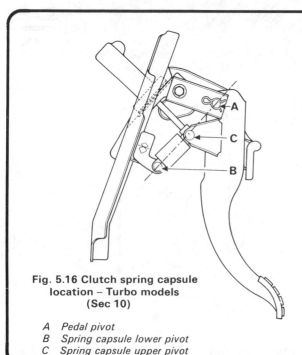

Fig. 5.16 Clutch spring capsule location – Turbo models (Sec 10)

A   Pedal pivot
B   Spring capsule lower pivot
C   Spring capsule upper pivot

Fig.   7 Sectional view of spring capsule (Sec 10)

B   Spring capsule lower pivot pin
C   Spring capsule upper pivot pin (connected to pushrod and pedal)

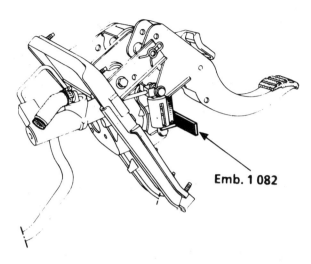

Fig. 5.18 Spring compressor tool located on spring capsule
(Sec 10)

---

11 Fault diagnosis – clutch

Symptom	Reason(s)
Judder when taking up drive	Loose engine or gearbox mountings Badly worn friction linings or contaminated with oil Worn splines on gearbox input shaft or driven plate (disc) hub
Clutch spin (failure to disengage) so that gears cannot be meshed*	Incorrect release bearing-to-pressure plate clearance Rust on splines (may occur after vehicle standing idle for long periods) Damaged or misaligned pressure plate assembly Cable stretched or broken (where applicable) Air in hydraulic system (where applicable)
Clutch slip (increase in engine speed does not result in increase in vehicle road speed – particularly on gradients)	Incorrect release bearing-to-pressure plate finger clearance Friction linings worn out or oil contaminated Air in hydraulic system (where applicable)
Noise evident on depressing clutch pedal (engine running)	Dry, worn or damaged release bearing Incorrect pedal adjustment Weak or broken pedal return spring (or spring capsule, as applicable) Excessive play between driven plate (disc) hub splines and input shaft splines Low fluid level or air in hydraulic circuit (where applicable) Incorrectly adjusted cable (where applicable)
Noise evident as clutch pedal released (engine running)	Distorted driven plate (disc) Broken or weak driven plate (disc) torsion springs Incorrect pedal adjustment Distorted or worn input shaft Release bearing loose on retainer hub

*This condition may also be due to the driven plate being rusted to the flywheel or pressure plate. It is possible to free it by applying the handbrake, depressing the clutch pedal, engaging top gear and operating the starter motor. If really badly corroded, then the engine will not turn over, but in the majority of cases, the driven plate will free. Once the engine starts, rev it up and slip the clutch several times to clear the rust deposits.

Chapter 6 Manual transmission

Contents

Specifications

Part A: JB3 transmission
General
Application .... 1.7 litre models

Ratios	JB3	JB3S*
1st	3.72:1	3.09:1
2nd	2.05:1	1.85:1
3rd	1.32:1	1.32:1
4th	0.96:1	0.96:1
5th	0.79:1	0.75:1
Reverse	3.54:1	3.54:1
Final drive	3.56:1	4.06:1

* RS model only

Differential bearing preload (see text)
New bearings .... 0 to 16 N (0 to 3.6 lbf)
Used bearings .... 16 to 32 N (3.6 to 7.2 lbf)

Lubrication
Capacity .... 3.4 litres (6.0 pints)
Lubricant type/specification .... Hypoid gear oil, viscosity SAE 80W to API GL5 (Duckhams Hypoid 80S)

Torque wrench settings

	Nm	lbf ft
Mounting nuts	40	30
Selector rod bolt	30	22
Primary shaft nut	135	100
Secondary shaft bolt:		
10 mm diameter	80	59
8 mm diameter	20	14
Housing bolts	25	18
5th gear detent unit	19	14
Crownwheel nut (taper bearing type)	130	95

Part B: NG9 transmission
General
Application .... 2.0 litre non-Turbo models
Ratios:
    1st 4.09:1
    2nd 2.17:1
    3rd 1.40:1
    4th 1.03:1
    5th 0.86:1
    Reverse 3.54:1
    Final drive 3.44:1

Differential bearing preload (see text) .... 10 to 13 N (2.3 to 2.9 lbf)

Crownwheel-to-pinion backlash .... 0.12 to 0.25 mm (0.005 to 0.010 in)

Lubrication
Capacity .... 2.2 litres (4.0 pints)
Lubricant type/specification .... Hypoid gear oil, viscosity SAE 80W to API GL5 (Duckhams Hypoid 80S)

Torque wrench settings

	Nm	lbf ft
Mounting nuts	40	30
Primary shaft nut	130	95
Secondary shaft (speedometer drive) nut	150	110
Rear casing bolts	15	11
Half-casing bolts	25	18
Reverse cable locknut	20	15
Crownwheel bolts	125	92

Part C: UN1 transmission
General
Application .... 2.0 litre Turbo models
Ratios:
    1st 3.36:1
    2nd 2.05:1
    3rd 1.38:1
    4th 1.03:1
    5th 1.21:1
    Reverse 3.54:1
    Final drive 3.44:1

Differential bearing preload (see text) .... 45 to 65 N (10.1 to 14.6 lbf)

Lubrication
Capacity .... 3.0 litres (5.2 pints)
Lubricant type/specification .... Hypoid gear oil, viscosity SAE 75W/90 (Duckhams Hypoid 75W/90S)

Torque wrench settings

	Nm	lbf ft
Primary shaft nut	135	100
Secondary shaft nut	200	147
Rear casing bolts	25	18
Half-casing bolts:		
8 mm diameter	25	18
10 mm diameter	50	37
Spacer plate bolts	50	37
Clutch bellhousing bolts	50	37
Reverse shaft swivel bolt	25	18
Crownwheel bolts	122	90

PART A: JB3 TRANSMISSION

1 General description

The JB3 transmission has five forward gears and one reverse gear. All forward gears have baulk ring synchromesh units fitted for ease of engagement.

The final drive (differential) unit is integral with the main gearbox and is located between the mechanism casing and clutch and differential housing. The gearbox and differential both share the same lubricating oil.

Gearshift is by means of a floor-mounted lever connected by a remote control housing and gearchange rod to the gearbox fork contact shaft.

If transmission overhaul is necessary, due consideration should be given to the costs involved, since it is often more economical to obtain a service exhange or good secondhand transmission rather than fit new parts to the existing unit.

2 Maintenance

1   At the intervals specified in *'Routine maintenance'*, inspect the transmission joint faces and oil seals for any signs of damage, deterioration or oil leakage.

2   At the same service interval, check and, if necessary, top up the transmission oil using the procedure described in Section 3.

3   At less frequent intervals (see *'Routine maintenance'*) the transmission should be drained and refilled with fresh oil, and this procedure is also described in Section 3.

4   It is also advisable to check for excess free play or wear in the gear linkage joints and rods and check the gear lever adjustment, as described in Section 14.

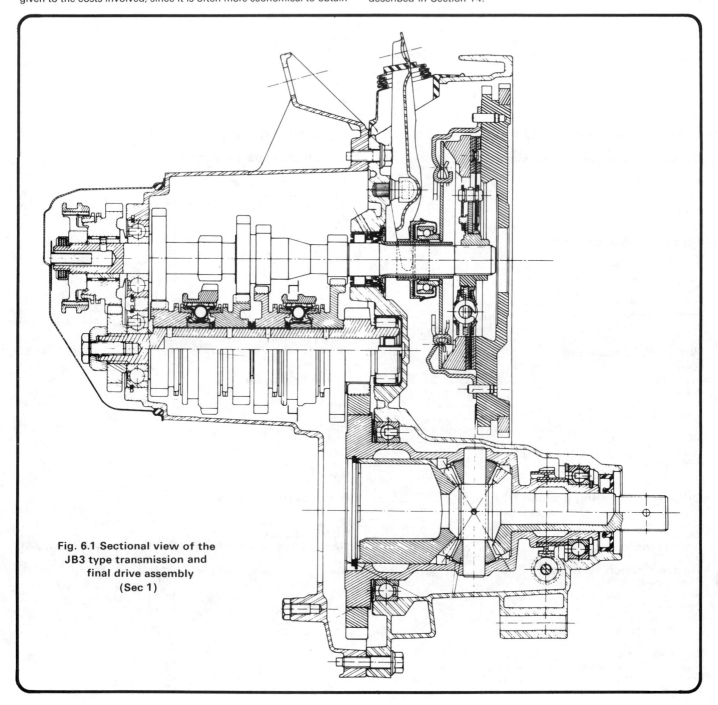

Fig. 6.1 Sectional view of the
JB3 type transmission and
final drive assembly
(Sec 1)

3 Transmission – draining and refilling

1 When draining the transmission oil, the vehicle will need to be standing level. If possible position the vehicle over an inspection pit, but failing this raise and support the vehicle at the front and rear on axle stands to allow access underneath the vehicle whilst at the same time keeping it level.

2 Remove the transmission undertray which is secured by bolts and pegs. Remove the transmission breather to ensure full draining.

3 Loosen the transmission drain plug using a suitable key, position a container under the plug, then remove the plug to drain the oil into the container (photo). When the oil has fully drained, refit the plug and wipe clean the area around the drain hole. Remove the container and dispose of the old oil (do not reuse it).

4 Refit the undertray.

5 Unscrew and remove the transmission filler/level plug.

6 Slowly refill the transmission using the specified grade of oil until the oil overflows from the filler plug orifice. Wait a few minutes to allow any trapped air to escape and then, if possible, add more oil. Repeat this process two or three times until no more oil can be added and then, with the level right to the top of the plug orifice, refit the filler plug. Take care over this operation as this type of transmission may take quite some time to fill.

7 Refit the transmission breather, then lower the vehicle (where applicable).

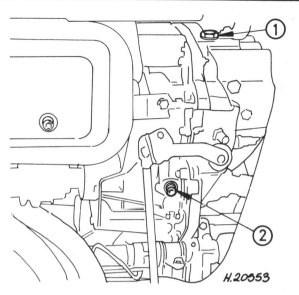

Fig. 6.2 Underside view of JB3 type transmission showing the filler/level plug (1) and the drain plug (2) (Sec 3)

3.3 Removing the transmission drain plug

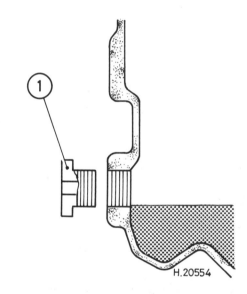

Fig. 6.3 Transmission oil level requirement and filler/level plug (1) (Sec 3)

4.4 Gearchange link rod joint

4 Transmission – removal and refitting

1 The transmission can be removed together with or separate from the engine. Removal with the engine and their subsequent separation is dealt with in Chapter 1. The method described in this Section is for removal of the transmission only, and leaves the engine in position in the vehicle.

2 After disconnecting all the relevant attachments, controls and services, the transmission is removed upwards and out of the engine compartment. Due to the weight of the unit, it will be necessary to have some form of lifting equipment available, such as an engine crane or suitable hoist to enable the unit to be removed in this way.

3 Begin by disconnecting the battery negative terminal and then refer to Section 3 and drain the transmission oil.

4 Unclip and pull back the rubber sleeve from the gearchange link rod joint, then disconnect the joint (photo).

5 Undo the retaining bolts and remove the engine/transmission U-shaped steady bar.

6   Remove the front roadwheel each side.

7   Unclip and remove the inner wing lower shield on the left-hand side.

8   Refer to Chapter 8 and detach the right and left-hand driveshafts from the transmission.

9   Position a jack under the engine with an interposed block of wood to prevent damage and raise it to support the weight of the engine. Alternatively, the manufacturers recommend the use of a special tool (WN 103) as shown in Figs. 6.4 and 6.5. The support stud is hooked through a fabricated bracket bolted to the air cleaner mounting studs. The support bar legs rest in the drain channels on each side of the engine compartment.

10 Disconnect the clutch cable from the release lever and the support bracket on top of the transmission. Move the cable out of the way.

11 Extract the speedometer cable wire retaining clip from its locating holes in the rear engine mounting bracket and gearbox casing. Note the fitted direction of the clip. Withdraw the speedometer cable from the gearbox.

12 Unbolt and detach the angular position/speed sensor unit from the top of the clutch housing. Detach its wiring connector from the top of the transmission and move the wiring and sensor out of the way (photo). Note that the retaining bolts are of a specific shouldered type and should not be replaced with ordinary bolts.

13 Detach the ignition coil HT lead and move it out of the way.

14 Remove the air cleaner unit as described in Chapter 3.

15 Disconnect the reversing light switch lead and the two transmis-

sion earth leads. Note the routeings and detach the leads from their retaining clips on the transmission and place them out of the way.

16 Disconnect the choke cable from the carburettor (Chapter 3).

17 Unbolt and detach the engine/transmission stabilizer unit – see Fig. 6.6.

18 Unbolt and remove the protector plate from the clutch housing.

19 Loosen but do not remove the engine mounting bolts.

20 Unscrew the transmission mounting nuts (front and rear), and the nut from the rear engine mounting from above.

21 Referring to Fig. 6.8, unscrew and remove the two studs using two nuts tightened against each other. A cranked spanner and a balljointed socket wrench will be needed to enable access.

22 Attach a suitable lift sling to the transmission and raise it so that the weight of the transmission is supported.

23 Undo the engine-to-transmission retaining bolts and withdraw them noting their lengths and positions (photo). These include the starter motor-to-clutch housing bolts, although the starter motor can be left attached to the engine by its end mounting bracket, and the solenoid wiring can be left attached.

24 Remove the front mounting, then slightly lower the engine.

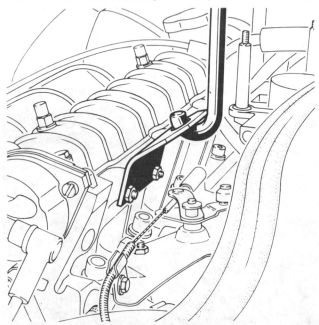

Fig. 6.5 Fabricated support bracket and support stud engagement (Sec 4)

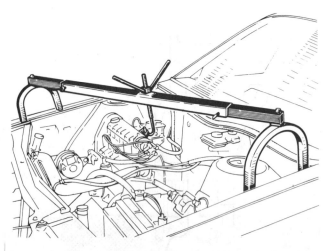

Fig. 6.4 Special engine support tool (WN 103) (Sec 4)

4.12 Unbolt the angular piston/speed sensor wiring connector from the transmission

4.23 Unscrew and remove the engine-to-transmission bolts (arrowed)

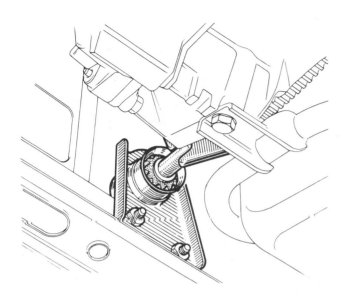

Fig. 6.6 Unbolt the engine/transmission stabilizer (Sec 4)

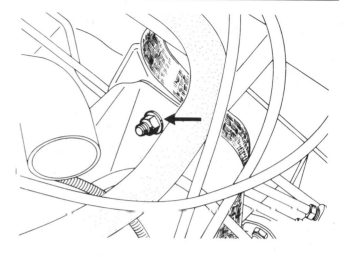

Fig. 6.7 Rear engine nut (arrowed) (Sec 4)

Withdraw the transmission from the engine ensuring that no pressure is applied to the input shaft, passing the 5th speed end housing between the sub-frame and the side members.

25 Raise the engine again to its normal position and twist the transmission to the left so that the final drive is free, then lift out the transmission.

26 Refitting is a reversal of the removal procedure, but note the following special points.

27 Before refitting the transmission unit, check that the driveshaft rollers are undamaged and that all the rollers are in position. Inspect the transmission differential housing to ensure that no bearing rollers have fallen into it.

28 Smear the input shaft splines with grease, and ensure that no pressure is applied to the input shaft as the engine and transmission are reconnected.

29 Fit the two studs each side of the bellhousing before refitting the transmission to the engine (see Fig. 6.8).

30 When refitting the engine-to-transmission retaining bolts, ensure that the retaining bolt (V) in Fig. 6.9 is correctly located.

31 Refit the driveshafts as described in Chapter 8.

32 Tighten the respective fastenings to their specified torque wrench settings.

33 Refill the transmission with the correct grade of oil as described in Section 3.

5 Transmission overhaul – general

Complete dismantling and overhaul of the transmission, particularly with respect to the differential and the bearings in the clutch and differential housing, entails the use of a hydraulic press and a number of special tools. For this reason it is not recommended that a complete overhaul be attempted by the home mechanic unless he has access to the tools required and feels reasonably confident after studying the procedure. However, the transmission can at least be dismantled into its major assemblies without too much difficulty, and the following Sections describe this and the overhaul procedure.

Before starting any repair work on the transmission, thoroughly clean the exterior of the casings using paraffin or a suitable solvent. Dry the unit with a lint-free rag. Make sure that an uncluttered working area is available with some small containers and trays handy to store the various parts. Label everything as it is removed.

After dismantling, all roll pins, circlips and snap-rings must be renewed, regardless of their condition, before reassembling.

Before starting reassembly all the components must be spotlessly clean and should be liberally lubricated with the recommended grade of gear oil during assembly.

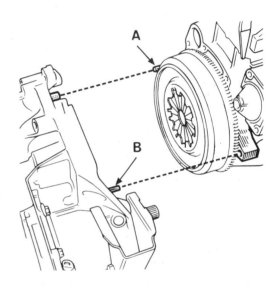

Fig. 6.8 Remove studs from positions A and B (Sec 4)

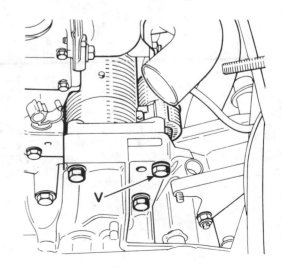

Fig. 6.9 Retaining bolt V must be correctly located (Sec 4)

6 Transmission – separating the housings

Note: *A puller will be required for this operation*

1 With the transmission on the bench, begin by removing the clutch release bearing and release fork, referring to Chapter 5 if necessary. Note that the release fork pivot is not removable.

2 Remove the rubber O-ring from the splines of the differential stub shaft (photo).

3 Unbolt and remove the rear cover. Remove the cover in a horizontal manner to avoid damaging the internal oil pipe fitted to some models. Recover the rubber O-ring seal.

4 Support the 5th speed selector shaft using a block of wood between the shaft and gears, then drive out the selector fork roll pin using a parallel pin punch.

5 Engage 1st gear by moving the gear linkage fork control shaft and engage 5th gear by moving the 5th speed selector fork. With the geartrain now locked, undo the 5th gear retaining nut on the end of the primary shaft. The 5th speed shift rod must not be withdrawn or the lock system will fall into the gearbox.

6 Return the geartrain to neutral.

7 Withdraw the 5th speed driving gear, synchroniser unit, and selector fork as an assembly using a suitable puller. Engage the puller legs over the flat strips of metal slid under the teeth of the driven gear.

8 Recover the needle roller bearing, bearing bush and the washer from the primary shaft.

9 Where fitted, undo the bolt then remove the washer and collar over the 5th speed driven gear on the secondary shaft.

10 Extract the 5th speed circlip and dished washer, then remove the gear, as described previously for the driven gear.

11 Extract the circlip and dished washer over the end of the primary shaft and secondary shaft.

12 Lift out the reverse shaft detent retaining plate, then remove the spring and ball. If the ball won't come out, leave it in place, but don't forget to retrieve it once the casing has been separated.

13 Unscrew the 5th speed detent assembly.

14 Unscrew the reversing lamp switch (photo).

15 Undo and remove the bolts securing the mechanism casing to the clutch and differential housing, noting their different lengths.

16 Pull the fork control shaft on the side of the gearbox out as far as it will go and then lift the mechanism casing, complete with 5th speed selector shaft, up and off the geartrain and housing. It may be necessary to tap the primary shaft down using a plastic mallet to free the casing and bearings from the shaft. As soon as the casing comes free, insert two bolts or suitable 13 mm diameter rods into the selector shaft holes and push them down firmly. These will retain the detent balls and springs and prevent them being ejected as the casing is lifted off (photo).

6.2 Remove the differential stub shaft O-ring

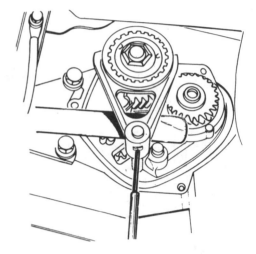

Fig. 6.10 Remove the 5th speed selector fork roll pin with a drift while supporting the shaft with a block of wood (Sec 6)

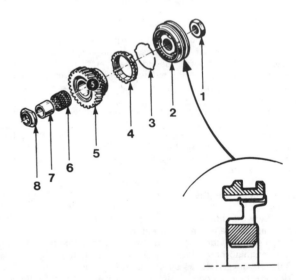

Fig. 6.11 5th speed driving gear components (Sec 6)

1	5th gear retaining nut	5	5th speed driven gear
2	5th speed synchroniser unit	6	Needle roller bearing
3	Spring clip	7	Bearing bush
4	Baulk ring	8	Washer

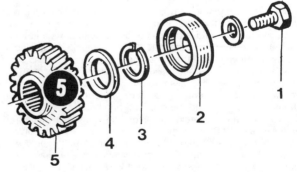

Fig. 6.12 5th speed driven gear components (Sec 6)

1	Bolt	4	Dished washer
2	Collar	5	5th speed driving gear
3	Circlip		

6.14 Remove the reversing lamp switch

7 Geartrains and differential unit – removal

1 Having separated the casings, the geartrain components can now be dismantled as follows:

6.16 Two bolts in position to retain the selector shaft detent balls and springs

2 Recover the detent plunger from the location in the clutch and differential housing vacated by the 5th speed selector shaft.
3 Using a parallel pin punch, drive out the roll pin securing the 3rd/4th selector fork to the shaft. Slip a tube of suitable diameter down over the shaft and support it while the roll pin is being driven out.

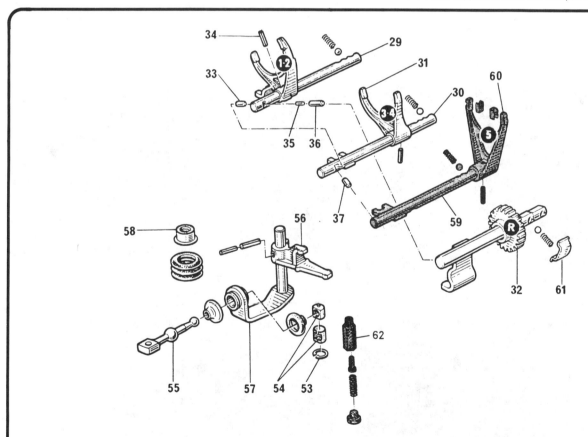

Fig. 6.13 Selector mechanism components (Sec 7)

29 1st/2nd selector shaft	34 Selector fork roll pin	54 Pivot arm bushes	59 5th speed selector shaft
30 3rd/4th selector shaft	35 Detent plunger	55 Pivot arm	60 5th speed selector fork
31 3rd/4th selector fork	36 Detent plunger	56 Fork finger	61 Reverse shaft detent
32 Reverse shaft	37 Detent plunger	57 Fork control shaft	retaining plate
33 Detent plunger	53 Circlip	58 Bush	62 5th speed detent assembly

4   Ensure that all the gears are in neutral, and then withdraw the 3rd/4th selector shaft, leaving the fork behind. It will be necessary to move the reverse shaft around slightly until the exact neutral position is found, otherwise the detent plungers will not locate properly in their grooves and it will be impossible to remove the 3rd/4th shaft. With the shaft removed, lift off the selector fork.

5   Recover the detent plunger from the shaft location in the housing (photo).

6   Using the same procedure as for the 3rd/4th shaft, remove the 1st/2nd selector shaft and fork. As the shaft is withdrawn, recover the small detent plunger from the hole in the centre of the shaft (photos).

7   Withdraw the long detent plunger from its location at the base of the housing (photo).

8   Take hold of the secondary shaft, primary shaft and reverse shaft geartrains and lift them as an assembly out of their locations in the clutch and differential housing.

9   Recover the magnet from the bottom of the housing (photo).

10 Although the differential unit can now be removed, it is recommended that this unit is left alone unless its removal is absolutely essential. If repairs to the differential unit are necessary, it is recommended that they are entrusted to a Renault dealer.

11 Two basic types of differential have been fitted. Although the same in design, one type runs in ball bearings whilst the second type runs in taper bearings. The outer profile of the bearing housing will indicate which type is fitted (Fig. 6.1 and 6.14 refer). The removal and refitting of each type differs and some special tools will be required, therefore read through the instructions before progressing to access the requirements and procedures.

12 Using a small punch and pliers, tip the oil seal in its location by tapping it down on one side. As the seal tips, prise it out using a screwdriver and pliers.

Ball bearing type differential

13 Place the differential crownwheel face down on a press bed, with a block of wood beneath it to spread the load.

14 Press the clutch and differential housing down and extract the circlip securing the differential to the outer bearing.

15 Support the housing on blocks of wood and remove the differential assembly by pressing on the splined stub shaft. Recover the dished and, where fitted, the plain thrust washer.

Taper bearing type differential

16 Referring to Fig. 6.18, lock the crownwheel as shown using the special Renault tool illustrated or a suitable fabricated equivalent. Take care not to damage the crownwheel and/or the differential housing.

17 With the crownwheel suitably locked and the housing securely supported (an assistant is useful here), unscrew and remove the retaining nut. Remove the locking tool.

18 Recover the bearing preload adjustment shims.

19 The differential assembly can now be removed by pressing or drifting the sunwheel to withdraw the assembly from the housing.

---

8   Transmission housings – overhaul

Gearbox casing

1   To renew the bearings in the casing, spread the retaining circlips with a pair of outward opening circlips pliers, and drive the bearings out towards the inside of the casing. Use a hammer and tube of suitable diameter to do this.

2   To fit the new bearings, first locate the circlips in their grooves in the casing so that their ends are together (photo).

3   Fit the bearings to the casing, ensuring that force is applied to the bearing outer race only. As the bearings are being fitted spread the circlips to allow the bearings to enter.

4   With the bearings in place, locate the circlips into the bearing grooves and ensure that the circlip ends are together (photo).

5   If it is necessary to renew the selector shaft detent balls and springs, remove the bolts or rods used to hold them in place during removal of the casing and withdraw the balls and springs as required.

6   Examine the condition of the fork control shaft and its mechanism for wear, particularly at the fork fingers, and renew these components if necessary as follows:

7.5 Recover the detent plunger (arrowed)

7.6A As 1st/2nd selector shaft is withdrawn, recover small detent plunger from hole (arrowed) ...

7.6B ... then remove the fork

7.7 Withdraw the long detent plunger (arrowed)

7.9 Recover the magnet

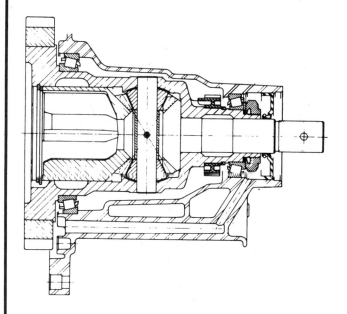

Fig. 6.14 Sectional view of the taper bearing type
differential unit and housing (Sec 7)

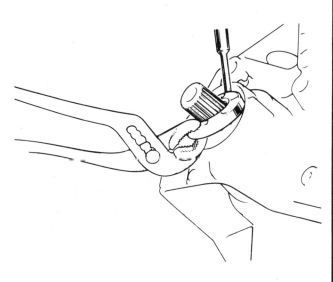

Fig. 6.15 Differential oil seal removal method (Sec 7)

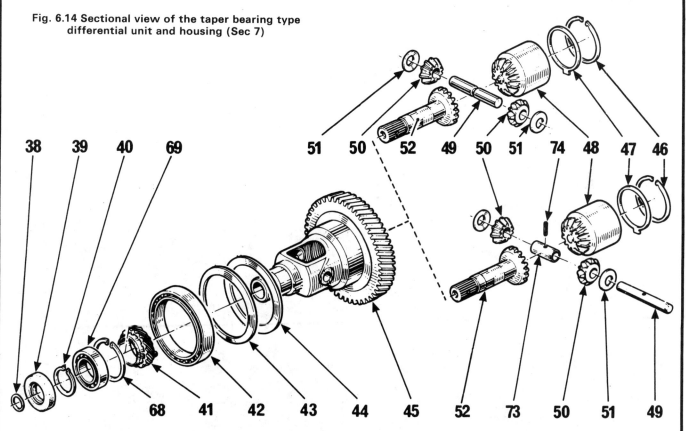

Fig. 6.16 Ball bearing type differential assembly (Sec 7)

38 O-ring
39 Oil seal
40 Circlip
41 Speedometer drive gear
42 Inner ball bearing

43 Plain thrust washer
44 Dished thrust washer
45 Crownwheel/differential
   housing
46 Snap ring

47 Shim
48 Spider sunwheel
49 Planet wheel shaft
50 Planet wheels

51 Thrust washers
52 Sun wheel and tall shaft
68 Circlip
69 Outer ball bearing

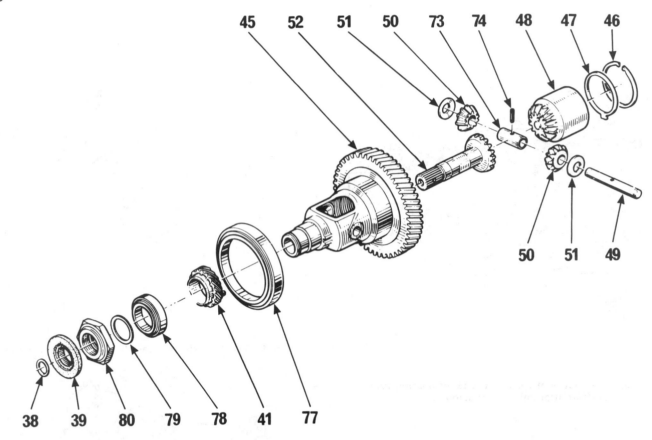

Fig. 6.17 Taper bearing type differential assembly (Sec 7)

38 O-ring
39 Oil seal
41 Speedometer drive gear
45 Crownwheel
46 Snap ring

47 Shim
48 Sun wheel
49 Planet wheel shaft
50 Planet wheel

51 Thrust washers
52 Sunwheel and tail shaft
73 Sleeve
74 Roll pin

77 Inner taper bearing
78 Outer taper bearing
79 Shim
80 Nut

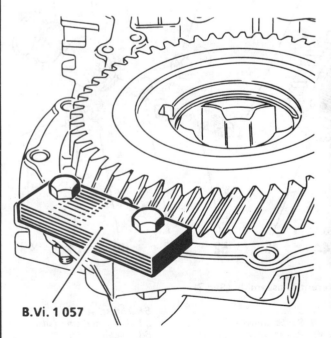

B.Vi. 1 057

Fig. 6.18 Crownwheel locking tool (Renault tool No BVi 1057) (Sec 7)

8.2 Secondary and primary shaft bearing circlips (arrowed)

8.4 Circlip ends (arrowed) must be together when the bearings are fitted

7   Extract the circlip (photo), then slide out the pivot arm bush and the arm.

8   Using a parallel pin punch, tap out the double roll pin, securing the fork finger assembly to the fork control shaft (photo). Withdraw the shaft and recover the fork and oil seal.

9   With the new components at hand, reassemble the fork control assembly using the reverse of the removal procedure.

10 If the oil flow guide is to be renewed bend flat the retaining lip edge on the guide and push it into the casing.

11 Push the new guide up into position and bend over the lip edge to lock it in place.

Clutch and differential housing

Ball bearing type differential

12 If a press is available the differential bearings can be removed quite easily. After removing the differential, as described previously, support the housing, bellhousing face downwards, and press the relevant bearing out. If the smaller bearing is to be removed, extract the circlip first. Fit the new bearings in the same way and use a new circlip to secure the smaller bearing. In each case the bearing must be fitted so that the bearing cage is orientated away from the crownwheel.

Taper bearing type differential

13 To remove the crownwheel bearing cone a puller/extractor of the type shown in Fig. 6.20. will be required. Unless this type of puller unit is available, entrust the bearing removal to a Renault dealer or garage with such equipment. The new bearing cone can be fitted by pressing or driving it onto the crownwheel shoulder using a tube drift of the type shown in Fig. 6.21.

14 To renew the taper bearing cap (essential if the cone is being renewed), press it from the housing using a suitable tube drift. Fit the new cup in the same way and ensure that the cup is flush with the housing shoulder when fitted.

15 The taper bearing cup of the sunwheel tail stock can be pressed off and renewed in a similar manner to the crownwheel bearing cup.

All differential types

16 If it is necessary to renew the secondary shaft support bearing, take the housing to a Renault dealer and have him renew the bearing for you using the Renault removal and refitting tools.

17 The gearbox primary shaft oil seal is part of a complete assembly containing the primary shaft roller bearing, and is located within a tubular housing. The complete assembly must be renewed if either the oil seal or the bearing require attention (photo).

18 To remove the assembly, extract it using tubes of suitable diameter with washers, a long bolt or threaded rod and nuts (photos). Tighten the nuts and draw the assembly out of its location and into the tube. Alternatively a press can be used, if available.

19 Refit the new oil seal and bearing assembly in the same way, but position it so that the bearing lubrication holes in the bearing assembly and clutch and differential housing will be directly in line after fitting (photo).

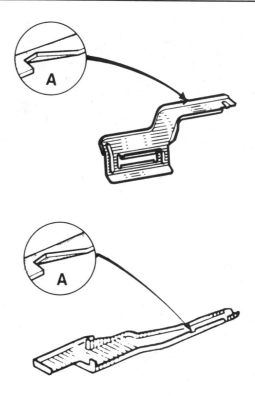

Fig. 6.19 Alternative types of oil flow guide fitted with the lip edge (A) indicated (Sec 8)

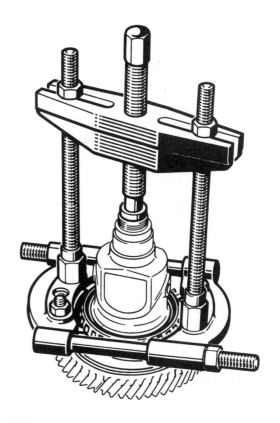

Fig. 6.20 Taper bearing cone removal from crownwheel (Sec 8)

8.7 Pivot arm retaining circlip (arrowed) ...

8.8 ... and fork finger retaining roll pin (arrowed)

8.17 Primary shaft oil seal and roller bearing assembly (arrowed)

8.18A Home-made tool consisting of a tube, threaded rod, nut and washers on one side of the housing ...

8.18B ... and a socket nut and washer on the other side for removal/refitting of the primary shaft oil seal and bearing

8.19 Primary shaft bearing lubrication hole and corresponding hole in housing (arrowed) must align

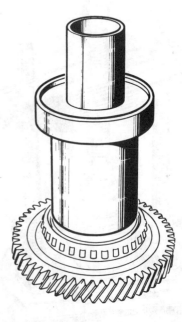

Fig. 6.21 Tube drift used to fit taper bearing cone (Sec 8)

9 Differential – overhaul

1   It is not advisable to dismantle the differential unless it is known that its components are suspect or require attention.

2   If dismantling is to be undertaken, remove the sun and planet wheels from the differential by referring to Fig. 6.16 or 6.17 as applicable. Keep the planet wheels together with their respective thrust washers and lay them out in strict order of removal.

3   If any of the sun wheels, planet wheels or thrust washers require renewal, it will be necessary to renew all the components as a matching set.

4   If the crownwheel is being renewed, obtain a replacement of the correct type. Take the crownwheel along to your supplier to obtain the correct crownwheel, bearings, shims and circlip replacements.

5   With the ball bearing type differential unit, if the crownwheel, bearings and/or planet and sun wheels are being renewed, take the old assembly along to a Renault parts supplier for identification of type. One of two crownwheel types will be fitted (shouldered or non-shouldered), and the spacer washer (shim) thickness requirement is dependent on the thickness of the bearing and the circlip being used. A Renault dealer will identify the components and advise on the replacement requirements necessary.

6   With the taper bearing type differential unit, alternative shim thicknesses may be required to adjust the bearing preload during reassembly.

7   Reassemble the differential using the reverse of the dismantling sequence.

10 Secondary shaft – overhaul

1   Support the secondary shaft in a vice with protected jaws and commence dismantling at the 4th gear end as follows.

2   Lift off the 3rd/4th gear and reverse synchroniser unit, complete

with the 4th gear baulk ring, 4th gear and the upper thrust washer as a complete assembly.

3   Extract the snap-ring and thrust washer, then lift off 3rd gear and its baulk ring.

4   Remove the thrust washer, snap-ring and second thrust washer, then lift off 2nd gear.

5   Remove the thrust washer and snap-ring above the 1st/2nd synchroniser unit and lift off 1st gear, the 1st/2nd synchroniser unit and the baulk ring as an assembly.

6   With the secondary shaft now completely dismantled, examine the gears and synchroniser units, as described in Section 11, then proceed with the reassembly as follows.

7   Place 1st gear on the secondary shaft with the flat face of the gear towards the pinion (photo).

8   Place the baulk ring over 1st gear and then position the 1st/2nd synchroniser unit over it (photos). Fit the synchroniser unit with the offset side of the hub and sliding sleeve towards 1st gear, and ensure that the lugs on the baulk ring engage with the roller grooves in the hub.

9   Place the 2nd gear baulk ring on the 1st/2nd synchroniser unit, then refit the snap-ring (photos).

10 Lay the thrust washer over the snap-ring, then slide 2nd gear onto the secondary shaft with its flat side facing away from the pinion end of the shaft (photos).

11 Fit the assembly of thrust washer, snap-ring and thrust washer to the secondary shaft, then slide on 3rd gear with its flat face towards the pinion end of the secondary shaft (photos).

12 Place a thrust washer over 3rd gear and secure it with the remaining snap-ring.

13 Fit the 3rd gear baulk ring to 3rd gear followed by the 3rd/4th and reverse synchroniser unit. The offset side of the hub and the selector fork groove in the sliding sleeve should face away from 3rd gear. Ensure that the lugs on the baulk ring engage with the roller grooves in the hub.

14 Fit the 4th gear baulk ring to the 3rd/4th synchroniser unit, then slide on 4th gear followed by the final thrust washer.

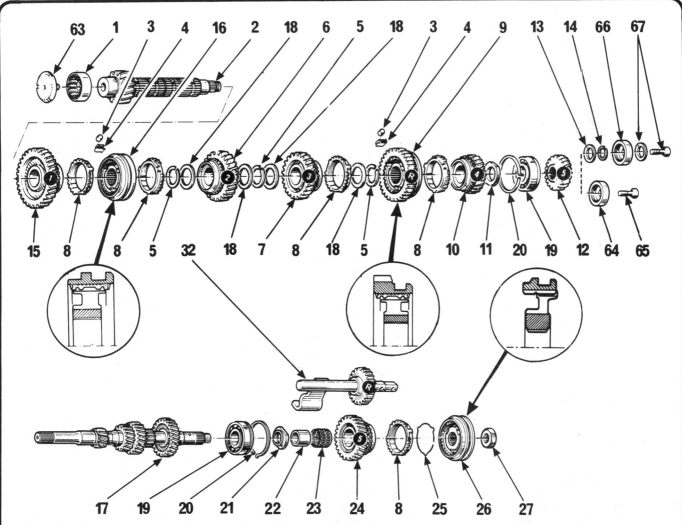

Fig. 6.22 Exploded view of the primary and secondary shaft gear assemblies (Sec 11)

1 Roller race	10 4th gear	19 Ball race	27 5th gear nut
2 Secondary shaft	11 Washer	20 Circlip	32 Reverse shaft and gear
3 Roller	12 5th gear (secondary)	21 Washer	63 Oil baffle
4 Roller spring	13 Washer	22 5th gear ring	64 Thrust washer
5 Circlip	14 5th gear circlip	23 Needle race	65 5th gear end bolt on
6 2nd gear	15 1st gear	24 5th gear (primary)	secondary shaft
7 3rd gear	16 1st/2nd gear hub	25 5th gear spring	66 Shouldered washer
8 Synchroniser ring	17 Primary shaft	26 5th gear hub	67 Retaining bolt and washer
9 3rd/4th gear hub	18 Splined ring		

Fig. 6.23 Spring key-to-circlip orientation (Sec 11)

10.7 Place 1st gear on the secondary shaft flat face towards the pinion

10.8A Place the baulk ring over the gear ...

10.8B ... followed by the 1st/2nd synchroniser unit

10.9A Locate the 2nd gear baulk ring on the synchroniser unit ...

10.9B ... then refit the snap-ring

10.10A Locate the thrust washer ...

10.10B ... then slide 2nd gear onto the secondary shaft

10.11A Locate the thrust washer ...

10.11B ... the snap-ring ...

10.11C ... and thrust washer to the secondary shaft ...

10.11D ... followed by 3rd gear

11 Shafts, gears and synchroniser units – inspection

1   With the gearbox completely dismantled, inspect the secondary, primary and reverse shafts for signs of damage, wear or chipping of the teeth, or wear or scoring of the shafts where they engage with their bearings (photos). If any of these conditions are apparent, the relevant shaft must be renewed.

2   If necessary, the synchroniser units can be dismantled for inspection by covering the assembly with a rag and then pushing the hub out of the sliding sleeve. Collect the spring keys and rollers which will have been ejected into the rag. Note that each synchroniser unit hub and sliding sleeve is a matched set and they must not be interchanged.

3   Check that the hub and sleeve slides over each other easily and that there is a minimum of backlash or axial rock. Examine the dog teeth of the sliding sleeve for excessive wear and renew the assembly if wear is obvious. Note that if the car had a tendency to jump out of a particular gear, then a worn synchroniser unit is the most likely cause and the relevant assembly should be renewed.

4   To reassemble the synchroniser units slide the hub into the sliding sleeve, noting that for the 1st/2nd unit the selector fork groove in the sleeve and the offset boss of the hub are on opposite sides. On the 3rd/4th unit, the selector fork groove and the hub offset boss are on the same side. On the 5th speed unit the chamfered outer edge of the sleeve is on the same side as the hub offset boss.

5   Place the synchroniser on the bench with the offset side of the hub facing downwards. Locate the end of the spring key, having the two tangs, against the circlip end of the hub and position the roller between the loop of the spring key and the side of the sleeve (photo).

6   Push down on the roller and key until they locate correctly with the roller located in the internal groove of the sliding sleeve (photo). Repeat this for the remaining rollers and spring keys.

7   Check the condition of the baulk rings by sliding them onto the land of the relevant gears and note whether they lock on the tapered land before reaching the gear shoulder. Also inspect the baulk rings for cracks or wear of the dog teeth and renew as necessary. It is recommended, having dismantled the gearbox this far, that all the baulk rings are renewed as a matter of course. The improvement in the gear changing action, particularly if the car has covered a considerable mileage, will be well worth the expense.

8   Finally check the selector fork clearance in the synchro-hub sliding sleeve groove; this should be minimal. If in doubt about the clearance, compare the forks with new ones and renew as necessary. Two contact pads fitted to the fork ends engage with the sleeve grooves and only these, not the complete fork, need to be renewed if wear has taken place.

9   Note that new roll pins must be fitted to the selector forks and shafts during reassembly.

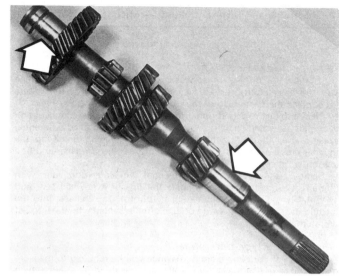

11.1A Inspect shafts for wear or scoring of teeth and bearing contact areas (arrowed) – typical

11.1B Check for chipped gear teeth (arrowed)

11.5 Locate the spring key and roller in the synchroniser unit ...

11.6 ... then push down to locate the roller in its groove

12 Geartrains and differential unit – refitting

1   The unit must be refitted according to type.

Ball bearing type differential

2   Position the dished thrust washer against the crownwheel face with the base of the dished face towards the crownwheel. Where fitted, place the flat thrust washer over the dished thrust washer.

3   Place a block of wood under the flat face of the crownwheel and locate this assembly on a press bed. Position the clutch and differential housing over the differential and press the housing on. Keep the housing pressed down to compress the dished thrust washer and fit a new outer retaining circlip.

4   Remove the clutch and differential housing, complete with differential, from the press, lubricate the lips of a new oil seal and carefully slide it over the splined shaft (photo). Tap the seal into the housing using a block of wood or tube until it is flush with the edge of the internal land.

Taper bearing type differential

5   A length of cord and a spring balance will be required to measure the turning torque of the crownwheel when it is fitted. The shim which fits under the nut must be selected as follows:

   (a) If the original crownwheel, bearings and housing are being refitted, fit the original shim

   (b) If the crownwheel, bearings and/or the housing have been renewed, select the thickest shim (2.52 mm) from the shim set supplied.

6   Lubricate the bearings lightly with grease, then fit the differential unit into position in the housing.

7   Support the crownwheel and housing, then fit the taper bearing to the tail shaft followed by the shim and nut, ensuring that the grooved face is towards the bearing.

8   Lock the crownwheel using the same method as used during removal, then initially tighten the retaining nut to a torque wrench setting of between 10 and 20 Nm (7 to 14 lbf ft). Remove the locking tool and rotate the crownwheel/differential unit to seat the bearings.

9   Refit the locking tool, firmly support the housing and further tighten the nut to the final specified torque wrench setting. Remove the locking tool and check the crownwheel turning torque as follows.

10   Rotate the crownwheel/differential a few times, then wind the cord round the crownwheel as shown in Fig. 6.25 and attach it to a spring balance. Pull on the spring balance and check the turning force. If the original bearings were refitted, the force should be between 0 and 16.0 N (0 and 3.6 lbf). If new bearings were fitted, the turning force should be between 16.0 and 32.0 N (3.6 and 7.3 lbf).

11   If the turning force is incorrect, select an alternative shim to suit as follows.

12   Adjustment shims are available in thicknesses from 2.225 mm to 2.525 mm in graduations of 0.05 mm. Select a suitable shim, bearing in mind that the preload of the bearings increases by approximately 7.0 to 8.0 N (1.58 to 1.80 lbf) when the shim thickness is reduced by 0.05 mm, and reduced by the corresponding amount when the shim thickness is increased.

13   Repeat the procedures outlined in paragraphs 8 to 10 inclusive until the correct shim thickness is obtained to provide the specified crownwheel turning force.

14   Ensure that the speedometer driveshaft rotates freely, then fit a new oil seal to the tailshaft (as described in paragraph 5).

All differential types

15   Place the magnet in its location in the bottom of the housing.

16   Hold the assembled secondary, primary and reverse shafts together and locate all three shafts as an assembly into the housing.

17   Insert the long detent plunger into its location and push it through into contact with the reverse shaft detent grooves using a screwdriver (photo).

18   Locate the 1st/2nd selector fork in its groove in the synchro sleeve and engage the 1st/2nd selector shaft into it. Turn the shaft so that the detent grooves at the top are towards the secondary shaft, insert the small detent plunger into the hole in the shaft and push the shaft down through the fork (photo). Manipulate the reverse shaft as necessary in the neutral position so that the 1st/2nd shaft can be pushed fully home.

19   Place the 3rd/4th selector fork into the groove in the synchro

sleeve with its thicker side towards the differential.

20   Locate the detent plunger in its groove in the housing, then slide the 3rd/4th selector shaft through the fork. Ensure that all the shafts are in neutral and push the 3rd/4th shaft fully home. It may take a few attempts to get all the shafts, particularly reverse, in just the right position so that the detent plungers all locate fully into their grooves enabling the 3rd/4th shaft to be fitted.

21   Support the selector shafts using a tube of suitable diameter and refit the 1st/2nd and 3rd/4th selector fork roll pins. Tap in the pins until they are flush with the side of the forks (photos). The roll pins must be orientated as shown in Fig. 6.26.

22   Refit the remaining detent plunger to its location in the housing.

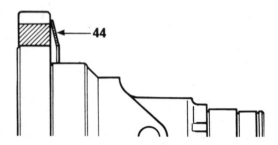

Fig. 6.24 Dished thrust washer (44)-to-crownwheel orientation (Sec 12)

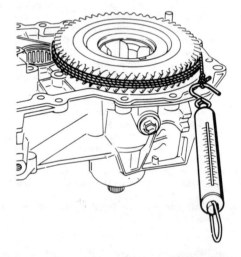

Fig. 6.25 Crownwheel timing load check method using cord and spring balance – taper bearing type differential (Sec 12)

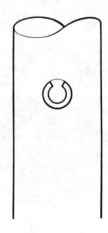

Fig. 6.26 Selector fork roll pin orientation in shaft (Sec 12)

12.4 Fit a new oil seal to the clutch and differential housing

12.17 Push the long detent plunger into its location using a screwdriver

12.18 Insert the small detent plunger (arrowed) into the 1st/2nd selector shaft

12.21A Refit the 1st/2nd selector fork roll pin ...

12.21B ... and 3rd/4th selector fork roll pin ...

12.21C ... tap the pins so that they are flush

13 Transmission – reassembling the housings

1   Make sure that the 5th speed selector shaft, detent ball and spring are in place in the mechanism casing.

2   Wipe clean the mating faces of the two housings, then apply a bead of jointing compound to both mating faces. *Note that no gasket is used.*

3   Make sure that all the shafts are in neutral and that the engagement slots on the 1st/2nd and 3rd/4th shafts are exactly in line.

4   Pull the fork control shaft on the mechanism casing outwards as far as it will go, then lower the mechanism casing over the geartrains. Align the selector shafts with the holes in the casing and, as the shafts protrude, remove the two bolts or rods used to retain the detent balls and springs.

5   As the primary and secondary shafts enter their bearings, tap the casing with a plastic mallet to assist entry.

6   Pass a hooked piece of wire through the aperture in the top of the casing. Lift up the reverse shaft and gear then retain the shaft with the detent ball, spring and retaining plate.

7   Fit two of the retaining bolts to secure the housings, then check that it is possible to engage all the gears.

8   Refit the 5th speed detent assembly. If a new 5th gear, housing or associated fittings have been used, the detent shim requirement should be checked using a depth gauge as shown in Fig. 6.28. To make the check, engage 4th gear and move the selector lever so that it contacts the 1st/2nd speed dog. Measure the depth 'X' as shown and select a shim (if necessary) of the required thickness.

9   Refit all the remaining housing retaining bolts and tighten to the specified torque.

10 Refit the 5th speed driven gear as follows according to type by referring to Fig. 6.29 and paragraphs 11 to 13 inclusive or Fig. 6.30 and paragraphs 14 and 15.

Type 1

11 Apply a few drops of Loctite FRENBLOC to the 5th speed driven

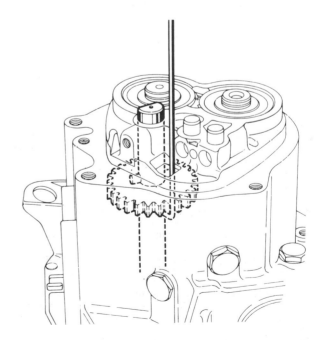

Fig. 6.27 Use a hooked piece of wire to lift the reverse gear and shaft (Sec 13)

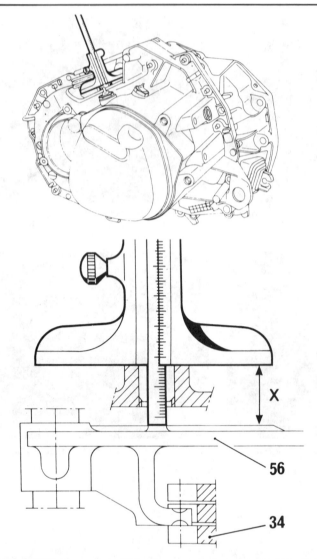

Fig. 6.28 5th speed detent shim requirement check (Sec 13)

34 1st/2nd gear dog
56 Selector lever
Depth X = 22.35 mm – No shim required
Depth X = 22.35 mm to 22.03 mm – 0.33 mm thick shim required
Depth X = 22.02 mm to 21.70 mm – 0.66 mm thick shim required

gear, fit the gear to the secondary shaft and push it fully onto the shaft using a socket with a bolt through its centre and screwed into the threaded end of the secondary shaft. Tighten the bolt and the socket will force the gear fully home.

12 Remove the socket and bolt, fit the dished washer and circlip, then compress the washer using the same bolt and socket method. As the washer is compressed the circlip will enter its groove.

13 Refit the collar, bolt and washer to the end of the secondary shaft after applying a few drops of locking compound to the bolt threads. Tighten the bolt to the specified torque wrench setting.

Type 2

14 Smear the inner bore of the 5th speed driven gear with Loctite FRENBLOC, then fit it onto the end of the secondary shaft, ensuring that it is fitted the correct way round.

15 Fit the shouldered washer over the end of the secondary shaft, then apply a little Loctite FRENBLOC to the threads of the retaining bolt and tighten the bolt to the specified torque setting.

All types

16 Fit the washer, bearing bush and needle roller bearing to the primary shaft, apply a few drops of thread locking compound to the 5th speed synchro-hub splines, then refit the driving gear, synchro-hub and selector fork as an assembly. Ensure that the offset boss of the

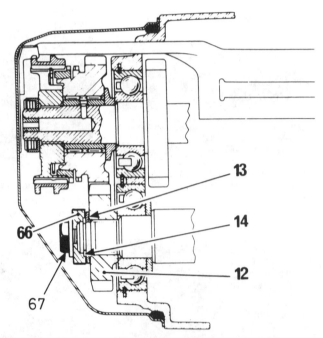

Fig. 6.29 Sectional view of the type 1 5th speed driven gear assembly (Sec 13)

12 5th speed driven gear	*66 Shouldered washer*
13 Washer	*67 8 mm bolt*
14 Circlip	

Fig. 6.30 Sectional view of the type 2 5th speed driven gear assembly (Sec 13)

64 Shouldered washer   *65 10 mm diameter bolt*

synchro-hub is towards the driven gear (see Fig. 6.11).

17 Engage 1st gear by moving the gear linkage fork control shaft, and engage 5th gear by moving the 5th speed selector fork. With the geartrain now locked, refit the 5th gear retaining nut, smearing the threads with Loctite FRENBLOC, and tighten to the specified torque.

18 Return the gears to neutral, then fit a new roll pin to secure the 5th gear selector fork on its shaft (photo). Apply the same method for fitting this pin as that used when removing the old pin (see Fig. 6.10).

13.18 General view of reassembled 5th gear and assembly

13.19A Fit a new O-ring seal ...

13.19B   and rear cover and retaining bolts

Ensure that the slot in the roll pin is towards the rear end of the housing.

19 Place a new rubber O-ring seal on the casing shoulder then refit the rear cover. Where applicable, engage the oil pipe in the primary shaft port and lubrication channel as the cover is fitted. Tighten the cover bolts to the specified torque wrench setting (photos).

20 Check that the respective gears can be positively engaged. If selection is a problem, check that 5th gear or reverse have not been selected accidentally.

21 Refit the O-ring to the splines of the differential stub shaft.

22 Refit the gearbox mounting bracket, then refer to Chapter 5 and refit the clutch release bearing and fork assembly.

23 The gearbox can now be refitted to the car, as described in Section 4.

14 Gear lever and remote control housing – removal, refitting and adjustment

1 To remove the gear lever and remote control housing first jack up the front of the car and support it on axle stands.

2 From underneath, unhook the tension spring fitted between the gearchange rod and the stud on the vehicle floor (photo).

3 Slacken the clamp bolt securing the gearchange rod to the gear lever yoke and withdraw the yoke from the rod (photo).

4 Refer to Chapter 11 and remove the centre console.

5 With the console removed, undo the four bolts securing the remote control housing to the floor and withdraw the assembly from the car (photo). Recover the sealing gasket.

6 If necessary the gear lever assembly may be dismantled by referring to the component locations shown in Fig. 6.32. Note that the gear lever knob is bonded with adhesive to the lever.

7 Reassembly and refitting are the reverse of the above procedures. Adjust the gear lever as follows before tightening the yoke clamp bolt.

8 Select 2nd gear at the gearbox by moving the fork control shaft.

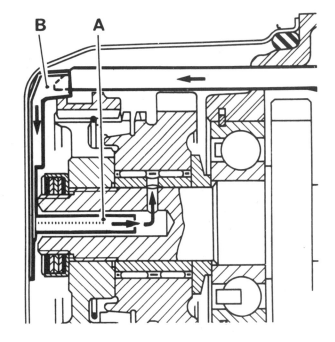

Fig. 6.31 Oil pipe (A) and lubrication channel (B) arrangement on certain models (Sec 13)

14.2 Gearchange rod tension spring

14.3 Gearchange rod and yoke

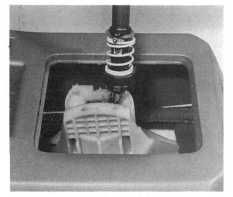

14.5 Gearlever remote control housing

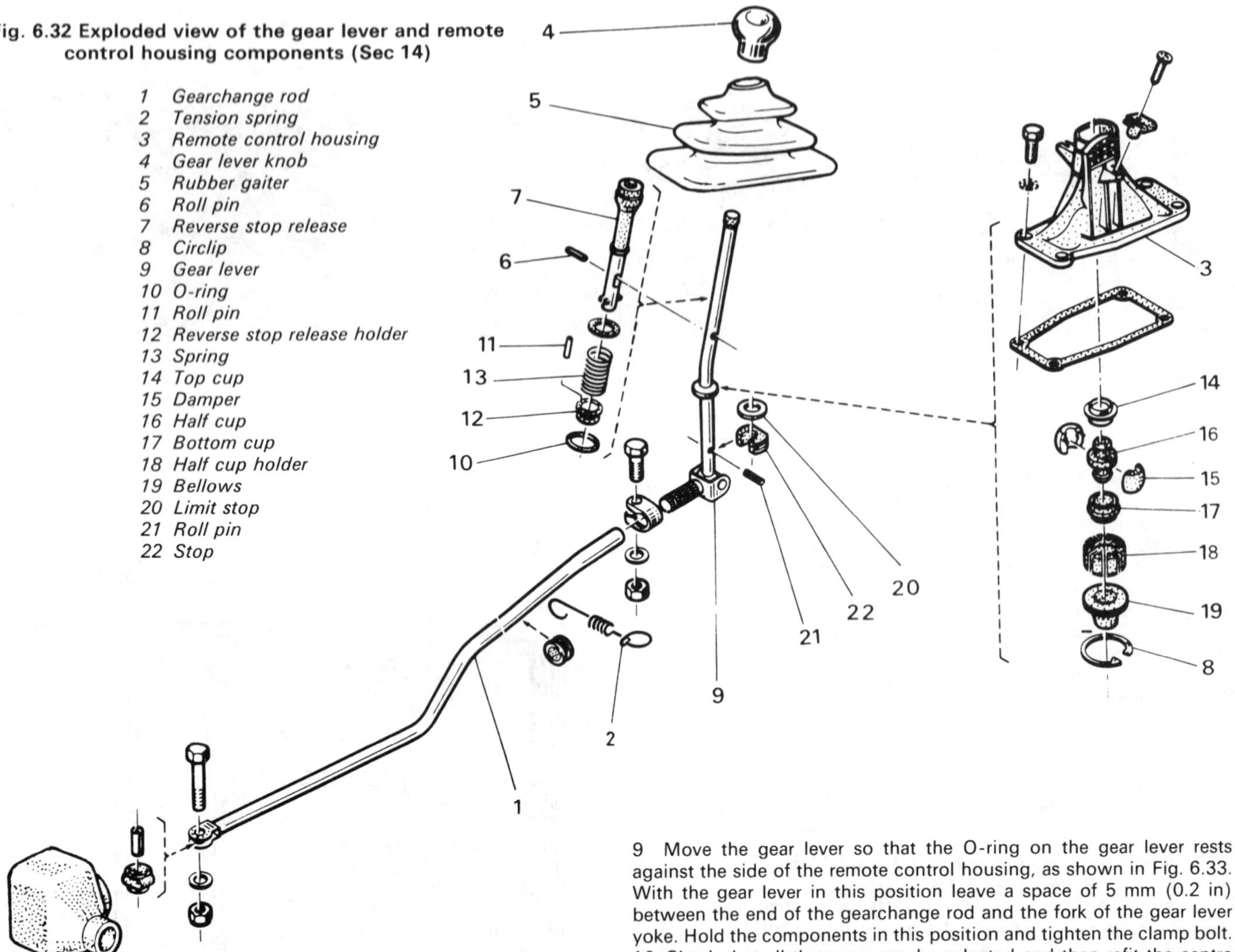

Fig. 6.32 Exploded view of the gear lever and remote control housing components (Sec 14)

1 Gearchange rod
2 Tension spring
3 Remote control housing
4 Gear lever knob
5 Rubber gaiter
6 Roll pin
7 Reverse stop release
8 Circlip
9 Gear lever
10 O-ring
11 Roll pin
12 Reverse stop release holder
13 Spring
14 Top cup
15 Damper
16 Half cup
17 Bottom cup
18 Half cup holder
19 Bellows
20 Limit stop
21 Roll pin
22 Stop

9 Move the gear lever so that the O-ring on the gear lever rests against the side of the remote control housing, as shown in Fig. 6.33. With the gear lever in this position leave a space of 5 mm (0.2 in) between the end of the gearchange rod and the fork of the gear lever yoke. Hold the components in this position and tighten the clamp bolt.
10 Check that all the gears can be selected and then refit the centre console, as described in Chapter 11, and lower the car to the ground.

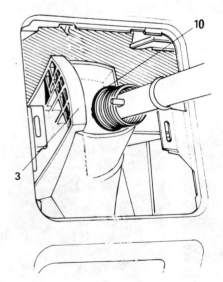

Fig. 6.33 Position the gear lever so that the O-ring (10) rests against the side of the remote control housing (3) (Sec 14)

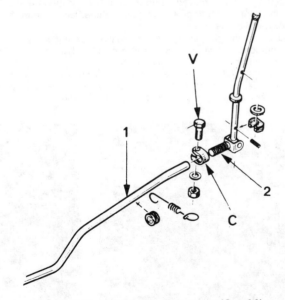

Fig. 6.34 Gear linkage adjustment (Sec 14)

1 Gearchange rod   C Gear lever yoke clamp
2 Gear lever yoke   V Clamp bolt

PART B: NG9 TRANSMISSION

15 General description

The NG9 transmission is located behind the engine in a similar manner to rear-wheel-drive cars but power is transmitted to the front roadwheels through driveshafts. The driveshafts are splined to the side gears of the differential/final drive which is integrated into the transmission casing.

Five forward synchromesh gears are provided with a reverse gear
The gearchange control is of floor-mounted type
The transmission casing is of four section type: the clutch bellhousing, the rear cover (which houses the selector finger and 5th gear), and the two main casing sections whch are split longitudinally.

16 Maintenance, draining and refilling

1 Proceed as described in Part A, Sections 2 and 3 of this Chapter, but refer to the accompanying photos and figure.

17 Transmission – removal and refitting

1 The transmission may be removed on its own as described in this Section, or together with the engine as described in Chapter 1.
2 Remove the transmission undertray. This is secured by a single screw on the left-hand side and locating pegs at the rear and on the right-hand side (see photo 16.1A).
3 Undo the drain plug and drain the transmission oil into a suitable container for disposal (see photo 16.1B).
4 Disconnect the battery earth lead.
5 Place the car over an inspection pit or raise and support it at the front end on safety stands at a height sufficient to allow access underneath and sufficient to enable the transmission to be lowered and removed from underneath.
6 Disconnect and remove the exhaust downpipe.
7 Disconnect both driveshafts from the transmission as described in Chapter 1, Part B, Section 50.
8 Disconnect the speedometer cable from the transmission by gripping the retaining pin with a pair of pliers and pulling it outwards to release the cable (photo).
9 Disconnect the gearbox earth strap and the reversing light leads at the in-line connector.
10 Disconnect the gearchange linkage at the transmission end as described in Section 28.
11 Undo the retaining bolts and remove the transverse rod from the subframe (photo).
12 Disconnect the clutch cable at the release lever and support bracket on the top of the bellhousing. See Chapter 5 for details.
13 Undo the retaining bolts and remove the angular position/speed sensor from the top of the bellhousing.
14 Unscrew the starter motor mounting bolts to release the starter motor from the flywheel housing.
15 Unscrew and remove the bolts which connect the transmission to the engine (photo).
16 Support the engine using a jack or hoist and place a second jack, preferably of trolley type, under the transmission.
17 Disconnect the transmission flexible mountings and brackets.
18 Raise the transmission slightly to clear the crossmember during withdrawal to the rear.
19 Remove the transmission from under the car.
20 Refitting is a reversal of removal, but observe the following points.
21 Make sure that the clutch driven plate has been centralised, as described in Chapter 5.
22 Tighten all nuts and bolts to the specified torque and renew those of self-locking type.
23 Adjust the clutch cable (Chapter 5).
24 Fill the transmission with oil of the specified type.

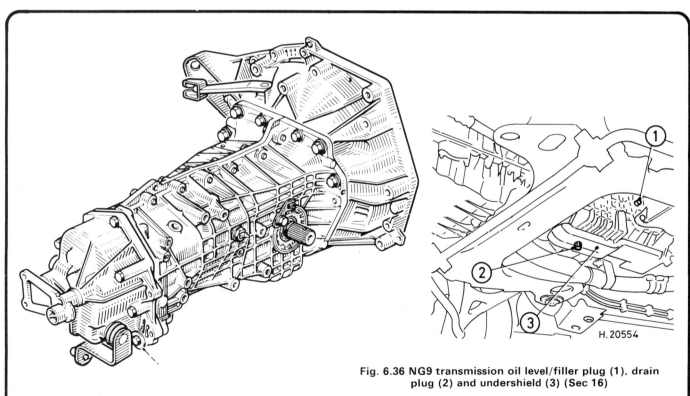

Fig. 6.35 NG9 type transmission (Sec 15)

Fig. 6.36 NG9 transmission oil level/filler plug (1), drain plug (2) and undershield (3) (Sec 16)

H. 20554

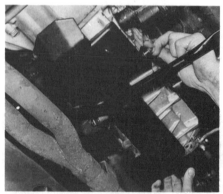

16.1A Remove the undershield from the NG9 transmission ...

16.1B ... for access to the drain plug (arrowed)

16.1C Oil level/filler plug (arrowed) – NG9 transmission

17.8 Disconnect the speedometer cable by pulling on the retaining pin (arrowed)

17.11 Unbolt the transverse rod

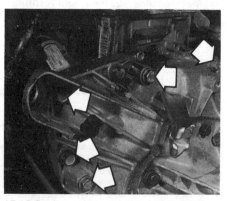

17.15 Engine-to-transmission bolts (arrowed)

18 Transmission overhaul – general

Refer to Part A, Section 5 of this Chapter.

19 Transmission – removal of major assemblies

1   With the transmission removed, clean away external dirt and grease using paraffin and a stiff brush, or a water-soluble solvent.

2   Place the unit on a bench or, if it must be dismantled on the floor, rest it on a sheet of hardboard.

3   Remove the clutch lever.

4   Unbolt and remove the clutch bellhousing and gasket.

5   Select 3rd or 4th gear, unscrew the 5th detent plug and extract the spring and ball.

6   Unbolt and remove the rear cover. Tilt the cover as it is withdrawn to disengage the selector finger. Remove the cover gasket. Note the bolt lengths and locations.

7   Unscrew the casing bolts, then position the transmission so that the crownwheel teeth point downwards and lift off the casing half-section.

8   Remove the differential/final drive.

9   Remove the primary and secondary geartrains.

10 With the major assemblies removed they can be inspected for wear and/or damage. If dismantling the gear assemblies, a bearing puller will be required.

20 Primary shaft – overhaul

Note: *A puller will be required for this operation*

1   Drive out the roll pin and separate the clutch shaft from the primary shaft. Remove the washer(s).

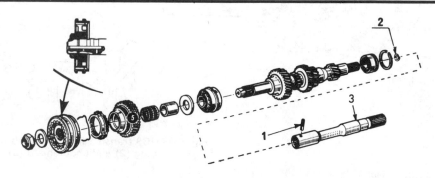

Fig. 6.37 Primary shaft components (Sec 20)

1   Roll pin   *2   Special washer*   *3   Clutch shaft*

2 Support the shaft vertically in a vice fitted with jaw protectors. Release the nut staking, and remove the nut (photo).

3 Withdraw the 5th gear and its synchro hub. It may be necessary to use a puller to withdraw this assembly, in which case engage the puller claws behind 5th gear and draw off 5th gear and the synchro hub together.

4 Extract the shaft bearings, again using the puller if necessary.

5 Examine all the components carefully and renew as necessary (photo).

6 Commence reassembly by sliding the new bearings into position. A double ball type bearing is used at the 5th gear end of the shaft and a roller bearing at the clutch shaft end. The bearings should be fitted so that their engraved marks are visible from the ends of the shaft (photos).

7 Fit the thick washer, needle bearing, bush, 5th gear and its baulk ring (photos). To fit the 5th gear synchro hub, support the 4th gear and press on the synchro hub with a load of not less than 100 kgf (220 lbf) or more than 1500 kgf (3300 lbf).

8 Finally, fit the washer, then apply a little locking fluid to the threads of a new nut before fitting it and tightening it to the specified torque. Lock the nut by staking (photo).

9 Locate the special washer, then fit the clutch shaft to the primary shaft and drive in the roll pin to secure (photos).

20.2 Release the nut staking

20.5 Primary shaft

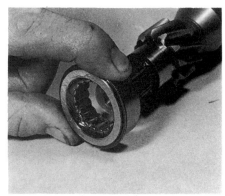
20.6A Fitting the roller bearing to the clutch shaft end of the primary shaft

20.6B Fit the inner ball race ...

20.6C ... the outer bearing track ...

20.6D ... and the inner ball race to the 5th gear end of the shaft

20.7A Fit the thick washer ...

20.7B ... the needle bearing ...

20.7C ... and its bush ...

20.7D ... followed by 5th gear ...

20.7E ... and its baulk ring

20.7F With the synchro hub fitted ...

20.8 ... locate the washer and retaining nut (staking arrowed)

20.9A Clutch shaft and special washer

20.9B Driving in the clutch shaft roll pin

21 Secondary shaft – overhaul

Note: *To dismantle and assemble the secondary shaft unit, Renault special tool No BVi 204.01 will be required*

1   Grip the shaft by 1st gear in a vice fitted with jaw protectors so that the shaft is vertical.
2   Select 1st gear by moving the synchro sleeve incorporating reverse gear teeth downwards.
3   Unscrew the speedometer drive gear nut using the special Renault spanner (No BVi 204.01) (photos).
4   Using a puller, remove 5th gear.
5   Remove the secondary shaft components in the order shown in Fig. 6.38. Extract the circlips before attempting removal. Mark the synchro hubs and sleeves in relation to each other to ensure correct refitting. Note that the roller bearing at the pinion end does not have an inner track, and to prevent the bearing falling apart a clip can be fitted over it (photo).
6   Renew any worn or damaged components, also the circlips and shaft nut. Modifications have been made to the following items, and it should be noted that later components are not directly interchangeable with the earlier types. Take this into account when ordering spare parts.

   (a) *1st gear has a larger rim on models produced from 1987 on (see Fig. 6.41)*
   (b) *3rd/4th gear synchro springs and the hub were modified in March 1987 (see Figs. 6.42, 6.43 and 6.44)*
   (c) *Alternative types of 5th gear are fitted. The earlier type can be identified by its inner splines (see paragraph 17)*

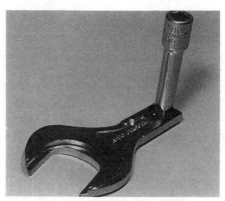

21.3A Renault special tool No BVi 204.01 is required ...

21.3B ... to unscrew the speedometer drive gear from the secondary shaft

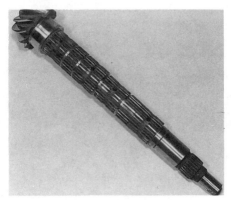

21.5 Secondary shaft dismantled for inspection

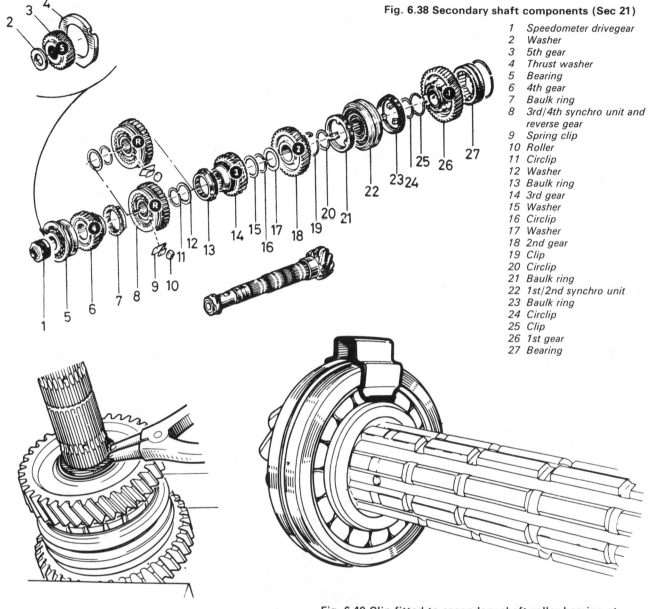

Fig. 6.38 Secondary shaft components (Sec 21)

1 Speedometer drivegear
2 Washer
3 5th gear
4 Thrust washer
5 Bearing
6 4th gear
7 Baulk ring
8 3rd/4th synchro unit and reverse gear
9 Spring clip
10 Roller
11 Circlip
12 Washer
13 Baulk ring
14 3rd gear
15 Washer
16 Circlip
17 Washer
18 2nd gear
19 Clip
20 Circlip
21 Baulk ring
22 1st/2nd synchro unit
23 Baulk ring
24 Circlip
25 Clip
26 1st gear
27 Bearing

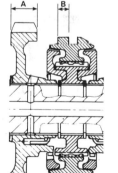

Fig. 6.39 Extracting the secondary shaft circlip (Sec 21)

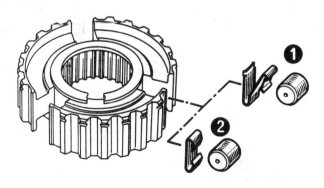

Fig. 6.40 Clip fitted to secondary shaft roller bearing at pinion end (Sec 21)

Fig. 6.41 1st gear and 1st/2nd gear synchro hub showing modification points on later models (Sec 21)

A = 19 mm (previously 17.5 mm)   B = 6.4 mm (previously 7.9 mm)

Fig. 6.42 Alternative types of synchro spring (Sec 21)

1 Earlier type spring   2 Later type spring

7   Reassemble the components in reverse order to removal. The synchro hubs are a sliding fit on the shaft splines, however, if the hub becomes tight, remove it, turn it, and engage it with different splines. Note the correct fitted positions of the synchro units shown in Fig. 6.45.

8   If necessary reassemble the pinion end roller bearing by greasing the rollers and inserting them into the bearing outer track, then fit the assembled bearing unit to the secondary shaft as shown (photos).

9   Ensure that the synchro spring is correctly fitted to 1st gear, then fit the gear into position on the secondary shaft (photos).

10 Fit the 1st gear baulk ring, 1st/2nd synchro hub, the retaining clip and 2nd gear baulk ring. Ensure that the clip is fully engaged in its groove (photos).

11 Fit 2nd gear, the splined washer and the retaining clip (photos).

12 Fit the 3rd gear splined washer, 3rd gear, baulk ring and the splined washer. Secure with a new retaining clip (photos).

13 Reassemble the rollers and springs to the 3rd/4th gear synchro hub (according to type – see paragraph 6), then fit the hub assembly onto the shaft (photos).

14 Fit the 4th gear baulk ring, then if applicable, slide the retaining clip and splined washer into position on the shaft (photo).

15 Slide 4th gear into position (photo).

16 Fit the inner taper roller bearing cone and spacer washer, the bearing cup and the outer bearing cone (photos).

17 Locate the spacer plate onto the bearing followed by 5th gear (photos). On this gearbox, one of two alternative types of 5th gear are fitted. With the first type having continuous inner splines apply a small amount of locking fluid to the splines before fitting the gear. The second type gear is free turning for three-quarters of its splines and the final splines must be pressed into position to give the correct preload to the double taper roller bearing. Position the assembly in the press as shown in Fig. 6.46 with a spring balance and cord around the bearing outer track. Press on the gear until the preload is between 1.5 and 4.0 kgf (3.4 and 9.0 lbf) and note that the press loading must not be less than 100 kgf (220 lbf) or more than 1500 kgf (3300 lbf).

18 Where applicable, fit the spacer washer, then select 1st gear. Smear the threads of the speedometer drive gear with locking compound and screw it onto the secondary shaft (photos). Tighten the nut to the specified torque wrench setting, then stake the nut over the flat section of the shaft to lock it.

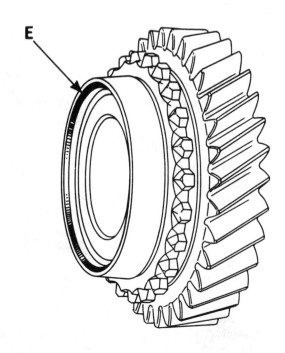

Fig. 6.43 3rd/4th gear synchro hub modification – 20° inlet chamfer at E to suit later synchro springs (Sec 21)

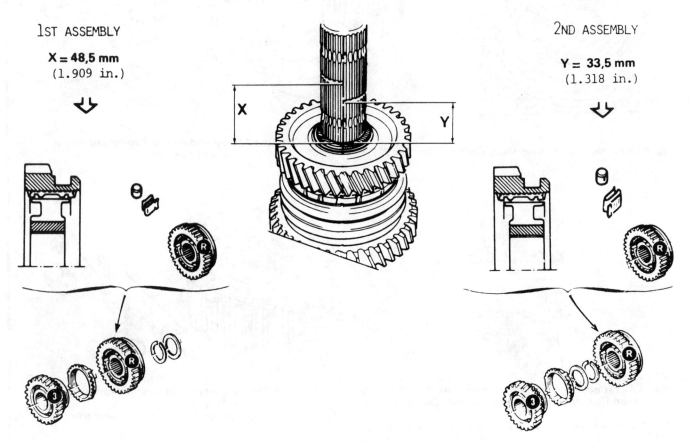

1ST ASSEMBLY

X = 48,5 mm
(1.909 in.)

2ND ASSEMBLY

Y = 33,5 mm
(1.318 in.)

Fig. 6.44 Identification of 3rd/4th synchro unit types (Sec 21)

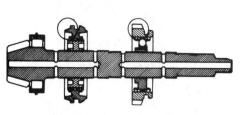

Fig. 6.45 The correctly fitted positions of the synchro units on the secondary shaft (Sec 21)

21.8A Grease the rollers to hold them in the bearing outer track ...

21.8B ... then fit the bearing

21.9A Synchro spring location in 1st speed gear

21.9B Fit the 1st speed gear ...

21.10A ... 1st gear baulk ring ...

21.10B ... 1st/2nd synchro hub ...

21.10C ... the hub retaining clip ...

21.10D ... and the 2nd gear baulk ring

21.11A Fit 2nd gear ...

21.11B ... the splined washer ...

21.11C ... and the retaining clip

21.12A Fit the 3rd gear splined washer ...

21.12B ... 3rd gear ...

21.12C ... 3rd gear baulk ring ...

21.12D ... the splined washer ...

21.12E ... and retaining clip

21.13A Assemble the rollers and springs to the 3rd/4th synchro hub

21.13B ... then fit the hub assembly

21.14 Fit the 4th gear baulk ring ...

21.15 ... and 4th gear

21.16A Fit the inner taper roller bearing cone and spacer washer ...

21.16B ... the bearing cup ...

21.16C ... and the outer bearing cone

21.17A Fit the spacer plate ...

21.17B ... and 5th gear

21.18A Fit the spacer washer (where applicable) ...

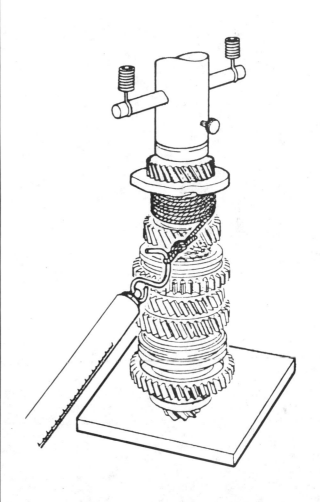

Fig. 6.46 Pressing 5th gear onto the secondary shaft
(Sec 21)

21.18B ... and the speedometer drive gear

22 Reverse idler shaft and gear – dismantling and reassembly

1   Extract the circlip, then withdraw the shaft followed by the gear, friction washer and guide. Recover the interlocking ball and spring.
2   To refit, locate the spring and ball in the casing.
3   Insert the shaft and locate the gear on it with the hub facing the differential end.
4   Fit the friction washer with the bronze face toward the gear.
5   Locate the guide in the bore, then push in the shaft and fit the circlip (photo).

23 Selector forks and shafts – dismantling and reassembly

1   Select neutral and then pull out the 5th gear selector shaft. Recover the locking ball.
2   Drive out the roll pin securing the selector forks.
3   Pull out the 3rd/4th selector shaft, remove the fork, and recover the detent ball and spring.
4   Remove the interlock disc and pull out the 1st/2nd selector shaft. Recover the detent ball and spring.
5   Unscrew the bolt and remove the reverse selector lever.
6   Pull out the reverse selector shaft.

7   When refitting the shaft, note that the slots on the roll pins must face the rear casing. The refitting procedure is a reversal of removal. After fitting the 5th gear shaft select 3rd or 4th to prevent the shaft moving when the rear cover is fitted (photo).
8   **Note:** A spring and ball are incorporated in the 1st/2nd selector shaft. When reassembling the fork to the shaft, make sure that the roll pin hole in the fork is nearest the rear cover. The slits in the roll pins must also be towards the rear cover.

Fig. 6.47 Reverse idler shaft components (Sec 22)

22.5 Reverse idler gear orientation to be as shown

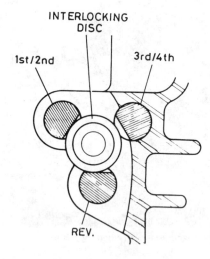

Fig. 6.48 Selector shaft interlock disc (Sec 23)

23.7 Selector forks and shafts

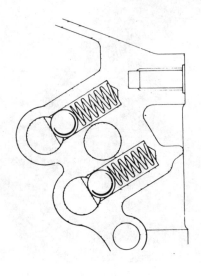

Fig. 6.49 Location of detent balls and springs (Sec 23)

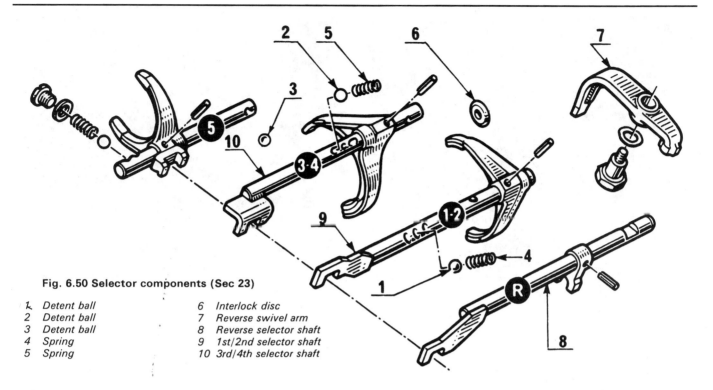

Fig. 6.50 Selector components (Sec 23)

1   Detent ball
2   Detent ball
3   Detent ball
4   Spring
5   Spring
6   Interlock disc
7   Reverse swivel arm
8   Reverse selector shaft
9   1st/2nd selector shaft
10 3rd/4th selector shaft

24 Rear cover – dismantling and reassembly

1   Drive out the roll pin(s) using a suitable punch (photo).
2   Extract the circlip and prise the bush from the selector lever shaft.
3   Unscrew the plug and extract the reverse shaft stop plunger and spring.
4   Remove the selector components.
5   To remove the speedometer drivegear, prise up the short arms and withdraw the shaft, followed by the gear. Note that the gear must be renewed after removal.
6   Extract the oil seals.
7   Remove any sharp edges from the ends of the shafts to prevent damage to the oil seals.
8   Reassembly is a reversal of dismantling, but fit new oil seals and make sure that the speedometer drivegear arms fully enter the groove in the shaft (photo).

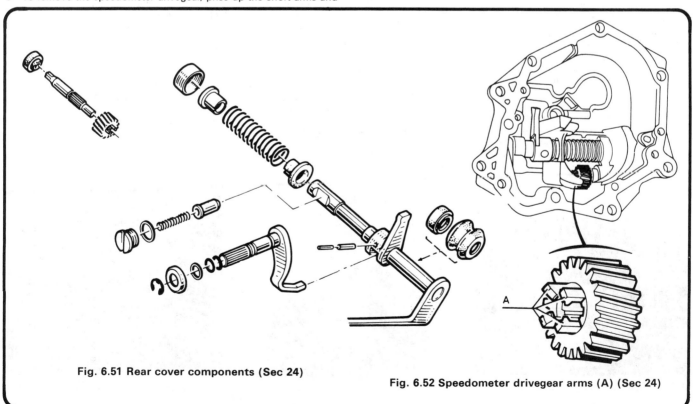

Fig. 6.51 Rear cover components (Sec 24)

Fig. 6.52 Speedometer drivegear arms (A) (Sec 24)

24.1 Selector lever shaft and roll pins (arrowed)

24.8 View showing selector lever, shaft assembly and speedometer drivegear

25 Transmission housing – inspection

Examine all housing sections for cracks, and renew oil seals as a matter of routine.

26 Differential – overhaul

Note: *A puller will be needed for this operation*

1   It is unlikely that the differential will require overhaul, but if the bearings or other components must be renewed, proceed in the following way.
2   Using a suitable puller, remove the tapered roller bearings (photos).
3   Unbolt and remove the crownwheel. If the crownwheel is renewed, then the secondary shaft must be renewed as well to ensure that the pinion gear is matched to the crownwheel (supplied as a matching pair).
4   Remove the sun wheels and planet gears and separate the differential components. The collar will be destroyed, so renew it.
5   Now turn your attention to the ring nuts in the transmission casing. Unscrew the lockbolt and remove the locktab (photo).

6   Make up a suitable tool to unscrew the ring nuts and remove them.
7   Remove the bearing outer tracks from the casing sections and fit the new ones.
8   Fit new oil seals and O-rings to the ring nuts. The oil seals are inserted from the rear face of the ring nut and pressed in until the seal face (2) is tight against the ring nut face (3 – Fig. 6.53).
9   Reassemble the differential and press on the new bearings. Always use new bolts on the crownwheel and tighten to the specified torque. Note that the bearing on the crownwheel side has a smaller diameter inner track than the opposite bearing.
20 If new differential bearings have been fitted the casing ring nuts must be adjusted to obtain the correct preload. First fit the differential in the casings without the primary or secondary shafts and tighten the casing bolts to the correct torque and in the correct sequence (Fig. 6.54).
11 Screw in the ring nuts turning the one on the differential housing side slightly more than the opposite side. Continue turning until the differential unit becomes hard to move.
12 Using a spring balance and cord (Fig. 6.55) check that the differential turns within the specified loadings, and adjust the ring nuts accordingly.
13 Separate the casings and remove the differential pending reassembly of the transmission.

26.2A Remove the taper roller bearings ...

26.2B ... from each end of the shaft

26.5 Lockbolt (1), lock tab (2) and ring nut (3)

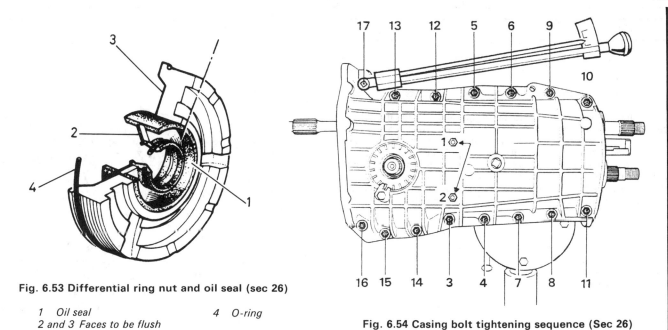

Fig. 6.53 Differential ring nut and oil seal (sec 26)

1   Oil seal   4   O-ring
2 and 3   Faces to be flush

Fig. 6.54 Casing bolt tightening sequence (Sec 26)

Fig. 6.55 Checking differential bearing preload (Sec 26)

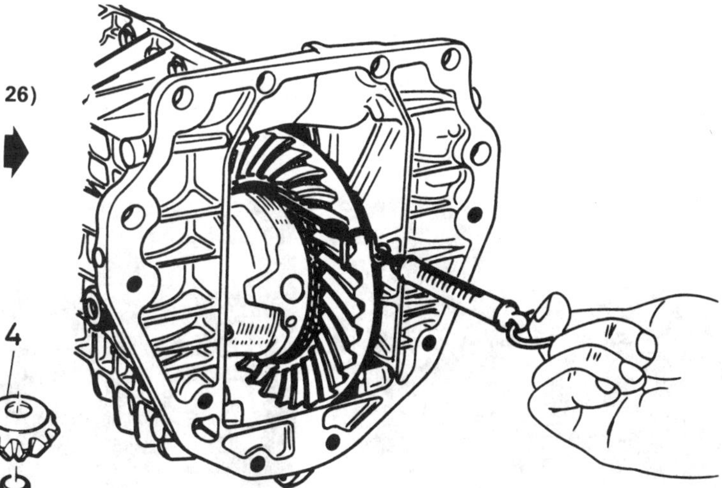

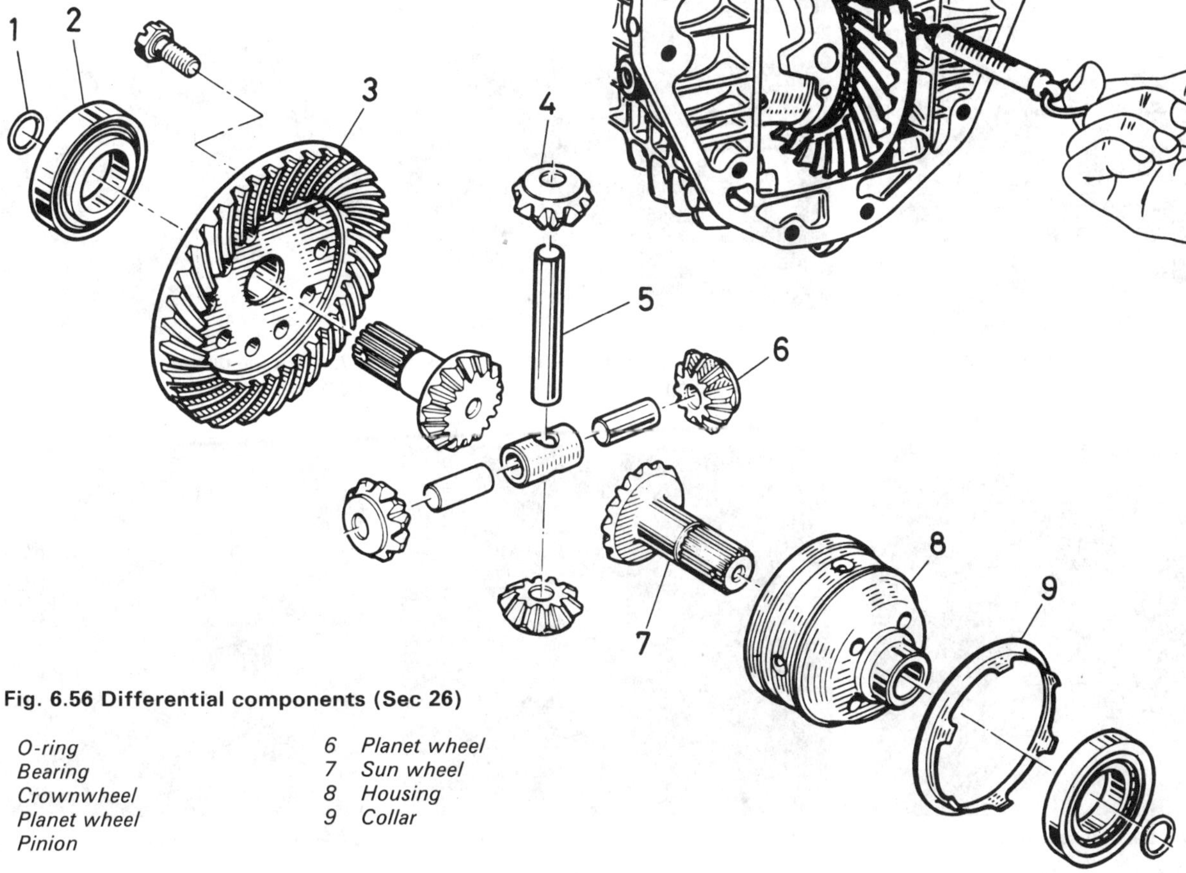

Fig. 6.56 Differential components (Sec 26)

1   O-ring   6   Planet wheel
2   Bearing   7   Sun wheel
3   Crownwheel   8   Housing
4   Planet wheel   9   Collar
5   Pinion

27 Transmission – reassembly

1   Locate the primary and secondary shaft assemblies in the right-hand casing. When fitting the secondary shaft into position, align the cut-out in the rear spacer plate with the selecto rod. Ensure that the bearing clips of the primary shaft engage with the slots in the casing (photos).

2   Fit the differential unit into the right-hand casing, then apply sealant to the mating faces of the casing halves. Refit the left-hand casing, then insert and tighten the retaining bolts to the specified torque wrench setting in the sequence shown in Fig. 6.54 (photos).

3   Using a dial gauge, as shown in Fig. 6.57 check that the backlash between the crownwheel and pinion is as given in the Specifications. If not, move the differential unit as necessary by turning the ring nuts by equal amounts. Note the unequal turning of the ring nuts will result in an incorrect bearing preload. Mark the ring nut positions after making the adjustment.

4   Fit the rear cover, together with a new gasket, then fit the bolts and tighten them to the specified torque (photos).

5   Insert the 5th gear detent ball and spring, then tighten the plug into the cover (photos).

6   Wrap adhesive tape lightly over the clutch shaft splines and smear with a little grease.

7   Refit the clutch housing using a new gasket and tighten the bolts. Remove the tape (photos).

8   Check that the ring nuts are positioned correctly, then fit the lockplates and tighten the bolts.

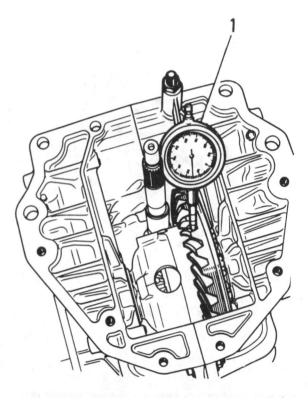

Fig. 6.57 Checking the crownwheel-to-pinion backlash using a dial gauge (1) (Sec 27)

27.1A Fit the primary shaft assembly and ...

27.1B ... secondary shaft assembly into the right-hand casing

27.2A Fit the differential unit into the right-hand casing

27.2B Apply a bead of sealant to the mating face ...

27.2C ... then fit the left-hand casing

27.4A Locate the gasket ...

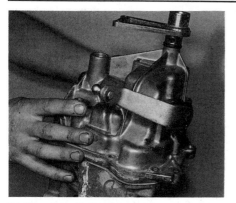
27.4B ... then fit the rear cover

27.5A Insert the 5th gear detent ball ...

27.5B ... spring ...

27.5C ... and plug

27.7A Locate the clutch housing gasket ...

27.7B ... then fit the clutch housing

28 Gearchange linkage – removal and refitting

1   The system consists of two remote control rods and a cable to release a locking finger when the ring on the gear lever is lifted during selection of reverse gear (photo). This is part of an interlock device to prevent engagement of reverse gear when shifting from 3rd to 2nd.
2   To disconnect the controls from the transmission, first unscrew the cable retaining union nut (photo).
3   To disconnect the control rod at the transmission end, prise free the balljoint using suitable pliers inserted as shown and used as a lever (photo).
4   To detach the framed balljoint, undo the retaining bolts and disconnect the joint coupling (photos).
5   Disconnection of the linkage rods at the gear lever end will necessitate the removal of the exhaust system for access (Chapter 3). Disconnect both rods from the base of the gearchange lever. One rod is secured by a nut, the other by a ball socket which is simply prised apart.
6   The cable can be released after unclipping its stop and removing the sleeve.
7   Working inside the car, remove the centre console (Chapter 11).
8   Unscrew and remove the gear lever knob.
9   Extract the four screws from the bellows retainer and withdraw the bellows.
10 Withdraw the gear lever.
11 Refitting is a reversal of removal, but smear the threads of the cable union with gasket cement before screwing it into the transmission casing. The balljoint connections can be reassembled using suitable grips as shown (photo).

PART C: UN1 TRANSMISSION

29 General description, maintenance, draining and refilling

1   The UN1 type transmission is similar to the NG9 type transmission described in Part B, Section 15 of this Chapter.

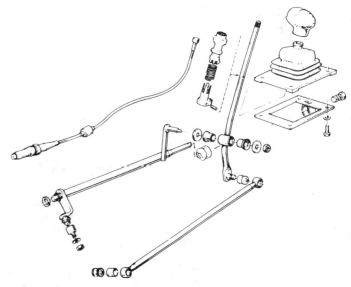
Fig. 6.58 Gearchange linkage (Sec 28)

28.1 Underside view showing gear selector rod, control rod and reverse cable (lever end)

28.2 Reverse gear interlock cable connection at the transmission

28.3 Separating the control rod balljoint

28.4A Undo the retaining bolts (arrowed) ...

28.4B ... to separate the framed balljoint

28.11 Reconnecting the control rod balljoint

2   The external features of the transmission as shown in Fig. 6.59.
3   The maintenance, draining and refilling procedures are the same as those described for the NG9 transmission in Part B, Section 16 of this Chapter.

30 Transmission – removal and refitting

1   The operations are similar to those described in Part B, Section 17

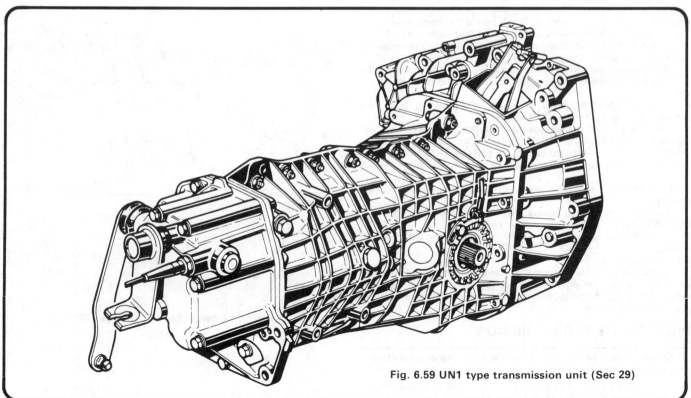

Fig. 6.59 UN1 type transmission unit (Sec 29)

of this Chapter, but the following differences must be taken into account.

2 Unbolt and remove the exhaust heat shield and unbolt the exhaust downpipe at the points indicated in Fig. 6.60.

3 Move the rigid cooling system pipes away from the clutch slave cylinder, then unbolt the slave cylinder and tie it up out of the way. There is no need to disconnect the hydraulic hose from the cylinder (see Chapter 5 for details).

4 When detaching the speedometer cable from the transmission, compress the clip shown in Fig. 6.62.

5 When the transmission is ready to be withdrawn, support it underneath with a trolley jack, and then undo the retaining bolts and remove the side mounting bracket on each side of the transmission – see Fig. 6.63. Withdraw the transmission rearwards and downwards.

6 Refit in the reverse order of removal. When the transmission is being reconnected to the engine, align it with and engage it on the dowels on the mating flange – see Fig. 6.64. The splines of the clutch thrust pad bore, clutch shaft and the sunwheels of the differential should be lightly lubricated with a suitable grease.

7 Tighten the retaining nuts and bolts to the specified torque wrench settings where given.

8 On completion, top up the transmission oil level as described in Part B, Section 16 of this Chapter.

31 Transmission overhaul – general

Refer to Part A, Section 5 of this Chapter.

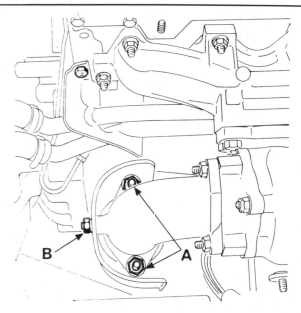

Fig. 6.60 Detach the exhaust downpipe – unbolt at points A and B (Sec 30)

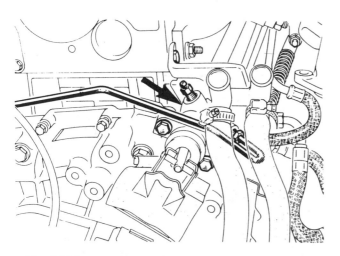

Fig. 6.61 Detach the clutch slave cylinder (arrowed) (Sec 30)

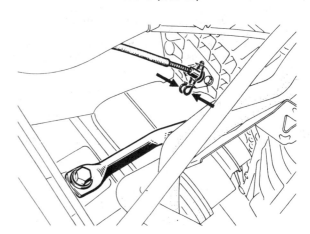

Fig. 6.62 Speedometer cable retaining clip (Sec 30)

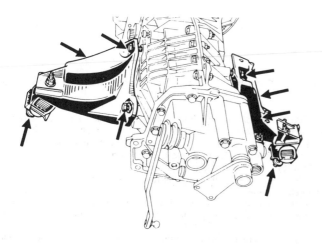

Fig. 6.63 Transmission mountings and retaining bolts (arrowed) (Sec 30)

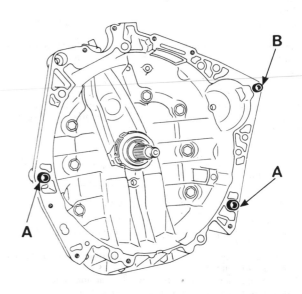

Fig. 6.64 Location dowel locations (A and B) on clutch housing flange face (Sec 30)

32 Transmission – removal of major assemblies

Note: *A puller will be needed for this operation*

1   With the transmission removed from the car, clean away external dirt and grease using paraffin and a stiff brush, or a water-soluble solvent.

2   Place the unit on a bench or, if it must be dismantled on the floor, rest it on a sheet of hardboard.

3   Remove the clutch release bearing and arm.

4   Unbolt and remove the bellhousing. Twelve bolts are used to hold it in position, two of them being longer and located at the positioning dowels.

5   Tap the bellhousing free if necessary using a soft-faced mallet. Peel off the old gasket.

6   Drive out the double roll pins and remove the selector arm and dust excluder from the selector rod.

7   From the side of the rear cover, unscrew the plug and extract 5th gear detent spring and ball. Use a pencil magnet if necessary to remove the ball.

8   Unscrew the rear cover fixing bolts.

9   Pull the cover off the transmission casing, at the same time pushing in the selector rod to free the cover.

10   Before separating the gearcase halves, consideration should be given as to whether or not the primary and secondary shaft assemblies are likely to require attention. If it is decided they will require attention, the respective primary and secondary shaft rear locknuts must be loosened. This is best done at this stage as the shafts can be prevented from turning by tapping the selector rods to 'in gear' positions to lock the shafts.

11   Once the shafts are locked, relieve the nut staking from the secondary and primary shafts. Get an assistant to steady the gearbox whilst you loosen off the primary, and secondary shaft locknuts.

12   Reset the selectors in the neutral mode.

13   From the primary shaft, take off the shaft nut and the dished washer (concave side to synchro unit).

14   Using a puller with thin claws, draw the locking gear from the primary shaft.

15   Take off the baulk ring and 5th gear synchro unit, complete with selector fork.

16   Remove 5th sliding gear, the split needle roller bearing, the bush and the thrust washer.

17   From the secondary shaft, remove the nut, dished washer (concave side to gear).

18   Using a puller, remove 5th gear. If it is difficult to engage the available puller behind the gear, leave it until the shaft is dismantled after removal; see paragraph 1, Section 34.

19   Unbolt the spacer plate.

20   Unscrew and remove the reversing light switch.

21   Unscrew all the bolts which hold the split casing sections together, noting that the centre two have their nuts to the reverse lamp switch side.

22   Position the transmission so that the teeth on the crownwheel are pointing down and remove the half-casing upwards.

23   Lift out the differential/final drive.

24   Remove the geartrains.

25   Remove the casing magnet.

26   Remove the reverse idler shaft and gear – see Section 35.

27   If necessary dismantle the selector components, as described in Section 36.

33 Primary shaft – overhaul

Note: *A puller will be needed for this operation*

1   Pull off the thrust guide tube.

2   Drive out the roll pin and separate the clutch shaft from the primary shaft.

3   Withdraw the oil seal, noting its orientation, then using circlip pliers, extract the circlip.

4   Place the claws of a puller behind 4th gear and pull the gear and the bearing from the shaft. Alternatively, use a press.

5   Note the concave side of the dished washer is against the gear.

6   Remove the split needle bearing.

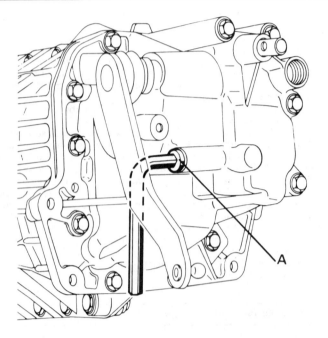

Fig. 6.65 5th gear selector shaft detent plug (A) (Sec 32)

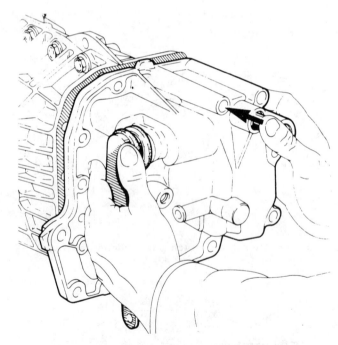

Fig. 6.66 Push in the selector rod and remove the rear cover (Sec 32)

7   Take off the baulk ring, the 3rd/4th synchro sleeve and three rollers.

8   Remove the thrust washer and extract the synchro-hub circlip.

9   Remove the synchro-hub and 3rd gear, with the baulk rings and split needle bearing. Remove the bearing from the threaded end of the shaft if it is worn or damaged (photo).

10   Clean and check all components for wear or damage and renew them as necessary.

11   If there has been a history of noisy gearchanging, certainly renew the baulk rings and the synchro assembly if the splines or teeth show signs of wear.

12   Commence reassembly by fitting 3rd gear and the split needle roller bearing to the non-threaded end of the primary shaft (photo). Apply oil as reassembly progresses.

13   Locate the baulk ring on the shaft and then fit 3rd/4th synchro hub

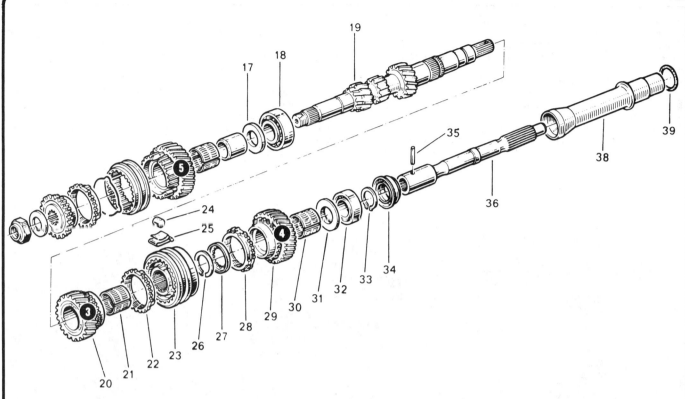

Fig. 6.67 Primary shaft components (Sec 33)

17 Thrust washer	23 3rd/4th synchro unit	28 4th gear baulk ring	34 Oil seal
18 Bearing	24 Roller	29 4th gear	35 Roll pin
19 Primary shaft	25 Roller spring clip	30 Split needle roller bearing	36 Clutch shaft
20 3rd gear	26 Circlip	31 Thrust washer	38 Guide tube
21 Split needle roller bearing	27 Washer	32 Bearing	39 O-ring
22 3rd gear baulk ring		33 Circlip	

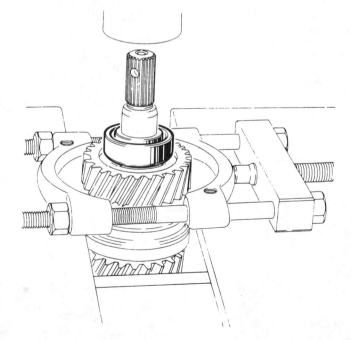

Fig. 6.68 4th gear removal from primary shaft using a press
(Sec 33)

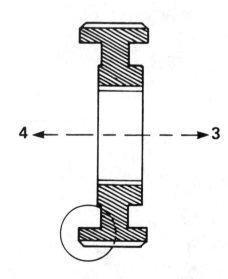

Fig. 6.69 3rd/4th gear synchro hub orientation (Sec 33)

(photo), making sure that it is positioned on the shaft as shown in Fig. 6.69. Fit a new hub circlip (photo).

14 Fit the synchro sleeve, the three rollers and spring clips (photos). Make sure that the extended tips of the spring clips are towards 4th gear.

15 Make sure that the large teeth of the baulk ring engage correctly in their synchro slots.

16 Fit the splined washer (photo).

17 Fit 4th gear baulk ring (photo).

18 Fit the split needle bearing and 4th gear (photo).

19 Fit the thrust washer, then the bearing, applying pressure only to its centre track (photos).

20 Fit a new bearing circlip (photo).

21 If the bearing was removed from the threaded end of the primary shaft, now is the time to press on a new one. Apply pressure to the bearing centre track only and fit the bearing so that the engraved marks are visible from the end of the shaft.

22 Fit a new oil seal (photo).

23 Reconnect the clutch shaft to the primary shaft and drive in a new roll pin (photo).

24 Fit the thrust guide tube (photo).

25 Place the primary shaft geartrain ready for assembling into the transmission casing.

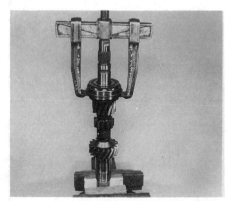
33.9 Primary shaft bearing removal using a puller

33.12 Fitting 3rd gear to the primary shaft

33.13A Fit the 3rd gear baulk ring ...

33.13B ... 3rd/4th synchro hub ...

33.13C ... and circlip

33.14A Fit 3rd/4th synchro sleeve ...

33.14B ... synchro unit rollers ...

33.14C ... and roller spring clips

33.16 Fit the splined washer ...

33.17 ... the 4th gear baulk ring ...

33.18 ... and the split needle roller bearing and 4th gear

33.19A Locate the thrust washer ...

33.19B ... followed by the bearing

33.20 Fit a new bearing circlip

33.22 Fitting the new oil seal

33.23 Connecting the clutch shaft to the primary shaft

33.24 Fitting the thrust guide tube

34 Secondary shaft – overhaul

Note: A puller will be required for this operation

1 If 5th gear was not removed earlier, place the claws of a puller behind the spacer plate and remove the gear from the shaft.
2 Using the puller, remove the double tapered roller bearing.
3 Remove 1st gear and the split needle roller bearing. Note the spring at the rear of the gear.
4 Remove the 2nd gear baulk ring.
5 If they are to be reused, mark the relative positions of the sliding sleeve, 2nd gear and hub as they are separated so that they can be refitted in their original positions during reassembly.
6 Remove the sliding sleeve (with reverse gear), then remove the snap ring securing the 2nd speed gear and hub unit.

7 Withdraw the 2nd speed gear/hub unit using a suitable puller or a press (photo). Separate the hub, baulk ring and spring ring (inside 2nd gear).
8 Remove the split needle roller bearing.
9 The remaining gears (3rd and 4th) are a shrink fit and cannot be removed from the shaft (photo).
10 Refer to Section 32, paragraphs 10 and 11. Renew the snap rings as a matter of course and where applicable, align the match marks of the gear, hub and sleeve as they are being assembled.
11 Commence reassembly by fitting the synchro spring inside 2nd gear so that the three slots are covered (photo).
12 Fit the split needle roller bearing and 2nd gear to the shaft (photos).
13 Locate the baulk ring (photo).
14 Warm 1st/2nd synchro hub in an oven or boiling water and press it

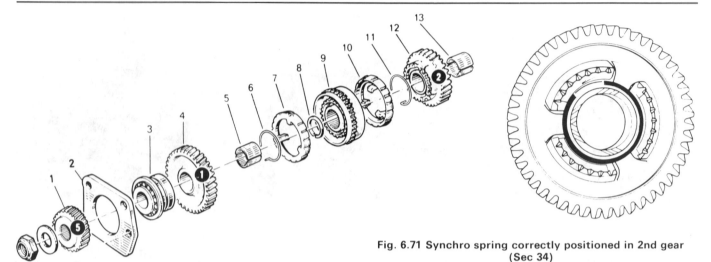

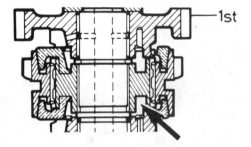

Fig. 6.71 Synchro spring correctly positioned in 2nd gear
(Sec 34)

Fig. 6.70 Secondary shaft components (Sec 34)

1   5th speed gear
2   Spacer plate
3   Double taper roller bearing
4   1st gear
5   Split needle roller bearing
6   Synchro spring
7   1st gear baulk ring
8   Circlip
9   1st/2nd synchro unit
10 2nd gear baulk ring
11 Synchro spring
12 2nd gear
13 Split needle roller bearing

Fig. 6.72 1st/2nd synchro hub orientation (Sec 34)

Deeper groove (arrowed) towards 2nd gear

or drive it onto the shaft using a length of tubing; orientate as shown in Fig. 6.72. Hold the baulk ring so that its lugs are not damaged during fitting of the hub (photos).
15 Fit the hub circlip (photo).
16 Fit the 1st/2nd synchro sleeve (with reverse gear) (photo).
17 Fit the baulk ring (photo).
18 Fit the split needle roller bearing and 1st gear (photos), making

sure that the synchro spring is in place inside it covering the three slots.
19 Fit the double tapered roller bearing so that the flange is towards the end of the shaft. Apply pressure only to the bearing centre track. Make sure that the spacer is between the races (photos).
20 Place the secondary shaft geartrain ready for assembling into the transmission casing.

34.7 Removing 1st/2nd synchro hub from secondary shaft

34.9 Secondary shaft stripped

34.11 2nd gear synchro spring (arrowed)

34.12A Fit the split needle roller bearing ...

34.12B ... and 2nd gear

34.13 Fit the baulk ring

34.14A 1st/2nd gear synchro hub

34.14B 1st/2nd synchro hub fitted

34.15 Fitting the hub circlip

34.16 1st/2nd synchro sleeve (and reverse gear)

34.17 Fit the baulk ring

34.18A Fit the 1st gear split needle roller bearing ...

34.18B ... and 1st gear

34.19A Using a piece of tubing to fit inner roller bearing race

34.19B Fit the bearing double track ...

34.19C ... and spacer ring ...

34.19D ... then the outer roller bearing race

35 Reverse idler shaft and gear – dismantling and reassembly

1   Remove the reverse idler shaft, gear and thrust washers.

2   The casing bushes cannot be renewed.

3   When refitting, note the location of the thinner and thicker thrust washers and make sure that the shaft roll pin locates in its cut-out (photos).

Fig. 6.73 Reverse idler gear components (Sec 35)

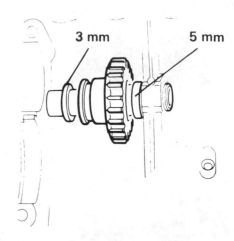

Fig. 6.74 Reverse idler shaft thrust washer locations (Sec 35)

35.3A Reverse idler shaft and gear

35.3B Reverse idler shaft locking roll pin (arrowed) located in cut-out

36 Selector forks and shafts – dismantling and reassembly

1   Move the selector forks and shafts as necessary to be able to drive out the fork securing roll pins. Withdraw the shafts and forks, noting carefully which way round the forks are fitted to the shafts. Take care to retrieve the detent balls and springs.
2   Unscrew the pivot bolt and remove the reverse selector swivel and shaft.
3   Inspect all components and pay particular attention to the selector forks for wear at their tips.
4   Reassemble 3rd/4th fork and shaft, then 1st/2nd followed by reverse. Apply thread locking fluid to the threads of the reverse swivel pivot bolt and tighten to the specified torque (photo).
5   Make sure that the slits in the roll pins face the rear cover, and note the different sizes of roll pins used on the 1st/2nd fork (Fig. 6.77).
6   The 5th gear selector fork was removed during withdrawal of 5th gear from the primary shaft, see Section 32.

37 Rear cover – dismantling and reassembly

1   Drive out the double roll pins from the swivel arm.
2   Using a forked tool, compress the coil spring, withdraw the shaft and remove the swivel arm.
3   Reassembly is a reversal of dismantling.

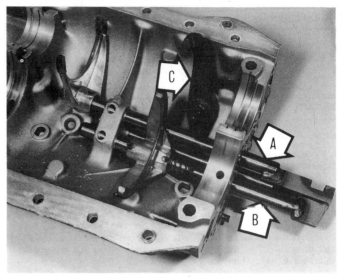

36.4 Selector shaft and fork arrangement
A 3rd/4th   B 1st/2nd   C Reverse swivel arm

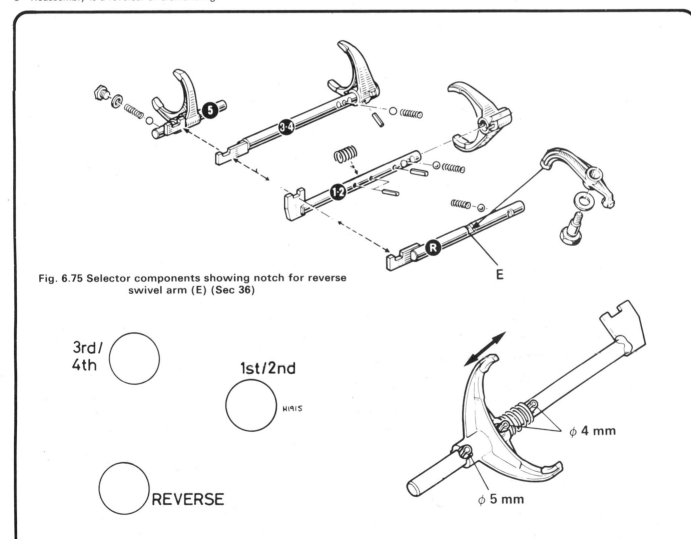

Fig. 6.75 Selector components showing notch for reverse swivel arm (E) (Sec 36)

Fig. 6.76 Selector shaft identification diagram (viewed from the differential end) (Sec 36)

Fig. 6.77 1st/2nd selector fork roll pins (Sec 36)

38 Transmission housing – inspection

1   Examine the transmission housing for any signs of damage or cracks. If any are found, the housing must be renewed.
2   Renew the housing oil seals as a matter of course.

39 Differential – overhaul

Note: *A puller will be required for this operation*

1   Unscrew the crownwheel fixing bolts. The bolts must be renewed at reassembly.
2   Remove the O-rings from the sun wheels and discard them.
3   Using a puller, remove the differential bearings.
4   Drive out the planet wheel roll pin.
5   Separate, clean and renew any worn components. The target wheel cannot be removed from the differential housing (photo).
6   If the crownwheel is being renewed, renew the secondary shaft as well to ensure that the pinion gear is matched to the crownwheel (supplied as a matching pair).

7   When reassembling, observe the following points. The groove in the anti-friction washer faces the sun wheel.
8   Make sure that the planet wheel roll pin is recessed by 5.0 mm (0.20 in) in the housing.
9   Apply thread locking fluid to clean threads of the new crownwheel bolts which must be tightened to the specified torque.
10   When fitting the new bearings, apply pressure only to the bearing centre track.
11   Use new sun wheel O-rings, the bearings have integral oil seals.
12   Always renew the bearing outer tracks in the casings. A piece of suitable diameter tubing makes a good removal and refitting tool.
13   The differential/final drive should now be fitted without the geartrains and the casing half-sections bolted together.
14   Only one bearing adjusting nut is fitted to this transmission. Turn the ring nut until any endfloat in the differential is eliminated.
15   Now adjust the bearing preload. Do this using a spring balance and cord (see Fig. 6.55). The differential should rotate under the load given in Specifications. Adjust the ring nut as necessary to achieve this, then mark the ring nut in relation to the casing. Unscrew and remove the ring nut, counting the number of turns required to remove it.
16   Separate the casings and remove the differential pending reassembly of the transmission.

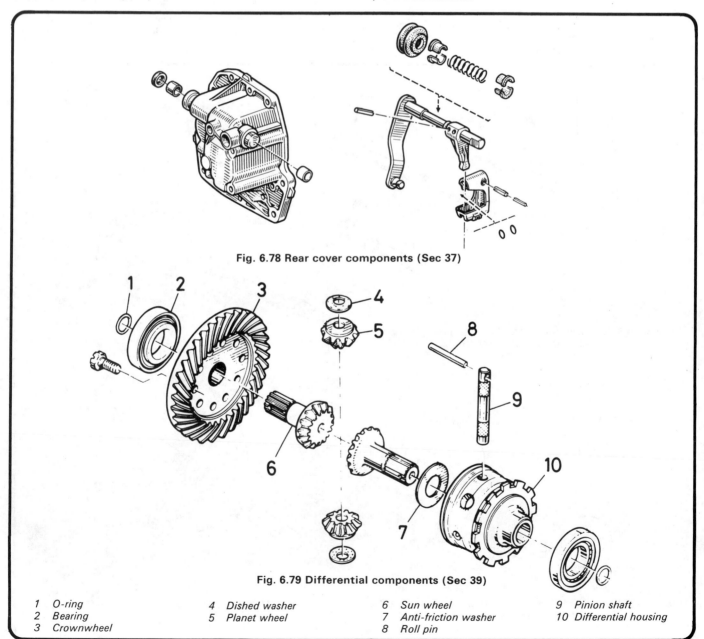

Fig. 6.78 Rear cover components (Sec 37)

Fig. 6.79 Differential components (Sec 39)

1 O-ring	4 Dished washer	6 Sun wheel	9 Pinion shaft
2 Bearing	5 Planet wheel	7 Anti-friction washer	10 Differential housing
3 Crownwheel		8 Roll pin	

39.5 Differential showing speedometer target wheel

40 Transmission – reassembly

1   Have the casings and components clean. Lubricate the parts as reassembly proceeds.
2   The reverse idler and selector components will have been reassembled as described in Sections 35 and 36.
3   Fit the casing magnet (photo).
4   Refit the geartrains, meshed together, into the right-hand half-casing (which has the adjustable differential bearing ring nut) (photo).
5   Lower the differential into position (crownwheel teeth pointing downward).
6   Smear the casing mating flanges with jointing compound and bolt them together (photos). Tighten to torque in the sequence shown in Fig. 6.81. The bolts (1 and 2) should be liberally smeared with jointing compound.
7   Smear the threads of the reversing light switch with jointing compound and screw it into position (photo).
8   Bolt the secondary shaft spacer plate into position (photo).
9   Fit 5th gear to the secondary shaft (photo).
10 Fit the dished washer and screw on a new nut, having applied thread locking fluid to its threads (photo).
11 To the primary shaft, fit the thrust washer, the bush, the needle roller bearing and 5th sliding gear (photos).
12 Fit the 5th gear synchro sleeve complete with selector fork and shaft (photo).
13 Fit the baulk ring (photo).
14 Fit the locking gear.
15 Fit the dished washer (concave side to gear) and screw on a new nut having applied thread locking fluid to its threads (photo).

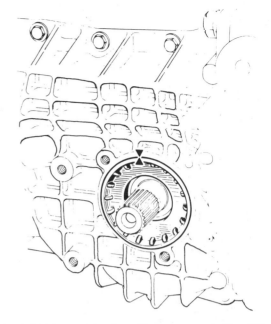

Fig. 6.80 Ring nut/casing alignment mark (Sec 39)

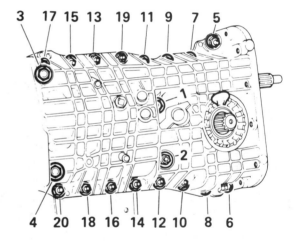

Fig 6.81 Casing bolt tightening sequence (Sec 40)

40.3 Casing magnet

40.4 Geartrains installed

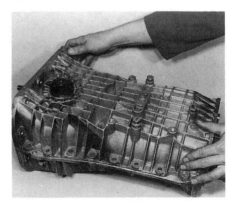

40.6A Connecting the casing sections

40.6B Tightening the casing bolts

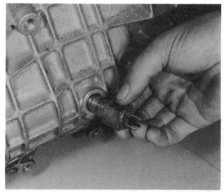

40.7 Fitting the reversing light switch

40.8 Secondary shaft spacer plate

40.9 5th gear fitted to secondary shaft

40.10 Fit the dished washer

40.11A Locate the primary shaft thrust washer ...

40.11B ... the 5th gear bush ...

40.11C ... the split needle roller bearing ...

40.11D ... and the 5th sliding gear on the primary shaft

40.12 Fit the 5th gear synchro sleeve, fork and shaft

40.13 5th gear baulk ring and locking gear

40.15A Locate the dished washer ...

16 Move the 5th and 2nd selector rods to engage two gears at once and so lock up the geartrains.

17 Tighten the two shaft nuts to the specified torque and lock them by staking. Reselect neutral (photos).

18 Fit the rear cover, having smeared the mating surfaces with sealant. It is important that the cover is tilted when offering it up to ensure that the selector arm engages positively in the selector shaft dog notches. Once the cover is fitted, tighten the bolts to the specified torque and check that all gears can be obtained. Fit the dust excluder, selector arm and double roll pins to secure it (photos).

19 Refit 5th gear interlock ball and spring. Apply sealant to the plug threads and screw it into position (photos).

20 Fit the dust excluder and selector arm using a new roll pin.

21 Using a new gasket, bolt the bellhousing into position (photos).

22 Fit the clutch release bearing and arm.

23 Refill the transmission with oil after it has been refitted to the car.

41 Gearchange linkage – removal and refitting

Refer to Part B, Section 28 of this Chapter.

40.15B ... then the new retaining nut

40.17A Tighten the nuts to the specified torque ...

40.17B ... and lock by staking

40.18A Fit the rear cover ...

40.18B ... and tighten the bolts

40.18C Locate the selector arm dust excluder ...

40.18D ... then fit the selector arm

40.18E Fit the selector arm double roll pins

40.19A Insert the 5th gear interlock ball ...

40.19B ... interlock spring ...

40.19C ... and retaining plug

40.21A Fit bellhousing to transmission casing

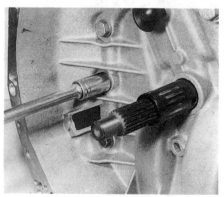

40.21B Tighten the bellhousing bolts

PART D – ALL TRANSMISSIONS

42 Fault diagnosis – manual transmission

Symptom	Reason(s)
Weak or ineffective synchromesh	Synchro baulk rings worn, split or damaged Synchromesh units worn, or damaged
Jumps out of gear	Gearchange mechanism worn Synchromesh units badly worn Selector fork badly worn Selector detent spring broken or jammed
Excessive noise	Incorrect grade of oil in transmission or oil level too low Gearteeth excessively worn or damaged Intermediate gear thrust washers or spacers worn allowing excessive end play Worn bearings
Difficulty in engaging gears	Worn synchromesh units Clutch pedal adjustment incorrect Gear lever out of adjustment
Noise when cornering	Wheel bearing or driveshaft fault Differential fault

Note: *It is sometimes difficult to decide whether it is worthwhile removing and dismantling the transmission for a fault which may be nothing more than a minor irritant. Transmissions which howl, or where the synchromesh can be beaten by a quick gearchange, may continue to perform for a long time in this state. A worn transmission usually needs a complete rebuild to eliminate noise because the various gears, if re-aligned on new bearings, will continue to howl when different bearing sufaces are presented to each other. The decision to overhaul, therefore, must be considered with regard to time and money available, relative to the degree of noise or malfunction that the driver has to suffer.*

Chapter 7 Automatic transmission

Contents

Specifications

General
Type .... Three-speed, with computerised control
Type number MJ3

Fluid
Capacity:
    From dry .... 6.0 litres (10.6 pints)
    At fluid renewal .... 2.5 litres (4.4 pints)
Fluid type .... Dexron type ATF (Duckhams D-Matic)

Torque wrench settings

	Nm	lbf ft
Driveplate-to-converter bolts	30	22
Fluid cooler pipe unions	19	14
Sump pan fixing screws	6	4
Filter retaining bolts	9	6
Torque converter housing-to-engine connecting bolts	54	40
Torque converter to crankshaft bolts	70	51
Mounting pad bolts	40	30

1 General description

The automatic transmission consists of three main assemblies: the torque converter, the final drive and the gearbox. A cutaway view of the transmission unit, with the three main assemblies sub-divided, is shown in Fig. 7.1.

The converter takes the place of the conventional clutch and transmits the drive automatically from the engine to the gearbox, providing increased torque when starting off.

Fully automatic gearchanging is provided without the use of a clutch, but override selection is still available to the driver.

The gearbox comprises an epicyclic geartrain giving three forward and one reverse gear, selection of which is dependent on the hydraulic pressure supplied to the respective clutches and brakes. The hydraulic pressure is regulated by the hydraulic distributor, and gear selection is determined by two solenoid valves. These are actuated by the electrically-operated governor/computer. The exact hydraulic pressure is regulated by a vacuum capsule and pilot valve operating according to engine loading.

The clutches (E1 and E2 in Fig. 7.4) and brakes (F1 and F2) are multi-disc oil bath type and, according to the hydraulic loading, engage or release the epicyclic geartrain components.

The governor is, in effect, a low output alternator which provides variable current to the computer. It is driven by a worm gear on the final drive pinion and its output depends on the vehicle speed and engine loading.

The computer or module is continually supplied with signals from the speed sensor, load potentiometer, multi-purpose switch, kickdown switch and its own control unit, and from this information it transmits signals to the pilot solenoid valves to select the correct gear range.

The kickdown switch is an integral part of the load potentiometer and a lower gear is selected when the pedal is fully depressed.

The multi-purpose switch is located on the rear of the transmission and is operated by the range selector lever. It controls the engine starting circuit, the reversing light circuit and the pilot solenoid valve circuit.

The load potentiometer is operated by the throttle valve and provides a variable voltage to the computer, dependent on the throttle position.

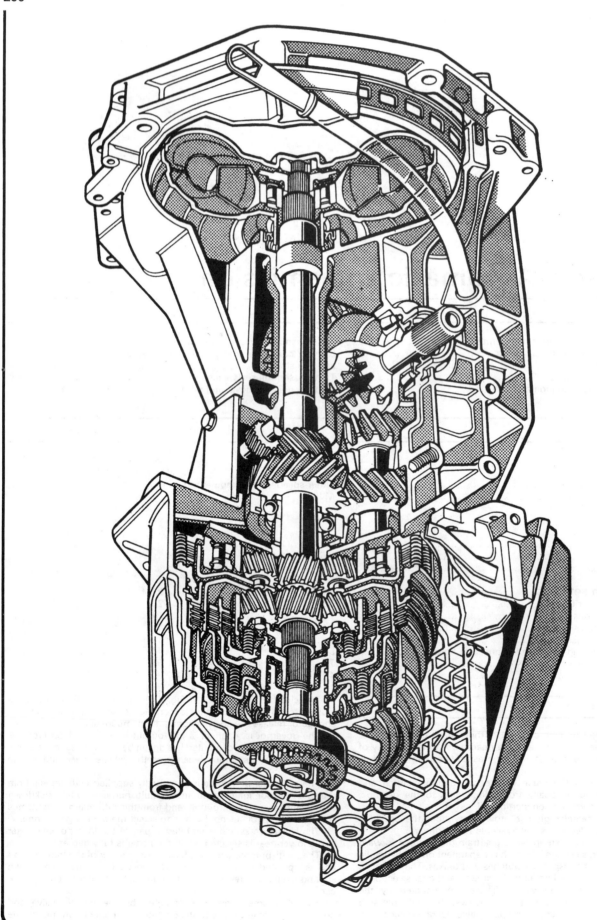

Fig. 7.1 Cutaway view of the MJ3 type automatic transmission (Sec 1)

The speed sensor is mounted on the left-hand side of the transmission and it provides an output signal dependent on the speed of the parking pawl wheel, which is proportional to the speed of the car.

A vacuum capsule is connected directly to the inlet manifold to regulate transmission fluid pressure according to engine loading.

The automatic transmission is a relatively complex unit and therefore, should problems occur, it is recommended that the fault be discussed with your Renault dealer, who should be able to advise you on the best course of action to be taken. Items that can be attempted by the home mechanic are given in the following Sections of this Chapter. To obtain trouble-free operation and maximum life expectancy from your automatic transmission, it must be serviced as described and not be subjected to abuse.

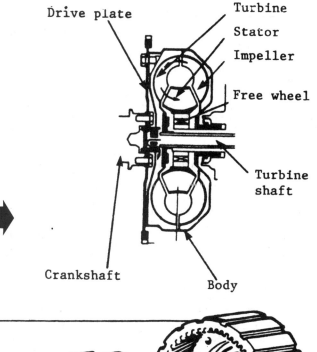

Fig. 7.2 Sectional view showing the driveplate and torque converter assembly (Sec 1)

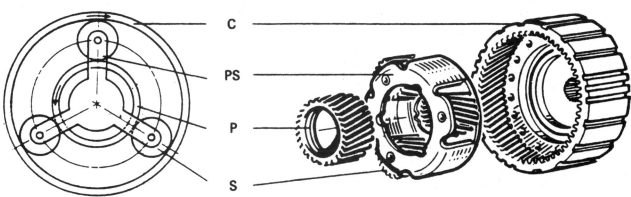

Fig. 7.3 Epicyclic gear train assembly (Sec 1)

C   Internal ring gear   P   Sunwheel
PS Planet wheel carrier   S   Planet wheels

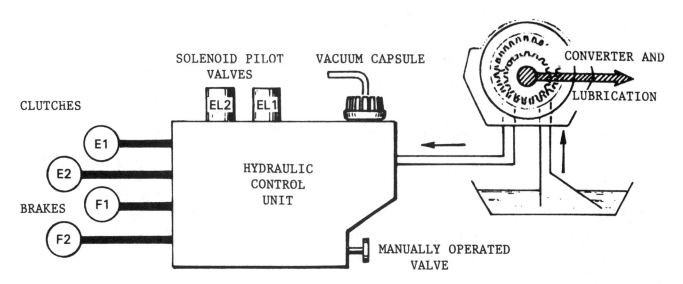

Fig. 7.4 Automatic transmission hydraulic control diagram (Sec 1)

2 Maintenance

1   At the intervals specified in 'Routine maintenance' check the fluid level in the following way.
2   The engine and transmission should be cold. Start the engine and allow it to run for a few minutes in order to fill the torque converter and cooler with fluid.
3   With the selector lever in P and the engine idling, withdraw the dipstick, wipe it clean, re-insert it and withdraw it for the second time. The fluid level should be between the 'min' and 'max' marks.
4   If necessary, top up with the specified fluid poured in through the dipstick guide tube.
5   The transmission will very rarely require topping-up, but if it does, check for leaks, probably at the torque converter or driveshaft oil seals in the transmission casing.
6   The transmission fluid should be drained, preferably hot, at the intervals specified in 'Routine maintenance'. Place a suitable container under the drain plug and then remove the plug. If the fluid is hot, take precautions against scalding.
7   Refit the drain plug, then fill the transmission to the specified level through the dipstick guide tube. Use only the specified type and quantity of fluid.

3 Fluid filter – renewal

1   This is not a routine service operation, but may be required if the transmission fluid has become contaminated or regular renewal has been neglected.
2   Drain the fluid as previously described, unbolt and remove the sump pan and gasket.
3   Undo the three filter unit retaining bolts and remove the filter.
4   Fit the new filter into position, ensuring that a new sealing ring is located as shown in Fig. 7.8. With reference to Fig. 7.9 initially locate the filter with the retaining bolt (1) to ensure that the filter is correctly positioned relative to the hydraulic control unit, then fit the remaining bolts (2 and 3) and tighten them to the specified torque wrench setting. Note that the number (2) bolt is shorter than the other two.
5   Clean the sump pan and check that the filter magnets are located as shown in Fig. 7.10, then refit the sump pan, ensuring that a new gasket is correctly located.
6   Check that the sump drain plug is tight, then refill the transmission as described in the previous Section.

4 Kickdown switch/load potentiometer – testing

1   The kickdown switch is incorporated in the load potentiometer on the throttle housing.
2   A defect in this unit is indicated by the gear shift speeds being constant, regardless of the position of the accelerator. On models fitted with an electronic fault warning lamp, the lamp will illuminate if a fault occurs in the transmission control system.
3   No further fault diagnosis is possible without the use of specialist test equipment. If a fault occurs, it is advisable to consult a Renault dealer who will have the specialist knowledge and tools available to rectify the fault.

5 Selector control lever and cable – removal, refitting and adjustment

1   Pull upwards on the selector lever handle to remove it from the lever.
2   Press the console trim to the left to release its retaining tags, whilst simultaneously lifting the console to remove it.
3   Raise and support the front of the vehicle on safety stands.
4   Remove the exhaust downpipe (Chapter 3), to provide access to the selector cable connections underneath.
5   Undo the four nuts securing the selector lever assembly to the floor.
6   Detach the selector light wire, then unclip the control cable from the relay unit balljoint.
7   Position a jack under the engine/transmission subframe, then

Fig. 7.5 Automatic transmission fluid level dipstick location (Sec 2)

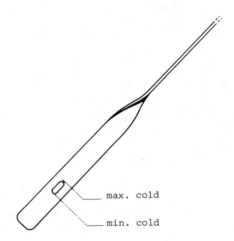

Fig. 7.6 Automatic transmission fluid level dipstick markings (Sec 2)

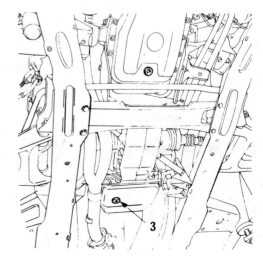

Fig. 7.7 Automatic transmission drain plug (3) (Sec 2)

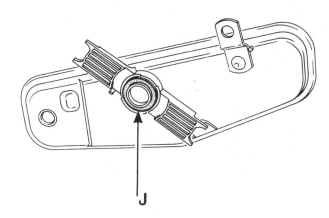

Fig. 7.8 Automatic transmission fluid filter seal (J) (Sec 3)

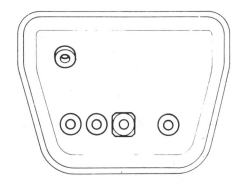

Fig. 7.10 Filter magnet locations (Sec 3)

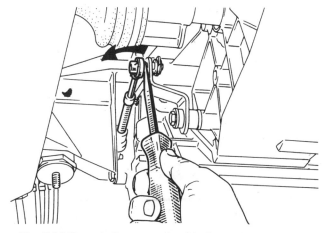

Fig. 7.12 Detach the control cable from the relay unit balljoint (Sec 5)

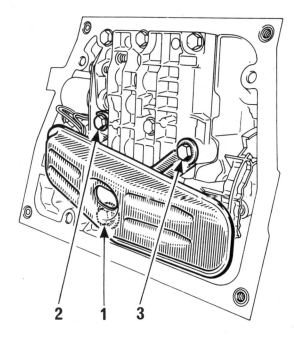

Fig. 7.9 Automatic transmission fluid filter retaining bolt locations (Sec 3)

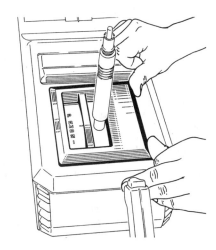

Fig. 7.11 Removing selector lever console trim (Sec 5)

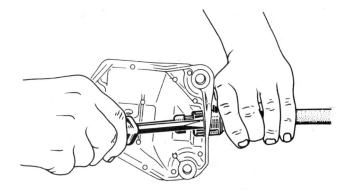

Fig. 7.13 Unclipping the control cable forward end from the mounting (Sec 5)

unscrew the two rear retaining bolts and lower the subframe by about 15 mm (0.6 in).

8   Unbolt and detach the transmission mounting on the right-hand side.

9   Detach the complete selector assembly.

10 To disconnect the cable for replacement, unclip it from the mounting at the forward end using a screwdriver. At the rear end, prise free the cover from the selector case, then unclip the joint from the bottom end of the lever and extract the retaining clip securing the cable to the case.

11 Refit in the reverse order of removal. Ensure that the rear retaining clip is fitted the correct way round as shown in Fig. 7.15.

12 To refit and adjust the control cable, relocate the right-hand

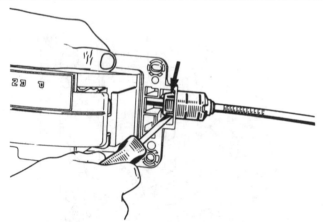

Fig. 7.14 Unclipping the control cable from the selector assembly case (Sec 5)

transmission mounting (with cable attached). Raise the subframe and tighten its securing bolts.

13 Using a suitable screwdriver as shown in Fig. 7.16, prise the cable lock clip at the mounting, then pull the cable rearwards from the adjuster.

14 Position the automatic transmission and the selector lever in the 'D' position, then attach the cable to the relay unit balljoint. Allow the selector assembly to hang free under the vehicle, then reattach the cable adjuster lock clip as shown in Fig. 7.17.

15 Refit the selector assembly (with gasket) and reattach the selector light wire.

16 Refit the console and the selector lever handle. Check the lever for satisfactory engagement to complete.

6 Transmission oil seals – renewal

Torque converter oil seal

1 This is accessible after having removed the transmission (or engine) and the torque converter.

2 Tap the front face of the old seal at one point with a punch so that it tilts and can be extracted.

3 Tap the new seal squarely into position using a suitable tube drift, having smeared its lips with petroleum jelly. Take care not to damage the shaft.

4 On refitting the torque converter, align it with the driveplate as shown in Fig. 7.24.

Driveshaft/transmission oil seals

5 The driveshaft removal and the oil seal removal details are given in Chapter 8.

7 Vacuum unit – removal and refitting

Note: *After removal and refitting of the unit, have the fluid pressure checked by a Renault dealer at the earliest opportunity.*

1 The transmission will have to be supported on a jack with a wooden block as an insulator so that the mounting can be removed to provide access to the vacuum unit.

2 Disconnect the vacuum pipe, remove the clamp plate and unscrew the unit.

3 Refitting is a reversal of removal. Lubricate the unit (black rubber) with fluid, screw the unit in by 2$^1/_2$ to 3 turns, then fit the clamp plate. Have the fluid pressure checked and if necessary adjusted by a Renault dealer at the earliest opportunity.

8 Automatic transmission – removal and refitting

1 A trolley jack will be useful during the removal and subsequent refitting of the transmission. Although not essential to drain the transmission fluid before removal, it is a task more easily achieved in

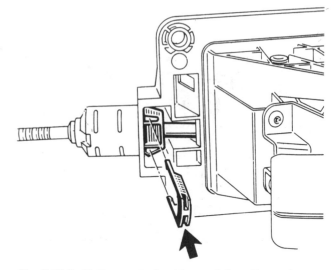

Fig. 7.15 Refit the control cable retaining clip as shown (Sec 5)

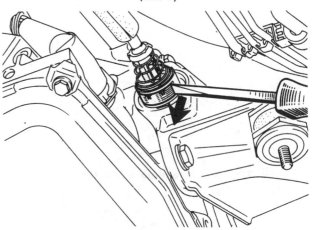

Fig. 7.16 Prise free the cable lock clip from the mounting (Sec 5)

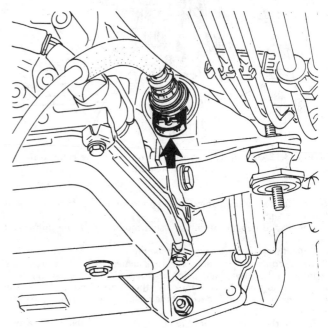

Fig. 7.17 Relocate the cable adjuster lock clip as shown (Sec 5)

the car and will help reduce the weight of the transmission.

2 Disconnect the battery earth lead.

3 Raise and support the vehicle at the front end on axle stands. Remove the front roadwheels.

4 Detach and remove the engine undershield.

5 Disconnect the angular position/speed sensor, the computer wiring plug, and the starter motor wiring. Unbolt and remove the starter motor (see Chapter 12).

6 Disconnect the vacuum pipe adjacent to the starter motor flange.

7 Disconnect the transmission fluid cooler pipes from the points indicated in Fig. 7.20. Plug them to prevent the ingress of dirt and fluid leakage.

8 Disconnect the driveshafts from the transmission as described in Chapter 8.

9 Detach and remove the exhaust downpipe as described in Chapter 3.

10 Working through the starter motor aperture, jam the driveplate to prevent it from turning, then undo the driveplate-to-torque converter retaining bolts. Loosen off each bolt in turn, then unscrew and remove them to detach the converter from the driveplate.

11 Unscrew and remove the upper engine-to-transmission bolts.

12 Disconnect the earth cable from the transmission.

13 Disconnect the selector control cable at the balljoint by levering it apart using a suitable screwdriver as shown in Fig. 7.12.

14 Position the trolley jack under the transmission to support its weight, then loosen off the engine/transmission subframe bolts and lower the subframe by about 15 mm (0.6 in).

15 Unbolt and remove the left-hand transmission mounting and support.

16 Remove the right-hand support.

17 Loosen off, but do not remove, the bolt securing the right-hand rubber pad, leaving the control cable attached.

18 Unscrew and remove the lower engine-to-transmission retaining bolts.

19 Lower the trolley jack and withdraw the transmission. Guide the computer out with the transmission. The engine should be supported safely on the front crossmember.

20 Secure the torque converter in position by bolting a retaining bar to a flange bolt hole as shown in Fig. 7.22.

21 Refitting is a reversal of removal, but observe the following points.

22 Check that the positioning dowels are in place before offering the transmission to the engine, also grease the recess in the crankshaft which accepts the torque converter.

23 Align the converter in relation to the driveplate, as shown in Fig. 7.24.

24 Tighten the driveplate bolts to the specified torque.

25 Tighten the exhaust flange bolts until the spring coils are coilbound.

26 Reconnect the driveshafts.

27 Check and top up the transmission fluid.

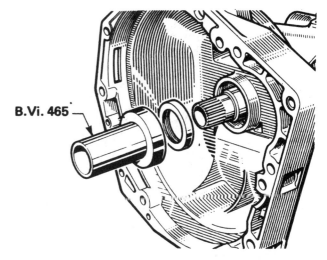

Fig. 7.18 Torque converter oil seal renewal – drive into position using a tube drift (Renault tool shown) (Sec 6)

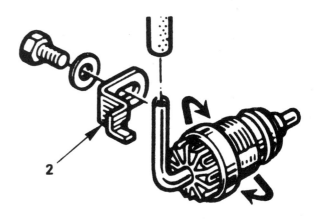

Fig. 7.19 Vacuum unit and lockplate (2) (Sec 7)

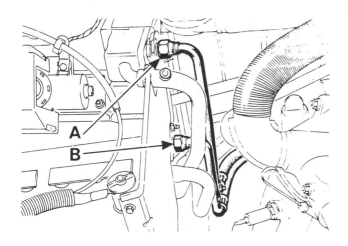

Fig. 7.20 Disconnect the fluid cooler pipes at A and B (Sec 8)

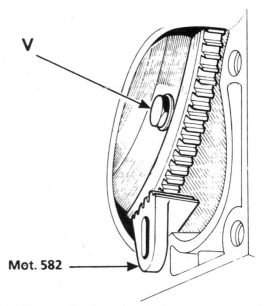

Fig. 7.21 Remove the driveplate-to-torque converter bolts (V) (Sec 8)

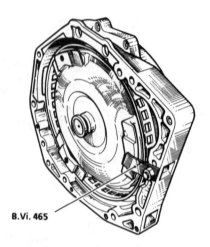

Fig. 7.22 Torque converter retaining bar in position (Renault tool shown) (Sec 8)

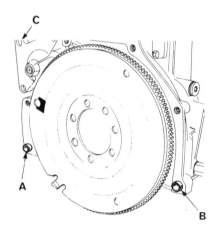

Fig. 7.23 Positioning dowels (Sec 8)

A   Engine locating dowel   C   Starter motor locating dowel
B   Engine locating dowel

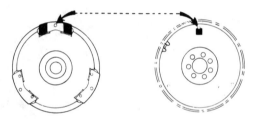

Fig. 7.24 Torque converter-to-driveplate alignment (Sec 8)

9 Fault diagnosis – automatic transmission

1   Automatic transmission faults are almost always the result of low fluid level or incorrect adjustment of the selector control cable.
2   If these items are checked and found to be in order, the fault is probably internal and should be diagnosed by your Renault dealer who is specially equipped to pinpoint the problem and effect any necessary repairs.
3   Do not allow any defect in the operation of the automatic transmission to go unchecked – it could prove expensive!
4   If the starter fails to function at any time, it is possible that the starter inhibitor switch is at fault but first check that (a) the selector control lever adjustment is correct and (b) the transmission wiring harness plugs and socket connections are secure. Check the starter circuit wiring for continuity to the switch plug. The inhibitor switch is situated beneath the transmission computer unit and within the hydraulic section of the unit. The sump plate would have to be removed to gain access to the switch and this is therefore best entrusted to your Renault dealer.
5   The following guide to simple faults should be regarded as being the limit of fault diagnosis for the home mechanic.

Symptom	Reason(s)
Engine stalling or rough idling	Leaking vacuum pipe
Loss of transmission fluid without visible leak	Faulty vacuum unit
Violent gearchanges	Faulty vacuum unit
'Creep' in N	Selector cable requires adjustment
Slip in D or R	Low fluid level
Incorrect gearchange speeds	Throttle requires adjustment or kickdown switch/load potentiometer fault
Jerk at speed selection	Fault in vacuum unit or pipe
No drive, or slipping during speed range changes	Clogged fluid filter

Chapter 8 Driveshafts, hubs, roadwheels and tyres

Contents

Specifications

Driveshafts
Type .... Tubular with CV joint at each end
Inboard joint .... GI 62 (tripod type) or RC 490 (tripod type)
Outboard joint .... GE 86 or GE 76 (tripod type) or UF 95/Lobro (6-ball type)

Hubs
Front .... Renewable split track ball bearing
Rear .... Renewable split track roller bearing
Endfloat (maximum):
    Front .... 0 to 0.05 mm (0 to 0.002 in)
    Rear .... 0 to 0.03 mm (0 to 0.001 in)

Roadwheels
Type .... Pressed steel or light alloy
Size (depending on model) 5.5B 13 4 CH36
    5.5J 14 4 CH36
    5.5B 13 4 FH36
    5.5J 14 4 FH36
    5.5J 14 4 CH36
    6.5J 15 5 CH42

Tyres
Type .... Radial ply, tubeless
Size (depending on model) .... 155 R 13T
    175/70 R 13T
    175/65 R 14H
    155/70 R 13T
    175/70 R 13H
    185/65 R 14H
    195/55 VR 15

Tyre pressures – cold *:	Front	Rear
Saloon models (except Turbo)	2.0 bar (29 lbf/in²)	2.2 bar (32 lbf/in²)
Savanna models	2.0 bar (29 lbf/in²)	2.6 bar (37 lbf/in²)
Turbo models	2.8 bar (40 lbf/in²)	2.5 bar (35 lbf/in²)

* Allow for an increase of 0.3 bar (4 lbf/in²) when tyres are hot after running

Torque wrench settings	Nm	lbf ft
Roadwheel bolts	90	66
Driveshaft nut	250	185
Rear hub nut	16	12
Rear stub axle bolts	7.5	5.5
Left-hand driveshaft inboard flange retaining bolts (1.7 litre models)	25	18

1 General description

1   The driveshafts which transmit power from the transmission final drive to the front roadwheels incorporate a constant velocity (CV) joint at each end.

2   The inboard joint is of tripod type while the outboard joint is of tripod or six-ball type, depending upon car model.

3   The design and construction of the driveshaft components is such that the only repairs possible are renewal of the rubber bellows and renewal of the inner joint spiders. Wear or damage to the outer constant velocity joints or the driveshaft splines can only be rectified by fitting a complete new driveshaft assembly.

2 Maintenance

1   A thorough inspection of the driveshafts and driveshaft joints should be carried out at the intervals given in 'Routine maintenance', using the following procedure.

2   Jack up the front of the car and support it securely on axle stands.

3   Slowly rotate the roadwheel and inspect the condition of the outer constant velocity joint rubber bellows. Check for signs of cracking, splits or deterioration of the rubber which may allow the grease to escape and lead to water and grit entry into the joint. Also check the security and condition of the retaining clips and then repeat these checks on the inner joint bellows. If any damage or deterioration is found the joints should be attended to immediately.

4   Continue rotating the roadwheel and check for any distortion or damage to the driveshafts. Check for any free play in the outer joints by holding the driveshaft firmly and attempting to turn the wheel. Any noticeable movement indicates wear in the joints, wear in the constant velocity joint or wheel hub splines, a loose driveshaft retaining nut or loose wheel bolts. Carry out any necessary repairs with reference to the appropriate Sections of this, and other applicable Chapters of this manual.

3 Driveshafts (1.7 litre models) – removal and refitting

1   Remove the roadwheel trim plate, then loosen off the driveshaft nut and the wheel bolts (photo).

2   Jack up the car at the front and support it on axle stands. Remove the appropriate roadwheel.

3   Undo the two bolts securing the brake caliper to the hub carrier. Slide the caliper, complete with pads, off the disc and tie it up using string or wire from a suitable place under the wheel arch.

4   Unscrew and remove the driveshaft nut and washer.

5   Disconnect the steering arm from the stub axle at the balljoint as described in Chapter 10.

6   Unscrew but do not remove the shock absorber-to-hub carrier retaining bolt nuts. Use a suitable mallet to drive against the end face of the bolts to release the serrated section under each bolt head from the shock absorber, then unscrew the nut from the upper bolt and

remove the bolt. The lower bolt can be left in position (see photos 4.4A and 4.4B).

7   The procedure now varies according to whether the left-hand or right-hand driveshaft is being removed.

Left-hand driveshaft

8   Refer to Chapter 6 and drain the transmission oil.

9   Undo the three bolts securing the rubber bellows retaining plate to the side of the transmission casing (photo).

10   Pivot the hub carrier outwards at the top and simultaneously withdraw the driveshaft from the inner joint spider in the transmission housing.

11   Withdraw the outer constant velocity joint stub axle from the wheel hub and remove the driveshaft from the car. If the stub axle is a tight fit in the wheel hub, tap it out using a plastic mallet or use a suitable puller.

Right-hand driveshaft

12   Using a parallel pin punch of suitable diameter, drive out the roll pin securing the driveshaft inner joint yoke to the differential stub shaft (photo). Note that the roll pin is in fact two roll pins, one inside the other.

13   Pivot the hub carrier outwards at the top and simultaneously withdraw the driveshaft from the differential stub shaft. If the inner end of the driveshaft is difficult to withdraw, carefully lever it free using a bar or screwdriver.

14   Proceed as described previously in paragraph 11.

Refitting

15   Refitting the left-hand or right-hand driveshaft is basically a reverse of the removal procedure with reference to the following additional points:

   (a) Lubricate the driveshaft joint splines with molybdenum disulphide grease

   (b) A rubber insulator washer may be fitted to the right-hand driveshaft at the transmission end, the details of which are described in Section 13. Where applicable, check that this washer is fitted. When fitting such driveshafts, press the shaft towards the differential housing to align the roll pin holes of the shafts. To ease roll pin insertion. a chamfer is machined in the roll pin hole at the top of a splined tooth on one side to provide a lead-in guide

   (c) On the right-hand side, position the inner joint splines so that the roll pin holes will align when the joint is pushed fully home. Position the two roll pins so that their slots are 90° apart

   (d) Ensure that all retaining nuts and bolts are tightened to the specified torque and that the hub carrier-to-shock absorber bolts are fitted with their bolt heads toward the rear of the car

   (e) If the left-hand driveshaft has been removed, refer to Chapter 6 and refill the transmission with oil

4 Driveshafts (2.0 litre models) – removal and refitting

1   Proceed as described in paragraphs 1 to 4 of the previous Section.

3.1 Loosen off the driveshaft nut and the wheel bolts

3.9 Remove the bellows retaining bolts (left-hand driveshaft)

3.12 Drive out the roll pins securing the right-hand driveshaft

3.14A Align the roll pin holes when fitting the right-hand driveshaft (arrowed) ...

3.14B ... and fit new roll pins

On Turbo models it is possible to leave the brake caliper unit attached to the hub carrier, but take care not to stretch the hydraulic hose.

2 Use a parallel pin punch of suitable diameter to knock out the driveshaft roll pins at the transmission end (photo). Note that there are two roll pins fitted, one inside the other.

3 On Turbo models detach the steering arm outer balljoint as described in Chapter 10.

4 Unscrew but do not remove the shock absorber-to-hub carrier bolt nuts. Use a suitable mallet to drift against the end face of the bolts to release the serrated section under each bolt head from the shock absorber, then remove the upper nut and bolt only (photo).

5 Pivot the hub carrier outwards at the top and simultaneously withdraw the driveshaft from the transmission (photos).

6 Withdraw the outer end of the driveshaft from the hub carrier and remove the shaft unit from the car. If the shaft is a tight fit in the hub carrier, tap it out using a plastic mallet or use a suitable puller.

7 Refitting is a reversal of removal, but observe the following points.

8 Smear the inboard shaft splines with molybdenum disulphide grease.

9 Use new roll pins (photo) and seal their ends with suitable sealant (hard setting type).

10 On non-Turbo models fitted with the NG9 type transmission, the transmission end of the driveshaft is fitted with an insulating washer. This washer is available in two thicknesses. Ensure that the correct type is fitted and in position when assembling the driveshaft to the differential stub shaft. Refer to Section 13 for identification details.

11 Apply thread locking fluid to the threads (clean) for the caliper fixing bolts (where applicable).

12 Tighten all nuts and bolts to the specified torque. Renew the driveshaft self-locking nut.

13 Apply the footbrake two or three times to position the disc pads against the disc (where applicable).

14 Refill the transmission with oil.

4.2 Drive out the roll pins securing the driveshafts at their inboard ends

4.4 Tap back the shock absorber-to-hub carrier bolts to expose their splines (arrowed)

4.5A Pivot the hub carrier as shown ...

4.5B ... and withdraw the driveshaft from the transmission

4.9 Fit new roll pins (arrowed)

5 Driveshaft bellows and spider (inboard tripod joint – type GI 62) – renewal

1   Remove the driveshaft, as described in the appropriate earlier Section (photo).
2   Remove the bellows retaining spring as shown in Fig. 8.2.
3   Cut the bellows along their length, and remove and discard them.
4   Lift the anti-separation plate tabs using pliers, then withdraw the yoke from the spider.
5   The needles, rollers and trunnions are matched in production so keep them as originally assembled by winding adhesive tape around the spider.
6   Remove the circlip, then use a three-legged puller to withdraw the spider (photo). Do not tap the shaft out of the spider as the rollers will be marked and the needles damaged.
7   Lubricate the driveshaft and slide the new bellows with small retaining ring into position on the shaft.
8   Use a suitable tube drift to drive the spider onto the driveshaft, then the circlip to secure.
9   Distribute the grease pack supplied between the bellows and the yoke.
10 Remove the adhesive tape from the spider, then fit the spider to the yoke.
11 Insert a 2.5 mm (0.10 in) thick metal wedge, fabricated to the dimensions shown in Fig. 8.5, between the anti-separation plate and the yoke. Carefully tap the anti-separation plate tabs into their original positions with a soft metal drift, then remove the wedge.

5.1 General view of the type G1 62 driveshaft joint

5.6 Remove the circlip (arrowed)

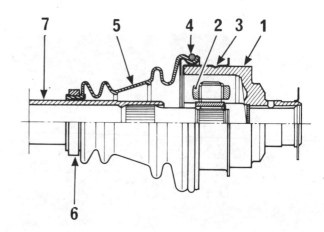

Fig. 8.1 Sectional view of the type GI 62 inboard tripod joint (Sec 5)

1 Yoke	5 Bellows
2 Spider	6 Bellows retaining ring
3 Metal cover	7 Driveshaft
4 Bellows retaining spring	

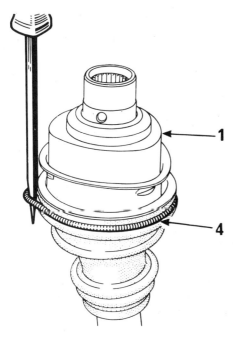

Fig. 8.2 Prise free the bellows retaining spring (4) from the yoke (1) (Sec 5)

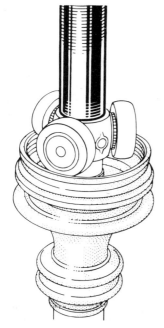

Fig. 8.4 Drive the spider onto the driveshaft using a tube drift (Sec 5)

12 Locate the bellows lips in the grooves in the driveshaft and the yoke.
13 Insert a rod under the bellows at the yoke end to restrict the amount of air retained in the bellows, and set the overall length of the bellows as shown in Fig. 8.6.
14 Remove the rod and fit the bellows retaining spring, taking care not to stretch the spring.

6 Driveshaft bellows and spider (inboard tripod joint – type RC 490) – renewal

1 The procedure is as described in Section 5 for the type GI 62 joint, but with the following differences.

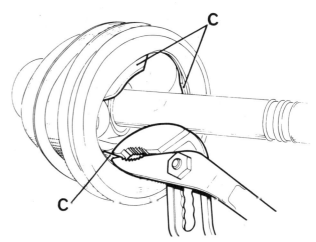

Fig. 8.3 Lift the anti-separation plate tabs (C) as shown (Sec 5)

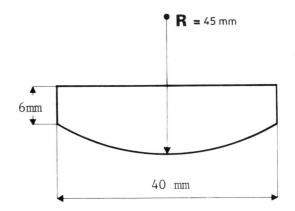

Fig. 8.5 Metal wedge used to retain shape of anti-separation plate (Sec 5)

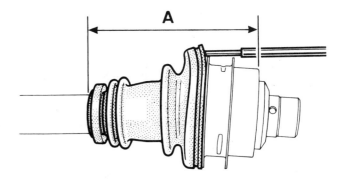

Fig. 8.6 Expel any trapped air by lifting bellows with a rod, then check distance A (Sec 5)

A = 152 to 154 mm (5.95 to 6.03 in)

2 The bellows are attached to the yoke by a metal ring which must be cut off and renewed on reassembly.
3 There is no anti-separation plate and therefore the spider can be slid straight out of the yoke.
4 On some models there is no spider retaining circlip. When refitting the spider on these models, punch the end of the shaft at 3 points 120° apart to retain the spider, as shown in Fig. 8.8.
5 Set the overall length of the bellows as shown in Fig. 8.9.
6 Crimp the new bellows metal retaining ring as shown in Fig. 8.10.

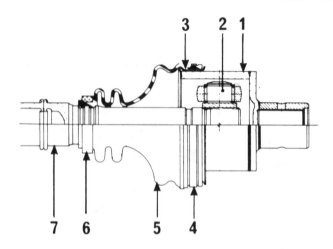

Fig. 8.7 Sectional view of the type RC 490 inboard tripod
joint (Sec 6)

1   Yoke   5   Bellows
2   Spider   6   Bellows retaining ring
3   Metal cover   7   Driveshaft
4   Bellows retaining collar

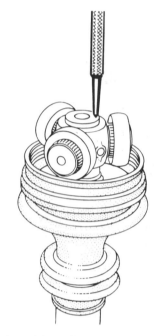

Fig. 8.8 Peen the spider using a centre punch of 3 points
120° apart to secure (Sec 6)

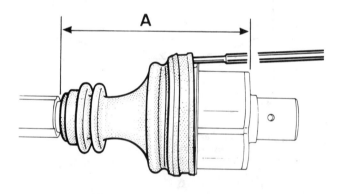

Fig. 8.9 Expel any trapped air by lifting bellows with a rod,
then check distance A (Sec 6)

A = 155.0 to 157.0 mm (6.05 to 6.12 in)

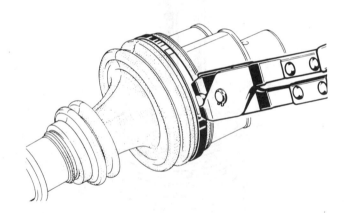

Fig. 8.10 Secure the bellows retaining ring using crimping
pliers (Sec 6)

7   Driveshaft bellows (outboard tripod joint) – renewal

Note: *If the bellows are to be renewed without removing the spider
from the inner joint, a special bellows expander tool will be required.
Tool No TAr 537-02 is required for the type GE 86 joint, and Tool No
TAr 586-01 is required for the type GE 76 joint*

1   If the spider at the inboard end of the driveshaft is removed the
outboard bellows can be slid off the shaft and renewed without the
need for a special expander. The choice is with the home mechanic
whether the extra work involved is worthwhile, so avoiding the need
for the special tool.
2   Remove the driveshaft as described in the relevant earlier Section.
3   Cut free the large diameter retaining clip from the bellows.
4   Pull back the bellows and wipe away as much grease as possible.
5   Prise up the starplate arms one by one and separate the stub axle
from the driveshaft. Take care not to bend the starplate arms.
6   Retain the thrust button, spring and axial clearance shim.
7   To fit the new bellows, a special expander will be required.
8   Grip the driveshaft in the jaws of a vice and locate the expander on

the end of the yoke. Deburr any edges at the joint – see Fig. 8.15.
9   Lubricate the expander and inside of the bellows and slide the
bellows up the expander, making sure that the first fold is fully
extended. Pull the bellows half way up the expander two or three times
to stretch the rubber and then pull them right over the shaft yoke.
10   If the driveshaft has an intermediate bush, locate the bush in the
shaft grooves.
11   Fit the spring and thrust button.
12   Locate the starplate so that each arm is centrally positioned
between the spider rollers.
13   Insert the driveshaft yoke into the bell-shaped stub axle.
14   Tilt the shaft to engage one starplate arm in its slot and then use a
screwdriver to engage the other two. Fit the thrust button shim (see
Fig. 8.19).
15   Distribute the sachet of grease evenly between the bellows and the
stub axle.
16   Locate the bellows lips in their grooves, insert a rod under the
smaller diameter neck of the bellows to expel any trapped air.
17   Fit the retaining ring and spring clip to the bellows. On some
models, crimped clips are used.

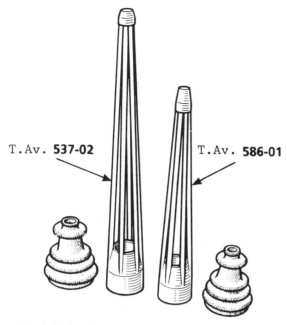

T.Av. **537-02**   T.Av. **586-01**

Fig. 8.11 Special bellows expander tools (Sec 7)

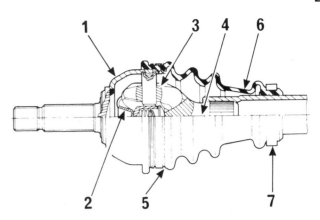

Fig. 8.12 Sectional view of the outboard tripod joint (Sec 7)

1 Stub axle
2 Starplate retainer
3 Spider
4 Yoke
5 Bellows retaining clip
6 Bellows
7 Bellows retaining clip

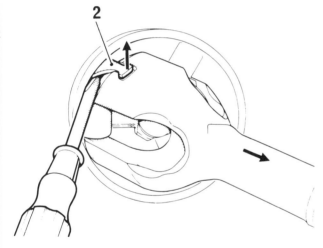

Fig. 8.13 Lift the starplate arms (2) to remove the stub axle (Sec 7)

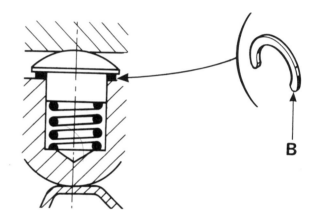

Fig. 8.14 Thrust button, spring and axial clearance shim (B) (Sec 7)

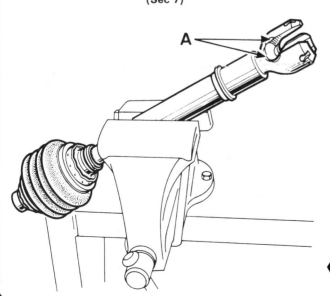

Fig. 8.15 Grip driveshaft in vice jaws as shown. Deburr any sharp edges at A (Sec 7)

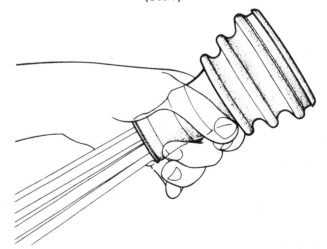

Fig. 8.16 Slide the bellows onto the expander tool (Sec 7)

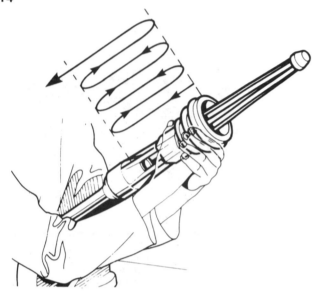

Fig. 8.17 Move bellows up and down the expander to stretch them prior to fitting on the yoke (Sec 7)

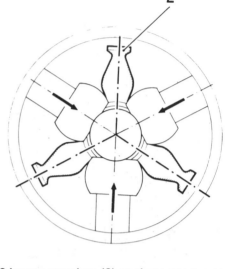

Fig. 8.18 Locate starplate (2) so that arms are positioned between spider rollers (Sec 7)

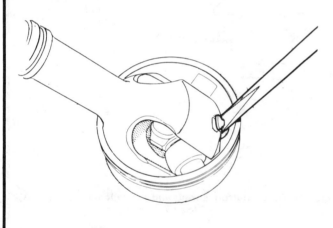

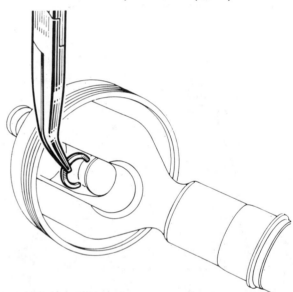

Fig. 8.20 Fit the thrust button shim (Sec 7)

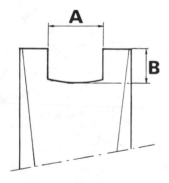

CORRECT   INCORRECT

Fig. 8.19 Grind end of screwdriver blade as shown to assist engagement of starplate arms (Sec 7)

A = 5 mm (0.195 in)   B = 3 mm (0.117 in)

Fig. 8.21 Sectional views showing correct bellows and retaining clips fitting (Sec 7)

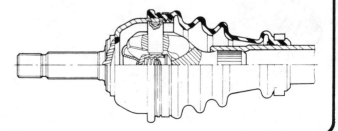

8   Driveshaft bellows (outboard six-ball type joint) – renewal

Note: *A bellows expander (Tool No. TAr 537-02) will be needed for this operation*

1   If the spider at the inboard end of the driveshaft is removed, the outboard bellows can be slid off the shaft and renewed without the need for a special expander. The choice is with the home mechanic whether the extra work involved is worthwhile, so avoiding the need for the special tool.
2   Remove the driveshaft as described in the appropriate earlier Section.
3   Grip the driveshaft in the jaws of a vice and remove the clips, cut the bellows and remove and discard them.
4   Wipe away as much grease as possible.
5   Expand the circlip (7 – Fig, 8.23), at the same time tapping the ball hub(s) with a plastic mallet. Withdraw the driveshaft from the coupling.
6   Slide the bellows retaining ring (A – Fig. 8.24) onto the shaft, followed by the bellows (3).
7   Spread the grease supplied with the new bellows inside them.
8   Slide the coupling, complete with circlip, onto the driveshaft until the circlip locks in its groove.
9   Locate the bellows so that their lips engage in the grooves of shaft and stub axle.
10   Fit the bellows retaining ring and the spring clip using drilled rods (see Fig. 8.25).

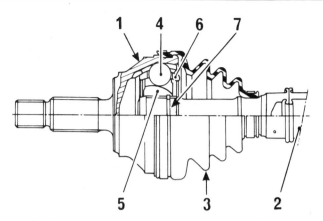

Fig. 8.22 Sectional view of the outboard six-ball type joint (Sec 8)

1 Stub axle	5 Ball hub
2 Driveshaft	6 Ball cage
3 Bellows	7 Circlip
4 Balls	

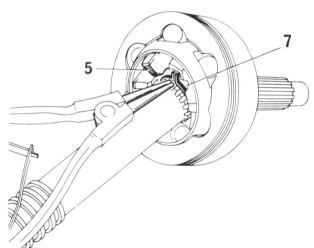

Fig. 8.23 Expand the circlip (7) and tap the ball hub (5) to remove the driveshaft (Sec 8)

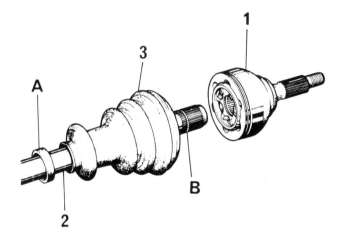

Fig. 8.24 Six-ball type driveshaft joint (Sec 8)

1 Six-ball coupling	A Bellows retaining ring
2 Driveshaft	B Circlip groove
3 Bellows	

9   Driveshaft coupling joints – renewal

Inboard tripod joint – type GI 62
1   The spider assembly can be renewed on this type of joint and is supplied with a plastic retainer.
2   Removal and refitting operations are described in Section 5.

Inboard tripod joint – type RC 490
3   The spider and yoke can be renewed on this type of joint
4   The spider is supplied with a plastic retainer and the removal and refitting procedure is described in Section 6.
5   The cover should be crimped to the yoke while the cover is under pressure and the yoke is fully home.
6   On cars fitted with the anti-lock braking system, the sensor target must be removed using a press before the cover is crimped. When refitting the target, apply Loctite Scelbloc before pressing it into position.

Outboard tripod joint
7   The joint components may be renewed after dismantling as described in Section 7.

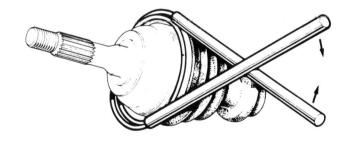

Fig. 8.25 Using drilled rods to fit the bellows spring clip (Sec 8)

Outboard six-ball joint
8   The driveshaft or the stub axle/coupling may be renewed after separation, as described in Section 8.
9   Dismantling of the ball cage serves no purpose as individual spare parts are not available.

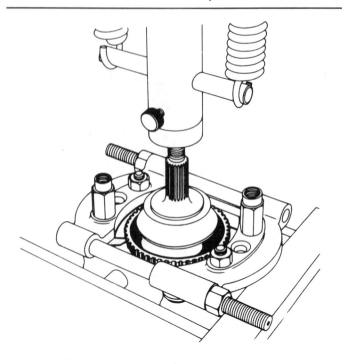

Fig. 8.26 Pressing off the anti-lock sensor target (Sec 9)

Fig. 8.27 Sensor target relocated on driveshaft joint (Sec 9)

10 Front hub bearings (1.7 litre models) – renewal

Note: *Hub bearing removal can only be achieved using suitable pullers, a press and some metal tubing of suitable diameter to press the old bearing out and the new bearing into the housing. For particulars read through before starting.*

1   Remove the front roadwheel trim plate on the side concerned, then loosen off the roadwheel bolts and the driveshaft nut.
2   Raise the car at the front and support it on axle stands. Remove the relevant roadwheel.
3   Remove the brake disc as described in Chapter 9.
4   Unscrew and remove the driveshaft nut and washer, then fit a suitable hub puller similar to that shown in Fig. 8.28. Withdraw the hub unit, then remove the puller from the hub.
5   To remove the inner bearing track ring, a puller of the type shown in Fig. 8.29 must be used.
6   Remove the hub carrier unit as described in Chapter 10.
7   Extract the bearing retaining ring from the carrier, then using a suitable tube drift, remove the bearing as shown in Fig. 8.30.
Thoroughly clean the hub and driveshaft before fitting a new bearing.
8   Leave the plastic ring in the new bearing bore, but remove the outer plastic protectors. Press the bearing into the housing using a tube with an outside diameter of 71 mm, and a 66 mm bore, so that it only rests on the bearing outer track ring end face. Do not press on the bearing inner track ring or it will be damaged.
9   Remove the inner plastic protective ring, then locate the retaining ring.
10   Smear the seal lips with a multi-purpose grease, and fit the thrust washer onto the hub, pressing it into position using a tube with an outside diameter of 48 mm and a bore of 43 mm.
Fit the thrust washer so that it is flush to the bearing inner track ring.
11   Refit the hub carrier to the car in the reverse order of removal as described in Chapter 10. Tighten the retaining nuts and bolts to their specified torque wrench settings.

11 Front hub bearings (2.0 litre models) – renewal

Note: *Refer to the note at the start of the previous Section. A T30 Torx bit will also be required*

1   Proceed as described in paragraphs 1 to 4 of the previous Section.

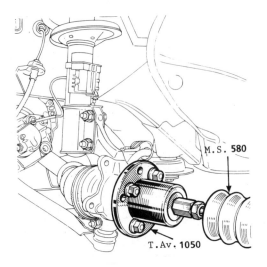

Fig. 8.28 Front wheel hub puller tool (Renault type shown) (Sec 10)

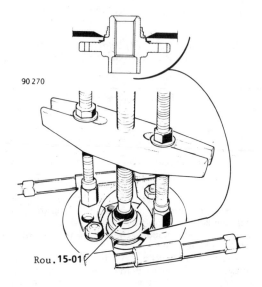

Fig. 8.29 Inner bearing track ring puller (Renault type shown) (Sec 10)

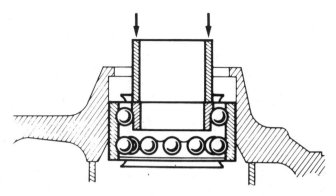

Fig. 8.30 Bearing removal from hub carrier using a tube drift (Sec 10)

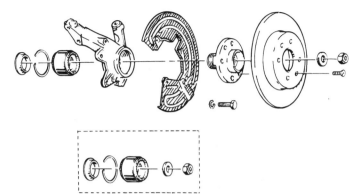

Fig. 8.31 Hub carrier and bearings (Sec 10)

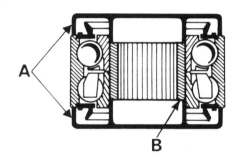

Fig. 8.32 Front hub bearing showing outer plastic protectors (A) and plastic ring (B) (Sec 10)

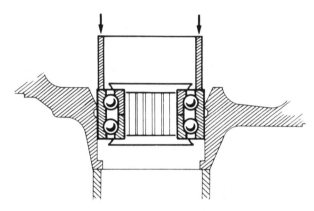

Fig. 8.33 Front hub bearing installation – press on areas indicated by arrows (Sec 10)

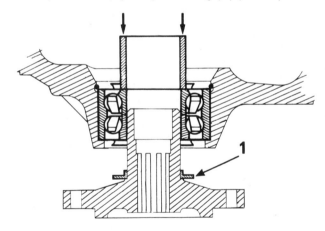

Fig. 8.34 Hub carrier installation – press on area indicated by arrows. Note thrust washer location (1) (Sec 10)

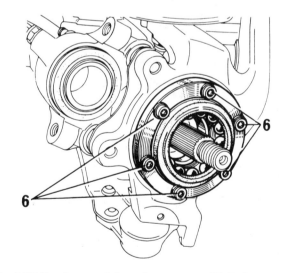

Fig. 8.35 Bearing retaining plate screws (6) (hub removed) (Sec 11)

2   One of two methods may be used to dismantle the hub.
3   Using two roadwheel bolts and two steel packing pieces (photo), screw in the bolts gradually and evenly to force the hub from the bearing retaining plate.
4   Remove the bearing plate screws using a Torx bit.
5   Remove the hub bearing from the hub (photo).
6   The inner half-section track must be removed from the hub. This is difficult without a bearing puller and the hub may have to be taken to your dealer for the track to be removed.
7   The alternative way to dismantle the hub is to unscrew the bearing retainer plate screws by inserting the Torx bit through the hole in the hub flange. The hub can then be removed with the bearing assembly. Seperate the hub from the bearing using the bolts and packing pieces as previously described.
8   Fit the tracks and bearing races and pack the balls with grease. The

hub can be tapped or pressed into the bearing, and the complete assembly fitted to the hub carrier by inserting the screws for the bearing retainer plate through the holes in the hub flange (photo).
9   Alternatively, fit the bearing and retainer plate and then offer the hub to the end of the driveshaft and tap it into position using a wooden or plastic mallet. Once several threads of the driveshaft are exposed, screw on a new driveshaft nut.
10 Refit the disc and caliper (Chapter 9). Continue screwing on the self-locking nut and tighten to the specified torque.
11 Refit the roadwheel and lower the car.

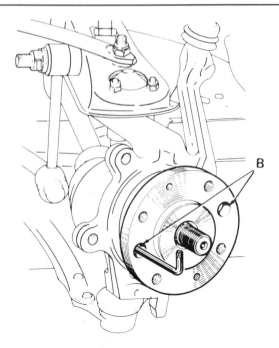

11.3 Forcing hub from bearing retaining plate using roadwheel bolts and packing pieces

Fig. 8.36 Extracting the bearing retaining plate screws using a Torx bit inserted through hub flange holes (B) (Sec 11)

11.5 Hub and bearing separated

11.8A Smear new inner bearing track with grease

11.8B Tapping hub into bearing

12 Rear hub bearings – renewal

1   Jack up the vehicle at the rear and support it on axle stands. Remove the relevant roadwheel.
2   Prise free and remove the hub cap (photo).
3   Remove the brake drum as described in Chapter 9. On 1.7 litre models the drum and hub are combined, but on 2.0 litre models they are separate. On 2.0 litre models, after removing the brake drum, unscrew and remove the hub nut then remove the hub (photo).
4   Extract the bearing retaining circlip from its groove in the hub bore, then using a suitable piece of tube with an outside diameter of 49 mm, press or drive out the bearing.
5   The circlip and hub nut must be renewed on reassembly.
6   Press the new bearing into position using a piece of tube with an outside diameter of 51 mm. Do not apply force to the inner race. When fitted, the bearing must be flush with the shoulder in the hub/drum bore.
7   Locate the new circlip into its groove to secure the bearing.
8   Lubricate the stub axle with SAE 80 oil, then fit the hub/drum onto it.
9   Fit the new locknut and tighten it to the specified torque wrench setting.

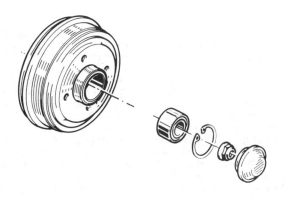

Fig. 8.37 Rear hub bearing components (Sec 12)

12.2 Prising free the hub cap (2.0 litre model shown)

12.3 Rear hub nut (2.0 litre model)

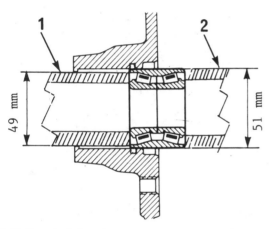

Fig. 8.38 Rear hub bearing removal and refitting (Sec 12)

1   Removal – use 49 mm
    diameter tubing

2   Refitting – use 51 mm
    diameter tubing

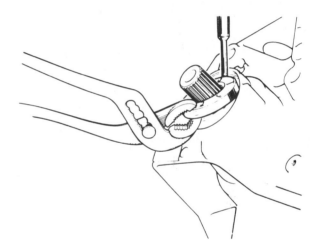

Fig. 8.39 Driveshaft/differential oil seal removal method
(Sec 13)

10 Tap the hub cap into position and refit the brake drum (Chapter 9).
11 Check that the wheel hub endfloat is as specified using a dial gauge, then adjust the brakes as described in Chapter 9.
12 Refit the roadwheel and lower the car to complete.

13 Driveshaft/differential oil seals – renewal

1   The driveshaft/differential oil seals can be renewed without having to remove the transmission from the car.
2   Refer to Section 3 or 4 as applicable, and detach the driveshaft from the transmission on the side concerned. It should not be necessary to remove the driveshaft from the hub carrier.
3   Remove the 0-ring seal from the differential stub shaft.
4   Prise and lever out the old oil seal from the differential housing, but take care not to damage the seal housing.
5   Before fitting the new oil seal into the housing, ensure that the replacement seal is the correct type by measuring its diameter. This is most important on automatic transmission models, since on later models not only do the right-hand and left-hand seals differ in diameter, but the seal diameter was also enlarged – see Fig. 8.40.
6   Refitting is a reversal of the removal procedure. Lubricate the lips of the new seal with grease before driving it into position (photo). Renew

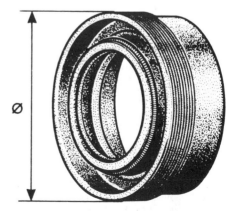

Fig. 8.40 Driveshaft oil seal identification on automatic
transmission models (Sec 13)

Early models (left and right-hand) – 42.2 mm diameter
Late models (left-hand) – 45.2 mm diameter
Late models (right-hand) – 43.7 mm diameter

the O-ring seal and lubricate it before fitting it onto the differential stub shaft (photo).

7 On 1.7 litre models fitted with the JB3 type transmission, and 2.0 litre models fitted with the NG9 type transmission, an insulator washer may be fitted at the differential sunwheel. The driveshaft butts against this washer, and when the driveshaft is refitted, it will need to be pressed in towards the differential to compress the washer and allow the retaining roll pins to be inserted. Two thicknesses of washer are available, and it is important that the correct type is fitted. The washer thickness is dependent on the differential sunwheel type as follows:

JB3 transmission .
Sunwheel without shoulder – no washer fitted
Sunwheel with 3 mm shoulder – 5 mm thick washer fitted

NG9 transmission
Sunwheel with 1 mm thick shoulder – 3 mm thick washer fitted
Sunwheel with 3 mm thick shoulder – 5 mm thick washer fitted

8 Where applicable, ensure that this washer is fitted at the base of the driveshaft yoke before fitting the driveshaft.
9 Refit the driveshaft as described in Section 3 or 4 as applicable.
10 Top up the transmission oil level as described in Chapter 6 for manual transmissions or 7 for automatic transmissions.

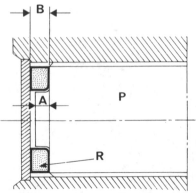

Fig. 8.41 Differential sunwheel/driveshaft insulation washer location in driveshaft – JB3 and NG9 transmission types (Sec 13)

P *Sunwheel*   A *Sunwheel shoulder width*
R *Insulating washer*   B *Washer width*

13.6A Driving the new oil seal into its housing using a socket

13.6B Renew the O-ring seal on the differential stub shaft

14 Wheels and tyres – general care and maintenance

Wheels and tyres should give no real problems in use provided that a close eye is kept on them with regard to excessive wear or damage. To this end, the following points should be noted.

Ensure that tyre pressures are checked regularly and maintained correctly. Checking should be carried out with the tyres cold and not immediately after the vehicle has been in use. If the pressures are checked with the tyres hot, an apparently high reading will be obtained owing to heat expansion. Under no circumstances should an attempt be made to reduce the pressures to the quoted cold reading in this instance, or effective underinflation will result.

Underinflation will cause overheating of the tyre owing to excessive flexing of the casing, and the tread will not sit correctly on the road surface. This will cause a consequent loss of adhesion and excessive wear, not to mention the danger of sudden tyre failure due to heat build-up.

Overinflation will cause rapid wear of the centre part of the tyre tread coupled with reduced adhesion, harsher ride, and the danger of shock damage occurring in the tyre casing.

Regularly check the tyres for damage in the form of cuts or bulges, especially in the sidewalls. Remove any nails or stones embedded in the tread before they penetrate the tyre to cause deflation. If removal of a nail *does* reveal that the tyre has been punctured, refit the nail so that its point of penetration is marked. Then immediately change the wheel and have the tyre repaired by a tyre dealer. Do *not* drive on a tyre in

such a condition. In many cases a puncture can be simply repaired by the use of an inner tube of the correct size and type. If in any doubt as to the possible consequences of any damage found, consult your local tyre dealer for advice.

Periodically remove the wheels and clean any dirt or mud from the inside and outside surfaces. Examine the wheel rims for signs of rusting, corrosion or other damage. Light alloy wheels are easily damaged by 'kerbing' whilst parking, and similarly steel wheels may become dented or buckled. Renewal of the wheel is very often the only course of remedial action possible.

The balance of each wheel and tyre assembly should be maintained to avoid excessive wear, not only to the tyres but also to the steering and suspension components. Wheel imbalance is normally signified by vibration through the vehicle's bodyshell, although in many cases it is particularly noticeable through the steering wheel. Conversely, it should be noted that wear or damage in suspension or steering components may cause excessive tyre wear. Out-of-round or out-of-true tyres, damaged wheels and wheel bearing wear/maladjustment also fall into this category. Balancing will not usually cure vibration caused by such wear.

Wheel balancing may be carried out with the wheel either on or off the vehicle. If balanced on the vehicle, ensure that the wheel-to-hub relationship is marked in some way prior to subsequent wheel removal so that it may be refitted in its original position.

General tyre wear is influenced to a large degree by driving style – harsh braking and acceleration or fast cornering will all produce more rapid tyre wear. Interchanging of tyres may result in more even wear, but this should only be carried out where there is no mix of tyre types on the vehicle. However, it is worth bearing in mind that if this is completely effective, the added expense of replacing a complete set of tyres simultaneously is incurred, which may prove financially restrictive for many owners.

Front tyres may wear unevenly as a result of wheel misalignment. The front wheels should always be correctly aligned according to the settings specified by the vehicle manufacturer.

Legal restrictions apply to the mixing of tyre types on a vehicle. Basically this means that a vehicle must not have tyres of differing construction on the same axle. Although it is not recommended to mix tyre types between front axle and rear axle, the only legally permissible combination is crossply at the front and radial at the rear. When mixing radial ply tyres, textile braced radials must always go on the front axle, with steel braced radials at the rear. An obvious disadvantage of such mixing is the necessity to carry two spare tyres to avoid contravening the law in the event of a puncture.

In the UK, the Motor Vehicles Construction and Use Regulations apply to many aspects of tyre fitting and usage. It is suggested that a copy of these regulations is obtained from your local police if in doubt as to the current legal requirements with regard to tyre condition, minimum tread depth, etc.

15 Fault diagnosis – driveshafts, hubs, roadwheels and tyres

Symptom	Reason(s)
Vibration	Driveshaft bent Worn CV joints Out of balance roadwheels
'Clonk' on taking up drive or on the over run	Worn CV joints Worn splines on driveshaft, hub or differential sun wheels Loose driveshaft nut or wheel bolts
Noise or roar when cornering	Worn hub bearings Loose driveshaft/hub nut
Rapid or uneven wear of tyre tread	Out of balance roadwheels Distorted roadwheel Incorrect front wheel alignment

Chapter 9 Braking system

Contents

Specifications

General

Type .... Servo-assisted, hydraulic, dual circuit. Front disc and rear drum brakes on all models except Turbo which has discs all round. ABS standard on Turbo models, optional on some others. Handbrake operates on rear wheels.

Front brakes

Disc diameter:
    1.7 litre models .... 238 mm (9.28 in)
    2.0 litre non-Turbo L483 models .... 265 mm (10.34 in)
    2.0 litre Turbo L485 models .... 285 mm (11.12 in)
Minimum disc thickness:
    1.7 litre L481 models .... 10.5 mm (0.41 in)
    1.7 litre L482 models .... 18.0 mm (0.70 in)
    2.0 litre non-Turbo L483 models .... 17.7 mm (0.69 in)
    2.0 litre Turbo L485 models .... 17.5 mm (0.68 in)
Minimum pad thickness:
    1.7 litre models .... 6.0 mm (0.23 in)
    2.0 litre models .... 6.5 mm (0.25 in)
Maximum disc run-out .... 0.07 mm (0.003 in)

Rear drum brakes

Drum diameter:
    1.7 litre models .... 180.25 mm (7.03 in)
    2.0 litre models .... 228.5 mm (8.91 in)
Maximum allowable drum diameter after refacing:
    1.7 litre models .... 181.25 mm (7.07 in)
    2.0 litre models .... 229.5 mm (8.95 in)
Minimum lining thickness (including shoe) .... 2.5 mm (0.10 in)

Rear disc brakes

Disc diameter .... 255.0 mm (9.95 in)
Minimum disc thickness .... 9.5 mm (0.37 in)
Maximum disc run-out .... 0.07 mm (0.003 in)

Hydraulic fluid

Type/specification .... Hydraulic fluid to SAE J1703F, DOT 3 or DOT 4 (Duckhams Universal Brake and Clutch Fluid)

Torque wrench settings

	Nm	lbf ft
Master cylinder/servo bolts	13	9
Servo unit bolts	20	15
Front brake caliper:		
Caliper mounting bolts	100	73
Caliper bracket mounting bolts (Bendix IV type)	65	48
Caliper guide bolts (Bendix IVM type)	25	18
Caliper guide bolts (Girling type)	35	26
Rear brake caliper:		
Caliper mounting bolts	65	48
ABS system:		
Wheel sensor mounting bolt	8	6
Hydraulic control unit nuts	20	14
Hydraulic system:		
Bleed screws	7	5
Brake pipe unions and associated fittings	13	9

1 General description

The braking system is of four wheel dual circuit type. On all models except those fitted with ABS (anti-lock braking system), the circuits are split diagonally. On models fitted with ABS, the circuits are split front to rear.

The front brakes are of ventilated disc type, with automatically adjusted drum brakes at the rear. On Turbo models, four wheel disc brakes are fitted, with ventilated discs at the front, and solid discs at the rear.

All models have servo assistance and a brake compensator system to balance the system in accordance with pressure and loading.

The handbrake is cable operated to the rear brakes, adjustment being automatic.

The removal and refitting of some brake system components requires the use of Torx type keys, therefore it is advisable to read through the instructions for a particular task before commencing, and examine the items on the vehicle to assess the tool requirements.

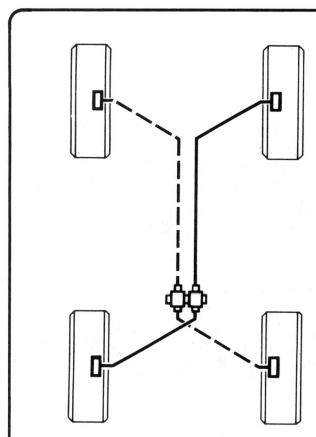

Fig. 9.1 Brake circuit diagram – 1.7 litre models with fixed compensators (Sec 1)

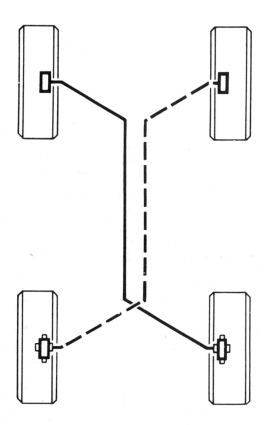

Fig. 9.2 Brake circuit diagram – 1.7 litre models with compensator integral in wheel cylinders (Sec 1)

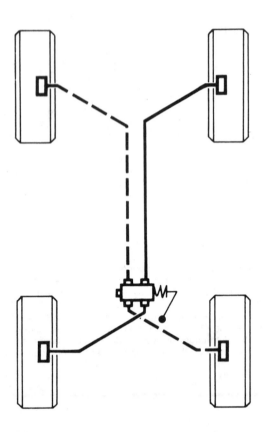

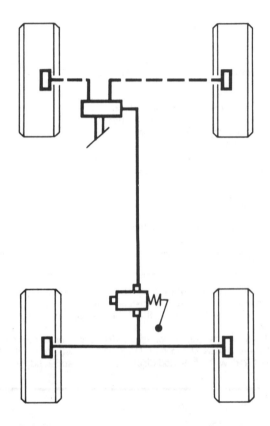

Fig. 9.3 Brake circuit diagram – 2.0 litre models with load
dependent compensator (Sec 1)

Fig. 9.4 Brake circuit diagram – 2.0 litre ABS models with
load dependent compensator (Sec 1)

2 Maintenance

1   Regularly check the fluid level in the brake master cylinder
reservoir. The need for topping-up should be very infrequent and then
only a small quantity should be required to compensate for friction
lining wear.
2   The fluid level should never be allowed to fall below the 'Minimum'
level marking on the front face of the reservoir, or topped up beyond
the 'Maximum' mark. Any loss of fluid will be due to a leak in the brake
hydraulic system (or possibly the clutch hydraulic system on Turbo
models, as both use the same reservoir) (photo).
3   When topping-up use only clean fluid of the correct type which has
been stored in an airtight container.
4   At the intervals specified in 'Routine maintenance' the following
service operations should be carried out on the braking system.
5   With the car raised on a hoist, over an inspection pit or supported
on ramps or axle stands, carefully inspect all the hydaulic pipes, hoses
and unions for chafing, cracks, leaks and corrosion. Details will be
found in Section 14.
6   Remove the front wheels and check the thickness of the front brake
pads. Renew the pads, as described in Section 3, if they are worn to the
specified minimum thickness.
7   Remove the rear wheels and inspect the rear brake linings, or pads
as applicable. With drum brakes it will be necessary to remove the
brake drum to make a full inspection of the brake linings. The wheel
cylinder can also be inspected for any signs of leakage at the same
time.
8   Check the operation of the handbrake on each rear wheel and
lubricate the exposed cables and linkages under the car.
9   At less frequent intervals (see 'Routine maintenance') the brake
servo air filter and non-return valve should also be renewed, using the
procedure described in Sections 17 and 18.

2.2 Brake fluid reservoir and fluid levels

3 Front disc pads – inspection and renewal

1   Raise the front of the car and support it securely.
2   Remove the front roadwheels.
3   Inspect the thickness of the friction material on the disc pads
(photo). If it has worn below the minimum specified, renew the pads
in the following way according to type.

Girling type

4 Unscrew the caliper guide bolts using a ring spanner and an open-ended spanner to lock the guide pins.

5 Lift off the caliper and support it or tie it up out of the way (photo).

6 Disconnect the sensor wire. Remove the disc pads and discard them (photos).

7 Brush away all dust and dirt, but *avoid inhaling it as it is injurious to health.*

8 The piston should now be pushed fully into its cylinder. Do this using a flat bar or a clamp similar to the one shown in Fig. 9.6. As the piston is depressed, the fluid will rise in the reservoir, so anticipate this by syphoning some out beforehand. An old battery hydrometer or poultry baster is useful for this, but make sure that they are clean. Do not syphon out fluid by mouth.

9 Fit the new pads; the inboard one being the one with the sensor wire.

10 Locate the springs correctly, then the caliper.

11 Fit the guide bolts, having applied thread locking fluid to their threads (photo).

12 Tighten the bottom guide bolts and then the upper one to the specified torque (photo). Proceed to paragraph 23.

Bendix IV type

13 Disconnect the pad wear sensor wire, then press piston into its caliper by sliding the caliper outwards (see paragraphs 7 and 8).

14 Note their location, then remove the retaining clip and wedge from the caliper housing. Withdraw the pads together with their anti-rattle springs. As they are removed, note the orientation of each pad. On the outer pad the wear groove is offset and towards the front of the car, whilst on the inner pad the offset groove is towards the rear. Brush away all dust and dirt, *but* avoid inhaling it as it is injurious to health.

15 If new pads are to be fitted, locate the anti-rattle springs as shown in Fig. 9.9.

16 Fit the brake pads into position ensuring that they are positioned as shown in Fig. 9.10. The pad wear sensor wire must be on the inboard side.

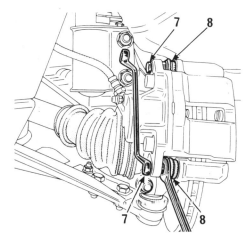

Fig. 9.5 Lock the guide pins (8) when unscrewing the caliper guide bolts (7) – Girling type (Sec 3)

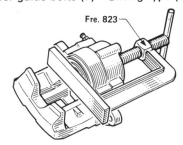

Fig. 9.6 Using a clamp to depress the caliper piston – Renault tool shown (Sec 3)

3.3 Front brake disc pad inspection window (Girling type)

3.5 Lift the caliper out of the way ...

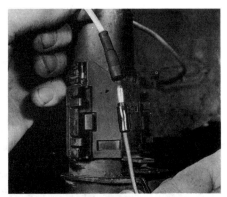

3.6A ... and detach the sensor wire ...

3.6B ... and remove the brake pads (Girling type)

3.11 Smear the bolt threads with locking compound ...

3.12 ... fit and tighten them to the specified torque (Girling type)

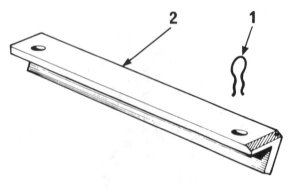

Fig. 9.7 Bendix IV type front brake pads retaining clip (1) and wedge (2) (Sec 3)

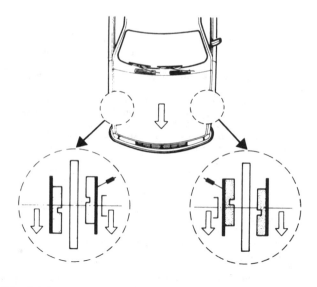

Fig. 9.8 Pad identification and orientation – Bendix IV type (Sec 3)

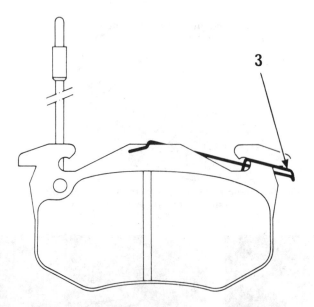

Fig. 9.9 Anti-rattle spring (3) fitted to pad – Bendix IV type (Sec 3)

17 Slide the wedge into position and then fit the retaining clip to the inboard side of the caliper. Proceed to paragraph 23.

3.19 Unscrew the caliper guide bolt using a Torx key (Bendix IV type) ...

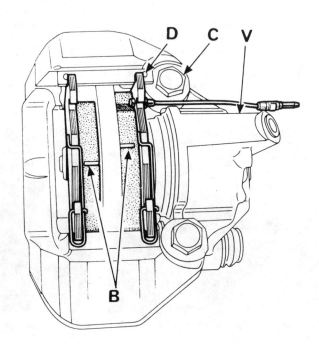

Fig. 9.10 Pad locations in Bendix IV type caliper (Sec 3)

B   Pad grooves are offset as shown
V   Pad with wear sensor wire to be on inside
D   Retaining clip location (inboard side)
C   Caliper bracket bolt

Bendix IVM type

18 Detach the brake pad wear sensor wire. Pull the caliper body outwards by hand to compress the piston into its cylinder.
19 Undo the caliper guide bolt using a T40 Torx key (photo). With the guide bolt detached from the caliper bracket, pivot the caliper body upwards and hold it in position to enable the pads to be withdrawn.
20 Withdraw the pads from the caliper bracket (photo).
21 Brush away all dust and dirt, *but avoid inhaling it, as it is injurious to health.* Remove and clean the spring (photo).
22 Refit in the reverse order of removal. Note that the pad with the wear sensor wire is fitted to the inboard side of the caliper. Tighten the guide bolt to the specified torque wrench setting.

All models
23 Renew the pads on the opposite wheel in a similar way.
24 Apply the footbrake several times to position the pads against the discs.
25 Fit the roadwheels and lower the car to the floor.
26 Top up the master cylinder reservoir to the correct level.
27 Ensure that the pad wear sensor wire is correctly routed and located (photos).

---

4 Rear disc pads – inspection and renewal

1 Raise the rear of the car, support it securely and remove the rear roadwheels.
2 Check the wear of the friction material on the pads. If it has worn below the minimum specified, renew the pads in the following way.
3 Disconnect the handbrake cable from the lever on the caliper, refer to Section 22.
4 Extract the two lockpins and then tap out the two sliding keys (photos).
5 Lift the caliper from the disc and tie it up out of the way.
6 Remove the disc pads and springs for inspection. Clean the caliper by carefully brushing away the dust and dirt, *but avoid inhaling it as it is injurious to health.*
7 Retract the piston fully into its cylinder prior to fitting new pads. Do this by turning the piston with the square section shaft of a screwdriver until the piston continues to turn but will not go in any further. As the piston goes in, the fluid level in the master cylinder reservoir will rise; anticipate this by syphoning out some fluid (see Section 3, paragraph 8). Finally set the piston so that the line (R – Fig. 9.11) is nearest to the bleed screw.
8 Locate the springs onto the pads and fit the pads (photos).
9 Fit the caliper by engaging one end of the caliper between the spring clip and the keyway on the bracket, compress the springs and engage the opposite end.

10 Insert the first key, then insert a screwdriver in the second key slot and use it as a lever until the slot will accept the key.
11 Fit new key retaining clips.
12 Renew the pads on the opposite wheel.
13 Reconnect the handbrake cable.
14 Apply the footbrake several times to position the pads against the discs.
15 Fit the roadwheels and lower the car to the floor.
16 Top up the master cylinder reservoir to the correct level.

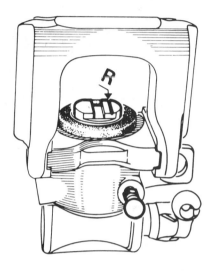

Fig. 9.11 Rear brake caliper piston orientation (Sec 4)

Line R to be nearest bleed screw

3.20 ... remove the pads ...

3.21 ... and spring (noting its orientation)

3.27A Pad wear sensor wire and retaining clip on caliper (arrowed)

3.27B Pad wear sensor connector (arrowed) and retainer on suspension strut (2.0 litre model)

4.4A Extract the lock pins (arrowed) ...

4.4B ... and remove the sliding keys

4.8A Locate the pad springs ...

4.8B ... and fit the pads

5 Front disc brake caliper – removal, overhaul and refitting

1   Raise the front of the car and remove the roadwheel.
2   Release the flexible brake hose from the caliper by unscrewing it no more than a quarter of a turn.
3   Remove the brake pads as described in Section 3.
4   Undo the two caliper unit-to-hub carrier bolts, then withdraw the caliper from the brake disc (photos).
5   Unscrew the caliper from the flexible hose and then cap the end of the hose or use a brake hose clamp to prevent loss of fluid (photo).
6   Clean away external dirt from the caliper on the Girling caliper, and remove the dust excluder and retaining ring.
7   Eject the piston from the cylinder by applying air pressure to the fluid inlet hole. Only low air pressure is required such as is generated by a foot-operated tyre pump. Remove the piston seal ring from its groove in the caliper bore.

8   Inspect the surfaces of the piston and cylinder. If there is evidence of scoring or corrosion, renew the caliper cylinder assembly complete.
9   If the components are in good condition, remove the seal and wash them in clean hydraulic fluid or methylated spirit – nothing else.
10 Obtain a repair kit which will contain all the necessary renewable items. Fit the new seal, using the fingers to manipulate it into its groove.
11 Dip the piston in clean hydraulic fluid and insert the piston into the cylinder.
12 On the Girling caliper, fit the dust excluder and retaining ring.
13 Screw the caliper onto the flexible hose and fit the caliper to its bracket, making sure that the piston is fully depressed into its cylinder.
14 Tighten the flexible hose union and bleed the hydraulic circuit (Section 15).
15 Refit the roadwheel and lower the car.
16 Apply the footbrake two or three times to settle the pads.

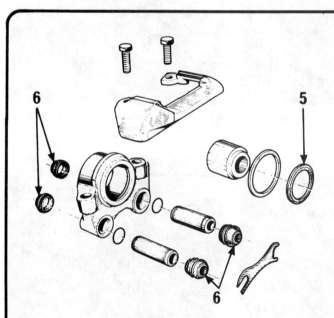

Fig. 9.12 Front disc brake caliper components, showing piston dust excluder (5) and gaiters (6) (Sec 5)

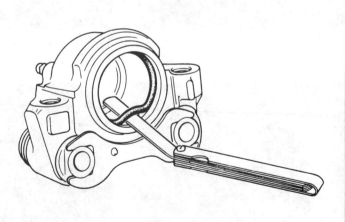

Fig. 9.13 Removing the piston seal ring from the caliper bore (Sec 5)

5.4A Brake caliper-to-hub carrier bolts (arrowed) – Girling type

5.4B Brake caliper-to-hub carrier bolts (arrowed) – Bendix type

5.6 Brake hose clamp in position

6 Rear disc brake caliper – removal, overhaul and refitting

1   Raise the rear of the car and remove the roadwheel.
2   Disconnect the handbrake cable from the lever on the caliper (see Section 22).
3   Release the flexible brake hose from the caliper by unscrewing it by no more than a quarter of a turn.
4   Remove the caliper from the disc as described in Section 4.
5   Unscrew the caliper from the hose and cap the end of the hose or use a brake hose clamp to prevent loss of fluid.
6   Clean away external dirt from the caliper and grip it in the jaws of a vice fitted with jaw protectors.
7   Remove the dust excluder from around the piston and then unscrew the piston, using the square section shaft of a screwdriver. Once the piston turns freely but does not come out any further, apply low air pressure to the fluid inlet hole and eject the piston. Only low air pressure is required such as is generated by a foot-operated tyre pump.
8   Inspect the surfaces of the piston and cylinder bore. If there is evidence of scoring or corrosion, renew the caliper cylinder.
9   To remove the cylinder a wedge will have to be made in accordance with the dimensions shown in Fig. 9.15.
10 Drive the wedge in to slightly separate the support bracket arms and so slide out the cylinder which can be done once the spring-loaded locating pin has been depressed (Figs. 9.16 and 9.17).
11 If the piston and cylinder are in good condition, then the cylinder will not have to be removed from the support bracket but overhauled in the following way.
12 Remove and discard the piston seal and wash the components in methylated spirit.
13 Obtain a repair kit which will contain all the necessary renewable

items. Fit the new seal using the fingers to manipulate it into its groove.
14 Dip the piston in clean hydraulic fluid and insert the piston into the cylinder.
15 Using the square section shaft of a screwdriver, turn the piston until it turns but will not go in any further. Set the piston so that the line (R – Fig. 9.11) is nearest the bleed screw.
16 Fit a new dust excluder.
17 If the handbrake operating mechanism is worn or faulty, dismantle it in the following way before renewing the piston seal.
18 Grip the caliper in a vice fitted with jaw protectors.
19 Refer to Fig. 9.18 and remove the dust excluder (1), the piston (2), dust cover (3), and the circlip (4).
20 Compress the spring washers (5) and pull out the shaft (6).
21 Remove the plunger cam (7), spring (8), adjusting screw (9), plain washer (10) and spring washer (5).
22 Refer to Fig. 9.19 and drive out the sleeve (12) using a drift, and remove the sealing ring (11).
23 Clean all components and renew any that are worn.
24 Reassembly is a reversal of removal but observe the following points.
25 Drive in the sleeve (12) until it is flush with face (A) in Fig. 9.20.
26 Make sure that the spring washers are fitted as shown, convex face to convex face.
27 Align the piston as previously described.
28 Refit the caliper after screwing it onto the hydraulic hose. Tighten the hose union.
29 Reconnect the handbrake cable.
30 Bleed the hydraulic circuit (Section 15).
31 Fit the roadwheel and lower the car.
32 Apply the footbrake several times and adjust the handbrake cable (Section 20).

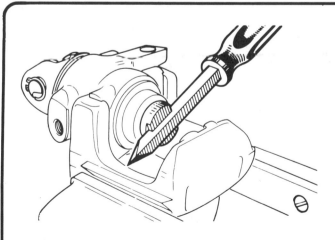

Fig. 9.14 Unscrewing the rear caliper piston using a screwdriver (Sec 6)

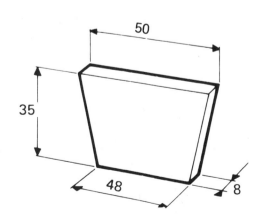

Fig. 9.15 Rear caliper support bracket arm wedge dimensions (in mm) (Sec 6)

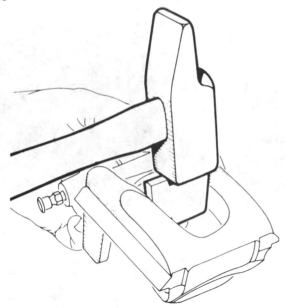

Fig. 9.16 Driving in the wedge to spread caliper support arm brackets (Sec 6)

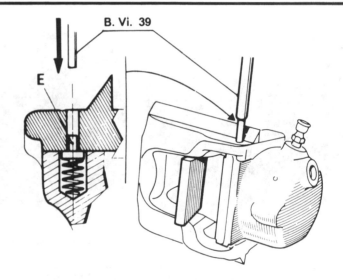

Fig. 9.17 Depressing cylinder spring-loaded locating pin (E) – Renault tool shown (Sec 6)

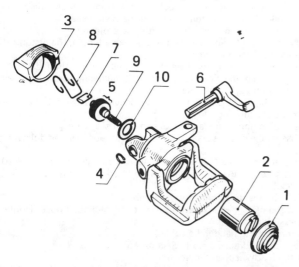

Fig. 9.18 Exploded view of rear caliper (Sec 6)

1 Dust excluder	6 Shaft
2 Piston	7 Plunger cam
3 Rear dust cover	8 Spring
4 Circlip	9 Adjusting screw
5 Spring washers	10 Washer

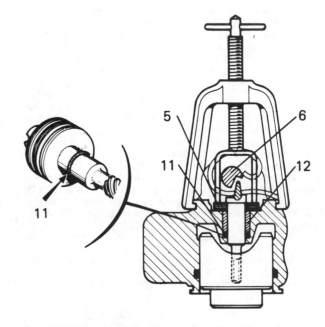

Fig. 9.19 Using a puller to compress spring washers in rear caliper. Inset O-ring (11) on adjusting screw (Sec 6)

5 Spring washer	11 O-ring
6 Shaft	12 Sleeve

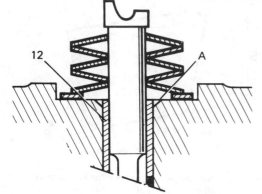

Fig. 9.20 Rear caliper sleeve (12) fitted flush with face (A) (Sec 6)

7 Brake disc – inspection, removal and refitting

Inspection
1 Whenever the disc pads are being checked for wear, take the opportunity to inspect the disc for deep grooving, scoring or cracks. Light scoring is normal.
2 Rust will normally build up on the edge of a disc and this should be removed periodically by holding a sharp tool against the disc whilst it is rotated (photo).
3 If there has been a history of brake judder, check the discs for run-out. Do this using a dial gauge or feeler blades between the disc and a fixed point while the disc is rotated. Run-out should be within the specified limit (see Specifications).
4 If the disc is grooved, cracked or distorted it must be renewed. Refinishing of a disc must not be carried out as this can cause the caliper piston to overextend when the brakes are applied. If a new disc is being fitted, new brake pads must also be fitted to both sides of the car.

Front disc renewal
5 Raise the front of the car and remove the roadwheel.
6 Unscrew and remove the two caliper bracket bolts (see photos 5.4A and 5.4B).
7 Lift the caliper off the disc and tie it up out of the way.
8 Unscrew the disc fixing screws; these are of Torx type so a special bit will be required.
9 Remove the disc.
10 Clean any protective coating from the new disc and locate it on the hub.
11 Screw in and tighten the fixing screws.
12 Clean the threads of the caliper bracket fixing bolts, apply thread locking fluid to them, locate the caliper and screw in the bolts, tightening them to the specified torque.
13 Apply the brake pedal several times to position the pads up against the disc, fit the roadwheel and lower the car.

Rear disc renewal
14 Raise the rear of the car and remove the roadwheel.
15 Refer to Section 4 and remove the disc pads and disconnect the handbrake cable. Tie the caliper up out of the way.
16 Unscrew and remove the two caliper bracket bolts (A – Fig. 9.21) and lift off the caliper bracket.
17 Using a Torx bit, unscrew and remove the two disc fixing screws and remove the disc (photo).
18 Fitting the disc is a reversal of removal, but remove any protective coating from the new disc, and apply thread locking fluid to clean the threads of the caliper bracket bolts.
19 Apply the brake pedal several times and adjust the handbrake.
20 Refit the roadwheel and lower the car.

8 Rear brake shoes (Bendix type) – inspection and renewal

1 Raise the vehicle at the rear end, support on axle stands and remove the roadwheels.
2 To inspect the shoe linings the brake drum will need to be removed. One of two brake drum types will be fitted, a monoblock type or a steel disc type. Remove the drum as follows according to type.
Steel disc type drum
3 With the handbrake fully applied, unscrew and remove the two Torx retaining screws, release the handbrake and withdraw the drum (photo). If it is tight, try gently tapping it with a plastic or copper-faced hammer. If this fails, remove the blanking plug on the rear face of the backplate to allow access to the automatic adjuster. On some models access to the adjuster is obtained through a vacant wheel bolt hole in the drum. Using a suitable screwdriver and a length of rod as shown, release the adjuster and unscrew the knurled adjuster wheel (photo). With the adjuster fully retracted, the drum will be released.
Monoblock type drum
4 A hub cap and inertia extractor or slide hammer will be required to remove this type of drum. Prise free the hub cap. If the cap is tight, use an extractor as shown in Fig. 9.22 and withdraw it from the centre of the hub. Unscrew the hub flange nut, then with the handbrake fully released, withdraw the brake drum. If it is tight, loosen off the secondary handbrake cable, then insert a screwdriver through one of

7.2 Remove rust deposits from outside edge of brake disc

7.17 Removing a rear brake disc

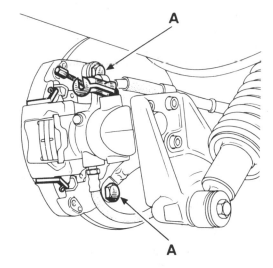
Fig. 9.21 Rear disc brake caliper bracket retaining bolts (A) (Sec 7)

8.3A Unscrewing a rear brake drum Torx retaining screw

8.3B Showing method employed to release the automatic adjuster – drum removed for clarity

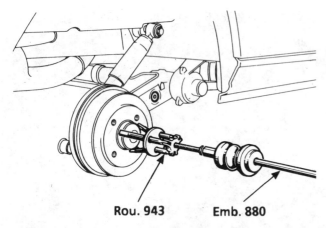

Fig. 9.22 Rear brake drum and hub cap removal tools – Renault tools shown (Sec 8)

the wheel bolt holes in the drum and press the handbrake operating lever down to release the shoe stud (E in Fig. 9.23). Push the lever rearwards to assist. Remove the drum.

All drum types

5 Brush away dust and dirt, *taking care not to inhale it as it is injurious to health.*

6 If the shoe friction linings have worn down to or below the specified minimum, then the shoes should be renewed.

7 Obtain factory relined shoes, do not attempt to reline the old shoes as this seldom proves satisfactory. Tap off the hub dust cap, unscrew the hub nut and remove the hub assembly.

8 Note carefully the position of the leading and trailing shoes and how the friction lining exposes more of the shoe web at one end than the other.

9 Note also into which holes in the shoe web the return springs engage.

10 Disconnect the upper and lower return springs.

11 Disconnect the handbrake cable from the trailing shoe.

12 Remove the two shoe hold-down springs. Do this by gripping the hold-down spring caps with a pair of pliers, then compressing the cap and spring. Simultaneously turn them through 90° to align the slotted hole in the cap with the T-head of the central retaining pin, then withdraw the cap and spring.

13 Remove the leading shoe and toothed adjuster quadrant, the trailing shoe and link unit.

14 When disconnecting the link from the trailing shoe, take care not to damage the automatic adjuster.

15 Remove the toothed adjuster quadrant and spring from the leading shoe.

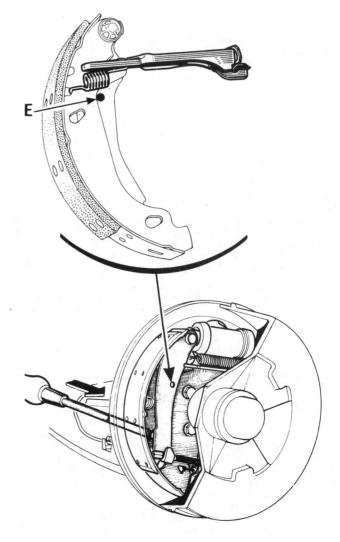

Fig. 9.23 Press on handbrake operating lever to release stud (E) (Sec 8)

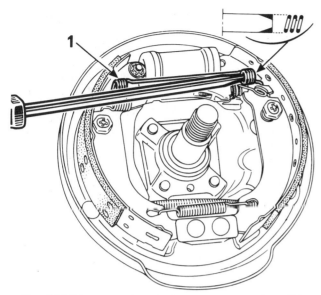

Fig. 9.24 Disconnecting the upper return springs (1) –
Bendix type (Sec 8)

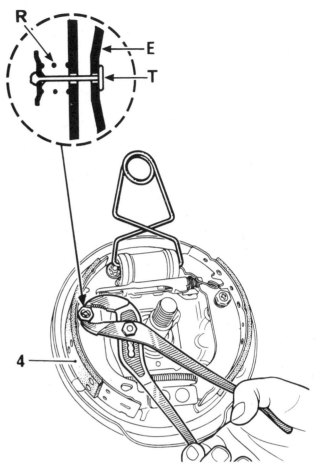

Fig. 9.25 Brake shoe hold-down spring removal – Bendix
type (Sec 8)

R   Spring   T   Retaining pin
E   Backplate   4   Trailing brake shoe

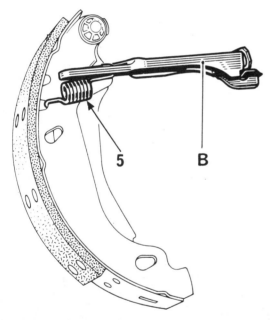

Fig. 9.26 Trailing brake shoe adjuster (B) and spring (5)
(Sec 8)

16 While the shoes are removed, do not touch the brake pedal or the
wheel cylinder pistons will be ejected. Keep the respective sub-
assemblies together for reference during reassembly, as the right and
left-hand assemblies differ and must not be interchanged.
17 Assemble the link and spring to the trailing shoe as shown in Fig.
9.26, and the toothed adjuster quadrant and spring to the leading shoe
as shown in Fig. 9.27. Move the knurled adjuster to the zero position.
18 Fit the new shoes by reversing the removal operations. Apply a
smear of high melting-point grease to the shoe-rubbing high spots on
the brake backplate, to the shoe lower anchor block recesses and to the
end faces of the wheel cylinder pistons. Take care not to get any grease
on the brake linings or the braking surfaces of the drum during
reassembly.
19 When fitting the leading shoe ensure that the toothed adjuster
quadrant engages with the link correctly before securing it.
20 When the brake shoes are fully refitted, adjust the diametrical
position of the shoes before fitting the brake drum. To do this, turn the
toothed adjuster quadrant to set the outside diameter of the brake
shoes to the specified setting shown in Fig. 9.28.

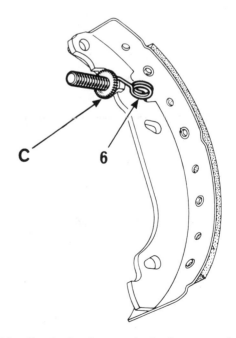

Fig. 9.27 Leading brake shoe toothed adjuster quadrant (C)
and spring (6) (Sec 8)

21 Clean the interior of the drum and fit it, together with the hub, taking care not to damage the oil seal. Tighten the hub nut to the specified torque (Chapter 8).
22 Refit the dust cap over the nut.
23 Refit the backplate plug (if applicable).
24 Repeat the operations on the opposite wheel.
25 Depress the brake pedal a few times to operate the automatic adjuster mechanism, then adjust the handbrake (Section 20).

9 Rear brake shoes (Girling type) – inspection and renewal

1   Raise the vehicle at the rear end, support on axle stands and remove the roadwheels.
2   Repeat the operations described in Section 8, paragraphs 2 to 9.
3   Prise free and remove the upper and lower brake shoe return springs.
4   Disconnect the handbrake cable from the trailing shoe (photos).
5   Disconnect the tension spring and remove the adjuster lever.
6   Grip one of the shoe hold-down caps with a pair of pliers, depress the cap and turn it through 90° so that it will pass over the T-shaped head of the hold-down pin. Remove the cap, spring and pin. Remove the hold-down assembly from the other brake shoe in a similar manner.
7   Detach and withdraw the leading brake shoe and thrust link.
8   Remove the trailing brake shoe.
9   While the shoes are removed, do not touch the brake pedal or the wheel cylinder pistons will be ejected.
10 Clean the backplate and inspect the brake assembly components. Keep the sub-assemblies separate, as the right and left-hand assemblies are different and must not be interchanged. The toothed adjuster screw units are colour-coded for identification as shown in Fig. 9.29. Clean the threads of the toothed adjusters and lightly grease them.
11 Apply a smear of high melting-point grease to the shoe-rubbing high spots on the brake backplate, to the shoe lower anchor block recesses and to the end faces of the wheel cylinder pistons.
12 Refitting is a reversal of the removal procedure. Take care not to get grease or oil onto the brake linings or the drum friction surface. Ensure that all connections are correctly and securely made (photo).
13 Prior to refitting the drum, adjust the diameter of the brake shoes to that specified in Fig. 9.30 by turning the toothed adjuster as required.
14 Refit the brake drums and carry out the operations given in paragraphs 21 to 25 of the previous Section to complete.

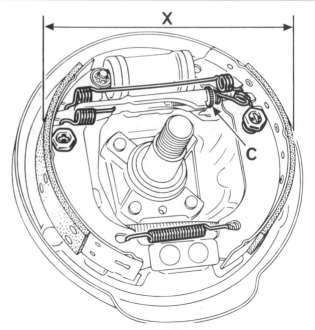

Fig. 9.28 Provisional brake shoes adjustment – Bendix type (Sec 8)

C   Toothed adjuster quadrant
X = 178.7 to 179.2 mm (6.97 to 6.99 in)

Fig. 9.29 Brake adjuster screw unit identification – Girling type (Sec 9)

Left-hand side – silver end piece (B)   *Right-hand side – gold end piece (B)*

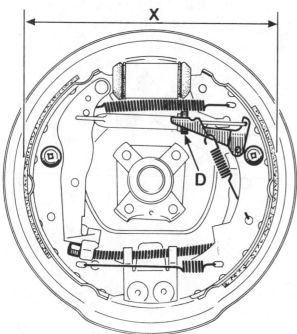

Fig. 9.30 Provisional brake shoes adjustment – Girling type (Sec 9)

D   Toothed adjuster quadrant   *X = 227.9 to 228.5 mm (8.89 to 8.91 in)*

9.4A Girling type rear drum brake
1   Wheel cylinder   3   Tension spring and adjusting lever
2   Upper return spring   4   Shoe hold down spring unit

9.4B Handbrake cable (arrowed) – Girling type rear drum brake

9.12 Reassembled Girling brake assembly

10 Rear wheel cylinder – removal, overhaul and refitting

1 Raise the rear of the car, support on axle stands and remove the roadwheel.
2 Remove the brake drum (according to type), as described in Section 8, paragraph 3 or 4 as applicable.
3 Prise and chock the upper ends of the brake shoes so that they are separated from the wheel cylinder pistons.
4 Clean the area around the hydraulic pipe union at the wheel cylinder connection on the inboard side of the backplate, then loosen off the union nut using a brake pipe spanner (photo).
5 Undo the two wheel cylinder mounting bolts and withdraw the cylinder. As the cylinder is withdrawn from the backplate, take care not to spill hydraulic fluid onto the brake linings or paintwork. Plug the hydraulic pipe to prevent spillage and the ingress of dirt.
6 If the wheel cylinder is defective, it must be renewed as a unit as no repair kits are available.
7 Refitting is a reversal of the removal procedure. Ensure that the hydraulic pipe connection at the wheel cylinder is clean. Do not fully tighten the nut until after the anchor plate bolts have been fitted.
8 Adjust the outside diameter of the brake shoes as described in Section 8 or 9, as applicable, before refitting the drum.

9 Refit the roadwheel, lower the car, then bleed the brake hydraulic system as described in Section 15. On 1.7 litre models fitted with wheel cylinders which incorporate a compensator, the system cut-off pressure should be checked. This task requires the use of a special pressure measuring gauge and must therefore be entrusted to a Renault dealer.

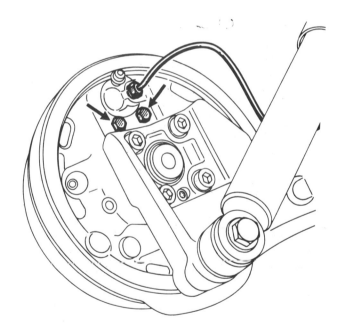

Fig. 9.31 Wheel cylinder mounting bolts (arrowed) (Sec 10)

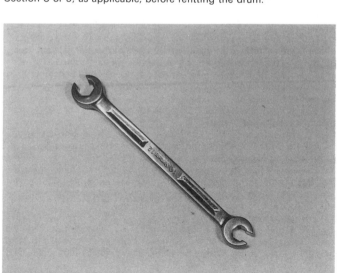

10.4 Brake pipe spanner

11 Brake drum – inspection and renovation

1 Whenever the brake drums are removed to examine the shoe linings for wear, take the opportunity to inspect the interior of the drums for grooving, scoring or cracks.
2 The drums may be machined to renovate them provided both drums are done at the same time and the internal diameter will not be increased to more than the specified maximum.

12 Master cylinder (non-ABS models) – removal and refitting

1   Syphon the fluid from the master cylinder reservoir. Use a syringe, a clean battery hydrometer or a poultry baster to do this, **never** use the mouth to suck the fluid out through a tube.

2   Disconnect the leads from the low level switch and pull the reservoir upwards out of the sealing grommets (photo).

3   Note the locations of the hydraulic pipes and then disconnect them from the master cylinder by unscrewing the unions. Catch any fluid which may drain out.

4   Unbolt the master cylinder from the front face of the servo unit and remove it.

5   A faulty master cylinder cannot be overhauled, only renewed, due to the fact that the internal roll pins cannot be extracted.

6   Before fitting the master cylinder, check the servo pushrod protrusion (X – Fig. 9.32). This must be as specified. Adjust if necessary by means of the pushrod nut.

7   Ensure that a new O-ring seal is fitted between the joint faces of the master cylinder and the servo unit.

8   Bolt the master cylinder into position and connect the fluid pipes.

9   Push the reservoir firmly into its grommets.

10 Fill the reservoir with clean fluid and bleed the complete hydraulic system (Section 15).

11 Check that dimension L in Fig. 9.32 is as specified and adjust if necessary by loosening the locknut at the clevis (C), then turning the rod to suit. Retighten the locknut to complete.

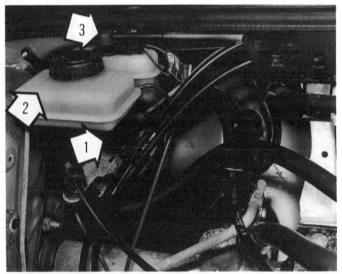

12.2 Brake master cylinder (1), fluid reservoir (2) and low level warning switch (3) – 2.0 litre model shown

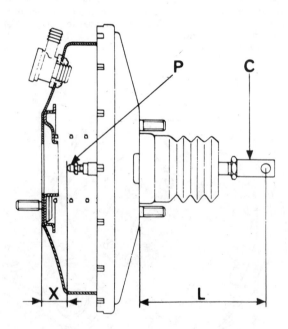

Fig. 9.32 Servo pushrod setting diagram (Secs 12 and 19)

X = 22.3 mm (0.87 in)   L = 105 mm (4.10 in)
P   Pushrod adjuster   C   Pedal pushrod adjuster
                              clevis

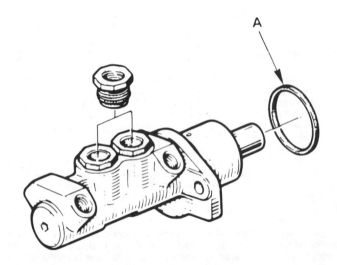

Fig. 9.33 Master cylinder and O-ring seal (A) (Sec 12)

13 Brake compensator – removal and refitting

1   Checking the operation of the brake compensator is not within the scope of the home mechanic as specialised equipment is required. However, a unit that is known to be faulty can be removed and renewed. It is important to ensure that the correct replacement compensator unit is obtained, as different types are fitted depending on model. Either a fixed or load-controlled type compensator will be fitted. On some models the fixed type compensator is integral with the rear wheel cylinders, and in this instance a fault in the compensator (or the cylinder) necessitates renewal of the relevant cylinder unit as described in Section 10.

2   The compensator unit on other models is located on the underside of the car, just to the right of centre, forward of the rear axle (photos).

3   Raise and support the vehicle at the rear on axle stands.

4   Clean the hydraulic pipe connections to the compensator, then undo the hydraulic pipe unions and disconnect the pipes. Plug them to prevent the ingress of dirt and leakage.

5   Unscrew and remove the compensator retaining bolt.

Fixed type compensator

6   Tilt the assembly, then withdraw it from the underside of the vehicle floor pan. Uncouple the compensator from the support.

Load-controlled type compensator

7   To remove this compensator, detach the control spring from the V-shaped profile, then pivot the compensator support and withdraw it from the underside of the car. **Do not** unscrew or reset the adjuster nut. Detach the compensator from its support.

All compensator types

8   Refitting for each type of compensator is a reversal of the removal procedure. Note that the hydraulic inlet pipe connections of the fixed type compensator are on the side with the smaller unions (see Fig. 9.35).

9   When the compensator is refitted, bleed the brake hydraulic system as described in Section 15.

10 On completion, have the compensator pressures checked by a Renault dealer as soon as possible.

13.2A Brake compensator – 2.0 litre non-Turbo model. Do not alter setting of nut (arrowed)

13.2B Brake compensator – 2.0 litre Turbo model. Do not alter setting of nut (arrowed)

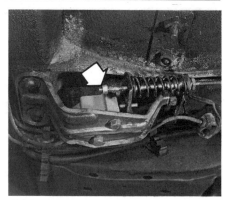

13.2C Brake compensator – 1.7 litre model. Do not alter setting of nut (arrowed)

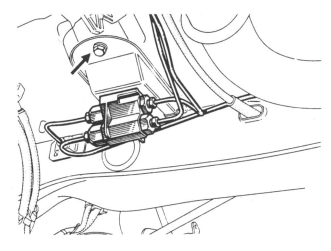

Fig. 9.34 Fixed type compensator unit and retaining bolt (arrowed) (Sec 13)

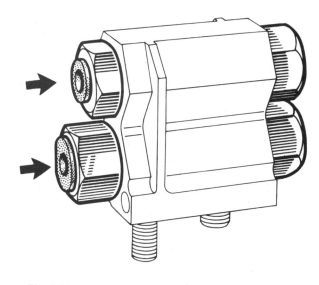

Fig. 9.35 Fixed type compensator and inlet unions (arrowed) (Sec 13)

14 Hydraulic pipes and hoses – inspection, removal and refitting

1   At intervals given in *'Routine maintenance'* carefully examine all brake pipes, hoses, hose connections and pipe unions (photo).

2   First check for signs of leakage at the pipe unions. Then examine the flexible hoses for signs of cracking, chafing and fraying.

3   The brake pipes must be examined carefully and methodically. They must be cleaned off and checked for signs of dents, corrosion or other damage. Corrosion should be scraped off and, if the depth of pitting is significant, the pipes renewed. This is particularly likely in those areas underneath the vehicle body where the pipes are exposed and unprotected.

4   If any section of pipe or hose is to be removed, first unscrew the master cylinder reservoir filler cap and place a piece of polythene over the filler neck. Secure the polythene with an elastic band ensuring that an airtight seal is obtained. This will minimise brake fluid loss when the pipe or hose is removed. On models fitted with ABS, ensure that the ignition is switched off and empty the accumulator by pumping the brake pedal twenty times. The brake pedal pressure should become hard.

5   Brake pipe removal is usually quite straightforward. The union nuts at each end are undone, the pipe and union pulled out and the centre section of the pipe removed from the body clips. Where the union nuts are exposed to the full force of the weather they can sometimes be quite tight. As only an open-ended spanner can be used, burring of the flats on the nuts is not uncommon when attempting to undo them. For this reason a self-locking wrench or special brake union split ring spanner should be used.

6   To remove a flexible hose, wipe the unions and brackets free of dirt

14.1 Flexible-to-rigid hydraulic brake pipe connection and retainer bracket – check for security and condition

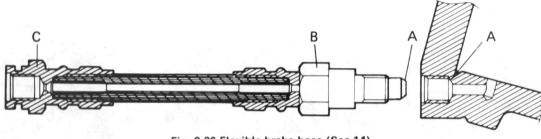

Fig. 9.36 Flexible brake hose (Sec 14)

A   Taper seat (no washer used)   *B   Union nut*   *C   End fittings*

Fig. 9.37 Rigid brake pipe flare cross-section (Sec 14)

and undo the union nut from the brake pipe end.

7   Next extract the hose retaining clip, or unscrew the nut, and lift the end of the hose out of its bracket. If a front hose is being removed, it can now be unscrewed from the brake caliper.

8   Brake pipes can be obtained individually, or in sets, from most accessory shops or garages with the end flares and union nuts in place. The pipe is then bent to shape, using the old pipe as a guide, and is ready for fitting to the car.

9   Refitting the pipes and hoses is a reverse of the removal procedure. Make sure that the hoses are not kinked when in position and also make sure that the brake pipes are securely supported in their clips. After refitting, remove the polythene from the reservoir and bleed the brake hydraulic system, as described in the next Section.

15   Brake hydraulic system – bleeding

Non-ABS systems

1   If the master cylinder or the pressure regulating valve has been disconnected and reconnected, then the complete system (both circuits) must be bled.

2   If a component of one circuit has been disturbed then only that particular circuit need be bled.

3   Bleed one rear brake and its diagonally opposite front brake. Repeat in this sequence on the remaining circuit if the complete system is to be bled.

4   Unless the pressure bleeding method is being used, do not forget to keep the fluid level in the master cylinder reservoir topped up to

prevent air from being drawn into the system which would make any work done worthless (photo).

5   Before commencing operations, check that all system hoses and pipes are in good condition with all unions tight and free from leaks.

6   Take great care not to allow hydraulic fluid to come into contact with the vehicle paintwork as it is an effective paint stripper. Wash off any spilled fluid immediately with cold water.

7   As the system incorporates a vacuum servo, destroy the vacuum by giving several applications of the brake pedal in quick succession.

Bleeding – two man method

8   Gather together a clean jar and a length of rubber or plastic tubing which will be a tight fit on the brake bleed screws.

9   Engage the help of an assistant.

10   Push one end of the bleed tube onto the first bleed screw and immerse the other end in the jar which should contain enough hydraulic fluid to cover the end of the tube (photos).

11   Open the bleed screw one half a turn and have your assistant depress the brake pedal fully then slowly release it. Tighten the bleed screw at the end of each pedal downstroke to obviate any chance of air or fluid being drawn back into the system.

12   Repeat this operation until clean hydraulic fluid, free from air bubbles, can be seen coming through into the jar. Tighten the bleed screw at the end of a pedal downstroke and remove the bleed tube.

13   Bleed the remaining screws in a similar way.

Bleeding – using one way valve kit

14   There are a number of one-man, one-way brake bleeding kits available from motor accessory shops. It is recommended that one of these kits is used whenever possible as it will greatly simplify the bleeding operation and also reduce the risk of air or fluid being drawn back into the system, quite apart from being able to do the work without the help of an assistant.

15   To use the kit, connect the tube to the bleed screw and open the screw one half a turn.

16   Depress the brake pedal fully and slowly release it. The one-way valve in the kit will prevent expelled air from returning at the end of each pedal downstroke. Repeat this operation several times to be sure of ejecting all air from the system. Some kits include a translucent

15.4 Topping-up master cylinder reservoir – 1.7 litre model shown

15.10A Front brake bleed screw (under dust cap – arrowed) – 2.0 litre Turbo model shown

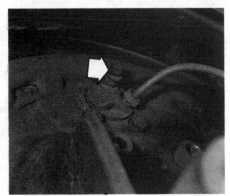

15.10B Rear drum brake bleed screw (under dust cap – arrowed) – 2.0 litre model shown

15.10C Rear disc brake bleed screw (under dust cap) – arrowed –
2.0 litre Turbo model

container which can be positioned so that the air bubbles can actually
be seen being ejected from the system.
17 Tighten the bleed screw, remove the tube and repeat the
operations on the remaining brakes.
18 On completion, depress the brake pedal. If it still feels spongy
repeat the bleeding operations as air must be trapped in the system.

Bleeding – using a pressure bleeding kit
19 These kits too are available from motor accessory shops and are
usually operated by air pressure from the spare tyre.
20 By connecting a pressurised container to the master cylinder fluid
reservoir, bleeding is then carried out by simply opening each bleed
screw in turn and allowing the fluid to run out, rather like turning on a
tap, until no air is visible in the expelled fluid.
21 By using this method, the large reserve of hydraulic fluid provides a
safeguard against air being drawn into the master cylinder during
bleeding which often occurs if the fluid level in the reservoir is not
maintained.
22 Pressure bleeding is particularly effective when bleeding 'difficult'
systems or when bleeding the complete system at a time of routine
fluid renewal.

All methods
23 It may also be necessary to bleed the clutch hydraulic circuit
(Chapter 5).
24 When bleeding is completed, check and top up the fluid level in the
master cylinder reservoir.
25 Check the feel of the pedal. If it feels at all spongy, air must still be
present in the system and further bleeding is indicated. Failure to bleed
satisfactorily after a reasonable period of the bleeding operation, may
be due to worn master cylinder seals.
26 Discard brake fluid which has been expelled. It is almost certain to
be contaminated with moisture, air and dirt making it unsuitable for
further use. Clean fluid should always be stored in an airtight container
as it absorbs moisture readily (hygroscopic) which lowers its boiling
point and could affect braking performance under severe conditions.

ABS system
27 On models fitted with ABS, the brake bleeding procedure should
be carried out as follows.
28 Before starting any dismantling or bleeding operations on the
hydraulic circuit it is essential to first ensure that the ignition is
switched off, and then to empty the pressure accumulator. To do this,
depress the brake pedal twenty times so that the brake pedal pressure
becomes noticeably hard. Ensure that the ignition is switched off at all
times during the following procedure, except where switching on of
the ignition is specified.
29 The front brake circuit must be bled first as follows. Ensure that the
pressure accumulator is empty, and that the ignition is switched off.

30 The front circuit should be bled using a pressure bleeding kit as
described previously for non-ABS models. The minimum pressure
recommended by Renault is 5 bar (72 lbf/in²), so a suitable
compressor will be required.
31 Ensure that the fluid reservoir is full, and open the compressed air
valve on the bleeding equipment.
32 Open the bleed screw on the right-hand wheel and wait for
approximately 20 seconds for the hydraulic fluid to drain out. Close the
bleed screw.
33 Repeat this procedure for the left-hand wheel.
34 The rear hydraulic circuit can now be bled as follows. Ensure that
the pressure accumulator is empty (see paragraph 28), and that the
ignition is switched off.
35 Connect one end of a hose to the bleed nipple on the right-hand
wheel and immerse the other end in a suitable container, containing
enough brake fluid to cover the open end of the hose.
36 It is most important to ensure that the following operations are
carried out in the order given.
37 Open the bleed screw. Press down lightly on the brake pedal.
Switch on the ignition.
38 Wait for a continuous stream of hydraulic fluid free from air bubbles
to flow into the container, then release the brake pedal.
39 Tighten the bleed screw. Switch off the ignition.
40 Repeat this procedure for the left-hand wheel.
41 Pressurise the pressure accumulator by switching on the ignition
and waiting for the pump to stop.
42 If necessary, top up the brake fluid level.

16 Vacuum servo unit – description and testing

1 A vacuum servo unit is fitted to the master cylinder, to provide
power assistance to the driver when the brake pedal is depressed
(photo).
2 The unit operates by vacuum obtained from the induction manifold
and comprises, basically, a booster diaphragm and a non-return valve.
3 The servo unit piston rod acts as the master cylinder pushrod. The
driver's braking effort is transmitted through another pushrod to the
servo unit piston and its built-in control system. The servo unit piston
does not fit tightly into the cylinder, but has a strong diaphragm to
keep its edges in constant contact with the cylinder wall, so assuring
an airtight seal between the two parts. The forward chamber is held
under vacuum conditions created in the inlet manifold of the engine
and, during periods when the brake pedal is not in use, the controls
open a passage to the rear chamber so placing it under vacuum. When
the brake pedal is depressed, the vacuum passage to the rear chamber
is cut off and the chamber opened to atmospheric pressure. The
consequent rush of air pushes the servo piston forward in the vacuum

16.1 Master cylinder and vacuum servo unit assembly – 1.7 litre
model

chamber and operates the main pushrod to the master cylinder. The controls are designed so that assistance is given under all conditions and, when the brakes are not required, vacuum in the rear chamber is established when the brake pedal is released. Air from the atmosphere entering the rear chamber is passed through a small air filter.

4 Operation of the servo can be checked in the following way.

5 With the engine off, depress the brake pedal several times. The pedal travel should remain the same.

6 Depress the brake pedal fully and hold it down. Start the engine and feel that the pedal moves down slightly.

7 Hold the pedal depressed with the engine running. Switch off the engine, holding the pedal depressed. The pedal should not rise nor fall.

8 Start the engine and run it for at least a minute. Switch off, then depress the brake pedal several times. The pedal travel should decrease with each application.

9 If the foregoing tests do not prove satisfactory, check the servo vacuum hose and non-return valve for security and leakage at the valve grommet.

10 If the brake servo operates properly in the test, but still gives less effective service on the road, the air filter through which air flows into the servo should be inspected. A dirty filter will limit the formation of a difference in pressure across the servo diaphragm.

11 The servo unit itself cannot be repaired and therefore a complete renewal is necessary if the measures described are not effective.

17 Vacuum servo air filter – renewal

1 Working under the facia panel, pull the dust excluder off the servo and slide it up the pushrod.

2 Using a scriber or similar tool, pick out the filter and cut it to remove it.

3 Cut the new filter as shown in Fig. 9.38 and push it neatly into position. Refit the dust excluding boot.

18 Vacuum servo non-return valve – renewal

1 Disconnect the vacuum hose from the connector on the front face of the servo unit.

2 Pull and twist the non-return valve elbow from its grommet.

3 Refitting is a reversal of removal; use a new grommet. A smear of rubber grease on the elbow spigot will ease its entry into the grommet. Do not force the elbow when fitting as it is possible to push the grommet into the interior of the servo.

19 Vacuum servo unit – removal and refitting

1 Remove the master cylinder, as described in Section 12.

2 Disconnect the vacuum hose from the servo unit.

3 Disconnect the pushrod from the brake pedal by extracting the split pin and the clevis pin.

4 Working inside the car unscrew the brake servo mounting nuts.

5 Withdraw the servo from the engine compartment.

6 When refitting the servo unit and the master cylinder, check the pushrod dimensions (X and L) as described in Section 12 and Fig. 9.32.

20 Handbrake – adjustment

All models

1 The handbrake will normally be kept in adjustment by the action of the drum brake automatic adjuster or the self-adjusting action of the rear disc calipers.

2 The handbrake should only be adjusted when new brake linings, new handbrake cables, or a new handbrake lever has been fitted.

3 Raise the car at the rear and support it on axle stands.

4 Fully release the handbrake, then, working under the vehicle, loosen off the primary rod locknut and completely unscrew the central linkage (photo).

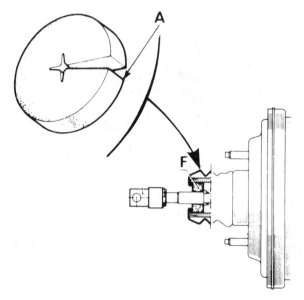

Fig. 9.38 Vacuum servo air filter (Sec 17)

A   Cut   F   Filter location

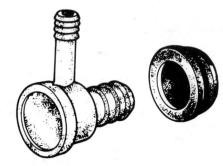

Fig. 9.39 Vacuum servo non-return valve and grommet (Sec 18)

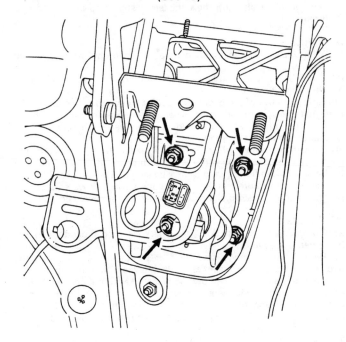

Fig. 9.40 Servo unit mounting nuts (arrowed) (Sec 19)

Drum brakes

5   Remove the two rear wheels, then the brake drum on each side.
6   Move the knurled automatic brake adjuster in each direction to ensure that it is operational, then loosen it off by 5 to 6 notches. Check that the cables slide freely and that the handbrake actuating lever is in contact with the brake shoes.
7   Now progressively tension the cables at the central adjuster so that the actuator lever of each rear brake unit starts to move at the 1st to 2nd notch position of the handbrake control lever travel. Retighten the primary rod locknut.
8   Fully release the handbrake, refit the brake drums and lower the vehicle.
9   Depress the brake pedal several times to settle the shoes. Apply the handbrake lever and check that it locks the rear wheels. The handbrake lever should fully apply the brakes when pulled over 9 notches.

Disc brakes

10 Remove the two rear wheels, then check that the handbrake actuating levers move without binding and move them as far as possible to the rear.
11 Progressively increase the tension of the cables from the central adjustment point. Adjust so that the cable end piece is just in contact with the actuator lever but does not actually move it (photo).
12 Now readjust the setting so that the actuating levers begin to move between the 1st and 2nd notch of the control lever travel, remaining lifted at the 2nd notch position. Retighten the primary rod locknut.
13 Refit the rear wheel and check the handbrake for satisfactory operation as described in paragraph 9, then lower the car.

---

21 Handbrake lever – removal and refitting

1   Chock the roadwheels, then fully release the handbrake.
2   Raise and support the vehicle at the rear on axle stands.
3   Working underneath the vehicle, extract the retaining clip from the cable clevis pin. Withdraw the clevis pin and detach the control rod from the central linkage.
4   Remove the trim cover from the safety belt anchors at the rear of the handbrake, then undo the two safety belt anchor bolts (photo).
5   Disconnect the handbrake switch wire, undo the handbrake lever retaining bolts, then withdraw the lever.
6   Refit in the reverse order of removal. Adjust the handbrake as described in Section 20 to give the correct lever travel.

---

22 Handbrake cables – removal and refitting

1   Raise the rear of the car and remove the rear roadwheels.
2   Fully release the handbrake.
3   On models with drum brakes, remove the drums and disconnect the cable(s) from the shoe lever(s).
4   On models with rear disc brakes, disconnect the cable(s) from the caliper lever(s).
5   If there is any difficulty in releasing the cable end fittings, slacken the adjuster on the handbrake primary rod right off.
6   Working at the central adjustment point, extract the clip, remove the clevis pin and disconnect the equaliser from the primary rod. Slip the cable out of the equaliser groove.
7   Disconnect the cables from their body clips.
8   Renew the cable by reversing the removal operations. Apply grease to the equaliser groove. Adjust as described in Section 20.

---

23 Brake pedal – removal and refitting

1   Working under the facia panel, undo the screws and remove the lower trim cover to expose the pedal arms and pushrods.
2   Disconnect the pushrod from the brake pedal arm by extracting the spring clip and pushing out the clevis pin (photo).
3   Disconnect the return and tension springs and remove the spring clip from the end of the pedal cross-shaft.
4   Push the cross-shaft out of the pedal bracket until the pedal can be removed.
5   Refitting is reversal of removal.

20.4 Handbrake cable central linkage with primary rod locknut arrowed

20.11 Handbrake cable endpiece (arrowed) – rear disc brake

21.4 View showing handbrake lever (A), switch (B) and safety belt anchor bolts (C)

23.2 Brake pedal pushrod clevis pin (A) and stop-lamp switch (B)

25.1 ABS sensor target wheel (arrowed) on the front driveshaft

26.1A Front ABS sensor unit and retaining bolt

24 Stop-lamp switch – adjustment

1   The stop-lamp switch should be adjusted by means of its locknut so that the stop-lamps come on when the switch plunger moves out about 1.0 mm (0.039 in) when the brake pedal is depressed (see photo 23.2).

25 Anti-lock braking system (ABS) – description

1   The hydraulic components used in this system are the same as those used in a conventional braking system but the following additional items are fitted. Refer to Fig. 9.41.

> A speed sensor (3) on each wheel
> Four targets (4) mounted at the front of the driveshafts and at the rear of the rear hubs (photo)
> An electronic computer (6) comprising a self-monitoring system, a hydraulic unit (1) which incorporates a pressure regulating valve, and a high pressure pump
> Two warning lamps are fitted to the instrument panel

2   The anti-lock braking system operates in the following way. As soon as the car roadspeed exceeds 6.0 kph (3.7 mph) the system becomes operational.
3   When the brakes are applied, the speed sensors detect the rapidly falling speed of any roadwheel which happens if it starts to lock. The computer operates a regulator valve to prevent hydraulic braking pressure rising and to reduce it until the particular roadwheel deceleration ceases.
4   As soon as this deceleration ceases, a reverse phase commences to again raise the hydraulic pressure to normal.
5   The anti-lock cycle can be repeated up to ten times per second.
6   In order to maintain even braking, one rear wheel locking will subject the opposite brake to the same pressure variation cycle.
7   The warning lamp indicates to the driver the fact that the system is non-operational. Should this happen, the normal braking system remains fully operational, but the fault in the ABS must be repaired at the earliest opportunity.
8   If the warning lamp illuminates intermittently, check that the wheel sensor lead connections are clean and secure.
9   The warning switch in the fluid reservoir is a two-stage type which first activates the handbrake warning lamp on the instrument panel when the fluid drops below the normal minimum level. If the fluid level continues to drop, the switch then activates a second warning lamp on the instrument panel.
10 When the second warning lamp is illuminated due to a further drop in the fluid level, the ABS continued to operate on the rear wheels only with normal braking to the front wheels.
11 In the event of both warning lamps operating simultaneously, it indicates that the pressure pump has a malfunction and is not working Again the system will operate the rear wheel brakes only, with normal braking to the front wheels.

26 ABS wheel sensors – removal and refitting

Front wheel sensor
1   Unscrew the sensor retaining bolt and detach the sensor from the brake unit, and the lead from the strut (photos).
2   Disconnect the sensor lead connector in the engine compartment adjacent to the top of the shock absorber turret. Detach the lead from its retainers and remove the sensor.
3   Refit in the reverse order of removal. Smear the sensor with a light coating of Molykote FB 180 grease before connecting it.

Front wheel sensor target
4   Remove the driveshaft as described in Chapter 8.
5   The sensor target can now be removed from the driveshaft by pressing it free as shown in Fig. 9.43.
6   Refit in reverse order of removal. Smear the target with Loctite Scelbloc before pressing it into position.

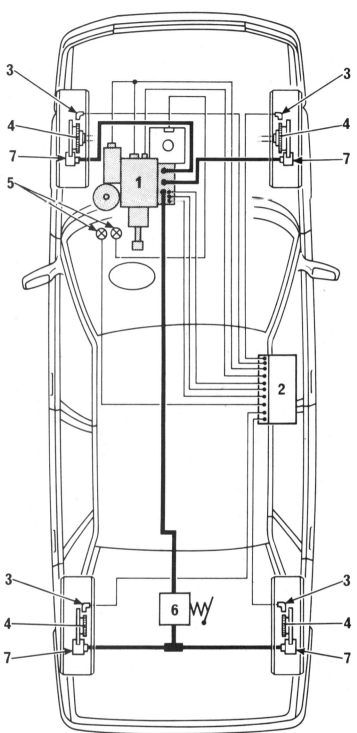

Fig. 9.41 Anti-lock braking system (ABS) layout (left-hand drive version shown) (Sec 25)

1	*Hydraulic unit*	5	*Instrument panel warning*
2	*Computer*		*lights*
3	*Speed sensor*	6	*Compensator*
4	*Sensor target*	7	*Disc brake units*

26.1B Front ABS sensor lead and attachment points (arrowed)

26.9 Rear ABS sensor and lead (arrowed)

Rear wheel sensor

7   Raise and support the car at the rear on axle stands. Remove the roadwheel on the side concerned.

8   Undo the sensor retaining bolt and detach the sensor unit, then unclip the sensor cable from its retainers.

9   Detach the rear axle fairing to gain access to the sensor lead connector. Disconnect the lead and remove the sensor (photo).

10 Refit in the reverse order of removal. Lubricate the sensor with a light smear of Molykote FB 180 grease before fitting. Ensure that the lead connections are clean and secure.

27 ABS computer unit – removal and refitting

1   The ABS computer is located under the carpet on the outboard side of the front passenger seat. Fold back the carpet for access (photo).

2   Disconnect the battery earth lead.

3   Undo the two retaining bolts and remove the cover from the computer unit. Lift the unit from its housing and detach the lead connector. Handle the computer with care.

4   Refit in the reverse order of removal. Ensure that the lead is securely connected.

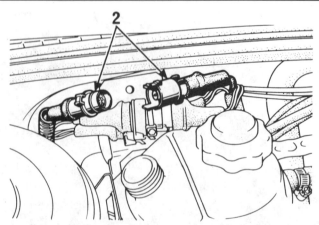

Fig. 9.42 ABS sensor lead connection (2) in engine compartment (Sec 26)

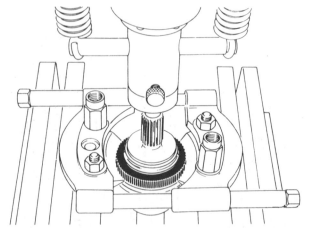

Fig. 9.43 Pressing sensor target from a driveshaft (Sec 26)

27.1 ABS computer unit location (carpet removed for access)

28.3 ABS hydraulic unit connections and reservoir

28 ABS hydraulic unit – removal and refitting

1   Disconnect the battery earth lead.
2   Depress the brake pedal twenty times in succession to reduce the pressure in the system. The pedal action will become hard.
3   Use a suitable syringe and empty the fluid from the reservoir (photo). Unclip the power steering fluid reservoir, move it downwards and detach its plastic mounting.
4   Disconnect the leads from the five connectors shown in Fig. 9.44. Also disconnect the earth lead and wiring mounting lug at (4).
5   Disconnect the clutch master cylinder hose and the rigid outlet pipes. Allow for fluid spillage and clean any from adjacent paintwork and fittings. Plug the hose and pipes to prevent further leakage and the ingress of dirt.
6   Remove the lower facia trim panels and the lower steering column covers.
7   Remove the retaining clip and withdraw the brake pedal pushrod clevis pin.
8   Undo the retaining nuts securing the hydraulic unit to the bulkhead, then remove the hydraulic unit and its seal from the bulkhead.
9   Refit in the reverse order of removal. Ensure that the seal is correctly located when fitting the hydraulic unit to the bulkhead. When connecting the hydraulic pipes, they should be positioned as shown in Fig. 9.45.
10 On completion, top up the brake fluid level and bleed the system as described in Section 15.

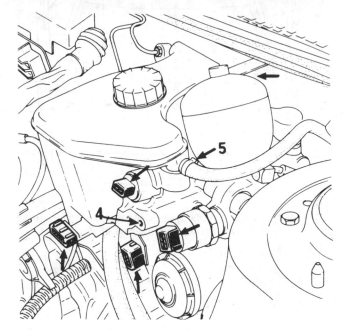

Fig. 9.44 ABS hydraulic unit lead connections (arrowed), earth lead mounting lug (4) and clutch master cylinder hose connection to the reservoir (5) (Sec 28)

Fig. 9.45 ABS hydraulic unit pipe identification (Sec 28)

29 ABS master cylinder/amplifier unit – removal and refitting

1   Remove the hydraulic unit as described in the previous Section.
2   Disconnect and remove the reservoir low pressure hose.
3   Disconnect the high pressure hose and plug the take-off ports.
4   Disconnect and remove the hydraulic pump connector.
5   Undo the pump retaining bolt, and remove the feed unit assembly and the master cylinder low pressure hose.
6   Remove the mounting lug, then unclip the reservoir and remove it.
7   Disconnect the master cylinder pipes from the regulator unit and plug their take-off ports.
8   Undo the retaining bolts and remove the regulator unit.
9   Renew as necessary, no repairs are possible.
10 Ensure that all parts are clean during reassembly. Start by refitting the low pressure hose to the master cylinder unit, then locate the regulator unit and rigid pipe connections. Smear the mounting bolt threads with locking fluid.
11 Refit the feed unit, ensuring that the 'silent-bloc' bushes are in good order. Apply some locking fluid to the retaining bolt threads.
12 Locate the high pressure hose and new O-ring seals.
13 The reservoir can now be fitted, but ensure that the anchor cups are in good condition and fit a new O-ring seal to the take-off port.
14 Refit the reservoir mounting lug, the hydraulic pump and the master cylinder low pressure hoses to the reservoir. Smear the mounting lug retaining bolt threads with locking fluid before fitting.
15 Refit the hydraulic unit as described in Section 28.

Fig. 9.47 Locate spacer and new O-ring seal (6) to the take-off port and high pressure hose unions (1). Smear bolt threads (2) with locking fluid (Sec 29)

Fig. 9.46 ABS hydraulic unit high pressure hose (I), pump retaining bolt (2), pump connector (1), reservoir mounting lug (7), and feed unit (E) – left-hand drive type shown (Sec 29)

30 ABS regulator unit – removal and refitting

1   Remove the hydraulic unit as described in Section 28.
2   Remove the reservoir mounting lug by undoing its retaining bolt, then unclip and remove the reservoir. Unclip the two low pressure hoses from the reservoir.
3   Remove the rigid hydraulic pipes from the master cylinder and regulator unit. Plug the take-off ports.
4   Undo the two retaining bolts and remove the regulator unit.
5   Refitting is a reversal of the removal procedure. Smear the retaining bolt threads with locking fluid before fitting, renew the take-off port

O-ring seals and ensure that the anchor cups are in good condition.
6   Refit the hydraulic unit as described in Section 28.

31 ABS hydraulic feed unit – removal and refitting

1   The feed unit can be removed with the hydraulic unit in position, but in this instance, the four bolts securing the hydraulic unit in position against the bulkhead must be removed in order to allow the pump retaining bolt removal.
2   Detach the wiring connector to the pressostat, then unscrew and remove the pressostat.
3   Detach the accumulator unit. If the hydraulic unit is in situ, release the pressure from the accumulator before removal. To do this follow the procedure given in Section 32, paragraph 1.
4   Disconnect the high pressure hose and plug its take-off port.
5   Undo the bolt securing the pump unit, then remove the feed unit. As it is withdrawn, detach the pump-to-reservoir hose.
6   Refit in the reverse order of removal. Renew the high pressure hose

O-ring seal and the bushes if they are worn or perished. Smear the threads of the feed unit bolt with locking fluid. The pressostat and the accumulator must also be fitted with new seals.
7   **Do not** switch on the ignition until after assembly is completed.

32 ABS accumulator – removal and refitting

1   Before removing the accumulator, ensure that the ignition is switched off, then pump the brake pedal twenty times to reduce the system pressure. The brake pedal operating pressure will increase. **Do not** switch the ignition on again until the accumulator is refitted.
2   Fit a suitable strap wrench over the accumulator (in a similar manner to that for oil filter removal), and remove the accumulator.
3   Refit in the reverse order of removal. Use a new O-ring seal.
4   Switch the ignition on, then when the pump is heard to stop, depress the brake pedal several times so that the pump is heard to restart and then stop again. Check the hydraulic fluid level in the reservoir and top up if necessary.

33 Fault diagnosis – braking system

Before diagnosing faults from the following chart, check that any braking irregularities are not caused by:
  Uneven and incorrect tyre pressures
  Wear in the steering mechanism
  Defects in the suspension and dampers
  Misalignment of the bodyframe

Symptom	Reason(s)
Pedal travels a long way before the brakes operate	Incorrect pedal adjustment Brake shoes set too far from the drums
Stopping ability poor, even though pedal pressure is firm	Linings, discs or drums badly worn or scored One or more wheel hydraulic cylinders seized, resulting in some brake shoes not pressing against the drums (or pads against disc) Brake linings contaminated with oil Wrong type of linings fitted (too hard)
Car veers to one side when the brakes are applied	Brake pads or linings on one side are contaminated with oil Hydraulic wheel cylinder on one side partially or fully seized A mixture of lining materials fitted between sides Brake discs not matched Unequal wear between sides caused by partially seized wheel cylinders
Pedal feels spongy when the brakes are applied	Air is present in the hydraulic system
Pedal feels springy when the brakes are applied	Brake linings not bedded into the drums (after fitting new ones) Master cylinder or brake backplate mounting bolts loose Severe wear in brake drums causing distortion when brakes are applied Discs out of true
Pedal travels right down with little or no resistance and brakes are virtually non-operative	Leak in hydraulic system resulting in lack of pressure for operating wheel cylinders If no signs of leakage are apparent the master cylinder internal seals are failing to sustain pressure
Binding, juddering, overheating	One or a combination of reasons given above Shoes installed incorrectly with reference to leading and trailing ends Broken shoe return spring Disc out-of-round Drum distorted Incorrect pedal or handbrake adjustment
Lack of servo assistance	Vacuum hose disconnected or leaking Non-return valve defective or incorrectly fitted Servo internal defect

Chapter 10 Suspension and steering

Contents

Specifications

Front suspension

Type .... Independent by MacPherson struts with coil springs, integral telescopic shock absorbers and anti-roll bar

Toe setting:
  1.7 litre models .... 1.0 ± 1.0 mm (0.039 ± 0.039 in) toe-out
  2.0 litre non-Turbo models .... 0 ± 1.0 mm (0 ± 0.039 in) toe-out
  2.0 litre Turbo models .... 2.0 ± 1.0 mm (0.078 ± 0.039 in) toe-out
Underbody height (H1–H2 – see Fig. 10.18):
  1.7 litre models .... 84.0 ± 7.5 mm (3.28 ± 0.29 in)
  2.0 litre non-Turbo models .... 98.0 ± 7.5 mm (3.82 ± 0.29 in)
  2.0 litre Turbo models .... 119.0 ± 7.5 mm (4.64 ± 0.29 in)

Rear suspension

Type .... Trailing arms with four-bar transverse link rods. Telescopic shock absorbers with coil springs on some models

Toe setting (all models) .... 2.0 to 5.0 mm (0.078 to 0.195 in) toe-in
Underbody height (H5–H4 – see Fig. 10.18):
    1.7 litre Saloon models .... 20.0 ± 7.5 mm (0.78 ± 0.29 in)
    2.0 litre non-Turbo Saloon models .... 30.0 ± 7.5 mm (1.17 ± 0.29 in)
    2.0 litre Turbo models .... 52.0 ± 7.5 mm (2.03 ± 0.29 in)
    Savanna models .... 10.0 ± 7.5 mm (0.39 ± 0.29 in)

Steering

Type .... Rack and pinion with collapsible safety column. Power assistance on some models

Power steering:
    Fluid type .... Dexron type ATF (Duckhams D-Matic)
    Fluid capacity .... 1.1 litres (1.9 pints)

Torque wrench settings

Front suspension

	Nm	lbf ft
1.7 litre models:		
Lower suspension arm inboard pivot nuts	80	59
Key bolt securing nut	60	44
Anti-roll bar bearing nuts (to subframe)	30	22
Anti-roll bar bearing nuts (to arm)	30	22
Lower balljoint nut	75	55
Hub carrier-to-shock absorber bolts	80	59
Shock absorber upper retaining nuts	25	18
Shock absorber cup nut	60	44
2.0 litre models (where different from 1.7 litre models):		
Key nut	55	40
Anti-roll bar bearing-to-arm nuts	80	59
Lower balljoint nuts	80	59
Shock absorber upper bolts	25	18
Shock absorber lower bolts	200	147

Rear suspension – all models

Shock absorber top mounting	80	59
Shock absorber lower mounting	85	62
Rear axle mounting	85	62

Steering

1.7 litre models:		
Steering arm (outer) balljoint nut	40	29
Suspension arm/hub carrier balljoint nut	60	44
Steering arm inner balljoint	50	37
Steering gear bolts	50	37
Steering wheel nut	40	29
Column universal joint coupling nuts	25	18
2.0 litre models (where different from 1.7 litre models):		
Steering arm sleeve locknuts	35	26
Steering arm-to-rack locknuts	35	26
Steering arm-to-rack bolts	40	29
Steering gear-to-shock absorber turret nuts	30	22
Steering gear-to-bulkhead nuts	50	37

1 General description

The front suspension is of independent type with coil springs and telescopic shock absorbers. An anti-roll bar is fitted to the front suspension on all models.

The rear suspension consists of a beam axle, trailing control arms and telescopic shock absorbers. On some models the shock absorber incorporates an external coil spring. Torsion bars and anti-roll bars are incorporated in the rear axle member on all models.

The steering gear is of rack and pinion type on all models, with power assistance fitted to some models. On some models the steering column incorporates a height adjustment mechanism.

2 Maintenance

1 At the specified intervals, check all suspension flexible bushes for wear.

2 Occasionally check the condition and security of all steering and suspension nuts, bolts and components.

3 Inspect the struts and shock absorbers for signs of fluid leakage. If anything more than a slight weep from the top gland is evident, then the unit must be renewed.

4 If the car tends to roll on bends or dip under heavy braking, check the action of the struts and shock absorbers by pressing the corner of the car downwards and then releasing it. The up and down momentum of the car should be damped out immediately. If the car oscillates up and down several times, the condition of the particular unit should be checked after removal from the car.

5 Inspect the steering rack bellows for splits and loss of lubricant. Look particularly closely at the bottom of the bellows pleats when the steering is at full lock. Splits here can often pass unnoticed.

6 With the help of an assistant, check for wear in the steering arm end balljoints. Move the steering wheel quickly a few degrees in each direction and observe the balljoints for shake or lost movement. If evident renew the balljoints.

7 Check the front suspension lower arm balljoint by inserting a lever

Fig. 10.1 Suspension and steering layout – 1.7 litre transverse engine models (Sec 1)

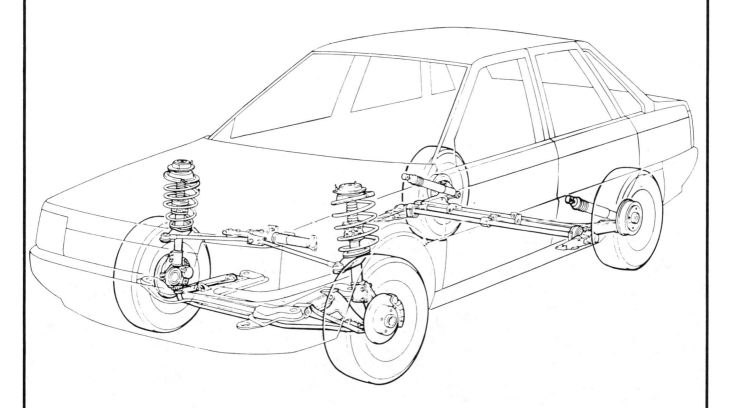

Fig. 10.2 Suspension and steering layout – 2.0 litre longitudinal engine models (Sec 1)

carefully between the arm and the hub carrier and checking for vertical movement.

8   At the specified intervals, check the front wheel alignment.

9   On models with power-assisted steering, check the fluid level in the reservoir at the intervals specified in *'Routine maintenance'*.

10 When necessary, top up the fluid level in the reservoir, but only use the specified fluid type (photo). The fluid level should be 10 mm (0.4 in) above the grille in the reservoir. Do not overfill or allow any dirt to enter the hydraulic system.

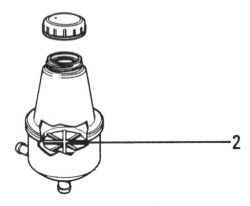

Fig. 10.3 Power steering fluid reservoir – maintenance fluid level 10 mm (0.4 in) above the grille (2) (Sec 2)

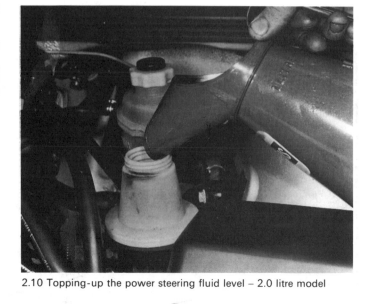

2.10 Topping-up the power steering fluid level – 2.0 litre model

---

3 Front anti-roll bar – removal and refitting

1   For improved access, raise the front of the vehicle and support on axle stands. Remove the engine undershield.

2   Undo the retaining bolts and detach the anti-roll bar from the subframe by removing its mounting block on each side (photos).

3   Undo the retaining nuts and remove the mounting block bracket from the suspension arm on each side (photo).

4   Remove the anti-roll bar from the vehicle. On 1.7 litre models, remove the left-hand roadwheel to allow access for anti-roll bar removal from that side of the vehicle.

5   On 2.0 litre models, the anti-roll bar mounting-to-subframe bolts also retain the lower balljoint and therefore to prevent the joint from moving, refit a nut to one of the bolts whilst the anti-roll bar is removed from the vehicle.

6   Renew the rubber bushes if they are perished or worn.

7   Refitting is a reversal of the removal procedure. Lubricate the bushes with molybdenum disulphide grease when fitting. Do not fully tighten the retaining nuts and bolts until the vehicle is lowered and free-standing. Tighten the nuts and bolts to their specified torque wrench settings.

8   Refit the engine undershield.

---

4 Front shock absorber and coil spring – removal and refitting

Note: *Overhaul of the shock absorber/coil spring unit must be entrusted to a Renault dealer*

1   Loosen off the front roadwheel bolts on the side concerned, raise the car at the front and support on axle stands. Remove the roadwheel.

2   On 2.0 litre models, disconnect the steering arm at the outboard end balljoint (see Section 12 for details).

3   Loosen off the two nuts on the shock absorber-to-hub carrier retaining bolts so that the end of each nut is flush with the end of its bolt (photo). Now tap the end face of each nut to drive the bolts out so that the serrated section under each bolt head is clear of the shock absorber. Remove the two nuts and withdraw the bolts.

4   Unscrew the three bolts securing the shock absorber strut to the upper mounting (photos).

5   Press down on the lower arm and remove the shock absorber/coil spring unit. Take care not to damage the driveshaft bellows as the unit is removed.

6   Dismantling of the coil spring/shock absorber unit is not considered a task to be undertaken by the home mechanic. The spring is fitted under a very high compression loading and it is essential that special Renault tools are used for the removal and refitting of the spring. A normal coil spring compressor is not suitable, and any attempt at dismantling without the correct tools and specialist knowledge will probably result in damage and/or personal injury. It is therefore recommended that the strut is taken to a Renault dealer for dismantling and replacement as necessary.

3.2A Anti-roll bar-to-subframe mounting – 1.7 litre model

3.2B Anti-roll bar-to-subframe mounting – 2.0 litre model

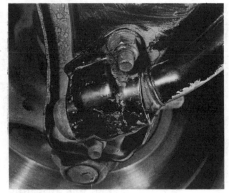

3.3 Anti-roll bar-to-suspension arm mounting – 2.0 litre model

7   Refitting is a reversal of the removal procedure. Ensure that the shock absorber-to-hub carrier bolts are fitted from the rear (with the nuts towards the front of the vehicle). Tighten the retaining bolts to their specified torque wrench settings.

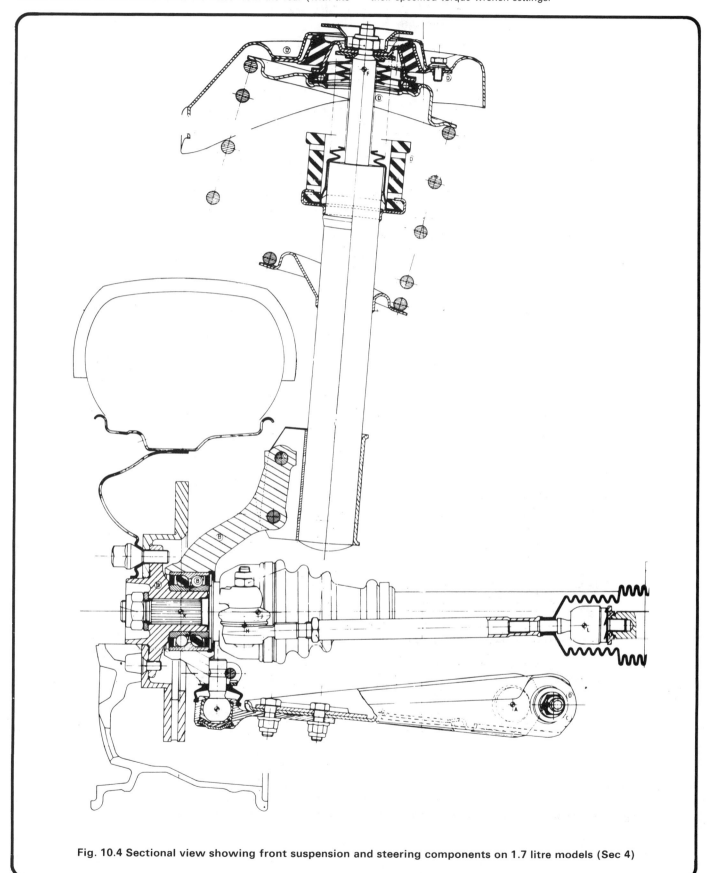

Fig. 10.4 Sectional view showing front suspension and steering components on 1.7 litre models (Sec 4)

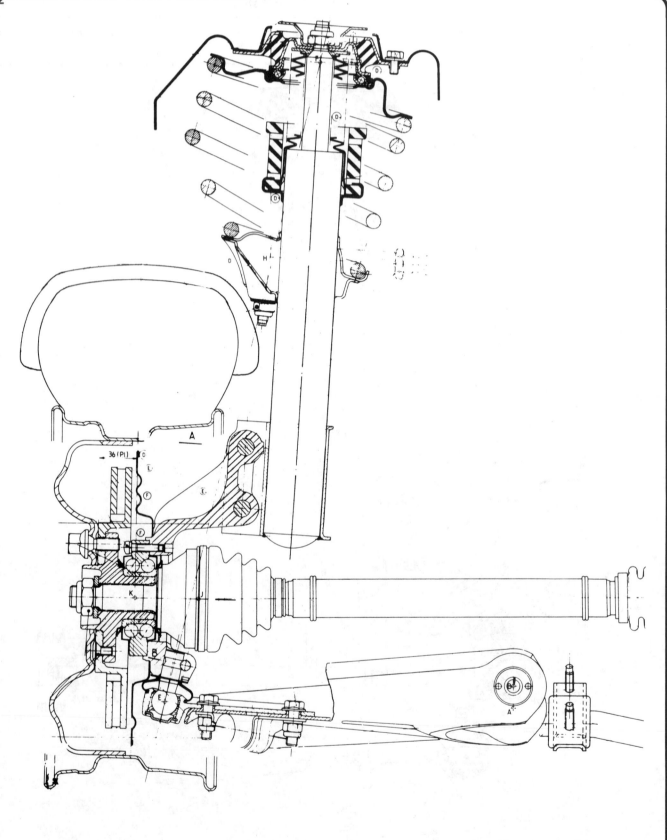

Fig. 10.5 Sectional view showing front suspension and steering components on 2.0 litre models (Sec 4)

4.3 Hub carrier-to-shock absorber retaining bolts – 1.7 litre model

4.4 Shock absorber upper mounting bolts (arrowed) – 2.0 litre non-Turbo model

5 Front lower suspension arm – removal and refitting

1 Unscrew the retaining nuts and disconnect the anti-roll bar from the lower suspension arm. On 2.0 litre models, the retaining bolts also secure the lower balljoint and one of the nuts should be refitted once the anti-roll bar is separated from the suspension arm to prevent the balljoint from moving. Press downwards on the anti-roll bar to separate it from the suspension arm (photos).

2 If not already done, raise the vehicle at the front end and support on axle stands.

3 Undo and remove the nut and washer, then withdraw the clamp bolt securing the lower suspension arm balljoint to the hub carrier (photo).

4 Undo and remove the two nuts, washers and pivot bolts securing the arm to the subframe (photos).

5 Pull the arm down to disengage the balljoint, then lever it out of its

inner pivot mountings. Recover the balljoint washer.

6 If the inner pivot bushes are to be renewed this can be done using suitable lengths of tube and a press or wide-opening vice. Renew the bushes one at a time so that the distance between the bush inner edges is maintained at 146.5 to 147.5 mm (5.77 to 5.81 in) for 1.7 litre models, or 189.5 to 190.5 mm (7.46 to 7.49 in) for 2.0 litre models (see Fig. 10.8). Note that the front and rear bushes differ on 2.0 litre models, so check that correct replacements are obtained.

7 Refitting the lower suspension arm is the reverse sequence to removal bearing in mind the following points:

   (a) Ensure that the plastic washer is in position over the balljoint shank before refitting the balljoint to the hub carrier

   (b) Tighten all nuts and bolts to the specified torque, but do not tighten the pivot bolts and anti-roll bar clamp bolts until the car has been lowered to the ground and rolled back and forth to settle the suspension

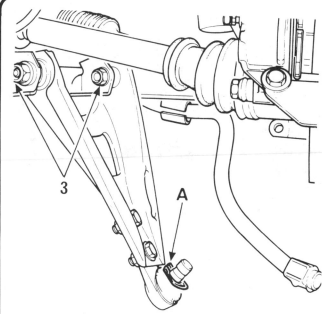

Fig. 10.6 Front lower suspension arm removal – 1.7 litre models (Sec 5)

   3   Arm-to-subframe pivot bolts
   A   Balljoint plastic protection washer

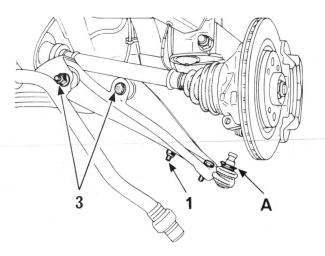

Fig. 10.7 Front lower suspension arm removal – 2.0 litre models (Sec 5)

   1   Balljoint unit retaining nut
   3   Arm-to-subframe pivot bolts
   A   Balljoint plastic protection washer

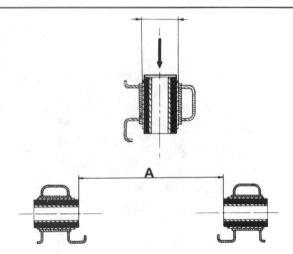

Fig. 10.8 Lower suspension arm inner pivot bush renewal
(Sec 5)

*Remove/refit bush using 30 mm (1.18 in) diameter tube for 1.7 litre
models or 34 mm (1.33 in) tube for 2.0 litre models. Dimension 'A'
between bush inner edges must be as specified (see text)*

5.1A Front suspension arm outboard end – 1.7 litre model
1   Anti-roll bar mounting bolt
2   Balljoint retaining bolts

5.1B Front suspension arm outboard end –
2.0 litre Turbo model

5.3 Lower suspension arm balljoint-to-hub
carrier clamp bolt – 2.0 litre model

5.4A Front suspension arm front inboard
pivot mounting – 1.7 litre model

5.4B Front suspension arm rear inboard
pivot mounting – 1.7 litre model

5.4C Front suspension arm front inboard
pivot mounting – 2.0 litre model

5.4D Front suspension arm rear inboard
pivot mounting – 2.0 litre model

6   Front lower suspension arm balljoint – removal and refitting

1   Proceed as described in the previous Section, paragraphs 1 to 5
inclusive, but do not fully remove the nuts and bolts securing the lower
suspension arm to the subframe, only loosen them.
2   If the balljoint gaiter is damaged, or the joint is worn, it must be
renewed as a unit. Unbolt it from the suspension arm for renewal.
3   Refitting is a reversal of the removal procedure. Ensure that the
plastic protector washer is fitted to the balljoint and tighten the

retaining bolts and nuts to the specified torque wrench settings.

7   Front hub carrier – removal and refitting

1   Loosen the hub nut, then raise the car at the front and support it on
safety stands. Remove the appropriate front wheel.
2   Remove the hub nut and recover the thrust washer.
3   Undo the two bolts securing the brake caliper to the hub carrier.
Slide the caliper, complete with pads, off the disc and tie it up using
string or wire from a convenient place under the wheel arch.

4   Undo the locknut securing the steering arm balljoint to the hub carrier. Using a suitable separator tool (see Section 12), release the balljoint and move the steering arm to one side.

5   At the base of the hub carrier, undo and remove the nut and washer, then withdraw the balljoint clamp bolt (see photo 5.3).

6   Undo and remove the nuts and washers, then withdraw the two bolts securing the shock absorber to the upper part of the hub carrier.

7   Release the hub carrier from the shock absorber and then lift it, while pushing down on the suspension arm, to disengage the lower balljoint. Withdraw the hub carrier from the driveshaft and remove it from the car. If the driveshaft is a tight fit in the hub bearings, tap it out using a plastic mallet, or use a suitable puller.

8   If the front hub bearings are to be renewed, refer to Section 10 or 11 (as applicable) of Chapter 8 for details.

9   Refitting is the reverse sequence to removal, bearing in mind the following points:

(a)   Ensure that the mating faces of the disc and hub flange are clean and flat before refitting the disc (if applicable)

(b)   Tighten all nuts and bolts to the specified torque

8   Rear shock absorber – removal and refitting

1   Jack up the rear of the car and support it on axle stands. Place a jack beneath the suspension trailing arm on the appropriate side of the car. Using the jack, raise the trailing arm slightly. Supplement the jack with an axle stand or blocks if necessary – ensure that the trailing arm is securely supported.

2   Remove the rear roadwheel on the side concerned.

3   Unscrew and remove the upper and lower rear shock absorber mounting bolts and remove the shock absorber (photos).

3   Examine the shock absorber body for signs of damage or corrosion, and for any trace of fluid leakage. Check the piston rod for distortion, wear, pitting or corrosion along its entire length. Test the operation of the shock absorber, while holding it in an upright position, by moving the piston rod through a full stroke and then through short strokes of 50 to 100 mm (2 to 4 in). In both cases the resistance felt should be smooth and continuous. If the resistance is jerky or uneven, or if there is any sign of wear or damage to the unit, renewal is necessary. Also check the condition of the upper and lower mounting bushes and renew them if there are any signs of deterioration or swelling of the rubber. Note that new shock absorbers are supplied complete with mounting bushes.

4   Before fitting a new shock absorber unit, hand pump the unit several times to ensure that it is fully primed.

5   Refit in the reverse order of removal. Smear the mounting bolt threads with thread locking compound before fitting. Do not fully tighten the retaining nut and bolt to the specified torque wrench setting until after the vehicle is lowered to the ground and is free-standing under its own weight.

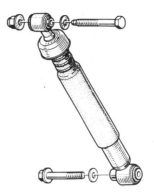

Fig. 10.9 Rear shock absorber unit, retaining bolts and washers (Sec 8)

Note: An external coil spring is fitted to the unit on some models

8.3A Rear shock absorber upper mounting bolt – 1.7 litre Savanna

8.3B Rear shock absorber lower mounting bolt – 1.7 litre Savanna

8.3C Rear shock absorber upper mounting bolt – 2.0 litre Saloon

8.3D Rear shock absorber lower mounting bolt – 2.0 litre Saloon

9 Rear axle – removal and refitting

1   A trolley jack and the aid of an assistant will be required to support and steady the axle unit during its removal and subsequent refitting.
2   Raise and support the vehicle at the rear on axle stands.
3   Remove the rear roadwheels.

4   Refer to Chapter 9 and disconnect the following brake system components from the rear axle:

   (a) The secondary handbrake cables
   (b) The hydraulic brake lines
   (c) The brake compensator (where applicable). On the load-controlled type compensator, take care not to change the setting of the preset adjuster nut (see Chapter 9)

5   Unbolt and disconnect the rear shock absorbers at their top or bottom ends.
6   Position the trolley jack under the centre of the axle and raise it to take the weight of the axle when the retaining bolts are removed. *It is important that the jack only supports the weight of the axle and is not raised to take the weight of the vehicle.*
7   Undo the retaining bolts on each side, check that the cables and hydraulic lines are clear, then carefully lower the axle unit and withdraw it from under the vehicle (photo). The aid of an assistant during this operation will be useful in steadying the axle as it is removed.
8   Refitting is a reversal of the removal procedure. Tighten the axle and shock absorber retaining bolts to their specified torque wrench settings, the latter only when the vehicle is lowered and standing under its own weight.
9   Reconnect the brake system components and bleed the hydraulic system with reference to the respective Sections of Chapter 9. On completion arrange to have the brake compensator adjustment checked at the earliest opportunity by a Renault dealer.

10 Rear axle torsion bars – removal and refitting

Note: *Unless the rear axle is being replaced as a unit, the removal and refitting of the torsion bars (suspension and anti-roll bars) is a task best entrusted to a Renault dealer due to the special tools and setting*

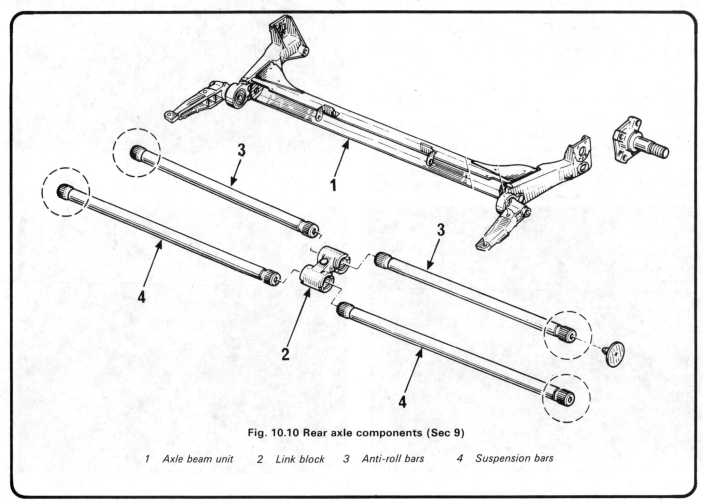

Fig. 10.10 Rear axle components (Sec 9)

1 Axle beam unit   2 Link block   3 Anti-roll bars   4 Suspension bars

9.7 Rear axle mounting bolts (arrowed) – 2.0 litre model

10.4 Remove cap from trailing arm mounting and extract clip (arrowed) – 2.0 litre model

10.7 Rear suspension anti-roll bar location (arrowed) – 2.0 litre Turbo model

procedures required. Read through this Section before starting so as to ensure awareness of the tool requirements and procedures involved

1   Raise and support the vehicle at the rear on axle stands.
2   Remove the rear roadwheels.
3   Remove the rear shock absorbers (Section 8).
4   Prise off the cap (where fitted) from the outer face of the trailing arm mounting bracket and extract the clip (photo).
5   The suspension bar can now be withdrawn outwards using a slide hammer such as Renault tool Emb 880 or a suitable alternative.
6   Once the splines of the bar are free, the bar can be withdrawn completely from its location. Repeat this procedure for the opposite suspension bar.
7   Remove an anti-roll bar from one side using the slide hammer as described for the suspension bars (photo).
8   Remove the link block, then the remaining anti-roll bar.
9   Before refitting the torsion bars it is necessary to position the trailing arm so that the correct underbody height of the car is obtained when it is lowered onto its wheels. This is done as follows:
10 Measure the distance from the centre of the shock absorber lower mounting stud on the trailing arm to the centre of the shock absorber upper mounting bolt under the wheel arch. Move the trailing arm up or down as necessary until the distance (X) in Fig. 10.12 is exactly as follows according to model:

    1.7 litre Saloon   X = 496 mm (19.5 in)
    2.0 litre Saloon   X = 485 mm (19.0 in)
    1.7 and 2.0 litre Savanna X = 475 mm (18.7 in)

If it was necessary to move the arm up to achieve the setting, support it in this position using a jack. If it was necessary to pull the arm down, support it with a length of wood cut to length and small packing pieces. Take care over this procedure as this is a critical dimension and will determine the success of subsequent operations.
11 Repeat this procedure to set the opposite trailing arm in the same manner.
12 An alignment index mark on the end face of the suspension bar bearing is used to set the initial fitted position of the suspension bar. If not already marked, an equivalent mark must also be made on the end face of the anti-roll bar bearing. This is achieved by aligning the hole centres as shown in Fig. 10.14 using a rule and making a mark adjacent to the bottom of a splined tooth.
13 The installation procedure for the bars now differs according to model.

1.7 litre Saloon models
14 Grease the splines of the left-hand anti-roll bar, then insert the bar so that the index mark on its end face is offset by five teeth to the index mark of the bearing end face, as shown in Fig. 10.15.
15 Fit the link block to the inner end of the anti-roll bar and centralise it within the V-section of the rear axle beam.
16 Now fit the opposing anti-roll bar with the index mark offset from its bearing end face index mark by five teeth in the opposite direction to the first anti-roll bar when viewed from the outer end.
17 Grease the left-hand suspension bar and fit it so that its index mark is offset by four teeth from its bearing index mark, as shown in Fig. 10.15. The link block on the inboard end of the anti-roll bars can be raised to ease engagement if necessary.

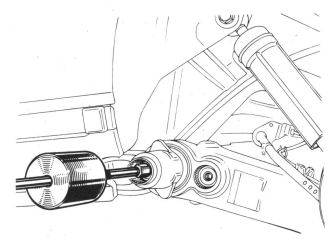

Fig. 10.11 Suspension bar removal using a slide hammer (Sec 10)

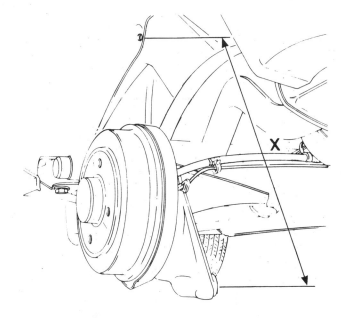

Fig. 10.12 Rear trailing arm setting – dimension 'X' should be set as specified in text according to model (Sec 10)

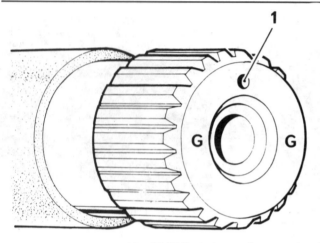
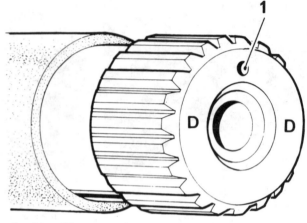

Fig. 10.13 End views of suspension bars showing identification marks (Sec 10)

1   Initial setting mark   G   Left-hand suspension bar identification mark   D   Right-hand suspension bar identification mark

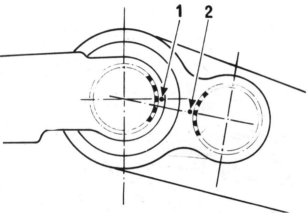

Fig. 10.14 End view of fitted suspension and anti-roll bars

(Sec 10)

*1   Suspension bar alignment   2   Anti-roll bar alignment index
    index mark   mark*

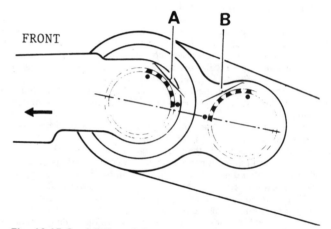

Fig. 10.15 On 1.7 litre Saloon models, offset the left-hand anti-roll and suspension bars as shown (Sec 10)

*A   Suspension bar – offset by   B   Anti-roll bar – offset by five
    four teeth   teeth*

18 Repeat this procedure with the opposing suspension bar, but align the index mark on the bar offset from its bearing end face index mark by four teeth in the opposite direction to the first suspension bar when viewed from its outboard end.

2.0 litre Saloon models
19 Proceed as described in paragraphs 14 to 18 inclusive, but when installing the suspension bars refer to Fig. 10.16 for the offset position of the left-hand bar relative to the bearing index mark. Offset the right-hand bar by an equal number of teeth in the opposite direction when viewed from the outer end.

Savanna models
20 Proceed as described in paragraphs 14 to 18 inclusive, but when installing the suspension bars refer to Fig. 10.17 for the offset position of the left-hand bar relative to the bearing index mark. Offset the right-hand bar by an equal number of teeth in the opposite direction when viewed from the outer end.

All models
21 Refit the shock absorbers as described in Section 8.
22 The vehicle body height must now be checked. Refit the roadwheels and lower the vehicle to the ground.
23 Roll the car back and forth and then bounce the body to settle the suspension. If the trailing arms were positioned correctly, as described in paragraph 10, the car should now be standing level and at the correct height (see Section 11). If this is not the case, then the setting procedure will have to be repeated, noting that a deviation of 3 mm (0.12 in) either side of the specified dimension will alter the suspension bar position on the relevant side of the vehicle by one spline. This will have a corresponding effect on the underbody height; increasing or decreasing it by 3 mm (0.12 in).

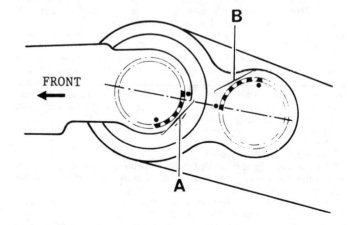

Fig. 10.16 On 2.0 litre Saloon models, offset the left-hand anti-roll and suspension bars as shown (Sec 10)

*A   Suspension bar – offset by   B   Anti-roll bar – offset by five
    four teeth   teeth*

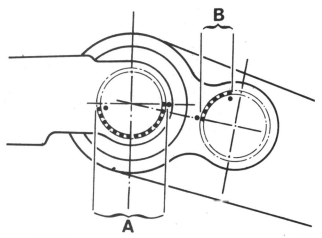

Fig. 10.17 On Savanna models, offset the anti-roll and suspension bars as shown (Sec 10)

A Suspension bar – offset by 13 teeth
B Anti-roll bar – offset by 5 teeth

11 Vehicle underbody height – checking and adjustment

1 Before carrying out the following checks, ensure that the fuel tank is full, the tyres are correctly inflated and the car is standing on level ground.
2 Refer to Fig. 10.18 and take measurements at the points shown.
3 Only the rear underbody height is adjustable, and this is achieved by repositioning the rear suspension bars in their mounting bracket splines. Repositioning the torsion bars by one spline either way from their original position will alter the height on the side concerned by 3 mm (0.12 in). The procedure for doing this is described in Section 10.
4 If the front underbody height is not within the specified tolerance, this will be caused by a weakening of the front coil springs. If this is the case renewal is necessary and, to maintain the side-to-side tolerance, the springs should be renewed in pairs. This procedure is covered in Section 4.
5 If any alteration to the rear underbody height is made, it will be necessary to adjust the headlamp aim as described in Chapter 12 and, where applicable, to have the brake pressure regulating valve adjusted by a Renault dealer.

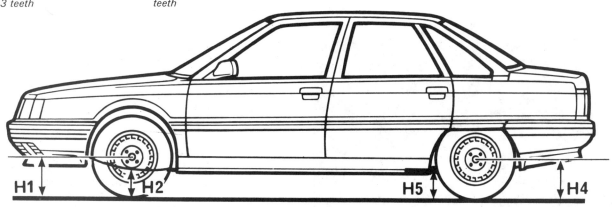

Fig. 10.18 Vehicle underbody height measuring points (Sec 11)

H1 Front wheel hub centreline to ground
H2 Front sidemember to ground (measured at wheel vertical centreline)

H4 Rear wheel hub centreline to ground
H5 Suspension bar centreline to ground

12 Steering arm outer balljoint – removal and refitting

1 Jack up the front of the car and support it on axle stands. Remove the appropriate front roadwheel.
2 Using a suitable spanner, slacken the balljoint locknut on the steering arm by a quarter of a turn (photos). Hold the steering arm with a second spanner engaged with the flats of the balljoint rod (1.7 litre models), or sleeve (2.0 litre models), to prevent it from turning.
3 Undo and remove the locknut securing the balljoint to the hub carrier (1.7 litre models) or the front shock absorber (2.0 litre models), and then release the tapered shank using a balljoint separator tool (photos).
4 Count the number of exposed threads between the end of the balljoint and the locknut and record this figure (photo).
5 Unscrew the balljoint from the steering arm and unscrew the locknut from the balljoint.
6 Screw the locknut onto the new balljoint and position it so that the same number of exposed threads are visible as was noted during removal.
7 Screw the balljoint onto the steering arm until the locknut just contacts the arm. Now tighten the locknut while holding the steering arm as before.
8 Engage the shank of the balljoint with the hub carrier or shock absorber (as applicable) and refit the locknut. Tighten the locknut to the specified torque. If the balljoint shank turns while the locknut is

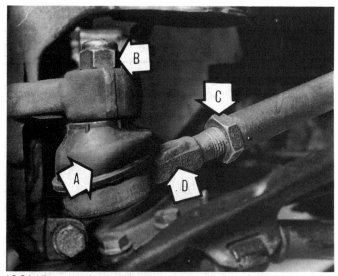

12.2A View showing steering arm outer balljoint – 1.7 litre model

A Balljoint
B Retaining nut
C Locknut
D Flats on balljoint

12.2B View showing steering arm outer balljoint – 2.0 litre Turbo model

12.3 Steering arm balljoint separation – 2.0 litre model

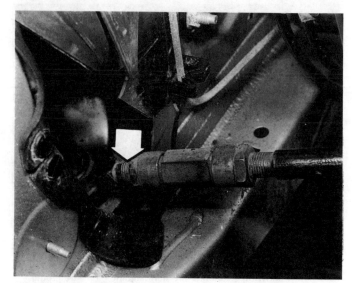

12.4 Steering arm balljoint adjuster sleeve – 2.0 litre model. Measure the exposed thread length (arrowed) before disconnecting

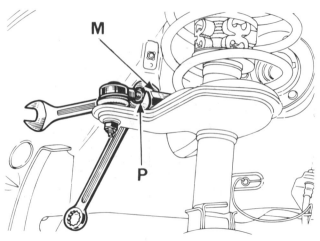

Fig. 10.19 Balljoint removal – 2.0 litre model (Sec 12)

P   Locknut   M   Sleeve

being tightened, on 1.7 litre models place a jack under the balljoint and raise it sufficiently to push the tapered shank fully into the hub carrier. The tapered fit of the shank will lock it and prevent rotation as the nut is tightened. On 2.0 litre models, reverse this process by pressing down on the joint as the nut is tightened.
9   On completion, remove the jack, refit the roadwheel and lower the car to the ground.
10   Check the front wheel alignment, as described in Section 26.

13 Steering gear rubber bellows – removal and refitting

1   Remove the steering arm outer balljoint as described in Section 12.
2   On 2.0 litre models, undo the two nuts and remove the two bolts securing the steering arm at its inboard end to the steering rack. If required, the steering arm can be withdrawn from the rack.
3   On 1.7 litre models with power steering, disconnect the bellows-to-bellows balance tube on the side concerned.
4   Release the retaining wire or unscrew the retaining clip screws and slide the bellows off the rack and pinion housing and steering arm.
5   Lubricate the inner ends of the new bellows with rubber grease and position it over the housing and steering arm.
6   Using new clips, or two or three turns of soft iron wire, secure the bellows in position.
7   Refit the outer balljoint, as described in the previous Section.

14 Steering arm and inner balljoint (1.7 litre models) – removal and refitting

1   Remove the outer balljoint and rubber bellows, as described in Sections 12 and 13 respectively.
2   Hold the thrust washer with grips to prevent the rack turning and unscrew the inner balljoint housing with a suitable wrench. Remove the balljoint housing and steering arm assembly under under the wheel arch.
3   With the components on the bench for inspection, identify the parts and note how they are fitted.
4   The steering arm and balljoint assembly may be refitted providing that it is in a satisfactory condition and that the balljoint serrations are undamaged. In both cases the lockplate and thrust washer must be renewed before refitting.
5   With new components of the correct type obtained, as necessary, reassemble as follows.
6   Refit the thrust washer and lockplate to the rack, ensuring that the two tabs on the lockplate are in line with the two flats on the end of the rack.
7   Apply a drop of locking compound to the threads of the balljoint and screw the balljoint housing and steering arm assembly into position. Tighten the housing securely.

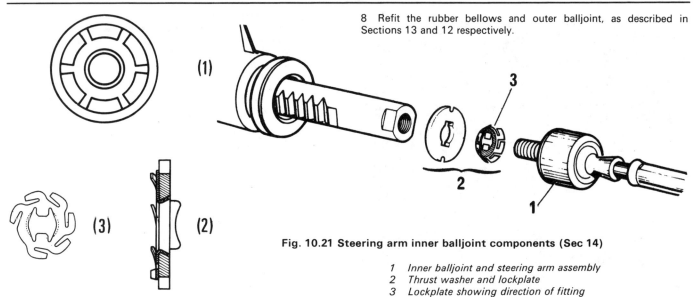

8 Refit the rubber bellows and outer balljoint, as described in Sections 13 and 12 respectively.

Fig. 10.21 Steering arm inner balljoint components (Sec 14)

1 Inner balljoint and steering arm assembly
2 Thrust washer and lockplate
3 Lockplate showing direction of fitting

Fig. 10.20 Steering arm inner balljoint assembly – 1.7 litre models (Sec 14)

1 End view of balljoint assembly
2 Side view of assembled thrust washer and lockplate
3 Lockplate

15 Steering arm (2.0 litre models) – removal and refitting

Proceed as described in Section 18, paragraphs 3 to 6 (to remove the arm) and paragraphs 16 and 19 (to reconnect the arm to the rack), and Section 12 to reconnect the outer balljoints.

16 Manual steering gear (1.7 litre models) – removal and refitting

1 Jack up the front of the car and support it on axle stands. Remove both front roadwheels.
2 Unscrew the locknuts securing the steering arm outer balljoints to the hub carriers, then release them using a balljoint separator tool.

3 Mark the position of the intermediate shaft lower universal joint in relation to the rack and pinion housing and also the two halves of the universal joint in relation to each other. Where necessary, unclip and remove the plastic cover from the joint – see Section 23 (photo).
4 Undo the nut and remove the bolt securing the lower part of the universal joint to the steering gear yoke.
5 Undo the two nuts and bolts securing the steering gear to the subframe, separate the universal joint and withdraw the steering gear sideways from under the wheel arch.
6 Refitting the steering gear is the reverse sequence to removal, bearing in mind the following points:

(a) Before fitting the steering gear unit into position, the pinion plunger setting must be checked for correct adjustment. To do this, prise back the lock tabs of the adjuster screw (A) in Fig. 10.23. Using a 10 mm hexagon key, tighten the plunger

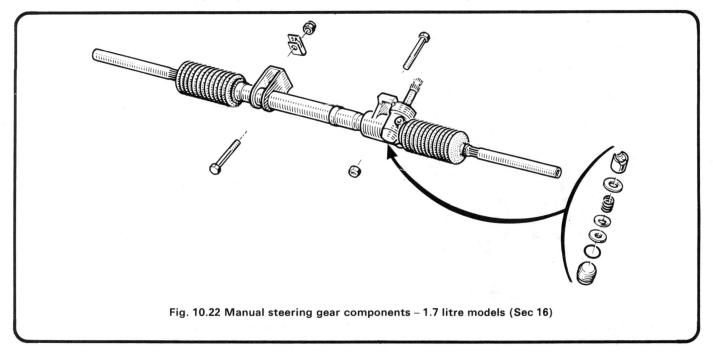

Fig. 10.22 Manual steering gear components – 1.7 litre models (Sec 16)

16.3 Remove the plastic cover for access to the universal joint
– 1.7 litre model with manual steering

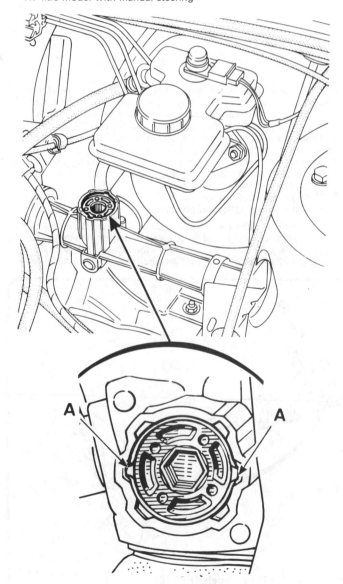

Fig. 10.23 Manual steering gear plunger adjuster lock tabs
(A) – 1.7 litre models (Sec 16)

adjustment nut by one notch ($^1/_8$th of a turn), then check
that the steering movement is free without any signs of
binding when moved from lock to lock. If necessary further
adjustment can be made to a maximum of two notches.
Secure the nut in the set position by peening over the lock
tabs on each side.

(b) Tighten all nuts and bolts to the specified torque
(c) When refitting the universal joint and steering gear yoke, align
the marks made during removal. If no marks are present due to
component renewal, set the steering wheel and steering gear
to the straight-ahead position before fitting
(d) If the steering arms or outer balljoints have been removed, or
their positions altered, check and adjust the front wheel
alignment, as described in Section 26.

17 Power-assisted steering gear (1.7 litre models) – removal and refitting

1 Proceed as described in paragraphs 1 to 3 of the previous Section.
2 Clamp the power steering hoses at the reservoir end, then detach
the hose support bracket. Disconnect the hoses at the reservoir and at
the rotary valve on the high pressure pump.
3 Undo the engine rear mounting nut.
4 Unbolt and remove the engine undertray.
5 Unbolt and detach the exhaust downpipe at the manifold and
under the vehicle at its central coupling (see Chapter 3).
6 Mark the relative fitted position of the gearchange control rod to
the lever, then disconnect them – see Fig. 10.27.
7 Unbolt and remove the rear engine mounting cover plate, then
undo the two engine mounting bolts and remove the mounting from
the subframe. Raise the engine and transmission as high as possible.
8 Unscrew the two lower bolts securing the steering gear unit to the
subframe. Move the rack to the left for access.
9 Unscrew and remove the steering gear unit upper retaining bolts,
then, supporting the unit, withdraw it from the left-hand side, under
the wheelarch.
10 Where a replacement steering gear unit is to be fitted, the steering
arm outer balljoints can be removed and fitted to the new unit as
described in Section 12.
11 When installing the steering gear unit, ensure that the engine and
transmission are raised as high as possible. Refitting is a reversal of the
removal procedure, but note the following significant points.
12 Align the positional index marks of the gearchange control rod and
lever, and also the universal joint index marks.
13 Tighten the retaining nuts and bolts to their specified torque
wrench settings.

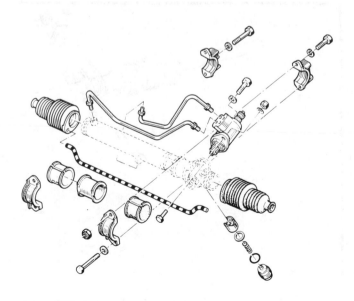

Fig. 10.24 Power steering gear and associated components –
1.7 litre models (Sec 17)

14 When the power steering hoses are reconnected, top up the hydraulic fluid level to the grille line in the reservoir, then turn the steering fully from lock to lock, first with the engine switched off, then with it running. Top up the fluid level if required. Check for any signs of fluid leakage from the system hoses and connections.

15 Finally, check the steering geometry to complete (Section 26).

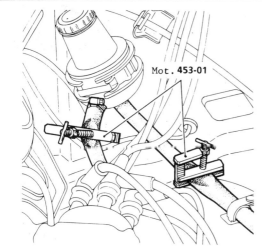

Fig. 10.25 Clamp the power steering hydraulic hoses (Renault tools shown) (Sec 17)

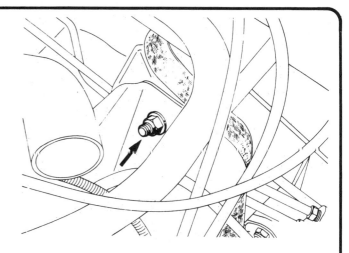

Fig. 10.26 Engine rear mounting nut – 1.7 litre models (Sec 17)

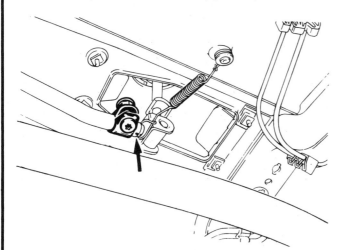

Fig. 10.27 Make alignment marks (arrowed) before disconnecting the gearchange control rod and lever – 1.7 litre models (Sec 17)

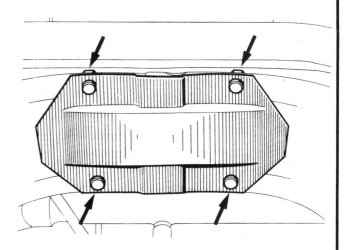

Fig. 10.28 Rear engine mounting cover plate and retaining bolts (arrowed) – 1.7 litre models (Sec 17)

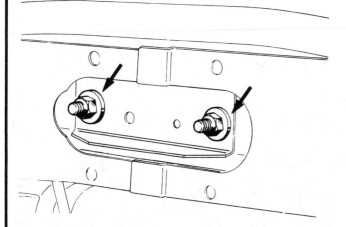

Fig. 10.29 Rear engine mounting bolts – 1.7 litre models (Sec 17)

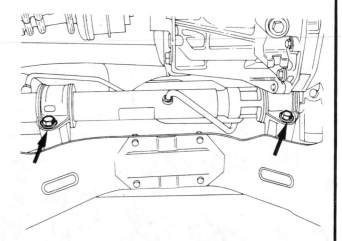

Fig. 10.30 Power steering gear-to-subframe lower mounting bolts – 1.7 litre models (Sec 17)

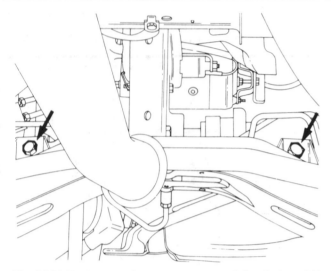

Fig. 10.31 Power steering gear upper retaining bolts – 1.7 litre models (Sec 17)

18 Manual and power-assisted steering gear (2.0 litre models) – removal and refitting

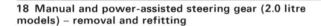

1 Disconnect the battery earth lead.
2 Detach and remove the lower facia trim panels on the driver's side.
3 Turn the steering to full right-hand lock and then unscrew the intermediate shaft-to-steering wheel shaft universal joint coupling bolt and nut.
4 Raise and support the vehicle at the front on axle stands. Remove the front roadwheels. On Turbo models, unbolt and remove the heat shield from the turbocharger unit.
5 Disconnect the steering arm balljoints on each side as described in Section 12.
6 Disconnect the ignition coil wiring and the diagnostic plug and mounting at the bulkhead in the engine compartment.
7 Undo the retaining nuts and unscrew the steering arm-to-rack bolts. Separate the steering arm from the rack on the right-hand side.
8 On models fitted with power steering, clamp the hydraulic hoses at the reservoir end, detach the hose support bracket, then disconnect the high pressure line from the valve union and the low pressure line from the pipe union (photos).
9 Undo the three steering unit-to-shock absorber turret nuts and withdraw the flange from the turret studs (photo).
10 Disconnect the relevant hoses, cables and wires as applicable from the steering unit.
11 Remove the PVC collar clip securing the bulkhead gaiter to the steering gear, where applicable.
12 Unscrew the retaining nuts from the main retaining clamps to the bulkhead, then carefully pull the steering gear forwards and away from

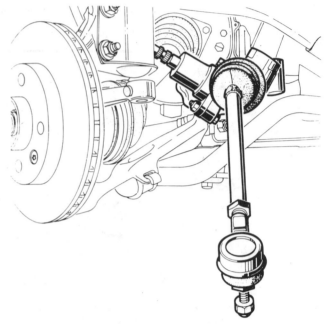

Fig. 10.32 Power steering gear unit removal – 1.7 litre models (Sec 17)

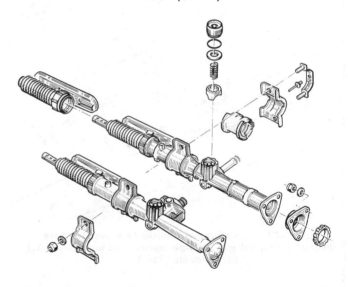

Fig. 10.33 Steering gear and associated components – 2.0 litre models (Sec 18)

18.8A View of right-hand end of power steering gear showing mounting bracket (arrowed) – 2.0 litre model

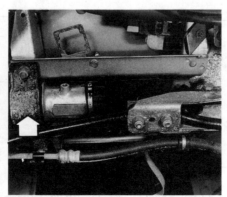

18.8B View of left-hand end of power steering gear showing mounting bracket (arrowed) – 2.0 litre model

18.9 Steering gear-to-shock absorber turret mounting – 2.0 litre model

Chapter 10 Suspension and steering 265

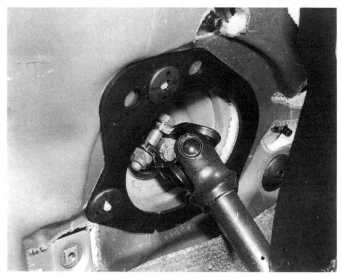

18.12 Lower steering column universal joint viewed from vehicle interior – 2.0 litre model

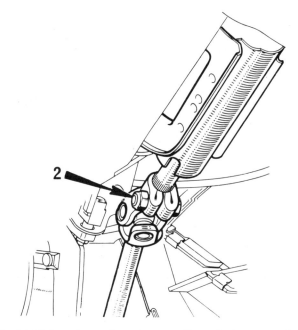

Fig. 10.34 Steering column intermediate shaft-to-steering wheel shaft coupling bolt and nut (Sec 18)

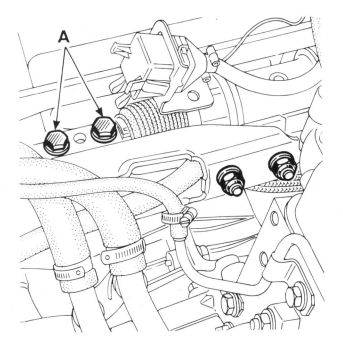

Fig. 10.35 Steering arm-to-rack bolts (A) – remove nuts first to allow bolts to be withdrawn (Sec 18)

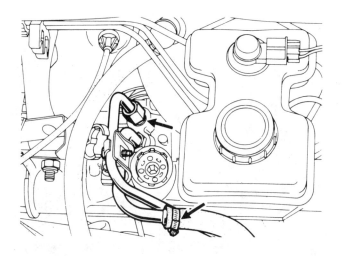

Fig. 10.36 Detach the power steering hydraulic connections at the points indicated (Sec 18)

the bulkhead so that the column intermediate shaft universal joint coupling (to the pinion shaft) is exposed (photo). Mark the relative positions of the intermediate shaft coupling and the pinion shaft, undo the through-bolt nut and remove the bolt.

13 Withdraw the steering gear unit from the intermediate shaft coupling, then when free, withdraw the unit sideways from under the wheel arch. Take care not to damage the angular position/speed sensor on the transmission bellhousing as the unit is removed.

14 Refitting is a reversal of the removal procedure, but note the following points.

15 When reconnecting the intermediate shaft coupling, ensure that the alignment marks made when dismantling correspond.

16 Use a new PVC collar to secure the bulkhead gaiter to the steering gear, where applicable.

17 Tighten all fixings to their specified torque wrench settings. This includes the steering arm-to-rack bolts (the rack being threaded).

18 When the unit is fitted on power steering models, reconnect the power steering hydraulic lines and then top up the fluid level in the power steering fluid reservoir. With the engine switched off, turn the steering fully from right to left-hand lock, then back. Now start the engine and repeat the procedure. Recheck the level of the fluid in the reservoir and top up as necessary.

19 With the steering gear refitted, check the pinion adjustment as described in Section 16, paragraph 6(a).

20 Finally check and if necessary adjust the steering geometry as described in Section 26.

19 Steering gear and power steering pump – overhaul

1 In view of the special tools and skills required, it is not recommended that the steering gear or, where applicable, the power steering pump be dismantled or overhauled, but renewed by obtaining a new or factory reconditioned unit.

2 If new steering gear is being refitted, then centre the rack by

placing a cardboard disc firmly on the pinion splines and count the number of turns required to turn the pinion from lock to lock. From full lock, turn the pinion half the number of turns counted and engage the pinion with the coupling (steering wheel in straight-ahead position).

20 Steering wheel height adjuster

1 The steering wheel height adjusting clamp lever can be adjusted for degree of tightness.
2 Remove the steering column shrouds.
3 Unscrew the locking lever nut (1 – Fig. 10.37) and lower the steering wheel as far as it will go. Remove the clamp lever.
4 Tighten the ring nut (2) and then refit the lever to its splined shaft so that (X) is 30.0 mm (1.2 in) from the column bracket.
5 Refit the nut and shrouds.

21 Steering wheel – removal and refitting

1 Set the front wheels in the straight-ahead position.
2 Ease off the steering wheel pad to provide access to the retaining nut (photo).
3 Using a socket and knuckle bar undo and remove the retaining nut and lockwasher.
4 Mark the steering wheel and steering column shaft in relation to each other and withdraw the wheel from the shaft splines. If it is tight, tap it upwards near the centre, using the palm of your hand. Refit the steering wheel retaining nut two turns before doing this, for obvious reasons.
5 Refitting is the reverse of removal, but align the previously made marks and tighten the retaining nut to the specified torque.

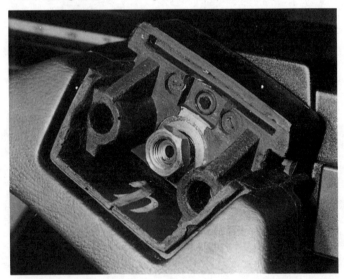

21.2 Steering wheel pad removed for access to retaining nut

22 Steering column – removal, overhaul and refitting

1 Disconnect the battery earth lead.
2 Remove the steering wheel as described in the previous Section.
3 Detach and remove the lower facia panels and the steering column upper and lower shrouds.
4 Unscrew and remove the steering wheel commutator screw (see Fig. 10.39).
5 Unscrew and remove the steering column intermediate shaft-to-steering wheel shaft coupling bolt.
6 Relocate the steering wheel and its retaining nut temporarily (do not tighten the nut), then pull on the wheel to release the shaft and upper bush. The steering lock must be freed during this operation. Remove the steering wheel when the column shaft and bush are free.
7 The steering column lock/ignition switch unit must now be

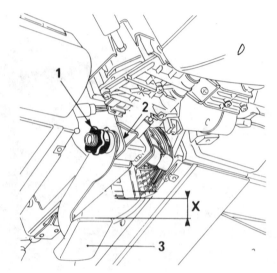

Fig. 10.37 Steering column locking lever setting diagram (Sec 20)

1 Nut   3 Lever
2 Ring nut   X = 30.0 mm (1.2 in)

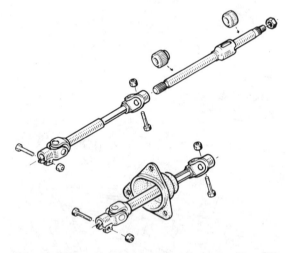

Fig. 10.38 Steering column components (Sec 22)

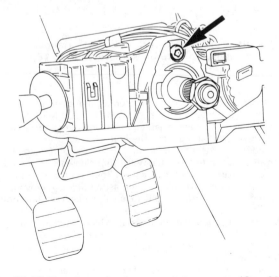

Fig. 10.39 Steering wheel commutator screw (Sec 22)

removed. Undo the retaining screw on the facia side, set the ignition key to the 'G' position, then depress the retaining pin on the underside of the unit and simultaneously withdraw the unit. Detach the wiring connector from the switch (photos).

8   Remove the steering column-to-dashboard retaining bolt, then the two nuts and two bolts securing the column support bracket (photo). Lower and remove the steering column.

9   The upper and lower column bushes can now be removed and

renewed. Drive the bushes out using a suitable length of 35 mm (1.37 in) diameter tubing. Smear the new bushes with grease before driving them into position.

10   Refitting is a reversal of the removal procedure. When the steering column shaft is being fitted to the intermediate shaft universal joint coupling, align the flat section with the slot centreline (see Fig. 10.41), then insert the key bolt.

11   Refit the steering wheel as described in Section 21.

22.7A Undo the retaining screw ...

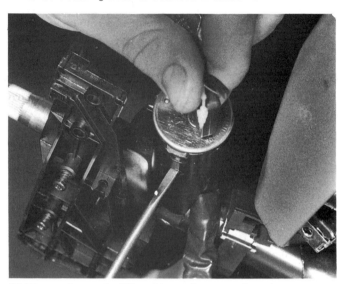

22.7B ... set key to the 'G' position and press retainer pin ...

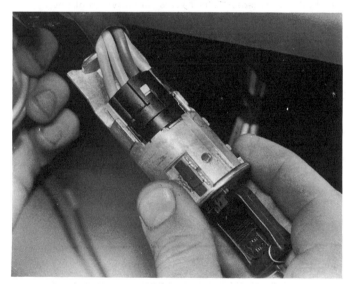

22.7C ... remove column lock/ignition switch unit

22.8 Steering column support bracket nuts and bolts (arrowed) – 2.0 litre model

23 Steering column intermediate shaft – removal and refitting

1.7 litre models

1   Detach and remove the lower trim panel from the facia on the driver's side.

2   Turn the steering to full right-hand lock so that the upper column-to-intermediate shaft coupling bolt is positioned as shown in Fig. 10.34. Unscrew the nut and withdraw the bolt.

3   Remove the lower universal joint coupling bolt working from the engine compartment side of the bulkhead. On some models the lower coupling is covered by a protective shield, and this must be removed

for access to the coupling. To remove the shield, carefully cut through the retaining clip and prise free the plastic clips. Be careful not to cut through the gaiter when removing the clip. Replace the foam seal when refitting.

4   With the coupling bolts removed, the intermediate shaft can be disengaged from the pinion at the lower end, and the column at the upper end, then removed. The bulkhead gaiter can be removed by undoing the three retaining nuts.

5   If the intermediate shaft is to be renewed, ensure that the correct replacement type is obtained, as the shafts differ in length according to model – see Fig. 10.44.

6   Refitting is a reversal of the removal procedure. When fitting the shaft, align the coupling bolt holes so that the bolts can be slid into

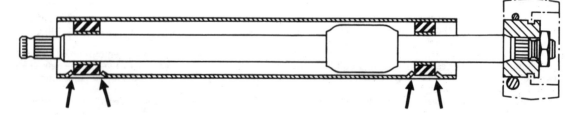

Fig. 10.40 Steering column upper and lower bush locations (arrowed) (Sec 22)

Fig. 10.41 Align column flat (A) with slot centreline when fitting the key bolt (Sec 22)

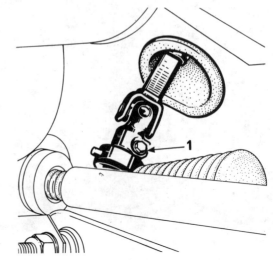

Fig. 10.42 Intermediate shaft lower universal joint coupling bolt (1) (Sec 23)

Fig. 10.43 Lower universal joint protective shield components (Sec 23)

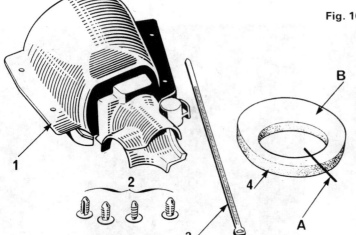

1 Shield
2 Clips (press-stud type)
3 Strap clip
4 Foam seal
A Cutting point for new seal
B Peel back protective paper from this face on new seal

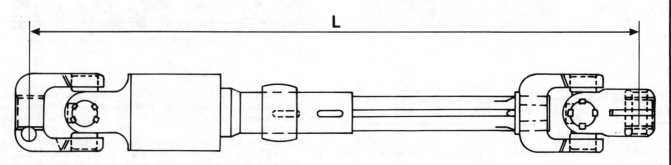

Fig. 10.44 Measure the intermediate shaft to check for correct replacement (Sec 23)

1.7 litre models with manual steering – L = 455.5 to 457.5 mm (17.76 to 17.84 in)
1.7 litre models with power steering – L = 425.5 to 427.5 mm (16.59 to 16.67 in)
All 2.0 litre models – L = 306.5 to 308.5 mm (11.95 to 12.03 in)

position without the need for force. Check the steering for satisfactory action on completion.

2.0 litre models

7   Proceed as described in paragraphs 1 and 2.

8   Raise and support the vehicle at the front end on axle stands.

9   Disconnect the steering arm balljoints as described in Section 12.

10 Unbolt but do not remove the steering gear unit, referring to Section 18 for details.

11 Withdraw the steering gear unit from the bulkhead just enough to allow the lower coupling bolt to be unscrewed and removed. Disengage the intermediate shaft from the lower and upper couplings and remove the shaft.

12 If required the gaiter can be removed from the bulkhead by undoing the three retaining nuts.

13 If the steering intermediate shaft is to be renewed, ensure that the correct replacement is obtained – see Fig. 10.44.

14 Refit in the reverse order to removal but note the following:

(a) *Align the intermediate shaft coupling bolt holes correctly so that the bolts can be inserted without force*

(b) *Refit the steering gear unit as described in Section 18*

(c) *Reconnect the steering arm balljoints as described in Section 12*

(d) *On completion check that the steering action is satisfactory*

24 Power steering pump – removal and refitting

1   On 1.7 litre models remove the alternator as described in Chapter 12.

2   Clamp the hydraulic hoses, the position a suitable container under the pump unit to catch the fluid. Detach the feed and high pressure hoses from the pump unit (photo).

3   On 1.7 litre models, undo the three retaining bolts and remove the pump unit.

4   On 2.0 litre models, refer to Fig. 10.46 and loosen off the drivebelt tensioner bolts of the alternator and power steering pump. Unscrew and remove the alternator lower retaining nut. Loosen bolts (C) and (D), also the pump rear mounting bolt (photo). Disengage the drivebelt, then remove the mounting bolts (C) and the rear mounting bolt. Withdraw the pump unit (photo).

5   In view of the special tools and skills required, it is not recommended that the power steering pump is dismantled or overhauled, but renewed by obtaining a new or factory reconditioned unit.

6   If the pump unit is to be renewed, the mounting bracket and pulley must be transferred to the new unit. As a special pulley withdrawal and refitting tool is required to change the pulley, it is a task best entrusted to a Renault dealer. Note that the mounting bracket must be in position when the pulley is fitted as it may not be possible to fit the bracket once the pulley is in position. In addition, the pulley position must be correctly set during assembly, or the drivebelt alignment will be incorrect.

7   Inspect the drivebelt and renew it if it is cracked or in poor general condition.

8   The refitting procedures for the power steering pump on both the 1.7 and 2.0 litre models are a reversal of the removal procedure, but note the following special points:

(a) *On 1.7 litre models refit the alternator as described in Chapter 12*

(b) *Adjust the drivebelt tension(s) as described in Chapter 2*

(c) *Connect up the hydraulic system hoses, then top up the fluid level and bleed the system as described in Section 25*

25 Power steering circuit – bleeding

1   This will only be required if any part of the hydraulic system has been disconnected.

2   Fill the reservoir to the brim with the specified fluid.

3   Turn the steering to full lock in both directions. Top up if required.

4   Start the engine and turn the steering slowly from lock to lock. Switch off and top up to the correct level.

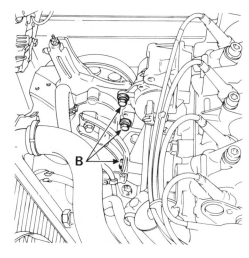

Fig. 10.45 Power steering pump bolts (B) – 1.7 litre models (Sec 24)

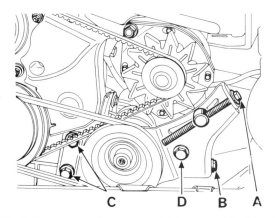

Fig. 10.46 Power steering pump – 2.0 litre models (Sec 24)

A Tensioner bolt (for alternator drivebelt)	*C Pump mounting bolts*
	D Pump mounting bolt
B Tensioner bolt (for power steering pump drivebelt)	

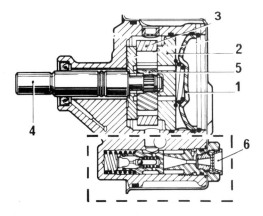

Fig. 10.47 Sectional view of the power steering pump unit (Sec 24)

1 Pressure closure plate	*4 Shaft*
2 Backplate	*5 Rotor*
3 Stator	*6 High pressure union*

24.2 Power steering pump unit and hydraulic hose connections – 2.0 litre model

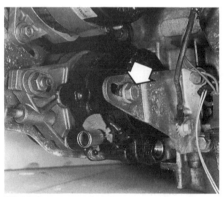

24.4A Power steering pump rear mounting bolt (arrowed) – 2.0 litre model

24.4B Removing the power steering pump unit – 2.0 litre model

26 Steering angles and front wheel alignment

1   Accurate front wheel alignment is essential to provide good steering and roadholding characteristics and to ensure slow and even tyre wear. Before considering the steering angles, check that the tyres are correctly inflated, that the front wheels are not buckled, the hub bearings are not worn or incorrectly adjusted and that the steering linkage is in good order, without slackness or wear at the joints.

2   Wheel alignment consists of four factors:

Camber, is the angle at which the road wheels are set from the vertical when viewed from the front or rear of the vehicle. Positive camber is the angle (in degrees) that the wheels are tilted outwards at the top from the vertical.

Castor, is the angle between the steering axis and a vertical when viewed from each side of the vehicle. Positive castor is indicated when the steering axis is inclined towards the rear of the vehicle at its upper end.

Steering axis inclination, is the angle when viewed from the front or rear of the vehicle between vertical and an imaginary line drawn between the top and bottom strut mountings.

Toe, is the amount by which the distance between the front inside edges of the roadwheel rims differs from that between the rear inside edges. If the distance between the front edges is less than that at the rear, the wheels are said to toe-in. If the distance between the front inside edges is greater than that at the rear, the wheels toe-out.

3   Owing to the need for precision gauges to measure the small angles of the steering and suspension settings, it is preferable that measuring of camber and castor is left to a service station having the necessary equipment.

4   The camber and steering axis inclination angles are set in production and cannot be adjusted. Where they differ from those specified, suspect collision damage or gross wear in the steering or suspension components.

5   To check the front wheel alignment, first make sure that the lengths of both steering arms are equal when the steering is in the straight-ahead position. Adjust if necessary by releasing the steering arm end locknuts and turning the steering arms until the lengths of the exposed threads are equal on each side.

6   Obtain a tracking gauge. These are available in various forms from accessory stores or one can be fabricated from a length of steel tubing suitably cranked to clear the sump and bellhousing and having a setscrew and locknut at one end.

7   With the gauge, measure the distance between the two wheel inner rims (at hub height) at the rear of the wheel. Push the vehicle forward to rotate the wheel through 180° (half a turn) and measure the distance between the wheel inner rims, again at hub height, at the front of the wheel. This last measurement should differ from the first by the appropriate toe-out according to specification (see Specifications).

8   Where the toe-out is found to be incorrect, release the steering arm balljoint locknuts and turn the steering arms equally. Only turn them a quarter of a turn at a time before re-checking the alignment.

9   Turn each steering arm in the same direction when viewed from the centre line of the car otherwise the rods will become unequal in length.

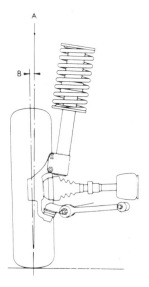

Fig. 10.48 Camber angle diagram (Sec 26)

A   Vertical   B   Camber angle (positive)

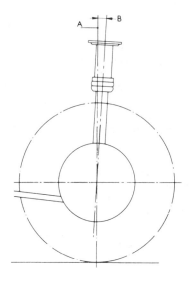

Fig. 10.49 Castor angle diagram (left-hand wheel) (Sec 26)

A   Vertical   B   Castor angle (positive)

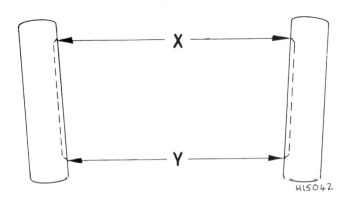

Fig. 10.50 Front wheel alignment diagram showing toe-out (Sec 26)

$$X - Y = toe\text{-}out$$

This would cause the steering wheel spoke position to alter and cause problems on turns with tyre scrubbing. On completion, tighten the steering arm locknuts without disturbing their setting, check that the balljoint is at the centre of its arc of travel.

27 Rear wheel alignment

1   All angles are set in production and cannot be adjusted.
2   Rear wheel alignment can be checked as described for the front wheels, but any deviation from the specified limits indicates rear suspension damage or wear, as the toe-setting is not adjustable.

28 Steering column lock/ignition switch – removal and refitting

1   Disconnect the battery.
2   Remove the steering column shroud.
3   The lock/ignition switch assembly can now be removed as described in paragraph 7 of Section 22.
4   Refit in the reverse order of removal. On completion check for satisfactory operation of the steering, ignition and steering lock.

29 Fault diagnosis – suspension and steering

Symptom	Reason(s)
Front suspension	
Vehicle wanders	Incorrect wheel alignment
	Worn front lower arm balljoints
Heavy or stiff steering	Incorrect front wheel alignment
	Incorrect tyre pressures
Wheel wobble or vibration	Roadwheels out of balance
	Roadwheel buckled
	Incorrect front wheel alignment
	Faulty shock absorber
	Weak coil spring
Excessive pitching or rolling on corners or during braking	Faulty shock absorber
	Weak or broken coil spring
Tyre squeal when cornering	Incorrect front wheel alignment
	Incorrect tyre pressures
Abnormal tyre wear	Incorrect tyre pressures
	Incorrect front wheel alignment
	Worn hub bearing
Rear suspension	
Poor roadholding and wander	Faulty shock absorber
	Weak coil spring (where applicable)
	Worn or incorrectly adjusted hub bearing
	Worn suspension arm bush
Manual steering gear	
Stiff action	Lack of rack lubrication
	Seized steering arm end balljoints
	Seized suspension lower balljoint
Free movement at steering wheel	Wear in steering arm balljoints
	Wear in rack teeth
Knocking when traversing uneven surface	Incorrectly adjusted rack slipper

29 Fault diagnosis – suspension and steering (continued)

Symptom	Reason(s)

Power-assisted steering
The symptoms and reasons applicable to manual steering gear will apply plus the following:

Symptom	Reason(s)
Stiff action or no return action	Slipping pump drivebelt Air in fluid Steering column out of alignment Castor angle incorrect due to damage or gross wear in bushes and mountings
Steering effort on both locks unequal	Leaking seal in steering gear Clogged fluid passage within gear assembly
Noisy pump	Loose pulley Kinked hose Low fluid level

Chapter 11 Bodywork and fittings

Contents

1 General description

The bodyshell and underframe are of all-steel welded construction, incorporating progressive crumple zones at the front and rear and a rigid centre safety cell. The assembly and welding of the main body unit is completed by computer-controlled robots, and is checked for dimensional accuracy using computer and laser technology.

The front and rear bumpers are of collapsible cellular construction to minimise minor accident damage and the front wings are bolted in position to facilitate accident damage repair.

2 Maintenance – bodywork and underframe

1   The general condition of a vehicle's bodywork is the one thing that significantly affects its value. Maintenance is easy but needs to be regular. Neglect, particularly after minor damage, can lead quickly to further deterioration and costly repair bills. It is important also to keep watch on those parts of the vehicle not immediately visible, for instance the underside, inside all the wheel arches and the lower part of the engine compartment.

2   The basic maintenance routine for the bodywork is washing – preferably with a lot of water, from a hose. This will remove all the loose solids which may have stuck to the vehicle. It is important to flush these off in such a way as to prevent grit from scratching the finish. The wheel arches and underframe need washing in the same way to remove any accumulated mud which will retain moisture and tend to encourage rust. Paradoxically enough, the best time to clean the underframe and wheel arches is in wet weather when the mud is thoroughly wet and soft. In very wet weather the underframe is usually cleaned of large accumulations automatically and this is a good time for inspection.

3   Periodically, except on vehicles with a wax-based underbody protective coating, it is a good idea to have the whole of the underframe of the vehicle steam cleaned, engine compartment included, so that a thorough inspection can be carried out to see what minor repairs and renovations are necessary. Steam cleaning is available at many garages and is necessary for removal of the accumulation of oily grime which sometimes is allowed to become thick in certain areas. If steam cleaning facilities are not available, there are one or two excellent grease solvents available which can be brush applied. The dirt can then be simply hosed off. Note that these methods should not be used on vehicles with wax-based underbody protective coating or the coating will be removed. Such vehicles should be inspected annually, preferably just prior to winter, when the underbody should be washed down and any damage to the wax coating repaired. Ideally, a completely fresh coat should be applied. It would also be worth considering the use of such wax-based protection for injection into door panels, sills, box sections, etc, as an additional safeguard against rust damage where such protection is not provided by the vehicle manufacturer.

4   After washing paintwork, wipe off with a chamois leather to give an unspotted clear finish. A coat of clear protective wax polish will give added protection against chemical pollutants in the air. If the paintwork sheen has dulled or oxidised, use a cleaner/polisher combination to restore the brilliance of the shine. This requires a little effort, but such dulling is usually caused because regular washing has been neglected. Care needs to be taken with metallic paintwork, as special non-abrasive cleaner/polisher is required to avoid damage to the finish. Always check that the door and ventilator opening drain holes and pipes are completely clear so that water can be drained out (photos). Bright work should be treated in the same way as paint work. Windscreens and windows can be kept clear of the smeary film which often appears by the use of a proprietary glass cleaner. Never use any form of wax or other body or chromium polish on glass.

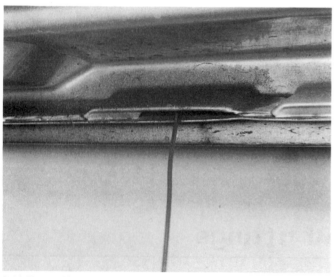

2.4A Use a thin gauge rod to clean out the door drain channels

2.4B Tailgate drain aperture – Savanna model

3 Maintenance – upholstery and carpets

Mats and carpets should be brushed or vacuum cleaned regularly to keep them free of grit. If they are badly stained remove them from the vehicle for scrubbing or sponging and make quite sure they are dry before refitting. Seats and interior trim panels can be kept clean by wiping with a damp cloth. If they do become stained (which can be more apparent on light coloured upholstery) use a little liquid detergent and a soft nail brush to scour the grime out of the grain of the material. Do not forget to keep the headlining clean in the same way as the upholstery. When using liquid cleaners inside the vehicle do not over-wet the surfaces being cleaned. Excessive damp could get into the seams and padded interior causing stains, offensive odours or even rot. If the inside of the vehicle gets wet accidentally it is worthwhile taking some trouble to dry it out properly, particularly where carpets are involved. *Do not leave oil or electric heaters inside the vehicle for this purpose.*

4 Minor body damage – repair

The photographic sequences on pages 278 and 279 illustrate the operations detailed in the following sub-sections.
Note: *For more detailed information about bodywork repair, the Haynes Publishing Group publish a book by Lindsay Porter called The Car Bodywork Repair Manual. This incorporates information on such aspects as rust treatment, painting and glass fibre repairs, as well as details on more ambitious repairs involving welding and panel beating.*

Repair of minor scratches in bodywork

If the scratch is very superficial, and does not penetrate to the metal of the bodywork, repair is very simple. Lightly rub the area of the scratch with a paintwork renovator, or a very fine cutting paste, to remove loose paint from the scratch and to clear the surrounding bodywork of wax polish. Rinse the area with clean water.

Apply touch-up paint to the scratch using a fine paint brush; continue to apply fine layers of paint until the surface of the paint in the scratch is level with the surrounding paintwork. Allow the new paint at least two weeks to harden: then blend it into the surrounding paintwork by rubbing the scratch area with a paintwork renovator or a very fine cutting paste. Finally, apply wax polish.

Where the scratch has penetrated right through to the metal of the bodywork, causing the metal to rust, a different repair technique is required. Remove any loose rust from the bottom of the scratch with a penknife, then apply rust inhibiting paint to prevent the formation of rust in the future. Using a rubber or nylon applicator fill the scratch with bodystopper paste. If required, this paste can be mixed with cellulose thinners to provide a very thin paste which is ideal for filling narrow scratches. Before the stopper-paste in the scratch hardens, wrap a piece of smooth cotton rag around the top of a finger. Dip the finger in cellulose thinners and then quickly sweep it across the surface of the stopper-paste in the scratch; this will ensure that the surface of the stopper-paste is slightly hollowed. The scratch can now be painted over as described earlier in this Section.

Repair of dents in bodywork

When deep denting of the vehicle's bodywork has taken place, the first task is to pull the dent out, until the affected bodywork almost attains its original shape. There is little point in trying to restore the original shape completely, as the metal in the damaged area will have stretched on impact and cannot be reshaped fully to its original contour. It is better to bring the level of the dent up to a point which is about ⅛ in (3 mm) below the level of the surrounding bodywork. In cases where the dent is very shallow anyway, it is not worth trying to pull it out at all. If the underside of the dent is accessible, it can be hammered out gently from behind, using a mallet with a wooden or plastic head. Whilst doing this, hold a suitable block of wood firmly against the outside of the panel to absorb the impact from the hammer blows and thus prevent a large area of the bodywork from being 'belled-out'.

Should the dent be in a section of the bodywork which has a double skin or some other factor making it inaccessible from behind, a different technique is called for. Drill several small holes through the metal inside the area – particularly in the deeper section. Then screw long self-tapping screws into the holes just sufficiently for them to gain a good purchase in the metal. Now the dent can be pulled out by pulling on the protruding heads of the screws with a pair of pliers.

The next stage of the repair is the removal of the paint from the damaged area, and from an inch or so of the surrounding 'sound' bodywork. This is accomplished most easily by using a wire brush or abrasive pad on a power drill, although it can be done just as effectively by hand using sheets of abrasive paper. To complete the preparation for filling, score the surface of the bare metal with a screwdriver or the tang of a file, or alternatively, drill small holes in the affected area. This will provide a really good 'key' for the filler paste.

To complete the repair see the Section on filling and re-spraying.

Repair of rust holes or gashes in bodywork

Remove all paint from the affected area and from an inch or so of the surrounding 'sound' bodywork, using an abrasive pad or a wire brush on a power drill. If these are not available a few sheets of abrasive paper will do the job just as effectively. With the paint removed you will be able to gauge the severity of the corrosion and therefore decide whether to renew the whole panel (if this is possible) or to repair the affected area. New body panels are not as expensive as most people think and it is often quicker and more satisfactory to fit a new panel than to attempt to repair large areas of corrosion.

Remove all fittings from the affected area except those which will act as a guide to the original shape of the damaged bodywork (eg headlamp shells etc). Then, using tin snips or a hacksaw blade, remove all loose metal and any other metal badly affected by corrosion. Hammer the edges of the hole inwards in order to create a slight depression for the filler paste.

Wire brush the affected area to remove the powdery rust from the surface of the remaining metal. Paint the affected area with rust inhibiting paint; if the back of the rusted area is accessible treat this also.

Before filling can take place it will be necessary to block the hole in some way. This can be achieved by the use of aluminium or plastic mesh, or aluminium tape.

Aluminium or plastic mesh is probably the best material to use for a large hole. Cut a piece to the approximate size and shape of the hole to be filled, then position it in the hole so that its edges are below the level of the surrounding bodywork. It can be retained in position by several blobs of filler paste around its periphery.

Aluminium tape should be used for small or very narrow holes. Pull a piece off the roll and trim it to the approximate size and shape required, then pull off the backing paper (if used) and stick the tape over the hole; it can be overlapped if the thickness of one piece is insufficient. Burnish down the edges of the tape with the handle of a screwdriver or similar, to ensure that the tape is securely attached to the metal underneath.

Bodywork repairs – filling and re-spraying

Before using this Section, see the Sections on dent, deep scratch, rust holes and gash repairs.

Many types of bodyfiller are available, but generally speaking those proprietary kits which contain a tin of filler paste and a tube of resin hardener are best for this type of repair. A wide, flexible plastic or nylon applicator will be found invaluable for imparting a smooth and well contoured finish to the surface of the filler.

Mix up a little filler on a clean piece of card or board – measure the hardener carefully (follow the maker's instructions on the pack) otherwise the filler will set too rapidly or too slowly. Using the applicator apply the filler paste to the prepared area; draw the applicator across the surface of the filler to achieve the correct contour and to level the filler surface. As soon as a contour that approximates to the correct one is achieved, stop working the paste – if you carry on too long the paste will become sticky and begin to 'pick up' on the applicator. Continue to add thin layers of filler paste at twenty-minute intervals until the level of the filler is just proud of the surrounding bodywork.

Once the filler has hardened, excess can be removed using a metal plane or file. From then on, progressively finer grades of abrasive paper should be used, starting with a 40 grade production paper and finishing with 400 grade wet-and-dry paper. Always wrap the abrasive paper around a flat rubber, cork, or wooden block – otherwise the surface of the filler will not be completely flat. During the smoothing of the filler surface the wet-and-dry paper should be periodically rinsed in water. This will ensure that a very smooth finish is imparted to the filler at the final stage.

At this stage the 'dent' should be surrounded by a ring of bare metal, which in turn should be encircled by the finely 'feathered' edge of the good paintwork. Rinse the repair area with clean water, until all of the dust produced by the rubbing-down operation has gone.

Spray the whole repair area with a light coat of primer – this will show up any imperfections in the surface of the filler. Repair these imperfections with fresh filler paste or bodystopper, and once more smooth the surface with abrasive paper. If bodystopper is used, it can be mixed with cellulose thinners to form a really thin paste which is ideal for filling small holes. Repeat this spray and repair procedure until you are satisfied that the surface of the filler, and the feathered edge of the paintwork are perfect. Clean the repair area with clean water and allow to dry fully.

The repair area is now ready for final spraying. Paint spraying must be carried out in a warm, dry, windless and dust free atmosphere. This condition can be created artificially if you have access to a large indoor working area, but if you are forced to work in the open, you will have to pick your day very carefully. If you are working indoors, dousing the floor in the work area with water will help to settle the dust which would otherwise be in the atmosphere. If the repair area is confined to one body panel, mask off the surrounding panels; this will help to minimise the effects of a slight mis-match in paint colours. Bodywork fittings (eg chrome strips, door handles etc) will also need to be masked off. Use genuine masking tape and several thicknesses of newspaper for the masking operations.

Before commencing to spray, agitate the aerosol can thoroughly, then spray a test area (an old tin, or similar) until the technique is mastered. Cover the repair area with a thick coat of primer; the thickness should be built up using several thin layers of paint rather than one thick one. Using 400 grade wet-and-dry paper, rub down the surface of the primer until it is really smooth. While doing this, the work area should be thoroughly doused with water, and the wet-and-dry paper periodically rinsed in water. Allow to dry before spraying on more paint.

Spray on the top coat, again building up the thickness by using several thin layers of paint. Start spraying in the centre of the repair area and then, using a circular motion, work outwards until the whole repair area and about 2 inches of the surrounding original paintwork is covered. Remove all masking material 10 to 15 minutes after spraying on the final coat of paint.

Allow the new paint at least two weeks to harden, then, using a paintwork renovator or a very fine cutting paste, blend the edges of the paint into the existing paintwork. Finally, apply wax polish.

Plastic components

With the use of more and more plastic body components by the vehicle manufacturers (eg bumpers, spoilers, and in some cases major body panels), rectification of more serious damage to such items has become a matter of either entrusting repair work to a specialist in this field, or renewing complete components. Repair of such damage by the DIY owner is not really feasible owing to the cost of the equipment and materials required for effecting such repairs. The basic technique involves making a groove along the line of the crack in the plastic using a rotary burr in a power drill. The damaged part is then welded back together by using a hot air gun to heat up and fuse a plastic filler rod into the groove. Any excess plastic is then removed and the area rubbed down to a smooth finish. It is important that a filler rod of the correct plastic is used, as body components can be made of a variety of different types (eg polycarbonate, ABS, polypropylene).

Damage of a less serious nature (abrasions, minor cracks etc) can be repaired by the DIY owner using a two-part epoxy filler repair material. Once mixed in equal proportions, this is used in similar fashion to the bodywork filler used on metal panels. The filler is usually cured in twenty to thirty minutes, ready for sanding and painting.

If the owner is renewing a complete component himself, or if he has repaired it with epoxy filler, he will be left with the problem of finding a suitable paint for finishing which is compatible with the type of plastic used. At one time the use of a universal paint was not possible owing to the complex range of plastics encountered in body component applications. Standard paints, generally speaking, will not bond to plastic or rubber satisfactorily. However, it is now possible to obtain a plastic body parts finishing kit which consists of a pre-primer treatment, a primer and coloured top coat. Full instructions are normally supplied with a kit, but basically the method of use is to first apply the pre-primer to the component concerned and allow it to dry for up to 30 minutes. Then the primer is applied and left to dry for about an hour before finally applying the special coloured top coat. The result is a correctly coloured component where the paint will flex with the plastic or rubber, a property that standard paint does not normally possess.

5 Major body damage – repair

Where serious damage has occurred, or large areas need renewal due to neglect, it means that completely new sections or panels will need welding in, and this is best left to professionals. If the damage is due to impact, it will also be necessary to check completely the alignment of the bodyshell structure. Due to the principle of construction, the strength and shape of the whole car can be affected by damage to one part. In such instances the services of an accident repair specialist or Renault dealer with special checking jigs are essential. If a body is left misaligned, it is first of all dangerous, as the car will not handle properly, and secondly uneven stresses will be imposed on the steering, engine and transmission, causing abnormal wear or complete failure. Tyre wear may also be excessive.

6 Maintenance – hinges and locks

1   Oil the hinges of the bonnet, boot or tailgate and door with a drop or two of light oil at regular intervals (see 'Routine maintenance').
2   At the same time, lightly oil the bonnet release mechanism and all door locks.
3   Do not attempt to lubricate the steering lock.

7 Door rattles – tracing and rectification

1   Check first that the door is not loose at the hinges, and that the latch is holding the door firmly in position. Check also that the door lines up with the aperture in the body. If the door is out of alignment, adjust it, as described in Section 15 or 22 as applicable.
2   If the latch is holding the door in the correct position, but the latch still rattles, the lock mechanism is worn and should be renewed.
3   If required the door striker can be adjusted for position by loosening with a suitable Torx key (photo).
4   Other rattles from the door could be caused by wear in the window operating mechanism, interior lock mechanism, or loose glass channels.

8 Bonnet – removal, refitting and adjustment

1   Open the bonnet and support it in the open position using the stay.
2   Disconnect the windscreen washer hose at the T-piece connector (photo).
3   Mark the outline of the hinges with a soft pencil, then loosen the four retaining bolts (photo).
4   With the help of an assistant, remove the stay, unscrew the four bolts and lift the bonnet off the car, together with any hinge shim plates.
5   Refitting is the reverse sequence to removal. Position the bonnet hinges within the outline marks made during removal, but alter its position as necessary to provide a uniform gap all round. Adjust the height of the lock mechanism if necessary, as described in Section 9.

9 Bonnet lock and release cable – removal, refitting and adjustment

Bonnet lock
1   Open and support the bonnet.
2   Remove the windscreen wiper arms (Chapter 12), then remove the grille panel from the base of the windscreen. This panel is secured by screws and clips (photos). Remove the seal and grille.

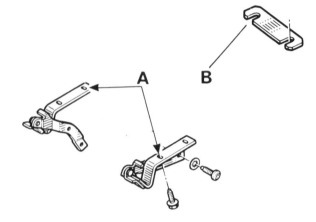

Fig. 11.1 Bonnet hinges (A) and adjuster shim plates (B) (Sec 8)

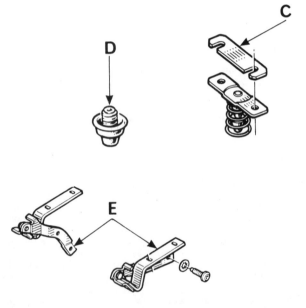

Fig. 11.2 Adjust bonnet lock height with shims (C) and bonnet fitted height with rubber stops (D) (Sec 9)

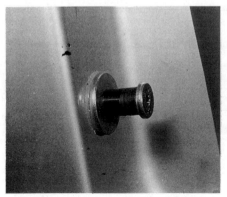

7.3 Door lock striker

8.2 Windscreen washer hoses T-piece connector

8.3 Bonnet hinge bolts

3 Unbolt and withdraw the bonnet lock (photo). Disconnect the cable.
4 Refitting is the reverse sequence to removal, but adjust the lock height so that the bonnet line is flush with the front wings and shuts securely without force.

Release cable
5 Remove the bonnet lock and disconnect the release cable from it,

as described in paragraphs 1 to 3.
6 From inside the vehicle, detach and remove the lower facia panel on the driver's side.
7 Undo the release cable handle retaining bolt, unclip the cable and withdraw it through the bulkhead (photo).
8 Refit in the reverse order of removal. When reconnected, check for satisfactory operation prior to refitting the facia and grille panels.

9.2A Remove the grille retaining screws (arrowed) ...

9.2B ... and peel back seal to remove grille ...

9.3 ... for access to bonnet lock and cable

9.7 Bonnet release cable and handle (lower facia panel removed)

10 Radiator grille – removal and refitting

1 Open the bonnet and support it in the raised position.
2 Undo the grille retaining screws, working from the front. Depending on type, tilt the grille and withdraw it from the vehicle, or if necessary lower the bonnet to allow sufficient clearance for grille removal.
3 Refit in the reverse order of removal. Engage the grille locating lugs before fitting the screws. When fitting a metal type grille, spring it into position between the bonnet (closed) and the bumper shield.

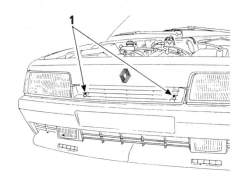
Fig. 11.3 Front grille retaining screw locations (Sec 10)

This sequence of photographs deals with the repair of the dent and paintwork damage shown in this photo. The procedure will be similar for the repair of a hole. It should be noted that the procedures given here are simplified — more explicit instructions will be found in the text

In the case of a dent the first job — after removing surrounding trim — is to hammer out the dent where access is possible. This will minimise filling. Here, the large dent having been hammered out, the damaged area is being made slightly concave

Now all paint must be removed from the damaged area, by rubbing with coarse abrasive paper. Alternatively, a wire brush or abrasive pad can be used in a power drill. Where the repair area meets good paintwork, the edge of the paintwork should be 'feathered', using a finer grade of abrasive paper

In the case of a hole caused by rusting, all damaged sheet-metal should be cut away before proceeding to this stage. Here, the damaged area is being treated with rust remover and inhibitor before being filled

Mix the body filler according to its manufacturer's instructions. In the case of corrosion damage, it will be necessary to block off any large holes before filling — this can be done with aluminium or plastic mesh, or aluminium tape. Make sure the area is absolutely clean before ...

... applying the filler. Filler should be applied with a flexible applicator, as shown, for best results; the wooden spatula being used for confined areas. Apply thin layers of filler at 20-minute intervals, until the surface of the filler is slightly proud of the surrounding bodywork

Initial shaping can be done with a Surform plane or Dreadnought file. Then, using progressively finer grades of wet-and-dry paper, wrapped around a sanding block, and copious amounts of clean water, rub down the filler until really smooth and flat. Again, feather the edges of adjoining paintwork

Again, using plenty of water, rub down the primer with a fine grade wet-and-dry paper (400 grade is probably best) until it is really smooth and well blended into the surrounding paintwork. Any remaining imperfections can now be filled by carefully applied knifing stopper paste

The top coat can now be applied. When working out of doors, pick a dry, warm and wind-free day. Ensure surrounding areas are protected from over-spray. Agitate the aerosol thoroughly, then spray the centre of the repair area, working outwards with a circular motion. Apply the paint as several thin coats

The whole repair area can now be sprayed or brush-painted with primer. If spraying, ensure adjoining areas are protected from over-spray. Note that at least one inch of the surrounding sound paintwork should be coated with primer. Primer has a 'thick' consistency, so will find small imperfections

When the stopper has hardened, rub down the repair area again before applying the final coat of primer. Before rubbing down this last coat of primer, ensure the repair area is blemish-free — use more stopper if necessary. To ensure that the surface of the primer is really smooth use some finishing compound

After a period of about two weeks, which the paint needs to harden fully, the surface of the repaired area can be 'cut' with a mild cutting compound prior to wax polishing. When carrying out bodywork repairs, remember that the quality of the finished job is proportional to the time and effort expended

11 Bumpers – removal and refitting

Front bumper

1   Raise the vehicle at the front end and support it on axle stands.
2   Refer to Fig. 11.4, (and photo) and remove the retaining screws and bolts from the points indicated. Note that screw (2) is accessible from the wheel arch side.
3   Repeat the procedure on the other side of the vehicle and remove the bumper.
4   Refit in the reverse order of removal. Check the bumper for correct alignment before fully tightening the retaining bolts and screws.

Rear bumper – Saloon

5   Raise and support the vehicle at the rear on axle stands.
6   Remove the trim panel from the left-hand side of the luggage area, then unscrew the bumper side fixing bolts.
7   Remove the mud baffle outer fastening.
8   Working from underneath the vehicle, undo the right-hand side fixing bolts from the wheel arch area, just to the rear of the fuel filler pipe.
9   Pull the bumper to the rear and remove it.
10 Refit in the reverse order of removal. Check for correct alignment before fully tightening the retaining bolts.

11 Rear bumper – Savanna

11 Proceed as described for the Saloon variants, but note the following additional points:

(a) Extract the foam plugs to gain access to the retaining bolts on the left-hand side of the luggage area
(b) Remove the plastic wheel arch protectors on each side
(c) Remove the upper retaining screws indicated in Fig. 11.7

12 Refitting is a reversal of the removal procedure. Check for correct alignment before fully tightening the retaining bolts.

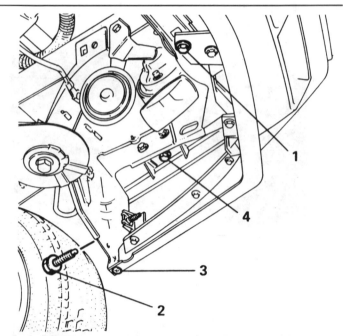

Fig. 11.4 Front bumper retaining screw and bolt locations (Sec 11)

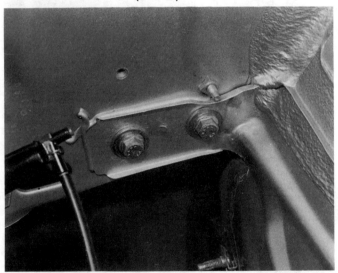

11.2 Front bumper side retaining bolts in engine compartment – Savanna model

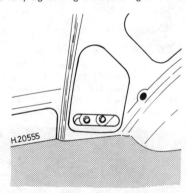

Fig. 11.5 Rear bumper side retaining bolts in luggage area – Saloon model (Sec 11)

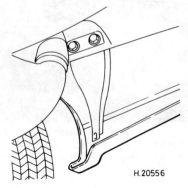

Fig. 11.6 Rear bumper side fastening bolts in wheel arch – Saloon model (Sec 11)

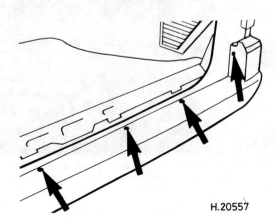

Fig. 11.7 Rear bumper upper retaining screw locations – Savanna model (Sec 11)

12 Front spoiler (and brake cooling ducts – Turbo models) – removal and refitting

Front spoiler

1   The type of front spoiler fitted is dependent on the vehicle model. Refer to the accompanying illustrations for typical examples and their fixings. The earlier type spoiler is identified by its integral air intake grille.
2   Raise and support the vehicle at the front end on axle stands.
3   According to type, undo the retaining screws, nuts or bolts, and where necessary drill out the pop rivets. Withdraw the spoiler.
4   Where applicable, separate the two halves of the spoiler by drilling out the pop rivets and/or removing the retaining screws.
5   On Turbo models, disconnect the brake cooling ducts.
6   Refit in the reverse order of removal, noting the reassembly sequence for the early type spoiler as shown in Fig. 11.11.

Brake cooling ducts (Turbo models)

7   Brake cooling ducts are fitted to Turbo models, the air being drawn in through the grille in the front face of the spoiler.
8   The ducts and protector shields are secured by screws and bolts as shown in the accompanying figures.
9   Removal of the shields will be necessary to allow access when undertaking certain repair and overhaul procedures on the front brakes and suspension components.

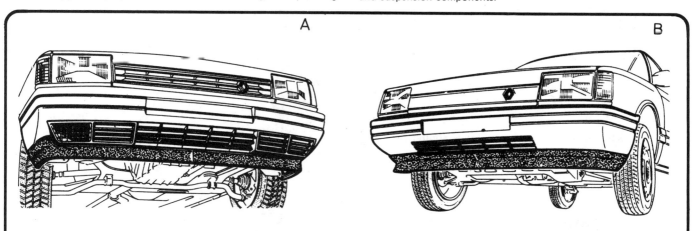

Fig. 11.8 Early (A) and late (B) type front spoiler (Sec 12)

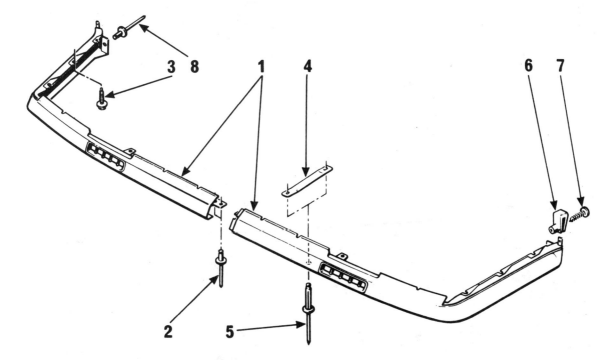

Fig. 11.9 Front spoiler components – Turbo model (Sec 12)

1	Right and left-hand spoiler sections	3	Shouldered screw (spoiler to wheel arch shield)	5	Bracket pop rivet	8	Pop rivet (spoiler to wheel arch shield)
2	Pop rivets	4	Bracket (to crossmember)	6	Clip		
				7	Screw		

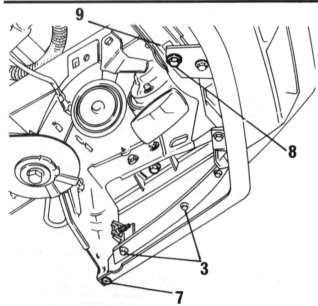

Fig. 11.10 Underside fixings of early type spoiler (Sec 12)

3	Bolts	8	Screw
7	Bolt	9	Nut

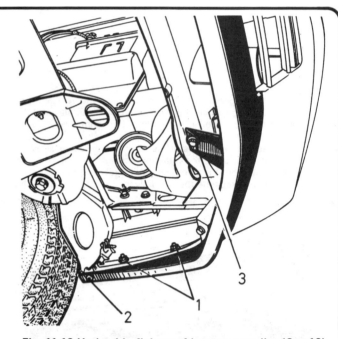

Fig. 11.12 Underside fixings of late type spoiler (Sec 12)

1	Nuts	3	Bolt
2	Pop rivet		

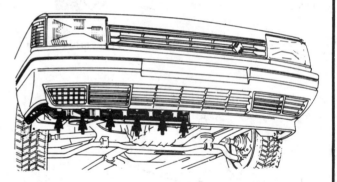

Fig. 11.13 Check for correct clip locations on late type spoiler (Sec 12)

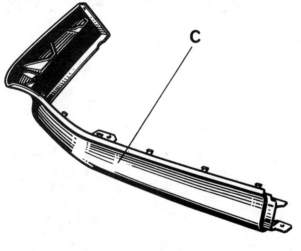

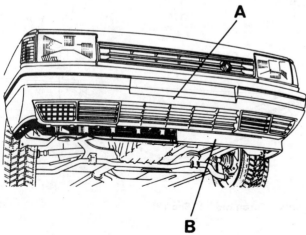

Fig. 11.11 Early type spoiler assembly sequence (Sec 12)

1	Fit B to A	3	Fit B to C
2	Fit C to A		

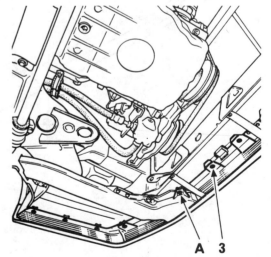

Fig. 11.14 Underside view of Turbo spoiler and brake cooling duct (Sec 12)

3	Spoiler retaining screw	A	Brake cooling duct retaining screw to spoiler

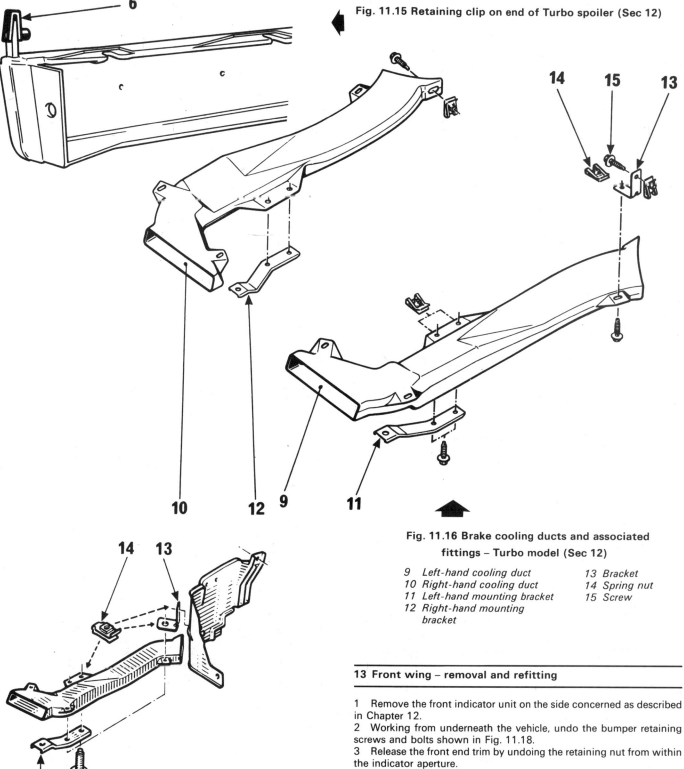

Fig. 11.15 Retaining clip on end of Turbo spoiler (Sec 12)

Fig. 11.16 Brake cooling ducts and associated fittings – Turbo model (Sec 12)

9 Left-hand cooling duct	13 Bracket
10 Right-hand cooling duct	14 Spring nut
11 Left-hand mounting bracket	15 Screw
12 Right-hand mounting bracket	

Fig. 11.17 Brake cooling duct and wheel arch shield components (Sec 12)

11 and 12 Cooling duct mountings	shield bracket
13 Cooling duct-to-wheel arch	14 Spring nut

13 Front wing – removal and refitting

1   Remove the front indicator unit on the side concerned as described in Chapter 12.

2   Working from underneath the vehicle, undo the bumper retaining screws and bolts shown in Fig. 11.18.

3   Release the front end trim by undoing the retaining nut from within the indicator aperture.

4   Refer to Fig. 11.19 and remove the various retainers from the points indicated. Prise free the wheel arch protector shield retaining clips. To remove side retaining screw (8), pivot the bumper outwards for access.

5   When all the retainers are removed, heat the inner wing section in the area marked (A) using a hot air gun (a hair dryer will suffice), but take care not to burn the paint if the wing is to be reused.

6   Refit in the reverse order of removal. If a new wing panel is being fitted, apply a suitable body sealant to the area marked (A).

7   Check for correct wing alignment before fully retightening the retaining bolts.

8   Check the indicators for correct operation on completion.

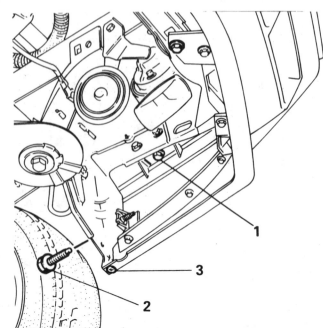

Fig. 11.18 Underside view showing front fixings (Sec 13)

1 Bolt   3 Screw
2 Bolt

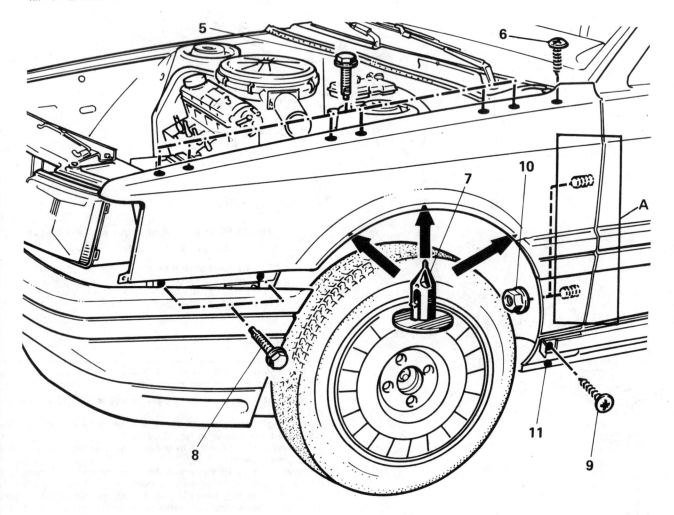

Fig. 11.19 Front wing fixings (Sec 13)

5 Top edge screws   7 Wheel arch shield clips   9 Moulding screw   11 Sill screw
6 Scuttle grille screw 8 Front bolts   10 Nuts

14 Door trim panels – removal and refitting

Front doors

1   Disconnect the battery earth lead.
2   Remove the door lock button by releasing its retainer as shown. Insert a suitable rod or a small screwdriver blade into the slot in the button and press to release the retainer (photo).
3   Undo the retaining screws and remove the lower trim/bin from the door panel (photo).
4   Remove the door-mounted speaker unit and door switches, if applicable, as described in Chapter 12.
Remove the speaker panel support and disconnect the wiring connectors (photos).

5   Undo the retaining screws and remove the door catch release (photos).
6   Prise free and remove the triangular trim panel from the door mirror adjuster (photo).
7   Where applicable, remove the door window regulator handle by prising free with a flat forked tool (photo).
8   Carefully prise free the trim panel from the door using a suitable tool as shown (photo).
9   Peel back the plastic insulator sheet from the inner door for access to the inner door fittings.
10 Refit in the reverse order of removal.

Rear doors

11 Proceed as described for the front door trim panels, but ignore paragraphs 3, 4 and 6. Refer to Fig. 11.21.

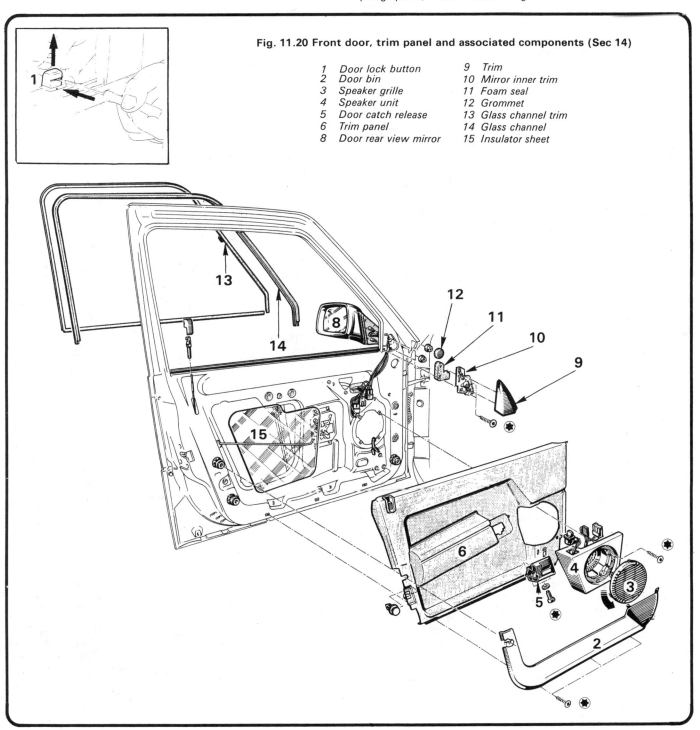

Fig. 11.20 Front door, trim panel and associated components (Sec 14)

1	Door lock button	9	Trim
2	Door bin	10	Mirror inner trim
3	Speaker grille	11	Foam seal
4	Speaker unit	12	Grommet
5	Door catch release	13	Glass channel trim
6	Trim panel	14	Glass channel
8	Door rear view mirror	15	Insulator sheet

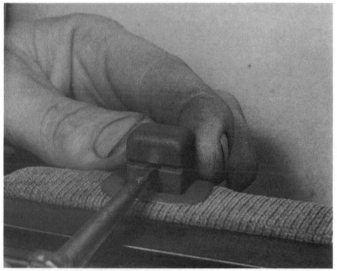

14.2 Door lock button removal

14.3 Door lower trim/bin retaining screws

14.4A Disconnect the door wiring connectors ...

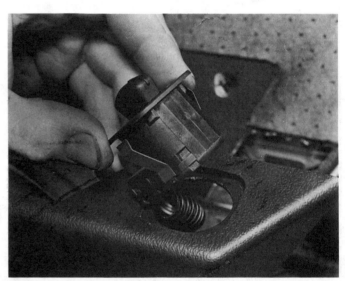

14.4B ... to remove the switches and speakers

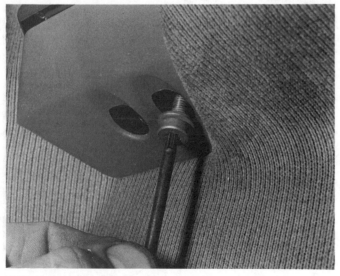

14.5A Undo the retaining screws ...

14.5B ... and detach the door catch release from the operating rod

14.6 Prise free the triangular trim panel

14.7 Removing a manual window regulator handle

14.8 Trim removal using a flat bladed tool with a forked end piece

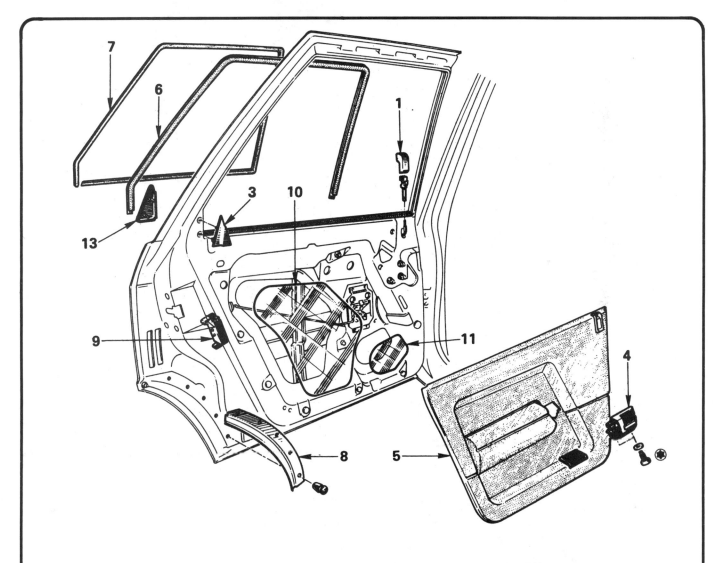
Fig. 11.21 Rear door, trim panel and associated components (Sec 14)

1	Lock button (inner)	5	Trim panel	8	Trim guard	11	Insulator sheet (small)
3	Triangular trim (inner)	6	Window channel	9	Window glass guide	13	Triangular trim (outer)
4	Door catch release handle	7	Channel trim	10	Insulator sheet (large)		

15 Doors – removal and refitting

1   Remove the trim panel and inner insulator sheet as described in Section 14, and disconnect the wiring from any retainers within the door. Withdraw the wiring harness from the door.
2   Release the door check strap by driving out the retaining pin with a drift (photo).
3   Support the door on blocks or with the help of an assistant.
4   Prise out the two caps covering each hinge pin, using a screwdriver.
5   Using a cranked metal rod suitable diameter as a drift, drive out the upper and lower hinge pins. Note that the hinge pins are removed towards each other, ie downwards for the lower pin.
6   With the hinge pins removed, carefully lift off the door.
7   Renew the hinge pins and bushes whenever the door is removed. Note that there are two hinge pin types available – see Fig. 11.22. Ensure that correct replacements are obtained.
8   Refitting is a reversal of the removal procedure.
9   If the door does not fit flush to the aperture, adjust by carefully bending the hinge arms using a suitable slotted lever bar. Ensure that the door wiring harness is correctly routed and secured – see Fig. 11.23 or 11.24 as applicable.

15.2 Door hinge and check strap

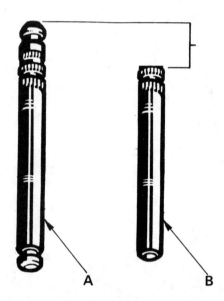

Fig. 11.22 Door hinge pin types (Sec 15)

A   Long pin   B   Short pin

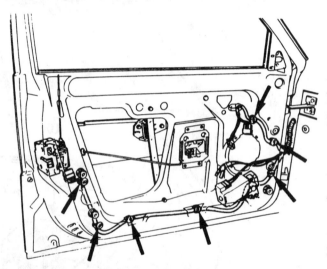

Fig. 11.23 Front door wiring harness routing and retaining clip locations (arrowed) (Sec 15)

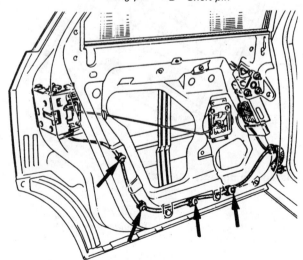

Fig. 11.24 Rear door wiring harness routing and retaining clip locations (Sec 15)

16 Door fittings – removal and refitting

1   Remove the door trim panel as described in Section 14.
2   With the door trim panel removed, the following items can be removed from the door as required. Unless otherwise stated, the refitting details are a reversal of the removal procedures.

Central door locking

3   The solenoids can be removed after disconnecting the lock link rods and wiring plugs. On models equipped with this system, door locking and unlocking is carried out by an infra red remote control device which is described in Chapter 12.

Exterior handle

4   The exterior handle is secured by a bolt accessible from within the door cavity. Undo the bolt, push the handle forward to release it from the door panel, then push the connecting link and clip down to release the upper end of the link from the door panel. The handle must be removed separately so that the clip is not damaged. Rotate the handle so that it is vertical, then disconnect the link.
5   If the link and its clips are separated, the amount by which the door handle opens will probably need adjustment. Refit the handle before clipping the link back in place.

Front door lock

6 Undo the two screws retaining the exterior handle, disconnect the link rod and remove the exterior handle.

7 Undo and remove the Torx screws securing the door lock, extract the rubber grommet, reach through the aperture and pull the lock towards the aperture. Detach the door catch release control rod from the lock, then withdraw the lock unit.

8 Refit in reverse order, ensuring that the connecting links are securely attached. Check the operation of the lock before refitting the trim panel.

Rear door lock

9 Remove the door window glass as described in paragraphs 16 to 19.

10 Unscrew the window guide rail screws to enable the link to pass between the winder rail and the door.

11 Detach the horizontal link rod from its retaining clip, remove the link retaining fork and push it into the door body.

12 Undo the three Torx retaining screws from the door lock unit, then withdraw the lock through the inner door aperture. As it is being removed, detach the control link.

13 Refit in reverse order, ensuring that the connecting links are securely attached.

Door window regulator

14 On models with manually-operated windows, undo the bolts securing the regulator mechanism and cable to the door (photo) and manipulate the regulator out of the door aperture.

15 On models with electrically-operated windows, disconnect the motor wiring connectors, undo the bolts securing the motor to the door, and the bolts securing the mechanism to the door.
Manipulate the assembly out of the door aperture (photo).

Window glass

16 With the glass fully down, pull off the inner glass weatherstrip. No clips are used to retain it.

17 Raise the glass fully and unscrew the two bolts from the glass bottom channel, accessible through the holes (photo).

18 Lower the mechanism (manual or power-operated), at the same time holding the glass in the raised position.

19 Swivel the glass and withdraw it towards the outside of the door.

20 If the glass is removed from its bottom channel, reset it in the channel in accordance with the dimension given in Fig. 11.32 or 11.33 as applicable.

21 When the glass is refitted, wind the glass up and down to check for smoothness of operation. If required, the bottom of the guides can be moved to centralise the glass.

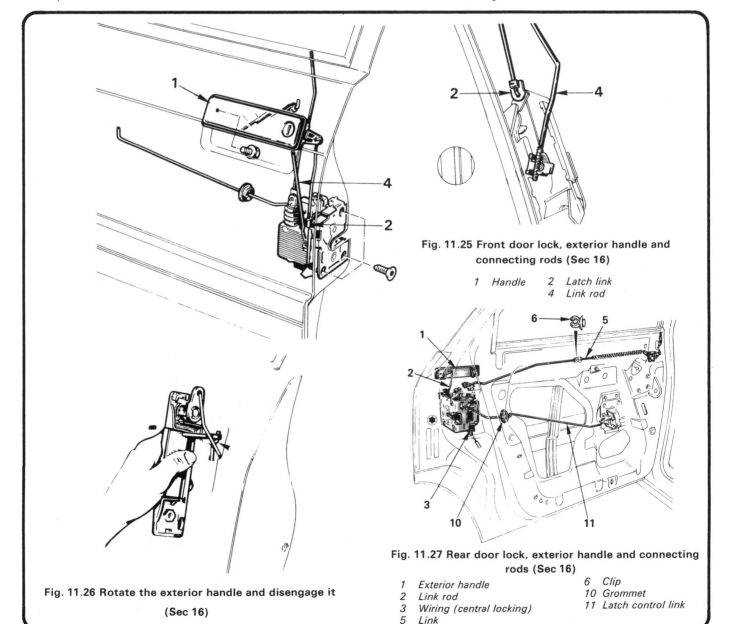

Fig. 11.25 Front door lock, exterior handle and connecting rods (Sec 16)

1	Handle	2	Latch link
		4	Link rod

Fig. 11.26 Rotate the exterior handle and disengage it

(Sec 16)

Fig. 11.27 Rear door lock, exterior handle and connecting rods (Sec 16)

1	Exterior handle	6	Clip
2	Link rod	10	Grommet
3	Wiring (central locking)	11	Latch control link
5	Link		

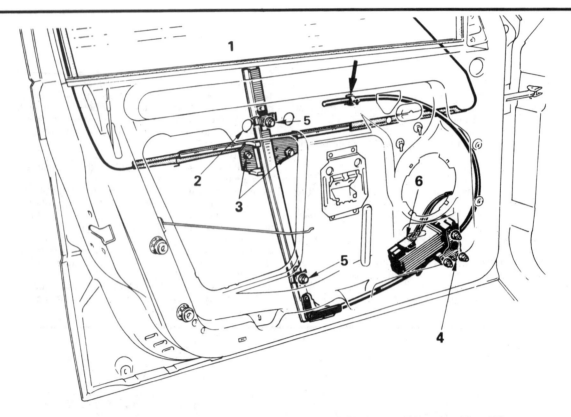

Fig. 11.28 Front door electric window regulator mechanism components (Sec 16)

1 Glass
2 Access holes (to glass fasteners)
3 Glass fasteners
4 Mechanism
5 Rail
6 Motor

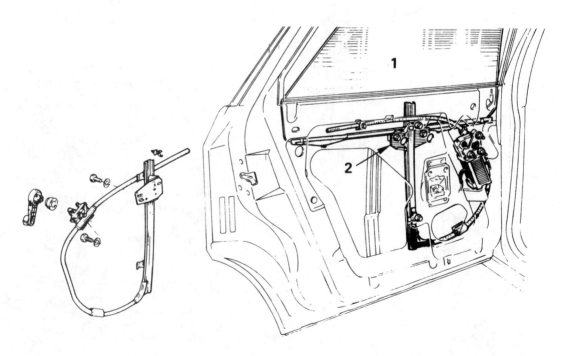

Fig. 11.29 Rear door window regulator mechanisms (electric type fitted) (Sec 16)

1 Glass
2 Access hole (for glass fasteners)

Fig. 11.30 Window glass (1) removal from front door
(Sec 16)

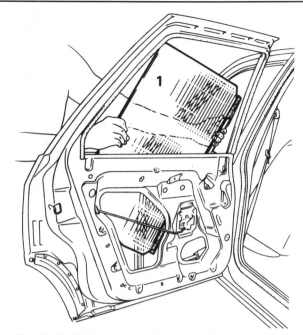

Fig. 11.31 Window glass (1) removal from rear door
(Sec 16)

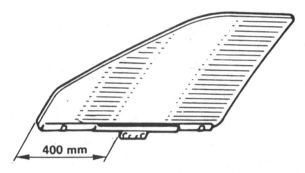

Fig. 11.32 Front door bottom channel-to-glass location
(Sec 16)

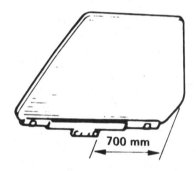

Fig. 11.33 Rear door bottom channel-to-glass location
(Sec 16)

16.14 Manual door window regulator
spindle and retaining bolt

16.15 Electric door window regulator
mechanism removal

16.17 Glass bottom channel bolt locations

17 Door rear-view mirror – removal and refitting

1 On models fitted with electric rear-view mirrors, disconnect the
battery earth lead, then remove the door speaker unit as described in
Chapter 12. Reach through the speaker aperture and disconnect the
wiring connector from the mirror.
2 Carefully prise free the plastic outer trim. Undo the mirror and

mirror adjuster retaining screws. Withdraw the adjuster unit and peel
back the insulation gasket (photos).
3 Extract the foam seal and on manual adjustment types, undo the
inner trim retaining screw. Undo the retaining nuts and remove the
mirror (photos).
4 Refit in the reverse order of removal. Check for satisfactory
operation on completion and adjust the mirror to suit.

17.2A Electric mirror adjuster and retaining screws

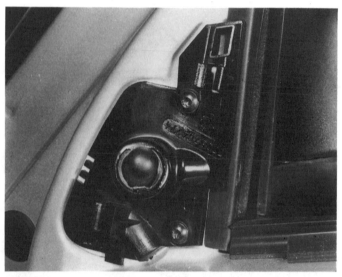

17.2B Manual mirror adjuster and retaining screws

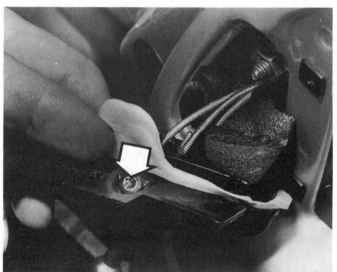

17.3A Manual mirror adjuster inner trim retaining screw (arrowed)

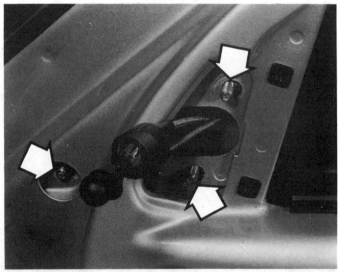

17.3B Manual mirror retaining studs (arrowed)

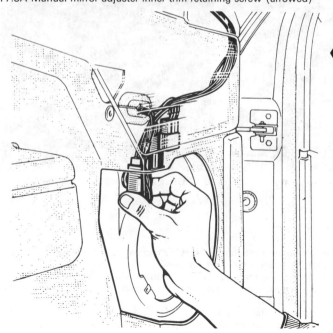

Fig. 11.34 Disconnecting the rear view mirror wing through the speaker aperture (Sec 17)

18 Boot lid – removal and refitting

1   Open the boot lid and mark the outline of the hinges using a soft pencil. Remove the plastic hinge cover for access where applicable (photo).

2   With the help of an assistant, undo the two bolts each side securing the boot lid to the hinge and carefully lift the boot lid away. As it is lifted clear, detach the number plate light and lock solenoid wiring connectors (where applicable).

3   Refitting is the reverse sequence to removal. Align the previously made outline marks or, if necessary, reposition the boot lid on each hinge to give a uniform gap all round.

4   To adjust the height of the boot lid, remove the trim panel for access, and reset the lock striker plate position to suit (photo).

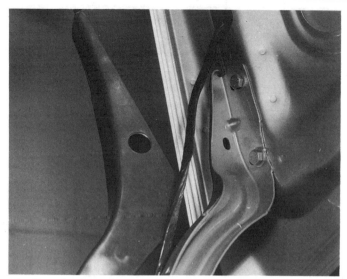

18.1 Boot lid hinge with plastic cover removed

18.4 Boot lid lock striker plate

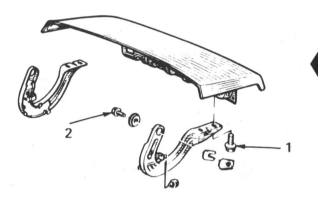

Fig. 11.35 Boot lid and hinges. Remove hinge bolts (1). Do not remove bolts (2) unless absolutely necessary (Sec 18)

19 Boot lid lock – removal and refitting

1   Open the boot lid and then remove the number plate and trim (photo).
2   Unclip and remove the lock unit connecting link, undo the retaining screws, then tilt the lock and remove it (photo).
3   To remove the lock barrel, drive out the retaining pin (1.5 mm diameter), then extract the barrel.
4   Where applicable, to remove the boot lid lock solenoid, detach the wiring and the connecting rod, then release and remove the solenoid unit (photo).
5   Refit in the reverse order of removal. Check for satisfactory operation on completion.

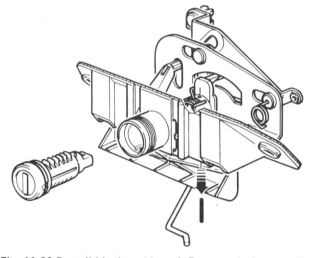

Fig. 11.36 Boot lid lock and barrel. Extract pin (arrowed) to remove barrel (Sec 19)

19.1 Boot lid lock shown with number plate and trim removed

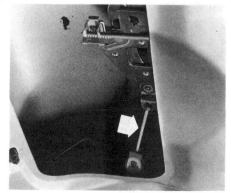

19.2 Boot lid lock connecting link (arrowed)

19.4 Boot lid lock solenoid removal

20 Tailgate support struts (Savanna models) – removal and refitting

1   Raise and support the tailgate, with the aid of an assistant if both struts are to be removed.
2   Using a screwdriver, carefully lever out the locking retainer at the strut ball end fitting (photo).
3   Withdraw the strut from the ball pegs and remove it from the car. **Do not** attempt to repair a defective strut, renew it.
4   Refitting is the reverse sequence to removal.

21 Tailgate (Savanna models) – removal and refitting

1   Remove the rear side trim panel from the luggage area for access to the rear window washer reservoir on the left-hand side.
2   Detach the tailgate wiring harness connectors and earth leads (photos).
3   Disconnect the rear window washer pipe from the reservoir allowing for a small amount of spillage. Plug the pipe and reservoir connector to prevent continuous fluid spillage whilst detached.
4   Tie the pipe tailgate wiring harness to a suitable length of strong cord, so that as the wiring and pipe are withdrawn through the rear corner panel, the cord follows and can be untied once clear of the rear panel and left in situ. The process can then be repeated in reverse order during refitting, the cord acting as a guide as it pulls the harness and pipe down through the corner panel.
5   Disconnect the support struts at the tailgate, as described in the previous Section.
6   Carefully prise free the headlining trim panel at the rear edge to gain access to the tailgate retaining nuts.
7   With the tailgate suitably supported, undo the retaining nuts and carefully remove the tailgate. Collect any adjustment shims from the hinges as they are withdrawn.
8   Refit in the reverse order or removal. Adjust the tailgate so that it is flush with the roof line using shims at the hinges.
9   If necessary, adjust the position of the tailgate striker as described in Section 22.

22 Tailgate lock and associated fittings (Savanna models) – removal, refitting and adjustment

1   Open the tailgate and remove the rear trim panel from it.
2   Undo the retaining screws from the lock unit, then disengage the control link from the lock to allow the lock to be withdrawn.
3   To remove the lock barrel, prise free the retaining clip, remove the control lever and withdraw the barrel.
Take care not to lose the barrel return spring which may eject as the barrel is removed.
4   To remove the number plate/light panel, disconnect the lock link and the latch control from the handle. Undo the four retaining nuts and remove the panel. Disconnect the light wires as it is withdrawn.
5   Refitting is a reversal of the removal procedure. If the barrel return

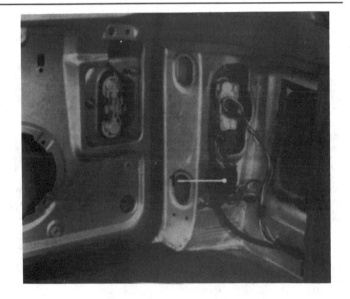

Fig. 11.37 Tailgate wiring harness connector location (1) behind rear side trim panel – Savanna models (Sec 21)

Fig. 11.38 Tailgate hinge retaining nuts are accessible on removing headlining trim panel (Sec 21)

20.2 Prising free a tailgate strut locking retainer

21.2A Tailgate heated rear window element connector

21.2B Tailgate wiring harness and rubber gaiter

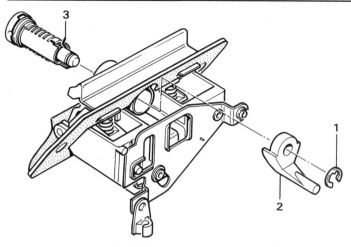

Fig. 11.39 Tailgate lock unit (Sec 22)

1   Retaining clip   3   Barrel and return spring
2   Control lever

spring was removed, refit it as shown in Fig. 11.39 prior to inserting the lock barrel. Check for satisfactory operation.
6   If required, adjust the striker plate by loosening off its retaining screws and adjusting it as required. Retighten the screws to complete.

23 Windscreen and fixed windows – removal and refitting

1   The removal and refitting of the windscreen and fixed windows (and the heated rear screen), are tasks which must be entrusted to a Renault dealer or a professional windscreen replacement specialist.
2   The glass is flush-mounted, and removal requires the use of a hot knife or wire to release the sealant plus the use of special bonding agents when refitting.

24 Centre console – removal and refitting

1   Disconnect the battery earth lead.
2   If fitted, remove the radio speaker unit as described in Chapter 12.
3   If fitted, lift out and remove the ashtray.
4   Unscrew and remove the console retaining screws.
5   Carefully prise free the gear lever gaiter from the console, pull it up and rotate it to allow it to pass over the gear lever. As the console is lifted clear, note any wiring connections to the console-mounted switches and/or the cigar lighter, and detach them.
6   Refit in the reverse order of removal.

25 Luggage area side trim panel – removal and refitting

1   Untwist and remove the side trim retaining clips, then withdraw the panel.
2   The left-hand side panel also retains the rear window washer reservoir and it is therefore necessary to detach the wire from the pump unit and the fluid supply hose (see Chapter 12).
3   To remove the reservoir from the panel, simply prise open the panel sides to release the reservoir.
4   Refit in the reverse order of removal.

24.2 Centre console, speaker grille and retaining screws

26 Facia panel – removal and refitting

1   Disconnect the battery earth lead.
2   Slide the front seats fully to the rear, or preferably unbolt and remove them to allow full access when removing the facia.
3   Remove the centre console as described in Section 24.
4   Undo the retaining screws from the positions indicated in Fig. 11.41 and remove the lower facia panels on the driver's side.
5   Remove the steering wheel and column as described in Chapter 10.
6   Remove the tweeter speaker from the facia on each side. To do this, prise free the small cover between the grilles, undo the retaining screw,

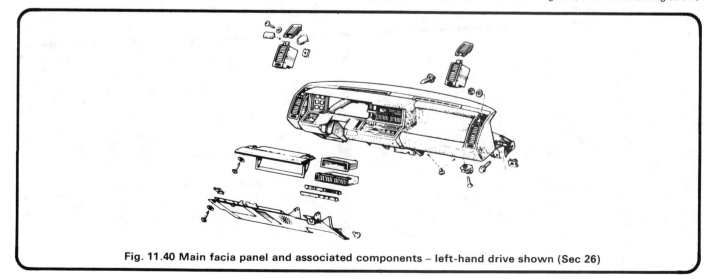

Fig. 11.40 Main facia panel and associated components – left-hand drive shown (Sec 26)

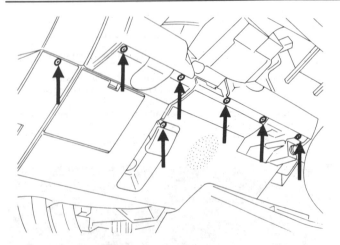

**Fig. 11.41 Remove the lower facia panel retaining screws –
left-hand drive shown (Sec 26)**

then withdraw the speaker and disconnect the wire. Repeat the
procedure and remove the speaker unit on the other side.

7   Remove the glovebox by releasing the retaining clip at the side of
each pivot whilst simultaneously lifting and withdrawing the glovebox
unit.

8   Detach and prise free the inner sill trim panel on each side. These
panels are a press fit into securing clips which also retain the wiring
harnesses each side. Disconnect the harnesses at their block
connectors and also unbolt the earth wires on the left-hand side.

9   Undo the facia retaining nut on each side from the positions shown
(photo).

10 Where applicable, disconnect and remove the manual choke
control (see Chapter 3).

11 Disconnect the heater control panel (see Chapter 3).

12 Remove the three facia-to-heater unit mounting screws.

13 The facia unit is now ready to be withdrawn. An assistant will be
required to help in supporting the weight of the unit and in guiding it
clear. As it is withdrawn, disconnect the relevant wiring connectors
from the rear face of the facia panel. Note the routeing of the wiring
harnesses and the radio antenna as they are disconnected to ensure
that they are correctly located when reassembling.

14 Refitting is a reversal of the removal procedure. Engage the facia
onto the centring peg and reconnect the wiring connectors, antenna
lead and speedometer cable as the unit is relocated (photo).

27 Seats – removal and refitting

Front seats

1   Move the seat to be removed fully forward, then undo the seat rail
retaining bolts at the rear. Now slide the seat fully to the rear and undo
the front rail retaining bolts (photos). Remove the seat.

2   Refit in the reverse order of removal.

Rear seat – saloon

3   Grip the seat retaining clip with a pair of pliers and withdraw it from
its location in the seat pivot. Remove the seat.

4   Refit in the reverse order of removal.

Rear 'intermediate' seat – Savanna

5   Tilt the seat forwards, unclip the gas support strut by prising free
the balljoint retaining clip and detach the strut.
Do not try to remove the clip from the balljoint.

6   Working from the inboard side of the seat, press down and remove
the retaining clip using a screwdriver as shown in Fig. 11.43, or pivot
down the trim cover and undo the hinge retaining bolts (photo).

7   Refit in the reverse order of removal.

26.9 Facia retaining nut – left-hand side viewed through tweeter
speaker aperture

26.14 Facia panel centring peg (arrowed)

27.1A Seat rail rear retaining bolts (arrowed) ...

27.1B ... and front retaining bolt

Rear 'occasional' seat – Savanna
8 Undo the seat hinge bolts, fold the seat down and remove it.
9 Refit in the reverse order of removal.

28 Headrests

The headrests are adjustable for height simply by moving them up and down.
2 To remove them, twist the bevelled plinth at the base of the right-hand headrest stem while pulling the headrest upwards.

29 Seat belts – maintenance, removal and refitting

1 Periodically inspect the seat belts for fraying or other damage. If evident, renew the belt.
2 The belts may be cleaned using warm water and liquid detergent. Do not use solvents of any kind.

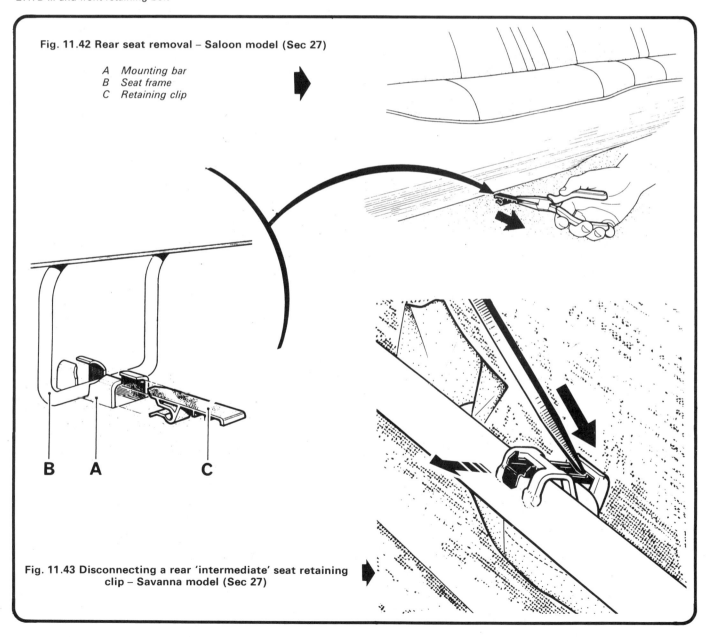

Fig. 11.42 Rear seat removal – Saloon model (Sec 27)

A Mounting bar
B Seat frame
C Retaining clip

B A C

Fig. 11.43 Disconnecting a rear 'intermediate' seat retaining clip – Savanna model (Sec 27)

27.6 Rear 'intermediate' seat hinge trim cover removed – Savanna model

29.5 Rear seat belt anchor bolt – Savanna model

3   If the car is involved in a front end collision and the belts have restrained the front or rear seat occupants, renew the belts.
4   When refitting, always maintain the original fitted sequence of washers and spacers.
5   The rear seat belt lower anchor bolts are accessible after removing the seat back (photo). The upper anchor bolts can be reached after removing the trim panel (Section 25).
6   On some models, a buzzer warning system is fitted with a timer relay to prevent driving off with the seat belts unfastened.

Chapter 12 Electrical system

Contents

Specifications

General
System type .... 12 volt, negative earth
Battery type .... Low maintenance or 'maintenance-free' sealed for life
Battery capacity .... 50 or 60 amp hr

Alternator
Make .... Paris-Rhône or Ducellier
Type:
    Paris-Rhône (models without air conditioning) .... A13N87, A13N88, A13N120 or A13N124
    Paris-Rhône (air conditioned models only) .... A14N73 or A14N76
    Ducellier 516067
    Maximum output .... 60 or 105* amps
    *air conditioned models only

Starter motor
Make/type number .... Paris-Rhône D9E85, D9E771, D10E88 or D10E92

Bulbs (typical)

	Wattage
Headlamp	60/55
Front foglamp	55
Front sidelight	4
Direction indicators	21
Stop/tail	21/5
Reversing lamp	21
Rear foglamp	21
Rear number plate lamp	5
Interior lamps	10
Switch and panel illumination	1.2 or 2
Warning lamps	1.2 or 2

Fuses

Fuse Number	Application	Rating (amps)
1	Heating (and rear window wiper/washer on Savanna model) ..	20
2	Engine cooling fan, radio	10
3	Heated rear window	20
4	Clock and interior lights. Also radio*, electronic instrument panel (before ignition)	5
5	Windscreen wiper/park timer*	10
6	Flasher unit and hazard warning lights (Savanna and Turbo) ...	10
7	Side and tail lamps (left-hand side) and front foglamps*	5
8	Side and tail lamps (right-hand side)	5
9	Cigar lighter	10
10	Stop lamps	10
11	Instrument panel, reversing lamp*	10
12	Windscreen wiper	15
13	Rear foglamp	7.5
14	Not used	—
15	Air conditioning*	30
16	Electric door locks*, electric rear view mirrors*	25
17	Window winder (left-hand side)*	30
18	Window winder (right-hand side)*, sunroof*	30
19	Anti-lock brakes*	3

Fitting depends on model and territory

---

1 General description

The electrical system is of the 12 volt negative earth type, and consists of a battery, alternator, starter motor and related electrical accessories, components and wiring.

The battery, charged by the alternator which is belt-driven from the crankshaft pulley, provides a steady amount of current for the ignition, starting, lighting and other electrical circuits. The battery may be a low maintenance type of a maintenance-free 'sealed for life' type, according to model.

The starter motor is of the pre-engaged type incorporating an integral solenoid. On starting, the solenoid moves the drive pinion into engagement with the flywheel ring gear before the starter motor is energised. Once the engine has started, a one-way clutch prevents the motor armature being driven by the engine until the pinion disengages from the flywheel.

Further details of the major electrical systems are given in the relevant Sections of this Chapter.

Caution: *Before carrying out any work on the vehicle electrical system, read through the precautions given in 'Safety First!' at the beginning of this manual and in Section 2 of this Chapter.*

---

2 Electrical system – precautions

It is necessary to take extra care when working on the electrical system to avoid damage to semiconductor devices (diodes and transistors), and to avoid the risk of personal injury. In addition to the precautions given in *'Safety First'* at the beginning of this manual, observe the following items when working on the system.

1 *Always remove rings, watches, etc before working on the electrical system.* Even with the battery disconnected, capacitive discharge could occur if a component live terminal is earthed through a metal object. This could cause a shock or nasty burn.

2 *Do not reverse the battery connections.* Components such as the alternator or any other having semiconductor circuitry could be irreparably damaged.

3 If the engine is being started using jump leads and a slave battery, connect the batteries *positive to positive* and *negative to negative*. This also applies when connecting a battery charger.

4 Never disconnect the battery terminals, or alternator wiring when the engine is running.

5 The battery leads and alternator wiring must be disconnected before carrying out any electric welding on the car.

6 Never use an ohmmeter of the type incorporating a hand cranked generator for circuit or continuity testing.

7 If an electronic instrument panel is fitted, refer to the precautionary notes given at the start of Section 24.

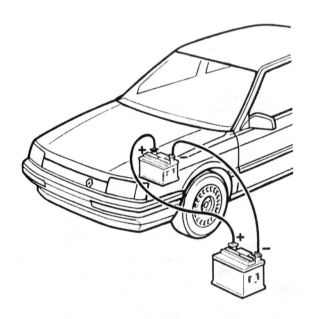

Fig. 12.1 Battery lead connections when using a slave battery (Sec 2)

---

3 Maintenance

1 At the intervals given in *'Routine maintenance'* the following service operations should be carried out on the electrical system components:

2 Check the operation of all the electrical equipment, ie wipers, washers, lights, direction indicators, horn etc. Refer to the appropriate Sections of this Chapter if any components are found to be inoperative.

3 Visually check all accessible wiring connectors, harnesses and retaining clips for security, or any signs of chafing or damage. Rectify any problems encountered.

4 Check the alternator drivebelt for cracks, fraying or damage. Renew the belt if worn or, if satisfactory, check and adjust the belt tension. These procedures are covered in Chapter 2.

5 Check the condition of the wiper blades and if they are cracked or show signs of deterioration, renew them, as described in Section 28. Check the operation of the windscreen, tailgate and headlamp washers, as applicable, and adjust the nozzle setting if necessary.

6 Top up the battery, on models where this is necessary, using distilled water until the tops of the cell plates are just submerged. Clean

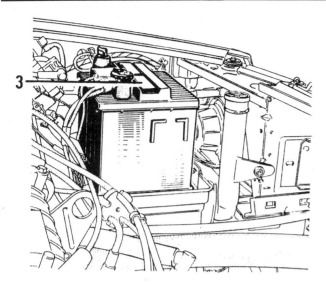

Fig. 12.2 Remove battery cell covers (3) to top up electrolyte level (low maintenance type battery) (Sec 3)

the battery terminals and case and, if necessary, check the battery condition using the procedures described in Section 4.

7   Top up the washer fluid reservoir and check the security of the pump wires and water pipes.

8   It is advisable to have the headlamp aim adjusted using optical beam setting equipment.

9   While carrying out a road test, check the operation of all the instruments and warning lights and the operation of the direction indicator self-cancelling mechanism.

4   Battery – general

1   According to model the battery may be of the low maintenance type in which the cell covers may be removed to allow periodic topping-up in the conventional way, or of the maintenance-free type which do not require topping up. The maintenance-free battery has a sealed top cover which must not under any circumstances be removed. If the seals are broken the battery warranty will be invalidated.

2   On low maintenance batteries, periodically lift off the cover and check the electrolyte level. The tops of the cell plates should be just covered by the electrolyte. If not, add distilled or demineralized water until they are. Do not add extra water with the idea of reducing the intervals of topping-up. This will merely dilute the electrolyte and reduce charging and current retention efficiency.

3   If the electrolyte level needs an excessive amount of replenishment but no leaks are apparent, it could be due to overcharging as a result of the battery having been run down and then left to recharge from the vehicle rather than from an outside source. If the battery has been heavily discharged for one reason or another it is best to have it continuously charged at a low amperage for a period of many hours. If it is charged from the car's system under such conditions, the charging will be intermittent and greatly varied in intensity. This does not do the battery any good at all. If the battery needs topping-up frequently, even when it is known to be in good condition and not too old, then the voltage regulator should be checked to ensure that the charging output is being correctly controlled. An elderly battery, however, may need topping-up more than a new one, because it needs to take in more charging current. Do not worry about this, provided it gives satisfactory service.

4   Keep the battery clean and dry all over by wiping it with a dry cloth. A dirty or damp top surface could cause tracking between the two terminal posts with consequent draining of power.

5   Periodically remove the battery and check the support tray clamp and battery terminal connections for signs of corrosion – usually indicated by a whitish green crystalline deposit. Wash this off with clean water to which a little ammonia or washing soda has been

added. Then treat the terminals with petroleum jelly and the battery mounting with suitable protective paint to prevent further corrosive action.

6   On maintenance-free batteries access to the cells is not possible and only the overall condition of the battery can be checked using a voltmeter connected across the two terminals. On the low maintenance type a hydrometer can be used to check the condition of each individual cell. The table in the following Section gives the hydrometer readings for the various states of charge. A further check can be made when the battery is undergoing a charge. If, towards the end of the charge, when the cells should be 'gassing' (bubbling), one cell appears not to be, this indicates the cell or cells in question are probably breaking down and the life of the battery is limited.

5   Battery – charging

1   In winter when a heavy demand is placed on the battery, such as when starting from cold and using more electrical equipment, it may be necessary to have the battery fully charged from an external source. *Note that both battery leads must be disconnected before charging in order to prevent possible damage to any semiconductor electrical components.*

2   The terminals of the battery and the leads of the charger must be connected *positive to positive* and *negative to negative*.

3   Charging is best done overnight at a 'trickle' rate of 1 to 1.5 amps. Alternatively, on low maintenance batteries, a 3 to 4 amp rate can be used over a period of 4 hours or so. Check the specific gravity in the latter case and stop the charge when the reading is correct. Maintenance-free batteries should not be charged in this way due to their design and construction. It is strongly recommended that you seek the advice of a Renault dealer on the suitability of various types of charging equipment before using them on maintenance-free batteries.

4   The specific gravities for hydrometer readings on low maintenance batteries are as follows:

Fully discharged	Electrolyte temperature	Fully charged
1.098	38°C (100°F)	1.268
1.102	32°C (90°F)	1.272
1.106	27°C (80°F)	1.276
1.110	21°C (70°C)	1.280
1.114	16°C (60°F)	1.284
1.118	10°C (50°F)	1.288
1.122	4°C (40°F)	1.292
1.126	−1.5°C (30°F)	1.296

6   Battery – removal and refitting

1   The battery is located in the engine compartment on the front right or left-hand corner, depending on model.

2   Open the bonnet and disconnect the battery negative (–) lead then the positive(+) lead in that order.

3   Unbolt the clamp from the lip at the base of the battery casing and lift the battery from its mounting platform (photo).

4   Refit by reversing the removal operations, connect the positive (+) lead and the negative (–) lead in that order.

5   On Renault original equipment batteries, the battery can be quickly disconnected simply by unscrewing the negative terminal thumbscrew through a few turns. There is no need to disconnect the cable from the battery terminal.

7   Alternator – precautions and maintenance

1   The alternator can be damaged if the following precautions are not observed.

2   Never connect the battery leads incorrectly.

3   Never run the engine with the alternator leads disconnected.

4   Do not pull off a battery lead as a means of stopping the engine.

5   When charging the battery from the mains, disconnect it from the car's electrical system or remove it.

6   When using electric welding equipment on the car, always

6.3 Battery retaining clamp and securing bolt – 1.7 litre model

disconnect both battery leads and the alternator leads.
7   Do not operate the starter motor if the engine earth lead is not connected.
8   Regularly inspect the condition of the alternator drivebelt and if frayed or cut, renew it, as described in Chapter 2.
9   The alternator has an integral voltage regulator.

8   Alternator – fault tracing and rectification

1   If the ignition warning lamp fails to illuminate when the ignition is switched on, first check the wiring connections at the rear of the alternator for security. If satisfactory, check that the warning lamp bulb has not blown and is secure in its holder. If the lamp still fails to illuminate check the continuity of the warning lamp feed wire from the alternator to the bulb holder. If all is satisfactory, the alternator is at fault and should be renewed or taken to an automobile electrician for testing and repair.
2   If the ignition warning lamp illuminates when the engine is running, ensure that the drivebelt is correctly tensioned (see Chapter 2), and that the connections on the rear of the alternator are secure. If all is so far satisfactory, check the alternator brushes and commutator, as described in Section 10. If the fault still persists, the alternator should be renewed, or taken to an automobile electrician for testing and repair.
3   If the alternator output is suspect even though the warning lamp functions correctly, the regulated voltage may be checked as follows:
4   Connect a voltmeter across the battery terminals and then start the engine.
5   Increase the engine speed until the reading on the voltmeter remains steady. This should be between 13.5 and 15 volts.
6   Switch on as many electrical accessories as possible and check that the alternator maintains the regulated voltage at between 13.5 and 15 volts.
7   If the regulated voltage is not as stated, the fault may be due to a faulty diode, a severed phase or worn brushes, springs or commutator. The brushes and commutator may be attended to, as described in Section 10, but if the fault still persists the alternator should be renewed, or taken to an automobile electrician for testing and repair.

9   Alternator – removal and refitting

1   Disconnect the battery earth lead.
2   On 2.0 litre models, access to the alternator is not good, but can be improved by raising the car at the front and removing the engine undershield to gain access from underneath, or by removing the radiator (see Chapter 2). If the former method is used, ensure that the vehicle is securely supported on axle stands.

3   Disconnect the leads from the terminals on the rear cover of the alternator (photos).
4   Remove the drivebelt as described in Chapter 2.
5   Unscrew and remove the mounting and adjuster link bolts and lift the alternator from its mounting bracket (photos).
6   Refit by reversing the removal operations.
7   Tension the drivebelt as described in Chapter 2.
8   On 2.0 litre models, refit the radiator and top up the cooling system (Chapter 2) and/or refit the undershield as applicable.

Fig. 12.3 Front view of alternator installation on 1.7 litre engine (Sec 9)

A   Belt tensioner   C   Adjuster bolt locking
B   Alternator mounting/pivot
    bolt

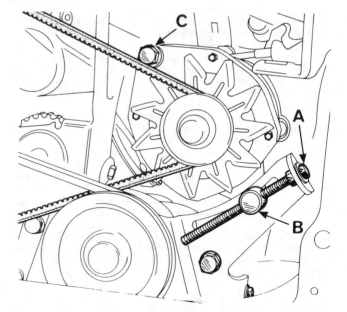

Fig. 12.4 Front view of alternator installation on 2.0 litre engine (Sec 9)

A   Belt tensioner adjuster bolt   C   Alternator mounting/pivot
B   Belt tensioner   bolt

9.3A Remove the rubber cover ...

9.3B ... and disconnect the leads from the rear of the alternator – 1.7 litre model

9.3C Detaching the alternator lead cover – 2.0 litre model

9.5A Alternator and adjuster/mounting bolts – 1.7 litre model

9.5B Alternator and adjuster/mounting bolts – 2.0 litre model

10 Alternator brushes – removal, inspection and refitting

Note: *Due to the specialist knowledge and equipment required to test and repair an alternator accurately, it is recommended that, if the performance is suspect, the alternator be taken to an automobile electrician who will have the facilities for such work. It is, however, a relatively simple task to attend to the brush gear and this operation is described below.*

1   On 1.7 litre engine models, brush removal can be carried out without removing the alternator from the engine, but in this instance the battery negative lead must first be disconnected, followed by the wiring connections to the alternator.
2   Remove the rear plastic cover.
3   Undo the two small bolts or nuts securing the regulator and brush box assembly to the rear of the alternator. Lift off the regulator and brush box, disconnect the electrical leads, noting their locations, then remove the regulator and brush box assembly from the alternator (photo).
4   Check that the brushes stand proud of their holders and are free to move without sticking (photo). If necessary clean them with a petrol-moistened cloth. Check that the brush spring pressure is equal for both brushes and gives reasonable tension. If in doubt about the condition of the brushes and springs compare them with new parts at a Renault parts dealer.
5   Clean the commutator with a petrol-moistened cloth, then check for signs of scoring, burning or severe pitting. If evident the commutator should be attended to by an automobile electrician.
6   Refitting the regulator and brush box assembly is the reverse sequence to removal.

10.3 Alternator regulator and brush box assembly removal

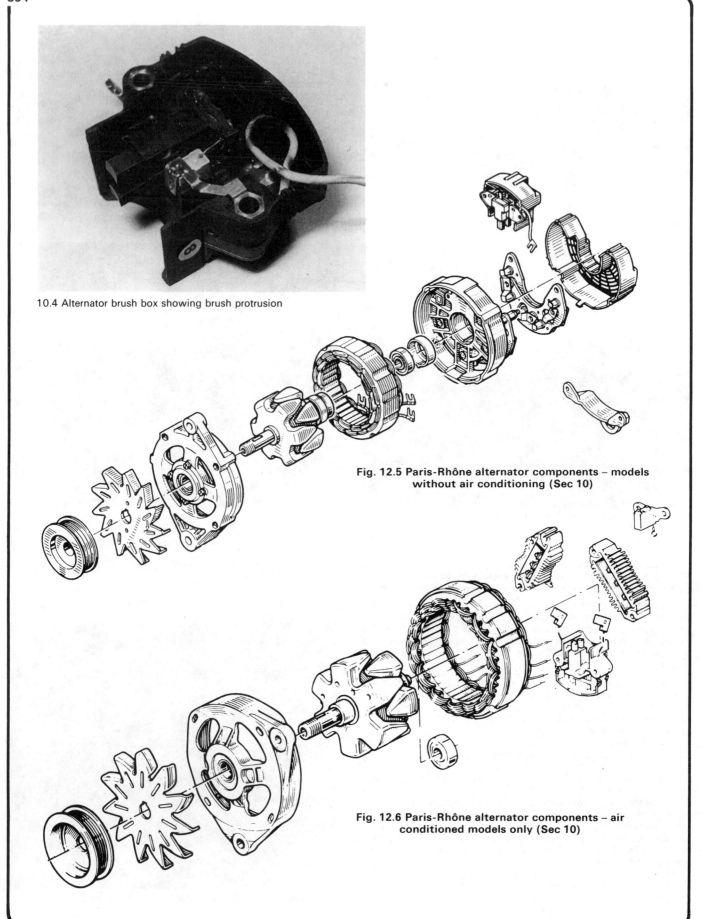

10.4 Alternator brush box showing brush protrusion

Fig. 12.5 Paris-Rhône alternator components – models without air conditioning (Sec 10)

Fig. 12.6 Paris-Rhône alternator components – air conditioned models only (Sec 10)

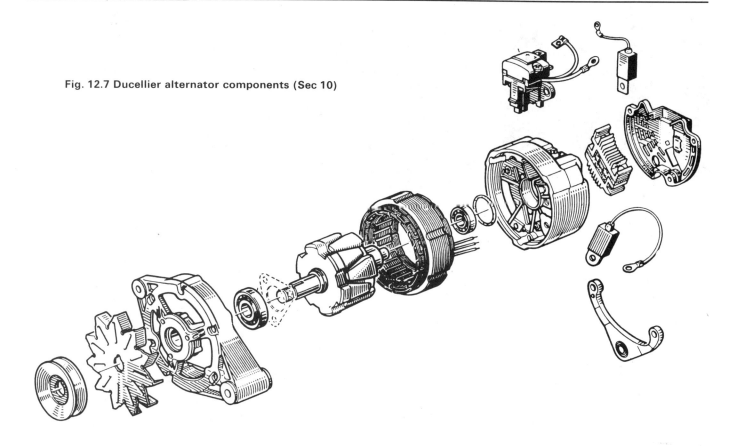

Fig. 12.7 Ducellier alternator components (Sec 10)

11 Starter motor – testing in the car

1   If the starter motor fails to operate, first check the condition of the battery by switching on the headlamps. If they glow brightly then gradually dim after a few seconds, the battery is in an uncharged condition.

2   If the battery is satisfactory, check the starter motor main terminal and the engine earth cable for security. Check the terminal connections on the starter solenoid, located on top of the starter motor.

3   Access to the starter motor and the wiring connections is poor on all models; refer to Section 12 for details.

4   If the starter still fails to turn, use a voltmeter, or 12 volt test lamp and leads, to ensure that there is battery voltage at the solenoid main terminal (containing the cable from the battery positive terminal).

5   With the ignition switched on and the ignition key in position D, check that voltage is reaching the solenoid terminal with the spade connector, and also the starter main terminal.

6   If there is no voltage reaching the spade connector, there is a wiring or ignition switch faulty. If voltage is available, but the starter does not operate, then the starter or solenoid is likely to be at fault.

12 Starter motor – removal and refitting

1   Disconnect the battery earth lead.

2   Access to the starter motor is poor on both the 1.7 and 2.0 litre models. In each case, access is best achieved from underneath, so raise and support the vehicle at the front on axle stands.

3   On 1.7 litre models, unbolt and disconnect the exhaust downpipe, and unbolt and remove the starter motor heat shield (photo).

4   On 2.0 litre models, detach and remove the engine undershield.

5   The procedure is now similar for both engine types.

6   Disconnect the electrical leads at the starter motor, noting their respective locations (photo).

7   Unscrew and remove the bolts securing the starter motor to the

clutch housing, and also the rear support bracket bolts (photo). Withdraw the starter motor.

8   Note the position of the locating dowel in the upper rear bellhousing bolt hole and make sure that it is in place when refitting (photo).

9   Refitting the starter motor is the reverse sequence to removal, but on 2.0 litre models, tighten the bellhousing bolts before the support bracket bolts.

12.3 Starter motor with heat shield (exhaust downpipe removed) – 1.7 litre model

12.6 Starter motor and lead connections (arrowed) – 2.0 litre model

12.7 Starter motor rear support bracket – 1.7 litre model

12.8 Refitting the starter motor – 1.7 litre model. Ensure that dowel (arrowed) is fitted to bellhousing

13 Starter motor – overhaul

Note: *Overhaul of the starter motor is normally confined to inspection and, if necessary, renewal of the brush gear components. Due to the limited availability of replacement parts, any other faults occurring on the starter usually result in renewal of the complete motor. However, for those wishing to dismantle the starter motor, this Section may be used as a guide. The procedure is essentially similar for all motor types and any minor differences can be noted by referring to the accompanying illustrations.*

1 Remove the starter motor from the car, as described in the previous Section.

2 Undo the two nuts and remove the mounting support bracket from the rear of the motor.

3 Undo the nut and disconnect the lead from the solenoid terminal (photo).

4 Where fitted, remove the cap plate on the rear cover and the bolt and washers between rear cover and armature.

5 Tap out the engine lever pivot pin from the drive end housing.

6 Undo the nuts securing the solenoid to the drive end housing.

7 Undo the through-bolts and withdraw the yoke, armature, solenoid and engaging lever as an assembly from the drive end housing.

8 Withdraw the solenoid and engaging lever, remove the rear cover with brushes, then slide the armature out of the yoke.

9 Slip the brushes out of their brush holders to release the rear cover.

10 If the pinion/clutch assembly is to be removed, drive the stop collar up the armature shaft and extract the circlip. Slide the stop collar and pinion clutch assembly off the armature (photo).

11 With the starter motor now completely dismantled, clean all the components with paraffin or a suitable solvent and wipe dry.

12 Check that all the brushes protrude uniformly from their holders and that the springs all provide moderate tension. Check that the brushes move freely in their holders and clean them with a petrol-moistened rag if there is any tendency to stick. If in doubt about the brush length or condition, compare them with new components and renew if necessary. Note that new field brushes must be soldered to their leads.

13 Check the armature shaft for distortion and the commutator for excessive wear, scoring or burrs. If necessary, the commutator may be lightly skimmed in a lathe and then polished with fine glass paper.

14 Check the pinion/clutch assembly, drive end housing, engaging lever and solenoid for wear or damage. Make sure that the clutch permits movement in one direction only and renew the unit if necessary.

15 Accurate checking of the armature, commutator and field coil windings and insulation requires the use of special test equipment. If the starter motor was inoperative when removed from the car and the previous checks have not highlighted the problem, then it can be assumed that there is a continuity of insulation fault and the unit should be renewed.

16 If the starter is in a satisfactory condition, or if a fault has been traced and rectified, the unit can be reassembled using the reverse of the dismantling procedure.

13.2A Starter motor and mounting support bracket – 1.7 litre model

13.2B Starter motor mounting support bracket – 2.0 litre model

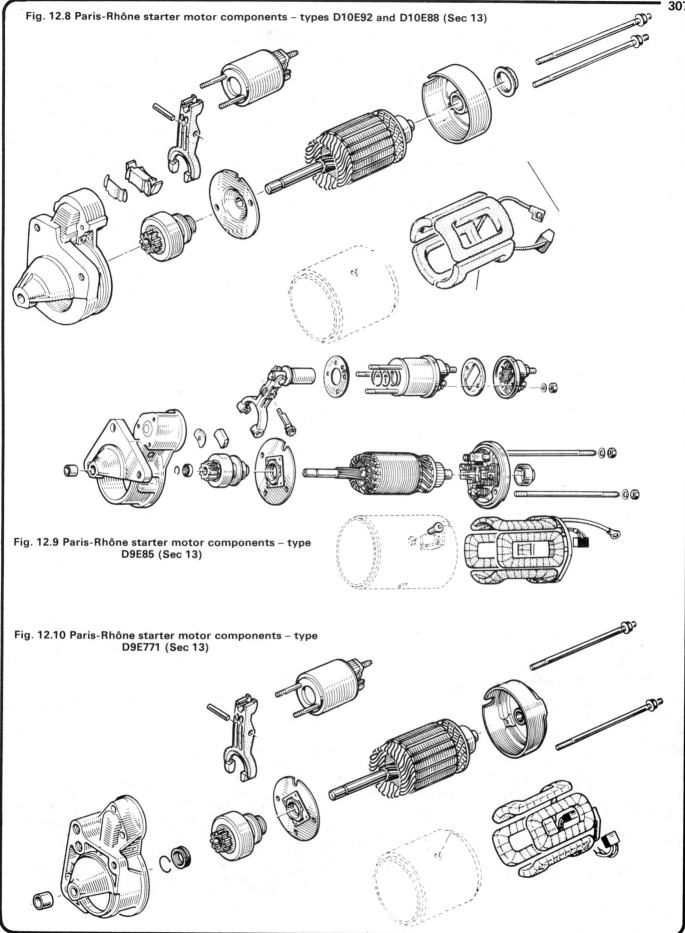

Fig. 12.8 Paris-Rhône starter motor components – types D10E92 and D10E88 (Sec 13)

Fig. 12.9 Paris-Rhône starter motor components – type D9E85 (Sec 13)

Fig. 12.10 Paris-Rhône starter motor components – type D9E771 (Sec 13)

13.3 Solenoid and wiring terminals on starter motor – 2.0 litre model

13.10 Starter motor pinion drive – 1.7 litre model

14 Fuses and relays – general

Fuses

1   The main fuse box unit is located in a hinged panel mounted on the lower facia trim panel. Press the two retainers to allow the fuse panel unit to pivot outwards (photo).

2   To remove a fuse from its location simply lift it upwards and out. The wire within the fuse is clearly visible and it will be broken if the fuse is blown.

3   Always renew a fuse with one of an identical rating. Never renew a fuse more than once without tracing the source of the trouble. The fuse rating is stamped on top of the fuse and spare fuses are located in a holder within the cover.

4   If a fuse continues to blow, the fault in the circuit(s) that it covers must be traced and rectified without delay. Refer to the Specifications at the start of this Chapter for the fuse numbers, their ratings and circuits covered.

Relays

5   The main relay block is located on a plate behind the lower facia panel. Disconnect the battery earth lead, then remove the panel for access to the relays (photos).

6   Further relays are located in the engine compartment on some models, the most notable being the ABS relay assembly on Turbo models. These relays are housed behind the ignition module unit on the bulkhead and access is gained after removing the housing top cover (photo).

7   The various relays can be removed from their respective locations by carefully pulling them upwards and out.

8   If a system controlled by a relay becomes inoperative and the relay is suspect, operate the system and if the relay is functioning it should be possible to hear it click as it is energized. If this is the case the fault lies with the components or wiring of the system. If the relay is not being energized then the relay is not receiving a main supply voltage or a switching voltage, or the relay itself is faulty.

9   To remove the main relay plate unit, undo the retaining screws and remove it from the dowels.

14.1 Fuse box assembly. Note spare fuses on left together with fuse remover

14.5A The main relays ...

14.5B ... and the front foglamp relay

14.6 ABS relays location – Turbo model

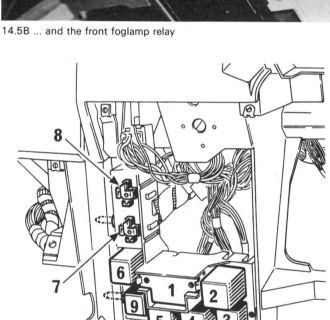

Fig. 12.11 Relay units and identification (Sec 14)

1	Windscreen wiper timer	6	Front foglight relay
2	Door lock timer	7	Rear foglight (shunt)
3	Heated rear window	8	Front foglight (shunt)
4	Lights on reminder buzzer	9	Headlight relay (where
5	Flasher unit		applicable)

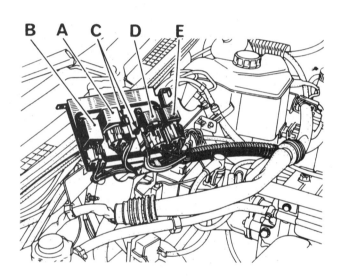

Fig. 12.12 ABS system relays and associated fittings in engine compartment (Sec 14)

A	Main relay	D	Diodes (in red based case)
B	Auxiliary relay	E	Pump relay
C	Protective fuses (30 amps)		

15 Direction indicator and hazard flasher system – general

1   The flasher unit is located on the accessory plate situated behind the fuse panel – see previous Section.
2   Should the flashers become faulty in operation, check the bulbs for security and make sure that the contact surfaces are not corroded. If one bulb blows or is making a poor connection due to corrosion, the system will not flash on that side of the car.
3   If the flasher unit operates in one direction and not the other, the fault is likely to be in the bulbs, or wiring to the bulbs. If the system will not flash in either direction, operate the hazard flashers. If these function, check the appropriate fuse and renew it if blown. If the fuse is satisfactory, renew the flasher unit.

16 Steering column switches – removal and refitting

1   Disconnect the battery earth lead.
2   Unscrew and remove the column shroud retaining screws from their recessed locations in the lower shroud. The screws are of Torx type. Remove the upper and lower shrouds.
3   Where fitted, the remote radio volume control can be removed from the end of the wiper switch by simply lifting it clear and detaching its cable.
4   To remove the ignition switch, refer to Chapter 10.
5   Withdraw the ignition switch cover.
6   Undo the switch retaining screws from the switch concerned and withdraw the switch. Detach its wire connector to remove it (photo).
7   Refit in the reverse order of removal. Check the operation of the switches and their various functions to complete.

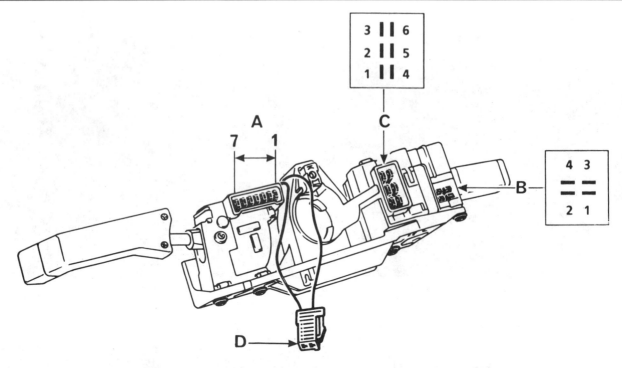

Fig. 12.13 Steering column switches and wiring terminals (Sec 16)

A   Windscreen wiper connector

| 1 | Timed input | 3 | Fast speed | 5 | Park/timer | 7 | Windscreen washer |
| 2 | + feed after ignition | 4 | Slow speed | 6 | + feed after ignition | | |

B   Lighting connector

| 1 | Headlamp main beam | 3 | + feed before ignition |
| 2 | Headlamp dipped beam | 4 | Side and tail lamps |

C   Direction indicators and horn connector

1	Horn	4	Right-hand indicator
2	Rear foglamp (if applicable)	5	Flasher
3	Horn feed + before ignition	6	Left-hand indicator

D   Trip computer switch

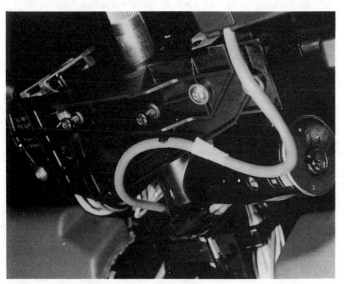

16.6 Underside view of the column switches and retaining screws

17 Switches (general) – removal and refitting

1   Disconnect the battery earth lead before disconnecting or removing a switch.

2   In most instances the switches and switch panels are held in position by plastic anchor tabs. If possible, reach behind the switch assembly and compress the tabs before prising the switch or plate from its location.

3   Withdraw the switch until the connecting plug can be disconnected (photo).

4   The interior and luggage area courtesy light switches are removed in a similar manner, but the door courtesy lamp switch has a rubber cover which must be prised free from the support panel to allow the switch to be withdrawn and disconnected (photo).

5   Refit in the reverse order of removal.

18 Timing relays – general

1   Timing relays are fitted to control the duration of operation of the following:

   Windsreen wiper (delay relay)
   Electric door locks
   Interior lights
   Seat belt (buzzer) warning system (certain operating territories only)

17.3 Removing a facia switch

17.4A Door courtesy lamp switch and connector

17.4B Boot lamp switch – Saloon model

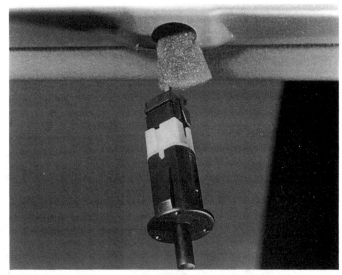

17.4C Luggage area lamp switch and wiring connector – Savanna model

Fig. 12.14 Timer relay with 2 to 4 second delay (Sec 18)

1   Opening switch
2   Earth
3   Closing switch
4   Motor
5   + feed before ignition
    (fuse)
6   Motor

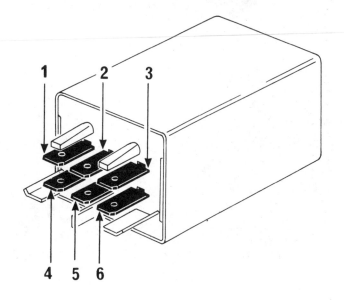

2   Should a fault develop in a timing relay, renewal is the only solution, as repair is not possible.

19 Bulbs (exterior) – renewal

Headlamp bulb

1   Open the bonnet, turn the plastic cover on the rear of the headlamp through a quarter of a turn and remove it.
2   Pull off the wiring plug.
3   Release the bulbholder spring clip and withdraw the bulbholder assembly (photos).
4   When fitting the new halogen type bulb avoid touching it with the fingers. If it is inadvertently touched, clean it with a tissue soaked in methylated spirit.
5   On models with dual headlamps, the bulb renewal procedure is

similar to that described above, but access is gained through the aperture in the top crossmember. After removing the plastic cover, release the clip and withdraw the bulbholder and lead. Detach the lead (photos).

Front parking lamp bulb
6   The bulb and holder are mounted in the headlamp reflector. Access is obtained as described for the headlamp bulb (photo).

Front direction indicator bulb
7   The bulb and holder are mounted in the direction indicator lamp reflector at the side of the headlamp. Twist the bulbholder through a quarter of a turn to remove it.

Side direction indicator bulb
8   Pull the lens free from the body panel, untwist the bulbholder from the lamp unit, then pull on the bulb to remove it from its holder (photo).

Rear lamp bulbs
9   Open the boot lid or tailgate, as applicable.
10 Remove the access trim panel (photo).
11 Unclip and release the bulbholder from the rear of the lamp unit. Remove the bulb from the holder for renewal. To remove the holder unit, detach the wiring connector from it (photos).
12 If required, the lens can be removed by undoing its retaining nuts (photos).

Rear number plate lamp bulb
13 Compress the retaining clips and remove the lamp unit. Detach the bulbholder from the rear of the unit, then remove the bulb from the holder (photos).

Front foglamp bulb
14 Undo the retaining screws and withdraw the lamp unit from the car.
15 Remove the cover cap, release the spring clip and extract the bulbholder (photo). Do not handle the bulb with the fingers as it is a halogen type. Hold it with a tissue or cloth. If accidentally touched, wipe the bulb clean with a tissue soaked in methylated spirits.
16 Refit the bulb and lamp unit in the reverse order of removal, then check the beam alignment.
17 If necessary, adjustment to the beam alignment can be made by turning the adjuster screw as required (photo).

19.3A Headlamp bulbholder and retaining clip – single headlamp model

19.3B Headlamp bulbholder removal – single headlamp model

19.5A Dual headlamp bulbholder and retaining clip

19.5B Dual headlamp bulb removal

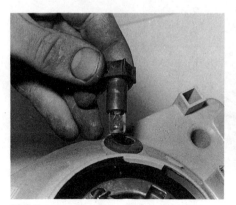

19.6 Front parking lamp bulb removal

19.8 Side direction indicator bulb replacement

19.10 Removing the access trim panel to renew a rear lamp bulb – Savanna model

19.11A Stop/tail and indicator lamp bulbs – Saloon model

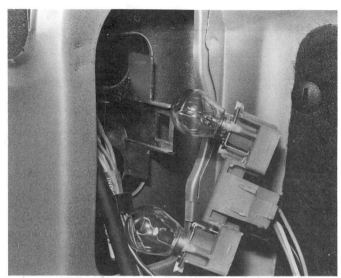

19.11B Stop/tail and indicator lamp bulbs – Savanna model

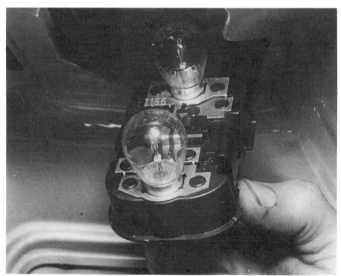

19.11C Reversing and foglamp bulbs – Saloon model

19.11D Reversing and foglamp bulbs – Savanna model

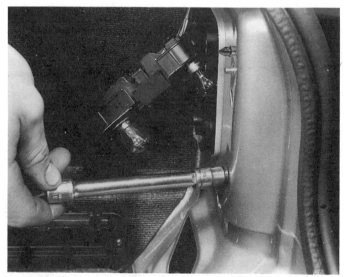

19.12A Lens retaining nuts removal from inside ...

19.12B ... allows lens removal – Saloon model

19.13A Rear number plate lamp (Saloon model) – compress clips at each end (arrowed) to remove

19.13B Number plate lamp removal – Savanna model

19.15 Front foglamp removed to show bulbholder

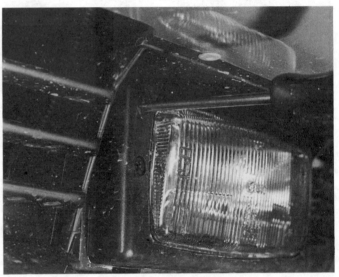

19.16 Front foglamp beam adjustment screw

20 Bulbs (interior) – renewal

Main interior lamp (standard type)
1　Insert a thin bladed tool around the periphery of the cover to compress and release the retaining clips, then lower the cover from the lamp unit frame. Detach and remove the frame unit from the roof. The festoon bulb can be removed from its holder for replacement (photos).

Map-reading and interior lamp
2　This unit can also retain the sliding roof control switch and the infra-red remote control unit, according to model.
3　Release the plastic cover from the front edge then undo the unit retaining screw on each side. Lower the unit from the roof and disconnect the appropriate wiring connectors (photo).
4　To renew the main interior light bulb, release the metal cover and pivot it down out of the way. Withdraw the festoon bulb from its holder (photo).
5　To remove the map-reading lamp, detach the wiring connector from the holder. Untwist and remove the holder to remove the bulb (photo).

6　To remove the lamp units from the frame, first detach and remove the infra-red remote control unit, then depress the lamp unit retaining lugs (photo).

Boot lamp bulb (Saloon models)
7　Open the boot lid, then reach through the access aperture, compress the lamp unit retaining clips and withdraw the lamp unit from the boot lid (photo).
8　Prise free the festoon bulb from its holder for replacement. To remove the unit, detach the wiring connector.

Luggage area lamp bulb (Savanna models)
9　Prise the lamp from its location and remove the festoon type bulb (photo).

Instrument panel bulbs
10　Remove the instrument panel, as described in Section 24.
11　The bulbholders can then be removed by twisting them and the wedge type bulbs removed simply by pulling them from their holders.

20.1A Release the cover from the interior lamp unit frame ...

20.1B ... and then withdraw the unit frame

20.3 Combined interior lamp and map reading lamp unit removed to show wiring connections

20.4 Interior lamp and festoon bulb

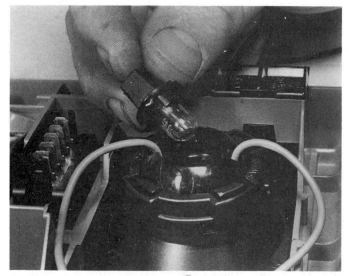

20.5 Map-reading lamp bulbholder removal

20.6 General view of the interior/map reading lamp unit incorporating a sliding roof control switch and infra-red remote control unit

20.7 Boot lamp unit removal – Saloon model

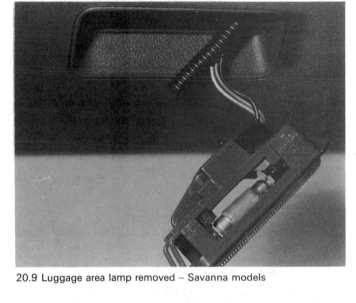

20.9 Luggage area lamp removed – Savanna models

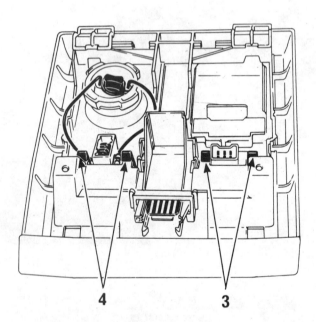

Fig. 12.15 Interior lamp retaining lugs (3) and map reading lamp retaining lugs (4) (Sec 20)

21 Headlamps – removal and refitting

Single headlamp unit

1   Disconnect the battery earth lead. Remove the battery if necessary for access.

2   Unscrew and remove the plastic cover from the rear of the headlamp unit, disconnect the wiring connector from the bulb and, where applicable, disconnect the remote control headlamp adjuster by untwisting at the balljoint (photos).

3   Release the retaining spring and withdraw the indicator unit. Disconnect its wiring connector (photos).

4   Remove the lower trim bar from the grille bumper by detaching its plastic retaining nut (photo).

5   Remove the upper and lower lamp unit retaining screws from the positions shown in Fig. 12.16 and the photograph. Remove the light unit (photo).

6   Refit in the reverse order of removal. When locating the headlamp into the body aperture, do not tighten the lower front retaining screw until the lamp unit is adjusted for position by the upper setting/ retaining bolts. The lamp unit should be flush with the surrounding bodywork. When refitting is complete, check the lamps for satisfactory operation of beam alignment.

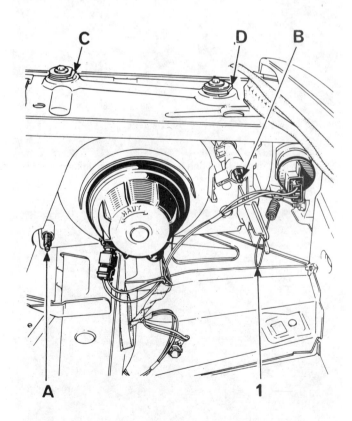

Fig. 12.16 Rear view of single headlamp unit (Sec 21)

1   Indicator lamp retaining spring
A and B Beam adjusting screws
C and D Bonnet height adjusters

Dual headlamp unit

7 Proceed as described in paragraphs 1 to 3.

8 Remove the two retaining screws and withdraw the front grille. Removal of the bonnet will give improved access (Chapter 11).

9 Undo the two upper and the single front retaining bolts, then raise the headlamp unit for access to the lower front retaining bolt – see Fig. 12.17 (photos). Undo the bolt and withdraw the lamp unit.

10 Refit in the reverse order of removal, but note the special points given in paragraph 6.

22 Headlamp beam load adjuster

1 A sealed hydraulic beam-adjusting device is fitted on some models so that the headlamp beams may be adjusted (over and above the normal basic setting) to compensate for variations in the vehicle load and so prevent dazzle and improve road illumination.

2 The device consists of a rotary adjustment knob and an actuating unit at the headlamp.

3 The control knob should be set in accordance with the following conditions:

0 *Driver alone or with front passenger, no luggage*
2 *Driver and four passengers, no luggage*
3 *Driver and four passengers plus luggage*
3 *Driver with luggage compartment full*

4 The adjuster control and the connecting cable can be removed, but must be renewed if defective. Remove the lower facia panel, pull free the control knob, then undo the retaining nuts from within the control unit dish (photos).

5 Disconnect the control unit from the support bracket at the facia end, detach the balljoint from the rear of the headlamps, then feed the cables through to the interior from the engine compartment for removal (photo).

6 Refit in reverse order, and check for satisfactory operation

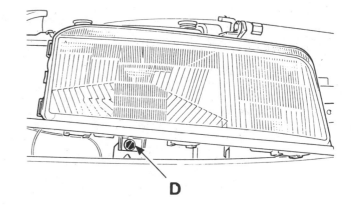

Fig. 12.17 Dual headlamp lower front retaining bolt (D) (Sec 21)

23 Headlamp beam – alignment

1 It is recommended that the headlamp beam alignment is carried out by your dealer or a service station having the necessary optical beam setting equipment.

2 As a temporary measure the headlamp beam adjusting screws may be turned in the required direction. If a beam load adjuster is fitted ensure that its adjustment knob is set at the 'O' position. The headlamp beam adjuster screws are shown in Fig. 12.16. On dual headlamp models, the adjuster at the top corner is accessible through the top panel aperture (photo).

21.2A Detach the headlamp rear cover ...

21.2B ... disconnect the wiring connector ...

21.2C ... and the headlamp adjuster remote control joint (if applicable)

21.3A Disengage the retaining spring (arrowed) ...

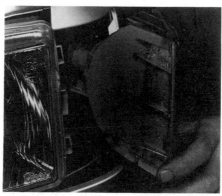

21.3B ... and remove the front indicator unit

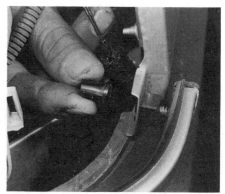

21.4 Remove the lower trim plastic retaining nut

21.5A Headlamp lower retaining screw

21.5B Removing a single headlamp unit

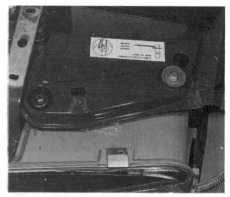

21.9A Dual headlamp unit upper retaining bolts

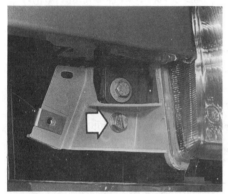

21.9B Dual headlamp unit front retaining bolt (arrowed)

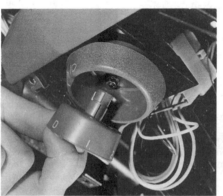

22.4A Pull free the headlamp beam load adjuster knob ...

22.4B ... and undo the retaining nuts

22.5 Detach the beam load adjuster control unit

23.2 Headamp beam adjuster screw – dual headlamp

24 Instrument panel – removal and refitting

Note: *An electronic type instrument panel, is fitted to some models. This is identifiable from its LCD display zone and a tell-tale warning light zone. In the event of the instrument panel receiving a malfunction signal from a sensor, it will display an error code in lieu of the speed reading. The fault will need to be diagnosed and rectified without delay by a Renault dealer. This type of instrument panel is not repairable – only the illumination bulbs can be renewed. The following special precautionary points should be noted to avoid damaging an electronic instrument panel:*

(a) Ensure that the panel wiring connections and associated items are correctly connected
(b) Do not make any checks on the unit or the sensors and probes using a test lamp

(c) Do not disconnect the battery or the instrument panel feed fuse with the ignition switched on
The removal and refitting procedures for the electronic and conventional instrument panels are otherwise the same

1   Disconnect the battery earth lead.
2   Where applicable, lower the steering column to its lowest setting.
3   Unscrew and remove the four instrument panel cowl retaining screws (photo).
4   Depress the hazard warning and rear window demister switches, insert a suitable screwdriver and depress the clips so that the cowl can be pivoted and removed (photos).
5   Unscrew the instrument panel retaining screws, then simultaneously lift and withdraw the panel outwards sufficiently to allow the wiring connectors and the speedometer cable to be detached from its rear face. As the panel is withdrawn get an assistant to feed the speedometer cable through the bulkhead from the engine compart-

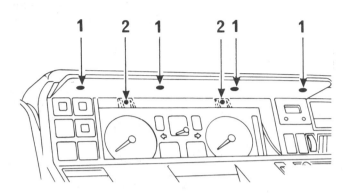

Fig. 12.18 Instrument panel cowl screws (1) and panel screws (2) (Sec 24)

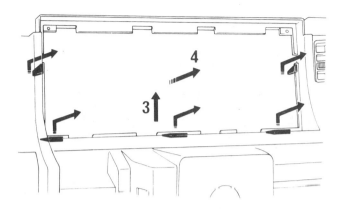

Fig. 12.19 Lift (3), then withdraw (4) the instrument panel from its aperture (Sec 24)

24.3 Instrument panel cowl retaining screws (arrowed)

24.4A Releasing the cowl retaining clips ...

24.4B ... to allow the cowl to be withdrawn

24.5A Instrument panel retaining screw

24.5B Speedometer cable (arrowed) and instrument panel wiring block connectors

24.6 Bulbholder removal from instrument panel

ment side just enough to allow the cable to be detached. Remove the instrument panel (photos).
6   Dismantling of the instrument panel is not recommended. Any tests or repairs which may be necessary should be entrusted to a Renault dealer. Illumination bulbs can be removed by untwisting the holder from the rear face of the panel (photo).
7   Refit in the reverse order of removal. Ensure that the wiring connections are correctly made and on completion check the operation of the various panel components.

25 Horns – removal and refitting

1   Electric or wind tone horns are fitted depending on model; in each case they are located on the forward chassis member (photos).

2   To remove the horn, disconnect the lead connector or air hoses (as applicable), then undo the mounting bracket bolt and withdraw the horn.
3   Note that with the wind tone horns, the filter on the end of the compressor intake pipe should be kept clean.
4   Refit in the reverse order of removal.

26 Cigar lighter – removal and refitting

1   Disconnect the battery earth lead.
2   Remove the panel in which the cigar lighter is mounted for access to the rear of the unit (photo).
3   Disconnect the lead connector and bulb wire. Unclip the unit and remove it from the panel. Note that the illumination bulb is not

renewable and therefore if this has blown or the unit is defective it must be renewed complete.

4   Refit in the reverse order of removal.

27 Clock – removal and refitting

1   On all models, the clock is a push-fit in its location aperture, and is

retained by plastic compression catches.

2   To remove the clock, first disconnect the battery negative terminal.

3   Carefully ease the clock from its location using a thin blunt instrument (photo).

4   Disconnect the wiring connections and remove the clock from the car (photo).

5   Refitting is the reverse sequence to removal.

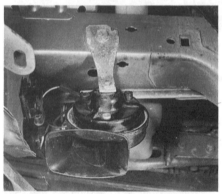
25.1A Horn and location bracket

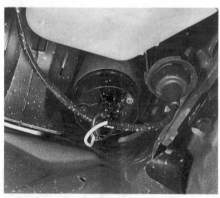
25.1B Wind tone horn and compressor unit

26.2 Cigar lighter unit location on underside of panel

27.3 Clock removal

27.4 Rear view of clock showing wiring connection and bulbholder

28 Wiper blades and arms – removal and refitting

1   The wiper blade is a snap fit in the groove at the end of the wiper arm.

2   Pull the wiper arm/blade away from the windscreen or tailgate glass until it locks, and pull the blade from the arm by giving the blade a sharp jerk (photo).

3   The wiper arm may be removed from its splined spindle by flipping up the nut cover, unscrewing the nut (photo) and prising the arm from the spindle. Before removing the arm, note the park position of the blade on the windscreen by marking with a felt tip pen or insulation tape which is easily removed. If the arm is tight, use two screwdrivers at opposite points under its eye as levers.

4   Refitting is a reversal of removal, but make sure that the alignment of the wiper blades and arms is correct.

5   Do not overtighten the wiper arm nuts.

29 Windscreen wiper motor and linkage – removal and refitting

1   Remove the wiper arms and blades as described in the preceding Section.

2   Open the bonnet and disconnect the battery.

3   Prise free the scuttle grille-to-bonnet seal, undo the scuttle

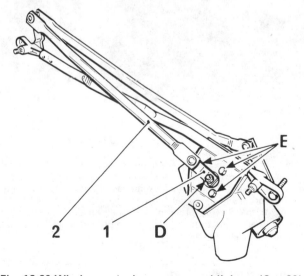
Fig. 12.20 Windscreen wiper motor and linkage (Sec 29)

1   Link arm   D   Drive link nut
2   Link arm   E   Motor retaining screws

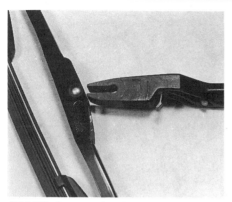

28.2 Windscreen wiper blade removal from wiper arm

28.3 Windscreen wiper arm to spindle nut

29.5 Windscreen wiper motor

retaining bolts and screws and remove the scuttle and lower windscreen trim.

4   Unplug the wiper motor.

5   Unbolt the wiper motor and the wiper linkage mounting plates (photo).

6   Release the wiper arm (spindle) wheel boxes and withdraw the motor and linkage from the scuttle recess.

7   To remove the linkage from the wiper motor, undo the drive link nut and remove the three motor retaining screws.

8   When reassembling the linkage to the wiper motor, first ensure that the motor is switched off and set in the 'parked' position, with the connecting links aligned as shown in Fig. 12.20.

9   Refitting is otherwise a reversal of the removal procedure.

30 Tailgate wiper motor (Savanna models) – removal and refitting

1   Remove the wiper arm and blade.

2   Open the tailgate and remove the trim panel as described in Chapter 11.

3   Unplug the wiper motor (photo).

4   Unscrew the wiper motor mounting bolts and remove the motor.

5   Refitting is a reversal of removal, but before bolting the motor into place, connect its plug and make sure that it is switched on and then off by means of its control switch so that it will be installed in the 'parked' position.

31 Windscreen, tailgate and headlamp washer systems

1   The windscreen washer reservoir is located in the engine compartment, and the tailgate washer reservoir (Savanna) is located in the left-hand side rear trim panel in the luggage area.

2   Check the reservoir(s) regularly and top up with a suitable cleaning fluid solution. Use a proprietary screen cleaning fluid in the water. **Do not** use cooling system anti-freeze in the cleaning solution.

3   The adjustment of the washer jets is carried out by inserting a pin in the jet nozzle and moving it to obtain the desired jet pattern on the screen.

4   To remove the windscreen washer reservoir, first syphon out its contents, then remove the battery for access. Undo the retaining bolts, and withdraw the reservoir so that the pump leads and washer hoses can be disconnected.

5   To remove the tailgate reservoir, disconnect the washer hose, wiring lead and the pump, and detach the reservoir from the trim panel (photo).

6   Refit in the reverse order of removal and check for satisfactory operation on completion.

7   Where fitted, the headlight washer system uses the same fluid reservoir as the windscreen washers.

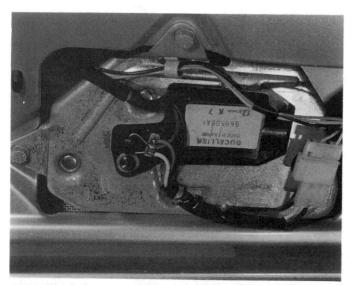

30.3 Tailgate wiper motor – Savanna model

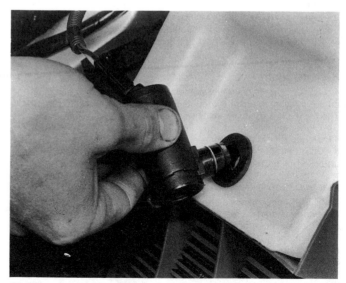

31.5 Pump unit removal from the tailgate washer reservoir – Savanna model

32 Engine oil level sensor

1   This device comprises a sensor unit mounted in the side of the cylinder block and a receiver unit at the instrument panel. It is not fitted to all models in the range.
2   If the sensor unit is to be removed for any reason, first partially drain the engine oil, then detach the wiring from the sensor. Unscrew and remove it.
3   Refit in reverse order, then top up the oil level and check the sensor for satisfactory operation as described in the driver's handbook.
4   The oil level receiver unit is mounted on the instrument panel. First remove the instrument panel unit for access as described in Section 24, then detach the receiver from it.
5   Once removed, the receiver can be checked by connecting the leads from an ohmmeter to the terminals on the rear face of the unit. The indicator needle should be seen to move.
6   Renew the receiver unit if it is defective and refit in the reverse order of removal.

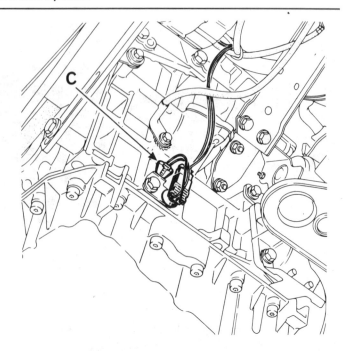

Fig. 12.21 Engine oil level sensor location (C) (Sec 32)

Fig. 12.22 Engine oil level sensor and wiring terminals (arrowed) (Sec 32)

33 Vehicle door locking – alternative systems

1   Each system enables the four doors, boot lid or tailgate (as applicable) and fuel filler cap to be unlocked.

Manual

2   Use the door key in the normal way to unlock one front door then unlock the remaining doors by pulling up the locking knob.
3   The key opens the boot lid or tailgate (as applicable) and fuel filler flap.

Remote control

4   The door is unlocked by pointing the remote control device at the infra red receiver which is mounted above the rear view interior mirror. The device has its own exclusive code for security reasons.
5   If the tell-tale lamp on the hand held sender unit does not illuminate, renew the batteries.
6   The fuel filler flap and the boot lid or tailgate (as applicable) are unlocked using the key.

Electric central door locking

7   This system enables all doors, fuel filler flap and boot lid or tailgate (certain versions) to be locked or unlocked using the key in a front door lock or the infra red remote control sender unit.
8   Alternatively, the doors can be locked or unlocked from inside the car using the switch on the centre console.
9   Should a fault develop which prevents the fuel filler flap opening, it may be unlocked manually by pulling the lever which is hidden behind the trim panel at the side of the luggage compartment.
10 Access to the central locking system lock solenoids is described in Chapter 11.

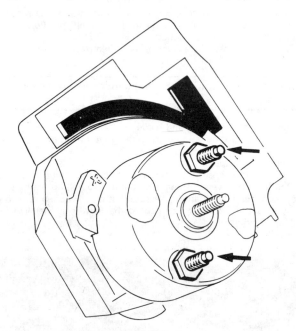

Fig. 12.23 Engine oil level receiver unit and wiring terminals (arrowed) (Sec 32)

34 Electric windows

1   Electrically-operated front and rear door windows are fitted to some models.
2   The control switches may be mounted in the centre console or in the door armrests. To remove a switch refer to Section 17.
3   Access to the window operating motors is described in Chapter 11.

35 Electric rear-view door mirror

1   The removal of this type of rear-view mirror is described in Chapter 11. If the mirror operation is defective in some way, remove the

appropriate door trim panels and check the various wires and their connectors to ensure that they are secure and in good condition.

2 The various wiring connections and their identifications are shown in Fig. 12.27.

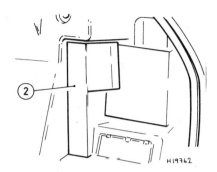

Fig. 12.24 Fuel filler flap emergency release lever location (2) – Saloon (Sec 33)

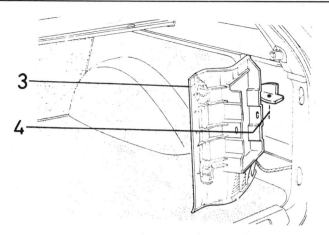

Fig. 12.25 Fuel filler flap emergency release lever location – Savanna (Sec 33)

(3) Access trim door   (4) Release lever

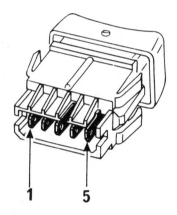

Fig. 12.26 Electric window switch and terminals (Sec 34)

1	Motor	4	Lighting
2	Earth	5	Motor
3	+ feed after ignition		

36 Radio/cassette player – general

1 All models are fitted with a stereo radio/cassette player as standard, but the type fitted is dependent on the vehicle model.

2 Similarly the speakers fitted and their locations are dependent on model. Speakers may be located in the console (woofer), in the facia upper corner above the ventilation grilles (tweeters), in the door panels, or in the rear parcel shelf.

3 All models are fitted with a roof-mounted radio aerial.

37 Radio/cassette player (Renault type) – removal and refitting

1 Insert two U-shaped rods of suitable gauge into the holes in the front face of the radio/cassette unit as shown (photo). Depress the retaining clips and simultaneously withdraw the radio/cassette unit.

2 Withdraw the unit sufficiently to disconnect the feed, earth, aerial and speaker leads (photo).

3 Refitting is a reversal of removal.

38 Radio aerial and speaker units – removal and refitting

Aerial

1 The radio aerial is roof-mounted above the windscreen and is a

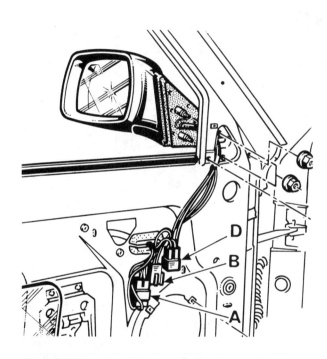

Fig. 12.27 Electric rear view door mirror and wiring connections (A, B and D) (Sec 35)

standard fitting on all models.

2 Remove the roof-mounted interior lamp unit as described in Section 20, and the radio/cassette unit as described in Section 37.

3 With the aerial lead disconnected from the radio, it will ease refitting if a suitable length of strong string or cord is tied to the end of the lead before it is withdrawn up through the windscreen pillar. The lower side trim and facia panel will also need to be removed for access during removal and refitting of the aerial lead.

4 Working through the small aperture in the headlining, unscrew the aerial mounting nuts while an assistant lifts off the aerial from outside the car (photo).

5 Carefully withdraw the aerial lead from the car, then once the radio/cassette end of the lead is clear, the string or cord can be detached from it.

6 Refit in the reverse order of removal. Trim the aerial on completion to obtain the best possible reception.

Speaker units

7   To remove the door or rear parcel shelf-mounted speaker units, untwist and remove the grille, undo the speaker retaining screws and withdraw the speaker. Detach the wires (photos).

8   To remove the tweeter speakers from their location above the vent grille, first prise free the intermediate trim panel. Undo the speaker unit retaining screw and withdraw the speaker. Detach the wire (photos).

9   Refit the speaker units in the reverse order of removal.

37.1 Insert U-shaped radio removal rods as shown to release side retaining clips ...

37.2 ... withdraw the unit and detach wiring and aerial connections

38.4 Aerial mounting nut viewed through headlining aperture

38.7A Untwist the door speaker grille ...

38.7B ... for access to the speaker mounting screws

38.7C Rear parcel shelf-mounted speaker

38.8A Remove the intermediate trim panel and screw

38.8B Withdraw the tweeter speaker from the facia

39 Radio interference and CB equipment

Radio/cassette case breakthrough

Magnetic radiation from dashboard wiring may be sufficiently intense to break through the metal case of the radio/cassette player. Often this is due to a particular cable routed too close and shows up as ignition interference on AM and cassette play and/or alternator whine on cassette play.

The first point to check is that the clips and/or screws are fixing all parts of the radio/cassette case together properly. Assuming good earthing of the case, see if it is possible to re-route the offending cable – the chances of this are not good, however, in most cars.

Next release the radio/cassette player and locate it in different positions with temporary leads. If a point of low interference is found, then if possible fix the equipment in that area. This also confirms that local radiation is causing the trouble. If re-location is not feasible, fit the radio/cassette player back in the original position.

Alternator interference on cassette play is now caused by radiation from the main charging cable which goes from the battery to the output terminal of the alternator, usually via the + terminal of the starter motor relay. In some vehicles this cable is routed under the dashboard, so the solution is to provide a direct cable route. Detach the original cable from the alternator output terminal and make up a new cable of at least 6 mm² cross-sectional area to go from alternator to battery with the shortest possible route. *Remember – do not run the engine with the alternator disconnected from the battery.*

Ignition breakthrough on AM and/or cassette play can be a difficult problem. It is worth wrapping earthed foil round the offending cable run near the equipment, or making up a deflector plate well screwed down to a good earth. Another possibility is the use of a suitable relay to switch on the ignition coil. The relay should be mounted close to the ignition coil; with this arrangement the ignition coil primary current is not taken into the dashboard area and does not flow through the ignition switch. A suitable diode should be used since it is possible that at ignition switch-off the output from the warning lamp alternator terminal could hold the relay on.

Connectors for suppression components

Capacitors are usually supplied with tags on the end of the lead, while the capacitor body has a flange with a slot or hole to fit under a nut or screw with washer.

Connections to feed wires are best achieved by self-stripping connectors. These connectors employ a blade which, when squeezed down by pliers, cuts through cable insulation and makes connection to the copper conductors beneath.

Chokes sometimes come with bullet snap-in connectors fitted to the wires, and also with just bare copper wire. With connectors, suitable female cable connectors may be purchased from an auto-accessory shop together with any extra connectors required for the cable ends after being cut for the choke insertion. For chokes with bare wires, similar connectors may be employed together with insulation sleeving as required.

VHF/FM broadcasts

Reception of VHF/FM in an automobile is more prone to problems than the medium and long wavebands. Medium/long wave transmitters are capable of covering considerable distances, but VHF transmitters are restricted to line of sight, meaning ranges of 10 to 50 miles, depending upon the terrain, the effects of buildings and the transmitter power.

Because of the limited range it is necessary to retune on a long journey, and it may be better for those habitually travelling long distances or living in areas of poor provision of transmitters to use an AM radio working on medium/long wavebands.

When conditions are poor, interference can arise, and some of the suppression devices described previously fall off in performance at very high frequencies unless specifically designed for the VHF band. Available suppression devices include reactive HT cable, resistive distributor caps, screened plug caps, screened leads and resistive spark plugs.

For VHF/FM receiver installation the following points should be particularly noted:

(a) Earthing of the receiver chassis and the aerial mounting is important. Use a separate earthing wire at the radio, and scrape paint away at the aerial mounting.

(b) If possible, use a good quality roof aerial to obtain maximum height and distance from interference generating devices on the vehicle.

(c) Use of a high quality aerial downlead is important, since losses in cheap cable can be significant.

(d) The polarisation of FM transmissions may be horizontal, vertical, circular or slanted. Because of this the optimum mounting angle is at 45° to the vehicle roof.

Citizens' Band radio (CB)

In the UK, CB transmitter/receivers work within the 27 MHz and 934 MHz bands, using the FM mode. At present interest is concentrated on 27 MHz where the design and manufacture of equipment is less difficult. Maximum transmitted power is 4 watts, and 40 channels spaced 10 kHz apart within the range 27.60125 to 27.99125 MHz are available.

Aerials are the key to effective transmission and reception. Regulations limit the aerial length to 1.65 metres including the loading coil and any associated circuitry, so tuning the aerial is necessary to obtain optimum results. The choice of a CB aerial is dependent on whether it is to be permanently installed or removable, and the performance will hinge on correct tuning and the location point on the vehicle. Common practice is to clip the aerial to the roof gutter or to employ wing mounting where the aerial can be rapidly unscrewed. An alternative is to use the boot rim to render the aerial theftproof, but a popular solution is to use the 'magmount' – a type of mounting having a strong magnetic base clamping to the vehicle at any point, usually the roof.

Aerial location determines the signal distribution for both transmission and reception, but it is wise to choose a point away from the engine compartment to minimise interference from vehicle electrical equipment.

The aerial is subject to considerable wind and acceleration forces. Cheaper units will whip backwards and forwards and in so doing will alter the relationship with the metal surface of the vehicle with which it forms a ground plane aerial system. The radiation pattern will change correspondingly, giving rise to break-up of both incoming and outgoing signals.

Interference problems on the vehicle carrying CB equipment fall into two categories:

(a) Interference to nearby TV and radio receivers when transmitting.

(b) Interference to CB set reception due to electrical equipment on the vehicle.

Problems of break-through to TV and radio are not frequent, but can be difficult to solve. Mostly trouble is not detected or reported because the vehicle is moving and the symptoms rapidly disappear at the TV/radio receiver, but when the CB set is used as a base station any trouble with nearby receivers will soon result in a complaint.

It must not be assumed by the CB operator that his equipment is faultless, for much depends upon the design. Harmonics (that is, multiples) of 27 MHz may be transmitted unknowingly and these can fall into other user's bands. Where trouble of this nature occurs, low pass filters in the aerial or supply leads can help, and should be fitted in base station aerials as a matter of course. In stubborn cases it may be necessary to call for assistance from the licensing authority, or, if possible, to have the equipment checked by the manufacturers.

Interference received on the CB set from the vehicle equipment is, fortunately, not usually a severe problem. The precautions outlined previously for radio/cassette units apply, but there are some extra points worth noting.

It is common practice to use a slide-mount on CB equipment enabling the set to be easily removed for use as a base station, for example. Care must be taken that the slide mount fittings are properly earthed and that first class connection occurs between the set and slide-mount.

Vehicle manufacturers in the UK are required to provide suppression of electrical equipment to cover 40 to 250 MHz to protect TV and VHF radio bands. Such suppression appears to be adequately effective at 27 MHz, but suppression of individual items such as alternators/dynamos, clocks, stabilisers, flashers, wiper motors, etc, may still be necessary. The suppression capacitors and chokes available from auto-electrical suppliers for entertainment receivers will usually give the required results with CB equipment.

Other vehicle radio transmitters

Besides CB radio already mentioned, a considerable increase in the use of transceivers (ie combined transmitter and receiver units) has taken place in the last decade. Previously this type of equipment was fitted mainly to military, fire, ambulance and police vehicles, but a large business radio and radio telephone usage has developed.

Generally the suppression techniques described previously will suffice, with only a few difficult cases arising. Suppression is carried out to satisfy the 'receive mode', but care must be taken to use heavy duty chokes in the equipment supply cables since the loading on 'transmit' is relatively high.

Glass-fibre bodied vehicles

Such vehicles do not have the advantage of a metal box surrounding the engine as is the case, in effect, of conventional vehicles. It is usually necessary to line the bonnet, bulkhead and wiring valances with metal foil, which could well be the aluminium foil available from builders merchants. Bonding of sheets one to another and the whole down to the chassis is essential.

Wiring harness may have to be wrapped in metal foil which again should be earthed to the vehicle chassis. The aerial base and radio chassis must be taken to the vehicle chassis by heavy metal braid. VHF radio suppression in glass-fibre cars may not be a feasible operation.

In addition to all the above, normal suppression components should be employed, but special attention paid to earth bonding. A screen enclosing the entire ignition system usually gives good improvement, and fabrication from fine mesh perforated metal is convenient. Good bonding of the screening boxes to several chassis points is essential.

40 Fault diagnosis – electrical system

Symptom	Reason(s)
No voltage at starter motor	Battery discharged Battery defective internally Battery terminals loose or earth lead not securely attached to body Loose or broken connections in starter motor circuit Starter motor switch or solenoid faulty
Voltage at starter motor – faulty motor	Starter brushes badly worn, sticking, or brush wires loose Commutator dirty, worn or burnt Starter motor armature faulty Field coils earthed
Starter motor noisy or rough in engagement	Pinion or flywheel gear teeth broken or worn Starter motor retaining bolts loose
Alternator not charging*	Drivebelt loose and slipping, or broken Brushes work, sticking, broken or dirty Brush springs weak or broken

*If all appears to be well but the alternator is still not charging, take the car to an automobile electrician for checking of the alternator

Battery will not hold charge for more than a few days	Battery defective internally Electrolyte level too low or electrolyte too weak due to leakage Plate separators no longer fully effective Battery plates severely sulphated Drivebelt slipping Battery terminal connections loose or corroded Alternator not charging properly Short in lighting circuit causing continual battery drain
Ignition light fails to go out, battery runs flat in a few days	Drivebelt loose and slipping, or broken Alternator faulty

Failure of individual electrical equipment to function correctly is dealt with alphabetically below

Fuel gauge gives no reading	Fuel tank empty Electric cable between tank sender unit and gauge earthed or loose Fuel gauge case not earthed Fuel gauge supply cable interrupted Fuel gauge unit broken
Fuel gauge registers full all the time	Electric cable between tank unit and gauge broken or disconnected
Horn operates all the time	Horn push either earthed or stuck down Horn cable to horn push earthed
Horn fails to operate	Blown fuse Cable or cable connection loose, broken or disconnected Horn has an internal fault
Horn emits intermittent or unsatisfactory noise	Cable connections loose Horn incorrectly adjusted
Lights do not come on	If engine not running, battery discharged Light bulb filament burnt out or bulbs broken Wire connections loose, disconnected or broken Light switch shorting or otherwise faulty
Lights come on but fade out	If engine not running, battery discharged

40 Fault diagnosis – electrical system (continued)

Symptom	Reason(s)
Lights give very poor illumination	Lamp glasses dirty
	Reflector tarnished or dirty
	Lamps badly out of adjustment
	Incorrect bulb with too low wattage fitted
	Existing bulbs old and badly discoloured
	Electrical wiring too thin not allowing full current to pass
Lights work erratically, flashing on and off, especially over bumps	Battery terminals or earth connections loose
	Contacts in light switch faulty
Wiper motor fails to work	Blown fuse
	Wire connections loose, disconnected or broken
	Brushes badly worn
	Armature worn or faulty
	Field coils faulty
Wiper motor works very slowly and takes excessive current	Commutator dirty, greasy or burnt
	Drive to spindles bent or unlubricated
	Drive spindle binding or damaged
	Armature bearings dry or unaligned
	Armature badly worn or faulty
Wiper motor works slowly and takes little current	Brushes badly worn
	Commutator dirty, greasy or burnt
	Armature badly worn or faulty
Wiper motor works but wiper blades remain static	Linkage disengaged or faulty
	Drive spindle damaged or worn
	Wiper motor gearbox parts badly worn

Example :

In the diagram below Unit 40 (L.H. door pillar switch) has a wire 133.OR/NO.2.41 which runs to unit 41.

Wire 133 is again found connected to Unit 41 (R.H. door pillar switch) but this time it is numbered 133.OR/NO.2.40.

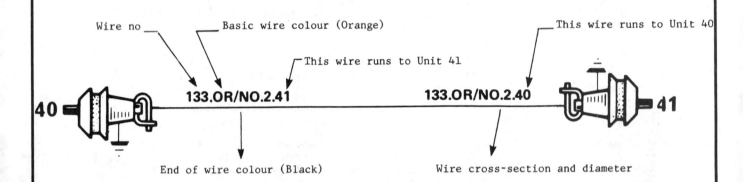

Wire no ──
Basic wire colour (Orange)
This wire runs to Unit 40
This wire runs to Unit 41

133.OR/NO.2.41   **133.OR/NO.2.40**

40   41

End of wire colour (Black)
Wire cross-section and diameter

Wire and connector colours.

BA	BE	BJ	CY	GR	JA	MA	NO	OR	RG	SA	VE	VI
White	Blue	Beige	Clear	Grey	Yellow	Brown	Black	Orange	Red	Pink	Green	Violet

Diameter and cross-section of the conductors

Number	1	2	3		4		5	6	7	8	9	10	11	12
Diameter (mm)	0.7	0.9	1	1.2		1.4	1.6	2	2.5	3	4.5	5	7	8
Cross-section (mm²)	0.4	0.6	0.8	1		1.5	2	3	5	7	15	20	40	50

General guide to use of wiring diagrams

Note: *Owing to the extremely large number of diagrams produced by the manufacturers for this range of vehicles, it has only been possible to include a typical selection*

Component/circuit locations for Fig. 12.28

For information on use and colour codes see page 328

Circuit	Diagram No
Anti-stall device (1.7 litre engine)	9
Boot lighting	24
Brake fluid level/pressure warning	18
Brake pad wear warning	14
Central door locking	30
Charging circuit (1.7 litre engine)	3
Charging circuit (2.0 litre engine)	4
Choke warning lamp	32
Cigar lighter	27
Clock	28
Cooling fan (1.7 litre engine)	10
Cooling fan (2.0 litre engine)	11
Cooling fan switch (1.7 litre engine)	7
Cooling fan switch (2.0 litre engine)	8
Coolant temperature sender (1.7 litre engine)	7
Coolant temperature sender (2.0 litre engine)	8
Dashboard switch lighting	37
Direction indicators	39
Electric windows	31
Electric window switch lighting	36
Front foglamps	20
Fuel gauge	41
Glovebox lamp	37
Handbrake warning lamp	18
Hazard warning lamps	39
Headlamps	35
Heated rear window	22
Heater	33
Horn	17
Ignition (1.7 litre engine)	10
Ignition (2.0 litre engine)	40
Injection (2.0 litre engine)	40
Instrument panel lighting	32
Interior lamps (with sunroof)	24
Interior lamps (without sunroof)	25
Lights on warning buzzer	24
Oil level sensor (1.7 litre engine)	5
Oil level sensor (2.0 litre engine)	6
Oil pressure switch (1.7 litre engine)	5
Oil pressure switch (2.0 litre engine)	6
Radio/cassette player	26
Rear foglamps	21
Rev counter	10
Reversing lamps (1.7 litre models)	1
Reversing lamps (2.0 litre models)	2
Speakers (radio/cassette)	26
Side and rear lamps	34
Side and rear lamps warning lamp	38
Starter circuit (1.7 litre engine)	12
Starter circuit (2.0 litre engine)	13
Stoplamps	29
Sunroof	23
Windscreen wash/wipe (1.7 litre models)	42
Windscreen wash/wipe (2.0 litre models)	19
Windscreen washer fluid level (1.7 litre models)	15
Windscreen washer fluid level (2.0 litre models)	16

Key to Fig. 12.28

Note: *Not all items are applicable to all models*

For information on use and colour codes see page 328

1	LH sidelamp and/or direction indicator
2	RH sidelamp and/or direction indicator
7	LH headlamp
8	RH headlamp
9	LH horn
12	Alternator
13	LH earth
14	RH earth
15	Starter
16	Battery
17	Engine cooling fan motor
20	Windscreen washer pump
21	Oil pressure switch
22	Fan motor No 1 activating thermal switch
24	LH front brake
25	RH front brake
26	Windscreen wiper motor
27	Brake fluid level/pressure warning
29	Instrument panel
30	Connector No 1 – instrument panel
31	Connector No 2 – instrument panel
32	Connector No 3 – instrument panel
33	Connector No 4 – instrument panel
34	Hazard warning lamps switch
35	Heated rear window switch
37	LH window switch
38	RH window switch
40	LH front door pillar switch
41	RH front door pillar switch
42	LH window motor
43	RH window motor
45	Junction block – front harness (accessories plate)
46	Junction block – front harness (accessories plate)
47	Junction block – front harness (accessories plate)
48	Junction block – front harness (accessories plate)
52	Stoplamps switch
53	Ignition/starter/anti-theft switch
54	Heating/ventilating controls illumination
55	Glove compartment lamp
56	Cigar lighter
58	Windscreen wiper/washer switch
59	Lighting and direction indicators switch
60	Direction indicator switch or connector
61	Terminal before ignition switch
64	Handbrake On warning lamp switch
65	Fuel gauge sender unit
66	Heated rear window
67	Luggage compartment lamp
68	LH rear lamp assembly
69	RH rear lamp assembly
70	Number plate lights
71	Choke On warning lamp
72	Reversing lamp switch

74	Flasher unit
75	Heating/ventilating fan switch
76	Instrument panel and warning lamp rheostat
77	Diagnostic socket
78	Rear window wiper motor
79	Rear window washer pump
80	Junction block – engine harness
81	Junction block – rear harness No 1
82	Junction block – console harness
84	Junction block – manual/automatic transmission harness
86	Lights On buzzer relay
90	Air conditioning compressor
97	Bodyshell earth
106	Rear foglamp switch
109	Angular position/speed sensor
110	Engine cooling fan motor relay
114	Windscreen wiper timer relay
118	Sunroof motor
120	Sunroof switch
123	Clock
127	Front centre speaker
129	Front foglamps switch
135	LH front door solenoid
136	RH front door solenoid
137	LH rear door solenoid
138	RH rear door solenoid
139	Front centre interior lamp
144	Wire junction – interior lamp
146	Temperature or thermal switch
150	LH front door speaker
151	RH front door speaker
152	Central door locking switch
155	Rear or LH rear interior lamp
156	LH rear door pillar switch
157	RH rear door pillar switch
159	LH rear window switch
161	RH rear window switch
164	Electric fuel pump
167	Heated rear window relay
171	Rear window wiper/washer switch
184	Luggage compartment lamp switch
185	Glove compartment lamp switch
189	Fuel filler flap solenoid
191	Tailgate lock solenoid
195	Idling cut-out
200	Heater plugs
201	Air pre-heating box
207	Anti-stall solenoid valve
208	Diesel fuel cut-off solenoid
209	Oil level indicator sensor
214	Relay No 1 – additional driving lamps
215	RH front foglamp
216	LH front foglamp
217	Electric rear view mirror – driver's side

Key to Fig. 12.28 (continued)

Note: *Not all items are applicable to all models*

For information on use and colour codes see page 328

220	Connector – heater crossmember harness
231	Junction – tailgate harness
233	Oil temperature switch
262	Heating and air conditioning control panel
263	No 2 engine cooling fan motor relay
264	No 2 engine cooling fan unit
265	Connector – No 2 engine cooling fan unit harness
267	Oxygen sensor
268	No 1 cylinder injector
269	No 2 cylinder injector
270	No 3 cylinder injector
271	No 4 cylinder injector
273	Flowmeter
274	Wire junction No 1
275	Electronic injection computer
278	Carburettor
282	EGR solenoid valve
286	Wire junction No 2
289	Wire junction No 3
290	Wire junction No 4
291	Pinking detector
297	Engine cooling fan cut-out
298	No 2 cooling fan motor thermal cut-out
301	Power steering pressure switch
306	Remote control door unlocking device
308	Junction No 2 – rear harness
310	Air conditioning – anti-stall diode
311	Connector – passenger door harness
321	Engine management module
341	External air temperature sensor
345	RH rear interior lamp
359	Pressure sensor
381	Injection relay
382	Connector – driver's door harness
402	Thermal switch – 115°C
404	Air conditioning compressor protecting diode
408	Electric rear view mirror control
409	Junction – number plate lamps harness
414	Advance corrector
415	Junction – additional front lamps harness
420	Electric rear view mirror control, passenger side
422	Rear window washer switch
423	Headlamp dipped beam intensity reducing resistor
425	Radio
432	Harness junction – dashboard to RH front
433	Harness junction – dashboard to LH front
434	LH speaker (tweeter)
435	RH speaker (tweeter)
438	Wire junction No 5
439	Wire junction No 6
440	Wire junction No 7
441	Wire junction No 8
455	Rear window wiper timer relay
456	Junction – engine cooling fan harness
460	Wire junction No 9
461	Wire junction No 10
462	Door locking timer relay
464	Wire junction No 11
467	Splicing No 12
474	LH rear window winder motor
475	RH rear window winder motor
476	Windscreen washer liquid level sensor
483	No 3 engine cooling fan motor relay
484	Splicing No 13
487	Splicing No 14
490	Air conditioning fan motor pressure switch
493	Fuel pump relay
494	Connection No 15
495	Connection No 16
496	Connection No 17
497	Connection No 18
498	Connection No 19
499	Connection No 20
500	Connection No 21
501	Connection No 22
502	Connection No 23
503	Connection No 24
504	Connection No 25
505	Connection No 26
506	Connection No 27
507	Connection No 28
508	Connection No 29
509	Connection No 30
510	Connection No 31
511	Connection No 32
512	Connection No 33
513	Water temperature sensor
514	Air intake temperature sensor
515	Full load switch
516	Idling speed potentiometer
517	LH front door pillar earth
518	RH front door pillar earth
535	Rear foglamp relay
542	Wire joint No 34
543	Wire joint No 35
544	Wire joint No 36
545	Wire joint No 37
559	Idling governor solenoid valve
567	Wire joint No 38
574	90°C temperature switch
580	Wire joint No 39
586	Dipped beam intensity reduction relay
596	Trip computer switch
597	Rear foglamp shunt
598	Front foglamp shunt
599	Rear window winder interdiction switch
600	No 2 oil pressure switch
601	Advance correction relay

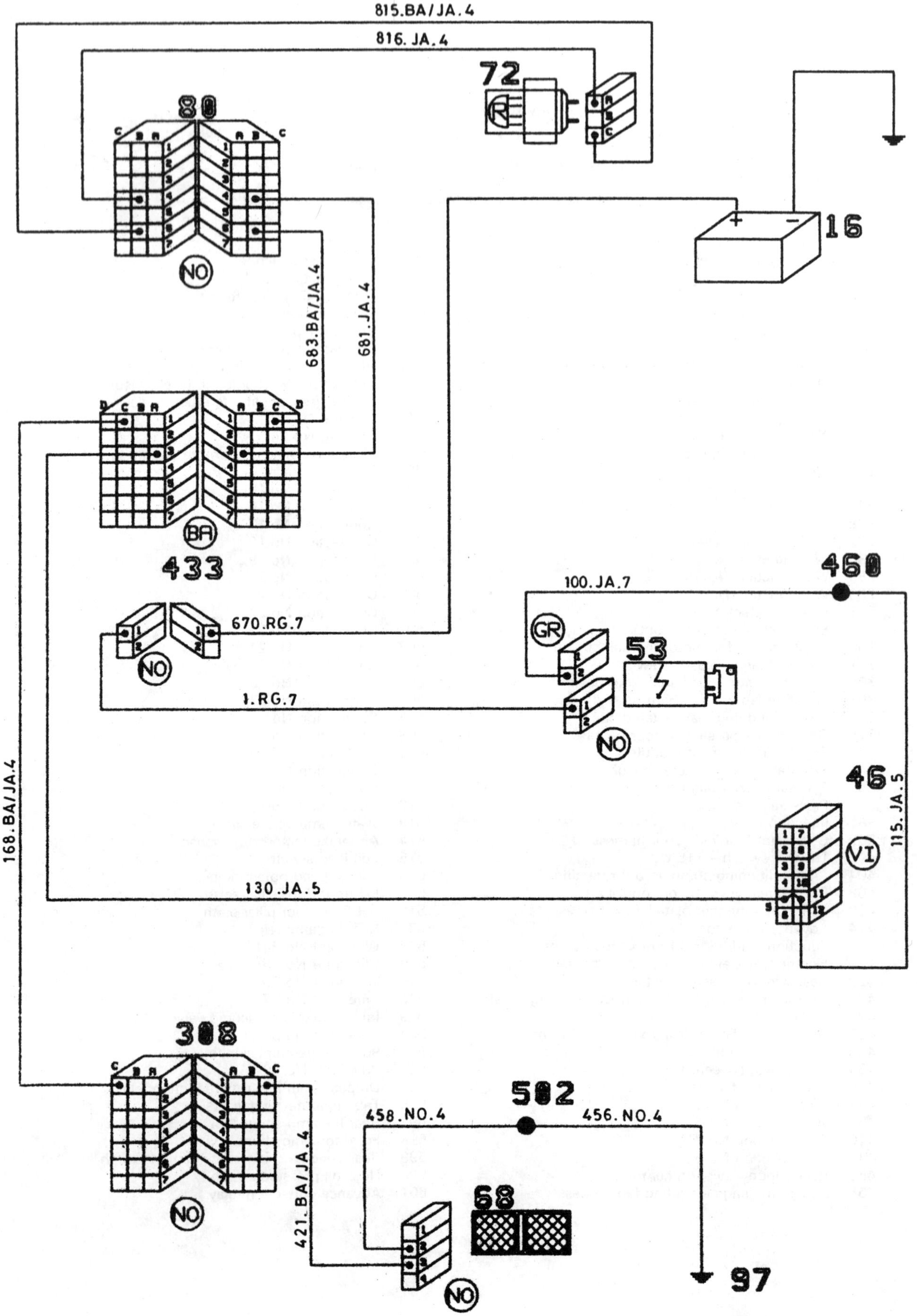

815.BA/JA.4

816.JA.4

72

80

NO

16

683.BA/JA.4

681.JA.4

433

BA

460

100.JA.7

670.RG.7

GR

53

NO

1.RG.7

NO

46

168.BA/JA.4

115.JA.5

VI

130.JA.5

308

502

458.NO.4

456.NO.4

NO

421.BA/JA.4

68

NO

97

Fig. 12.28 Typical wiring diagram for 1987 Renault 21 models – Diagram 1

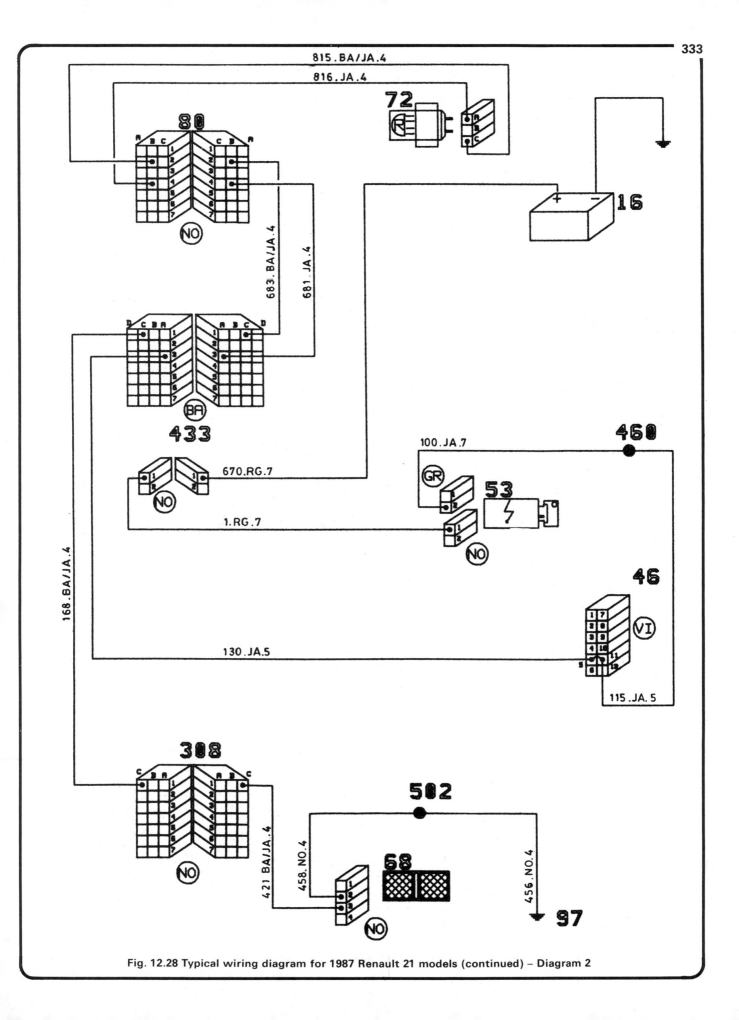

Fig. 12.28 Typical wiring diagram for 1987 Renault 21 models (continued) – Diagram 2

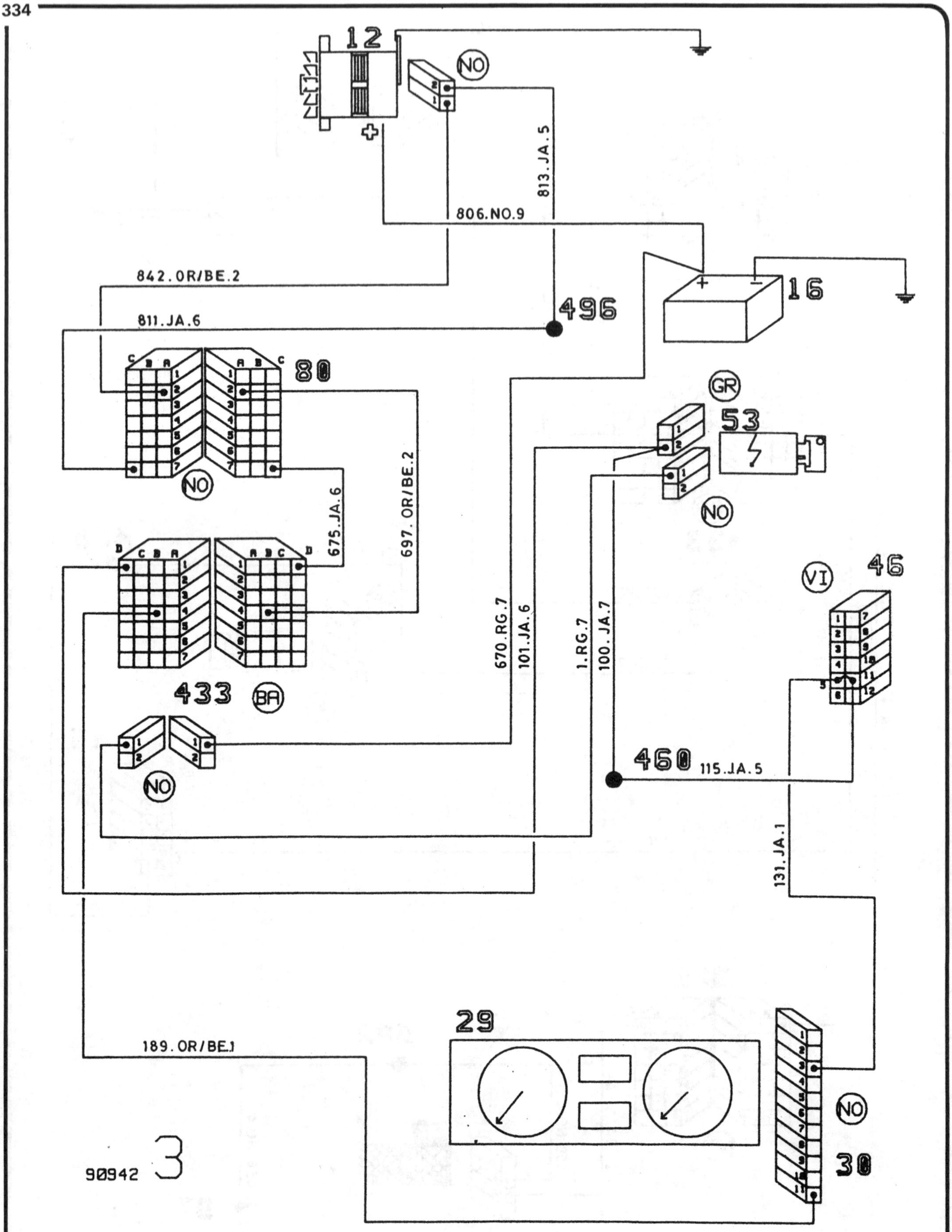

12

NO

813.JA.5

806.NO.9

842.OR/BE.2

811.JA.6

496

16

GR

53

80

NO

675.JA.6

697.OR/BE.2

433 **BA**

NO

670.RG.7

101.JA.6

1.RG.7

100.JA.7

VI **46**

460 115.JA.5

131.JA.1

189.OR/BE.1

29

NO

30

90942 **3**

Fig. 12.28 Typical wiring diagram for 1987 Renault 21 models (continued) – Diagram 3

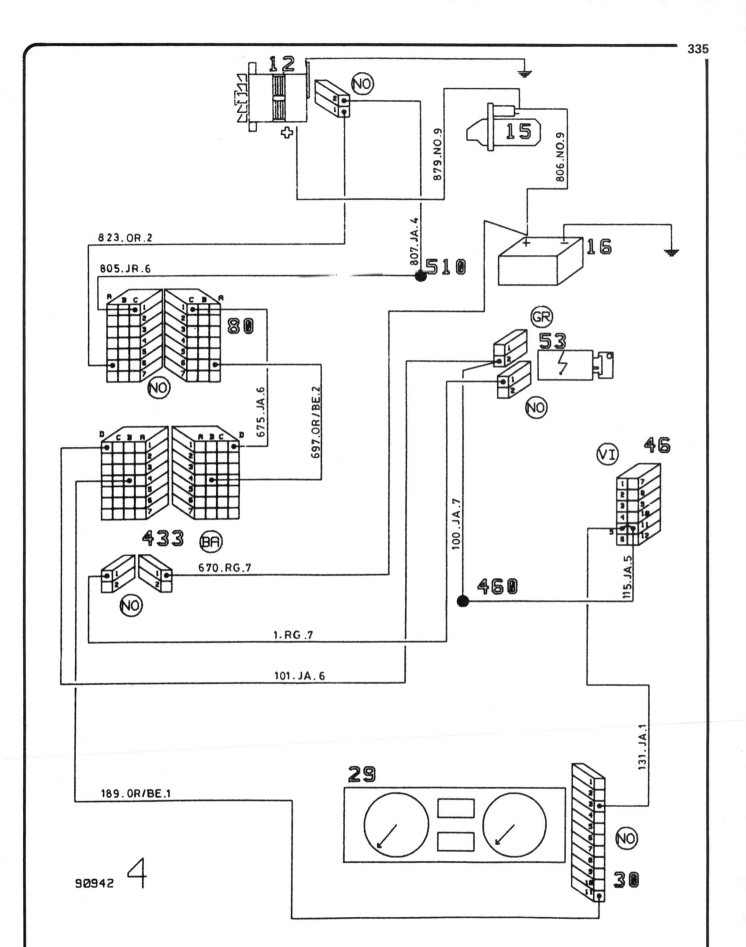

Fig. 12.28 Typical wiring diagram for 1987 Renault 21 models (continued) – Diagram 4

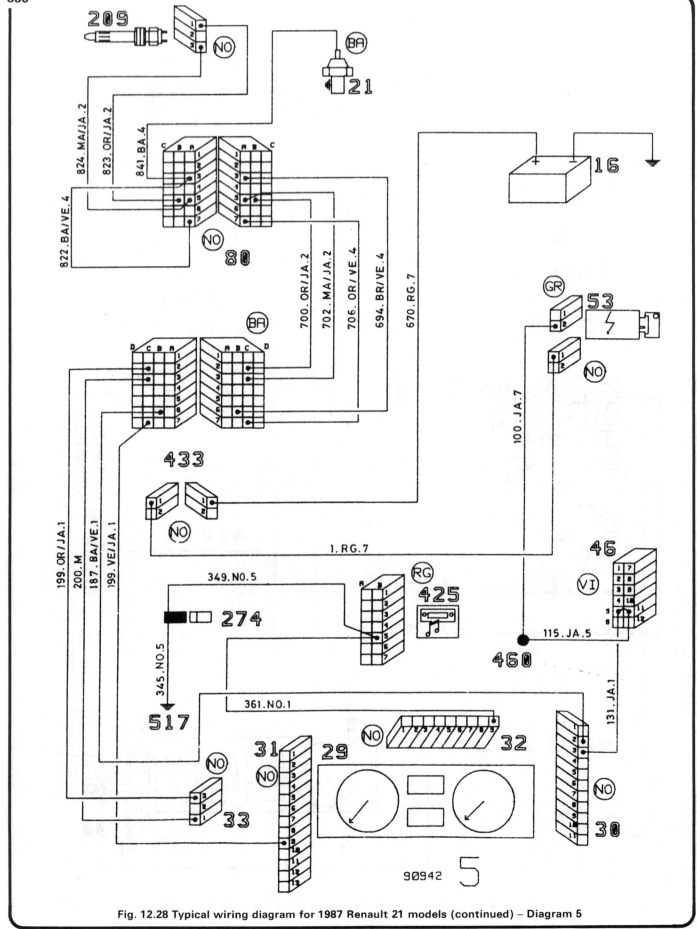

Fig. 12.28 Typical wiring diagram for 1987 Renault 21 models (continued) – Diagram 5

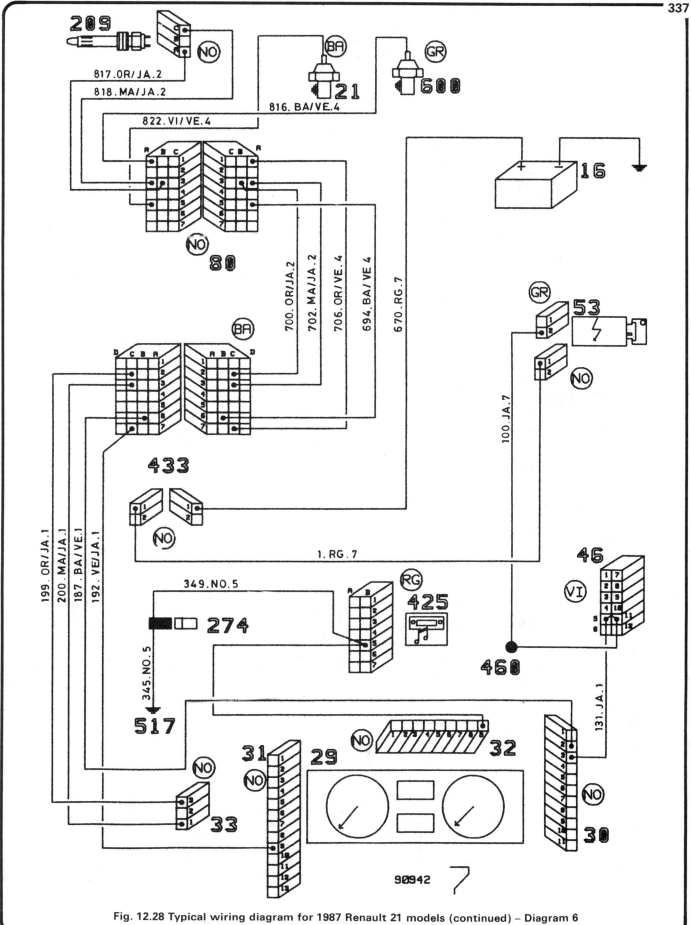

Fig. 12.28 Typical wiring diagram for 1987 Renault 21 models (continued) – Diagram 6

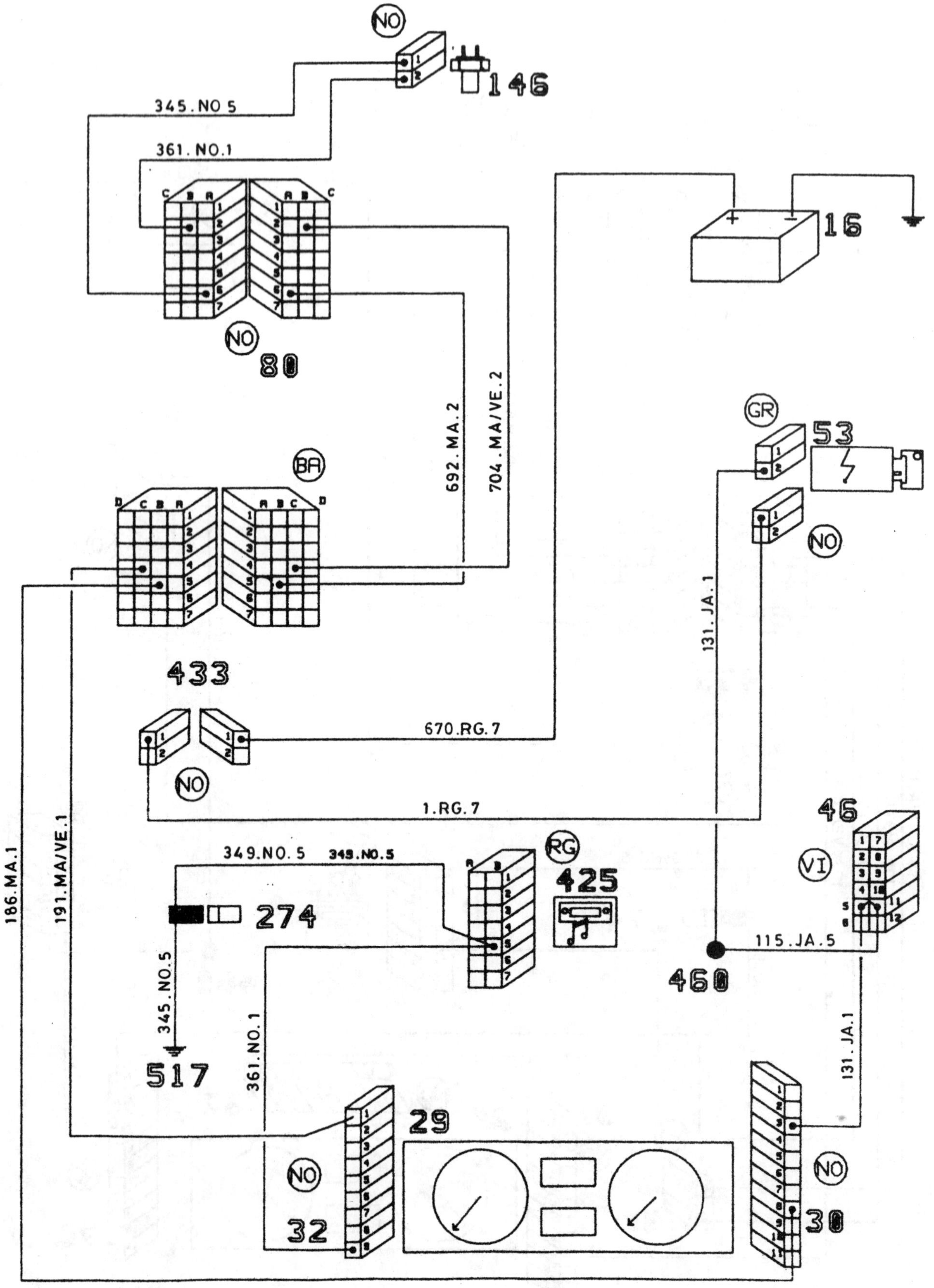

338

Fig. 12.28 Typical wiring diagram for 1987 Renault 21 models (continued) – Diagram 7

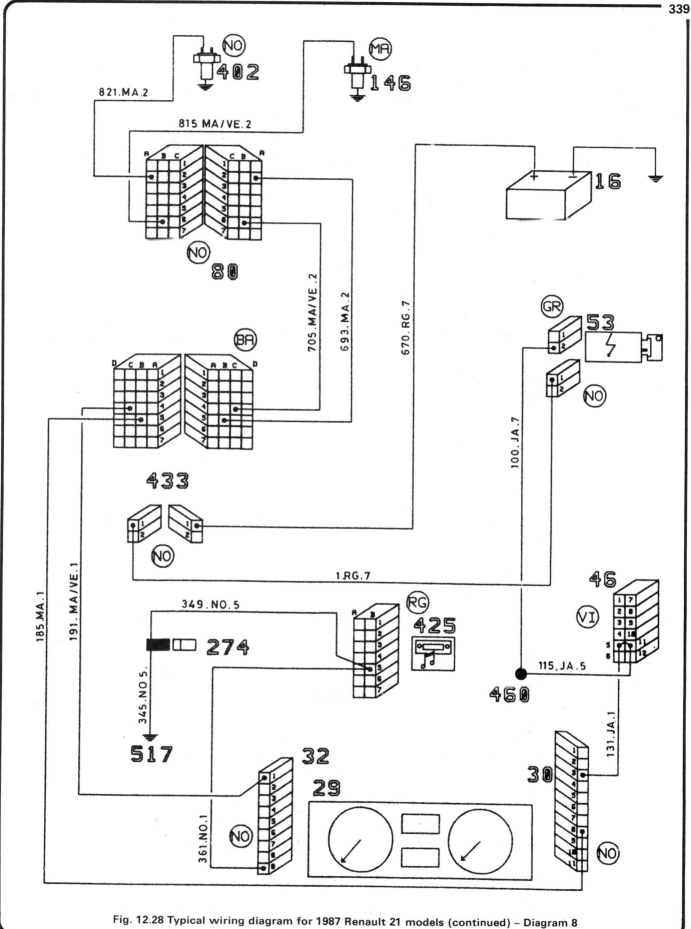

Fig. 12.28 Typical wiring diagram for 1987 Renault 21 models (continued) – Diagram 8

207

12

843.NO.4

844.BR.4

NO

846.JA.4

301

496

811.JA.5

16

NO

80

675.JA.5

GR

53

7

BA

NO

433

670.RG.7

NO

1.RG.7

101.JA.6

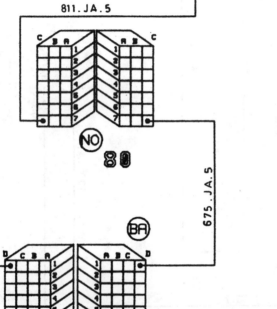
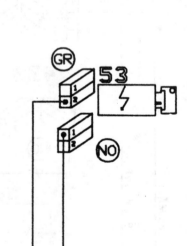
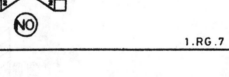

Fig. 12.28 Typical wiring diagram for 1987 Renault 21 models (continued) – Diagram 9

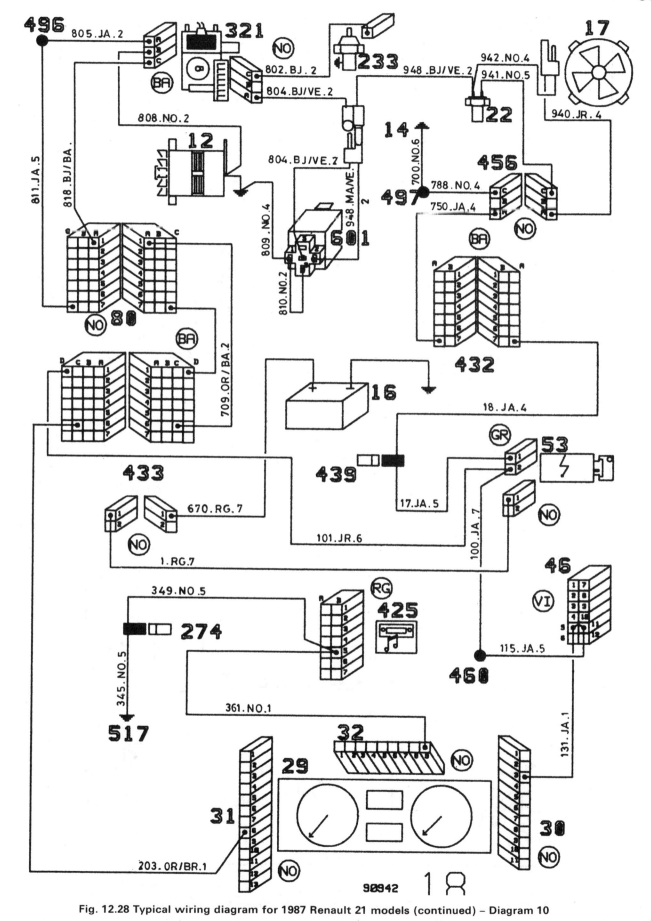

Fig. 12.28 Typical wiring diagram for 1987 Renault 21 models (continued) – Diagram 10

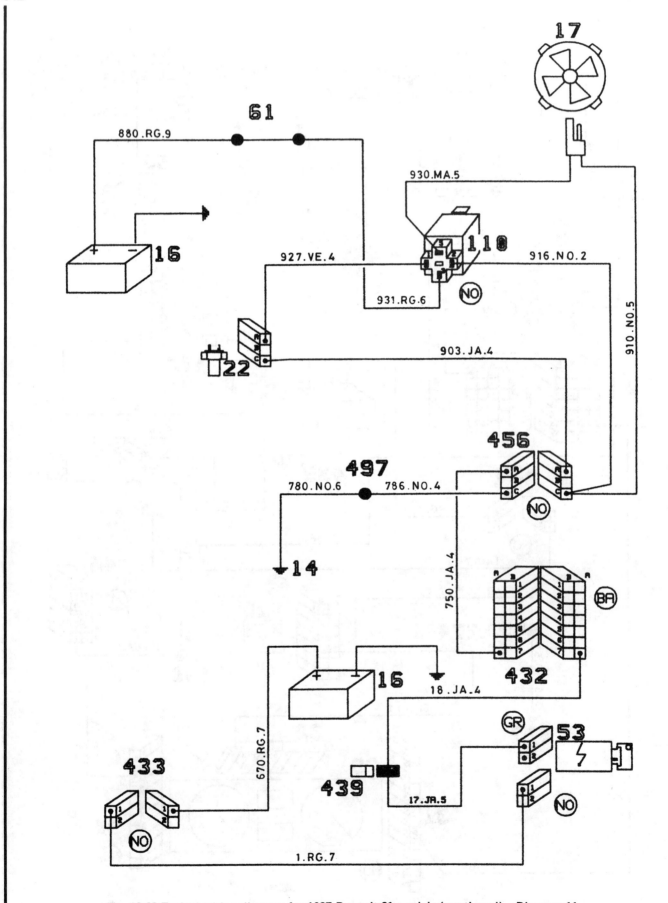

Fig. 12.28 Typical wiring diagram for 1987 Renault 21 models (continued) – Diagram 11

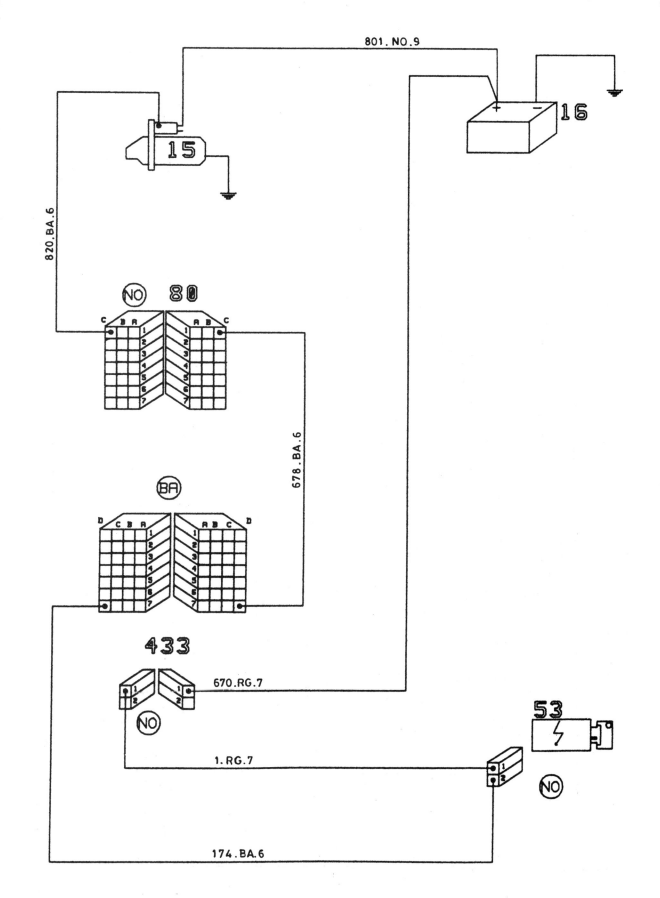

Fig. 12.28 Typical wiring diagram for 1987 Renault 21 models (continued) – Diagram 12

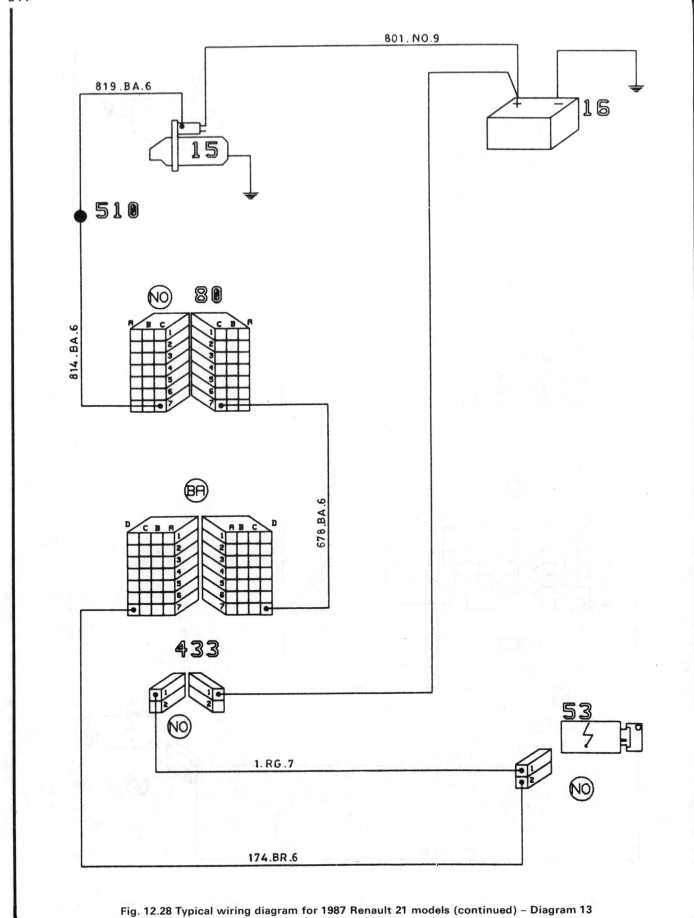

Fig. 12.28 Typical wiring diagram for 1987 Renault 21 models (continued) – Diagram 13

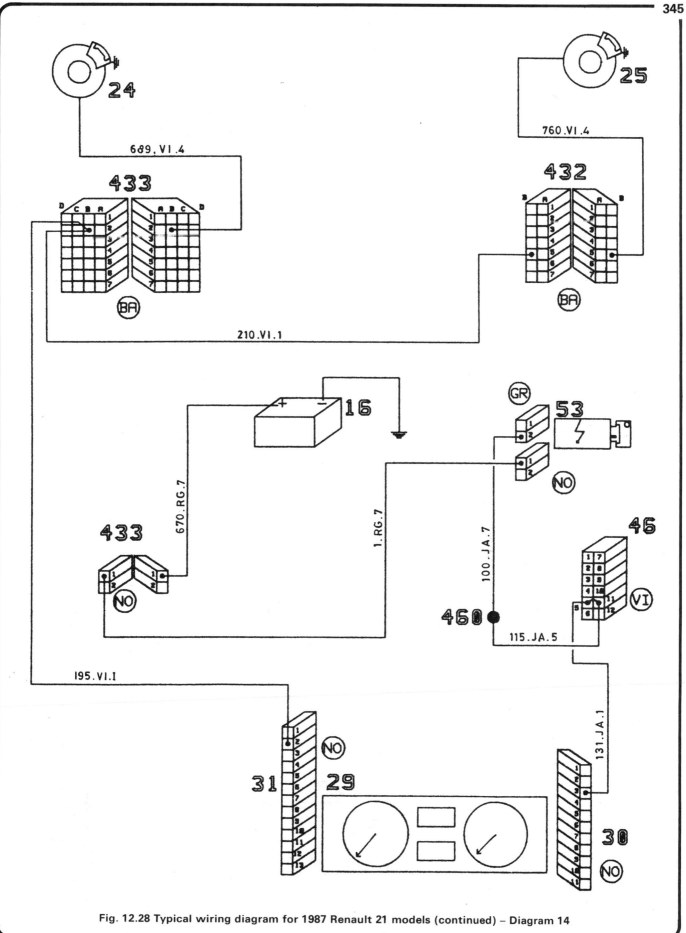

Fig. 12.28 Typical wiring diagram for 1987 Renault 21 models (continued) – Diagram 14

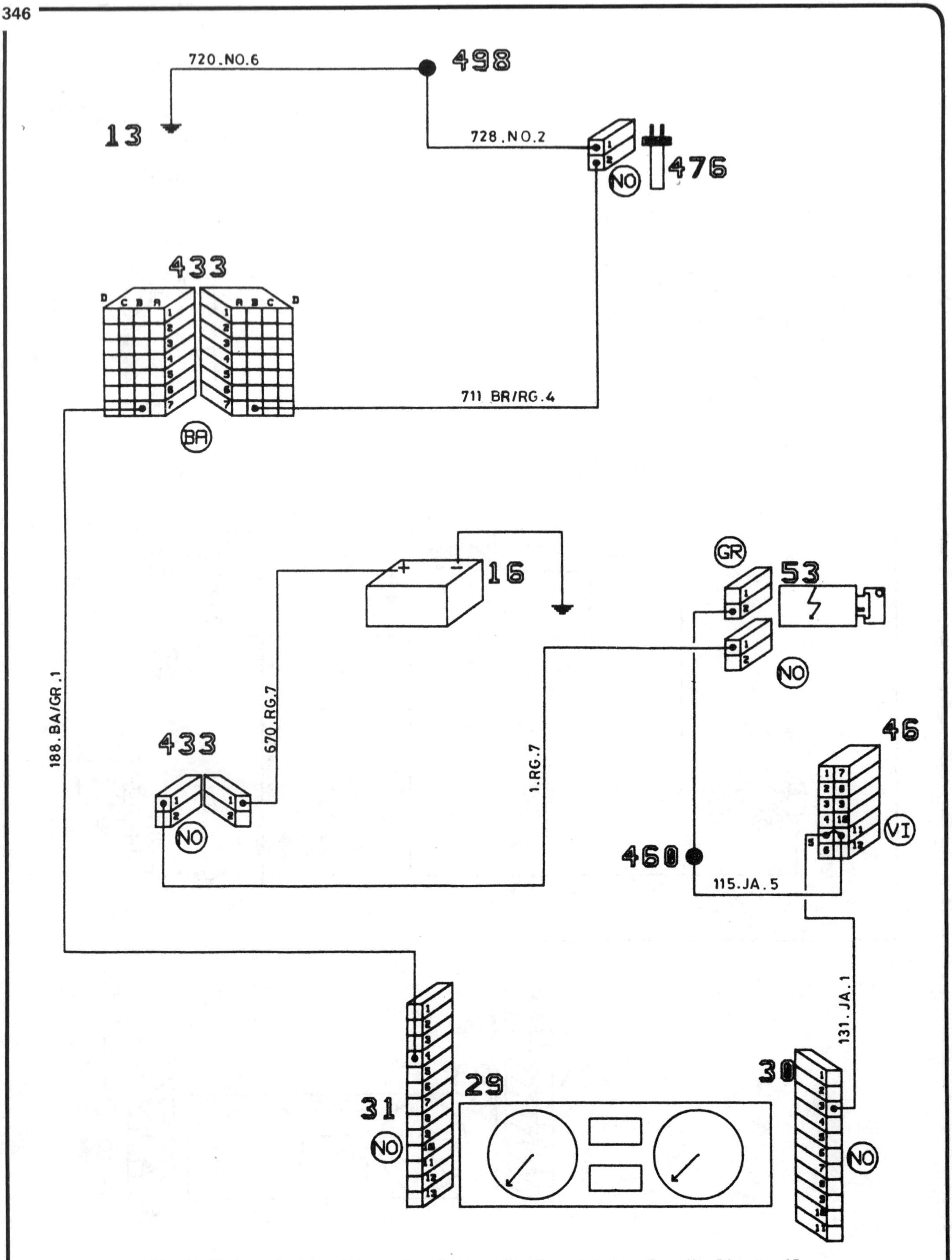

720.NO.6

498

13

728.NO.2

476

NO

433

D C B A
A B C D

1
2
3
4
5
6
7

BA

711 BR/RG.4

GR

53

NO

16

46

188.BA/GR.1

570.RG.7

1.RG.7

433

NO

460

115.JA.5

VI

131.JA.1

31

NO

29

30

NO

Fig. 12.28 Typical wiring diagram for 1987 Renault 21 models (continued) – Diagram 15

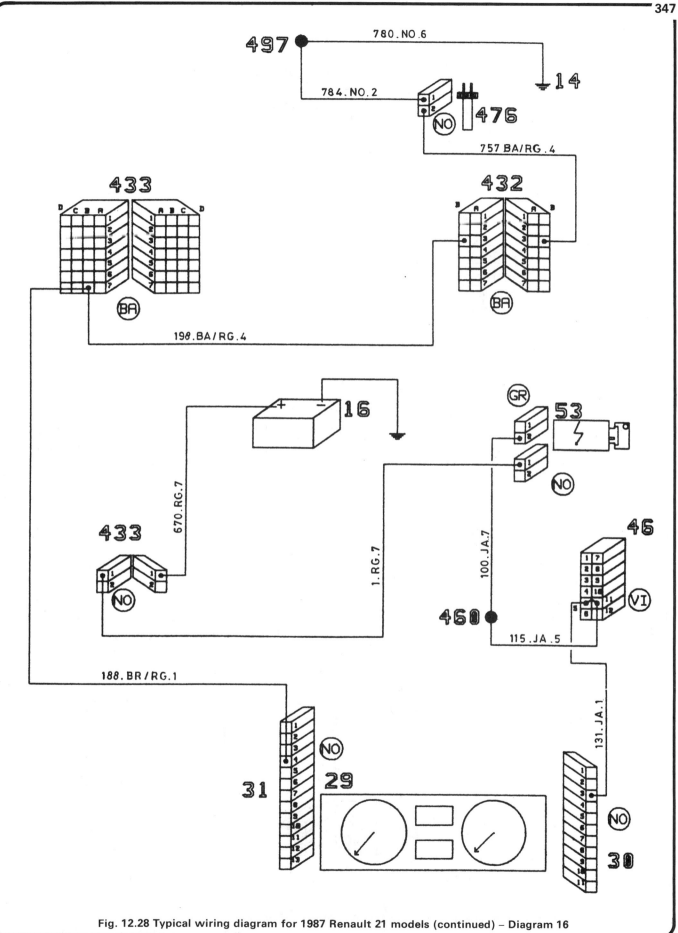

Fig. 12.28 Typical wiring diagram for 1987 Renault 21 models (continued) – Diagram 16

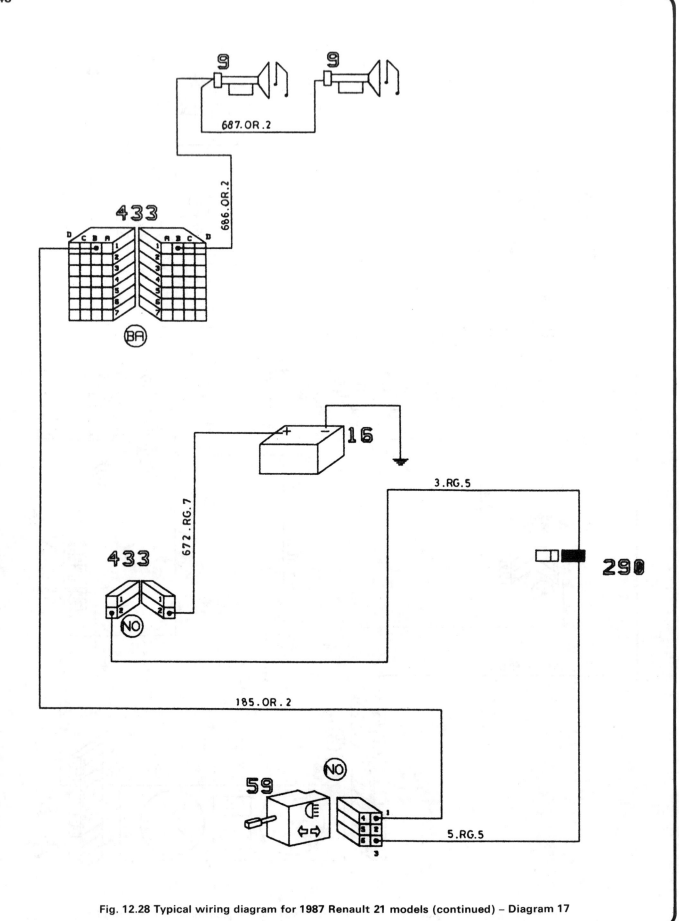

Fig. 12.28 Typical wiring diagram for 1987 Renault 21 models (continued) – Diagram 17

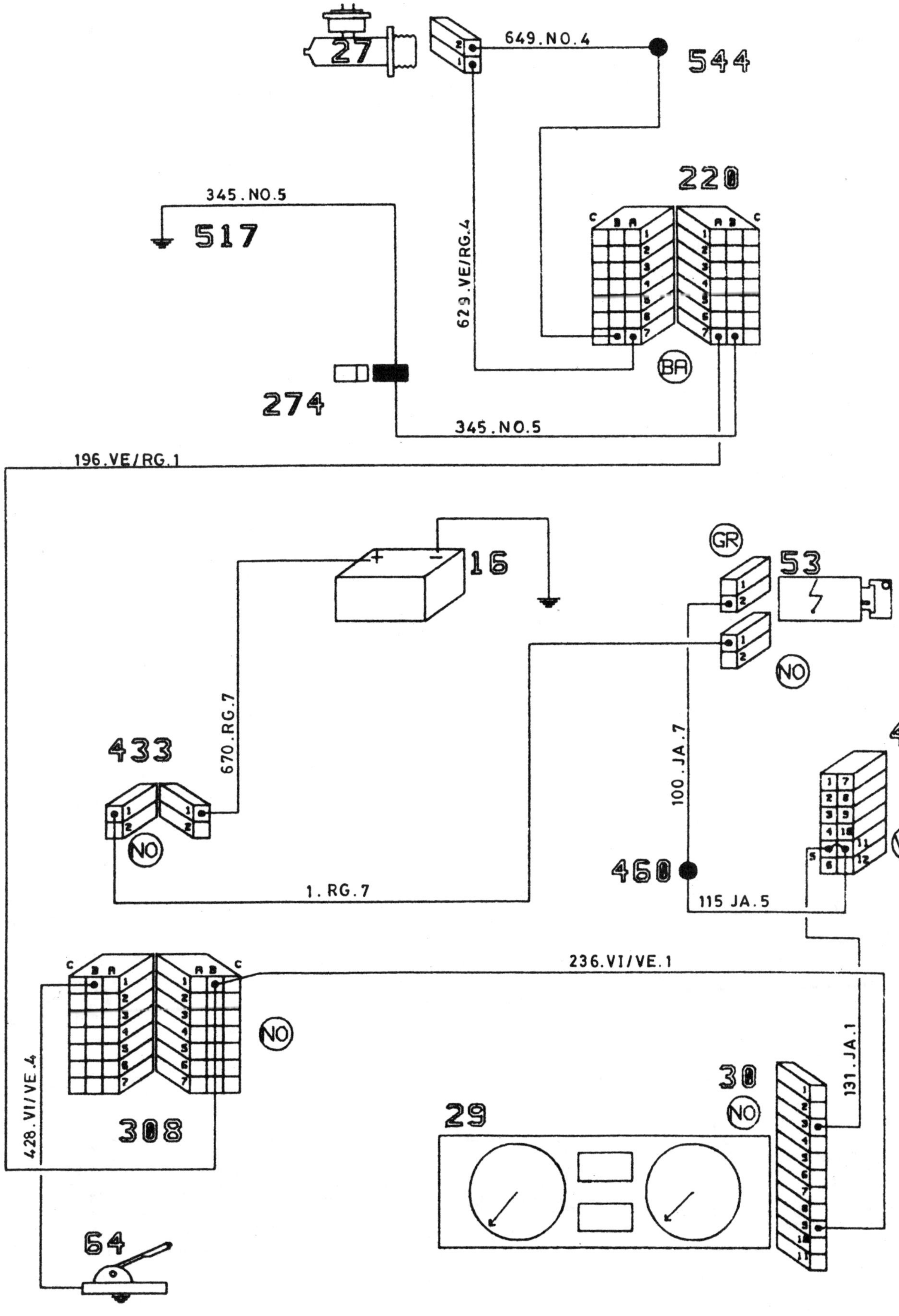

27

649.NO.4

544

345.NO.5

517

629.VE/RG.4

220

C B A | 1 2 3 4 5 6 7 | A B C

BA

274

345.NO.5

196.VE/RG.1

16 + −

GR

53 7

NO

433

670.RG.7

NO

100.JA.7

46

VI

460

1.RG.7

115 JA.5

236.VI/VE.1

C B A | A B C

NO

428.VI/VE.4

308

131.JA.1

29

30

NO

64

Fig. 12.28 Typical wiring diagram for 1987 Renault 21 models (continued) – Diagram 18

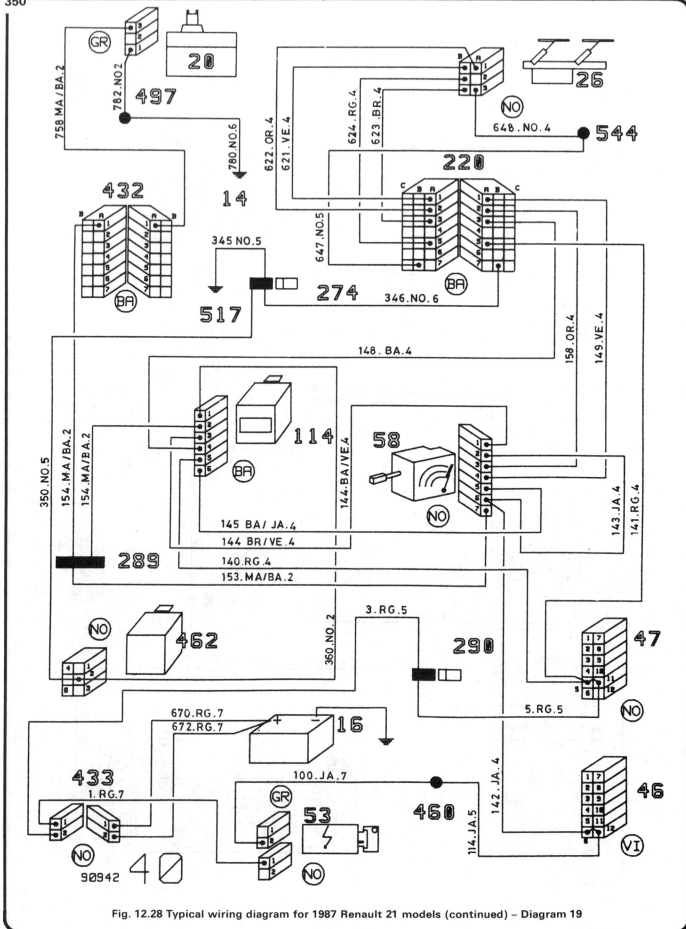

Fig. 12.28 Typical wiring diagram for 1987 Renault 21 models (continued) – Diagram 19

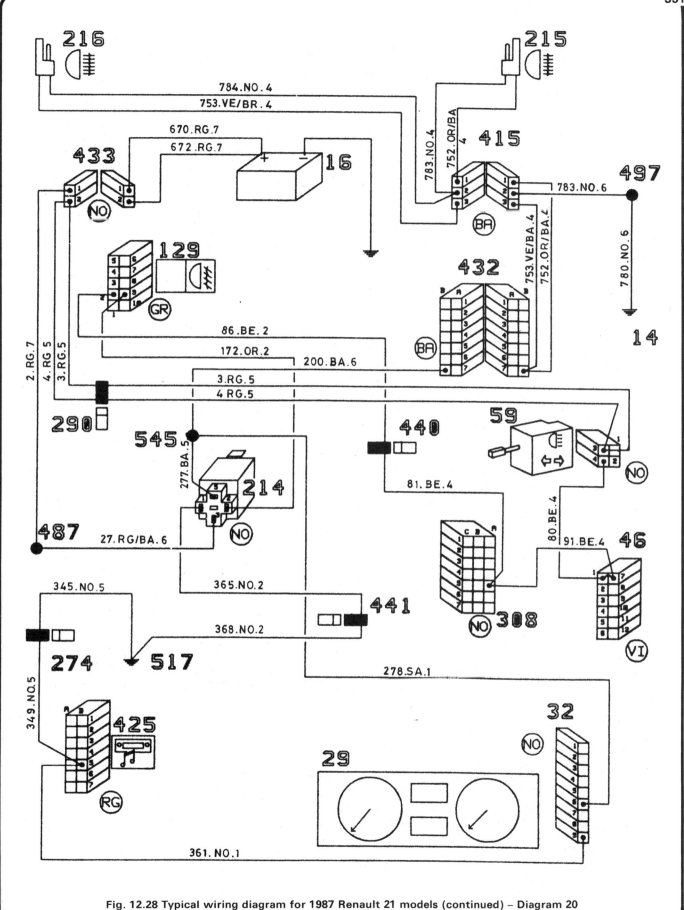

Fig. 12.28 Typical wiring diagram for 1987 Renault 21 models (continued) – Diagram 20

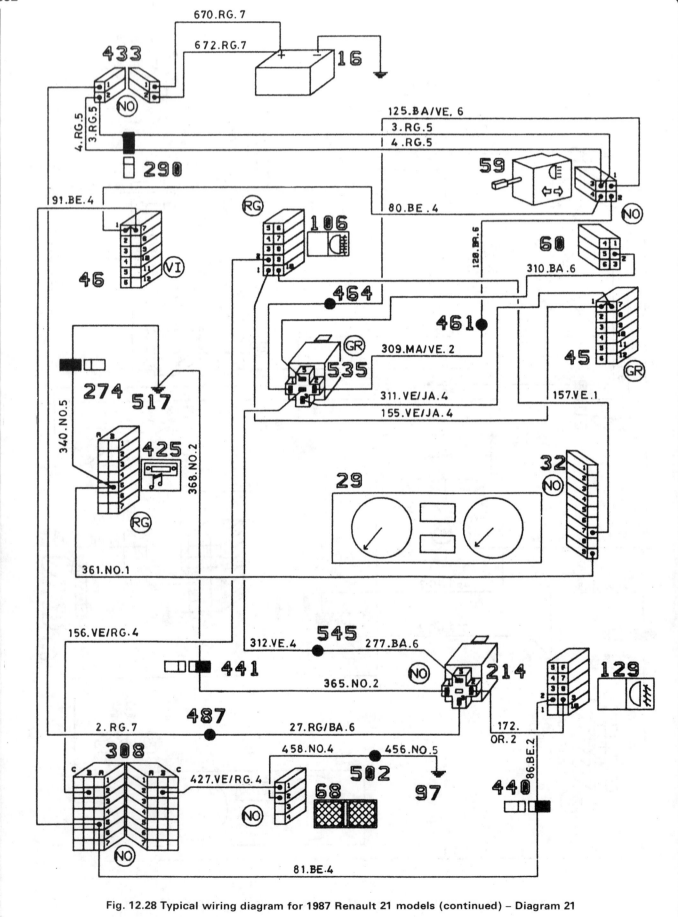

Fig. 12.28 Typical wiring diagram for 1987 Renault 21 models (continued) – Diagram 21

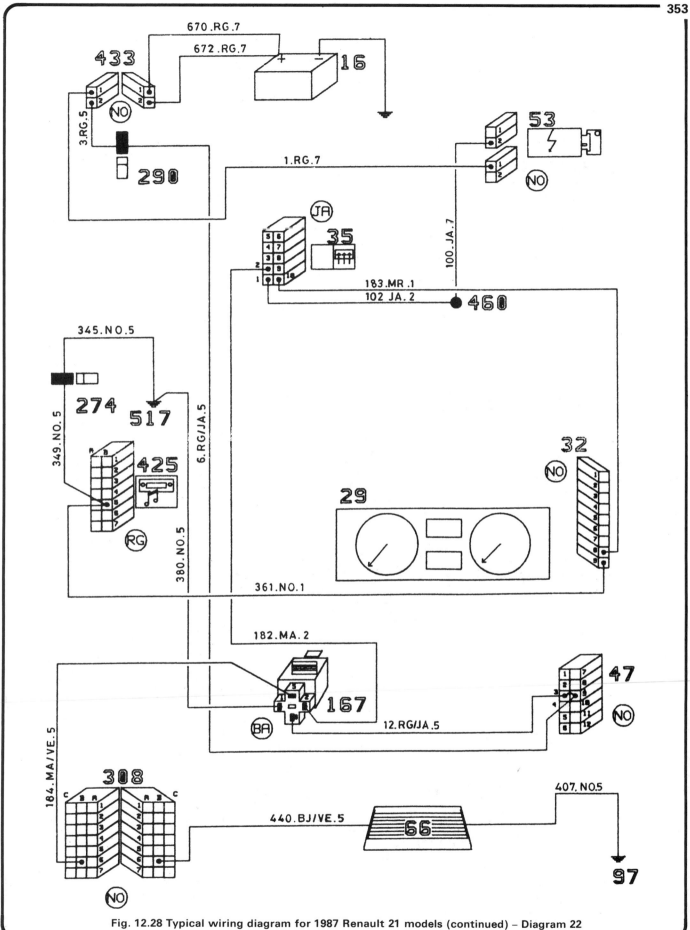

Fig. 12.28 Typical wiring diagram for 1987 Renault 21 models (continued) – Diagram 22

354

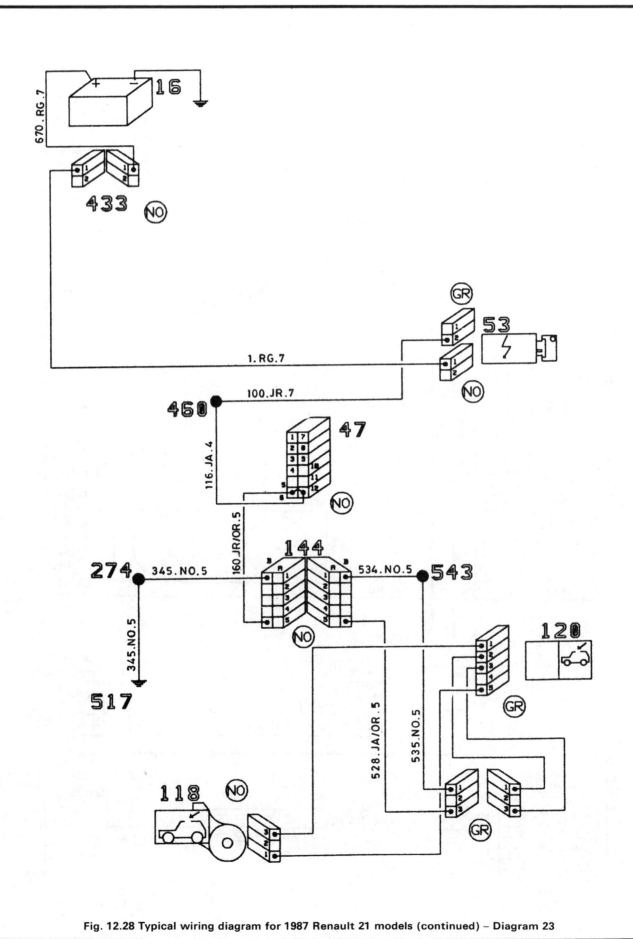

Fig. 12.28 Typical wiring diagram for 1987 Renault 21 models (continued) – Diagram 23

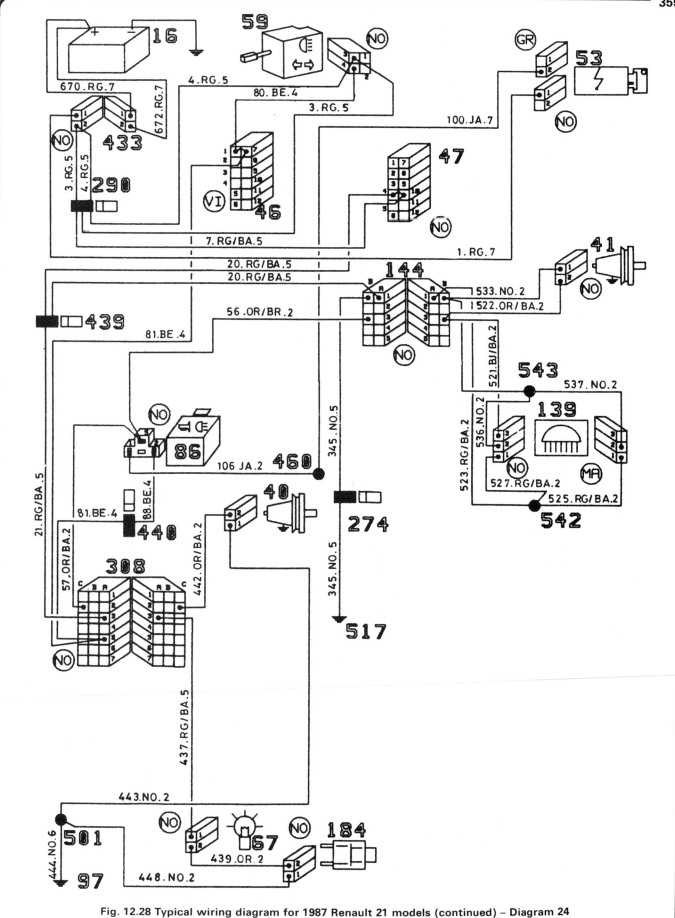

Fig. 12.28 Typical wiring diagram for 1987 Renault 21 models (continued) – Diagram 24

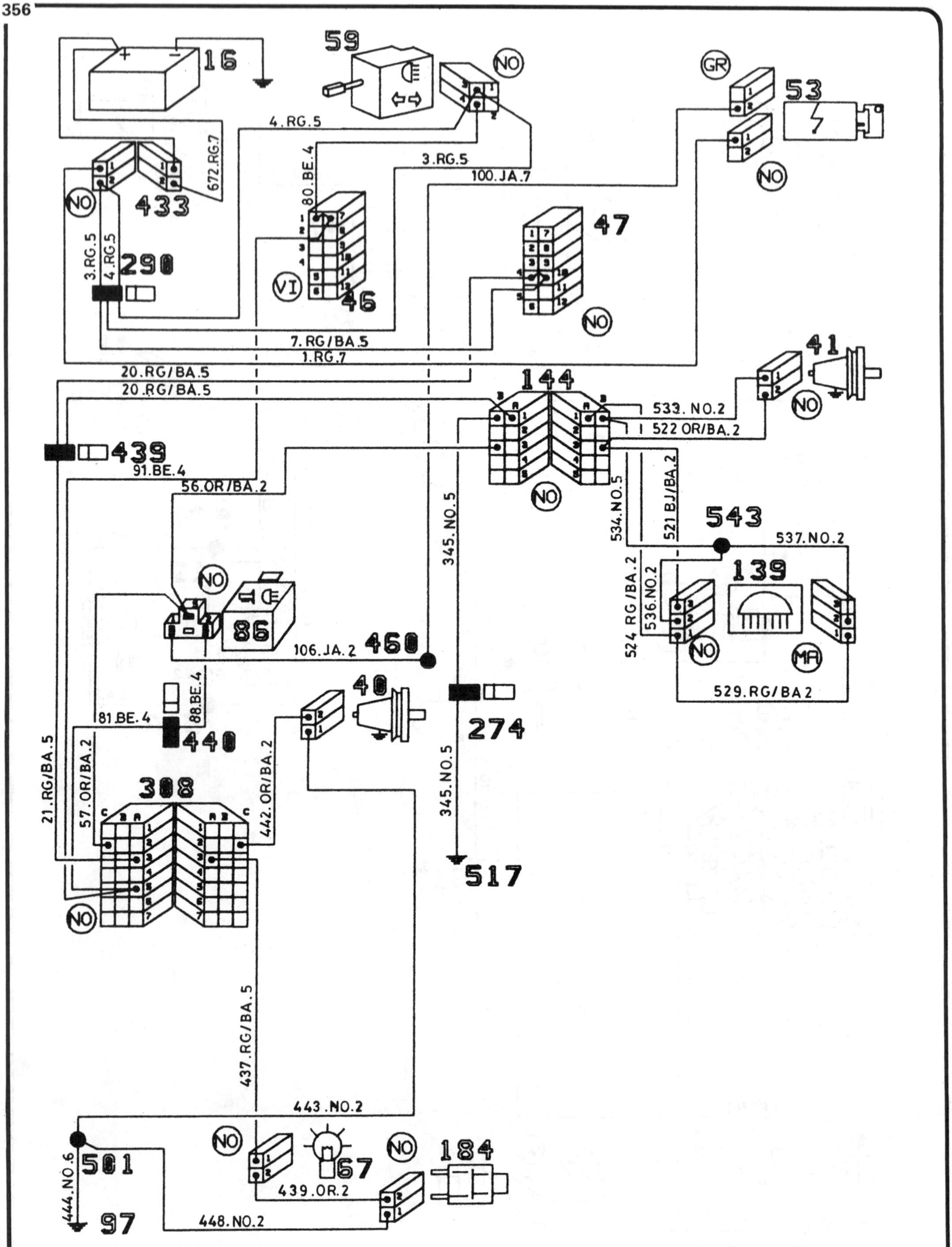

Fig. 12.28 Typical wiring diagram for 1987 Renault 21 models (continued) – Diagram 25

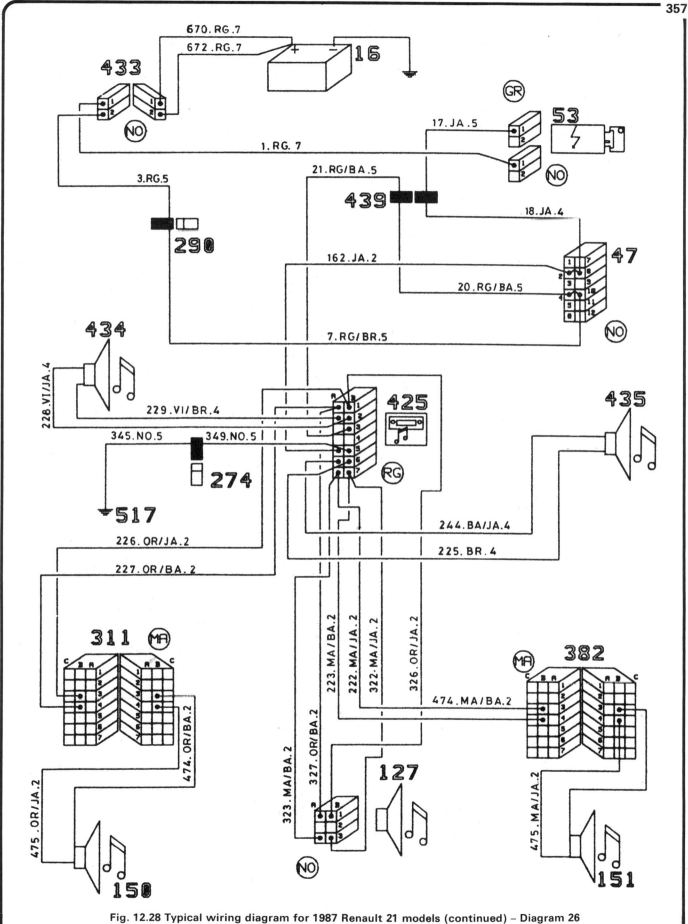

Fig. 12.28 Typical wiring diagram for 1987 Renault 21 models (continued) – Diagram 26

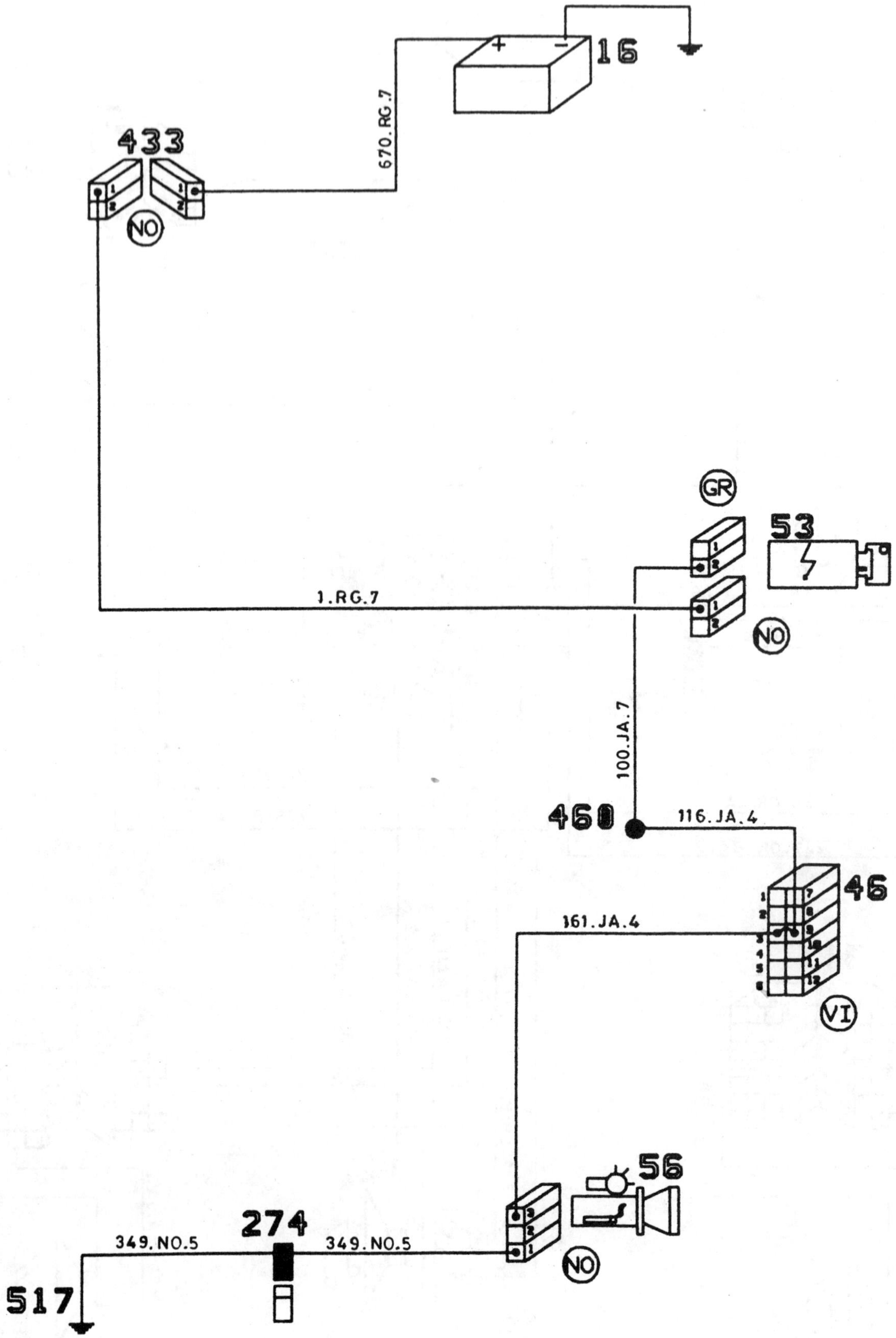

433

NO

670.RG.7

16

+ −

GR

53

NO

1.RG.7

100.JA.7

460

116.JA.4

46

VI

161.JA.4

56

349.NO.5

274

349.NO.5

NO

517

Fig. 12.28 Typical wiring diagram for 1987 Renault 21 models (continued) – Diagram 27

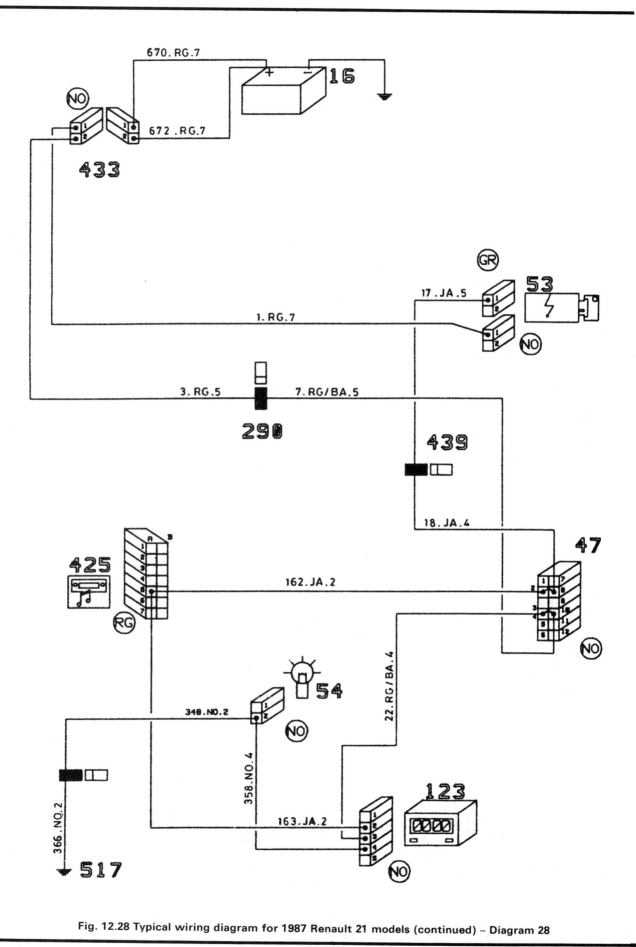

Fig. 12.28 Typical wiring diagram for 1987 Renault 21 models (continued) – Diagram 28

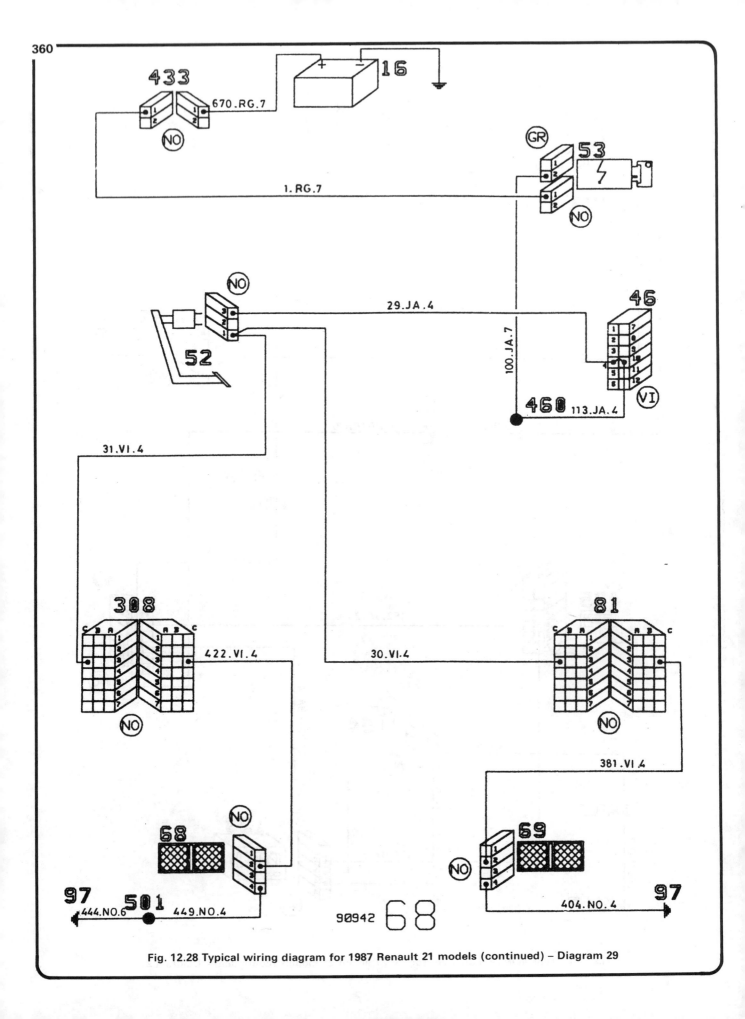

Fig. 12.28 Typical wiring diagram for 1987 Renault 21 models (continued) – Diagram 29

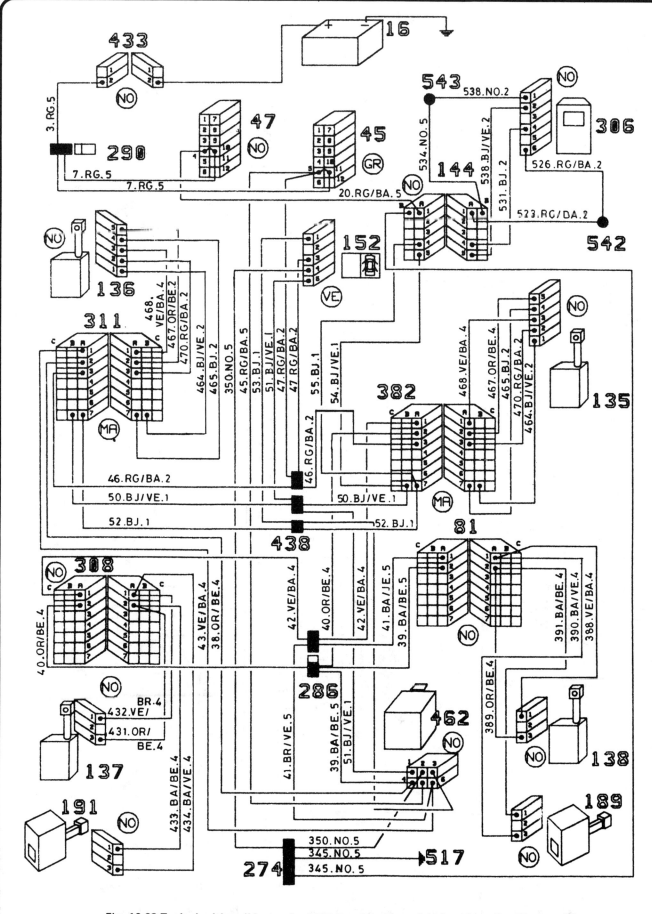

Fig. 12.28 Typical wiring diagram for 1987 Renault 21 models (continued) – Diagram 30

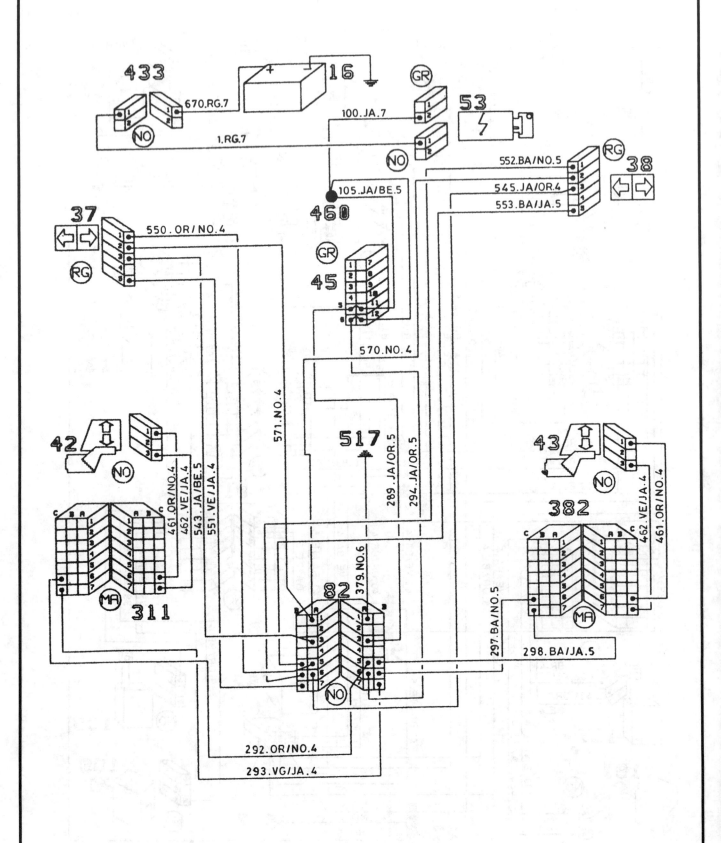

Fig. 12.28 Typical wiring diagram for 1987 Renault 21 models (continued) – Diagram 31

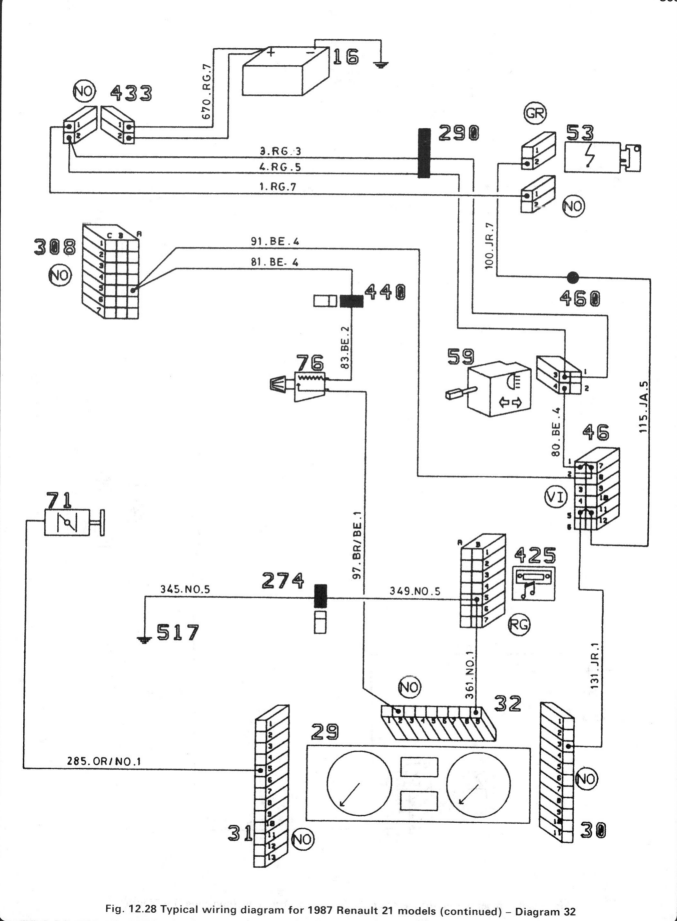

Fig. 12.28 Typical wiring diagram for 1987 Renault 21 models (continued) – Diagram 32

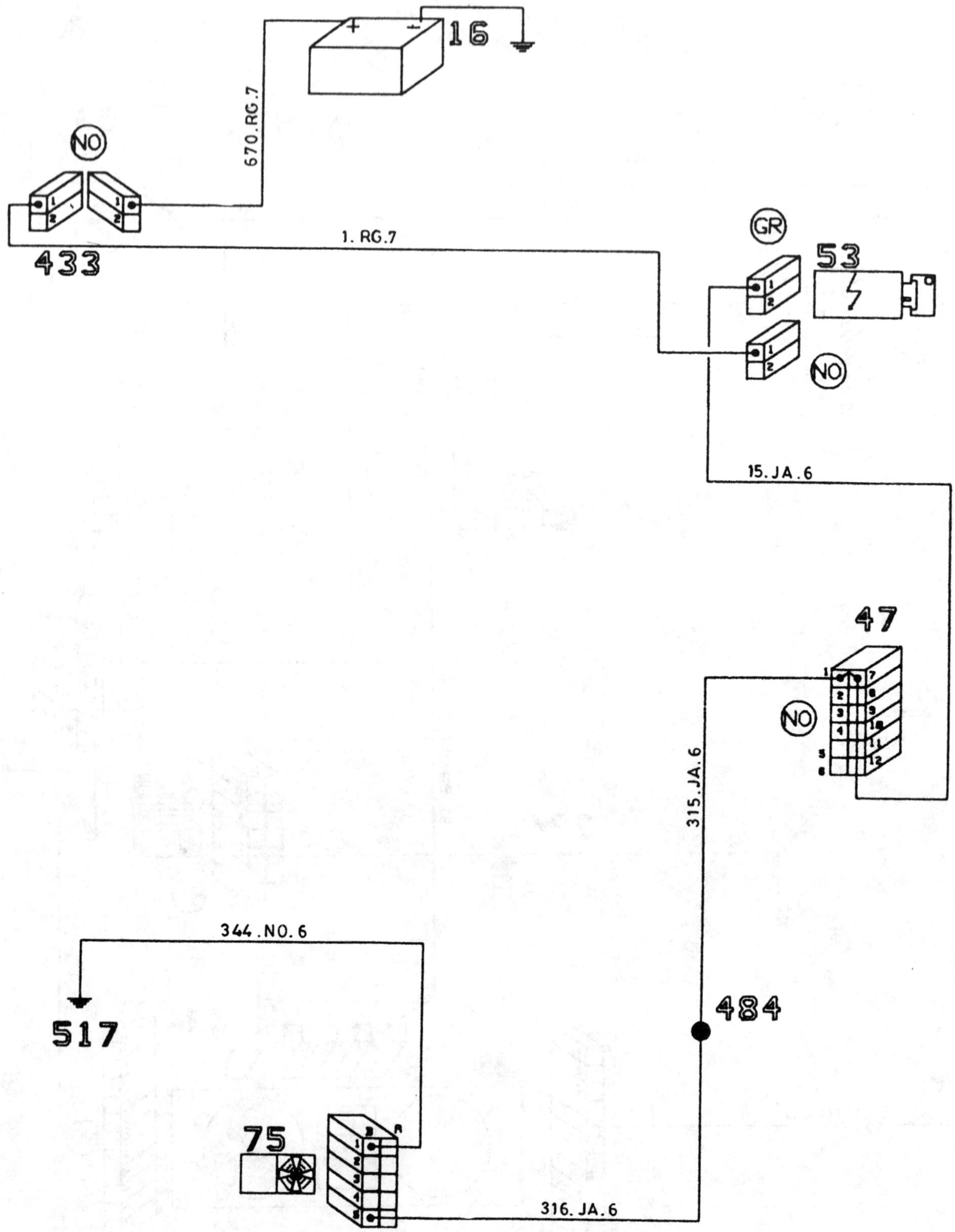

16

670.RG.7

NO

1
2

1
2

433

1. RG.7

GR

53

NO

1
2

1
2

15.JA.6

47

NO

1 7
2 8
3 9
4 10
5 11
6 12

344.NO.6

517

315.JA.6

484

75

3 8
1
2
3
4
5

316.JA.6

Fig. 12.28 Typical wiring diagram for 1987 Renault 21 models (continued) – Diagram 33

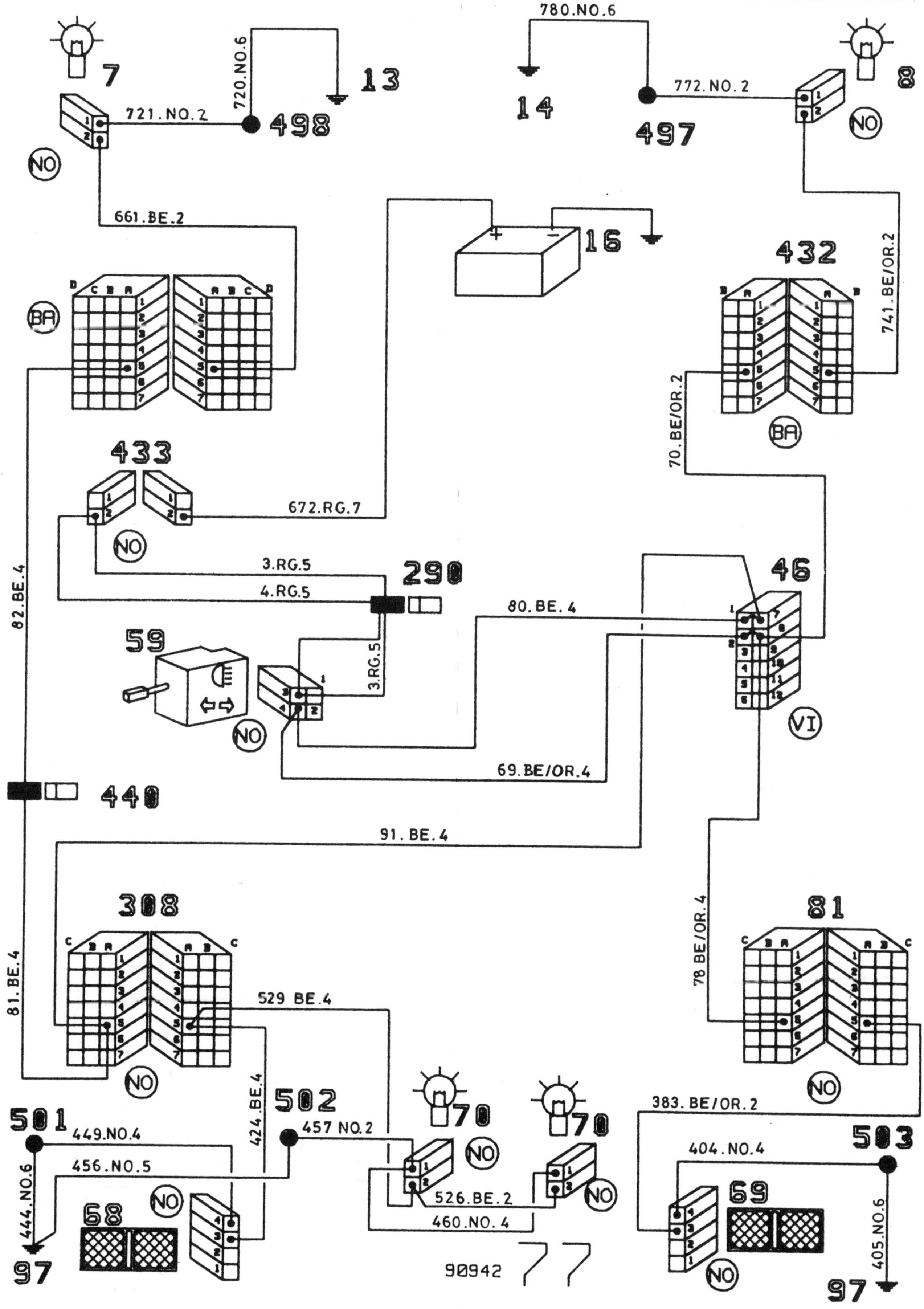

780.NO.6

720.NO.6

7

721.NO.2 498

13

14 497

772.NO.2

8

NO

NO

661.BE.2

16

432

BA

741.BE/OR.2

70.BE/OR.2

BA

433

672.RG.7

NO

3.RG.5

4.RG.5

290

80.BE.4

46

59

3.RG.5

NO

69.BE/OR.4

VI

440

91.BE.4

82.BE.4

308

81

78 BE/OR.4

C B A R B C

C B A R B C

NO

NO

529 BE.4

81.BE.4

424.BE.4

502

457 NO.2

70

70

383.BE/OR.2

501

449.NO.4

526.BE.2

404.NO.4

503

456.NO.5

460.NO.4

NO

NO

444.NO.6

68

NO

59

405.NO.6

97

90942

77

NO

97

Fig. 12.28 Typical wiring diagram for 1987 Renault 21 models (continued) – Diagram 34

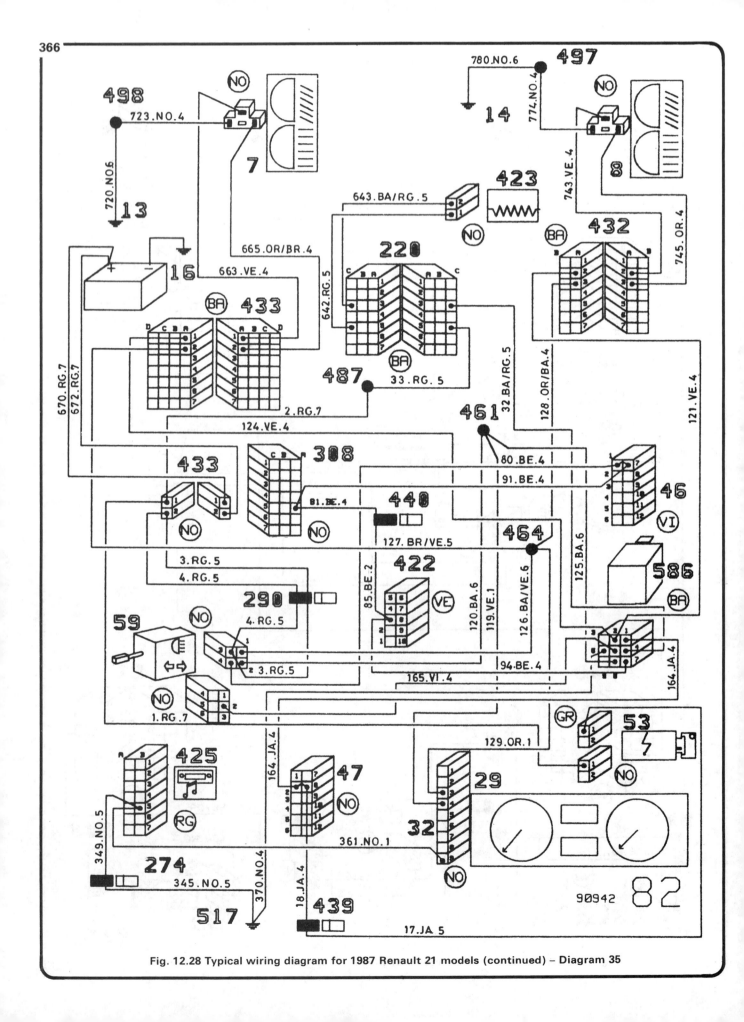

Fig. 12.28 Typical wiring diagram for 1987 Renault 21 models (continued) – Diagram 35

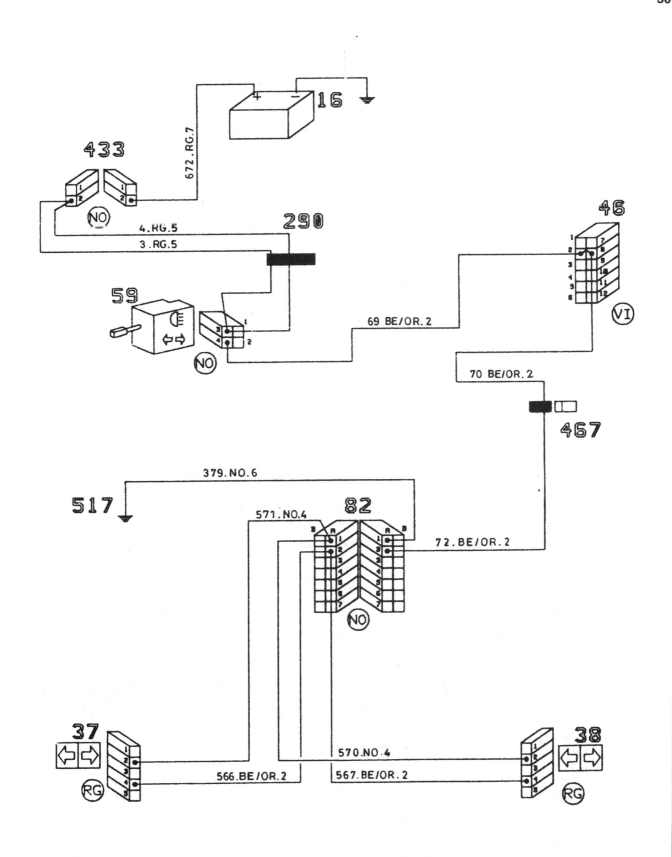

Fig. 12.28 Typical wiring diagram for 1987 Renault 21 models (continued) – Diagram 36

Fig. 12.28 Typical wiring diagram for 1987 Renault 21 models (continued) – Diagram 37

90942 85

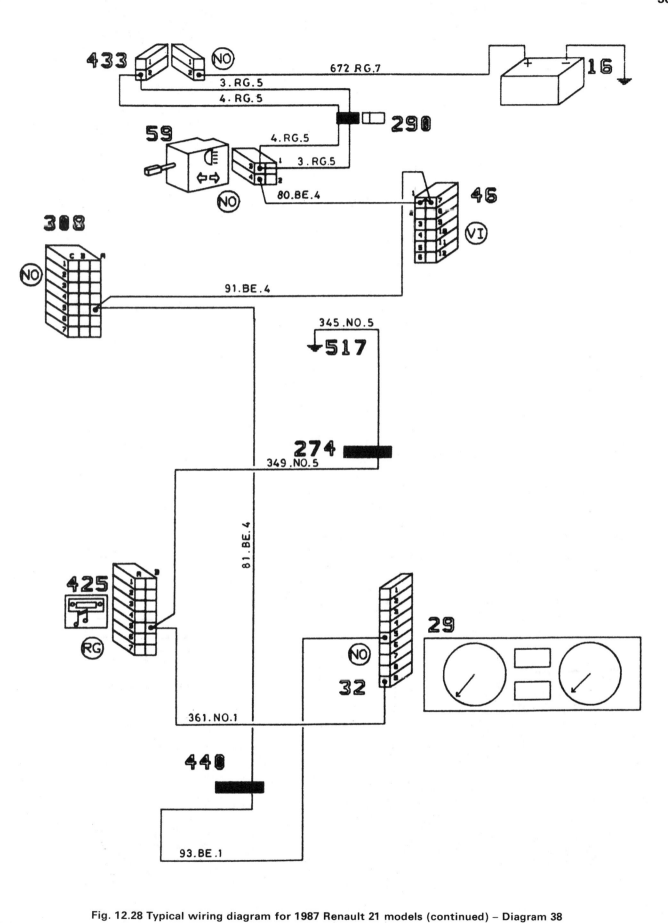

Fig. 12.28 Typical wiring diagram for 1987 Renault 21 models (continued) – Diagram 38

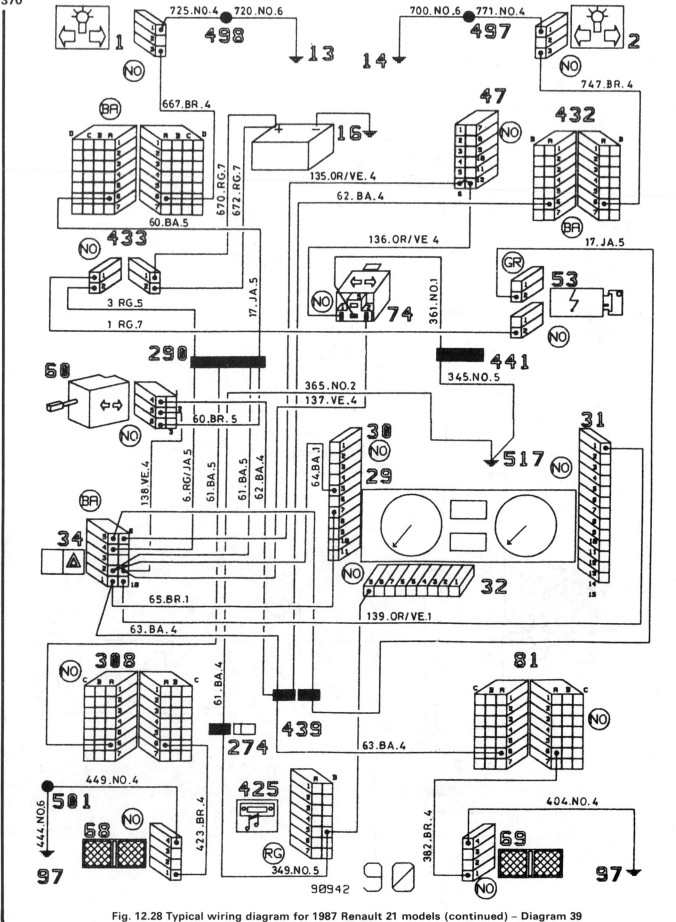

Fig. 12.28 Typical wiring diagram for 1987 Renault 21 models (continued) – Diagram 39

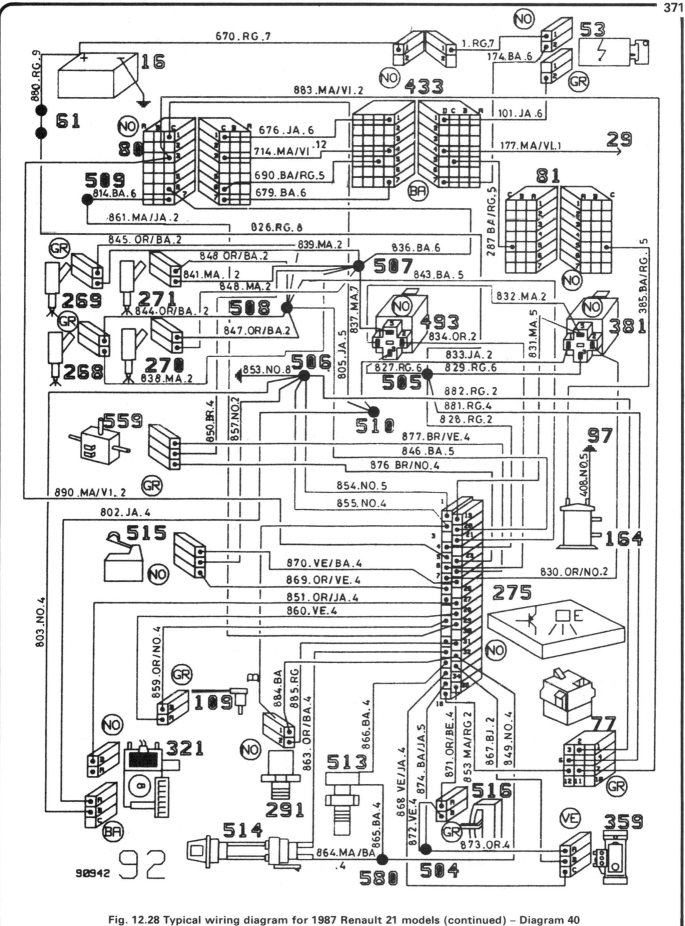

Fig. 12.28 Typical wiring diagram for 1987 Renault 21 models (continued) – Diagram 40

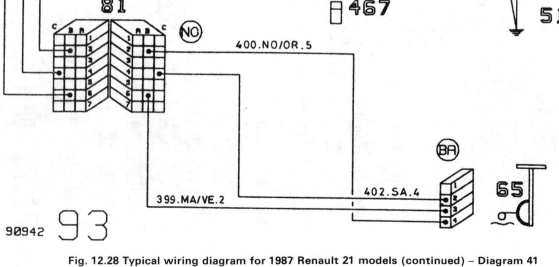

670.RG.7

16

433

GR
53

NO

100.JA.7

46

VI

450

115.JA.5

131.JA.1

1.RG.7

180.VE.1

361.NO.1

425

RG

31

29

NO

32

30

NO

NO

179.SA.1

349.NO.5

274

365.NO.2

366.NO.2

467

366.NO.2

517

81

NO

400.NO/OR.5

BA

399.MA/VE.2

402.SA.4

65

90942 93

Fig. 12.28 Typical wiring diagram for 1987 Renault 21 models (continued) – Diagram 41

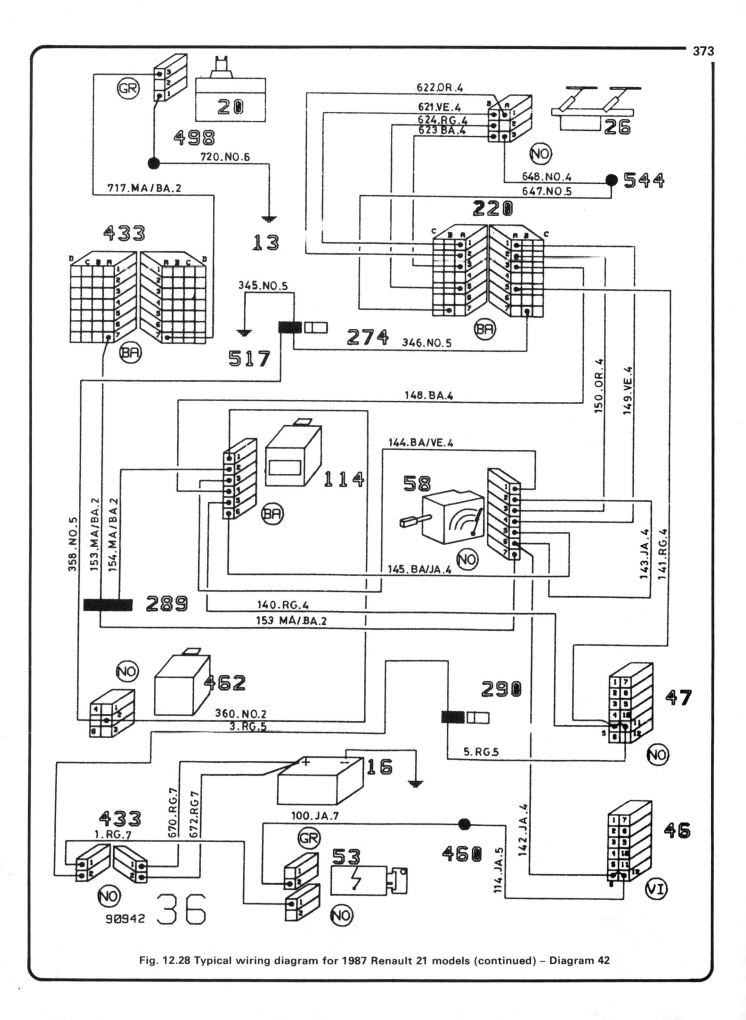

Fig. 12.28 Typical wiring diagram for 1987 Renault 21 models (continued) – Diagram 42

Index